# General Liability Insurance Coverage

# General Liability Insurance Coverage

## Key Issues in Every State

Randy J. Maniloff

Jeffrey W. Stempel

OXFORD

UNIVERSITY PRESS

# OXFORD
UNIVERSITY PRESS

*Oxford University Press, Inc., publishes works that further Oxford University's objective of excellence in research, scholarship, and education.*

Oxford    New York
Auckland    Cape Town    Dar es Salaam    Hong Kong    Karachi    Kuala Lumpur    Madrid
Melbourne    Mexico City    Nairobi    New Delhi    Shanghai    Taipei    Toronto

With offices in
Argentina    Austria    Brazil    Chile    Czech Republic    France    Greece    Guatemala    Hungary
Italy    Japan    Poland    Portugal    Singapore    South Korea    Switzerland    Thailand
Turkey    Ukraine    Vietnam

Copyright © 2011 by Oxford University Press, Inc.

Published by Oxford University Press, Inc.
198 Madison Avenue, New York, New York 10016

Oxford is a registered trademark of Oxford University Press
Oxford University Press is a registered trademark of Oxford University Press, Inc.

Library of Congress Cataloging-in-Publication Data
Maniloff, Randy J.
    General liability insurance coverage : key issues in every state / Randy J. Maniloff, Jeffrey Stempel.
        p. cm.
    Includes bibliographical references and index.
    ISBN 978-0-19-538151-1 ((pbk.) : alk. paper)
    1.    Liability Insurance—United States—States.    I. Stempel, Jeffrey W. II. Title.
    KF1215.M36 2011
    346.73'0865—dc22

                                                            2010037534

3  4  5  6  7  8  9

Printed in the United States of America on acid-free paper

**Note to Readers**
This publication is designed to provide accurate and authoritative information in regard to the subject matter covered. It is based upon sources believed to be accurate and reliable and is intended to be current as of the time it was written. It is sold with the understanding that the publisher is not engaged in rendering legal, accounting, or other professional services. If legal advice or other expert assistance is required, the services of a competent professional person should be sought. Also, to confirm that the information has not been affected or changed by recent developments, traditional legal research techniques should be used, including checking primary sources where appropriate.

*(Based on the Declaration of Principles jointly adopted by a Committee of the
American Bar Association and a Committee of Publishers and Associations.)*

You may order this or any other Oxford University Press publication by
visiting the Oxford University Press website at www.oup.com

*To Lisa and Ella – Whom I love without terms, conditions, limitations, or exclusions*

– R.J.M.

*To Ann, Ryan, Shanen, and Reed – The Ultimate Coverage Team*

– J.W.S.

# About the Authors

Randy J. Maniloff is a partner at White and Williams, LLP in Philadelphia. He concentrates his practice in the representation of insurers in coverage disputes over primary and excess obligations under a host of policies, including commercial general liability and various professional liability policies. For the past ten years, Mr. Maniloff has published a year-end article in *Mealey's Litigation Report: Insurance* that addresses the ten most significant insurance coverage decisions of that year. Mr. Maniloff has also written for such influential organizations as The Federalist Society, Manhattan Institute, and Washington Legal Foundation. Mr. Maniloff is a frequent lecturer at industry seminars and has been quoted on insurance coverage topics by such media as *The Wall Street Journal, The New York Times, USA Today, Dow Jones Newswires, Associated Press, A.M. Best, Business Insurance, National Underwriter, Insurance Journal, The Philadelphia Inquirer, The Times-Picayune,* and *The National Law Journal.* Mr. Maniloff received his B.S., with distinction, in 1988 from Pennsylvania State University and his J.D. in 1991 from Temple University School of Law in Philadelphia.

Jeffrey W. Stempel, the Doris S. & Theodore B. Lee Professor of Law, teaches legal ethics, civil procedure, insurance, and contracts at the William S. Boyd School of Law, University of Nevada Las Vegas. He is the author or co-author of many law journal articles and six previous books, including *Fundamentals of Litigation Practice* (2010), *Fundamentals of Pretrial Litigation* (7th ed. 2008), *Stempel on Insurance Contracts* (3d ed. 2006) and *Foundations of the Law* (1994). A member of the bar in both Minnesota and Nevada, he served on the State Bar of Nevada Committee on Ethics and Professional Responsibility and served on the Bar's Ethics 2000 Committee. Prior to joining the UNLV law faculty in 1999, he taught at Florida State University College of Law and Brooklyn Law School and has been a practicing attorney and judicial clerk. He is a graduate of the University of Minnesota and the Yale Law School.

# Acknowledgments

Just as it perhaps "takes a village" to raise a child, a book-length project inevitably is based on the work of many persons in addition to the named authors. This book in particular would not exist without the commitment and enthusiasm of our editor, Matt Gallaway, and his colleagues at Oxford University Press, including Alden Domizio, Michelle Lipinski, Maria Pucci, Ninell Silberberg, Mary Rosewood and Pushpa Giri (Glyph International). Support from White and Williams, LLP and the William S. Boyd School of Law at the University of Nevada Las Vegas was also essential. In addition, our wives and children displayed more than their usual extraordinary patience and tolerance regarding our fascination with insurance coverage matters.

More generally, we have both benefited enormously from the lawyers, legal scholars, insurance claims professionals, and clients with whom we have worked over the years. Their insights and opportunities to engage in real-world insurance disputes have been in many ways the backbone of our understanding of the often complex (and usually state-variant) issues of insurance coverage law. Although this group is by definition too numerous for giving adequate recognition to all of its members, certain persons stand out for the degree to which their scholarship and practice has enriched our understanding of insurance coverage and other areas of law.

Randy thanks his parents, whose love, unwavering support, and reminder to never forget the lesson of Coca-Cola have brought him to this point; his partner, Gale White, whose support for this book has been immeasurable; Celestine Montague, Tony Miscioscia, and Larry Bistany, colleagues at White and Williams who helped shoulder his burden during this project; Barbara Bryer, his fantastic secretary; Susan Warren and Peggy Killeen, for their humor, counsel and encouragement along the way; Brenda and Howard Axel, for being such supportive and understanding in-laws; Amy Trojecki, for her endless amusement; Sarah Burger (Villanova University School of Law Class of 2010) for her significant contribution as a research assistant; and the gang at Saxbys in One Liberty for keeping him caffeinated. Lastly, special gratitude is owed to Sarah Damiani (Temple University School of Law Class of 2010) for her monumental contribution to the final product.

In addition to his family, Jeff thanks in particular research assistants Shannon Rowe (Boyd Law Class of 2010) and Kathleen Wilde (Boyd Law Class of 2011) and David McClure, Jeanne Price, and the entire crew of the Weiner-Rogers Law Library as well as the Boyd Law administration and Dean John White and Associate Deans Kay Kindred and Steve Johnson. Thanks also to Ken Abraham, Aviva Abramovsky, Josh Aiklen, Corby Arnold, Gene Backus, Tom Baker, Pat Barald, Roger Baron, Hazel Beh, Michelle Boardman, Pat Byrne, Drew Cass, Curtis Coulter, Cary Donham, Robert Eglet, Cory Eschweiler, Jim Fischer, David Gardner, Scott Godes, Steve Guy, Laird Hart, Marjorie Hauf, Gary Haugen, Paul Hejmanowski, Roger Henderson, David Herr, David Hyman, Bob Jerry, Dennis Kennedy, John Kennedy, Erik Knutsen, Gene Leverty, Phil Lorenzo, Leo Martinez, Bill Maupin, Jay Mootz, Brad Myers, Johnny Parker, Steve Parsons, Mike Raibman, Jerry Randolph, Jim Reece, Brad Richardson, John Rivkin, Adam Scales, Dan Schwarz, Peter Seligman, Matt Sharp, Charles Silver, Rick Stempel, Peter Swisher, Kent Syverud, Bob Thavis, Jeff Thomas, Todd Touton, Jim Whitmire, and Bob Works.

Randy J. Maniloff
Jeff Stempel
October 2010

# Preface

Those involved with insurance claims, such as risk managers, brokers, insurance company claims professionals, and coverage counsel all respond to a new claim scenario with the same three words: Is it covered? [That may also be the last time that they agree on anything.] General liability insurance claims are complex and the answer to that three-word question can be vexing.

On one hand, insurance is a business built on standardization. The vast majority of insurance policies are standardized documents, particularly for property/casualty risks, where the leading forms—including the commercial general liability (CGL) policy—are authored by the Insurance Services Office (ISO). But despite the relative uniformity of policies, states can differ widely in their interpretation and application of insurance policies. Whether a claim is covered under a CGL policy can depend a great deal on whether the case arises on one side of the street (or river or mountain) or another.

For example, in Arkansas a policyholder's late notice of a claim against it is fatal to insurance coverage, so long as the policy identified prompt notice as a "condition precedent" to coverage, regardless of whether the insurer's ability to respond to the claim was prejudiced by the late notice. In Tennessee, similarly late notice negates coverage only if the insurer can prove it was prejudiced by the delay. In Connecticut, the policyholder can get coverage even if it gave late notice—but only if it can shoulder the burden to prove absence of prejudice to the insurer. In Nevada, the effect of late notice is not entirely clear. Older precedent suggests that prejudice is irrelevant and late notice voids coverage, but a good argument can be made that the older decisions have been superseded by administrative regulations and that the current state supreme court would follow Tennessee's approach, which is the majority view. Illinois follows a hybrid approach that considers prejudice to the insurer and several other factors in determining whether the notice to the insurer was in fact "late."

All this uncertainty exists in an area of insurance law where there is a fairly clear majority rule in favor of the "notice-prejudice" approach, usually with the burden to prove prejudice on the insurer. Time and again it is proven that coverage counsel and claims professionals cannot be safe in assuming that a given state follows the "normal" approach to a coverage question.

But despite this uncertainty, general liability claims, even the most challenging, usually involve one or more schools of thought that govern their resolution. The task for courts is often to identify and examine these various schools and decide in which one they want to enrol. This process, while convenient, leads to fractures among states over how to handle the most important coverage issues. This can be so even in the case of claims that involve virtually identical policy language and facts. In this book, we identify the various schools of thought that govern the most important coverage issues, and provide the type of state-specific knowledge that is essential to enable counsel, claims professionals and all those involved in a claim to more efficiently and accurately assess a coverage controversy.

In some instances this book will provide the answer with as much certainty as possible—such as a situation where the instant claim involves facts and policy language that are not materially different from those that have been addressed by the relevant state supreme court. In other instances the answer will be less clear—such as situations where the law is unsettled or the instant claim involves facts or policy language that can be distinguished from otherwise settled law. But even where the book cannot provide certainty to the "is it covered" question, it will provide guidance on the issues that must be resolved to get to that answer. This may also enable the stakeholders in the claim to handicap their chances of prevailing.

With this one volume, the reader is armed with the tools to address the key coverage issues of the day for each state. Although the book is aimed at attorneys and insurance professionals with some degree of experience, it is accessible to entry-level readers as well. Chapter 1 provides an overview of the CGL policy and the general ground rules of insurance law and policy construction. In addition, each chapter contains an overview of the nature, background, development, and competing schools of thought concerning the issue addressed in that chapter's fifty-state survey of the law. Most important, however, readers will get a comprehensive state-by-state summary of relevant law on the coverage issue, including the latest cases and developments.

This book has its roots in our own frustrations when addressing areas of insurance law. Although there are several good treatises on insurance law, many of which include listings of many of the cases, none had the sort of thorough, nuanced, and specific state-by-state focus of the critical issues that can best aid the insurance professional and claims attorney in knowing and understanding the law applicable to a particular dispute. We hope to bridge that gap—not to mention with the convenience of a single paperback volume. In future editions, we will address developments in the states on these key issues, providing up-to-date assistance to those handling coverage matters.

Because this book is a collaborative effort, the viewpoints expressed are not necessarily those of White and Williams, LLP, the University of Nevada Las Vegas, or any of its clients or constituents. Indeed, because of the collaborative nature of this book, the views expressed herein may not be held by both authors. The same holds true for the employers or home institutions of any additional contributors to this volume. Notwithstanding this disclaimer, we have endeavored to "play it straight" throughout this book and to keep our own preferences out of our reporting of the state of the law of key coverage issues. State-by-state case law is reported impartially, without any intent to slant descriptions in favor of policyholders, insurers, brokers, or others with a stake in coverage disputes.

The bulk of this book was written from May 2008 to June 2010. Some additional content was added through early October 2010, as new decisions were issued during the production process. The coverage landscape is constantly changing. And sometimes rapidly so. Therefore, by its very nature, writing a book of this sort comes with a built-it challenge to keep it current. While attempts were made to update the book throughout the writing process, care should be taken to ensure that the law is current at the time that it is being examined.

We hope you will find the book a useful, perhaps even essential, addition to the coverage toolbox. But never lose sight that this is a reference book (a hopefully dog-eared one) and not a substitute for a subscription to Lexis or Westlaw or the advice of experienced counsel. We welcome questions or comments.

October 2010

Randy J. Maniloff
White and Williams, LLP
1650 Market Street
One Liberty Place, Suite 1800
Philadelphia, PA 19103
215-864-6311
215-789-7608 (fax)
maniloffr@whiteandwilliams.com

Jeffrey W. Stempel
Doris S. & Theodore B. Lee Professor of Law
William S. Boyd School of Law – UNLV
4505 South Maryland Parkway, Box 451003
Las Vegas, NV 89154-1003
702-895-2361
702-895-2482 (fax)
jeff.stempel@unlv.edu

# Contents

# CHAPTER
# 1

# Commercial General Liability Insurance— an Overview

## The Structure and Development of General Liability Coverage

Liability coverage provides the policyholder and others insured under the policy with protection, including a defense, against lawsuits and liability that may result in judgments or settlements. The most common type of liability insurance is "general" liability insurance that provides protection for bodily injury or property damage claims that arise from the alleged negligence of the policyholder.

The commercial general liability (CGL) policy is the dominant general liability policy in the United States. In addition to providing coverage for "bodily injury" and "property damage" claims generally sounding in negligence, the standard CGL form also provides coverage for "personal injury" claims such as defamation or trespass and "advertising injury" claims such as when the policyholder's advertising disparages the product of a competitor.

The extent of coverage, of course, is defined by the insuring agreement as tailored by various exclusions contained in the CGL form. But the question oftentimes does not end there. In addressing insurance construction and coverage, it is important to note that state law can differ dramatically on how the policy language is interpreted. It is not unusual for virtually identical facts and policy language to result in a finding of no coverage whatsoever in one state and full coverage in another. Consequently, choice-of-law methodology in a given state can have an enormous impact on the ultimate resolution of a coverage dispute, as demonstrated in this book.

This book focuses on state-by-state treatment of important CGL coverage issues. By "coverage," we mean the question whether the insurance policy is obligated to provide protection under the facts and circumstances of the claim. While the specifics of more specialized types of liability insurance—such as Directors and Officers, Errors and Omissions, and Professional Liability—are outside the scope of this book, some of the CGL issues addressed in this volume are relevant to these other forms of liability insurance.

For the most part, liability insurance provides protection against these claims without regard to the fault or blameworthiness of the policyholder so long as the policyholder did not intend to harm the claimant or the policyholder's conduct does not trigger a specific fault-based exclusion such as one forbidding coverage if the injury is the result of criminal acts by the policyholder.

Liability insurance is a relatively recent development, one most scholars define as beginning with general accident and specific risk liability policies sold to manufacturers and merchants in the late nineteenth century. Liability coverage expanded significantly with automobile liability policies in the late nineteenth and early twentieth centuries. These policies were arranged to provide coverage for damages against the policyholder resulting from an "accident." Liability insurance expanded to other areas gradually but took root as a form of commercial insurance protection in the 1920s and 1930s. The liability policies of that era continued to define coverage in terms of claims arising out of an "accident."

Early liability policies also tended to be policies designed to provide coverage against liability for a particular premises or operations hazards of the policyholder. Employers Liability Insurance was created to cover claims for work-related injuries and today continues but in modified form as an adjunct to workers compensation policies. Public Liability Insurance came into use and covered claims made against policyholders by injured customers or passersby, the type of classic "slip-and-fall" claims that are staples of the first-year torts class. Public Liability Insurance was reasonably broad in scope but not as comprehensive as the modern CGL policy. There was also Owners, Landlords, and Tenants liability insurance, Manufacturers' Public Liability Insurance, Contractor's Public Liability Insurance as well as more narrow insurance products like Elevator Liability Insurance and Product

Liability Insurance. Separate liability insurance for contractors and builders also developed and was commonly called Owners' Protective Liability Insurance or Contractors' Protective Liability Insurance. *See generally* ELMER W. SAWYER, COMPREHENSIVE LIABILITY INSURANCE (1943).

Prior to the advent of the CGL policy, various specific types of liability insurance were each sold and purchased as separate insurance policies. This presented difficulties for both insurers and policyholders. Insurers disliked the increased potential for adverse selection by policyholders, who might purchase only a coverage more likely to be needed while refusing to buy other coverages, thereby depriving insurers of potential premium dollars. It also raised pricing problems and issues of fairness in that some customers subsidized the coverages of others. It was also thought that presenting this much choice to some policyholders would encourage unduly risky behavior as policyholders gambled on the types of coverages they would need. Rating the multiple coverages was also difficult because of the narrow focus of risk assumed and the smaller pools of premiums for collection and investment.[1] In response to the problems of splintered policies and coverages, the liability insurance industry developed the CGL policy.

In the late 1930s and early 1940s, insurers began offering a "comprehensive" commercial liability policy that also included a "duty to defend" claims irrespective of whether the claims were meritorious. This provided the policyholder not only indemnity protection for adverse judgments or settlements but also with legal representation to defend the claim. *See* Chapter 4 for a discussion of the Duty to Defend.

The standard form CGL policy provides that the insurer controls the litigation and resolution of the claim and will supply counsel. That the insurer selects counsel has led to numerous disputes between insurers and policyholders that are unsatisfied with the insurer's choice. In addition, the relationship between attorney, policyholder, and insurer can lead to significant legal ethics issues for counsel—for which a complex body of law has developed. States vary in their responses to these situations. These issues are addressed in Chapter 5. For further information in these areas, *see* ALLAN WINDT, INSURANCE CLAIMS AND DISPUTES § 4.19 (5th ed. 2007); JEFFREY W. STEMPEL, STEMPEL ON INSURANCE CONTRACTS § 10.07[B] (3d ed. 2006 & Supp. 2009); RONALD E. MALLEN & JEFFREY M. SMITH, LEGAL MALPRACTICE §§ 30:3–5 (4th ed. 1996).

The initials CGL initially stood for "comprehensive" general liability policy. Insurers subsequently renamed the CGL a "commercial" general liability policy to avoid the implication that the CGL covered "everything" (or more than the insurer intended). The CGL policy was still written on an accident

---

1. *See* ELMER W. SAWYER, COMPREHENSIVE LIABILITY INSURANCE (1943).

basis until 1966, when the "occurrence" language was introduced (although "occurrence" coverage for "bodily injury" was the subject of an advisory endorsement in the late 1950s). During the 1980s, CGL coverage, particularly for product liability, was increasingly written on a claims-made basis,[2] but the occurrence-basis form remains most popular. The first standardized CGL form, crafted by the National Bureau of Casualty and Surety Underwriters and the Mutual Casualty Insurance Rating Bureau, was issued in 1941.[3] A revised standard form CGL issued in 1943 became widely used. The CGL policy was again revised in 1947 and significantly revised in 1955, 1966, 1973, and 1986.[4] Still further versions of the CGL policy followed, this time more frequently and with less significant changes. The two rating bureaus that crafted the CGL policy eventually merged into the Insurance Services Office (ISO), an organization that continues today and is responsible for the more recent revisions to the CGL policy.

The original CGL policy provided coverage where injury giving rise to a liability claim was "caused by accident." The term "accident" was not defined in the original CGL policy, the 1943 CGL form, the 1947 form, or the 1955 form. Courts were divided significantly on the question whether an injury-producing event must be discrete and isolated in order to constitute an "accident." The majority of courts concluded that an "accident" need not be confined in time and space and could be an injury-producing event taking place over a longer time span.

Many insurers were opposed to this judicial trend, arguing that an "accident" needed to be an event confined in time and space.[5] During the 1955 to 1966 period, these insurers either came to change their views or to accept the judicial interpretation of the "accident" trigger of coverage as inevitable. In addition, some individual insurers were offering "occurrence" basis coverage that was an attractive competing product because it clearly provided coverage for liability that resulted from ongoing conditions. In response, as part of the insurance industry's 1966 revision to the standard CGL policy, the term "occurrence" was substituted for the term "accident," with an "occurrence" being defined as "an accident, including injurious exposure to conditions,

---

2. *See* Donald S. Malecki & Arthur L. Flitner, Commercial General Liability (8th ed. 2005) (describing revisions of CGL during past thirty years and current structure and content of CGL).

3. *See* Sawyer, *supra* note 1.

4. *See* Eugene R. Anderson, Jordan S. Stanzler, & Lorelie S. Masters, Insurance Coverage Litigation § 1.02 (2d ed. 2000) (also noting less significant revisions in 1988, 1990, and 1993).

5. *See, e.g.,* John J. Tarpey, *The New Comprehensive Policy: Some of the Changes,* 33 Ins. Couns. J. 223 (1966) ("The principal reason given for revision of the policies was adverse court decisions.").

which results, during the policy period, in bodily injury or property damage neither expected nor intended from the standpoint of the insured."

The fundamental requirement of the CGL policy, that bodily injury and property damage must occur during the policy period (although such requirement is no longer located in the definition of "occurrence"), has led to an enormous amount of coverage litigation. This seemingly simple question can sometimes be far from it, as evidenced by the fact that this issue is the subject of not just one, but two, chapters in this book. *See* Chapters 15 and 16.

Under the terms of an occurrence basis CGL policy, the insurer ordinarily establishes a limit of its liability, generally known as a "per occurrence" limit, which is usually set forth on the declarations page of the CGL policy and constitutes the maximum amount that the CGL insurer will pay for any one occurrence. Today, most occurrence basis CGL policies also provide an "aggregate limit" that sets forth the maximum amount of the CGL insurer's liability irrespective of the number of occurrences. However, aggregate limits for general liability claims did not become part of the standard ISO form until 1986. For products hazard coverage, however, insurers had employed aggregate limits well prior to the 1980s, largely because of the greater risk of cascading liability that was effectively beyond the control of the policyholder or insurer once products were in the field or structures were in use by third parties. That the limit of the CGL policy's liability is provided on a "per occurrence" basis had led to much litigation over the "number of occurrences" at issue in a claim. In many cases, more "occurrences" means more limits of liability available. *See* Chapter 8.

## The Organization of the CGL Form

The CGL policy, like most insurance policies, has a relatively targeted objective for insuring risks. It is designed to protect commercial entities from litigation and liability arising out of their business operations. The CGL policy is not designed to guarantee the quality of the policyholder's work or the successful completion of its business activities. *See* Chapter 11 for a discussion of the dispute between insurers and policyholders over coverage for faulty workmanship.

Because even broad coverages are at some point limited in scope, an effective risk management plan for businesses (and for individuals) usually includes a package of coverages that match up and may even overlap. Effective risk-management leaves no "gaps" in the coverage of purchased policies unless the policyholder consciously intends to self-insure or "go bare" as to the risk that falls in the gap. A general liability policy will accordingly seek to cover only general liability. More specific liabilities that may be seen by the underwriters as presenting different sorts of risks are often excluded from the

CGL but usually can be insured through the purchase of another type of policy.

The boundary disputes between the CGL policy and other forms of insurance coverage can become vexing where the loss is of a type that either does not clearly fall on one side of the line or where the policyholder can make a nonfrivolous argument that it reasonably expected coverage or that the loss at issue is properly characterized as a claim stemming from general operations. Commentators may refer to some of these cases as involving "tough" exclusions or policy language. Both policyholder and insurer may have good arguments for or against coverage.

Organizationally, the CGL policy has a declarations page giving the basic information summary of the policy, usually including the policyholder(s) and insurer names (and entities comprising any syndicates on the risk), the limits of insurance, the coverage period, a summary of the risk insured, and the premiums charged. The declarations page may also list the various forms that make up the policy, although it has become popular to relegate the list of forms to its own page—evidence, no doubt, that insurance policies are growing in size. Indeed, the 1955 version of the standard CGL form was five pages and the most current one is sixteen.

Until the late 1960s, CGL policies were written with an annual policy period and hence obvious annualized limits on the policy. Aggregate limits and multiyear policy periods began to arrive in the late 1960s and 1970s and were common by the 1980s. In coverage actions involving older policies (e.g., asbestos or environmental liability actions), there can arise a question whether the limits of a multiyear policy are annualized or apply only once for the entire multiyear period (usually three years). There is mixed case law on the issue, with some cases taking the view that a multiyear declarations page has a "plain meaning" that makes the limit a collective three-year limit rather than three one-year limits. Regarding the CGL language, one commentator has concluded: "[w]here a contract is issued for a period of three years, the limits of the insurer's liability apply separately to each *consecutive* annual period thereof."[6]

Section I of the CGL policy outlines its "coverages": Coverage A for "bodily injury and property damage liability"; Coverage B for "personal and advertising injury liability"; and Coverage C for "medical payments" available in connection with bodily injury claims. Each of the three coverages has its own "insuring agreement" setting forth the nature of the coverage and the insurer's obligation as well as a list of exclusions that apply to that particular coverage.

In addition, the policy provides for some essentially minor supplementary coverages for injury claims. By length and verbiage alone, bodily injury is clearly the focus of the CGL. Coverages A and C both deal with bodily injury,

---

6. C. A. Kulp & John W. Hall, Casualty Insurance 143 (4th ed. 1968).

but Coverage B is brief. However, the bulk of the length of Coverage A results from the long list of exclusions, which is why policyholders may seek to characterize claims as sounding in Coverage B, thereby avoiding such long list of exclusions to bodily injury and property damage coverage in Part A.

Section II of the CGL defines who is an "insured," and Section III sets forth the "limits of insurance," making reference to the declarations page for the precise dollar amounts of the policy in question. An important, but to some extent implicit, concept in liability insurance is that the CGL policy ordinarily covers actions by third parties seeking monetary relief but does not provide coverage for purely injunctive claims against the policyholder.

Section IV establishes a number of CGL conditions that the policyholder must satisfy to successfully invoke coverage (e.g., notice and cooperation) as the insurance policy's "no action" clause limits policyholder actions against the insurer as well as "other insurance" ground rules for coordination of coverage. Failure to give prompt notice of a claim is a commonly litigated issue in insurance disputes as is allocation of responsibility among insurers (and insurers and policyholders). *See* Chapters 3 and 17 respectively.

Finally, in Section V, one finds the definitions of the policy. These provisions are often more than cosmetic. For example, Section V of the CGL form defines such important terms as "personal and advertising injury," "bodily injury," "property damage," and "occurrence." Although any phrase in a policy can become important in particular litigation, coverage litigation often focuses on the meaning of a definition or exclusion in dispute.

As noted above, much coverage litigation involves claims for occurrences of bodily injury. The CGL defines bodily injury as "bodily injury [to be sure, insurance policies have their share of redundancies], sickness, or disease sustained by a person, including death resulting from any of these at any time," while an occurrence "means an accident, including continuous and repeated exposure to substantially the same general harmful conditions." However, "accident" is not defined. CGL Coverage Part A brings the two terms together by stating that the coverage applies only if the bodily injury or property damage "is caused by an 'occurrence' that takes place in the coverage territory" and if the bodily injury or property damage "occurs during the policy period."

The Coverage A exclusion list includes many of the classic sticking points of insurance coverage litigation: the expected or intended exclusion; contractual liabilities; alcohol-induced injury; pollution; vehicular injuries (auto insurers are supposed to cover this); war; the "owned property" exclusion; and exclusions for the insured's own work and product. These exclusions may prompt the policyholder to characterize a claim as sounding in something other than bodily injury. The Coverage B exclusions are fewer in number and tend to focus on intentional conduct, breach of contract, and date of loss. But, of course, one reason the exclusion list can be so short is because Coverage B itself is not nearly so expansive as Coverage A.

## Construction and Interpretation of Insurance Policies: Rules of Policy Construction Generally

Because insurance policies are contracts, the general rules of contract formation and construction apply to the CGL form. Relatively little insurance litigation concerns issues of contract formation. In almost all coverage disputes, there is no question that a policy was issued (the exception being life or health insurance conditional receipt cases or property insurance binder cases in which a claim is made for a loss that took place during the underwriting process, and the insurer contests whether there is coverage during this period under the terms of the conditional receipt). There is also a significant amount of insurance litigation concerning possible rescission of an issued policy on grounds of fraud or misrepresentation. For the most part, however, cases involve whether an admittedly operative policy provides coverage for a particular third party's claim against the policyholder or other person or entity that qualifies as an "insured" under the policy.

In construing insurance policies, courts strive to give effect to the intent of the parties. Normally, the text of the agreement provides the best indication of that intent. Consequently, clear policy text will usually be enforced unless the term is unconscionable or violates a statute, regulation, or public policy as announced by courts or legislatures. To be unconscionable, an insurance policy provision must be unreasonably favorable to one side or the agreement obtained through misconduct. Many courts require a showing of both this latter "procedural" unconscionability as well as "substantive" unconscionability in that the provision is too one-sided. Disputes also arise over clear policy text when insureds argue that the policy is "illusory" because it excludes coverage for a significant portion of the insured's operations. Insureds arguing that a policy is illusory often face a demanding standard as courts often reject the argument when the policy provides some coverage in some fashion—even if not what the insured in essence needed from the policy.

Because insurance is so heavily regulated, a policy term approved by or permitted by regulators is unlikely to be deemed substantively unconscionable. Policyholders have had more success contending that insurance policy provisions violate public policy. For example, auto insurance provisions limiting coverage may be held to unduly undermine state requirements that all drivers have adequate liability insurance because of the strong state policy in demanding at least minimal financial responsibility by drivers. Public policy arguments are less successful in CGL litigation because the policies are not usually required by law and are by definition purchased by often sophisticated businesses rather than less sophisticated consumers. However, the insurability of punitive damages under the CGL policy often gives rise to public policy arguments. *See* Chapter 19.

Even when text is reasonably clear, a court may examine other evidence of party intent or the purpose of the insurance policy in order to inform its construction of disputed words in the policy. For the most part, however, courts consider intent or purpose seriously only when the words are unclear. *See* Chapter 21. If a policy term is ambiguous, then the general rule of *contra proferentem* ("against the drafter") is that the language will be construed against the party that authored the problematic language and in favor of the nondrafter.

As Maniloff likes to say in jest, all policyholders seem to "speak Latin" in coverage cases as they are often quick to invoke the principle of *contra proferentem*, arguing that contested language is sufficiently ambiguous such that it should be construed to favor them rather than the insurer, who is almost always the author of the policy, particularly in the case of CGL policies. Although all courts follow the *contra proferentem* principle, various jurisdictions and individual judges vary in their eagerness to invoke the maxim. A few courts will immediately rule against the insurer if ambiguity is shown. A few are highly resistant to conceding any textual ambiguity and will conduct extensive linguistic analysis seeking to find the true meaning of text that initially may seem unclear.

Most courts take a middle approach. If policy text is not clearly and easily read to resolve a dispute, the court then examines extrinisic evidence of party intent and policy purpose, perhaps looking at underwriting documents, promotional material, correspondence, e-mails, drafting history, claims history, or other material in an attempt to resolve textual ambiguity. Only if these other indicia of meaning fail does the court usually use the ambiguity principle or *contra proferentem* as a tiebreaker to decide the case. In a small number of cases, such as when a policyholder or its broker authors or insists upon certain language in the policy, the ambiguity principle may actually favor the insurer.

For more extensive discussion of contract doctrine and insurance policy construction, *see generally* JOSEPH M. PERILLO, CALAMARI AND PERILLO ON CONTRACTS (6th ed. 2009); BARRY R. OSTRAGER & THOMAS R. NEWMAN, HANDBOOK ON INSURANCE COVERAGE DISPUTES (14th ed. 2008); JEFFREY W. STEMPEL, STEMPEL ON INSURANCE CONTRACTS (3d ed. 2006 & Supp. 2010); EMERIC FISCHER, PETER NASH SWISHER, & JEFFREY W. STEMPEL, PRINCIPLES OF INSURANCE LAW Ch. 2 (3d ed. 2004 and Supp. 2006); E. ALLAN FARNESWORTH, CONTRACTS (4th ed. 2004); EUGENE ANDERSON, JORDAN STANZLER, & LORELIE S. MASTERS, INSURANCE COVERAGE LITIGATION (2d ed. 2004); PETER KALIS, THOMAS M. REITER, & JAMES R. SEGERDAHL, POLICYHOLDER'S GUIDE TO INSURANCE COVERAGE § 10.04 (1997 & Supp. 2004).

## Occurrence Policies as Contrasted with Claims-Made Policies

An occurrence basis policy operates differently from a claims-made policy. Under the occurrence basis CGL, an action seeking damages against the policyholder for bodily injury or property damage is covered if it results from an occurrence and causes damage during the policy period. The triggering point is the time of the alleged injury or damage. If the claimant is successful in demonstrating the time of loss alleged, the CGL insurer on the risk at that time must provide coverage for the damages obtained (absent the applicability of an exclusion or the exhaustion of policy limits). Once a CGL policy is "triggered," the insurer remains on the risk even if the injury continues into a subsequent policy period. The key point is the time of the precipitating injury. The occurrence (e.g., negligence, defective manufacture) need not take place at the same time as the injury. For example, negligent manufacture may cause harm that does not take place for years. But when it does, the occurrence CGL policy on the risk *at that time* is triggered. Consequently, occurrence CGL policies are sometimes described as providing almost unlimited "prospective" coverage. As noted, this "timing" issue can be more complex than it seems. *See* Chapters 15 and 16.

By contrast, a claims-made CGL is not triggered until there is a claim made and reported to the insurer during the policy period—even if the claim is based on long-ago events. In theory, this could make the claims-made CGL provide almost unlimited retroactive coverage. Insurers avoid such unlimited retroactive coverage by including a "retroactive date," which provides that the insurance will not cover claims caused in whole or in part by occurrences taking place prior to the retroactive date.

Another significant difference between occurrence and claims-made policies is their treatment of late notice. While prejudice is almost always required for an insurer to disclaim coverage for late notice under an occurrence policy, the opposite is usually true in the case of claims-made policies.

## Coverage for Claims of "Bodily Injury"

Because of the frequency of litigation over Coverage A (bodily injury and property damage), the contours of bodily injury and property damage coverage are also comparatively well established. For example, a shorthand aphorism describing CGL coverage is that bodily injury coverage is construed to extend to tort claims against the policyholder but not to breach of contract liability. However, this aphorism can be misleading. For example, the CGL policy provides coverage for liability assumed under certain types of contracts.

There is also some division over the question whether bodily injury coverage includes damages for emotional distress. Most courts read the term "bodily injury" to require at least some detectible physical injury in order to trigger coverage,[7] although the term has been described as ambiguous.[8] Many courts have found that pure emotional injury qualifies as bodily injury when there is physical manifestation of the emotional injury, such as chest pains. A perhaps obvious point that can occasionally be forgotten is that "bodily injury" must involve a human body. The extent to which emotional injury may qualify as bodily injury is the subject of Chapter 10.

## Coverage for "Property Damage"

Similarly, the meaning of "property damage" under Coverage A of the basic CGL policy is also viewed as relatively well settled. For example, numerous cases hold that the property damage alleged must affect tangible property. Economic losses such as those connected with investments or anticipated profits do not count.[9] However, where economic loss occurs as a fairly traceable consequence of tangible physical injury, property damage coverage is likely to be available.

---

7. *See, e.g., Jacobsen v. Farmers Mut. Ins. Co.*, 87 P.3d 995, 999 (Mont. 2004) ("We… conclude that the term "bodily injury" as defined in [the instant policy], is limited to physical injury to a person caused by an accident and does not include emotional and psychological injuries stemming therefrom"); *SL Indus., Inc. v. American Motorists Ins. Co.*, 128 N.J. 188, 205, 607 A.2d 1266, 1275 (1992); *National Cas. Co. v. Great Southwest Fire Ins. Co.*, 833 P.2d 741, 746 (Colo. 1992). *See generally* OSTRAGER & NEWMAN § 7.03[a].

8. *See, e.g., Lavanant v. General Accident Ins. Co. of Am.*, 79 N.Y.2d 623, 630, 584 N.Y.S.2d 744, 747, 595 N.E.2d 819, 822 (1992).

9. *See, e.g., Kazi v. State Farm Fire & Cas. Co.*, 24 Cal. 4th 871, 103 Cal. Rptr. 2d 1, 15 P.3d 223 (2001) (impairment of easement is not claim alleging physical injury to tangible property); *Miller v. Triad Adoption & Counseling Servs., Inc.*, 65 P.3d 1099 (N.M. App. 2003) (financial injury not property damage); *Whitman Corp. v. Commercial Union Ins. Co.*, 782 N.E.2d 297 (Ill. App. 2002) (economic injury from breach of asset purchase agreement not property damage); *Scottsdale Ins. Co. v. International Protective Agency, Inc.*, 19 P.3d 1058 (Wash. App. 2001) (where restaurant sued security agency over negligent admission of a minor, which led to loss of liquor license, restaurant had not stated a claim for property damage against policyholder security agency).

## Exclusions from Bodily Injury and Property Damage Coverage

Although the scope of the insuring agreement of the CGL is quite broad, the typical CGL form contains a list of exclusions significantly restricting coverage for "bodily injury" and "property damage" claims. Among the standard exclusions are:

- Expected or Intended injury or damage
- Liability assumed in a contract or agreement (but with significant exceptions)
- Liquor Liability
- Workers Compensation claims
- Employer's Liability
- Pollution (*See* Chapters 13 and 14)
- Aircraft, Automobile, or Watercraft claims
- Claims arising from the transportation of mobile equipment
- Claims arising out of war, including civil war, insurrection, rebellion or revolution
- Claims for damage to the policyholder's own property
- Claims for damage to the policyholder's own product
- Claims for damage to the policyholder's own work (heavily litigated in construction defect cases, with an exception "if the damaged work or the work out of which the damage arises was performed on your [the insured's] behalf by a subcontractor")
- Damage to "Impaired Property" or property that was not physically injured
- Product recall
- Personal and Advertising Injury (which is covered, subject to its own set of exclusions, in Part B of the policy, as discussed below)
- Loss of electronic data
- Telephone Consumer Protection Act ("junk fax") and other statutes that prohibit or limit the distribution of material

## The Parameters of Personal Injury and Advertising Injury Coverage

The bulk of modern liability insurance coverage litigation has centered on the "bodily injury" and "property damage" coverage of the standard commercial general liability policy, when it occurred, what constitutes an "occurrence" under that coverage, and whether certain key exclusions in Part A of the CGL form are applicable. Increasingly, policyholders have focused on the other facets of the CGL, particularly the advertising injury and personal injury coverages. For the most part, this has been an effort to find coverage for claims that, at first blush, had traditionally been viewed as excluded bodily injury claims or uninsured events. The policyholder effort to expand the scope of the CGL, through a common law of claims characterized as personal injury or advertising injury matters, has enjoyed some success.

The standard CGL defines "personal and advertising injury" as injury that arises out of one or more of the following:

(a) False arrest, detention, or imprisonment;

(b) Malicious prosecution;

(c) The wrongful eviction from, wrongful entry into, or invasion of the right of private occupancy of a room, dwelling, or premises that a person occupies, committed by or on behalf of the owner, landlord, or lessor;

(d) Oral or written publication, in any manner, of material that slanders or libels a person or organization or disparages a person's or organization's goods, products, or services;

(e) Oral or written publication, in any manner, of material that violates a person's right of privacy (*See* Chapter 18);

(f) The use of another's advertising idea in your "advertisement"; or

(g) Infringing upon another's copyright, trade dress, or slogan in your "advertisement."

Unlike the CGL itself and the "bodily injury" and "property damage" provisions of Coverage A, which is broadly drafted, personal and advertising injury coverage is written more narrowly, with focus on specified risks. However, where a loss arises out of one of the claimed enumerated offenses, emotional injury is usually covered.[10]

The personal injury provisions of Part B of the CGL contain exclusions for:

- Knowing violation of rights of another;
- Material published with knowledge of falsity;
- Material first published prior to the policy period;
- Criminal acts;
- Contractual liability;
- Breach of contract;
- Failure of goods to measure up to promised quality;
- Wrong description of prices;

---

10. *See, e.g., Artcraft of N.H., Inc. v. Lumberman's Mut. Cas. Co.*, 126 N.H. 844, 497 A.2d 1195, 1196 (1985).

- Infringement of copyright; patent, trademark, or trade secret;
- Insureds in media and internet type businesses;
- Electronic chatrooms or bulletin boards;
- Unauthorized use of another's name or product;
- Pollution (added to the policy form as a reaction to judicial decisions that found pollution liability claims to fall under the "trespass" or "wrongful entry" portion of personal injury coverage), including a specific exclusion for pollution-related expenses such as government-mandated cleanup;
- War; and
- Telephone Consumer Protection Act ("junk fax") and other statutes that prohibit or limit the distribution of material.

In general, courts have taken a relatively strict view of personal and advertising injury coverage, reading the enumerated items strictly and construing other actions according to their similarity or "fit" with the covered torts. This approach of confined construction of the coverage has been tested by policyholder efforts to obtain coverage for sexual harassment claims,[11] discrimination claims,[12] breach of contract claims,[13] pollution-related claims[14] and has raised whether the "wrongful entry" provisions apply to claims that a policyholder is unfairly usurping another's property rights.

---

11. *See* OSTRAGER & NEWMAN, § 7.04[A] (12th ed. 2004).
12. *See, e.g., Groshong v. Mutual of Enumclaw Ins. Co.*, 329 Or. 303, 985 P.2d 1284 (1999) (prospective tenant's claim of discrimination by policyholder landlord in failing to rent unit does not fall within CGL personal injury coverage for "wrongful eviction" or "invasion of the right of private occupancy" because claimant never had acquired possession and thus could not be evicted nor have right of occupancy invaded). *Accord. Westfield Ins. Group v. J.P.'s Wharf, Ltd.*, 859 A.2d 74 (Del. 2004); *Rockgate Mgmt Co. v. CGU Ins., Inc.*, 88 P.3d 798 (Kan. Ct. App. 2004).
13. *See, e.g., Holly Mountain Resources, Ltd. v. Westport Ins. Corp.*, 104 P.3d 725 (Wash. Ct. App. 2005) (claims of timber trespass and breach of contract not covered under property damage Part A of CGL form, which had specific timber trespass exclusion; policyholder apparently did not argue for personal injury or advertising injury coverage); *City of Arvada v. CIRSA*, 988 P.2d 184 (Colo. App. 1999), *aff'd*, 19 P.3d 10 (Colo. 2001) (tenant's suit for breach of contract, interference with prospective contractual relations, and misappropriation of business opportunity does not come within personal injury coverage as "infringement of property" (the contract); third-party claim sounds in breach of contract rather than interference with possessory right and is therefore outside scope of CGL).*See also Robinson Helicopter Co., Inc. v. Dana Corp.*, 34 Cal. 4th 979, 102 P.3d 268 (Cal. 2004) (economic loss doctrine does not bar tort of misrepresentation in connection with sale of product and performance of contract; cases like this may lead to subsequent coverage litigation).
14. *See, e.g., Connecticut Specialty Ins. Co. v. Loop Paper Recycling, Inc.*, 824 N.E.2d 1125 (Ill. Ct. App. 2005) (absolute pollution exclusion bars personal injury coverage). *But see Brucia v. Hartford Accident & Indem.*, 307 F.Supp. 2d 1079 (N.D. Calif. 2003) (successful use of personal injury section of CGL to obtain coverage in pollution case). State divergence in application of both the absolute pollution exclusion and its predecessor qualified pollution exclusion is discussed later in this book.

Courts generally have required that there be some selling or promotion or marketing of a product to third parties in order to fall within the coverage for advertising injury. Courts divide as to whether there must be "mass media" type of advertising or whether any sales promotion is sufficient to fall within coverage in view of the insurance industry's failure to use a more explicit and narrow definition of advertising in the CGL.[15] The current CGL definition of an "advertisement" is surprisingly not all that helpful in resolving the dispute. It provides that an advertisement is "a notice that is broadcast or published to the general public or specific market segments" about the policyholder's business "for the purpose of attracting customers or supporters." The definition expressly includes electronic postings and certain portions of websites. This language can be read as including business marketing such as kiosk postings, distribution of handbills, or similar "narrowcasting" sorts of advertising/marketing/solicitation, but insurers generally contend that these sorts of marketing efforts are not "advertisements."

To be covered, the claims made against the policyholder must arise from advertising activity.[16] A highly attenuated connection to advertising is not sufficient to create coverage.[17] If courts were to view any advertisement connected to a tort claim as triggering coverage, the same logic would make product liability claims covered under the advertising injury provisions of the policy (Coverage B), rather than the bodily injury policy provisions (Coverage A), any time the offending product was advertised. Although efforts to shoehorn intellectual property claims into advertising injury are not as stretched (the advertising has a greater relation to public perceptions of product identity than it bears to the product's physical danger to users), the link is uncomfortably close for many courts.

For further discussion regarding the CGL policy form and its scope of coverage, one may consult insurance law treaties. *See generally* JEFFREY W. STEMPEL, STEMPEL ON INSURANCE CONTRACTS (3d ed. 2006 & Supp. 2010); BARRY R. OSTRAGER & THOMAS R. NEWMAN, HANDBOOK ON INSURANCE COVERAGE DISPUTES (14th ed. 2008); EUGENE ANDERSON, JORDAN STANZLER,

---

15. *See Hameid v. National Fire Ins. of Hartford*, 31 Cal. 4th 16, 71 P.3d 761 (2003) (advertising connotes widespread activity directed to public at large); *Monumental Life Ins. Co. v. United States Fid. & Guar. Co.*, 94 Md. App. 505, 617 A.2d 1163, *cert. denied*, 330 Md. 319, 624 A.2d 491 (1993) (advertising must be public to qualify as advertising within common sense of the word); *Smartfoods, Inc. v. Northbrook Prop. & Cas. Co.*, 35 Mass. App. Ct. 239, 618 N.E.2d 1365 (1993) (letter sent to third party may have discussed product attributes but was not advertising).

16. *See Sentry Ins. v. R. J. Weber Co.*, 2 F.3d 554 (5th Cir. 1993) (applying Texas law); *Bank of the West v. Superior Ct.*, 2 Cal. 4th 1254, 1276–1277, 833 P.2d 545, 559–560, 10 Cal. Rptr. 2d 538, 552–553 (1992).

17. *See The Frog, Switch & Mfg. Co., Inc. v. Travelers Ins. Co.*, 193 F.3d 742, 744 (3d Cir. 1999) (applying Pennsylvania law) ("This case involves allegations that the insured stole various ideas and then advertised the results of that theft; the question is whether the advertising converts the theft into 'advertising injury.' We conclude that it does not.").

& LORELIE S. MASTERS, INSURANCE COVERAGE LITIGATION (2d ed. 2004); PETER KALIS, THOMAS M. REITER, & JAMES R. SEGERDAHL, POLICYHOLDER'S GUIDE TO INSURANCE COVERAGE §10.04 (1997 & Supp. 2004); ALLAN WINDT, INSURANCE CLAIMS AND DISPUTES (5th ed. 2007). In addition, a number of insurance textbooks used outside of law practice or law schools can provide a useful overview of the CGL and of other insurance policies, terms, and concepts. *See, e.g.*, HAROLD D. SKIPPER & W. JEAN KWON, RISK MANAGEMENT AND INSURANCE (2007); MARK S. DORMAN, INTRODUCTION TO RISK MANAGEMENT AND INSURANCE (8th ed. 2005); GEORGE E. REJDA, PRINCIPLES OF RISK MANAGEMENT AND INSURANCE (9th ed. 2005); JAMES S. TREISCHMANN, ROBERT E. HOYT, & DAVID W. SOMMER, RISK MANAGEMENT & INSURANCE (12th ed. 2005); EMMETT J. VAUGHAN & THERESE VAUGHAN, FUNDAMENTALS OF RISK AND INSURANCE (8th ed. 1999).

CHAPTER

# 2

# Choice of Law for Coverage Disputes

By Steven M. Klepper[1]

50-State Survey: Choice of Law for Coverage Disputes          23

Any attempt to use this book's various fifty-state surveys begs a threshold question: *Which* state's law do I use? Since claims and lawsuits do not always arise in the same state in which the insurance policy was issued, the answer is not always obvious.

For several reasons, few insurance coverage professionals likely place choice of law on their list of favorite issues. Thanks to its complexity, choice of law can be time-consuming (or tedious) to analyze. Even worse, it is not unusual that, even after this time-consuming or tedious analysis is complete, policyholders and insurers still cannot say for certain which state's law applies. Some coverage issues combine generally undisputed facts with well-defined legal tests to lead to reasonable predictability of the outcome. Choice of law is not one of these.

With that said, there are thankfully two main situations where the reader can skip this chapter. First, if the policy declarations show an address for the named insured and the broker in one state, the person seeking coverage is the named insured (or some other entity in that same state), and the claim arose and the underlying lawsuit are pending in that same state, then that state's law should control absent some unusual circumstance.[2]

---

1. Mr. Klepper is a principal at Kramon & Graham, P.A., in Baltimore, Maryland. His practice focuses on insurance coverage and appellate advocacy. He is a graduate of Goucher College (B.A., 1997) and the University of Virginia (M.A., 1998; J.D., 2001). He frequently publishes and lectures on insurance, choice of law, legal history, and other topics.
2. Even in this situation, creative advocacy can lead to anomalous results, such as *TPLC v. United Nat. Ins. Co.*, 796 F. Supp. 1382 (D. Colo. 1992), *aff'd*, 44 F.3d 1484 (10th Cir. 1995), in which the policyholder convinced the court to apply the law of Pennsylvania, where the *insurer* was

Second, if the substantive law is the same in all jurisdictions whose law could possibly apply, there is no need to undertake a choice-of-law analysis.[3] "When certain contacts involving a contract are located in two or more states with identical local law rules on the issue in question, the case will be treated for choice-of-law purposes as if these contacts were grouped in a single state." Restatement (Second) of Conflict of Laws § 186 (1971), cmt. c. *See, e.g., Glidden Co. v. Lumbermens Mut. Cas. Co.*, 861 N.E.2d 109, 115 (Ohio 2006); *Talen v. Employers Mut. Cas. Co.*, 703 N.W.2d 395, 408–09 (Iowa 2005). Although courts sometimes use the term "false conflict" to describe a situation in which two jurisdictions' laws are identical, the term "no conflict" more accurately applies. *Hammersmith v. TIG Ins. Co.*, 480 F.3d 220, 229–30 (3d Cir. 2007). The term "false conflict" connotes that, upon application of a Second Restatement–type analysis, a court has determined that "only one jurisdiction's governmental interests would be impaired by the application of the other jurisdiction's laws." *Id.* at 229 (quoting *Lacey v. Cessna Aircraft Co.*, 932 F.2d 170, 187 (3d Cir. 1991)). If more than one jurisdiction has an interest in applying its own law, a "true conflict" exists, requiring a court to weigh those competing interests. *Id.* at 230.

To decide if a choice-of-law analysis is necessary, the parties must consider all jurisdictions where a coverage action could be brought and then analyze how each of those states would resolve choice of law—with a state court applying its own choice-of-law rule[4] and a federal court applying the choice-of-law rule of the state in which it sits. *Klaxon Co. v. Stentor Elec. Mfg. Co.*, 313 U.S. 487, 496 (1941).

The party invoking another state's law bears the burden of establishing a material difference from forum law; otherwise, the court will apply forum

---

domiciled, instead of the law of Colorado, where the policyholder was domiciled, to the question whether the insurer needed to demonstrate prejudice to disclaim coverage on the basis of late notice.

3. "When certain contacts involving a contract are located in two or more states with identical local law rules on the issue in question, the case will be treated for choice-of-law purposes as if these contacts were grouped in a single state." Restatement (Second) of Conflict of Laws § 186 (1971), cmt. c. *See, e.g., Glidden Co. v. Lumbermens Mut. Cas. Co.*, 861 N.E.2d 109, 115 (Ohio 2006); *Talen v. Employers Mut. Cas. Co.*, 703 N.W.2d 395, 408–09 (Iowa 2005). Although courts sometimes use the term "false conflict" to describe a situation in which two jurisdictions' laws are identical, the term "no conflict" more accurately applies. *Hammersmith v. TIG Ins. Co.*, 480 F.3d 220, 229–30 (3d Cir. 2007). The term "false conflict" connotes that, upon application of a Second Restatement–type analysis, a court has determined that "only one jurisdiction's governmental interests would be impaired by the application of the other jurisdiction's laws." *Id.* at 229 (quoting *Lacey v. Cessna Aircraft Co.*, 932 F.2d 170, 187 (3d Cir. 1991)). If more than one jurisdiction has an interest in applying its own law, a "true conflict" exists, requiring a court to weigh those competing interests. *Id.* at 230.

4. Restatement (First) of Conflict of Laws § 332 (1934); Restatement (Second) of Conflict of Laws § 6 (1971).

law. *See, e.g., Excess Underwriters at Lloyd's v. Frank's Casing Crew & Rental Tools, Inc.*, 246 S.W.3d 42, 53 (Tex. 2008).

In theory, two provisions of the U.S. Constitution—the "full faith and credit" clause of Article IV and the "due process" clause of the Fourteenth Amendment—limit a state's ability to apply its own law to an insurance contract. But the U.S. Supreme Court has adopted a standard so permissive that, in practice, choice of law rarely raises constitutional concerns. "[F]or a State's substantive law to be selected in a constitutionally permissible manner, that State must have a significant contact or significant aggregation of contacts, creating state interests, such that choice of its law is neither arbitrary nor fundamentally unfair." *Allstate Ins. Co. v. Hague*, 449 U.S. 302, 312–13 (1981).

Until the 1970s, virtually all courts resolved choice-of-law disputes by applying the common law doctrine of *lex loci contractus*, which is Latin for "the law of the place of the contract." Under this doctrine, "a contract is governed by the law of the jurisdiction within which the contract is made." *Lifestar Response of Ala., Inc. v. Admiral Ins. Co.*, 17 So. 3d 200, 213 (Ala. 2009). While many states dismiss *lex loci contractus* as an outdated nineteenth-century doctrine, a substantial number of states, all of which have running water, continue to apply the rule.[5] The Supreme Court of Florida conceded that *lex loci contractus* is inflexible but defended that inflexibility as "necessary to ensure stability in contract arrangements." *State Farm Mut. Auto. Ins. Co. v. Roach*, 945 So. 2d 1160, 1164 (Fla. 2006). Under *lex loci contractus*, the law of the state where the insurer delivered the policy to the named insured ordinarily will control. *Admiral Ins. Co. v. G4S Youth Servs.*, 634 F. Supp. 2d 605, 611–12 (E.D. Va. 2009).

The vast majority of jurisdictions have abandoned *lex loci contractus* in favor of the flexible "most significant relationship" analysis set forth in the American Law Institute's Restatement (Second) of Conflict of Laws, usually called the "Second Restatement" for short. The overarching framework of that analysis appears at Section 6, which provides that, absent a controlling statutory directive regarding choice of law, courts look to:

> (a) the needs of the interstate and international systems, (b) the relevant policies of the forum, (c) the relevant policies of other interested states and the relative interests of those states in the determination of the particular issue, (d) the protection of justified expectations, (e) the basic policies underlying the particular field of law, (f) certainty, predictability and uniformity of result, and (g) ease in the determination and application of the law to be applied.

---

5. See the state summaries for Alabama, Arkansas, Florida, Georgia, Kansas, Maryland, New Mexico, North Carolina, Oklahoma, South Carolina, Tennessee, and Virginia.

Restatement (Second) of Conflict of Laws § 6. As a matter of practical application to insurance contracts, however, the "underlying principles or guideposts" of Section 6 are of "secondary importance" to the more specific provisions of Sections 188 and 193. *Zurich Am. Ins. Co. v. Goodwin*, 920 So. 2d 427, 433–34 (Miss. 2006).

Section 193 enunciates the cardinal rule for insurance contracts:

> The validity of a contract of fire, surety or casualty insurance and the rights created thereby are determined by the local law of the state which the parties understood was to be the principal location of the insured risk during the term of the policy, unless with respect to the particular issue, some other state has a more significant relationship... to the transaction and the parties, in which event the local law of the other state will be applied.

Restatement (Second) of Conflict of Laws § 193.

Second Restatement jurisdictions frequently disagree whether a liability policy, applying to injury occurring anywhere in the United States, has a "principal location of the insured risk," and, if so, where that risk is located. Some courts, usually in the context of coverage for environmental contamination, find that each state where a claim arises is the principal location of the insured risk. *Reichhold Chems., Inc. v. Hartford Acc. & Indem. Co.*, 703 A.2d 1132, 1138 (Conn. 1997).[6] Other courts have reasoned that the policyholder's principal place of business, as the place where the policyholder faces the ultimate economic risk, doubles as the principal location of the insured risk. *Babcock & Wilcox Co. v. Arkwright-Boston Mfg. Mut. Ins. Co.*, 867 F. Supp. 573, 580 (N.D. Ohio 1992).

More frequently, courts hold that there is no principal location of the insured risk under a policy covering the insured's liability in any state where a claim may arise. *Compagnie des Bauxites de Guinee v. Argonaut-Midwest Ins. Co.*, 880 F.2d 685, 690 (3d Cir. 1989). Indeed, a comment to Section 193 provides that "the location of the risk has less significance... where the policy covers a group of risks that are scattered throughout two or more states," and that a court should instead look to the considerations that govern choice of law for contracts generally. Restatement (Second) of Conflict of Laws § 193 cmt. b.

Section 188 sets forth these general considerations, which govern in the absence of a principal location of the insured risk, or which in some cases may even outweigh the principal location of the insured risk. These considerations include: "(a) the place of contracting, (b) the place of negotiation of the

---

6. In reviewing a state's choice-of-law precedents, it is important to note whether a given decision involved environmental contamination. Decisions involving environmental contamination may have rested on considerations that do not apply in other contexts. *Fantis Foods, Inc. v. N. River Ins. Co.*, 753 A.2d 176, 178 (N.J. Super. Ct. App. Div. 2000).

contract, (c) the place of performance, (d) the location of the subject matter of the contract, and (e) the domicil, residence, nationality, place of incorporation and place of business of the parties." Restatement (Second) of Conflict of Laws § 188. Because these factors focus on the relationship of the parties to the contract at the time of contracting, they will in most cases point to the state where the policyholder maintained its principal place of business during the policy period.[7]

Whatever approach a court takes to choice of law, a court's analysis frequently leads back to the application of its own law.[8] But, as the Supreme Court of North Dakota observed, applying forum law to protect "North Dakota residents whenever North Dakota has any contacts with a controversy... is the kind of 'chauvinistic parochialism' sought to be avoided by modern choice-of-law analysis." *Plante v. Columbia Paints*, 494 N.W.2d 140, 142 (N.D. 1992) (quoting Robert A. Leflar, *The Nature of Conflicts Law*, 81 COLUM. L. REV. 1080 (1981)).

Sometimes, albeit rarely, a liability policy will contain a clause specifying which state's law governs the interpretation of the policy. The Second Restatement, however, is much less friendly toward choice-of-law clauses than one might anticipate: "Effect will frequently not be given to a choice-of-law provision in a contract of fire, surety, or casualty insurance which designates a state whose local law gives the insured less protection than he would receive under the otherwise applicable law." Restatement (Second) of Conflicts of Law § 193 cmt. e. *See, e.g., Industrial Indem. Ins. Co. v. United States*, 757 F.2d 982 (9th Cir. 1985) (declining to apply Illinois choice-of-law clause to policy having no relationship to Illinois).

It is important to review a state's statutes, not just its case law, to determine applicable law. In California, for instance, a statute has long provided that a "contract is to be interpreted according to the law and usage of the place where it is to be performed; or, if it does not indicate a place of performance, according to the law and usage of the place where it is made." CAL. CIV. CODE § 1646. But only recently did California decisions addressing choice-of-law for liability policies begin to cite that statute or to recognize its effect on the

---

7. *See, e.g., St. Paul Fire & Marine Ins. Co. v. Bldg. Constr. Enters., Inc.*, 526 F.3d 1166, 1168–69 (8th Cir. 2008); *Certain Underwriters at Lloyd's v. Foster Wheeler Corp.*, 822 N.Y.S.2d 30, 35 (Sup. Ct. App. Div. 2006); *Liggett Group, Inc. v. Affiliated FM Ins. Co.*, 788 A.2d 134, 138 (Del. Super. Ct. 2001).

8. *Compare Nat. Union Fire Ins. Co. v. Standard Fusee Corp.*, 917 N.E.2d 170, 179–81 (Ind. Ct. App. 2009) (applying one view of Section 193 to apply Indiana law to coverage for contaminated site in Indiana), *with Am. Employers Ins. Co. v. Coachmen Indus., Inc.*, 838 N.E.2d 1172, 1181 (Ind. Ct. App. 2005) (applying different view of Section 193 to apply Indiana law to coverage for contaminated site in Texas).

analysis.[9] Montana and Oklahoma courts have treated identical statutes as a mere factor in a "most significant relationship" analysis,[10] even though the Second Restatement expressly provides that the multifactor analysis applies only in the absence of a statutory directive on choice of law. Restatement (Second) of Conflicts of Law § 6.

In any choice-of-law regime—statutory, *lex loci contractus*, or Second Restatement—different considerations may apply in disputes that turn on details of the performance of the insurer's contractual obligations, as opposed to whether an obligation exists in the first instance. Distinguishing Mississippi decisions looking to the law of the policyholder's headquarters to interpret the insurance contract, the Fifth Circuit held that Mississippi law governed whether an insurer faced a conflict of interest in controlling the defense of a Louisiana policyholder in a Mississippi tort action: "Mississippi's interest here involves the power of its courts to enforce its conflict of interest rules in litigation in order to protect parties and the judicial process." *Hartford Underwriters Ins. Co. v. Foundation Health Servs, Inc.*, 524 F.3d 588, 599 (5th Cir. 2008). Applying Kansas *lex loci contractus* decisions, the Tenth Circuit held that the law of Missouri, where a lawsuit was pending, governed details of the insurer's defense of its policyholder, but that the law of the policyholder's home state of Kansas governed whether an obligation arose to settle that lawsuit within policy limits. *Moses v. Halstead*, 581 F.3d 1248, 1252–54 (10th Cir. 2009).

The lesson is that whenever a policyholder headquartered in one state is sued or has a claim arise in a different state, there frequently will be room for argument as to which state's law applies to the interpretation of the insurance policy. If the two states have reached differing interpretations of the policy language at the center of the dispute, and if the two states have differing approaches to choice of law, the resulting uncertainty may force the insurer or the policyholder to file suit to determine the controlling law.[11] In the event of coverage litigation, a party advocating the application of another state's law should raise that issue in a timely manner, at the risk of waiving such contention.[12]

---

9. *Compare Frontier Oil Corp. v. RLI Ins. Co.*, 63 Cal. Rptr. 3d 816, 836–37 (Ct. App. 2007), *and Costco Wholesale Corp. v. Liberty Mut. Ins. Co.*, 472 F. Supp. 2d 1183, 1197–98 (S.D. Cal. 2007), *with Downey Venture v. LMI Ins. Co.*, 78 Cal. Rptr. 2d 142, 164 (Ct. App. 1998).

10. *Bohannan v. Allstate Ins. Co.*, 820 P.2d 787, 797 (Okla. 1991) (applying 15 OKLA. STAT. ANN. § 162); *Tucker v. Farmers Ins. Exchange*, 215 P.3d 1, 7–8 (Mont. 2009) (citing cases addressing MONT. CODE ANN. § 28-3-102).

11. *See generally* Steven M. Klepper, *Choice of Law for CGL Insurance Policies: Toward a Uniform Rule*, 45 TORT TRIAL & INS. PRAC. L.J. 31 (2009).

12. *See, e.g., Wood v. Mid-Valley Inc.*, 942 F.2d 425, 426 (7th Cir. 1991).

## 50-State Survey: Choice of Law
## for Coverage Disputes

**Alabama:** "Alabama law follows the traditional conflict-of-law principles of *lex loci contractus*," under which "a contract is governed by the law of the jurisdiction within which the contract is made." *Lifestar Response of Ala., Inc. v. Admiral Ins. Co.*, 17 So. 3d 200, 213 (Ala. 2009). Thus, where the policyholder was a citizen of Georgia at the time of the issuance of the policy, Georgia law controlled even though the policyholder had moved to Alabama by the time of the accident. *Am. Interstate Ins. Co. v. Holliday*, 376 So. 2d 701, 702 (Ala. 1979). Where the parties stipulated that a CGL policy was executed in South Carolina, South Carolina law governed whether the insurer's issuance of a reservation of rights letter gave rise to an enhanced duty of good faith. *Twin City Fire Ins. Co. v. Colonial Life & Acc. Ins. Co.*, 839 So. 2d 614, 616–17 (Ala. 2002).

**Alaska:** The Supreme Court of Alaska applies the contractual choice-of-law provisions of Section 188 of the Second Restatement. *Long v. Holland America Line Westours, Inc.*, 26 P.3d 430, 432–33 (Alaska 2001). Its Second Restatement decisions have not involved insurance contracts. An Alaska District Court applied Alaska law to an E&O policy issued to an Alaska-based real estate broker. *CNA Ins. Co. v. Lightle*, 364 F. Supp. 2d 1068, 1072 (D. Alaska 2005).

**Arizona:** The Supreme Court of Arizona has adopted the Second Restatement, but its decisions have not involved the application of Sections 188 and 193 to CGL policies. It applied the tort choice-of-law principles of Sections 145 and 146 of the Second Restatement to determine the law applicable to a claim for bad-faith denial of no-fault automobile benefits. *Bates v. Superior Court*, 749 P.2d 1367, 1369–72 (Ariz. 1988) (applying law of Arizona, where plaintiff lived at time of denial of benefits, not law of Michigan, where plaintiff lived at time of purchasing policy and of automobile accident). Nonbinding decisions have applied Sections 188 and 193 to CGL policies, with differing results. *Compare Bell v. Great Am. Ins. Co.*, No. 1 CA-CV 07-0445, 2008 WL 3010063 (Ariz. Ct. App. 2008) (applying Arizona law in action addressing coverage under Texas policy for Arizona additional insured who built homes only in Arizona), *with Smith v. Hughes Aircraft Co. Corp.*, 783 F. Supp. 1222, 1228 (D. Ariz. 1991) (applying law of California as policyholder's headquarters and as the location of the greatest part of the risk), *rev'd in part on other grounds*, 22 F.3d 1432, 1436 (9th Cir. 1993) (declining to reach choice-of-law question).

**Arkansas:** "Choice-of-law questions regarding insurance coverage have traditionally been resolved by applying the law of the state where the insurance contract was made." *S. Farm Bur. Cas. Ins. Co. v. Craven*, 89 S.W.3d 369, 372 (Ark. Ct. App. 2002) (citing older *lex loci contractus* decisions and finding that, in any event, result would not change if Second Restatement applied to claim for no-fault automobile benefits). A federal decision held that Wisconsin law governed a CGL policy which was made in Wisconsin with a Wisconsin policyholder, and which had substantial contacts with Wisconsin. *Ferrell v. West Bend Mut. Ins. Co.*, 393 F.3d 786, 794 (8th Cir. 2005) (noting parties agreed as to application of Wisconsin law).

**California:** A California choice-of-law statute provides that a "contract is to be interpreted according to the law and usage of the place where it is to be performed; or, if it does not indicate a place of performance, according to the law and usage of the place where it is made." CAL. CIV. CODE § 1646. Apparently overlooking this statute, a number of decisions from the 1990s applied a Second Restatement § 193 analysis, holding that a "liability insurance policy issued on a nationwide basis may be construed in accordance with the law of the jurisdiction in which a particular claim arises.... Thus, the same policy language may receive different construction and application in different jurisdictions." *Downey Venture v. LMI Ins. Co.*, 78 Cal. Rptr. 2d 142, 164 (Ct. App. 1998). *See Stonewall Surplus Lines Ins. Co. v. Johnson Controls, Inc.*, 17 Cal. Rptr. 2d 713, 719–21 (Ct. App. 1993) (applying law of California, where car battery was manufactured and injured California resident, not law of insured manufacturer's home state of Wisconsin). More recent decisions, however, have held that the California choice-of-law statute controls in contract actions. *Frontier Oil Corp. v. RLI Ins. Co.*, 63 Cal. Rptr. 3d 816, 835 (Ct. App. 2007). An intermediate appellate decision held that, with respect to endorsements to a Texas-made CGL policy specifically covering certain California locations, the policy contemplated California law as the place of performance of the insurer's defense obligation, and that California law controlled over Texas law in determining whether an underlying California pollution lawsuit triggered a defense obligation. *Id.* at 836–37. But a California federal decision, finding that a CGL policy covering multistate risks failed to specify a place of performance, held that Connecticut law controlled coverage for bodily injury sustained in Pennsylvania, where the insurer delivered the policy to the insured's Connecticut-based parent corporation in Connecticut. *Costco Wholesale Corp. v. Liberty Mut. Ins. Co.*, 472 F. Supp. 2d 1183, 1197–98 (S.D. Cal. 2007).

**Colorado:** The Supreme Court of Colorado has adopted the Second Restatement in selecting the law governing contracts, but its decisions have not involved the application of Sections 188 and 193 to CGL policies. *Wood Bros. Homes, Inc. v. Walker Adjustment Bur.*, 601 P.2d 1369, 1372–73 (Colo. 1979) (looking to § 188 and to subsequent sections that "apply to specific types of contracts"); *Ackerman v. Foster*, 974 P.2d 1, 3 (Colo. Ct. App. 1998) (applying § 193 to automobile insurance contract, finding that California law applied, even though purported omnibus insured moved to Colorado). The Colorado Court of Appeals held that, under a homeowner's policy issued to Colorado policyholders with respect to a Colorado home, Colorado law controlled the application of the policy's liability coverage to a Florida lawsuit alleging that the policyholders' son, while a student in Florida, violated Florida privacy laws. *Fire Ins. Exchange v. Bentley*, 953 P.2d 1297, 1300 (Colo. Ct. App. 1998) ("all significant contacts are in Colorado"). In one of the only decisions nationwide ever to find that the law of the insurer's home state controlled an insurance coverage dispute, the Tenth Circuit held that Pennsylvania law controlled the question of whether a Pennsylvania insurer asserting a late-notice defense needed to show prejudice to disclaim coverage for a Missouri lawsuit alleging that a Colorado-based policyholder defectively manufactured a pacemaker. *Telectronics, Inc. v. United Nat. Ins. Co.*, 796 F. Supp. 1382, 1389–90 (D. Colo. 1992), *aff'd sub nom.*, *TPLC, Inc. v. United Nat. Ins. Co.*, 44 F.3d 1484, 1490–91 (10th Cir. 1995). *But see Berry & Murphy, P.C. v. Carolina Cas. Ins. Co.*, 586 F.3d 803 (10th Cir. 2009) (finding that Colorado law applied to construction of legal malpractice policy because the "contract was apparently negotiated and entered into in Colorado and the insured's place of business is in Colorado"); *Nicholls v. Zurich Am. Ins. Group*, 244 F. Supp. 2d 1144, 1152 (D. Colo. 2003) (Colorado law controlled construction of directors' and officers' liability policy issued with respect to Colorado-based corporation, even though the policy was issued by California-based producer to California-based broker).

**Connecticut:** Applying a Second Restatement analysis to CGL policies, the Supreme Court of Connecticut has held that the law of the polluted waste site is presumed to control. *Reichhold Chems., Inc. v. Hartford Acc. & Indem. Co.*, 703 A.2d 1132, 1138 (Conn. 1997) (applying law of Washington as place of contaminated site rather than law of New York as policyholder's headquarters). The application of Connecticut choice-of-law rules outside the environmental context is unsettled. Like most states, Connecticut does not consider the insurer's domicile to be a significant contact. *Interface Flooring Sys., Inc. v. Aetna Cas. & Sur. Co.*, 804 A.2d 201, 207 (Conn. 2002). A Connecticut trial court decision held that New York law governed an insurer's duty to defend a New York policyholder in an antitrust action, and that Connecticut law governed the duty to defend its Connecticut subsidiary; because neither party challenged the point on appeal, the Connecticut Supreme Court affirmed that holding. *QSP, Inc. v. Aetna Cas. & Sur. Co.*, 773 A.2d 906, 912 n. 8 (Conn. 2001).

**Delaware:** The Supreme Court of Delaware has applied the Second Restatement to tort claims, but its decisions have not involved choice of law for contracts. *Turner v. Lipschultz*, 619 A.2d 912, 914 (Del. 1992). The Superior Court of Delaware, addressing coverage for over 1,000 tobacco health-related lawsuits, under in excess of 100 liability insurance policies issued over a 28-year span, applied a Second Restatement analysis to hold that the law of North Carolina controlled. The policyholder maintained its principal place of business in North Carolina for most of the relevant period, and the manufacturing operations and marketing functions giving rise to the alleged liability were centered in North Carolina for the entire period. The fact that many of the policies were negotiated through New York brokers was a relatively insignificant contact that did not require the application of New York law. *Liggett Group, Inc. v. Affiliated FM Ins. Co.*, 788 A.2d 134, 137–44 (Del. Super. Ct. 2001).

**Florida:** The Supreme Court of Florida has "long adhered to the rule of lex loci contractus," which "provides that the law of the jurisdiction where the contract was executed governs the rights and liabilities of the parties in determining an issue of insurance coverage." *State Farm Mut. Auto. Ins. Co. v. Roach*, 945 So. 2d 1160, 1164 (Fla. 2006) (automobile coverage). Florida courts have carved out a narrow exception to the *lex loci* rule, for the purpose of necessary protection of a Florida citizen, or to enforce some paramount rule of public policy. "This has become known as the public policy exception. It requires *both* a Florida citizen in need of protection *and* a paramount Florida public policy." *Roach* at 1165 (emphasis in original); *see also USF&G v. Liberty Surplus Insurance Company*, No. 6:06-cv-1180-Orl-31UAM, 2007 WL 3024345, at *4, n.7 (M.D. Fla. Oct. 15, 2007) ("Although *Roach* was an automobile insurance case, the court did not in any way suggest that its pronouncements were limited to such policies."). The Eleventh Circuit predicted that Florida courts would, with respect to a multiple-risk policy providing liability and other coverage for nightclubs located in multiple states, apply a Second Restatement analysis under which coverage would depend on the law in which each club was located. *Shapiro v. Associated Int'l Ins. Co.*, 899 F.2d 1116, 1119–20 (11th Cir. 1990). No Florida state court has adopted *Shapiro*, and one Florida District Court decision held that *Shapiro* was restricted to the multi-risk policy at issue. *CNL Hotels & Resorts, Inc. v. Houston Cas. Co.*, 505 F. Supp. 2d 1317, 1320–21 (M.D. Fla. 2007) (applying *lex loci contractus* to directors and officers liability policy). In 2008, the Eleventh Circuit certified to the Supreme Court of Florida the question whether *lex loci contractus* applied to a construction defect coverage dispute regarding a commercial general liability policy issued in Massachusetts to a contractor headquartered there, *see U.S. Fid. & Guar. Co. v. Liberty Surplus Ins. Corp.*, 550 F.3d 1031, 1034–35 (11th Cir. 2008), but the parties settled before resolution of that question.

**Georgia:** Georgia courts adhere to the common law rule of *lex loci contractus*, under which the law of the place of the delivery of the insurance contract controls. *O'Neal v. State Farm Mut. Auto. Ins. Co.*, 533 S.E.2d 781, 782 (Ga. Ct. App. 2000). *But cf. Amica Mut. Ins. v. Bourgault*, 429 S.E.2d 908, 911 (Ga. 1993) (citing Second Restatement § 193 in interpreting scope of statute).

**Hawaii:** "Hawaii's choice-of-law approach creates a presumption that Hawaii law applies unless another state's law would best serve the interests of the states and persons involved." *Mikelson v. United Services Auto. Ass'n*, 111 P.3d 601, 607 (Haw. 2005). The Supreme Court of Hawaii held that, under the Second Restatement factors, Hawaii had the most significant interest in coverage for environmental contamination in Hawaii, notwithstanding that

California was the place of contracting and the principal place of business of the insurer and the policyholder. *Del Monte Fresh Produce (Haw.), Inc. v. Fireman's Fund Ins. Co.*, 183 P.3d 734, 740–41 & n.12 (Haw. 2007).

**Idaho:** Idaho applies the "most significant relationship" test of the Second Restatement. *Ryals v. State Farm Mut. Auto. Ins. Co.*, 1 P.3d 803, 805–06 (Idaho 2000) (Idaho law controlled coverage for New York accident under policy issued in Idaho with respect to vehicle principally garaged in Idaho). Idaho courts have not applied this test outside the context of automobile insurance.

**Illinois:** In determining the law governing an insurance policy, the Supreme Court of Illinois looks to "the location of the subject matter, the place of delivery of the contract, the domicile of the insured or of the insurer, the place of the last act to give rise to a valid contract, the place of performance, or other place bearing a rational relationship to the general contract." *Lapham-Hickey Steel Corp. v. Protection Mut. Ins. Co.*, 655 N.E.2d 842, 845 (Ill. 1995). Thus, in a dispute under a liability component of an all-risk policy insuring property in six different states, the law of Illinois, as the policyholder's home state, controlled whether an insurer was obligated to defend a claim for pollution at a Minnesota site. *Id.* Illinois intermediate appellate decisions generally have applied the law of the policyholder's home state in determining the law governing CGL policies. *Westchester Fire Ins. Co. v. G. Heileman Brewing Co., Inc.*, 747 N.E.2d 955, 961–64 (Ill. App. Ct. 2001) (citing Second Restatement § 193); *Maremont Corp. v. Cheshire*, 681 N.E.2d 548, 551 (Ill. App. Ct. 1997) ("Other than being the location of the polluted site, South Carolina had nothing to do with the negotiating, purchasing, delivering or performing of the insurance policies.").

**Indiana:** The Supreme Court of Indiana, applying Section 193 of the Second Restatement, has held that an "insurance policy is governed by the law of the principal location of the insured risk during the term of the policy." *Dunn v. Meridian Mut. Ins. Co.*, 836 N.E.2d 249, 251 (Ind. 2005). The application of that test to CGL policies is unsettled. A number of decisions from the Court of Appeals of Indiana followed a "uniform-contract-interpretation approach," under which the law of a single state governed the construction of a CGL policy. In such cases involving insurance coverage for environmental contamination, Section 193 of the Second Restatement created a rebuttable presumption that the governing law was that of the state where the greatest number of insured sites were located. *Am. Employers Ins. Co. v. Coachmen Indus., Inc.*, 838 N.E.2d 1172, 1181 (Ind. Ct. App. 2005); *Employers Ins. of Wausau v. Recticel Foam Corp.*, 716 N.E.2d 1015, 1025 (Ind. Ct. App. 1999); *Travelers Indem. Co. v. Summit Corp. of Am.*, 715 N.E.2d 926, 933 (Ind. Ct. App. 1999); *Hartford Acc. & Indem. Co. v. Dana Corp.*, 690 N.E.2d 285, 293–94 (Ind. Ct. App. 1997). But in 2009, a panel of the court expressly disagreed with those prior decisions and held, in a coverage dispute regarding a Maryland-based manufacturer's CGL policy, that Indiana law controlled coverage for contamination at an Indiana facility, and that California law controlled coverage for contamination at a California facility. *National Union Fire Ins. Co. v. Standard Fusee Corp.*, 917 N.E.2d 170, 176–81 (Ind. Ct. App. 2009).

**Iowa:** The Supreme Court of Iowa applies Sections 188 and 193 of the Second Restatement to questions of coverage under insurance contracts. *Gabe's Constr. Co., Inc. v. United Capitol Ins. Co.*, 539 N.W.2d 144, 146–47 (Iowa 1995). *Gabe's* rejected the contention that Minnesota law governed an Iowa general contractor's claim for coverage as an additional insured under a Minnesota subcontractor's CGL policy with respect to bodily injury sustained at an Iowa construction site. Because the "general liability coverage applied separately to each insured," and because the general contractor sought coverage under an endorsement issued solely with respect to the Iowa job site, the principal location of the insured risk was Iowa. *Id.* If a party does not sufficiently plead and prove that another state's law controls, an Iowa court will apply Iowa law. *Talen v. Employers Mut. Cas. Co.*, 703 N.W.2d 395, 408–09 (Iowa 2005).

**Kansas:** The Kansas Supreme Court has held, in cases not involving CGL policies, that "Kansas follows the general rule that the law of the state where the insurance contract is made controls." *Safeco Ins. Co. of Am. v. Allen*, 941 P.2d 1365, 1372 (Kan. 1997). Surveying Kansas *lex loci contractus* decisions, the Tenth Circuit recognized that the First Restatement sometimes looks to the law of the place of performance, but "only when the question goes to the manner and method of performance." *Moses v. Halstead*, 581 F.3d 1248, 1252 (10th Cir. 2009). Construing that exception narrowly, the Tenth Circuit held that the law of Missouri, where a lawsuit was pending, governed details of the insurer's defense of its policyholder, but that the law of the policyholder's home state of Kansas governed whether an obligation arose to settle that lawsuit within policy limits. *Id.* at 1252–54.

**Kentucky:** The Supreme Court of Kentucky applies Sections 188 and 193 of the Second Restatement to questions of coverage under insurance contracts. *Lewis v. Am. Family Ins. Group*, 555 S.W.2d 579, 581–82 (Ky. 1977). None of its Second Restatement decisions have involved CGL policies. Applying Kentucky choice-of-law principles to coverage under a construction manager's professional liability policy for defective work on a Kentucky golf course, the Sixth Circuit held that Tennessee law applied because the policy "was issued to Tennessee citizens, was negotiated by a Tennessee citizen with an insurance agent located in Tennessee, and was issued by an insurer authorized to do business in Tennessee." *Security Ins. Co. v. Kevin Tucker & Assocs., Inc.*, 64 F.3d 1001, 1006 (6th Cir. 1995). *See also Cincinnati Ins. Co. v. Crossmann Communities P'ship*, No. 05-470-KSF, 2008 WL 852133 (E.D. Ky. Mar. 28, 2008) (applying same analysis to CGL policy issued to Indiana-based general contractor).

**Louisiana:** Under the Louisiana Civil Code, "an issue of conventional obligations is governed by the law of the state whose policies would be most seriously impaired if its law were not applied to that issue." LA. CIV. CODE ANN. art. 3537. The Court of Appeals of Louisiana held that the law of Belgium, not Louisiana, governed coverage for an asbestosis injury claim involving asbestos products delivered across the United States and Canada. Louisiana was merely "one location among many that could be considered the object of the contract.... A contrary conclusion could subject this policy to 50 different interpretations based on the state in which a plaintiff files suit, thereby destroying any predictability or uniformity of application." *Murden v. ACandS, Inc.*, 921 So. 2d 165, 172 (La. Ct. App. 2005). *See also Norfolk S. Corp. v. Cal. Union Ins. Co.*, 859 So. 2d 167, 181 (La. Ct. App. 2003) (CGL policies "intended to provide indemnity to [policyholder] for liability arising out of the conduct of its business, regardless of the location of the risk").

**Maine:** The Maine Supreme Judicial Court, applying a Second Restatement analysis, held that Maine law governed CGL coverage for a New Hampshire–based contractor doing business in Maine, New Hampshire, and Vermont, with respect to the construction of a school located in Maine. *Baybutt Constr. Corp. v. Commercial Union Ins. Co.*, 455 A.2d 914, 918 (Me. 1983), *rev'd on other grounds*, *Peerless Ins. Co. v. Brennon*, 564 A.2d 383 (Me. 1989). "In no way in the instant case can the mere fact... that the construction company was a New Hampshire corporation and that the insurance contract was issued in New Hampshire be considered of greater significance, whether by reason of state contact or governmental interest, than the location, here in Maine, of the insured risk." *Id. But see Am. Employers' Ins. Co. v. DeLorme Pub. Co., Inc.*, 39 F. Supp. 2d 64, 72 (D. Me. 1999) ("Maine law is applicable because the insured's risk—the business of [the insured]—is located in Maine").

**Maryland:** Although Maryland follows the *lex loci contractus* rule, the Court of Appeals of Maryland, the state's highest court, has recognized the "limited *renvoi*" exception, under which Maryland will apply its own law to an insurance contract made in another state if and only if that other state's choice-of-law rules favor the application of Maryland law. *Am. Motorists Ins. Co. v. ARTRA Group, Inc.*, 659 A.2d 1295, 1304 (Md. 1995). Thus, Maryland law governed CGL coverage for pollution in Maryland where, although the insurance contract was formed in Illinois, the Maryland Court of Appeals determined that an Illinois court would apply the law of Maryland. *Id.* at 1302–03.

**Massachusetts:** Applying the Second Restatement, the Supreme Judicial Court of Massachusetts held that New York law governed coverage for asbestos claims against a New York manufacturer because whether "there is a duty to defend or to indemnify under a nationwide comprehensive general liability policy as to such a claim should not depend on the law of the jurisdiction governing that particular claim but rather should be determined by the law governing the interpretation of the insurance policy and its issuance." *W.R. Grace & Co. v. Hartford Acc. & Indem. Co.*, 555 N.E.2d 214, 221–22 (Mass. 1990). *See also W.R. Grace & Co. v. Md. Cas. Co.*, 600 N.E.2d 176, 179

(Mass. App. Ct. 1992) (applying law of New York, rather than law of Massachusetts, where environmental contamination occurred), *rev. denied*, 604 N.E.2d 35 (Mass. 1992). *But see Stonewall Ins. Co. v. Travelers Cas. & Sur. Co.*, 677 F. Supp. 2d 420, 422 (D. Mass. 2010) (without citing *W.R. Grace* decisions, holding that Texas law governed an insurer's claim for contribution under a policy issued to a Florida-based parent corporation because the subsidiary at issue was based in Texas, the majority of defense costs were incurred in Texas, and a Texas law firm generated over 70 percent of the defense costs).

**Michigan:** The Supreme Court of Michigan applies a Second Restatement analysis to determine the law governing a contract. *Chrysler Corp. v. Skyline Indus. Servs., Inc.*, 528 N.W.2d 698, 703 (Mich. 1995). Intermediate state appellate decisions have applied Section 193 to insurance policies, although the cases have not involved CGL policies. *Farm Bur. Ins. Co. v. Abalos*, 742 N.W.2d 624, 626–27 (Mich. Ct. App. 2007) (law of Michigan, where vehicle was principally garaged, controlled coverage under automobile policy with respect to accident in Ohio). A Michigan District Court, engaging in an extensive choice-of-law analysis, held that the law of a single state governs the construction of an insurance contract under the Second Restatement and, therefore, Michigan law controlled coverage under a Michigan-based corporation's CGL policy for environmental contamination occurring in California. *Aetna Cas. & Sur. Co. v. Dow Chem. Co.*, 883 F. Supp. 1101, 1104–10 (E.D. Mich. 1995). *See also Mill's Pride, Inc. v. Continental Ins. Co.*, 300 F.3d 701, 708–09 (6th Cir. 2002) (law of Ohio, as policyholder's headquarters and place of negotiation of policy, controlled coverage under CGL policy for Michigan trademark action, where settlement with underlying Michigan plaintiff ended any Michigan interest in contract dispute).

**Minnesota:** The choice-of-law regime in Minnesota is unsettled. In a 1973 tort action, the Supreme Court of Minnesota applied a multifaceted choice-of-law analysis that looked to: (1) predictability of results, (2) maintenance of interstate order, (3) advancement of the forum's governmental interests, (4) application of the better rule of law, and (5) simplification of the judicial task. *Milkovich v. Saari*, 203 N.W.2d 408 (Minn. 1973). Yet in 2004, the Supreme Court of Minnesota held that the *Milkovich* "better rule of law" analysis was restricted to cases where "respect for certainty and the parties' expectations" was not important. The court instead applied a Second Restatement analysis to determine the law applicable to the assertion of the physician-patient privilege in a criminal prosecution. *State v. Heaney*, 689 N.W.2d 168, 174–75 (Minn. 2004). One unpublished intermediate appellate decision held that Section 188 of the Second Restatement controlled in a noninsurance contract dispute. *Lerner v. Lerner*, Nos. C2-90-2138, C8-90-2595, 1991 WL 132760 (Minn. Ct. App. July 23, 1991) (prenuptial agreement). Minnesota's unsettled choice-of-law rule has led to divergent results in insurance coverage actions. The Court of Appeals of Minnesota, finding that it "strains credulity to believe that either party to this contract of insurance could have intended" that "the law of each state where [the policyholder's] properties are located could potentially control," held that the law of either the policyholder's home state of Minnesota or of the insurer's home state of Illinois, not the law of Georgia, as the site of environmental contamination, controlled the interpretation of an "owned property" exclusion in an environmental impairment liability policy. *Cargill, Inc. v. Evanston Ins. Co.*, 642 N.W.2d 80, 89–90 (Minn. Ct. App. 2002) (proceeding to find no conflict between Minnesota and Illinois law). But an earlier decision of the same court, focusing on the "simplification of the judicial task" prong of *Milkovich*, held that Minnesota law governed coverage for asbestos-related property damage under CGL policies issued to a New York asbestos manufacturer doing business nationwide. *Board of Regents of Univ. of Minn. v. Royal Ins. Co. of Am.*, 503 N.W.2d 486, 490–91 (Minn. Ct. App. 1993), *rev'd in part on other grounds*, 517 N.W.2d 888 (Minn. 1994) (not addressing choice of law). *See also Am. States Ins. Co. v. Mankato Iron & Metal, Inc.*, 848 F. Supp. 1436, 1443 (D. Minn. 1993) (applying law of Minnesota, noting regulatory interest in coverage under Minnesota policyholder's CGL policy for environmental contamination occurring in Nebraska and Illinois).

**Mississippi:** Although a statute provides that "[a]ll contracts of insurance on property, lives, or interests in this state shall be deemed to be made therein," MISS. CODE ANN. § 83-5-7, modern Mississippi choice-of-law decisions do not cite this statute. The Supreme Court of Mississippi has held that Sections 188 and 193 of the Second Restatement determine the law governing the construction of an insurance contract, with Section 188 assuming greater importance outside the context of coverage for "immovables and chattel whose location [is] geographically localized." *Zurich Am. Ins. Co. v. Goodwin*, 920 So. 2d 427, 434 (Miss. 2006). Thus, Iowa law governed coverage for an accident in Mississippi under a commercial automobile policy issued to an Iowa-based policyholder with respect to a fleet of trucks mostly garaged in Iowa. *Id.* at 436–37 ("The public policy, of adequate compensation to injured [Mississippi] motorists is not strong enough to override the contracting parties' expectations of which state's substantive law will apply."). A Mississippi District Court held that the law of Texas, as the location of the policyholder's headquarters and of thirteen of its plants, or the law of Iowa, as the state of contracting and the location of four covered plants, controlled CGL coverage for environmental contamination at the single covered plant in Mississippi, even though Mississippi was also the policyholder's state of incorporation. *Employers Mut. Cas. Co. v. Lennox Int'l, Inc.*, 375 F. Supp. 2d 500, 508–09 (S.D. Miss. 2005). *Cf. Hartford Underwriters Ins. Co. v. Foundation Health Servs, Inc.*, 524 F.3d 588, 599 (5th Cir. 2008) (distinguishing decisions involving interpretation of insurance contract, finding that Mississippi had primary interest in whether insurer faced a conflict of interest in controlling the defense of a Louisiana policyholder in Mississippi tort action).

**Missouri:** The Supreme Court of Missouri held that Pennsylvania was the principal location of the insured risk under Section 193 of the Second Restatement, and that Pennsylvania law therefore governed coverage for asbestos claims, where Pennsylvania was the place of the policyholder's incorporation, of its insurance department, of its brokers, and of the delivery of the policies. *Viacom, Inc. v. Transit Cas. Co.*, 138 S.W.3d 723, 725 (Mo. banc 2004). The Eighth Circuit held that, in a lawsuit against a Missouri contractor for defective work in Kansas, Missouri law controlled. It rejected the contention that an endorsement creating separate limits of liability for each project was the equivalent of creating a separate Kansas-specific policy controlled by Kansas law. *St. Paul Fire & Marine Ins. Co. v. Bldg. Constr. Enters., Inc.*, 526 F.3d 1166, 1168–69 (8th Cir. 2008).

**Montana:** A Montana statute provides that a "contract is to be interpreted according to the law and usage of the place where it is to be performed or, if it does not indicate a place of performance, according to the law and usage of the place where it is made." MONT. CODE ANN. § 28-3-102. Nevertheless, the Supreme Court of Montana has adopted the Second Restatement analysis to determine the applicable state law in determining a choice-of-law conflict in contract disputes. *Tucker v. Farmers Ins. Exchange*, 215 P.3d 1, 7 (Mont. 2009) (automobile insurance). Montana courts have not applied this test outside the context of automobile insurance.

**Nebraska:** The Supreme Court of Nebraska applies Sections 188 and 193 of the Second Restatement to questions of coverage under insurance contracts. *Johnson v. U.S. Fid. & Guar. Co.*, 696 N.W.2d 431, 441–42 (Neb. 2005). None of its Second Restatement decisions have involved CGL policies. A Nebraska District Court held that, under a policy issued to an Illinois parent corporation, Nebraska law controlled coverage for a Nebraska-based subsidiary (also a named insured) held liable for a polluted site in Nebraska: "Nebraska has the most significant interest in determining who will pay for the cleanup of a contaminated site within the state's borders." *Lindsay Mfg. Co. v. Hartford Acc. & Indem. Co.*, 911 F. Supp. 1249, 1254 (D. Neb. 1995), *rev'd on other grounds*, 118 F.3d 1263, 1265 (8th Cir. 1997) (agreeing that Nebraska law controlled).

**Nevada:** The Supreme Court of Nevada applies Sections 188 and 193 of the Second Restatement to questions of coverage under insurance contracts. *Sotirakis v. United Serv. Auto. Ass'n*, 787 P.2d 788, 790–91 (Nev. 1990). None of its Second Restatement decisions have involved CGL policies. A Nevada District Court decision held that, notwithstanding a provision that the policies conformed to Illinois law, Nevada law governed the construction of healthcare liability policies issued to a Nevada rest home through a Nevada broker and covering risks located only in Nevada. *Prime Ins. Syndicate, Inc. v. Damaso*, 471 F. Supp. 2d 1087, 1094–95 (D. Nev. 2007). Two other Nevada District Court decisions have held that, in the context of environmental contamination within the state, Nevada had the most significant interest in the availability of insurance for remedial measures. *Mont. Refining Co. v. Nat. Union Fire Ins. Co.*, 918 F. Supp. 1395, 1397 (D. Nev. 1996); *Pioneer Chlor Alkali Co., Inc. v. Nat. Union Fire Ins. Co.*, 863 F. Supp. 1237, 1241 (D. Nev. 1994) (applying Texas choice-of-law rules after transfer from Southern District of Texas).

**New Hampshire:** The Supreme Court of New Hampshire applies Sections 188 and 193 of the Second Restatement to questions of coverage under insurance contracts. *Cecere v. Aetna Ins. Co.*, 766 A.2d 696, 698–700 (N.H. 2001). Applying these principles to a CGL policy issued to a Massachusetts-based company that sold and maintained forklifts, the Supreme Court of New Hampshire held that Massachusetts law governed coverage for a forklift accident occurring in New Hampshire. Massachusetts was the principal location of the insured risk because the CGL policy "was intended to insure [the policyholder], rather than its customers, from liability." *Marston v. U.S. Fid. & Guar. Co.*, 609 A.2d 745, 748 (N.H. 1992). A New Hampshire District Court applied the same analysis to CGL coverage for contamination from a manufacturing facility in New Hampshire, finding that the law of the policyholder's home state of Massachusetts controlled. *See also K.J. Quinn & Co., Inc. v. Continental Cas.*, 806 F. Supp. 1037, 1041 (D.N.H. 1992) ("The fact that one of [the policyholder's] facilities was located in New Hampshire does not dictate the application of New Hampshire law to this policy any more than would be the case with the law of Missouri or the several provinces of Canada where other [of its] facilities are located.").

**New Jersey:** The Supreme Court of New Jersey applies Sections 188 and 193 of the Second Restatement to determine the law governing a CGL policy. A trio of 1998 decisions from New Jersey's top court, expressing a preference for applying the law most favorable to coverage for environmental contamination, rejected the notion that the law of a single state controls the construction of a CGL policy. *Pfizer, Inc. v. Employers Ins. of Wausau*, 712 A.2d 634, 642–43 (N.J. 1998) (law of policyholder's home state of New York controlled, except that, in event of demonstrated conflict with law of any of nineteen states where contamination occurred, law of site controlled coverage for that site); *HM Holdings, Inc. v. Aetna Cas. & Sur. Co.*, 712 A.2d 645, 649 (N.J. 1998) (where, although policies had no connection to New Jersey at time of contracting, policyholder subsequently moved from New York to New Jersey, "New Jersey law or the law of the waste sites should govern the late-notice issues," but if "the law of the waste sites is similar to New York's, it should yield to New Jersey's unless the insurance companies are domestic companies of the waste sites"); *Unisys Corp. v. Ins. Co. of N. Am.*, 712 A.2d 649, 652–53 (N.J. 1998) (construing CGL policies issued to New York policyholder, holding that "in the case of New Jersey sites, New Jersey law should govern; in the case of the other sites, the law of the waste sites should govern if it differs from New Jersey's"). Subsequent intermediate appellate authority indicates that the Second Restatement analysis applies differently outside the context of coverage for environmental contamination, but that analysis remains malleable and unpredictable. *Fantis Foods, Inc. v. N. River Ins. Co.*, 753 A.2d 176, 178 (N.J. Super. Ct. App. Div. 2000) (under New Jersey policyholder's general liability policy issued with respect to buildings located in several states, law of New York controlled coverage for imminent collapse of particular building in New York).

**New Mexico:** The Supreme Court of New Mexico has generally adhered to the *lex loci contractus* rule, applying the law of the state of contracting in insurance disputes, but it has applied a Second Restatement "most significant relationship" test in certain cases that require a flexible approach. *Ferrell v. Allstate Ins. Co.*, 188 P.3d 1156, 1173 & n.3 (N.M. 2008) ("We conclude that the Restatement (Second) is a more appropriate approach for multi-state contract class actions."). New Mexico courts further deviate from *lex loci contractus* where the law of the state of contracting contravenes New Mexico public policy. *State Farm Mut. Auto. Ins. Co. v. Ballard*, 54 P.3d 537, 542 (N.M. 2002) ("step down" provision of automobile policy void as against New Mexico public policy). *See also Valencia v. Colo. Cas. Ins. Co.*, 560 F. Supp. 2d 1080, 1085–86 (D.N.M. 2007) (applying Colorado law to Colorado policy because insured had not "advanced a public policy ground sufficient to overcome the general rule" of *lex loci contractus*). The decisions addressing departures from *lex loci contractus* have not involved CGL policies.

**New York:** The Court of Appeals of New York, the state's highest court, applies Sections 188 and 193 of the Second Restatement to CGL policies, but it has declined to "shape an abstract rule of general applicability concerning the location of the risk in general liability contracts where the insured party conducts business in many States." *Zurich Ins. Co. v. Shearson Lehman Hutton, Inc.*, 642 N.E.2d 1065, 1068–69 (N.Y. 1994). As a matter of practical application, however, New York intermediate appellate courts have held that "where it is necessary to determine the law governing a liability insurance policy covering risks in multiple states, the state of the insured's domicile should be regarded as a proxy for the principal location of the insured risk. As such, the state of domicile is the source of applicable law." *Certain Underwriters at Lloyd's v. Foster Wheeler Corp.*, 822 N.Y.S.2d 30, 35 (Sup. Ct. App. Div. 2006) (in dispute regarding coverage for asbestos liabilities in multiple states, New Jersey law governed New Jersey–based policyholder's CGL policies, which were negotiated in New York). *See also Liberty Surplus Ins. Corp. v. Nat. Union Fire Ins. Co.*, 888 N.Y.S.2d 35, 36 (Sup. Ct. App. Div. 2009) (law of Connecticut governed as state of policyholder's principal place of business). New York federal courts have applied a similar analysis. *Fed. Ins. Co. v. Am. Home Assur. Co.*, 664 F. Supp. 2d 397, 404–05 (S.D.N.Y. 2009) (Florida law governed CGL policies where Florida-based parent was named insured); *Md. Cas. Co. v. Continental Cas. Co.*, 332 F.3d 145, 153–55 (2d Cir. 2003) (law of policyholder's home state of New York controlled CGL coverage for environmental contamination in multiple states).

**North Carolina:** North Carolina courts adhere to the common law doctrine of *lex loci contractus*, which "mandates that the substantive law of the state where the last act to make a binding contract occurred, usually delivery of the policy, controls the interpretation of the contract." *Huber Engineered Woods, LLC v. Canal Ins. Co.*, 690 S.E.2d 739, 743 (N.C. Ct. App. 2010) (quoting *Fortune Ins. Co. v. Owens*, 526 S.E.2d 463, 465–66 (N.C. 2000)). Nevertheless, pursuant to N.C. Gen. Stat. § 58-3-1, which provides that "[a]ll contracts of insurance on property, lives, or interests in this State shall be deemed to be made therein... and are subject to the laws thereof," North Carolina law may control "where a close connection exists between [North Carolina] and the interests insured by an insurance policy." *Fortune*, 526 S.E.2d at 466 (Florida law controlled automobile policy issued to cover vehicle principally garaged in Florida at time of contracting, even though policyholder had temporary address in North Carolina at the time of North Carolina accident, because mere presence in state insufficient to trigger statute) (citing *Collins & Aikman Corp. v. Hartford Acc. & Indem. Co.*, 436 S.E.2d 243 (N.C. 1993) (applying North Carolina law to policy made in California because vast majority of insured fleet of trucks were principally garaged in North Carolina)). *See also NAS Sur. Group v. Precision Wood Prods., Inc.*, 271 F. Supp. 2d 776, 780 (M.D.N.C. 2003) ("The North Carolina courts have explicitly held that where the fortuity of an accident within the state is the only connection to the state, that is not sufficient to make North Carolina's law applicable.").

**North Dakota:** North Dakota applies the "significant contacts approach... in cases with 'multi-state factual contacts.'" *Schleuter v. N. Plains Ins. Co.*, 772 N.W.2d 879, 885 (N.D. 2009) (quoting *Plante v. Columbia Paints*, 494 N.W.2d 140, 142 (N.D. 1992)). In an action addressing coverage for an explosion in North Dakota allegedly caused by defective paint, Washington law controlled the construction of a CGL policy issued to the Washington-based policyholder to cover its retail and manufacturing functions in five states. The parties were "more likely to have thought that the coverage provided would be determined in accordance with the law of Washington, where the contract was negotiated, the policy was delivered, and the premiums were paid, than in accordance with the law of any other state." *Plante*, 494 N.W.2d at 143. "The most compelling North Dakota contact here is that the injured parties are North Dakota residents. Protecting North Dakota residents whenever North Dakota has any contacts with a controversy, however, is the kind of 'chauvinistic parochialism'... sought to be avoided by modern choice-of-law analysis." *Id.* (quoting Robert A. Leflar, *The Nature of Conflicts Law*, 81 COLUM. L. REV. 1080 (1981)).

**Ohio:** The Supreme Court of Ohio applies Sections 188 and 193 of the Second Restatement to determine the law governing an insurance contract. *Ohayon v. Safeco Ins. Co.*, 747 N.E.2d 206, 211 (Ohio 2001) (automobile policy). Ohio intermediate appellate decisions have reached divergent results in applying the Second Restatement analysis to CGL policies. *Compare Gen. Acc. Ins. Co. v. Ins. Co. of N. Am.*, 590 N.E.2d 33, 36–37 (Ohio Ct. App. 1990) (law of Ohio, as headquarters of policyholder and additional insureds, governed coverage for defective coke battery installed at plant in Maryland), *and Nationwide Ins. Co. v. Phelps*, 2003-Ohio-497, 2003 WL 220418, at *3 (Ct. App. Jan. 31, 2003) (law of West Virginia, where insured homebuilder was located and performed most work, governed coverage for claim arising out of a house built in Ohio), *with Morton Int'l, Inc. v. Aetna Cas. & Sur. Co.*, 666 N.E.2d 1163, 1167–68 (Ohio Ct. App. 1995) (applying law of Washington, as location of polluted site, rather than law of Pennsylvania, as state of contracting and policyholder's headquarters). Ohio federal decisions have reached similarly divergent results. *Compare Babcock & Wilcox Co. v. Arkwright-Boston Mfg. Mut. Ins. Co.*, 867 F. Supp. 573, 580 (N.D. Ohio 1992) ("the principal location of the insured risk... is the principal location of that insured's assets"), *with Int'l Ins. Co. v. Stonewall Ins. Co.*, 863 F. Supp. 599 (S.D. Ohio 1994) (insured risk "was the possibility of adverse tort judgments against [the policyholder], a risk that necessarily depends upon the law of the state that governs the tort claim"), *aff'd*, 86 F.3d 601, 606 (6th Cir. 1996).

**Oklahoma:** An Oklahoma statute adopts the *lex loci contractus* rule, providing that "[a] contract is to be interpreted according to the law and usage of the place where it is to be performed, or, if it does not indicate a place of performance, according to the law and usage of the place where it is made." 15 OKLA. STAT. § 162. The Supreme Court of Oklahoma has "carved an exception to application of the *lex loci contractus* rule for choice-of-law questions in motor vehicle insurance cases that deal with conflicting state laws." *Bernal v. Charter County Mut. Ins. Co.*, 209 P.3d 309, 315 & n.25 (Okla. 2009) (citing *Bohannan v. Allstate Ins. Co.*, 820 P.2d 787, 795–97 (Okla. 1991)). "In those instances, the traditional *lex loci contractus* rule governs the validity, interpretation, application and effect of the motor vehicle insurance contracts **except** where (1) the provisions would violate Oklahoma public policy or (2) the facts demonstrate another jurisdiction has the most significant relationship to the subject matter and the parties." *Id.* at 315–16 (emphasis in original). This hybrid First Restatement/Second Restatement approach appears to be limited by its terms to automobile insurance. The *lex loci contractus* rule appears to continue to apply to CGL policies. *Bituminous Cas. Corp. v. St. Clair Lime Co.*, 69 F.3d 547 (Table), 1995 WL 632292 (10th Cir. Oct. 27, 1995).

**Oregon:** The Supreme Court of Oregon applies a Second Restatement analysis to determine the law governing an insurance contract. *Davis v. State Farm Mut. Auto. Ins. Co.*, 507 P.2d 9 (Or. 1973) (Michigan law governed automobile policy that "was entered into in Michigan under the authority of a Michigan statute and was issued to Michigan residents," as "place of plaintiff's injury [in Oregon] was fortuitous"). An Oregon intermediate appellate decision, finding that "Oregon has a substantial interest in the regulation of insurance contracts and in determining the rights and liabilities of the parties who enter into those contracts in Oregon," applied Oregon law to CGL coverage for contamination in California and Oregon by an Oregon-based operator of wood treatment plants. *St. Paul Fire & Marine Ins. Co., Inc. v. McCormick & Baxter Creosoting Co.*, 870 P.2d 260, 263–64 (Or. Ct. App. 1994). *See also Industrial Indem. Co. v. Pac. Maritime Ass'n*, 777 P.2d 1385, 1387 n.2 (Or. Ct. App. 1989) ("Because [the policyholder] transacts business in three states, the parties would face the anomaly of three potential varying interpretations of their [CGL policy], if the law of the forum were applied.").

**Pennsylvania:** Pennsylvania courts apply a Second Restatement analysis, and the few decisions actually applying that test generally support an analysis under which the controlling law typically will be that of where the policyholder maintained its headquarters during the policy period. *Hammersmith v. TIG*, 480 F.3d 220 (3d Cir. 2007); *Chemetron Investments, Inc. v. Fid. & Cas. Co.*, 886 F. Supp. 1194 (W.D. Pa. 1994); *Gould Inc. v. Continental Cas. Co.*, 822 F. Supp. 1172, 1176 (E.D. Pa. 1993). There is, however, a paucity of state-court authority. Indeed, notwithstanding the Third Circuit's recent reminder that Pennsylvania has in fact adopted the Second Restatement, other federal decisions inaccurately state that Pennsylvania follows the common law rule of *lex loci contractus*, under which the governing law is that of the state where the contract was made. *Compare Hammersmith*, 480 F.3d at 228–29 & n.4, *with Century Indem. Co. v. Certain Underwriters at Lloyd's*, 584 F.3d 514, 533 (3d Cir. 2009).

**Rhode Island:** The Supreme Court of Rhode Island has adopted the Second Restatement "most significant relationship" analysis, at least in tort actions. *Busby v. Perini Corp.*, 290 A.2d 210, 211–12 (R.I. 1972). It has yet to apply Sections 188 or 193, but it appears likely that these principles control in contract actions. *See DeFontes v. Dell, Inc.*, 984 A.2d 1061, 1066–67 (R.I. 2009) (citing Second Restatement § 187(2)(a) regarding enforceability of contractual choice-of-law clause); *General Acc. Ins. Co. of Am. v. Budget Rent a Car Sys., Inc.*, No. 94-5616, 1999 WL 615737, at *2 (R.I. Super. Ct. Aug. 2, 1999) (applying § 193). Applying this "interest weighing" approach, a Rhode Island District Court held, in a dispute regarding allegedly defective work in Rhode Island, that Massachusetts law governed a CGL policy issued in Massachusetts to a Massachusetts-based contractor. *Hartford Cas. Ins. Co. v. A & M Assocs., Ltd.*, 200 F. Supp. 2d 84, 87 (D.R.I. 2002).

**South Carolina:** "Section 38-61-10 of the South Carolina Code provides that '[a]ll contracts of insurance on property, lives, or interests in this state are considered to be made in the state… and are subject to the laws of this state.'" *Sangamo Weston, Inc. v. National Sur. Corp.*, 414 S.E.2d 127, 130 (S.C. 1992). The Supreme Court of South Carolina held that, under this statute, South Carolina law controlled CGL coverage for contamination at a site in South Carolina, even though the policy was made outside the state and covered the policyholder's risk of liability at locations through the country. *Id.* In cases not controlled by the statute, South Carolina courts look to the law of the state where the policy was delivered to the policyholder. *Companion Prop. & Cas. Ins. Co. v. Airborne Exp., Inc.*, 631 S.E.2d 915, 916 (S.C. Ct. App. 2006) (Georgia law controlled CGL policy delivered to Georgia corporation in Georgia).

**South Dakota:** A statute provides that a "contract is to be interpreted according to the law and usage of the place where it is to be performed or, if it does not indicate a place of performance, according to the law and usage of the place where it is made." S.D.C.L. § 53-1-4. The Supreme Court of South Dakota has held that, in an action to determine coverage under an insurance policy that does not specify a place of performance, the controlling law is that of the state of delivery of the policy, which is the last act necessary to complete the contract. *Great W. Cas. Co. v. Hovaldt*, 603 N.W.2d 198, 201 (S.D. 1999) (automobile policy). *See also St. Paul Reinsurance Co., Ltd. v. Baldwin*, 503 F. Supp. 2d 1255, 1261 (D.S.D. 2007) (South Dakota law controlled CGL policy delivered to South Dakota broker for South Dakota policyholder).

**Tennessee:** "In Tennessee, absent a valid choice of law provision, the rights and obligations under an insurance policy are governed by the law of the state where the insurance policy was 'made and delivered.'" *Charles Hampton's A-1 Signs, Inc. v. Am. States Ins. Co.*, 225 S.W.3d 482, 485 n.1 (Tenn. Ct. App. 2006) (quoting *Ohio Cas. Ins. Co. v. Travelers Indem. Co.*, 493 S.W.2d 465, 467 (Tenn. 1973)). Thus, Missouri law controlled coverage under a Missouri subcontractor's CGL policy for defective welding on sign poles at restaurants located in multiple states. A Tennessee statute modifies this *lex loci contractus* rule, providing that "[e]very policy of insurance, issued to or for the benefit of any citizen or resident of this state... shall be held as made in this state and construed solely according to the laws of this state." TENN. CODE § 56-7-102.

**Texas:** Although a Texas statute provides that "[a]ny contract of insurance payable to any citizen or inhabitant of this State by any insurance company or corporation doing business within this State shall be held to be a contract made and entered into under and by virtue of the laws of this State relating to insurance, and governed thereby," TEX. INS. CODE ART. 21.42, Texas courts apply that statute only to insurance policies delivered in Texas to Texas citizens in the course of insurers' Texas business. *Austin Bldg. Co. v. Nat. Union Fire Ins. Co.*, 432 S.W.2d 697, 701 (Tex. 1968) (applying Kansas law to policy negotiated in Kansas to cover Kansas property, even though insured was a Texas resident); *Scottsdale Ins. Co. v. National Emergency Servs., Inc.*, 175 S.W.3d 284, 292–93 (Tex. Ct. App. 2004) (statute inapplicable to medical liability policy where named insured not a Texas resident, even though Texas subsidiaries and physicians were insureds); *Reddy Ice Corp. v. Travelers Lloyds Ins. Co.*, 145 S.W.3d 337, 341 (Tex. Ct. App. 2004) (statute applied to CGL policy only if policyholder incorporated in Texas, even if principal place of business in Texas). *But see Am. Home Assur. Co. v. Safway Steel Prods. Co., Inc.*, 743 S.W.2d 693, 697 (Tex. Ct. App. 1987) (umbrella liability policy became payable to Texas citizens under Art. 21.42 upon entry of judgment against out-of-state policyholders). In cases where no statute controls, the Supreme Court of Texas employs a Second Restatement analysis to determine the law governing a contract. *Sonat Exploration Co. v. Cudd Pressure Control, Inc.*, 271 S.W.3d 228, 231 (Tex. 2008). Texas courts applying the Second Restatement to CGL policies generally have found that the governing law is that of the state where the policyholder maintained its principal place of business during the policy period, even if the injury occurred in a different state. *Reddy Ice*, 145 S.W.3d at 345–46 (under §§ 188 and 193, Texas law controlled CGL policy issued to policyholder headquartered in Texas and doing business mostly in Texas, even though dispute involved coverage for pollution at Louisiana site); *Pennzoil-Quaker State Co. v. Am. Int'l Specialty Lines Ins. Co.*, 653 F. Supp. 2d 690, 702–03 (S.D. Tex. 2009) (applying Texas law to pollution legal liability policy covering Texas policyholder as to sites in sixteen states, even though coverage dispute involved only Louisiana sites).

**Utah:** The Supreme Court of Utah applies Sections 188 and 193 of the Second Restatement to questions of coverage under insurance contracts. *Am. Nat. Fire Ins. Co. v. Farmers Ins. Exchange*, 927 P.2d 186, 188–92 (Utah 1996). Although Utah state courts have yet to apply these principles to CGL policies, *American National*, which involved an automobile policy, provides a strong indication that the law of a single state would control such a case: "To protect justified expectation and predictability of result as intended by Restatement of Conflict section 6, we must hold that the parties to an automobile insurance contract cannot change their bargain or have the bargain changed for them every time they drive across a state line." *Id.* at 192. Some pre–*American National* decisions from Utah federal courts applied the law of Utah to CGL coverage for injury occurring in Utah. *See Anaconda Minerals Co. v. Stoller Chem. Co., Inc.*, 773 F. Supp. 1498, 1504 n.8 (D. Utah 1991) (finding that Second Restatement factors favored application of law of Utah, as location of polluted site, in CGL coverage dispute where parties did not brief choice of law); *Mountain Fuel Supply v. Reliance Ins. Co.*, 933 F.2d 882, 888 (10th Cir. 1991) (choosing between state of injury and state of negotiation of policies, as neither party looked to state of policyholder's headquarters). *See also Rupp v. Transcontinental Ins. Co.*, 627 F. Supp. 2d 1304, 1314–16 (D. Utah 2008) (applying tort choice-of-law principles of Second Restatement § 145 to find that Utah law governed claim for bad-faith failure to settle Utah lawsuit).

**Vermont:** The Supreme Court of Vermont applies the contractual choice-of-law provisions of Second Restatement § 188. *Pioneer Credit Corp. v. Carden*, 245 A.2d 891, 894 (Vt. 1968). Its Second Restatement decisions have not involved insurance contracts. Vermont federal decisions have applied conflicting Second Restatement analyses to CGL policies. One decision held that the law of Vermont—as the policyholder's headquarters, the place where the policies where negotiated and delivered, and the place where the policyholder did most of its business—governed coverage under CGL policies for pollu-tion in Missouri. *Village of Morrisville Water & Light Dept. v. U.S. Fid. & Guar. Co.*, 775 F. Supp. 718, 723 (D. Vt. 1991). But a second decision expressly declined to follow *Village of Morrisville*, which it interpreted as applying a *lex loci contractus* approach: "While the traditional rule of 'lex loci contractus' may better apply to cases involving multiple sites, judicial economy and pre-dictability dictate that in single site cases courts apply the law of the state where the site is located." *E.B. & A.C. Whiting Co. v. Hartford Fire Ins. Co.*, 838 F. Supp. 863, 865–66 (D. Vt. 1993), *disapproved on other grounds, Maska U.S., Inc. v. Kansa Gen. Ins. Co.*, 198 F.3d 74 (2d Cir. 1999). Although "the insurance policies were all negotiated, executed and paid for in states other than Vermont," Vermont, "as the state in which the toxic waste site is located... has the strongest interest in how the policies are interpreted because resolution of insurance issues impacts directly on Vermont environmental policies." *Id.* at 866. *Cf. City of Burlington v. Hartford Steam Boiler Inspection & Ins. Co.*, 190 F. Supp. 2d 663, 678 (D. Vt. 2002) (applying *E.B. & A.C. Whiting* site-specific approach to property policy).

**Virginia:** Virginia adheres to the common law rule of *lex loci contractus*, under which an insurance policy is "governed by the law of the place where made." *Lexie v. State Farm Mut. Auto. Ins. Co.*, 469 S.E.2d 61, 63 (Va. 1996). *See CACI Int'l, Inc. v. St. Paul Fire & Marine Ins. Co.*, 566 F.3d 150 (4th Cir. 2009) (applying Virginia law to CGL policies delivered in Virginia to govern-ment contractor accused of torture and abuse at prison in Iraq). "Under Virginia law, a contract is made when the last act to complete it is performed, and in the context of an insurance policy, the last act is the delivery of the policy to the insured." *Resource Bankshares Corp. v. St. Paul Mercury Ins. Co.*, 407 F.3d 631, 635–36 (4th Cir. 2005).

**Washington:** "Since 1967, Washington courts have adhered to and applied the most significant relationship test to contract choice of law issues." *Mulcahy v. Farmers Ins. Co.*, 95 P.3d 313, 317 (Wash. 2004) (applying Second Restatement § 188). The Supreme Court of Washington has held that, for a CGL policy covering potential risk in multiple states, with the location of the risk therefore unidentifiable at the time of contracting, the "principal location of the insured risk" principle of Section 193 of the Second Restatement is inapplicable. *Fluke Corp. v. Hartford Acc. & Indem. Co.*, 34 P.3d 809, 815–16 (Wash. 2001). Thus, Washington law controlled coverage under a Washington-based policyholder's CGL policy with respect to a malicious prosecution action filed in California. *Id. See also N. Ins. Co. v. Allied Mut. Ins. Co.*, 955 F.2d 1353 (9th Cir. 1992) (applying same analysis to conclude that California law controlled question of whether insurer needed to pay for independent *Cumis* counsel for California-based policyholder in lawsuit in Washington).

**West Virginia:** The Supreme Court of Appeals of West Virginia has adopted a hybrid of *lex loci contractus* and the Second Restatement—the law of the state of the formation of the insurance contract governs, unless another state has a more significant relationship to the transaction and the parties, or the law of the other state is contrary to West Virginia public policy. *Liberty Mut. Ins. Co. v. Triangle Indus., Inc.*, 390 S.E.2d 562, 566–67 (W. Va. 1990). Thus, New Jersey law governed coverage for a New Jersey corporation, which owned plants in multiple states, for a suit alleging that waste transported from its West Virginia plant contaminated a landfill in Ohio. The court reasoned that "it is infinitely more practicable to permit one policy to cover the numerous contracts rather than to require both [the policyholder] and the insurance companies to negotiate individual policies based upon each state where an insured risk is located." *Id. See also APAC-Atl., Inc. v. Protection Servs., Inc.*, 397 F. Supp. 2d 792, 796–97 (N.D. W. Va. 2005) (in CGL coverage action arising out of motorist's death at highway construction site in West Virginia, law of Pennsylvania, as state where policy was issued to subcontractor, controlled whether general contractor was entitled to defense as additional insured).

**Wisconsin:** Wisconsin courts apply a "grouping-of-contacts" analysis that follows Sections 188 and 193 of the Second Restatement. *Utica Mut. Ins. Co. v. Klein & Son, Inc.*, 460 N.W.2d 763, 767 (Wis. Ct. App. 1990). Thus, Wisconsin law controlled coverage under a Wisconsin insurance broker's errors and omissions policy with respect to a lawsuit filed in Minnesota because the insured risk had its principal location at the insured's offices. *Id.* "The place of the accident is irrelevant in deciding which law governs a contract, including an insurance agreement." *Lampe v. Genuine Parts Co.*, 463 F. Supp. 2d 928, 935 (E.D. Wis. 2006).

**Wyoming:** Wyoming has close to no authority on choice-of-law for insurance policies, and none for liability policies. Wyoming apparently applies a Second Restatement analysis. *Resource Tech. Corp. v. Fisher Scientific Co.*, 924 P.2d 972, 975 (Wyo. 1996). *See also Cal. Cas. & Fire Ins. Co. v. Brinkman*, 50 F. Supp. 2d 1157, 1166 (D. Wyo. 1999) (applying Wyoming law to automobile liability policy issued with respect to a vehicle principally garaged in Wyoming and involved in an accident in Colorado).

policyholder/tortfeasor is stripped of otherwise applicable insurance for failing to give prompt notice, the injured victim suffers as much or more than the policyholder, perhaps leading to increased victim claims for public health or welfare benefits.

Against these arguments, insurer counsel defending the traditional rule point out that the insurance policy is often characterized as a unilateral or reverse-unilateral contract in which the policyholder performs first by paying the premium but the insurer is only required to perform if established conditions precedent take place. The typical insurance policy lists prompt notice as a condition that must occur before the promise is activated. Therefore, according to the traditional argument, late notice fails to satisfy an essential condition precedent to coverage and excuses the insurer from the contract regardless of prejudice and regardless of working a forfeiture upon the policyholder.

Regardless of the rule used in a given jurisdiction, there will always be the question whether notice is in fact "late." Even notice coming long after an accident may be considered timely if the policyholder had no reason to expect a claim. For example, a policyholder's houseguest may slip in the bathroom but seem fine. Months later, the guest may develop back pains or headaches and attribute them to the fall, bringing a claim. In this sort of case, the clock usually begins ticking (for late notice purposes) upon the policyholder's receipt of the claim rather than from the time of the guest's fall. However, specific insurance policy deadlines based on any incident may change this approach if the court does not view the notice requirements as confusing or unfair to the policyholder. In addition, the insurer may require notice of any event that *may* lead to a claim, strengthening the notice obligations contained in the policy.

As one might expect, common sense is usually the courts' guide in these areas. However, even notice years after an incident may not be "late" depending on the circumstances. Because law "abhors a forfeiture" of contract benefits, the traditional rule/"no prejudice required" jurisdictions often exhibit reluctance to label notice as "late," perhaps because to do so conclusively strips the policyholder of coverage.

Alternatively, even concededly late notice may also be considered excused under apt circumstances. For example, wind may blow off a roof of a home or burst plumbing may flood a neighbor's condominium on a lower floor. If the policyholder was not present at the time, most courts will suspend the running of the clock for late notice purposes, at least for some reasonable time and perhaps even until the policyholder becomes consciously aware of the problem. Conversely, insurers will argue, with mixed success, that the policyholder must take at least some steps to be reasonably informed about the condition of its property or the consequences of its business operations or property upon others.

The trend toward a prejudice requirement in occurrence-based insurance policies is in more than a little tension with the use of claims-made policy forms for many types of liability insurance. The claims-made form is particularly popular for Professional Liability (e.g., legal and medical malpractice), Errors and Omissions coverage generally, Directors and Officers liability insurance, and has seen intermittent use for General Liability insurance. Under the law of most states involving typical claims-made forms, there must be quite strict compliance with the deadlines set forth in the policy, which usually require that the policyholder give notice to the insurer of claims made against it during the policy period prior to the expiration of that same policy period or any extended reporting period provided in the policy. It is generally not necessary for the insurer to prove that it has been prejudiced by the policyholder's failure to comply with a claims-made policy's notice requirements. Indeed, it is not at all unusual for a state to place a demanding prejudice requirement on insurers seeking to disclaim coverage for late notice under occurrence basis policies but then do a complete about-face and allow the insurer to disclaim coverage for late notice under claims-made basis policies based on the slimmest of violations by the policyholder and without any showing of prejudice by the insurer. At the margin, however, notice regarding claims-made policies can become less cut-and-dried. This chapter deals only with notice regarding occurrence policies.

For further discussion of the late notice defense, *see generally* JEFFREY W. STEMPEL, STEMPEL ON INSURANCE CONTRACTS § 9.01 (3d ed. 2006 & Supp. 2009); BARRY R. OSTRAGER & THOMAS R. NEWMAN, HANDBOOK ON INSURANCE COVERAGE DISPUTES Ch. 4 (14th ed. 2008); EUGENE ANDERSON, JORDAN STANZLER, & LORELIE S. MASTERS, INSURANCE COVERAGE LITIGATION Ch. 5 (2d ed. 2004); Richard L. Suter, *Insurer Prejudice: An Analysis of an Expanding Doctrine in Insurance Coverage Law*, 46 ME. L. REV. 221 (1994); F. Warren Jacoby, Comment, *The Materiality of Prejudice to the Insurer as a Result of the Insured's Failure to Give Timely Notice*, 74 DICK. L. REV. 260 (1970); Comment, 68 HARV. L. REV. 1436 (1955).

## 50-State Survey: Late Notice Defense Under "Occurrence" Policies: is Prejudice to the Insurer Required?

**Alabama:** No prejudice required for primary insurers to successfully invoke the late notice defense but excess insurers must show prejudice from late notice to defeat coverage. *See Midwest Employers Cas. Co. v. E. Ala. Health Care*, 695 So. 2d 1169, 1173 (Ala. 1997) (workers' compensation claim involving an employee whose initial diagnosis after suffering an injury on the job was a sprained ankle, but later required back surgery due to a herniated disc; claim exceeded the primary insurance policy limits, and the excess insurer complained of late notice when it did not receive notice until two years after the initial injury; burden to prove prejudice in excess cases is on the insurer) (prejudice also may be a factor in determining whether notice is deemed to be late). "[P]rejudice to the insurer is a factor to be considered, along with the reasons for delay and the length of delay, in determining the overall reasonableness of a delay in giving notice of an accident." *Id.*; *see also State Farm Mut. Auto. Ins. Co. v. Burgess*, 474 So. 2d 634, 637 (Ala. 1985) (holding that, although no prejudice is required for late notice to vitiate liability coverage, in uninsured motorist cases the insurer can use prejudice to show that the policyholder did not give notice within a reasonable amount of time, and prejudice is required if the insurer denies coverage because of late notice); *Overstreet v. Safeway Ins. Co. of Ala.*, 740 So. 2d 1053, 1059 (Ala. 1999) ("If the [excess] insurer fails to present evidence as to prejudice, then the insured's failure to give notice will not be a bar to his recovery" but finding prejudice and breach due to policyholder settlement of claim without insurer consent); *Progressive Specialty Ins. Co. v. Steele*, 985 So. 2d 932, 937–38 (Ala. Civ. App. 2007) (holding that an injured pedestrian's uninsured motorist claim should be assessed under a *Burgess* analysis); *Lemuel v. Admiral Ins. Co.*, 414 F. Supp. 2d 1037, 1056 (M.D. Ala. 2006) ("[As with a primary insurer] the length of the delay and the reasons for the delay also must be considered in the context of excess insurer's assertion of late notice. Alabama [courts]… impose an additional requirement upon an excess insurer; an excess insurer also must demonstrate that it was prejudiced by the late notice.").

**Alaska:** Prejudice required. *See Weaver Bros., Inc. v. Chappel*, 684 P.2d 123, 125 (Alaska 1984) (finding that the insurer was not notified of the accident implicating the policy until six years after it occurred; because notice provision intended to protect the insurer from prejudice, prejudice must be demonstrated to deny coverage because of untimely notice) ("In the absence of prejudice, regardless of the reasons for the delayed notice, there is no justification for excusing the insurer from its obligations under the policy."). Burden to prove prejudice on insurer. *Id.* at 126; *see also Estes v. Alaska Ins. Guar. Ass'n*, 774 P.2d 1315 (Alaska 1989) (finding a policy provision requiring action within one year of loss unenforceable absent prejudice to insurer from delay in a case where the policyholder reported fire loss one year and seven days after fire); *Long v. Holland Am. Line Westours, Inc.*, 26 P.3d 430, 435 (Alaska 2001) (reasoning that public policy barred enforcement of a time limit clause where a cruiseline was not prejudiced and an injured tourist received notice of the provision days before a scheduled journey) ("[I]t would be inequitable to enforce these [time limit] clauses unless prejudice could be demonstrated" by the party asserting the defense); *Tush v. Pharr*, 68 P.3d 1239, 1250 (Alaska 2003) (citing *Weaver* for the proposition that "absent prejudice, regardless of the reasons for the delayed notice, there is no justification for excusing the insurer from its obligations under the policy") (quotation omitted).

**Arizona:** Prejudice required. *See Lindus v. N. Ins. Co. of N.Y.*, 438 P.2d 311, 315 (Ariz. 1968) (involving a policyholder that waited two years to notify insurer of car accident but no prejudice resulted; insurer could not deny coverage) ("[A]n insurance company is not relieved of its contractual liability because of the insured's failure to give notice unless it can show that it has been prejudiced thereby."). Burden to prove prejudice on insurer. *Id.*; *see also Salerno v. Atl. Mut. Ins. Co.*, 6 P.3d 758 (Ariz. Ct. App. 2000) (policyholder failed to give notice of injury because she did not become aware coverage existed for her medical bills until after the time limit expired but insurer could not prove prejudice); *U.S. Fid. & Gaur. Co. v. Powercraft Homes*, 685 P.2d 136 (Ariz. Ct. App. 1984) (finding that a delay in answer alone is insufficient prejudice); *Penn-American Ins. Co. v. Sanchez*, 202 P.3d 472, 480 (Ariz. Ct. App. 2008) (citing *Lindus* for the rule that, in the absence of actual prejudice to the insurer, late notice will not bar the insured's claim).

**Arkansas:** No prejudice required—if notice provision in policy sufficiently demarcated as a "condition precedent." *See Fireman's Fund Ins. Co. v. Care Mgmt., Inc.*, No. 09-662, 2010 WL 744994, __ S.W.3d __ (Ark. Mar. 4, 2010) (finding no coverage for medical malpractice claim where policyholder notified insurer more than two years after complaint served on policyholder). "In sum, it is well-settled law in Arkansas that an insured must strictly comply with an insurance policy provision requiring timely notice where that provision is a condition precedent to recovery. Failure to do so constitutes a forfeiture of the right to recover from the insurance company, regardless of whether the insurance company was prejudiced by the failure. On the other hand, if notice is not a condition precedent, the insurance company must show it was prejudiced by any delay in notice in order to be relieved of liability."; *accord Am. Gen. Life Ins. Co. v. First Am. Nat'l Bank*, 716 S.W.2d 205 (Ark. 1986) (reasoning that, because notice of disability within one year was a condition precedent to coverage, it was unreasonable for policyholder to give notice more than a year after accident and insurer could deny coverage); *Campbell & Co. v. Utica Mut. Ins. Co.*, 820 S.W.2d 284 (Ark. Ct. App. 1991) (finding that an insurer must show prejudice in occurrence policy unless prompt notice is identified as a condition precedent to coverage). Burden to show prejudice on insurer if prejudice is required. *Id.* at 288. *But see Kimbrell v. Standard Ins.*, 207 F.3d 535 (8th Cir. 2000) (applying Arkansas law) (finding insurer estopped from using notice defense where its conduct induced policyholder's delay in providing notice).

**California:** Prejudice required. *See Clemmer v. Hartford Ins. Co.*, 22 Cal. 3d 865, 882 (Cal. 1978) (finding that because insurer of murderer could show no prejudice in late notice from widow and son of a murder victim, insurer's defense of late notice failed) ("[P]rejudice must be shown with respect to breach of notice clause."); *see also Campbell v. Allstate Ins. Co.*, 384 P.2d 155, 156 (Cal. 1963) (holding there was insufficient evidence to show prejudice from late notice and insurer had to pay default judgment to persons injured by policyholder). Burden to prove prejudice on insurer. *Campbell*, 384 P.2d at 157; *Rosen v. State Farm Gen. Ins. Co.*, 70 P.3d 351, 368–69 (Cal. 2003) (noting California's longstanding notice-prejudice rule); *Safeco Ins. Co. of Am. v. Parks*, 88 Cal. Rptr. 3d 730, 740 (Cal. Ct. App. 2009) (rejecting late notice defense in personal injury case where insurer failed to show actual prejudice) ("The insurer must show actual prejudice, not the mere possibility of prejudice."). For excess insurance, the judicial inquiry tends to focus on whether the policyholder acted reasonably in giving notice in view of the practicality that an excess insurance policy is generally implicated only by claims with a potential for sizeable recovery. *Providence Wash. Ins. Co. v. Container Freight, Inc.*, 68 Cal. Rptr. 2d 776 (Cal. 1997).

   **Colorado:** Prejudice required. See *Clementi v. Nationwide Mut. Fire Ins. Co.*, 16 P.3d 223, 230 (Colo. 2001) (holding that uninsured motorist carrier did not show prejudice when state trooper failed to give timely notice of injury so insurer could not deny coverage). "[I]nsurer prejudice should now be considered when determining whether noncompliance with a UIM policy's notice requirements vitiates coverage." *Id.* Burden to prove prejudice is usually on the insurer, but not always. *Clementi*, 16 P.3d at 230; *see also Lauric v. USAA Cas. Ins. Co.*, 209 P.3d 190, 193 (Colo. Ct. App. 2009) (remanding to reassess an uninsured motorist vehicle claim with a presumption of prejudice where the insured failed to notify the insurer until after settlement). "When an insured settles in breach of notice and consent-to-settle clauses, we conclude that there must be a presumption of prejudice." *Id.*

   **Connecticut:** Prejudice required. See *Aetna Cas. & Sur. Co. v. Murphy*, 538 A.2d 219, 223 (Conn. 1988) ("[A] proper balance between the interests of the insurer and the insured requires a factual inquiry into whether, in the circumstances of a particular case, an insurer has been prejudiced by its insured's delay in giving notice of an event triggering insurance coverage."). Burden to prove lack of prejudice appears to be on insured. See *Nat'l Pub. Co., Inc. v. Hartford Fire Ins. Co.*, 949 A.2d 1203, 1208 (Conn. 2008) (upholding a lower court's refusal to give a jury instruction on the special defense of late notice where the plaintiff met the burden of proving lack of prejudice).

   **Delaware:** Prejudice required. See *Nationwide Mut. Ins. Co. v. Starr*, 575 A.2d 1083, 1088 (Del. 1990) (insurer must provide coverage in uninsured motorist claim even though claimant failed to promptly notify insurer of judgment against insured because insurer could not prove prejudice). "To prevail on its claim, [the insurer] must show both that the policy was breached and that it was prejudiced by the violation of the policy." *Id.* Burden to prove prejudice on insurer. *Id.*; *State Farm Mut. Auto. Ins. Co. v. Johnson*, 320 A.2d 345 (Del. 1974) (finding that where policyholder failed to show compliance with notice provision, insurer had burden of showing prejudice before coverage could be denied); *Falcon Steel Co. v. Md. Cas. Co.*, 366 A.2d 512 (Del. Super. Ct. 1976) (finding a nine-month delay unreasonable, but finding that the insurer must still provide coverage because insurer could not show prejudice because of delay). *See also Wausau Bus. Inc. Co. v. IdleAire Techs. Corp.*, 2010 Bkrcy LEXIS 436 (Bkrcy. Del., Feb. 17, 2010) (six-month delay in notifying insurer of product liability claim does not void coverage in absence of insurer showing of prejudice; notice-prejudice rule firmly established in Delaware).

**Florida:** Prejudice required. *See Bankers Ins. Co. v. Macias*, 475 So. 2d 1216, 1218 (Fla. 1985) (finding that substantial prejudice was required in case involving a personal injury policy the insured tried to activate two years after a car accident). "If the insured breaches the notice provision, prejudice to the insurer will be presumed." *Id.*; *Tiedtke v. Fid. & Cas. Co. of N.Y.*, 222 So. 2d 206, 209 (Fla. 1969). Burden to prove absence of prejudice on policyholder. *Bankers Ins. Co. v. Macias*, 475 So. 2d 1216, 1218 (Fla. 1985) (finding that presumption of prejudice against the insurer arises because of late notice; policyholder has burden of disproving); *Robinson v. Auto-Owners Ins. Co.*, 718 So. 2d 1283 (Fla. Dist. Ct. App. 1998) (same). *See also Liberty Mut. Ins. Group v. Cifuentes*, 760 So. 2d 230 (Fla. 2000) (finding that the insurer should be relieved of liability if insurer is prejudiced by the policyholder's failure to comply with the timely notice requirement); *Martinez-Claib v. Bus. Men's Assurance Co. of Am.*, No. 2:06-cv-479-FtM-34SPC, 2008 WL 4791318, at *5 (M.D. Fla. Sept. 9, 2008) (holding that the policyholder's disability insurance claim was barred where she waited two years to notify insurer of her disability). "Florida law provides that prejudice to the insurer is presumed 'when a policy makes a compliance with a written notice provision a condition precedent to the insurer's liability.'" *Id.*

**Georgia:** No prejudice required. *See Yarborough v. Dickinson*, 359 S.E.2d 235, 237 (Ga. 1987) (involving an uninsured motorist action subject to duty to defend and finding that the notice requirement allows insurer to protect its interest in "assuring a minimal or zero judgment"); *Caldwell v. State Farm Fire & Cas. Ins. Co*, 385 S.E.2d 97, 99 (Ga. Ct. App. 1989) (holding that the notice requirement allows the insurer to prepare its defense while the facts are fresh and the witnesses are available). *See also Royer v. Murphy*, 625 S.E.2d 544, 545 (Ga. Ct. App. 2006) (holding that the insured's two-year delay in reporting an automobile accident was unreasonable and discharged the insurer's obligation). "[F]ailure to meet this condition precedent [providing notice] is fatal to [the] action." *Id.*; *Travelers Indem. Co. v. Douglasville Dev., LLC*, No. 1:07-CV-0410-JOF, 2008 WL 4372004, at *3 (N.D. Ga. Sept. 19, 2008) (involving a property damage dispute, the court found untimely notice doubt as to coverage is not an excuse for not giving notice). "The Georgia courts have repeatedly held that where no valid excuse exists, failure to give written notice for periods in the range of four to eight months is unreasonable as a matter of law." *Id. accord. Am. Ins. Co. v. Evercare Co.*, No.1:09-cv-2608-TCB, 2010 WL 1814675, at *4 (N.D. Ga. May 5, 2010) (finding policyholder's explanation for late notice of competitor's Lanham Act claim unreasonable as a matter of law). "Under Georgia law, 'timely notice to the insurer of a claim or occurrence is a condition precedent to the insurer's duty to defend or pay.'" *Id.* "The duty to provide notice is triggered when [the policyholder] knew or *should have known* that it might be liable for an occurrence that fell within [the policyholder's] coverage periods." *Id.* at *5.

**Hawaii:** Prejudice required. *See Standard Oil Co. of Cal. v. Hawaiian Ins. & Guar. Co.*, 654 P.2d 1345, 1348 n.4 (Haw. 1982) (involving an insurer that failed to defend when heirs of plane crash victims sued policyholder; holding that for late notice to bar coverage, insurer must be prejudiced). "The function of the notice requirement... is simply to prevent the insurer from being prejudiced, not to provide a technical escape-hatch... ." *Id.* Opinion suggests insurer has the burden of proving prejudice. *See also Hawaii Mmgt. Aliance Ass'n v. Ins. Comm'r*, 100 P.3d 952, 960 (Haw. 2004) (involving a dispute over attorney's fees after a cancer patient's successful claim for coverage; comparing independent review standards with late notice rules) ("An insurer will not be relieved of liability based on an insured's untimely notice of a claim unless the insurer demonstrates that it has been prejudiced as a result of the late notice.").

**Idaho:** No prejudice required. *See Viani v. Aetna Ins. Co.*, 501 P.2d 706, 713–14 (Idaho 1972) (overruled in part on other grounds); *Sloviaczek v. Estate of Puckett*, 565 P.2d 564, 568 (Idaho 1977) (in case where policyholder failed to give notice of suit until after an adverse judgment was entered, no showing of prejudice was required; insurer prejudiced because it had no chance to defend the claims). Burden of proving prejudice rests on the insurer. *See Union Warehouse & Supply Co. v. Ill. R.B. Jones, Inc.*, 917 P.2d 1300, 1306 (Idaho 1996) (finding that notice provisions are reasonable requirements to a contract, but the insurer bears the burden of providing prejudice in a case involving insurance coverage dispute arising from the sale of contaminated winter wheat seed). "[T]he insurer is required to establish prejudice without benefit of a presumption." *Id.*

**Illinois:** Hybrid rule. Insurer need only show that notice was late to defeat coverage but whether the insurer was prejudiced is a factor in determining whether notice was sufficiently late to be fatal to coverage. *See Country Mut. Ins. Co. v. Livorsi Marine, Inc.*, 856 N.E.2d 338, 346 (Ill. 2006) (recognizing Illinois's notice/prejudice rule and holding that even if there was no prejudice to the insurer, the policyholder must still give reasonable notice in accordance with the terms of the policy) (involving a trademark dispute and a finding that the insurer had no duty to defend or indemnify pursuant to a general commercial liability policy where the policyholder waited over twenty-one months to give notice). "[L]ack of prejudice may be a factor in determining... whether a reasonable notice was given in a particular case yet it is not a condition which will dispense with the requirement." *Id.* at 343. *Accord. Simmon v. Iowa Mut. Cas. Co.*, 121 N.E.2d 509, 512 (Ill. 1954) (same). *See also Berglind v. Paintball Bus. Ass'n*, 921 N.E.2d 432, 441 (Ill. App. Ct. 2009) (finding that fact issues precluded summary judgment for insurer despite policyholder's eleven-month delay in giving notice when paintball facility sued by injured patron) ("[A] lengthy passage of time in notification is not an absolute bar to a claim of defense or indemnity under an insurance policy, even under the 'as soon as practicable' provision.") (finding that the factors relevant to determining whether notice was unreasonably late included "(1) the specific language of the policy's notice provision; (2) the degree of the insured's sophistication in the world of commerce and insurance; (3) the insured's awareness that an occurrence as defined under the terms of the policy has taken place; (4) the insured's diligence and reasonable care in ascertaining whether policy coverage is available once the awareness has occurred; and (5) any prejudice to the insurance company") (citing *Livorsi Marine*); *Am. Standard Ins. Co. v. Slifer*, 919 N.E.2d 372, 374, 377 (Ill. App. Ct. 2009) (concluding that late notice strips an insured of coverage for failure to report 2002 hit-and-run fatality while driving insured vehicle where policyholder/ perpetrator not apprehended and sued until 2007 and that the policy at issue required "prompt" notice of "an auto accident or loss" regardless of severity or existence of claim). *See, e.g., West American Ins. Co. v. Yorkville Nat'l Bank*, __ N.E.2d __, No. 108285, 2010 Ill. LEXIS 1069, at *10 (Ill. Sept. 23, 2010) (In 6-1 decision, Supreme Court reverses appellate court finding of notice twenty-seven months after defamation lawsuit against bank as late as a matter of law and upholds fact-based trial court determination of sufficiently timely notice as "not against the manifest weight of the evidence"). Applying the *Livorsi Marine* factors, the *Yorkville Bank* Court found (1) the policy language inconclusive; (2) the Bank was a sophisticated policyholder, which weighed in favour of a late notice finding; (3) the Bank was aware of an occurrence, which weighed in favour of a late notice finding; (4) the Bank had been sufficiently diligent and had been misinformed by a broker and the insurer regarding coverage, a key factor weighing against a finding of late notice; and (5) that there was no showing of prejudice by the insurer, a factor militating against a finding of late notice). *Id.* at *9-16. Although notice was given shortly before scheduled trial, the insurer hurt its chances of prevailing on a late notice defense by failing to investigate and failing to seek a continuance. *Id.* at *15. "After considering all relevant factors, we find that, under the circumstances in the present case, Yorkville's written notice of the lawsuit to West American was giving within a reasonable time and did not violate the notice provision in the Policy." *Id.* at *17-18.

**Indiana:** Prejudice required but prejudice presumed if notice is late. *See Ind. Ins. Co. v. Williams*, 463 N.E.2d 257, 260–61 (Ind. 1984) (involving a policyholder that did not give notice of car accident until six months after it occurred; court held prejudice can be presumed from unreasonable delay in giving notice) ("The requirement of prompt notice gives the insurer an opportunity to make a timely and adequate investigation of all the circumstances surrounding the accident or loss. This adequate investigation is often frustrated by a delayed notice. Prejudice to the insurance company's ability to prepare an adequate defense can therefore be presumed by an unreasonable delay in notifying the company about the accident or about the filing of the lawsuit. This is not in conflict with the public policy theory that the court should seek to protect the innocent third parties from attempts by insurance companies to deny liability for some insignificant failure to notify."). The burden to prove a prima facia case of no prejudice is placed on the on policyholder or third-party claimant, with the ultimate question of prejudice thereafter a question of fact. *Ind. Ins. Co. v. Williams*, 463 N.E.2d 257, 260–61 (Ind. 1984); *Wolf Lake Terminals, Inc. v. Mut. Marine Ins. Co.*, 433 F. Supp. 2d 933, 952 (N.D. Ind. 2005) (stating that the presumption of prejudice "is rebutted by evidence that the insureds' 'adequately safeguarded' the [insurers'] interests by assuming the defense of the contamination claims" made against policyholder). *See also P.R. Mallory & Co. v. Am. Cas. Co of Reading, Pa.*, 920 N.E.2d 736, 748–55 (Ind. Ct. App. 2010) (concluding that policyholder's delay of approximately twenty years in providing notice to insurers despite being aware of environmental contamination was unreasonably late and created presumption of prejudice that policyholder must factually rebut to obtain coverage; instant policyholder failed to shoulder burden, supporting summary judgment for insurer); *Dreaded, Inc. v. St. Paul Guardian Ins. Co.*, 904 N.E.2d 1267, 1271–72 (Ind. 2009) (concluding that the policyholder was not entitled to reimbursement for pre-notice and tender defense costs where policyholder failed to give notice until three years after onset of environmental liability claim); *Askren Hub States Pest Control Servs., Inc. v. Zurich Ins. Co.*, 721 N.E.2d 270, 278–79 (Ind. Ct. App. 1999) (finding a delay of six months unreasonable); *Ind. Farmers Mut. Ins. Co. v. N. Vernon Drop Forge, Inc.*, 917 N.E.2d 1258 (Ind. Ct. App. 2009) (concluding that policyholder's delay of eighteen months in giving notice of contamination claims was unreasonably late but that it did not prejudice insurer when fact of contamination and identity of responsible party not in dispute; extent of injury unclear but can be determined at trial, with amount of insurer responsibility, if any, assessed accordingly). Relatedly, an insurance policy may shorten the time for commencing suit to obtain benefits as long as a reasonable time is afforded, except where there is fraud, duress, or similar misconduct by insurer. *See Bradshaw v. Chandler*, 916 N.E.2d 163 (Ind. 2009) (construing two-year limitations period favorably to policyholder because his underinsured motorist complaint was filed within two years of the accident as required by the plain language of the policy).

**Iowa:** Prejudice required. *See Grinnell Mut. Reins. Co. v. Jungling*, 654 N.W.2d 530, 542 (Iowa 2002) (holding that if policyholder cannot show substantial compliance with the notice requirement, prejudice is presumed) ("Unless the insured shows such substantial compliance [with a notice requirement], excuse, waiver, or lack of prejudice to the insurer, prejudice must be presumed."). Burden to prove lack of prejudice is on policyholder. *Grinnell*, 654 N.W. at 542; *see also Simpson v. United States Fid. & Guar. Co.*, 562 N.W.2d 627, 631–32 (Iowa 1997) (finding that where policyholder can demonstrate excuse for late notice, burden to prove prejudice placed upon insurer); *Met-Coil Sys. Corp. v. Columbia Cas. Co.*, 524 N.W.2d 650, 654 (Iowa 1994) (same); *Fireman's Fund Ins. Co. v. ACC Chem. Co.*, 538 N.W.2d 259, 264 (Iowa 1995) (same).

**Kansas:** Prejudice required. *See Atchison, Topeka & Santa Fe Ry. Co. v. Stonewall Ins. Co.*, 71 P.3d 1097, 1139 (Kan. 2003) (holding there is better reasoning in support of requiring prejudice than not requiring it and finding late notice defense unsuccessful in case involving request for indemnification for a large quantity of work-related injuries) "[U]ntimely notice... is not alone sufficient to excuse performance of the insurer or relieve the insurer of its obligation to provide coverage when coverage otherwise should be afforded. Kansas also requires a showing of actual prejudice as a result of the untimely notice." *Id.* at 1137. *Nat'l Union Fire Ins. Co. v. FDIC*, 957 P.2d 357, 368 (Kan. 1998) (applying the notice-prejudice rule to proof-of-loss requirements in a fidelity bond). "Given that insurance contracts are not negotiated agreements, no compelling reason appears for allowing the insurer to avoid performing a duty purchased by the insured's premium unless the insured's delay caused loss to the insurer." *Id.* at 368. Burden to prove prejudice on insurer. *Id.* at 368. *See also Sheldon v. Kan. Pub. Employees. Ret. Sys.*, 189 P.3d 554, 564–66 (Kan. Ct. App. 2008) (discussing varying approaches and rationales behind the late-notice defense in the context of a disability income dispute). "Policy provisions respecting notice of claim or occurrence should be liberally construed in favor of the insured." *Id.* at 564.

**Kentucky:** Prejudice required. *See Jones v. Bituminous Cas. Corp.*, 821 S.W.2d 798, 803 (Ky. 1991) (holding insurer could not deny coverage because of six-month delay before notification of explosion implicating policy because insurer could not prove prejudice). "We view the question of prejudice in terms of whether it is reasonably probable that the insurance carrier suffered substantial prejudice from the delay in notice." *Id. See also Best v. W. Am. Ins. Co.*, 270 S.W.3d 398, 405 (Ky. Ct. App. 2008) (finding that the insurer was still obligated to pay on an anti-theft automobile policy where the insured waited two months before providing notice). "[A]n insurer may not deny coverage because the insured failed to provide prompt notice of loss unless the insurer can prove that it is reasonably probable that it suffered substantial prejudice from the delay in notice." *Id.* (also suggesting that insurer presented no evidence of prejudice to the court). Burden to prove prejudice on insurer. *Jones*, 821 S.W.2d at 803.

**Louisiana:** Prejudice required. *See Miller v. Marcantel*, 221 So.2d 557, 559 (La. Ct. App. 1969) (insurer suffered no prejudice when employee failed to inform employer of accident implicating policy until five months later; insurer could not deny coverage). "[U]nless the insurer is actually prejudiced by the insured's failure to give notice immediately, the insurer cannot defeat its liability." *Id. See also Smith v. Reliance Ins. Co. of Ill.*, 807 So.2d 1010 (La. Ct. App. 2002) (insured liable for counsel fees and costs where the insurer denied coverage; residents sued due to injuries caused by a malfunction at a waste plant). "[I]nsurance policies are simply to prevent the insurer from being prejudiced… [but] whether to strictly apply the notice requirements of a Limited Buy Back Endorsement, is an issue upon which the trial court has not yet ruled [justifying appellate court's refusal to address issue notwithstanding that notice was concededly later than the deadline set forth in the policy]." *Id.* at 1023 (Daley, J., concurring). Burden to prove prejudice on insurer. *Gully & Assocs. v. Wausau Ins. Cos.*, 536 So. 2d 816 (La. Ct. App. 1988); *Moskau v. Ins. Co. of N. Am.*, 366 So. 2d 1004 (La. Ct. App. 1978). *See also State v. Nat'l Union Fire Ins. Co.*, 984 So. 2d 91, 97 (La. Ct. App. 2008) (finding summary judgment inappropriate where material questions of prejudice to the insurer were not addressed) ("[A]n insurer cannot escape liability unless it suffers prejudice either in fact or as a matter of law from the late notice.").

**Maine:** Prejudice required. *Main Mut. Fire Ins. Co. v. Watson*, 532 A.2d 686 (Me. 1987); *Lanzo v. State Farm Mut. Auto. Ins.*, 524 A.2d 47, 50 (Me. 1987) (concluding that notice a year and a half after an accident was adequate where insurer failed to show prejudice). "[T]o avoid liability as a result of a failure of notice, a liability insurer must show that the notice provision was breached *and* that the insurer was prejudiced by the insured's delay." *Id.* *Accord. Ouellette v. Mw. Bonding & Cas. Co.*, 495 A.2d 1232, 1235 (Me. 1985). *See also Acadia Ins. Co. v. Keiser Indus., Inc.*, 793 A.2d 495 (Me. 2002). Burden to prove prejudice on insurer. *Marquis v. Farm Family Mut. Ins. Co.*, 628 A.2d 644, 649 (Me. 1993). *Jackson v. N. E. Ins. Co.*, No. 07–178, 2009 Me. Super. Lexis 165, *11 (Me. Super. Ct. Nov. 10, 2009) (insurer had duty to defend despite late notice of a vehicular accident claim because it was not prejudiced because it became aware of accident and had ability to investigate within two months of event even though default judgment entered against insured) (personal injury action arising under a commercial garage policy) ("The purpose of a notice provision… is to allow the insurer an opportunity to investigate the circumstances surrounding an accident giving rise to a claim reasonably soon after the accident has occurred."). *Accord, Michoud v. Mut. Fire, Marine & Inland Ins. Co.*, 505 A.2d 786, 787 (Me. 1986) (insurer failed to demonstrate prejudice despite learning of claim eight months after entry of default but before hearing on damages; insurer failed to participate in damages hearing despite knowledge of the claim).

**Maryland:** Prejudice required. *See Prince George's County v. Local Gov't Ins. Trust*, 879 A.2d 81, 93–95 (Md. 2005) (finding that a trust participating in an excess insurance pool not required to indemnify the state in a police brutality suit because it successfully met its burden of proving prejudice). "[Insurer must] establish by a preponderance of the evidence that it suffered 'actual prejudice' from the lack of notice before [it] may deny coverage." *Id.* at 92. *Accord. Commercial Union Ins. Co. v. Porter Hayden Co.*, 698 A.2d 1167 (Md. 1997); *Sherwood Brands, Inc. v. Hartford Accident & Indem. Co.*, 698 A.2d 1078, 1084 (Md. 1997); *Prince George's Count v. Local Gov't Ins. Trust,*

879 A.2d 81, 92–93 (Md. 2005); *St. Paul Fire & Marine Ins. Co. v. House*, 554 A.2d 404 (Md. 1989). *See also McNeill v. Md. Auto. Ins. Fund*, 927 A.2d 418 (Md. Ct. Spec. App. 2007) (finding the insurer responsible for coverage in a tort action because the injured plaintiff did not have enough information to feasibly meet notice requirement).

**Massachusetts:** Prejudice required. *See Johnson Controls, Inc. v. Bowes*, 409 N.E.2d 185, 187 (Mass. 1980) (Court departed from previous common law requiring that the insured follow strict compliance with contract provisions regarding notice, reasoning that an insurance contract is not a negotiated contract because the insurer dictates most terms aside from the monetary amount of coverage) (late notice defense unsuccessful where attorney provided untimely notice of professional negligence claim to legal malpractice insurer). "[W]here an insurance company attempts to be relieved of its obligations... on the ground of untimely notice, [it] will be required to prove both that the notice provision was in fact breached and that the breach resulted in prejudice to its position." *Id. See also Bellanti v. Boston Pub. Health Comm'n*, 874 NE.2d 439, 447 (Mass. App. Ct. 2007) (noting that while Massachusetts law is usually forgiving of late notice, prejudice is not required where written presentment to an executive officer required) ("In the context of presentment, however, it has been held that [i]t is irrelevant that the defendant may not have suffered any prejudice by reason of the lack of actual notice."). Burden to prove prejudice on insurer. *Bellanti*, 874 NE.2d at 447. The insurer is also required to prove that the notice provision was in fact breached. *Id. See also Pilgrim Ins. Co. v. Molard*, 897 N.E.2d 1231, 1240 (Mass. App. Ct. 2008) (finding that an insurer must prove delayed notice, which materially prejudiced the company and that generalities and even extreme time delays are generally not sufficient to prove prejudice, the court found that further proceedings were required to decide if delayed notice was prejudicial where an injured taxicab passenger spent approximately eight months locating the negligent driver that caused her injuries).

**Michigan:** Prejudice required. *See Koski v. Allstate Ins. Co.*, 572 N.W.2d 636, 639 (Mich. 1998) (finding that the insurer was prejudiced, and thus relieved from obligation, where the policyholder did not provide notice until after entry of default judgment) (involving a personal injury allegedly covered by a homeowner's policy) ("[A]n insurer who seeks to cut off responsibility on the ground that its insured did not comply with a contract provision requiring notice immediately or within a reasonable time must establish actual prejudice to its position."). Burden to prove prejudice is on the insurer. *Koski*, 572 N.W.2d at 639; *Wendel v. Swanberg*, 185 N.W.2d 348, 353 (Mich. 1971). *See also Factory Mut. Ins. Co. v. Westport Ins. Corp.*, No. 09–12761, 2010 U.S. Dist. Lexis 51634 (E.D. Mich. May 26, 2010) (one-year time limit for actions under insurance policy not a violation of public policy but policyholder met deadline; insurer must prove prejudice to prevail on generalized late notice defense); *Westport Ins. Corp. v. Al Bourdeau Ins. Servs.*, No. 287920,

2010 WL 1507785, at **5–6 (Mich. Ct. App. Apr. 15, 2010 (finding that failure to report claim within policy period eliminates claims-made coverage and that prejudice otherwise required for late notice) (granting summary judgment to insurer and suggesting that reporting claim after adverse judgment is sufficiently prejudicial to negate coverage); *Tenneco Inc. v. Amerisure Mut. Ins. Co.*, 761 N.W.2d 846, 859 (Mich. Ct. App. 2008) (finding that notice of any suits or demands is different from notice of an occurrence because of insurer interest in contesting liability in a case involving a policyholder that gave notice of a potential occurrence, but failed to provide notice of a claim until after settlement relieved insurer of duties) ("[P]rejudice to the insurer is a material element in determining whether notice is reasonably given and the burden is on the insurer to demonstrate such prejudice." *Id.*

**Minnesota:** Prejudice required. *See L&H Transp. v. Drew Agency*, 369 N.W.2d 608, 611 (Minn. 1985) (finding dismissal inappropriate where an insurer failed to show prejudice from late notice and denying cleanup costs included within a cargo insurance policy after an accident caused property damage) ("In the absence of prejudice to the insurer, untimely notice will not absolve the insurer of liability."); *Reliance Ins. Co. v. St. Paul. Ins. Cos.*, 239 N.W.2d 922, 924–25 (Minn. 1976) (involving an insured attorney who waited eighteen months before notifying insurer of claim, concluding that this did not render policies unenforceable absent showing of prejudice). Burden to prove prejudice on insurer. *John Deere Ins. Co. v. Shamrock Indus., Inc.*, 929 F.2d 413, 418 (8th Cir. 1991) (applying Minnesota law); *L&H Transp. v. Drew Agency*, 403 N.W.2d 223, 224 (Minn. 1987); *Grain Dealers Mut. Ins. v. Cady*, 318 N.W.2d 247, 251 (Minn. 1982). *See also Hans Hagen Homes, Inc. v. City of Minnetrista*, 713 N.W.2d 916, 922 (Minn. Ct. App. 2006) (finding that coverage was preserved where governing body was nine days late in providing a written denial of an application for rezoning the application was approved as a matter of Minnesota statutory law) ("Plain meaning is the governing principle in applying all statutory language.").

**Mississippi:** Prejudice required. *Bolivar County Bd. of Supervisors v. Forum Ins. Co.*, 779 F.2d 1081, 1085–86 (5th Cir. 1986) (applying Mississippi law) (but finding prejudice as a matter of law where insured provided notice five months after event and after trial of matter but before entry of judgment). *See also Mimmitt v. Allstate County Mut. Ins. Co.*, 928 So.2d 203, 207 (Miss. Ct. App. 2003) (finding that the insurer did not have a duty to defend in a suit arising out of an automobile accident where the insured never provided notice) ("Without notice the insurance carrier cannot be expected to provide a defense.") *Id. But see Ingalls Shipbuilding v. Fed. Ins. Co.*, 410 F.3d 214 (5th Cir. 2005) (policy required notice "as soon as practicable," but delay of more than four months in giving notice "was neither unreasonable nor prejudicial to [insurer's] ability to defend [insured]. Burden to prove prejudice on insurer." *Rampy v. State Farm Mut. Auto Ins. Co.*, 278 So. 2d 428, 434 (Miss. 1973) (finding that an insurer must show substantial prejudice when insured fails to perform the terms of the contract). *See also Spann v. Allstate Prop. & Cas. Ins. Co.*, No. 4:08cv95-DPJ-JCS, 2009 WL 3633879, at *3 (S.D. Miss Oct. 28, 2009) (concluding that the insurer could not show prejudice because default judgment was not final in a case involving a policyholder that claimed uninsured motorist benefits after his vehicle was struck by another driver that failed to appear for legal proceedings) ("[A] showing of prejudice is required before forfeiture will be sanctioned."). In addition, late notice may be excused where the insured was not negligent or responsible for the delay in notification. *See Harris v. Am. Motorists Ins. Co.*, 126 So.2d 870, 873 (Miss. 1961).

**Missouri:** Prejudice required. *See Weaver v. State Farm Mut. Auto. Ins. Co.*, 936 S.W.2d 818, 820–21 (Mo. 1997) (finding that delay alone was insufficient to prove prejudice in a case involving a policyholder that waited a year before requesting benefits from an uninsured motorist policy) ("[T]he insurer must establish prejudice to forfeit the coverage to which the insured would otherwise be entitled."); *Mo. Prop. Ins. Placement Facility*, 705 S.W.2d 104 (Mo. Ct. App. 1986). *Accord. Billings Mut. Ins. Co. v. Cameron Mut. Ins. Co.*, 229 S.W.3d 138, 148 (Mo. Ct. App. 2007) (engaging in a detailed explanation of late notice policy and holding that the insurer suffered prejudice where insured failed to provide notice of a house fire until after jury verdict.) ("A showing of untimely notice is not enough; the insurer must also prove that it was prejudiced by that late notice.") Burden to prove prejudice on insurer. *Weaver v. State Farm Mut. Auto. Ins. Co.*, 936 S.W.2d 818, 821 (Mo. 1997). *See also Greer v. Zurich Ins. Co.*, 441 S.W.2d 15 (Mo. 1969) (finding that notice given after judgment, even though only days after policyholder learned of potential coverage, was too late and prejudicial as a matter of law). *See also Bolin v. Progressive Nw. Ins. Co.*, No. 2:07CV0049 AGF, 2009 WL 1010770, at *10 (E.D. Mo. Apr. 9, 2009) (concluding that a fifteen-month delay in reporting motorcycle accident insufficient to show prejudice) ("[S]howing of untimely notice [by an insured] is not enough; the insurer must also prove that it was prejudiced by that late notice.").

**Montana:** No instructive state court case law. *But see J.G. Link & Co. v. Cont'l Cas. Co.*, 470 F.2d 1133 (9th Cir. 1972) (applying Montana law) (predicting that Montana would adopt notice-prejudice rule and holding that a seven-month delay not unreasonable). *See also Mont. Petroleum Tank Release Comp. Bd. v. Gen. Ins. Co.*, No. ADV-2004–646, 2009 Mont. Dist. Lexis 561 (Mont. Dist. Ct. Dec. 9, 2009) (claims excluded from coverage where the policyholder waited more than two years without justification to inform the insurer of a pending case; general insurer sought indemnification from individual insurers to cover oil spill cleanup costs).

**Nebraska:** Prejudice required. *See Herman Bros., Inc. v. Great W. Cas. Co.*, 582 N.W.2d 328, 334–35 (Neb. 1998) (concluding that the insurer was prejudiced when insured waited twenty months before giving notice under a contract term that required notice "as soon as practicable" and that insurer did not have adequate notice to be able to "meaningfully protect its interests").

*See also Steffensmeier v. Le Mar Mut. Ins. Co.*, 752 N.W.2d 155, 161 (Neb. 2008) (concluding that the insurer was prejudiced where it did not receive notice of a pending lawsuit in time to intervene) ("[P]rejudice from an unreasonable and unexcused delay in giving notice of a claim 'is established by examining whether the insurer received notice in time to meaningfully protect its interests.'"). Burden to prove prejudice on insurer. *Herman Bros.*, 582 N.W.2d at 334–35; *MFA Mut. Ins. Co. v. Sailors*, 141 N.W.2d 846 (Neb. 1966). *Accord. Dutton-Lainson Co. v. Cont'l Ins. Co.*, 716 N.W.2d 87, 102 (Neb. 2006) (case involving an insurer's contesting indemnification of environmental cleanup costs; court concludes summary judgment was inappropriate where insurer failed to prove prejudice caused by lack of notice).

**Nevada:** Older case law follows traditional rule of no prejudice required. *State Farm Mut. Auto Ins. Co. v. Cassinelli*, 216 P.2d 606, 616 (Nev. 1950); *Las Vegas Star Taxi v. St. Paul Fire & Marine Ins. Co.*, 714 P.2d 562 (1986) (following traditional rule but not citing *Cassinelli*). However, Nevada Administrative Code §§ 686A.660 and 686A.625 requires prejudice in order for late notice to bar coverage and there is no recent state supreme court case law on the issue. *See also Am. Fid. Fire Ins. Co. v. Adams*, 625 P.2d 88 (Nev. 1981) (finding that a policyholder's good faith belief that no action would be filed may mitigate or excuse delay in providing notice).

**New Hampshire:** Prejudice required. *See Dover Mills P'ship v. Commercial Union Ins. Cos.*, 740 A.2d 1064, 1067 (N.H. 1999) (holding that the three factors considered in determining if delay bars a claim are (1) length of delay, (2) reasons for the delay, and (3) prejudice to the insured). Burden to prove prejudice is on the insurer. *See id.* at 1066–67. *See also Wilson v. Progressive No. Ins. Co.*, 868 A.2d 268, 271 (N.H. 2005) (finding that a seven-month delay in reporting a hit-and-run accident in itself insufficient to show prejudice). *But see Lumbermens Mut. Cas. Co. v. Oliver*, 335 A.2d 666, 668 (N.H. 1975) (finding that policyholder had burden to prove that notice was given as soon as reasonably possible).

**New Jersey:** Prejudice required. *See Cooper v. Gov't Employees Ins. Co.*, 237 A.2d 870, 874 (N.J. 1968) (finding the late notice defense unavailing because policyholders acted in good faith because they reasonably believed a claim would not arise, and no prejudice resulted from delay). *See also Hager v. Gonsalves*, 942 A. 2d 160, 163 (N.J. Super. Ct. App. Div. 2008) (concluding that the prejudice standard used for notice also applies to the duty of cooperation in a case where insured and person injured in an automobile accident failed to cooperate with insurer efforts to gather information) ("[T]he carrier may not forfeit the bargained-for protection unless there are both a breach of the notice provision and a likelihood of appreciable prejudice."). Burden to prove prejudice on insurer. *Cooper*, 237 A.2d at 874.

**New Mexico:** Prejudice required. *See Found. Reserve Ins. Co. v. Esquibel*, 607 P.2d 1150, 1152 (N.M. 1980) (involving an insurer that brought suit against policyholder for money paid under a policy claiming material breach for delay in notice, court required a showing of prejudice). *See also State Farm Mut. Auto. Ins. Co. v. Fennema*, 110 P.3d 491, 493 (N.M. 2005) (discussing policy concerns and late notice defenses relevant to uninsured motorist policies) ("[F]ailure by an insurer to show substantial prejudice [due to] an insured's breach will frustrate the insured's reasonable expectation that coverage will not be denied arbitrarily."); *Sheldon v. Hartford Ins. Co.*, 189 P.3d 695 (N.M. 2008) (concluding that the insurer was not obligated to provide benefits where policyholder gave delayed notice of an accident and did not update policy to reflect marriage to a regular vehicle user). Burden to prove prejudice on insurer. *See Esquibel*, 607 P.2d at 1152; *Worth v. Sedillo Title Guar.*, 512 P.2d 667 (N.M. 1973).

**New York:** Until recently New York followed the rule that no prejudice was required for late notice to defeat coverage. *See Sec. Mut. Ins. Co. of N.Y. v. Acker-Fitzsimons Corp.*, 293 N.E.2d 76, 78 (N.Y. 1972) (involving an insured that waited nineteen months to notify insurer of fire damage, the court held that this constituted late notice under "as soon as practicable" clause). Traditional rule applied for excess insurers as well. *Am. Home Assur. Co. v. Int'l Ins. Co.*, 684 N.E.2d 14 (N.Y. 1997). However, reinsurers are required to prove prejudice from late notice to avoid coverage. *See Unigard Sec. Ins. Co. v. North River Ins. Co.*, 594 N.E.2d 571, 579–80, 584 (N.Y. 1992). In January 2009, New York enacted § 3420(a) of the New York Insurance Law to require that liability insurance policies covering bodily injury contain a provision that provides, "that failure to give notice within the prescribed time will not invalidate any claim made by the insured, injured person, or any other claimant, unless the failure to provide timely notice has prejudiced the insurer." It is not clear where the burden lies. For an extensive examination of the statute, see Eric Tausend, Note, *"No Prejudice" No More: New York and the Death of the No-Prejudice Rule*, 61 HASTINGS L.J. 497 (2009). Note that there remain in the litigation "pipeline" cases where the incidents took place prior to the effective date of the statute. *See, e.g., Lehigh Constr. Group, Inc. v. Lexington Ins. Co.*, 894 N.Y.S.2d 299 (N.Y. App. Div. 2010); *See also Sevenson Envtl. Servs., Inc. v. Sirius Am. Ins. Co.*, 64 A.D.3d 1234, 1236 (N.Y. App. Div. 2009) (finding a fifteen-month delay in reporting an on-the-job accident involving insured's employee was unreasonable as a matter of law) (discussing old rule and applicability of new statute)

**North Carolina:** Prejudice required. *See Great Am. Ins. Co. v. C.G. Tate Constr. Co.*, 279 S.E.2d 769, 775 (N.C. 1981) (finding that because policyholder acted in good faith despite late notice, insurer had burden to show that delay materially prejudiced its ability to investigate and defend the claim to deny coverage in a case involving a policyholder that did not notify insurer of an accident because he did not believe he was potentially at fault). *See also Richardson v. Maxim Healthcare Allegis Group*, 669 S.E.2d 582, 663 (N.C. 2008) (involving an employee who failed to supply a written notice of an injury within a required time period but was excused from the requirement because she provided telephone notice) ("[A]n employee may be excused from [notice requirements] by providing a reasonable excuse for failing to give notice and by showing that the employer has not been prejudiced."). Burden to prove prejudice on insurer. *See C.G. Tate*, 279 S.E.2d at 776.

**North Dakota:** Prejudice required. *See Finstad v. Steiger Tractor, Inc.*, 301 N.W.2d 392, 398 (N.D. 1981) (requiring insurer to prove that insured breached notice provision and that breach resulted in "likelihood of appreciable prejudice" to insurer when insured employee failed to report work injury due to lack of knowledge of policy); *see also Hasper v. Ctr. Mut. Ins. Co.*, 723 N.W.2d 409, 416 (N.D. 2006) (finding summary judgment proceedings are not conducive to determining insurer prejudice because prejudice a question of fact in case where injured policyholder did not inform his uninsured motorist insurer until after settlement, nearly a year after an accident). A UIM insurer that "seeks to deny coverage based upon the insured's failure to notify the insurer of a proposed settlement with the tortfeasor must demonstrate that it suffered actual prejudice resulting from the lack of notice." *Id.* Burden to prove prejudice on insurer. *Finstad v. Steiger Tractor*, 301 N.W.2d at 398; *see also D.E.M. v. Allickson*, 555 N.W.2d 596, 602 (N.D. 1996) (concluding that policyholder need not notify insurer of impending settlement where insurer has refused to defend claim); *Blackburn, Nickels & Smith, Inc. v. Nat'l Framers Union Prop. & Cas. Co.*, 482 N.W.2d 600 (N.D. 1992) (finding policyholder excused from late notice where insurer never provided copy of policy).

**Ohio:** Prejudice required but prejudice presumed from late notice. *See Ferrando v. Auto-Owners Ins. Co.*, 781 N.E.2d 827, 944–45 (Ohio 2002) (reviewing case law in Ohio and other jurisdictions and noting "modern trend" in favor of notice-prejudice rule, with most jurisdictions requiring insurer to show prejudice; also applying similar analysis to consent to settle provisions and preservation of insurer's subrogation rights) ("[W]e hold that when an insurer's denial of UIM coverage is premised on the insured's breach of a prompt notice provision in a policy of insurance, the insurer is relieved of the obligation to provide coverage if it is prejudiced by the insured's unreasonable delay in giving notice. An insured's unreasonable delay in giving notice is presumed prejudicial to the insurer absent evidence to the contrary."); *Champion Spark Plug Co. v. Fid. & Cas. Co. of N.Y.*, 687 N.E.2d 785, 791 (Ohio Ct. App. 1996) (concluding that a delay of one year before notifying insurer of possible liability for pollution cleanup failed to meet policy requirements of notification "as soon as possible" where policyholder gave no reasonable explanation for an unreasonable delay prejudice was presumed with potential for rebuttal by the policyholder). *See also Thomas v. Nationwide Mut. Ins. Co.*, 895 N.E.2d 217, 230 (Ohio Ct. App. 2008) (concluding that lower court erred in giving a directed verdict where reasonable minds could differ as to insurer prejudice where policyholder called her insurer after an accident but did not submit written notice as required by her policy). In either a breach of a prompt-notice provision or a consent-to-settle or other subrogation provision, [*Ruby v. Midwestern Indem. Co.* provides] that the breach is "presumed prejudicial to the insurer absent evidence to the contrary." *Id.* Burden to prove absence of prejudice on policyholder. *See Ferrando v. Auto-Owners Ins. Co.,* 781 N.E.2d 827, 944–45 (Ohio 2002); *Sanborn Plastics Corp. v. St. Paul Fire & Marines Ins. Co.,* 616 N.E.2d 988 (Ohio 1993); *Patrick v. Auto-Owners Ins. Co.,* 449 N.E.2d 790 (Ohio 1982). *See, e.g., McCann v. Nationwide Mut. Fire Ins. Co.,* No. 88CA004433, 1989 WL 52635, at *5 (Ohio May, 17 1989) (finding the presumption of prejudice to insurer from late notice overcome where despite tardy notice, insurer retained adequate time to investigate facts and defend suit against policyholder). In *Penn. Gen. Ins. Co. v. Park-Ohio Industries,* 930 N.E.2d 800 (Ohio 2010), the Supreme Court applied the state's law of notice in an allocation matter. Pursuant to *Goodyear Tire & Rubber Co. v. Aetna Cas. & Sur. Co.,* 769 N.E.2d 835 (Ohio 2002), Ohio is an "all sums" state (see Chapter 17 regarding state-by-state difference regarding allocation of insurer responsibility in cases of consecutively triggered coverage) that allows the a policyholder facing claims implicating several policy periods of multiply triggered policies to approach particular insurers for coverage, with the targeted insurer then permitted to seek pro rata contribution from other triggered insurers. In the 2010 *Park-Ohio* opinion, the court faced the issue of whether insurers facing an indemnity request could assert a late notice defense and concluded that they could—but that such defenses would not be successful unless the insurer was prejudiced by the delay. In what may be a departure from the general law of late notice, the *Park-Ohio* opinion can be read as suggesting that in multiyear contribution cases of this sort, the insurer bears the burden to show prejudice from any delay in seeking contribution. On the merits, the *Park-Ohio* Court found that the delay in notifying in notifying the insurers was not unreasonable and was "as soon as practicable" under the circumstances of the long-tail asbestos liability at issue in the underlying case. "If the failure to notify non-targeted insurers pursuant to the relevant insurance policies results in prejudice to the nontargeted insurers, then the nontargeted insurers will not be required to contribute to the targeted insurer. In cases in which the nontargeted insurers have not been prejudiced by a failure to notify, the equitable nature of the all sums approach requires that those nontargeted insurers will still be liable in a contribution action brought by the targeted insurer." *See Park-Ohio,* 930 N.E.2d at 807.

**Oklahoma:** Prejudice required. *See Fox v. Nat'l Sav. Ins. Co.,* 424 P.2d 19, 25 (Okla. 1967) (policyholder waited six months to notify insurer of car accident implicating policy; court remanded case because lower court did not assess whether the insurer satisfied its burden of proving prejudice). "[I]t is in accord with the public policy of this State… to place the burden upon the insurer to show prejudice from noncompliance with the policy's provisions concerning written notice." *Id. See also Ass'n of County Comm'rs of Okla. v. Nat'l Am. Ins. Co.,* 116 P.3d 206 (Okla. Civ. App. 2005). Burden to prove prejudice on insurer. *See Fox v. Nat'l Sav. Ins. Co.*, 424 P.2d 19, 25 (Okla. 1967) (holding that the burden should be on the insured "where the evidence shows that the insurer has received actual notice, or knowledge" of a claim). *Accord. Indep. Sch. Dist. No. 1 v. Jackson*, 608 P.2d 1153, 1155 (Okla. 1980); *First Bank v. Fid. & Deposit Ins. Co. of Md.*, 928 P.2d 298 (Okla. 1996).

**Oregon:** Prejudice required. *See Lusch v. Aetna Cas. & Sur. Co.*, 538 P.2d 902, 904 (Or. 1975) (concluding that where an insurer could not show any prejudice it must provide coverage and holding that even if insurer is prejudiced by the late notice it must still provide coverage if the policyholder was excused from prompt notice requirement because it acted reasonably in failing to give notice at an earlier time where policyholder reported car accident after other party to accident reported it to insurer). *See also Employers Ins. of Wausau, A Mut. Co. v. Tektronix, Inc.*, 156 P.3d 105, 112 (Or. 2007) (concluding that late notice cases require two inquiries: (1) was the insurer prejudiced by the late notice and (2) was the insured's delay in reporting reasonable; notice argument moot because the court held insurer not required to defend or indemnify because of "sudden and accidental" exception) (involving policyholder costs associated with hazardous waste and environmental cleanup). "If the insured does not give notice immediately after the accident or if notice is given by a third party, the initial question should be whether the notice is given in time for the insurer to adequately investigate the potential claim and thus protect itself and the insured." *Id.* Burden to prove prejudice on insurer. *Halsey v. Fireman's Fund Ins. Co.*, 681 P.2d 168 (Or. 1984); *Lusch v. Aetna Cas. & Sur. Co.*, 538 P.2d 902 (Or. 1975).

**Pennsylvania:** Prejudice required. *See Brakeman v. Potomac Ins. Co.*, 371 A.2d 193, 196 (Pa. 1977) (departing from prior decisions and holding that an insurer must prove breach of notice provision and prejudice as a result of that breach to avoid coverage obligation). "[T]he insurance company will be required to prove that the notice provision was in fact breached and that the breach resulted in prejudice to its position." *Id.* at 198. *Accord Nationwide Ins. Co. v. Schneider*, 960 A.2d 442, 451 (Pa. 2008); *Metal Bank of Am., Inc., v. Ins. Co. of N. Am.*, 520 A.2d 493 (Pa. 1987); *Nationwide Ins. Co. v. Lehman*, 743 A.2d 933, 940 (Pa. Super. Ct. 1999).

**Rhode Island:** Prejudice required. *See Canavan v. Lovett, Schefrin and Harnett*, 862 A.2d 778, 785 (R.I. 2004) (sustaining client's professional malpractice claim against lawyer where legal malpractice insurer refused to pay claim due to late notice of at least three and perhaps as much as six years). The insurance carrier has the "burden to show that it was prejudiced" by the insured's late notice before it can "declare a forfeiture of the bargained-for protection." *Id.* Burden of proving prejudice on insurer. *Pa. Gen.*, 475 A.2d at 1035. *But see Avco Corp. v. Aetna Cas. & Sur. Co.*, 679 A.2d 323 (R.I. 1996) (finding that insurer's claim of unrebutted claim of prejudice established sufficient prejudice). *See also Pa. General Ins. Co. v. Becton*, 475 A.2d 1032, 1035 (R.I. 1984) (concluding that insurer was prejudiced when policyholder notified insurer almost three years after incident, when policyholder found out about policy).

**South Carolina:** Prejudice required. *See Vt. Mut. Ins. Co. v. Singleton*, 446 S.E.2d 417, 421 (S.C. 1994) (concluding that insurer failed to show substantial prejudice to defeat coverage when policyholder waited four months to report eye injury implicating homeowners policy). "The purpose of a notification requirement is to allow for investigation of the facts and to assist the insurer in preparing a defense." *Id.*; *see also Cowan v. Allstate Ins. Co.*, 594 S.E.2d 275, 277 (S.C. 2004) (finding that, pursuant to state statutory law, insurer was still obligated to policyholder where insurer's first notice of lawsuit arising out of an automobile accident was a letter of default judgment). "[D]espite an insured's failure to… forward pleadings, the insurer must honor all its obligations under the policy if it has actual notice of those pleadings." *Id.* Burden of proving prejudice on insurer. *See Vt. Mut.*, 446 S.E.2d at 421–22 (finding that insurer must show "substantial prejudice."). *Accord. Floyd v. St. Paul Fire & Marine Ins. Co.*, 328 S.E.2d 132 (S.C. 1985).

**South Dakota:** Prejudice required. *See Auto-Owners Ins. Co. v. Hansen Housing, Inc.*, 604 N.W.2d 504, 513 (S.D. 2000) (finding insurer prejudiced given insured's failure to give prompt notice where insured waited two years to notify insurer of burglary). "Where the insurance company's interests have not been harmed by a late notice, even in the absence of extenuating circumstances to excuse the tardiness, the reason behind the notice condition in the policy is lacking." *Id. Union Pac. R.R. v. Certain Underwriters at Lloyd's London*, 771 N.W.2d 611 (S.D. 2009) (concluding insurer was prejudiced and granting insurer summary judgment due to policyholder's late notice, which occurred after cleanup of website pursuant to EPA pressure and after seven-figure expenditures by policyholder) ("[Insurer] articulated specific facts and reasons for the claim of actual prejudice and demonstrated that its interests were actually harmed"). *But see Union Pac. R.R.*, 771 N.W.2d at 618 (Meierhenry, J., concurring) (arguing that Illinois law should apply but that result would be the same in that where notice is late, prejudice need not be shown). South Dakota law is somewhat unclear regarding the burden of proof but appears to place it on the insurer. *Union Pac. R.R.*, 771 N.W.2d at 618.

**Tennessee:** Prejudice required. *See Alcazar v. Hayes*, 982 S.W.2d 845, 856 (Tenn. 1998) (departing from previous precedent and holding that prejudice must be shown to sustain coverage denial when policyholder waited one year to give notice to recover uninsured motorist benefits). "[I]t is inequitable for an insurer that has not been prejudiced by a delay in notice to reap the benefits flowing from the forfeiture of the insurance policy." *Id.* at 852; *see also Brick Church Transmission, Inc. v. So. Pilot Ins. Co.*, 140 S.W.3d 324, 334 (Tenn. Ct. App. 2003) (finding dismissal appropriate where insured waited two years to make a claim under a loss-by-theft policy making it barred by statute of limitations clause). "We, therefore, hesitate to hold that limitation of suit clauses can be enforced only in the absence of prejudice to the carrier." *Id.* Delayed notice creates a presumption of prejudice that the insured bears the burden of rebutting. *Alcazar*, 982 S.W.2d at 856.

**Texas:** Prejudice required. *See PAJ, Inc. v. Hanover Ins. Co.*, 243 S.W.3d 630, 636–37 (Tex. 2008) (finding prejudice when insured jewelry manufacturer did not notify insurer of copyright infringement suit brought against it until six months after litigation commenced); *Harwell v. State Farm Mut. Auto. Ins. Co.*, 896 S.W.2d 170, 174 (Tex. 1995); *Hernandez v. Gulf Group Lloyds*, 875 S.W.2d 691, 692 (1994) (concluding that breach of notice provision was an immaterial breach of insurance contract unless insurer prejudiced). Burden of proving prejudice on insurer. *See PAJ*, 243 S.W.3d at 636–37.

**Utah:** Prejudice required. *See State Farm Mut. Auto. Ins. Co. v. Green*, 89 P.3d 97, 104 (Utah 2003) (finding that policyholder's late notice acted as a bar to coverage if it "results in actual, rather than theoretical, impairment of an insurer's ability to recover," and concluding that breach of consent to settle provision in sufficient to show prejudice where insurer settled claim prior to notifying insurer). Burden of proving prejudice on insurer. *State Farm Mut. Auto. Ins. Co. v. Green, supra*, 89 P.3d at 104. *But see Busch Corp. v. State Farm*, 743 P.2d 1217 (Utah 1987) (finding a five-year delay in providing notice prejudicial as a matter of law).

**Vermont:** Prejudice required. *See Coop. Fire Ins. Ass'n of Vt. v. White Caps, Inc.*, 694 A.2d 34, 38 (Vt. 1997) (finding that because insurer failed to prove substantial prejudice from policyholder restaurant's eighteen-month delay in giving notice of slip-and-fall incident implicating policy, insurer could not deny coverage). "When faced with a claim for coverage, it is not sufficient for the carrier to merely sit back and engage in cursory investigation, seeking excuses for lack of information." *Id.* at 29; *see also Hardwick Recycling & Salvage, Inc. v. Acadia Ins. Co.*, 869 A.2d 82 (Vt. 2004) (holding that insurer was required to provide defense in environmental cleanup case because insurer did not prove prejudice occurred where policyholder waited five years to make a claim). "[A]n insurer must show prejudice from an insured's late notice before it can avoid its obligations under an insurance policy." *Id.* at 96. Burden to prove prejudice on insurer. *Coop. Fire*, 694 A.2d at 38.

**Virginia:** No prejudice required. *See State Farm Fire & Cas. Co. v. Scott*, 372 S.E.2d 383, 385 (Va. 1983) (allowing the jury to consider prejudice when deciding whether a ten-week delay in reporting an uninsured motorist claim was a breach of the notice provision, but finding that the insurer does not have to show prejudice to deny coverage where late notice is established). *See also Osborne v. Nat'l Union Fire Ins. Co.*, 465 S.E.2d 835 (Va. 1996) (concluding that an insurer could deny uninsured motorist coverage on the grounds that the insured settled with another insurer without the insurer's consent where insured settled with his personal insurer after an automobile accident on the job, but did not provide notice to his employer's insurer). "[W]hen an insured fails to comply with a policy provision requiring timely notice of an accident, we have said that 'the insurance company need not show that it was prejudiced by such a violation.'" *Id. See also Modern Cont'l S. v. Fairfax County Water Auth.*, 70 Va. Cir. 172 (Va. Cir. 2006) (holding that contractor not entitled to additional work where he gave notice two days later than the five-day required reporting time). "Under Virginia law, a court must 'enforce the contract… as written, and the contract becomes the law of the case unless the contract is repugnant to some rule of law or public policy.'" *Id.* at 192.

**Washington:** Prejudice required. *See Or. Auto Ins. Co. v. Salzberg*, 535 P.2d 816, 819 (Wash. 1975) (concluding that coverage was required where insurer received notice of injuries implicating policy three months after accident, but demonstrated no prejudice). "[A]n alleged breach of a cooperation clause… may effect a release of an insurer from its responsibilities *only* if the insurer was actually *prejudiced* by the insured's actions or conduct." *Id.* at 819. Burden to prove prejudice on insurer. *Thompson v. Grange Ins. Ass'n*, 660 P.2d 307, 314 (Wash. 1983); *Felice v. St. Paul Fire & Marine Ins. Co.*, 711 P.2d 1066, 1070 (Wash. App. 1985) (insurer asserting prejudice has burden of demonstrating prejudice, which insurer did where notified of claim only two days before running of time for appeal, depriving insurer of adequate opportunity to investigate and evaluate matter). *See also S & K Motors, Inc. v. Harco Nat. Ins. Co.*, 213 P.3d 630, 636 (Wash. Ct. App. 2009) (finding that late notice did not bar coverage where insurer failed to prove prejudice and engaged in bad faith, thereby breaching the contract after it refused to provide benefits under an employee theft provision). "Harco must perform under its insurance contract unless it can show actual and substantial prejudice due to the late notice." *Id. But see Pulse v. Nw. Farm Bureau Ins. Co.*, 566 P.2d 577 (Wash. 1977) (finding that where notice extremely late or policyholder without justification, burden may shift to policyholder).

**West Virginia:** Prejudice required. *See Colonial Ins. Co. v. Barrett*, 542 S.E.2d 869, 875 (W. Va. 2000) (concluding that coverage was required where six-day delay in reporting car accident resulted in no prejudice to insurer). Burden of proof on policyholder, but if the delay is reasonable in light of the insured's circumstances then the burden shifts and the insurer must show prejudice caused by the delay. *Id. See also Dairyland Ins. Co. v. Voshel*, 428 S.E.2d 542, 545 (W. Va. 1993) ("[R]egardless of the language used [in the policy]… the courts are generally in agreement that reasonable notice is sufficient."); *State Farm Mut. Auto. Ins. Co. v. Milam*, 438 F. Supp. 227, 232 (S.D. W. Va. 1977) ("The test to apply is whether the insurer would be in a better position… [if] it [had] been furnished notice within a reasonable time."); *State Farm Fire & Cas. Co. v. Walton*, 396 S.E. 2d 737, 742 (W. Va. 1990) ("The particular language used in the automobile insurance policy as to the time in which notice must be given is not controlling."); *Arch Specialty Ins. Co. v. Go-Mart, Inc.*, No. 2:08–0285, 2009 WL 5214916, at *9 (S.D. W. Va. Dec. 28, 2009) (insurer was unduly prejudiced as a matter of law where convenience store/policyholder waited thirty-two months to provide notice of a customer's injuries) ("When the delay is determined to be unreasonable, prejudice need not be determined" through fact adjudication and court may find prejudice to insurer as a matter of law).

**Wisconsin:** Prejudice required. Insurer has burden to show prejudice. *See Gerrard Realty Corp. v. Am. States Ins. Co.*, 277 N.W.2d 863, 871 (Wis. 1979) (applying Wis. Stat. § 631.81) (finding insurer did not owe coverage to policyholder where policyholder did not notify insurer until twenty-two months after commencement of a suit against it as such late notice resulted in prejudice). "[T]he circumstances of the particular case must be considered in ascertaining whether notice was given 'as soon as practicable.'" *Id.* at 870. *See also Int'l Flavors & Fragrances, Inc v. Valley Forge Ins. Co.*, 738 N.W.2d 159, 162 (Wis. Ct. App. 2007) (concluding that insurer was not prejudiced where it received notice of a multiple personal injuries caused by exposure to "butter popcorn flavoring" before trial was imminent). "[F]ailure to provide timely notice as required by the policy does not defeat coverage unless the insurer is prejudiced thereby." *Id.*

**Wyoming:** Appears to follow traditional rule but recent case law lacking. *See Pacheco v. Cont'l Cas. Co.*, 476 P.2d 166, 169 (Wyo. 1970) (concluding that notice given three years after the date of an accident at work was not given as soon as "reasonably possible" and deprived the insurer of the opportunity to investigate). "[A] beneficiary's demand must be made within a reasonable time for the insurer to investigate the claim." *Id. See also State Farm Mut. Auto. Ins. Co. v. Hollingsworth*, 668 F. Supp. 1476 (D. Wyo. 1987) (finding an eight-month delay in notice defeats coverage as such notice was unreasonable as a matter of law).

# 4

# Duty to Defend Standard: "Four Corners" or Extrinsic Evidence?

If coverage issues were stocks, the duty to defend would be Blue Chip. Just as investors purchase such stocks in hopes of steady and consistent returns, the rules concerning an insurer's duty to defend have long been unwavering.

This is why it comes as a surprise to no one when a court states that the duty to defend is broader than the duty to indemnify. After all, this has been the case for decades. *Goldberg v. Lumber Mut. Cas. Ins. Co. of N.Y.*, 77 N.E.2d 131, 133 (N.Y. 1948) ("The courts have frequently remarked that the duty to defend is broader than the duty to pay."). Likewise, it does not make news when a court declares that an insurer is obligated to defend even groundless, false, or fraudulent claims. This too has been the case for a very long time. *Patterson v. Standard Accident Ins. Co.*, 144 N.W. 491, 492 (Mich. 1913) (describing a provision in an automobile liability policy that obligated the insurer to defend any suits alleging injuries and demanding damages even if the allegations or demands were "wholly groundless, false or fraudulent"). Still another duty to defend truism is that "the appropriate starting point" for such a determination are the allegations contained in the complaint filed against the insured. *Essex Ins. Co. v. Fieldhouse, Inc.*, 506 N.W.2d 772, 775 (Iowa 1993). And, of course, no citation is needed for the test for determining an insurer's duty to defend: whether a claim in the complaint is potentially covered under the policy.

Given that these principles are so universally held, they are not candidates for a fifty-state survey. Any such survey would be the proverbial broken record. But there is a duty to defend issue about which courts do not agree. While all courts may begin their duty to defend determination by reviewing the complaint filed against the insured and comparing it to the policy, they often part ways on whether such examination also ends there. There is wide variation between courts over whether, and, if so, the extent to which, information contained outside the complaint—so-called "extrinsic evidence"—can be considered when deciding if an insurer's duty to defend has been triggered. Such wide disparity between the states concerning this issue, makes it an appropriate one for a fifty-state survey.

In some states, the answer is simple—No. Courts are not permitted to consider extrinsic evidence when evaluating whether an insurer is obligated to defend. This is sometimes referred to as the "complaint" rule, "comparison test," "four corners" rule, or "eight corners" rule. *Pompa v. Am. Family Mut. Ins. Co.*, 520 F.3d 1139, 1145 (10th Cir. 2008) (applying Colorado law). While the rule is, by definition, constraining, it is applied with adherence to certain principles that are designed to benefit policyholders. Where there is some doubt as to whether the complaint against the insured alleges a risk insured against, that doubt should be resolved in favor of the insured. *Pac. Ins. Co. v. Liberty Mut. Ins. Co.*, 956 A.2d 1246, 1255 (Del. 2008). Further, any ambiguity in the pleadings should be resolved against the insurer. *Id.*

Depending on the situation, a rule that limits a court's duty to defend determination to only a comparison between the complaint and the policy can favor policyholders or insurers. For example, the Supreme Court of Connecticut's application of the "four corners" rule favored a policyholder in *Hartford Casualty Insurance Co. v. Litchfield Mutual Fire Insurance Co.*, 876 A.2d 1139, 1144 (Conn. 2005). The court held that an insurer was obligated to defend an insured if the complaint alleged a covered claim, *even if* the insurer obtained information from the insured or anyone else that the claim was not in fact covered. On the other hand, the Supreme Court of Pennsylvania's adherence to the "four corners" rule in *Kvaerner Metals Div. of Kvaerner U.S., Inc. v. Commercial Union Ins. Co.*, 908 A.2d 888, 895 (Pa. 2006) resulted in the opposite outcome for the policyholder. Here the policyholder was denied a defense because the court would not consider extrinsic evidence that the lower court concluded triggered a defense obligation.

While many states adhere to the "four corners" rule, about twice as many do not and have concluded that extrinsic evidence can be considered by a court in its duty to defend determination. *Miller v. Westport Ins. Corp.*, 200 P.3d 419, 424 (Kan. 2009) (quoting *Spivey v. Safeco Ins. Co.*, 865 P.2d 182, 188 (Kan. 1993)) ("If these known or reasonably discoverable extrinsic facts give rise to potential liability on the insured's part, the insured (sic) has a duty to defend... . This approach has become known as the 'extrinsic evidence' approach or rule. Under [this] approach, the insurer's duty to defend still hinges on the potential for coverage, but the universe of information from which that potential must be ascertained is much greater [than the universe used in an approach limited to the 'eight corners' of a pleading and the applicable insurance policy].") (alteration in original).

Courts that have rejected the "four corners" rule have done so based on various rationales. New York's highest court was troubled by the "four corners" rule, reasoning that the denial of a defense, notwithstanding the existence of extrinsic evidence proving that a defense was owed, would eliminate the breadth of the duty to defend. *Fitzpatrick v. Am. Honda Motor Co.*, 575 N.E.2d 90, 92 (N.Y. 1991) ("[W]here the insurer is attempting to shield itself from the responsibility to defend despite its actual knowledge that the lawsuit involves a covered event, wooden application of the 'four corners of the complaint' rule would render the duty to defend narrower than the duty to indemnify—clearly an unacceptable result. For that reason, courts and commentators have indicated that the insurer must provide a defense if it has knowledge of facts which potentially bring the claim within the policy's indemnity coverage.").

Courts have also rejected the "four corners" rule on the basis that notice pleading often provides few facts upon which to assess an insurer's duty to defend. *Talen v. Employers Mut. Cas. Co.*, 703 N.W.2d 395, 406 (Iowa 2005); *but see Transcon. Ins. Co. v. Jim Black & Assocs., Inc.*, 888 So. 2d 671, 675 (Fla. Dist. Ct. App. 2004) ("Even under the more liberal federal pleading requirements, a third-party plaintiff's claims against an insured should be sufficiently described to allow a determination of whether a duty to defend arises under the allegations of the complaint.").

The permissibility of extrinsic evidence to establish an insurer's duty to defend has also been justified on the basis that liability insurance is in effect "litigation insurance" to protect the insured from the expense of defending suits brought against it. *Aetna Cas. & Sur. Co. v. Cochran*, 651 A.2d 859, 865 (Md. 1995). Therefore, "[a]llowing an insured the opportunity to establish a defense to tort allegations which may provide a potentiality of coverage under an insurance policy prior to the insured incurring expenses associated with maintaining a defense in that tort action is precisely what the insured bargained for under the insurance contract." *Id.* This rationale is tied to an insured's reasonable expectations that the insurer will defend it whenever there is a potential for coverage. *Id.; see also Ball v. Wilshire Ins. Co.*, 221 P.3d 717, 723 (Okla. 2009) ("The defense duty is measured by the nature and kinds of risks covered by the policy as well as by the reasonable expectations of the insured.").

Extrinsic evidence has also been permitted in a duty to defend determination "to avoid permitting the pleading strategies, whims, and vagaries of third party claimants to control the rights of parties to an insurance contract." *M. Mooney Corp. v. U.S. Fid. & Guar. Co.*, 618 A.2d 793, 797 (N.H. 1992).

Some states that have adopted an exception to the "four corners" rule sometimes refuse to apply such exception when extrinsic evidence is sought to be used by an insurer to deny a defense that is otherwise owed under the four corners of the complaint. *Woo v. Fireman's Fund Ins. Co.*, 164 P.3d 454, 459 (Wash. 2007) ("The insurer may not rely on facts extrinsic to the complaint to deny the duty to defend—it may do so only to trigger the duty."); *see also Dairy Road Partners v. Island Ins. Co., Ltd.*, 992 P.2d 93, 113 (Haw. 2000) (noting a split of authority nationally on the permissibility of an insurer's use of extrinsic evidence to disclaim a duty to defend and concluding that the majority forbid it).

But even when courts permit an insurer to use extrinsic evidence to disclaim a defense, they sometimes do so narrowly—allowing consideration of extrinsic evidence solely in specific situations. For example, the Supreme Court of Hawaii held that an insurer may only disclaim a duty to defend based on extrinsic facts by showing that none of such facts relied upon might be resolved differently in the underlying lawsuit. *Dairy Road Partners*, 992 P.2d at 117 n. 17 ("One example of an extrinsic fact upon which an insurer might rely pursuant to the new rule arises when an insurer argues that an occurrence was outside of the effective period of the policy. In such a case, the factual issue regarding the parameters of the effective period of the policy would not normally be subject to dispute in the underlying action."); *see also Pompa v. Am. Family Mut. Ins. Co.*, 520 F.3d 1139, 1147 (10th Cir. 2008) (applying Colorado law) (predicting that the Supreme Court of Colorado would adopt an exception to the complaint rule, explaining that "[w]hen the extrinsic facts relied on by the insurer are relevant to the issue of coverage, but do not affect the third party's right of recovery, courts occasionally have held that the insurer may refuse to defend third-party actions, even though the allegations in the complaint suggest that coverage exists") (quotation and internal citation omitted).

Another example of extrinsic evidence being permissible to disclaim a defense, but narrowly so, is where a complaint pleads "negligence," but, despite such label, the conduct at issue was unquestionably intentional. *Peerless Ins. Co. v. Viegas*, 667 A.2d 785, 788–89 (R.I. 1995) (holding that, notwithstanding that the duty to defend is determined by the "pleadings test," an insurer was not obligated to defend an insured that sexually abused a minor, even if the allegations in the complaint were described in terms of negligence).

Some courts may also permit the consideration of extrinsic evidence, as a basis to disclaim a defense obligation, when such evidence addresses a threshold issue concerning coverage under the policy. *Nateman v. Hartford Cas. Ins. Co.*, 544 So. 2d 1026, 1027 (Fla. App. Ct. 1989) ("While, as a general rule, the obligation to defend an insured against an action, whether groundless or not, must be measured and determined by the allegations of the petition rather than the outcome of the litigation, an obvious exception must be made in those instances where, notwithstanding allegations in the petition to the contrary, the insurer successfully urges the alleged insured is not in fact an insured under the policy.").

While the use of extrinsic evidence to disclaim a defense is oftentimes, at most, permitted solely in narrow circumstances, courts often speak in broad terms when addressing the allowance of extrinsic evidence to establish an insurer's defense obligation. However, such pronouncements are sometimes general and lacking in guidance. *Talen*, 703 N.W.2d at 406 (Iowa 2005) ("The scope of inquiry [for the duty to defend]... [includes] the pleadings of the injured party and any other admissible and relevant facts in the record.") (citations and internal quotation omitted); *Am. Bumper & Mfg. Co. v. Hartford*

*Fire Ins. Co.*, 550 N.W.2d 475, 481 (Mich. 1996) ("The insurer has the duty to look behind the third party's allegations to analyze whether coverage is possible."); *Garvis v. Employers Mut. Cas. Co.*, 497 N.W.2d 254, 258 (Minn. 1993) (stating that the determination of the duty to defend includes consideration of facts of which the insurer is "aware"); *Farmland Mut. Ins. Co. v. Scruggs*, 886 So. 2d 714, 719 n.2 (Miss. 2004) (holding that, in determining whether an insurer has a duty to defend, an insurer may consider those "true facts [that] are inconsistent with the complaint," the insured brought to the insurer's attention); *Peterson v. Ohio Cas. Group*, 724 N.W.2d 765, 773–74 (Neb. 2006) (finding that a duty to defend exists where the "actual facts" reveal such a duty exists); *Am. Gen. Fire & Cas. Co. v. Progressive Cas. Co.*, 799 P.2d 1113, 1116 (N.M. 1990) ("The duty of an insurer to defend arises from the allegations on the face of the complaint or from the known but unpleaded factual basis of the claim."); *State Farm Fire & Cas. Co. v. Harbert*, 741 N.W.2d 228, 234 (S.D. 2007) ("[T]he issue of whether an insurer has a duty to defend is determined by… 'other evidence of record.'").

Courts also vary in the nature of the insurer's effort that is required to obtain extrinsic evidence that could trigger a defense obligation. *Scottsdale Ins. Co. v. MV Transp.*, 115 P.3d 460, 466 (Cal. 2005) ("[T]hat the precise causes of action pled by the third party complaint may fall outside policy coverage does not excuse the duty to defend where, under the facts alleged, reasonably inferable, or otherwise known, the complaint could fairly be amended to state a covered liability."); *Colonial Oil Indus. v. Underwriters Subscribing to Policy Nos. TO31504670 & TO31504671*, 491 S.E.2d 337, 338–39 (Ga. 1997) ("The insurer is under no obligation to independently investigate the claims against its insured… A different rule, however, applies when the complaint on its face shows no coverage, but the insured notifies the insurer of factual contentions that would place the claim within the policy coverage."); *Garvis*, 497 N.W.2d at 258 ("[I]f the insurer is aware of facts indicating that there may be a claim, either from what is said directly or inferentially in the complaint, or if the insured tells the insurer of such facts, or if the insurer has some independent knowledge of such facts, then the insurer must either accept tender of the defense or further investigate the potential claim."); *Revelation Indus., Inc. v. St. Paul Fire & Marine Ins. Co.*, 206 P.3d 919, 926 (Mont. 2009) (holding that insurers are not required to "look at facts beyond the allegations in the complaint" and that those that do, "do so at their own risk as they will be required to defend and/or indemnify based on the information discovered"); *Waste Mgmt. of Carolinas, Inc. v. Peerless Ins. Co.*, 340 S.E.2d 374, 377–78 (N.C. 1986) (finding that an insurer's investigation includes investigation into any facts it "knows or could reasonably ascertain"); *First Bank of Turley v. Fid. & Deposit Ins. Co.*, 928 P.2d 298, 303 (Okla. 1996) ("The insurer's defense duty is determined on the basis of information gleaned from the petition (and other pleadings), from the insured and from other sources available to the insurer at the time the defense is demanded.").

As these decisions demonstrate, whether an insurer is in the "four corners" or "extrinsic evidence" camp is only the first duty to defend question—and the easiest one. Where the complexity arises is when it comes to extrinsic evidence states and determining the nature of such evidence to be considered by the insurer, as well as the manner in which such evidence is obtained by the insurer. These are oftentimes extremely fact-intensive determinations with case law providing guidance but not a definitive answer.

## 50-State Survey: Duty to Defend Standard: "Four Corners" or Extrinsic Evidence?

**Alabama:** The Supreme Court of Alabama held that the determination of the duty to defend is not limited to the allegations in the complaint. *Hartford Cas. Ins. Co. v. Merchs. & Farmers Bank*, 928 So. 2d 1006, 1009–10 (Ala. 2005) ("Whether an insurance company owes its insured a duty to provide a defense in proceedings instituted against the insured is determined primarily by the allegations contained in the complaint. If the allegations of the injured party's complaint show an accident or an occurrence within the coverage of the policy, then the insurer is obligated to defend, regardless of the ultimate liability of the insured. However, this Court has rejected the argument that the insurer's obligation to defend must be determined solely from the facts alleged in the complaint in the action against the insured.") (citations and internal quotation omitted). "[I]f there is any uncertainty as to whether the complaint alleges facts that would invoke the duty to defend, the insurer must investigate the facts surrounding the incident that gave rise to the complaint in order to determine whether it has a duty to defend the insured." *Blackburn v. Fid. & Deposit Co. of Md.*, 667 So. 2d 661, 668 (Ala. 1995).

**Alaska:** The Supreme Court of Alaska held that the determination of the duty to defend is not limited to the allegations in the complaint. *Great Divide Ins. Co. v. Carpenter*, 79 P.3d 599, 616 (Alaska 2003) ("The allegations of the complaint provide the initial guide to whether an insurance company has a duty to defend. The duty to defend arises if the complaint on its face alleges facts which, standing alone, give rise to a possible finding of liability covered by the policy. If the complaint does not contain allegations indicating coverage, there is nonetheless a duty to defend if facts underlying the complaint are within, or potentially within, the policy coverage and are known or reasonably ascertainable by the insurer.") (citations and internal quotation omitted). Extrinsic evidence may not be resorted to by an insurer to disclaim a defense that is otherwise owed based on the complaint. *Afcan v. Mut. Fire, Marine & Inland Ins. Co.*, 595 P.2d 638, 645 (Alaska 1979) ("[E]ven though facts extrinsic to the pleadings may show that there will be no ultimate liability under the policy, if the complaint on its face alleges facts which, standing alone, give rise to a possible finding of liability covered by the policy, the insured has the contractual right to a proper defense at the expense of the insurer.").

**Arkansas:** The Supreme Court of Arkansas held that the determination of the duty to defend is not limited to the allegations in the complaint. *Commercial Union Ins. Co. of Am. v. Henshall*, 553 S.W.2d 274, 276 (Ark. 1977) ("[T]here may be situations where the insurance company's duty to defend cannot be determined simply from the allegations of the complaint. This is such a case. The insurance company may not close its eyes to facts it knew or should have known, because they were easily ascertainable. Information from the insured and a simple inspection of the property would have disclosed facts which would have raised questions."); *see also Watkins v. Southern Farm Bureau Cas. Ins. Co.*, __ S.W.3d __, No. CA 09–120, 2009 WL 3400697 (Ark. Ct. App. Oct. 21, 2009) (citing *Henshall* and providing as an example of the permissible use of extrinsic evidence claims involving self-defense, in response to allegations of assault and battery, because plaintiffs can not be expected to allege that they were assaulted by the insured while the insured was protecting life or property); *Silverball Amusement, Inc. v. Utah Home Fire Ins. Co.*, 842 F. Supp. 1151, 1156–57 (W.D. Ark. 1994) (recognizing that "[t]here are exceptions to the general rule that the complaint determines the duty to defend" and outlining a few of the "myriad cases on [the] subject").

**Arizona:** The Supreme Court of Arizona held that the determination of the duty to defend is not limited to the allegations in the complaint. *U.S. Fid. & Guar. Corp. v. Advance Roofing & Supply Co., Inc.*, 788 P.2d 1227, 1231 (Ariz. Ct. App. 1989) (quoting *Kepner v. W. Fire Ins. Co.*, 509 P.2d 222, 224 (Ariz. 1973)) ("[T]he duty to defend should focus on the facts rather than solely upon the allegations of the complaint, and that there was no duty to defend where the alleged facts ostensibly bring the case within the policy coverage but other facts which are not reflected in the complaint plainly take the case outside the policy coverage.") (citation and internal quotation omitted); *see also Lennar Corp. v. Auto-Owners Ins. Co.*, 151 P.3d 538, 547 (Ariz. Ct. App. 2007) ("Even assuming the complaint did not otherwise identify any specific subcontractor as negligent sufficient to create in its insurer an obligation to defend Lennar as an additional insured, according to Arizona law, once an insured makes some factual showing that the suit is actually one for damages resulting from events that fall under policy terms, an insurer has a duty to investigate those facts and provide a defense when indicated.").

**California:** The Supreme Court of California held that the determination of the duty to defend is not limited to the allegations in the complaint. *Scottsdale Ins. Co. v. MV Transp.*, 115 P.3d 460, 466 (Cal. 2005) ("Determination of the duty to defend depends, in the first instance, on a comparison between the allegations of the complaint and the terms of the policy. But the duty also exists where extrinsic facts known to the insurer suggest that the claim may be covered. Moreover, that the precise causes of action pled by the third party complaint may fall outside policy coverage does not excuse the duty to defend where, under the facts alleged, reasonably inferable, or otherwise known, the complaint could fairly be amended to state a covered liability."); *see also Golden Eagle Ins. Corp. v. Cen-Fed, Ltd.*, 56 Cal. Rptr. 3d 279, 284 (2007) ("If any facts stated or fairly inferable in the complaint, or otherwise known or discovered by the insurer, suggest a claim potentially covered by the policy, the insurer's duty to defend arises and is not extinguished until the insurer negates all facts suggesting potential coverage. On the other hand, if, as a matter of law, neither the complaint nor the known extrinsic facts indicate any basis for potential coverage, the duty to defend does not arise in the first instance.").

**Colorado:** Colorado has adopted several rules related to the determination of the duty to defend. "[I]f the insurer wishes to avoid the cost of a defense before the underlying litigation has concluded—either by simply refusing to defend or by bringing a declaratory judgment action while the litigation is proceeding—its duty to defend is determined under the complaint rule." *Pompa v. Am. Family Mut. Ins. Co.*, 520 F.3d 1139, 1146 (10th Cir. 2008) (applying Colorado law and citing *Cotter Corp. v. Am. Empire Surplus Lines Ins. Co.*, 90 P.3d 814, 828–29 (Colo. 2004)). However, the Tenth Circuit Court of Appeals in *Pompa* predicted that the Colorado Supreme Court would adopt an exception to the complaint rule, explaining that "[w]hen the extrinsic facts relied on by the insurer are relevant to the issue of coverage, but do not affect the third party's right of recovery, courts occasionally have held that the insurer may refuse to defend third-party actions, even though the allegations in the complaint suggest that coverage exists." *Id.* at 1147 (quotation and internal citation omitted). Lastly, if an insurer believes that it has no obligation to defend its insured, it may defend but reserve its rights to seek reimbursement should the facts at trial prove that the incident resulting in liability was not covered by the policy, or file a declaratory judgment action after the underlying case has been adjudicated. *Cotter*, 90 P. 3d at 827 (discussing *Hecla Mining v. N.H. Ins. Co.*, 811 P.2d 1083, 1089 (Colo. 1991)). Under these circumstances, the insurer may rely on facts outside of the complaint to determine whether it can recover its defense costs from the insured. *Id.* The Colorado Supreme Court was creating an incentive for insurers to defend by allowing them to subsequently seek reimbursement. *Id.* at 818; *see also Apartment Investment and Management Co. v. Nutmeg Ins. Co.*, 593 F.3d 1188, 1196 (10th Cir. 2010) (applying Colorado law) (discussing *Cotter, Hecla,* and *Pompa* and concluding that, for purposes of making a duty to defend determination, "an insurer cannot view the allegations contained in a single complaint in isolation when it is aware multiple complaints arising from a common core of operative facts have been filed against the insured.").

**Connecticut:** The Supreme Court of Connecticut held that the determination of the duty to defend is limited to the allegations in the complaint.

*Hartford Cas. Ins. Co. v. Litchfield Mut. Fire Ins. Co.*, 876 A.2d 1139, 1144 (Conn. 2005) ("[I]t is well established… that a liability insurer has a duty to defend its insured in a pending lawsuit if the pleadings allege a covered occurrence, even though facts outside the four corners of those pleadings indicate that the claim may be meritless or not covered.") (citation and internal quotation omitted). "[I]t is irrelevant that the insurer may get information from the insured, or from anyone else, which indicates, or even demonstrates, that the injury is not in fact covered." *Id.* On the other hand, when it comes to the use of extrinsic evidence to establish the duty to defend, the Connecticut high court chose to follow New York's rule that "'the sounder approach is to require the insurer to provide a defense when it has actual knowledge of facts establishing a reasonable possibility of coverage.'" *Id.* at 1146 (quoting *Fitzpatrick v. Am. Honda Motor Co., Inc.*, 575 N.E.2d 90, 93 (N.Y. 1991)).

**Delaware:** The Supreme Court of Delaware held that the determination of the duty to defend is limited to the allegations in the complaint. *Pac. Ins. Co. v. Liberty Mut. Ins. Co.*, 956 A.2d 1246, 1254–55 (Del. 2008) ("In construing an insurer's duty to indemnify and/or defend a claim asserted against its insured, a court typically looks to the allegations of the complaint to decide whether the third party's action against the insured states a claim covered by the policy, thereby triggering the duty to defend. The test is whether the underlying complaint, read as a whole, alleges a risk within the coverage of the policy. Determining whether an insurer is bound to defend an action against its insured requires adherence to the following principles: (1) where there is some doubt as to whether the complaint against the insured alleges a risk insured against, that doubt should be resolved in favor of the insured; (2) any ambiguity in the pleadings should be resolved against the carrier; and (3) if even one count or theory alleged in the complaint lies within the policy coverage, the duty to defend arises.") (citations and internal quotation omitted).

**Florida:** The Supreme Court of Florida held that the determination of the duty to defend is limited to the allegations in the complaint. *Higgins v. State Farm Fire & Cas. Co.*, 894 So. 2d 5, 10 (Fla. 2004) ("[A]n insurer's obligation to defend is determined solely by the claimant's complaint if suit has been filed."). The *Higgins* Court also noted that, as a result of this, "there generally is no need for a declaratory action in respect to the insurer's obligation to defend." *Id.* However, the Florida high court also pointed out that an exception exists where the duty to defend is based on factual issues that would not normally be alleged in the underlying complaint, such as late notice. *Id.* at 10 n.2; *see also Transcon. Ins. Co. v. Jim Black & Assocs., Inc.*, 888 So. 2d 671, 675 (Fla. Dist. Ct. App. 2004) ("[A]n insurer's duty to defend a complaint depends solely on the allegations in the complaint filed by a third party against the insured. Even under the more liberal federal pleading requirements, a third-party plaintiff's claims against an insured should be sufficiently described to allow a determination of whether a duty to defend arises under the allegations of the complaint.") (citations and internal quotation omitted).

**Georgia:** The Supreme Court of Georgia held that the determination of the duty to defend is not limited to the allegations in the complaint. *Colonial Oil Indus. v. Underwriters Subscribing to Policy Nos. TO31504670 & TO31504671*, 491 S.E.2d 337, 338–39 (Ga. 1997) ("The generally accepted view is that in making a determination of whether to provide a defense, an insurer is entitled to base its decision on the complaint and the facts presented by its insured. The insurer is under no obligation to independently investigate the claims against its insured… . A different rule, however, applies when the complaint on its face shows no coverage, but the insured notifies the insurer of factual contentions that would place the claim within the policy coverage… . [I]n this situation the insurer has an obligation to give due consideration to its insured's factual contentions and to base its decision on 'true facts.' The requirement that an insurer base its decision on true facts will necessitate that the insurer conduct a reasonable investigation into its insured's contentions."); *see also Allstate Ins. Co. v. Harkleroad*, No. 409CV011, 2010 WL 2076941 (S.D. Ga. May 24, 2010) (following *Colonial Oil*).

**Hawaii:** The Supreme Court of Hawaii adopted a rule that an "insurer may only disclaim its duty to defend by showing that none of the facts upon which it relies might be resolved differently in the underlying lawsuit." *Dairy Road Partners v. Island Ins. Co., Ltd.*, 992 P.2d 93, 117 (Hawaii 2000). "One example of an extrinsic fact upon which an insurer might rely pursuant to the new rule arises when an insurer argues that an occurrence was outside of the effective period of the policy. In such a case, the factual issue regarding the parameters of the effective period of the policy would not normally be subject to dispute in the underlying action." *Id.*, n.14; *see also Allstate Ins. Co. v. Davis*, 430 F. Supp. 2d 1112, 1125–26 (D. Hawaii 2000) ("[W]here the facts at issue can no longer be disputed in the underlying lawsuit because they have already been conclusively established for the purposes of those proceedings prior to the resolution of the declaratory judgment, we see no reason why evidence of such facts should not be available in the declaratory judgment action.") (quoting *Dairy Road Partners* at 117, n.14); *State Farm Fire & Cas Co. v. Thompson*, No. 09–00530, 2010 WL 2017101, *6 (D. Hawaii May 20, 2010) (following *Dairy Road Partners*).

**Idaho:** The Supreme Court of Idaho held that the determination of the duty to defend is limited to the allegations in the complaint. *Hoyle v. Utica Mut. Ins. Co.*, 48 P.3d 1256, 1264 (Idaho 2002) ("Despite [notice pleading], it makes little sense to require an insurer to defend a lawsuit simply because a complaint, with no covered claims, could potentially be amended to include covered claims. If this were true, an insurer would be required to defend every lawsuit regardless of the allegations. The better rule is that if there is a subsequent change in the pleadings, a duty to defend may arise and the issue of the duty to indemnify would likewise come before the court again."); *see also Amco Ins. Co. v. Tri-Spur Inv. Co.*, 101 P.3d 226, 231 (Idaho 2004) (quoting *Hoyle*, 48 P. 3d at 1264).

**Illinois:** The Supreme Court of Illinois held that the determination of the duty to defend is not limited to the allegations in the complaint. *Pekin Ins. Co. v. Wilson*, 930 N.E.2d 1011, 1020 (Ill. 2010) ("It is certainly true that the duty to defend flows in the first instance from the allegations in the underlying complaint; this is the concern at the initial stage of the proceedings when an insurance company encounters the primary decision of whether to defend its insured. However, if an insurer opts to file a declaratory proceeding, we believe that it may properly challenge the existence of such a duty by offering evidence to prove that the insured's actions fell within the limitations of one of the policy's exclusions. The only time such evidence should not be permitted is when it tends to determine an issue crucial to the determination of the underlying lawsuit... If a crucial issue will not be determined, we see no reason why the party seeking a declaration of rights should not have the prerogative to present evidence that is accorded generally to a party during a motion for summary judgment in a declaratory proceeding.") (quoting *Fidelity & Cas. Co. of New York v. Envirodyne Engineers, Inc.*, 461 N.E.2d 471, 473–74 (Ill. Ct. App. 1983)) (alteration in original). The Illinois high court also cited *American Economy Ins. Co. v. Holabird and Root*, 886 N.E.2d 1166 (Ill. App. Ct. 2008), *appeal allowed* 897 N.E.2d 249 (Ill. 2008), as setting forth a proper consideration for a circuit court's use of extrinsic evidence to determine the duty to defend: "[C]onsideration of a third-party complaint in determining a duty to defend is in line with the general rule that a trial court may consider evidence beyond the underlying complaint if in doing so the trial court does not determine an issue critical to the underlying action." *Wilson* at 1020-21 (quoting *Holabird and Root* at 1178) (alteration in original); *see also Konstant Products, Inc. v. Liberty Mut. Fire Ins. Co.*, No. 1–09–0080, 2010 WL 1796809 (Ill. Ct. App. May 4, 2010) (decided two weeks prior to *Wilson* and interpreting *Holabird and Root* as limiting the consideration of extrinsic evidence to true but unpleaded facts about which the insurer is aware); *Amerisure Mut. Ins. Co. v. Microplastics, Inc.*, ___ F.3d ___, No. 09-3764, 2010 WL 3619785 (7th Cir. 2010) (applying Illinois law) (declining to permit an insured from triggering a duty to defend a vaguely drafted complaint by hypothesizing situations which, if alleged or true, would bring the claim within the scope of coverage).

**Indiana:** The Supreme Court of Indiana held that the determination of the duty to defend is not limited to the allegations in the complaint. *Freidline v. Shelby Ins. Co.*, 774 N.E.2d 37, 43 n.6 (Ind. 2002) ("Where an insurer's independent investigation of the facts underlying a complaint against its insured reveals a claim is patently outside of the risk covered by the policy, the insurer may properly refuse to defend."). On the other hand, in *Transamerica Insurance Services v. Kopko*, 570 N.E.2d 1283, 1285 (Ind. 1991), the Supreme Court of Indiana stated that "[t]he duty to defend is determined solely by the nature of the complaint." However, numerous decisions from the Court of Appeals of Indiana and Indiana federal courts have either declined to follow *Kopko*, distinguished it or ignored it. *See, e.g., Monroe Guar. Ins. Co. v. Monroe*,

677 N.E.2d 620, 624 (Ind. Ct. App. 1997) ("[A]s a matter of law the Insurer has a duty to conduct a reasonable investigation into the facts underlying the complaint before it may refuse to defend the complaint."); *Ace Rent-A-Car, Inc. v. Empire Fire & Marine Ins. Co.*, 580 F. Supp. 2d 678, 689 (N.D. Ill. 2008) ("Several Indiana courts have questioned the validity of this statement of law [*Kopko's* statement that the duty to defend is determined solely by the nature of the complaint], or have simply ignored it and have continued to hold that the duty to defend is determined not only by the underlying complaint, but by a reasonable investigation on the part of the insurer."); *Fed. Ins. Co. v. Stroh Brewing Co.*, 127 F.3d 563, 566 (7th Cir. 1997) (applying Indiana law and finding that "[w]hile Indiana's courts may use differing language to describe the standard, we believe there is essentially only one standard—that the allegations of the complaint, including the facts alleged, give rise to a duty to defend whenever, if proved true, coverage would attach").

**Iowa:** The Supreme Court of Iowa held that the determination of the duty to defend is not limited to the allegations in the complaint. *Talen v. Employers Mut. Cas. Co.*, 703 N.W.2d 395, 406 (Iowa 2005) ("The scope of inquiry [for the duty to defend], however, must sometimes be expanded beyond the petition, especially under 'notice pleading' petitions which often give few facts upon which to assess an insurer's duty to defend. Quoting from an earlier case, we stated that an insurer has no duty to defend if after construing both the policy in question, the pleadings of the injured party and any other admissible and relevant facts in the record, it appears the claim made is not covered by the indemnity insurance contract. We find this principle to be especially relevant when the basis for withholding coverage is a policy exclusion the application of which is not readily ascertainable from the allegations of the petition and will not necessarily be determined in the tort litigation.") (citations and internal quotation omitted).

**Kansas:** The Supreme Court of Kansas held that the determination of the duty to defend is not limited to the allegations in the complaint. *Miller v. Westport Ins. Corp.*, 200 P.3d 419, 424 (Kan. 2009) (quoting *Spivey v. Safeco Ins. Co.*, 865 P.2d 182, 188 (Kan. 1993)) ("Under Kansas law, lawsuit pleadings are merely a starting point for the duty to defend analysis. They are not dispositive. An insurer must additionally consider actual facts of which it is or should be aware when evaluating its duty to defend. The insurer 'must look beyond the effect of the pleadings and must consider any facts brought to its attention or any facts which it could reasonably discover in determining whether it has a duty to defend.' If these known or reasonably discoverable extrinsic facts give rise to potential liability on the insured's part, the insured (sic) has a duty to defend.... This approach has become known as the 'extrinsic evidence' approach or rule. Under [this] approach, the insurer's duty to defend still hinges on the potential for coverage, but the universe of information from which that potential must be ascertained is much greater [than the universe used in an approach limited to the 'eight corners' of a pleading and the applicable insurance policy].") (alteration in original); *see also Allied Mut. Ins. Co. v. Moeder*, 48 P.3d 1, 4 (Kan. Ct. App. 2002) (quoting *Quality Painting, Inc. v. Truck Ins. Exch.*, 988 P.2d 749 (Kan. Ct. App. 1999)) (quoting *Spivey*, 865 P.2d at 188 (Kan. 1993)) ("The insurer determines if there is a potential of liability under the policy by examining the allegations in the complaint or petition and considering any facts brought to its attention or which it could reasonably discover.").

**Kentucky:** The Supreme Court of Kentucky held that the determination of the duty to defend is limited to the allegations in the complaint. *James Graham Brown Foundation, Inc. v. St. Paul Fire & Marine Ins. Co.*, 814 S.W.2d 273, 279 (Ky. 1991) ("The insurer has a duty to defend if there is any allegation which potentially, possibly or might come within the coverage of the policy. The insurance company must defend any suit in which the language of the complaint would bring it within the policy coverage regardless of the merit of the action. The determination of whether a defense is required must be made at the outset of the litigation.") (citations omitted). Some Kentucky federal courts have stated that the determination of whether a defense is required must be made at the outset of the litigation by reference to the complaint *and known facts. E.g., Lenning v. Commer. Union Ins. Co.*, 260 F.3d 574, 581 (6th Cir. 2001); *Pizza Magia Int'l, LLC v. Assurance Co. of Am.*, 447 F. Supp. 2d 766, 778–79 (W.D. Ky. 2006). While these courts cite to *James Graham Brown* for this proposition, the "known facts" requirement is not contained in the Supreme Court of Kentucky's decision.

**Louisiana:** The Supreme Court of Louisiana held that the determination of the duty to defend is limited to the allegations in the complaint. *Elliott v. Cont'l Cas. Co.*, 949 So. 2d 1247, 1250 (La. 2007) ("The insurer's duty to defend suits brought against its insured is determined by the allegations of the plaintiff's petition, with the insurer being obligated to furnish a defense unless the petition unambiguously excludes coverage. Accordingly, the insurer's obligation to defend suits against its insured is generally broader than its obligation to provide coverage for damage claims. Thus, if, assuming all of the allegations of the petition to be true, there would be both coverage under the policy and liability of the insured to the plaintiff, the insurer must defend the insured regardless of the outcome of the suit. An insured's (*sic*) duty to defend arises whenever the pleadings against the insured disclose even a possibility of liability under the policy.") (citations omitted); *see also Sibley v. Deer Valley Homebuilders, Inc.*, 32 So. 3d 1034 (La. Ct. App. 2010) (describing *Elliott*) ("This review of the petition and the policy has been referenced as the 'four corners' rule for the determination of the existence of the duty to defend.").

**Maine:** The Supreme Judicial Court of Maine held that the determination of the duty to defend is limited to the allegations in the complaint. *York Ins. Group v. Lambert*, 740 A.2d 984, 985 (Me. 1999) ("The longstanding rule is that we determine the duty to defend by comparing the allegations in the underlying complaint with the provisions of the insurance policy. A duty to defend exists if a complaint reveals a *potential* that the facts ultimately proved may come within the coverage.") (citations and internal quotation omitted) (emphasis in original). The Maine high court explained the rationale for its rule as follows: "If we were to look beyond the complaint and engage in proof of actual facts, then the separate declaratory judgment actions... would become independent trials of the facts which the [insured] would have to carry on at his expense....We see no reason why the insured, whose insurer is obligated by contract to defend him, should have to try the facts in a suit against his insurer in order to obtain a defense." *Id.* (quoting *Elliott v. Hanover Ins. Co.*, 711 A.2d 1310, 1312 (Me. 1998)).

**Maryland:** The Court of Appeals of Maryland has addressed the use of extrinsic evidence to determine an insurer's duty to defend and set forth rules for different circumstances. An insurer may not use extrinsic evidence to avoid a duty to defend if the underlying complaint establishes a potential for coverage. *Brohawn v. Transamerica Ins. Co.*, 347 A.2d 842, 850 (Md. 1975). However, an insured may use extrinsic evidence to establish that an insurer has a duty to defend a complaint that does not, on its face, give rise to the potential for coverage. *Aetna Cas. & Sur. Co. v. Cochran*, 651 A.2d 859, 864 (Md. 1995) ("*Brohawn* in no way intimates that reference to outside sources is prohibited if that reference is necessary to determine whether there is a potentiality of coverage under an insurance policy where the tort plaintiff's complaint neither conclusively establishes nor negates a potentiality of coverage."); *see also Moscarillo v. Prof'l Risk Mgmt. Servs.*, 921 A.2d 245, 252 (Md. 2007) (reaffirming the rules established by *Brohawn* and *Cochran* and addressing in detail the use of extrinsic evidence).

**Massachusetts:** The Supreme Judicial Court of Massachusetts held that the determination of the duty to defend is not limited to the allegations in the complaint. *Herbert A. Sullivan, Inc. v. Utica Mut. Ins. Co.*, 788 N.E.2d 522, 531 (Mass. 2003) ("The scope of an insurer's duty to defend is based on the facts alleged in the complaint and those facts which are known to the insurer. Specifically, the process is one of envisaging what kinds of losses may be proved as lying within the range of the allegations of the complaint, and then seeing whether any such loss fits the expectation of protective insurance reasonably generated by the terms of the policy.") (citations and internal quotation omitted); *see also Open Software Found., Inc. v. U.S. Fid. & Guar. Co.*, 307 F.3d 11, 16 (1st Cir. 2002) (discussing extrinsic facts as "an aid to interpreting" an underlying complaint and not serving as "independent grounds for a duty to defend"); *House of Clean Inc. v. St. Paul Fire & Marine Ins. Co.*, 705 F. Supp. 2d 102, 109 (D. Mass. 2010) ("Known or knowable extrinsic facts, such as those set forth in demand letters, therefore, serve to aid the interpretation of the underlying pleadings and can add substance and meaning to otherwise skeletal third-party claims. Extrinsic evidence cannot, however, provide independent grounds for a duty to defend.") (citing *Open Software*).

**Michigan:** The Supreme Court of Michigan held that the determination of the duty to defend is not limited to the allegations in the complaint. *Am. Bumper & Mfg. Co. v. Hartford Fire Ins. Co.*, 550 N.W.2d 475 (Mich. 1996) ("An insurer has a duty to defend, despite theories of liability asserted against any insured which are not covered under the policy, if there are any theories of recovery that fall within the policy. The duty to defend cannot be limited by the precise language of the pleadings. The insurer has the duty to look behind the third party's allegations to analyze whether coverage is possible. In a case of doubt as to whether or not the complaint against the insured alleges a liability of the insurer under the policy, the doubt must be resolved in the insured's favor.") (citations and internal quotation omitted).

**Minnesota:** The Supreme Court of Minnesota held that the determination of the duty to defend is limited to the allegations in the complaint, unless the insurer is aware of facts indicating that there may be a covered claim. *Garvis v. Employers Mut. Cas. Co.*, 497 N.W.2d 254, 258 (Minn. 1993) ("This court has consistently stated that where the insurer has no knowledge to the contrary, it may make an initial determination of whether or not it is obligated to defend from the facts alleged in the complaint against its insured. Where the pleadings do not raise a claim arguably within the scope of coverage, the insurer has no duty to defend or investigate further to determine whether there are other facts present which trigger such a duty. Of course, if the insurer is aware of facts indicating that there may be a claim, either from what is said directly or inferentially in the complaint, or if the insured tells the insurer of such facts, or if the insurer has some independent knowledge of such facts, then the insurer must either accept tender of the defense or further investigate the potential claim.") (citations omitted); *see also Western Nat. Mut. Ins. Co. v. Structural Restoration, Inc.*, No. A09–1598, 2010 WL 1753336, *3 (Minn. Ct. App. May 4, 2010) ("An insurance company may not rely on the allegations of the underlying complaint without investigating the facts, once the insured has come forward and made some factual showing that the suit is actually one for damages resulting from events which do fall into policy terms.") (citation and internal quotes omitted).

**Mississippi:** The Supreme Court of Mississippi held that the determination of the duty to defend is limited to the allegations in the complaint, but a true facts exception exists. *Farmland Mut. Ins. Co. v. Scruggs*, 886 So. 2d 714, 719 n.2 (Miss. 2004). "A liability insurance company has an absolute duty to defend a complaint which contains allegations covered by the language of the policy, but it has absolutely no duty to defend those claims which fall outside the coverage of the policy." *Id.* at 719. However, the *Scruggs* Court also acknowledged that "an insurer does have a duty to defend where a complaint fails to state a cause of action covered by policy but the insured informs the insurer that the true facts are inconsistent with the complaint, or where the insured learns from an independent investigation that the true facts present the potential liability of insured the insured (*sic*)." *Id.* at 719 n.2; *see also QBE*

*Ins. Corp. v. Brown & Mitchell, Inc.*, 591 F.3d 439, 444–45 (5th Cir. 2009) (applying Miss. law) (concluding that the "true facts" raised by the insured did not trigger a duty to defend).

**Missouri:** The Supreme Court of Missouri held that the determination of the duty to defend is not limited to the allegations in the complaint. *Marshall's U.S. Auto Supply v. Md. Cas. Co.*, 189 S.W.2d 529, 531 (Mo. 1945) ("We do not think that an insurance company can ignore actual facts (known to it or which could be known from reasonable investigation) in determining its liability to defend."); *see also Stark Liquidation Co. v. Florists' Mut. Ins. Co.*, 243 S.W.3d 385, 392 (Mo. Ct. App. 2007) (quoting *Truck Ins. Exch. v. Prairie Framing, LLC*, 162 S.W.3d 64, 83 (Mo. Ct. App. 2005)) ("The insurer has a duty to defend if the complaint merely alleges facts that give rise to a claim potentially within the policy's coverage. An insurer, however, may not merely rest upon the allegations contained within the petition. 'Rather it must also consider the petition in light of facts it knew or could have reasonably ascertained.'") (internal citations omitted).

**Montana:** The Supreme Court of Montana held that the determination of the duty to defend is not limited to the allegations in the complaint. *Burns v. Underwriters Adjusting Co.*, 765 P.2d 712, 713 (Mont. 1988) (upholding an insurer's disclaimer of a duty to defend a complaint that alleged negligence, based upon extrinsic evidence of an insured's guilty plea to felony aggravated assault). The *Burns* Court stated that "the proper focus of inquiry [for the duty to defend] is the acts giving rise to coverage, not the language of the complaint." *Id.* Then, in *Revelation Industries, Inc. v. St. Paul Fire & Marine Ins. Co.*, 206 P.3d 919 (Mont. 2009), the Montana high court—characterizing *Burns* as permitting an insurer to look beyond the allegations in the complaint to deny a duty to defend—held that the same rule applies when a complaint on its face does not trigger a duty to defend, but the insurer nonetheless has information that could give rise to a duty to defend and indemnify. *Id.* at 926. The court noted that, while an insurer need not seek out such information, it is not entitled to simply ignore factual information supplied to it by its insured, but not alleged in the complaint, which would trigger a duty to defend. *Id.* "[I]nsurers that look at facts beyond the allegations in the complaint do so at their own risk as they will be required to defend and/or indemnify based on the information discovered." *Id.*

**Nebraska:** The Supreme Court of Nebraska held that the determination of the duty to defend is not limited to the allegations in the complaint. *Peterson v. Ohio Cas. Group*, 724 N.W.2d 765, 773–74 (Neb. 2006) ("An insurer's duty to defend an action against the insured must, in the first instance, be measured by the allegations of the petition against the insured. In determining its duty to defend, an insurer must not only look to the petition or complaint filed against its insured, but must also investigate and ascertain the relevant facts from all available sources. An insurer is obligated to defend if (1) the allegations of the complaint, if true, would obligate the insurer to indemnify, or (2) a reasonable investigation of the actual facts by the insurer would or does disclose facts that would obligate the insurer to indemnify. An insurer, therefore, bears a duty to defend its insured whenever it ascertains facts which give rise to the potential of liability under the policy."); *see also Mortgage Express, Inc. v. Tudor Ins. Co.*, 771 N.W.2d 137 (Neb. 2009) (reaffirming the standard set out in *Peterson*).

**Nevada:** The Supreme Court of Nevada held that the determination of the duty to defend is not limited to the allegations in the complaint. *United Nat'l Ins. Co. v. Frontier Ins. Co.*, 99 P.3d 1153, 1158 (Nev. 2004) ("The duty to defend is broader than the duty to indemnify. There is no duty to defend where there is no potential for coverage. In other words, an insurer… bears a duty to defend its insured whenever it ascertains facts which give rise to the potential of liability under the policy. Once the duty to defend arises, this duty continues throughout the course of the litigation. If there is any doubt about whether the duty to defend arises, this doubt must be resolved in favor of the insured. The purpose behind construing the duty to defend so broadly is to prevent an insurer from evading its obligation to provide a defense for an insured without at least investigating the facts behind a complaint.") (citations and internal quotation omitted); *see also McClain v. Nat'l Fire & Marine Ins. Co.*, No. 2:05-cv-00706-LRH-RJJ, 2008 U.S. Dist. LEXIS 50874, at *14–*15 n.4 (D. Nev. June 23, 2008) ("*United National Insurance* contemplates the consideration of facts outside of the complaint in order to compel an insurer to defend its insured. However, if an insurer seeks to avoid defending its insured, that insurer may only do so by demonstrating that the complaint shows there is no potential for coverage when compared with the insurer's policy.") (citation omitted).

**New Hampshire:** The Supreme Court of New Hampshire held that the determination of the duty to defend is not limited to the allegations in the complaint. *Webster v. Acadia Ins. Co.*, 934 A.2d 567, 570 (N.H. 2007) ("It is well-settled in New Hampshire that an insurer's obligation to defend its insured is determined by whether the cause of action against the insured alleges sufficient facts in the pleadings to bring it within the express terms of the policy. In considering whether a duty to defend exists based upon the sufficiency of the pleadings, we consider the reasonable expectations of the insured as to its rights under the policy. We have said, [a]n insurer's obligation is not merely to defend in cases of perfect declarations, but also in cases where by any reasonable intendment of the pleadings liability of the insured can be inferred, and neither ambiguity nor inconsistency in the underlying plaintiff's complaint can justify escape of the insurer from its obligation to defend.") (citations and internal quotation omitted).

**New Jersey:** The Superior Court of New Jersey, Appellate Division, rejected the insured's argument that extrinsic evidence may only be considered to support coverage rather than to prove that the claims are not covered by the policy. *Polarome Intern., Inc. v. Greenwich Ins. Co.*, 961 A.2d 29, 48

(N.J. Super. Ct. App. Div. 2008). "If an insurer believes that the evidence indicates that the claim is not covered, the insurer is not always required to provide a defense." *Id.* The Supreme Court of New Jersey has held that, if the trial in the underlying action "will leave the question of coverage unresolved so that the insured may later be called upon to pay, or if the case may be so defended by a carrier as to prejudice the insured thereafter upon the issue of coverage, the carrier should not be permitted to control the defense." *Burd v. Sussex Mutual Insurance Co.*, 267 A.2d 7, 10 (N.J. 1970); *see also Flomerfelt v. Cardiello*, 997 A.2d 991, 999 (N.J. 2010) ("In short, in circumstances in which the underlying coverage question cannot be decided from the face of the complaint, the insurer is obligated to provide a defense until all potentially covered claims are resolved, but the resolution may be through adjudication of the complaint or in a separate proceeding between insured and insurer either before or after that decision is reached.") (discussing *Burd* at length). "[T]he practical effect of *Burd* is that an insured must initially assume the costs of defense itself, subject to reimbursement by the insurer if it prevails on the coverage question." *Trustees of Princeton University v. Aetna Cas. & Sur. Co.*, 680 A.2d 783, 787 (N.J. Super. Ct. App. Div. 1996) (quoting *Hartford Accident Indem. Co. v. Aetna Life & Cas. Ins. Co.*, 483 A.2d 402, 407 n.3 (N.J. 1984)). Further, such reimbursement obligation can be limited, when feasible, solely to those costs that were incurred to defend covered claims. *SL Indus. Inc. v. Am. Motorists Ins. Co.*, 607 A.2d 1266 (N.J. 1992). *See also* Chapter 5 addressing the requirement, under New Jersey law, for an insurer that wishes to retain counsel to defend its insured under a reservation of rights.

**New Mexico:** The Supreme Court of New Mexico held that the determination of the duty to defend is not limited to the allegations in the complaint. *Am. Gen. Fire & Cas. Co. v. Progressive Cas. Co.*, 799 P.2d 1113, 1116 (N.M. 1990) ("The duty of an insurer to defend arises from the allegations on the face of the complaint or from the known but unpleaded factual basis of the claim that brings it arguably within the scope of coverage. The duty may arise at the beginning of litigation or at some later stage if the issues are changed so as to bring the dispute within the scope of policy coverage.") (citations omitted); *see also G & G Servs., Inc. v. Agora Syndicate, Inc.*, 993 P.2d 751 (N.M. Ct. App. 1999) (discussing in detail the scope of an insurer's duty to investigate whether it is obligated to defend).

**New York:** The Court of Appeals of New York held that the determination of the duty to defend is not limited to the allegations in the complaint. *Fitzpatrick v. Am. Honda Motor Co., Inc.*, 575 N.E.2d 90, 92 (N.Y. 1991) ("[T]he courts of this State have refused to permit insurers to look beyond the complaint's allegations to avoid their obligation to defend and have held that the duty to defend exists if the complaint contains any facts or allegations which bring the claim even potentially within the protection purchased. The holdings thus clearly establish that an insurer's duty to defend is at least broad enough to apply when the four corners of the complaint suggest the reasonable possibility of coverage. However, to say that the duty to defend is at least broad enough to apply to actions in which the complaint alleges a covered occurrence is a far cry from saying that the complaint allegations are the sole criteria for measuring the scope of that duty. Indeed, in these circumstances, where the insurer is attempting to shield itself from the responsibility to defend despite its actual knowledge that the lawsuit involves a covered event, wooden application of the 'four corners of the complaint' rule would render the duty to defend narrower than the duty to indemnify—clearly an unacceptable result. For that reason, courts and commentators have indicated that the insurer must provide a defense if it has knowledge of facts which potentially bring the claim within the policy's indemnity coverage.").

**North Carolina:** The Supreme Court of North Carolina held that the determination of the duty to defend is not limited to the allegations in the complaint. *Waste Mgmt. of Carolinas, Inc. v. Peerless Ins. Co.*, 340 S.E.2d 374, 377–78 (N.C. 1986) ("Where the insurer knows or could reasonably ascertain facts that, if proven, would be covered by its policy, the duty to defend is not dismissed because the facts alleged in a third-party complaint appear to be outside coverage, or within a policy exception to coverage… .[Many] jurisdictions have recognized that the modern acceptance of notice pleading and of the plasticity of pleadings in general imposes upon the insurer a duty to investigate and evaluate facts expressed or implied in the third-party complaint as well as facts learned from the insured and from other sources. Even though the insurer is bound by the policy to defend 'groundless, false or fraudulent' lawsuits filed against the insured, if the facts are not even arguably covered by the policy, then the insurer has no duty to defend.").

**North Dakota:** The Supreme Court of North Dakota held that the determination of the duty to defend is not limited to the allegations in the complaint. *Ohio Cas. Ins. Co. v. Clark*, 583 N.W.2d 377, 380 (N.D. 1998). In *Ohio Cas. Ins. Co. v. Clark*, the North Dakota high court upheld the decision of an insurer to deny a defense for an underlying claim that alleged intentional conduct but plead it as negligence. *Id.* The court reasoned that "labeling Daniel Clark's conduct [conviction for manslaughter] as negligent does not alter its true nature." *Id.* (internal quotation omitted). *But see Bullis v. Minn. Lawyers Mut. Ins. Co.*, No. 3:06-cv-102, 2007 WL 4353760, at *4 (D.N.D. Dec. 10, 2007) ("Although [the insured] is correct that *Clark* allowed for a limited investigation beyond the pleadings by the trial court to determine whether the insured's acts were intentional or unintentional, generally, the Court is limited to the face of the complaint."); *First Nat'l Bank & Trust Co. v. St. Paul Fire & Marine Ins. Co.*, 971 F.2d 142, 144 (8th Cir. 1992) ("In the absence of other proceedings, it is presumed that information outside the complaint is not available to the insurer for the purposes of determining whether a duty to defend arises. This presumption should not, however, relieve St. Paul of an obligation to consider other information provided to it.") (citation omitted).

**Ohio:** The Supreme Court of Ohio held that the determination of the duty to defend is not limited to the allegations in the complaint. *Willoughby Hills v. Cincinnati Ins. Co.*, 459 N.E.2d 555, 558 (Ohio 1984). The Supreme Court of Ohio held that "the pleadings alone may not provide sufficient factual information to determine whether the insurer has an obligation to defend the insured. It remains true that where the pleadings unequivocally bring the action within the coverage afforded by the policy, the duty to defend will attach. However, where the insurer's duty to defend is not apparent from the pleadings in the case against the insured, but the allegations do state a claim which is potentially or arguably within the policy coverage, or there is some doubt as to whether a theory of recovery within the policy coverage had been pleaded, the insurer must accept the defense of the claim. Thus, the 'scope of the allegations' may encompass matters well outside the four corners of the pleadings." *Id.* In *Ferro Corp. v. Cookson Group*, 561 F. Supp. 2d 888 (N.D. Ohio 2008), the Ohio District Court examined numerous decisions that have interpreted *Willoughby Hills*. The court concluded that "the inquiry into the insurer['] duty to defend must naturally begin with a close scrutinization of the allegations of the disputed complaint. If such a review reveals claims which 'potentially' or 'arguably' fall within the purview of the policy, then, and only then, does *Willoughby Hills* dictate that a court look to extraneous matters to determine whether a defense is required of the insurer." *Id.* at 899 (alteration in original) (citations and internal quotation omitted). "Courts will not,... impose a duty to defend based on allegations outside the complaint, where the complaint does not state a claim that arguably triggers coverage." *Id.* at 900 (alteration in original) (citations and internal quotation omitted).

**Oklahoma:** The Supreme Court of Oklahoma held that the determination of the duty to defend is not limited to the allegations in the complaint. *First Bank of Turley v. Fid. & Deposit Ins. Co.*, 928 P.2d 298, 303 (Okla. 1996) ("The defense duty is measured by the nature and kinds of risks covered by the policy as well as by the reasonable expectations of the insured. An insurer has a duty to defend an insured whenever it ascertains the presence of facts that give rise to the potential of liability under the policy. The insurer's defense duty is determined on the basis of information gleaned from the petition (and other pleadings), from the insured and from other sources available to the insurer at the time the defense is demanded (or tendered) rather than by the outcome of the third-party action.") (citations omitted). The *Turley* Court stated: "The duty to defend cannot be limited by the precise language of the pleadings. The Insurer has the duty to look behind the third party's allegations to analyze whether coverage is possible." *Id.* at 303 n.15.

**Oregon:** The Supreme Court of Oregon held that the determination of the duty to defend is limited to the allegations in the complaint. *Ledford v. Gutoski*, 877 P.2d 80, 82 (Or. 1994) ("Whether an insurer has a duty to defend an action against its insured depends on two documents: the complaint and the insurance policy. An insurer has a duty to defend an action against its insured if the claim against the insured stated in the complaint could, without amendment, impose liability for conduct covered by the policy.") (citation omitted); *see also Isenhart v. Gen. Cas. Co.*, 377 P.2d 26, 28–29 (Or. 1962) ("If a contrary rule were adopted, requiring the insurer to take note of facts other than those alleged, the insurer frequently would be required to speculate upon whether the facts alleged could be proved. We do not think that this is a reasonable interpretation of the bargain to defend."). *But see Fred Shearer & Sons, Inc. v. Gemini Ins. Co.*, 0507-07126, 2010 WL 3768022, __P.3d__ (Or. App. Ct. 2010) (distinguishing *Ledford* and concluding that, when the question is whether the insured is being held liable for conduct that falls within the scope of the policy, it makes sense to look exclusively to the complaint; but the same cannot be said with respect to whether a party seeking coverage is an "insured") (allowing a party to use extrinsic evidence to establish its status as an insured under a vendor's endorsement).

**Pennsylvania:** The Supreme Court of Pennsylvania held that the determination of the duty to defend is limited to the allegations in the complaint. *Kvaerner Metals Div. of Kvaerner U.S., Inc. v. Commercial Union Ins. Co.*, 908 A.2d 888, 896 (Pa. 2006) ("The Superior Court erred in looking beyond the allegations raised in Bethlehem's Complaint to determine whether National Union had a duty to defend Kvaerner and in finding that the Battery's damages may have been the result of an 'occurrence.' In doing so, it departed from the well-established precedent of this Court requiring that an insurer's duty to defend and indemnify be determined solely from the language of the complaint against the insured. We find no reason to expand upon the well-reasoned and long-standing rule that an insurer's duty to defend is triggered, if at all, by the factual averments contained in the complaint itself.") (citations omitted); *see also American & Foreign Ins. Co. v. Jerry's Sport Center, Inc.*, 2 A.3d 526, 541 (Pa. 2010) ("An insurer is obligated to defend its insured if the factual allegations of the complaint on its face encompass an injury that is actually or potentially within the scope of the policy."). However, Pennsylvania courts will look beyond the four corners of the complaint to deny a defense for intentional conduct that is plead as negligence. *Erie Ins. Exch. v. Fidler*, 808 A.2d 587, 590 (Pa. Super. Ct. 2002) ("If we were to allow the manner in which the complainant frames the request for damages to control the coverage question, we would permit insureds to circumvent exclusions that are clearly part of the policy of insurance.").

**Rhode Island:** The Supreme Court of Rhode Island held that the determination of the duty to defend is limited to the allegations in the complaint. *Am. Commerce Ins. Co. v. Porto*, 811 A.2d 1185, 1191 (R.I. 2002). In *Am. Commerce Ins. Co. v. Porto*, the court noted that the duty to defend is determined by applying the "pleadings test," which it defined as requiring "the trial court to look at the allegations contained in the complaint, and if the pleadings recite facts bringing the injury complained of within the coverage of the insurance policy, the insurer must defend irrespective of the insured's ultimate liability to the plaintiff." *Id.* (internal quotation omitted). However, the Supreme Court of Rhode Island carved out an exception in *Peerless Ins. Co. v. Viegas*, 667 A.2d 785 (R.I. 1995), where the court inferred an intent to cause harm and injury in cases involving the sexual molestation of a minor. *Id.* at 788–89. Thus, notwithstanding that the duty to defend is determined by the "pleadings test," the Supreme Court of Rhode Island held that, if the policy contains an intentional act exclusion, an insurer is not obligated to defend an insured that sexually abuses a minor, even if the allegations in the complaint are described in terms of negligence. *Id.*; *see also Narragansett Jewelry Co., Inc. v. St. Paul Fire & Marine Ins. Co.*, 555 F.3d 38, 41–42 (1st Cir. 2009) (applying R.I. law) (strictly applying the "pleadings test").

**South Carolina:** The Supreme Court of South Carolina held that the determination of the duty to defend is limited to the allegations in the complaint. *Collins Holding Corp. v. Wausau Underwriters Ins. Co.*, 666 S.E.2d 897, 899 (S.C. 2008). The court reiterated South Carolina law that the obligation of a liability insurer to defend is determined by the allegations in the complaint and if the facts alleged in the complaint fail to bring a claim within the policy's coverage, the insurer has no duty to defend. *Id.* However, the *Collins Holding* Court also adopted the rule that if "a complaint mischaracterizes intentional conduct as negligent conduct, a court may find no duty to defend despite the label of negligence in the complaint." *Id.* at 900.

**South Dakota:** The Supreme Court of South Dakota held that the determination of the duty to defend is not limited to the allegations in the complaint. *State Farm Fire & Cas. Co. v. Harbert*, 741 N.W.2d 228, 234 (S.D. 2007) ("Under South Dakota law, a liability insurer's duty to defend extends to any third party claim asserted against an insured that arguably falls within the policy's coverages. If disputed, the issue of whether an insurer has a duty to defend is determined by the third party's complaint and 'other evidence of record.'").

**Tennessee:** The Supreme Court of Tennessee held that the determination of the duty to defend is limited to the allegations in the complaint. *Travelers Indem. Co. of Am. v. Moore & Assocs., Inc.*, 216 S.W.3d 302, 305 (Tenn. 2007) (citing *St. Paul Fire & Marine Ins. Co. v. Torpoco*, 879 S.W.2d 831, 835 (Tenn. 1994)) ("We previously have held that whether a duty to defend arises depends solely on the allegations contained in the underlying complaint. Accordingly, the insurer has a duty to defend when the underlying complaint alleges damages that are within the risk covered by the insurance contract and for which there is a potential basis for recovery.") (internal citation omitted).

**Texas:** The Supreme Court of Texas held that, "[u]nder the eight-corners rule, the duty to defend is determined by the claims alleged in the petition and the coverage provided in the policy." *Pine Oak Builders, Inc. v. Great American Lloyds Ins. Co.*, 279 S.W.3d 650, 654 (Tex. 2009). "[I]n deciding the duty to defend, the court should not consider extrinsic evidence from either the insurer or the insured that contradicts the allegations of the underlying petition. The duty to defend depends on the language of the policy setting out the contractual agreement between insurer and insured." *Id.* at 655. In *GuideOne Elite Ins. Co. v. Fielder Road Baptist Church*, 197 S.W.3d 305 (Tex. 2005), the Supreme Court of Texas declined to adopt a narrow exception to the "eight-corners" rule, as some courts have, that allows for the consideration of extrinsic evidence that "goes solely to a fundamental issue of coverage which does not overlap with the merits of or engage the truth or falsity of any facts alleged in the underlying case." *Id.* at 308–09. The court likewise rejected, as an exception to the eight-corners rule, extrinsic evidence that is relevant both to coverage and the merits of the underlying action—so-called overlapping evidence. *Id.* at 309. In *D.R. Horton-Texas, Ltd. v. Markel International Ins. Co., Ltd.*, 300 S.W.3d 740 (Tex. 2009), the Supreme Court of Texas held that "the duty to indemnify is not dependent on the duty to defend and that an insurer may have a duty to indemnify its insured even if the duty to defend never arises." *Id.* at 741.

**Utah:** The Supreme Court of Utah held that "whether extrinsic evidence is admissible to determine whether an insurer has a duty to defend an insured turns on the parties' contractual terms. If the parties make the duty to defend dependent on the *allegations* against the insured, extrinsic evidence is irrelevant to a determination of whether a duty to defend exists. However, if, for example, the parties make the duty to defend dependent on whether there is actually a 'covered claim or suit,' extrinsic evidence would be relevant to a determination of whether a duty to defend exists." *Fire Ins. Exch. v. Estate of Therkelsen*, 27 P.3d 555, 561 (Utah 2001) (emphasis in original); *see also Mid-America Pipeline Co., LLC v. Mountain States Mut. Cas. Co.*, No. 2:05-CV-153, 2006 WL 1278748, at *2 (D. Utah May 8, 2006) (recognizing that "the Utah Supreme Court identified two categories of insurance provisions creating a duty to defend": first, where "an insurance contract requires an insurer to defend an insured against a suit 'alleging liability within the coverage afforded by the policy,'" extrinsic evidence is irrelevant and inadmissible, and second, where "an insurance contract provides that an insurer will defend a 'covered suit,'" it requires a court to "examine extrinsic evidence to determine if a particular suit is covered").

**Vermont:** The Supreme Court of Vermont held that a court "determine[s] whether the insurer has a duty to defend by comparing the allegations in the underlying claim to the policy's coverage terms." *Hardwick Recycling & Salvage, Inc. v. Acadia Ins. Co.*, 869 A.2d 82, 87 (Vt. 2004) (citing *City of Burlington v. Nat'l Union Fire Ins. Co.*, 655 A.2d 719, 721 (Vt. 1994)). However, "[o]ccasionally, [Vermont courts] have looked to the known facts underlying a plaintiff's complaint to understand the application of policy provisions or exclusions." *Garneau v. Curtis & Bedell, Inc.*, 610 A.2d 132, 134 (Vt. 1992).

**Virginia:** The Supreme Court of Virginia acknowledged that, in several prior decisions, it applied the rule that only the allegations in the complaint and the terms of the policy can be considered in deciding if there is a duty to defend. *Copp v. Nationwide Mut. Ins. Co.*, 692 S.E.2d 220, 224 (Va. 2010) (quoting several cases including *Brenner v. Lawyers Title Ins. Corp.*, 397 S.E. 2d 100 (Va. 1990)). However, the court noted that none of the prior decisions involved the situation before it—applicability of an exception to the "expected or intended" exclusion if the insured acted in self-defense. *Id.* at 225. Despite allowing the consideration of self-defense evidence in its duty to defend determination, it does not appear that the court created an exception to the four corners rule. Rather, the court's decision appears to be that the self-defense evidence must be considered in order to give effect to the "expected or intended" exception, which "is found in one of the four corners of the insurance contract and stands on an equal footing with other provisions thereof." *Id.*; *see also CACI Intern., Inc. v. St. Paul Fire and Marine Ins. Co.*, 566 F.3d 150, 156 (4th Cir. 2009) (applying Va. law) ("[B]ecause Virginia courts have not signaled a readiness to look beyond the underlying complaint, we will decline to consider those documents attached to the complaints or on which the complaints in the underlying action rely.").

**Washington:** The Supreme Court of Washington held that the determination of the duty to defend is not limited to the allegations in the complaint. *Woo v. Fireman's Fund Ins. Co.*, 164 P.3d 454, 459 (Wash. 2007) ("There are two exceptions to the rule that the duty to defend must be determined only from the complaint, and both the exceptions favor the insured. First, if it is not clear from the face of the complaint that the policy provides coverage, but coverage could exist, the insurer must investigate and give the insured the benefit of the doubt that the insurer has a duty to defend... .Second, if the allegations in the complaint conflict with facts known to or readily ascertainable by the insurer, or if the allegations... are ambiguous or inadequate, facts outside the complaint may be considered. The insurer may not rely on facts extrinsic to the complaint to deny the duty to defend—it may do so only to trigger the duty.") (citations and internal quotations omitted); *see also Campbell v. Ticor Title Ins. Co.*, 209 P.3d 859 (Wash. 2009) (same) (quoting *Woo*).

**West Virginia:** The Supreme Court of Appeals of West Virginia held that the determination of the duty to defend is limited to the allegations in the complaint. *Bowyer v. Hi-Lad, Inc.*, 609 S.E.2d 895, 912 (W. Va. 2004) ("An insurance company has a duty to defend an action against its insured if the claim stated in the underlying complaint could, without amendment, impose liability for risks the policy covers. If, however, the causes of action alleged in the plaintiff's complaint are entirely foreign to the risks covered by the insurance policy, then the insurance company is relieved of its duties under the policy. Included in the consideration of whether an insurer has a duty to defend is whether the allegations in the complaint are reasonably susceptible of an interpretation that the claim may be covered by the terms of the insurance policy.") (citation and internal quotation omitted). In *Bruceton Bank v. United States Fidelity & Guaranty*

*Insurance Co.*, 486 S.E.2d 19 (W. Va. 1997), the Supreme Court of Appeals of West Virginia stated that the court's mandate in *Farmers & Mechanics Mutual Fire Insurance Co. v. Hutzler*, 447 S.E.2d 22 (W. Va. 1994), to conduct a reasonable inquiry into the facts behind the allegations of the complaint, was clarified to the extent that it differed from the aforementioned duty to defend standard. *Bruceton Bank*, 486 S.E.2d at 23.

**Wisconsin:** The Supreme Court of Wisconsin held that the determination of the duty to defend is limited to the allegations in the complaint. *Fireman's Fund Ins. Co. v. Bradley Corp.*, 660 N.W.2d 666, 673 (Wis. 2003) ("An insurer's duty to defend an insured is determined by comparing the allegations of the complaint to the terms of the insurance policy. An insurer's duty to defend the insured in a third-party suit is predicated on allegations in a complaint which, if proven, would give rise to the possibility of recovery that falls under the terms and conditions of the insurance policy. The duty to defend is based solely on the allegations contained within the four corners of the complaint, without resort to extrinsic facts or evidence.") (citations and internal quotation omitted).

**Wyoming:** The Supreme Court of Wyoming held that the determination of the duty to defend is limited to the allegations in the complaint. *First Wyo. Bank, N.A. v. Cont'l Ins. Co.*, 860 P.2d 1094, 1097 (Wyo. 1993) ("[T]he duty of an insurer to defend a claim is broader than the duty of the insurer to indemnify. Analysis of the duty to defend is not made based on the ultimate liability of the insurer to indemnify the insured or on the basis of whether the underlying action is groundless or unsuccessful. Instead, we analyze the duty to defend by examining the facts alleged in the complaint that the claim is based upon.") (citations omitted); *see also Reisig v. Union Ins. Co.*, 870 P.2d 1066, 1071 (Wyo. 1994) (declining to adopt a duty to defend standard based on extrinsic evidence); Employers *Mut. Cas. Co. v. Bartile Roofs, Inc.*, __ F.3d __, Nos. 08-8064 and 08-8068, 2010 WL 3473382, at *12 (10th Cir. Sept. 7, 2010) (addressing Wyoming and Utah law) ("[W]e look only to the allegations of the Complaint filed by [the third-party complainant] to see if there is alleged a loss caused by an occurrence as required by the CGL policy.") (alteration in original) (quoting *Reisig*).

# Insured's Right to Independent Counsel

The question whether an insurer is obligated to provide a defense to its insured, for a suit filed against it, turns on whether the claim is potentially covered under the terms of the policy. It is a substantive question and one that can sometimes be the subject of significant analysis and dispute over the answer. Once the insurer determines that it has a defense obligation, the focus shifts to a seemingly easier task and, indeed, one that sounds ministerial—picking up the phone and hiring a lawyer. But it is sometimes far from it. Just as the question whether a defense was owed in the first place can be complex, and a source of great dispute between insurer and insured, so too can be the question of which lawyer to hire to represent the insured.

After an insured has been sued and served with the complaint, the clock begins to tick on the time available under the applicable court rules for the insured to file an answer or other type of responsive pleading. Since time is of the essence, it makes sense that insurance companies maintain lists of law firms that have been prescreened as acceptable to represent their insureds in the various type of legal proceeding in which they find themselves. By maintaining lawyers at the ready—often referred to as "panel counsel"—the insurer can act quickly to protect its insured's interests. Much time is saved because the insurer knows that the law firm it is hiring is qualified to handle the type of case at issue, at a previously agreed upon hourly rate or other payment arrangement, and has familiarity concerning the insurer's various guidelines on billing, reporting, and litigation management.

While the use of panel counsel makes sense in a lot of ways, not all insureds are content being represented by the defense counsel selected by the insurer. This is particularly the case when the defense is being provided by the insurer under a reservation of rights. In this situation, the insurer has agreed to hire counsel to represent its insured, but, at the same time, has informed the insured that some or all of any damages that may be awarded against it may not be covered under the terms of the policy.

This situation is created by the so-called tripartite relationship:

> In the usual tripartite insurer-attorney-insured relationship, the insurer has a duty to defend the insured, and hires counsel to provide the defense. So long as the interests of the insurer and the insured coincide, they are both the clients of the defense attorney and the defense attorney's fiduciary duty runs to both the insurer and the insured. The insurance defense attorney is placed in a position of conflict, however, when issues of coverage are asserted by the insurer through a reservation of rights.

*Kroll & Tract v. Paris & Paris*, 72 Cal. App. 4th 1537, 1542 (Cal. App. Ct. 1999).

Facing the prospect of uninsured liability for some or all of the damages at issue, some insureds conclude that they would prefer to have a say in choosing the lawyer whose job will be to prevent or minimize their exposure—with the cost of such defense being borne by the insurer, just as if the insurer had hired panel counsel. In other words, while a liability insurer usually has the right to control the defense, some insureds argue that a different rule should apply when it is the insured's own money that is on the line. Under these circumstances, insureds sometimes demand the right to choose defense counsel, usually referred to as "independent counsel," based on the insured's belief that the lawyer, because it was selected by the insurance company, is not independent.

The motivation for insureds to demand that they be allowed to hire independent counsel is that they look at the relationship between insurers and their panel counsel with a jaundiced eye. As they see it, the law firm is in a position to receive future assignments from the insurer when other insureds are named as defendants in the jurisdictions in which the firm practices. Indeed, some law firms have served as panel counsel for certain insurers for years, receiving hundreds, if not thousands, of case assignments. Insureds may conclude that, because of this arrangement, the lawyer hired to represent it is not truly independent because it has, as its principal concern, making sure that it does nothing to jeopardize the steady stream of work that comes from serving as panel counsel. Since the defense is being provided under a reservation of rights, the possibility exists that, when the case is over, some or all of any damages awarded may not be covered by the insurer, and, hence, would become the personal responsibility of the insured. Under this scenario, the concern for insureds may be that, in handling the case, the lawyer's objective will be to minimize the extent to which any damage award is covered by the terms of the insurer's policy.

This risk was explained—without any sugar coating and with support from, some might say, a higher authority than any court—by the Eighth Circuit Court of Appeals in *U.S. Fid. & Guar. Co. v. Louis A. Roser Co.*, 585 F.2d 932, 938 n.5 (8th Cir. 1978) (applying Utah law):

Even the most optimistic view of human nature requires us to realize that an attorney employed by an insurance company will slant his efforts, perhaps unconsciously, in the interests of his real client the one who is paying his fee and from whom he hopes to receive future business the insurance company. Although it has perhaps become trite, the biblical injunction found in Matthew 6:24 retains a particular relevancy in circumstances such as these, "No man can serve two masters... ."

The classic example of an asserted conflict of interest, giving rise to a demand by an insured for independent counsel, is a suit alleging that the insured's liability is based on intentional or negligent conduct (or some other alternative causes of action where one is covered and one is not):

Under a typical liability insurance policy, coverage is available for negligent acts but not for intentional acts. The insurer therefore would benefit from either a defense verdict or a finding of intentional wrongdoing. The insured, on the other hand, would benefit from either a defense verdict or a finding of negligence. Absent informed consent of both the insurer and the insured, an attorney trying to represent both the insured and the insurer would face an insurmountable conflict of interest.

*Armstrong Cleaners, Inc. v. Erie Ins. Exch.*, 364 F. Supp. 2d 797, 806 (S.D. Ind. 2005).

In this situation, an insured may fear that its counsel, wanting to please the insurer, in hopes of continuing to benefit from its status as panel counsel, will handle the case in such a way that any damage award is based on intentional, rather than negligent, conduct. This is the so-called "steering" argument: "the insurer may steer result to judgment under an uninsured theory of recovery." *CHI of Alaska, Inc. v. Employers Reinsurance Corp.*, 844 P.2d 1113, 1118 (Alaska 1993). "[I]f a plaintiff alleged both negligence and an intentional tort as alternative theories of recovery, an insurer operating under a reservation of rights might covertly frame its defense to achieve a verdict based upon commission of the intentional tort, so that it could later assert that the defendant was not covered, since the policy provided no coverage for intentional torts. In the absence of a reservation of rights agreement, however, the insurer would be liable for indemnification regardless of whether the verdict established negligence or an intentional tort, and thus would be more likely to defend vigorously on both grounds." *Continental Ins. Co. v. Bayless and Roberts, Inc.*, 608 P.2d 281, 289–90 (Alaska 1980).

Another possible conflict of interest arises if "the insurer knows it can later assert non-coverage, it... may offer only a token defense of its insured. If the insurer does not think that the loss on which it is defending will be covered under the policy, it may not be motivated to achieve the lowest possible settlement or in other ways treat the interests of its insured as its own." *Id.* at 289.

There is nothing new about this conundrum. To the contrary, the potential conflict of interest among the liability insurance company, the insured, and the insurance defense attorney has been referred to as the law's "eternal triangle." *Id.* at 801. "[T]he ethical dilemma thus imposed upon the carrier-employed defense attorney would tax Socrates, and no decision or authority we have studied furnishes a completely satisfactory answer." *Hartford Accdent. & Indem. Co. v. Foster*, 528 So. 2d 255, 273 (Miss. 1988).

There is no consensus solution for resolving asserted conflicts of interest under these circumstances, and reasonable minds can differ on the best approach. *See Finley v. The Home Ins. Co.*, 975 P.2d 1145, 1151 (Haw. 1998) ("The magnitude of the difficulty in resolving the issue is reflected in the volume of litigation nationwide, and, in the instant case, the number of amicus curiae briefs representing divergent views."). As the following fifty-state survey reveals, courts have responded with several methods for addressing conflicts of interest and they vary widely. In addition, some states have turned to their legislatures for the solution.

In addition to the perceived conflict of interest, insureds sometimes object to the insurer's selection of counsel for other reasons, such as a belief that the insurer's selected counsel is not qualified, lacks sufficient knowledge of the insured's business or, when the dispute has a lengthy pre-suit history, the insurer's chosen counsel lacks the necessary background knowledge. In general, when a defense is provided under a reservation of rights, causing an insured to have skin in the game, insureds may assert a host of reasons why they object to being defended by counsel selected by the insurance company. But perhaps the insured's motivation for demanding choice of counsel actually comes down to something as simple as this: "[W]hatever his estimate of lawyers in general, a man usually has faith in 'my lawyer.' This intangible is a valuable right." *Merchants Indem. Corp. v. Eggleston*, 179 A.2d 505, 511 (N.J. 1962).

The simplest solution to an insured's demand for independent counsel is for the court to adopt a blanket rule. Some have done so by concluding that a defense provided under a reservation of rights creates a per se conflict of interest—no questions asked—thereby entitling the insured to independent counsel at the insurer's expense. *Moeller v. Am. Guarantee & Liab. Ins. Co.*, 707 So. 2d 1062, 1071 (Miss. 1996) (quoting *State Farm Mut. Auto. Ins. Co. v. Commercial Union Ins. Co.*, 394 So.2d 890, 894 (Miss. 1981)) ("A law firm which cannot be one hundred percent faithful to the interests of its clients offers no defense at all. 'There is no higher ethical duty in the legal profession than complete absolute fidelity to the interest of the client.'").

Some courts have adopted a blanket rule in the other direction—a reservation of rights does not create a conflict of interest in any case. In *Finley v. Home Ins. Co.*, 975 P.2d 1145 (Haw. 1998), the Supreme Court of Hawaii concluded that, because of the safeguards inherent in the Rules of Professional Conduct, as well as alternate remedies existing in the case of attorney misconduct, an attorney retained by an insurer can represent the insured without the insured's informed consent. *Id.* at 1154. Using a different method, but achieving the same result, the Supreme Court of South Dakota in *St. Paul Fire & Marine Ins. Co. v. Engelmann*, 639 N.W.2d 192 (S.D. 2002) concluded that, because the insurer and insured are not estopped to litigate in a subsequent coverage action facts that were determined in the underlying action, no conflict was created by the insurer's choice of defense counsel. *Id.* at 200.

As the following fifty-state survey of the issue reveals, the majority of courts confronted with the conflict of interest issue have declined to adopt a black-and-white rule one way or the other. Rather, they conclude that the circumstances of each case must be examined to determine whether a conflict exists:

> Whether the potential conflict of interest is sufficient to require the insured's consent is a question of degree that requires some predictions about the course of the representation. If there is a reasonable possibility that the manner in which the insured is defended could affect the outcome of the insurer's coverage dispute, then the conflict may be sufficient to require the insurer to pay for counsel of the insured's choice. Evaluating that risk requires close attention to the details of the underlying litigation. The court must then make a reasonable judgment about whether there is a significant risk that the attorney selected by the insurance company will have the representation of the insureds significantly impaired by the attorney's relationship with the insurer.

*Armstrong Cleaners*, 364 F. Supp. 2d at 808.

When determining if the manner in which the insured is defended could affect the outcome of the insurer's coverage dispute, thereby requiring the insurer to pay for counsel of the insured's choice, courts look to various possibilities:

> First, if the insurer knows that it can later assert non-coverage, or if it thinks that the loss which it is defending will not be covered under the policy, it may only go through the motions of defending: "it may offer only a token defense… .[I]t may not be motivated to achieve the lowest possible settlement or in other ways treat the interests of the insured as its own." Second, if there are several theories of recovery, at least one of which is not covered under the policy, the insurer might conduct the defense in such a manner as to make the likelihood of a plaintiff's verdict greater under the uninsured theory. Third, the insurer might gain access to confidential or privileged information in the process of the defense which it might later use to its advantage in litigation concerning coverage.

*CHI of Alaska, Inc. v. Employers Reinsurance Corp.*, 844 P.2d 1113, 1116 (Alaska 1993) (alteration in original) (citations omitted).

Once the determination has been made that the insured is entitled to select its own counsel, to be paid for by the insurer, it is not uncommon for a dispute to arise over the hourly rates to be paid to counsel. The source of such dispute is almost always that the hourly rates charged by the insurer's panel counsel are less than—and sometimes significantly so—the rates charged by independent counsel retained by the insurer.

The insurer usually maintains that it will pay independent counsel reasonable rates, which it asserts are the same rates it would have paid panel counsel, if there had been no need to retain independent counsel. The typical insured response is that panel counsel's hourly rates are lower than market rates (i.e., the rates sought to be charged by independent counsel) because panel counsel is willing to work at a discount—in exchange for the volume of work that is receives on account of serving as panel counsel.

While California and Alaska statutorily permit an insurer to pay independent counsel the same rates as panel counsel, discussed *infra*, most of the time clear-cut answers to the rate issue do not exist. The case law on the subject is relatively sparse and that which does exist is fact specific and does not make general pronouncements. For guidance on the rate issue, *see PhotoMedex, Inc. v. St. Paul Fire & Marine Ins. Co.*, No. 07–0025, 2008 WL 324025, at \*19 (E.D. Pa. Feb. 6, 2008) ("The determination of a reasonable fee is a fact-intensive inquiry, requiring competent evidence.") (scheduling a trial to determine whether the insured's counsel's fees were reasonable) (rate disparity of $685 and $360 per hour for insured's counsel versus $175 per hour for insurer's selected counsel); *HK Systems, Inc. v. Admiral Ins. Co.*, No. 03 C 0795, 2005 WL 1563340, at \*18 (D. Wis. June 27, 2005) (simply because the insured was paying its counsel's rates does not establish that it would have done so if there were no hope of recovering such payments) (rate disparity of $495 per hour for insured's counsel versus $105 to $145 per hour for insurer's selected counsel); *Watts Water Techs. v. Fireman's Fund Ins. Co.*, No. 05–2604-BLS2, 2007 WL 2083769, at \*11 (Mass. Super. Ct. July 11, 2007) (noting that there are many factors for determining the reasonableness of legal fees incurred by the insured, one of which is "'the usual price charged for similar services by other attorneys in the same area,' *not* the usual price paid *by insurance companies* to other attorneys for similar services in the same area") (citation omitted) (emphasis in original); *Employers Ins. Co. of Wausau v. Harleysville Ins. Co. of N.J.*, No. 05–4900, 2008 WL 5046838, at \*4 (D.N.J. Nov. 20, 2008) (agreeing with insurer that basic legal services should have been delegated by senior attorneys to associates or paralegals) ("Michelangelo should not charge Sistine Chapel rates for painting a farmer's barn.") (citation omitted).

## 50-State Survey: Insured's Right to Independent Counsel

**Alabama:** The Supreme Court of Alabama specifically adopted the Supreme Court of Washington's test, set forth in *Tank v. State Farm Fire & Cas. Co.*,

715 P.2d 1133 (Wash. 1986), discussed *infra*, for determining whether an insured being defended under a reservation of rights is entitled to independent counsel at the insurer's expense. *L & S Roofing Supply Co. v. St. Paul Fire & Marine Ins. Co.*, 521 So. 2d 1298, 1304 (Ala. 1987). "The standard set forth in *Tank, supra*, requiring an *enhanced obligation of good faith* coupled with the specific criteria that must be met by both the insurer as well as the defense counsel retained by the insurer, provides an adequate means for safeguarding the interests of the insured without, at the same time, engaging in the presumption that any and all defense counsel retained by the insurance industry to represent its insureds under a reservation of rights are conclusively unable to do so without consciously or unconsciously compromising the interests of the insureds." *Id.* at 1304 (emphasis added); *see also Aetna Cas. & Sur. Co. v. Mitchell Brothers, Inc.*, 814 So. 2d 191, 193 (Ala. 2001) (addressing whether an insurer has met its "enhanced obligation of good faith" required under *L & S Supply*); *State Farm and Cas. Co. v. Myrick*, 611 F. Supp. 2d 1287, 1295-99 (M.D. Ala. 2009) (same).

**Alaska:** "If an insurer has a duty to defend an insured under a policy of insurance and a conflict of interest arises that imposes a duty on the insurer to provide independent counsel to the insured, the insurer shall provide independent counsel to the insured unless the insured in writing waives the right to independent counsel." ALASKA STAT. § 21.89.100(a) (2009). It sets forth certain scenarios that do not constitute a conflict of interest, requires that independent counsel have certain experience and malpractice insurance, and provides that the fee charged by independent counsel is limited to the rate paid by the insurer for similar actions in the community in which the claim arose or is being defended. *Id.* The statute also contains an allocation provision: "In providing independent counsel, the insurer is not responsible for the fees and costs of defending an allegation for which coverage is properly denied and shall be responsible only for the fees and costs to defend those allegations for which the insurer either reserves its position as to coverage or accepts coverage. The independent counsel shall keep detailed records allocating fees and costs accordingly." *Id.* at § 21.89.100(d). In general the statute shares several similarities with California's *Cumis* statute. *See Great Divide Ins. Co. v. Carpenter*, 79 P.3d 599, 617 (Alaska 2003) (discussing statute); *CHI of Alaska v. Employers Reinsurance Corp.*, 844 P.2d 1113, 1116 (Alaska 1993) (discussing insured's right to counsel pre-statute).

**Arkansas:** An Arkansas District Court held that a reservation of rights creates a per se conflict that allows the insured to choose its own counsel to be paid for by the insurer. *Union Ins. Co. v. The Knife Co.*, 902 F. Supp. 877, 880 (W.D. Ark. 1995). *The Knife Company* Court concluded that a conflict cannot be eliminated so long as the insurer chooses defense counsel. *Id.* at 881. "It is simply a matter of human nature." *Id.* The court called the insurer's suggestion for addressing any conflict—the insured can always sue the insurer's chosen counsel for malpractice if he engages in misconduct—"cavalier." *Id.*

**Arizona:** The Supreme Court of Arizona held that an insurer with a good faith coverage defense may appropriately comply with its contractual duty to defend while simultaneously reserving the right to later assert the defense. *Parking Concepts, Inc. v. Tenney*, 83 P.3d 19, 22 (Ariz. 2004). However, an insurer that chooses this course of action faces the prospect of its insured entering into a *Morris* agreement [*United Servs. Auto Ass'n v. Morris*, 741 P.2d 246 (Ariz. 1987)]. *Tenney*, 83 P.3d at 22. A *Morris* agreement is a reasonable and prudent settlement that is entered into by an insured that is being defended under a reservation of rights. *Id.* Specifically, the insured stipulates to a judgment, assigns his policy rights to the claimant and, in return, receives a covenant that the claimant will not execute against it. *Id.* at 20, n.1. Under these circumstances, the insured will not be deemed to have violated the cooperation clause's prohibition against the insured settling a case without the insurer's consent. *Id.* at 21–22. A *Morris* agreement must be preceded by notice to the insurer to provide it with the opportunity to withdraw the reservation of rights and unconditionally assume liability under the policy. *Id.* at 22.

**California:** The California legislature adopted CAL. CIV. CODE ANN. § 2860 (Westlaw 2009) to address an insured's right to independent counsel. The statute is a codification of the Court of Appeal of California's decision in *San Diego Navy Fed. Credit Union v. Cumis Ins. Soc'y*, 208 Cal. Rptr. 494 (Cal. Ct. App. 1984). California's answer to the conflict issue is well known, so much so that "independent counsel" is sometimes referred to colloquially as "*Cumis* counsel"—even when describing independent counsel outside of California.

Section 2860(b) provides that "when an insurer reserves its rights on a given issue and the outcome of that coverage issue can be controlled by counsel first retained by the insurer for the defense of the claim, a conflict of interest may exist." If a conflict does exist, the insurer must provide independent counsel to the insured, unless the insured waives its right. CAL. CIV. CODE ANN. § 2860 (a), (f). Section 2860 does not answer whether a disqualifying conflict exists. That determination is left to the courts. Substantial litigation has been brought in California on that subject, and it has produced no simple answers. *See Gulf Ins. Co. v. Berger*, 93 Cal. Rptr. 2d 534, 79 Cal. App. 4th 144, 131 (Cal. Ct. App. 2000) (alteration in original) ("There is no talismanic rule that allows a facile determination of whether a disqualifying conflict of interest exists. Instead, "[t]he potential for conflict requires a careful analysis of the parties" respective interests to determine whether they can be reconciled... or whether an actual conflict of interest precludes insurer-appointed defense counsel from presenting a quality defense for the insured.""). The issue must be addressed on a case-by-case basis, in conjunction with an examination of how other conflict situations have been addressed by California courts and whether they were determined to be disqualifying. For additional guidance on whether a disqualifying conflict exists, *see James 3 Corp. v. Truck Ins. Exch.*, 111 Cal. Rptr. 2d 181 (Cal. Ct. App. 2001); *Dynamic*

*Concepts, Inc. v. Truck Ins. Exch.*, 71 Cal. Rptr. 2d 882 (Cal. Ct. App. 1998); *Blanchard v. State Farm*, 2 Cal. Rptr. 2d 884 (Cal. Ct. App. 1991); and *Native Sun Inv. Group v. Ticor Title Ins. Co.*, 235 Cal. Rptr. 34 (Cal. Ct. App. 1987).

California Civil Code § 2860 also addresses other facets of the independent counsel issue, such as: a conflict does not exist with respect to allegations for which an insurer denies coverage or punitive damages or because the insured is sued for an amount in excess of its policy limits, § 2860(b); the insurer can require that independent counsel have errors and omissions insurance and at least five years of civil litigation experience, including substantial relevant experience, § 2860(c); the fees to be paid to independent counsel shall be limited to the rates paid by the insurer to its panel counsel to defend similar claims in the community where the claim arose or is being defended, § 2860(c); independent counsel must timely report to the insurer and disclose all information concerning the action except privileged materials relevant to coverage disputes, § 2860(d); and counsel selected by the insurer and independent counsel shall both be allowed to participate in all aspects of the litigation and they shall exchange information subject to each counsel's ethical and legal obligations to the insure, § 2860(f).

**Colorado:** No instructive authority. *See Hecla Mining Company v. N.H. Ins. Co.*, 811 P.2d 1083, 1098 n.7 (Colo. 1991) (Mullarkey, J., dissenting) ("The issue of whether the insurers would be involved in a conflict of interest requiring them to provide independent counsel, possibly of [the insured's] choosing, or to obtain [the insured's] consent to allow the insurers to conduct the defense is not before us. I would therefore leave this issue to the trial court to resolve.").

**Connecticut:** No instructive authority.

**Delaware:** A Delaware trial court held that "[i]f an insurer has a conflict of interest, either real or potential, it is not relieved of its duty to defend. The insurer must either provide independent counsel to represent its insured, or pay the cost of defense incurred by the insured." *Int'l Underwriters, Inc. v. Stevenson Enters., Inc.*, No. 80C-SE-82, 1983 Del. Super. LEXIS 649, at *7 (Del. Super. Ct. Oct. 4, 1983). The *Stevenson Enterprises* Court provided no explanation of its decision. However, the court characterized the counsel retained by the insurer as "independent." *Id.* The court also cited to *U.S. Fidelity & Guaranty Co. v. Louis A. Roser Co.*, 585 F.2d 932 (8th Cir. 1978) and *Broham v. Transamerica Insurance Co.*, 347 A.2d 842 (Md. 1975) as support for its decision. *Id.* (both discussed *infra*.)

**Florida:** A Florida District Court held that there was no conclusive presumption that defense counsel chosen by the insurer was unable to fully represent its client, the insured, without consciously or unconsciously compromising the insured's interests. The court concluded that the rules governing the Florida bar were sufficient to protect the insured's interests. *Travelers Indem. Co. v. Royal Oak Enters., Inc.*, 344 F. Supp. 2d 1358, 1373 (M.D. Fla. 2004). The *Royal Oak* Court stated that "[m]embers of the Florida bar are charged with the responsibility of properly determining whether an actual conflict of interest exists, and if so, whether withdrawal from the representation is required. If counsel fails to do so and violates his or her duty of loyalty, he or she may face disciplinary actions and malpractice liability." *Id.* at 1375; *see also Ernie Haire Ford, Inc. v. Universal Underwriters Ins. Co.*, Nos. 6:07-cv-288-Orl-28DAB, 6:07-cv-595-Orl-28DAB, 2008 WL 2047936, at *7–8 (M.D. Fla. May 13, 2008) (following *Royal Oak*); *BellSouth Telecommunications, Inc. v. Church & Tower of Florida, Inc.*, 930 So. 2d 668, 670-71 (Fla. App. Ct. 2006) ("It is well-settled law that, when an insurer agrees to defend under a reservation of rights or refuses to defend, the insurer transfers to the insured the power to conduct its own defense, and if it is later determined that the insured was entitled to coverage, the insured will be entitled to full reimbursement of the insured's litigation costs."); FLA. STAT. ANN. § 627.426(2)(b)(3) (Westlaw 2009) (addressing a liability insurer's obligation to retain independent counsel which is mutually agreeable to the parties, with reasonable counsel fees agreed upon by the parties or set by the court).

**Georgia:** The Eleventh Circuit Court of Appeals concluded that "'where a conflict of interest exists between the insurer and the insured in the conduct of the defense of the action brought against the insured, the insured has the right to refuse to accept an offer of the counsel appointed by the insurer[.] In such circumstances, [the insurer] would have been obligated to pay for [the insured's] defense.'" *Am. Family Life Assurance Co. v. U.S. Fire Co.*, 885 F.2d 826, 831 (11th Cir. 1989) (citations omitted); *see also Utility Serv. Co., v. St. Paul Travelers Ins. Co.*, No. 5:06-CV-207, 2007 WL 188237, at *4 (M.D. Ga. Jan. 22, 2007) ("*Am. Family Life* held that the presence of a conflict of interest may enable the insured to retain independent counsel at the expense of the insurer.").

**Hawaii:** The Supreme Court of Hawaii concluded that if an attorney retained by an insurer follows the Hawaii Rules of Professional Conduct, he or she will be sufficiently independent. The court declined to accept an assumption that the attorney will slant its representation to the determine of the insured. *Finley v. Home Ins. Co.*, 975 P.2d 1145, 1154 (Haw. 1998). The *Finley* Court explained its decision as follows: "Although it is incontrovertible that the insurer and the insured have divergent economic interests in the outcome of the litigation, HRPC Rule 1.7 bars the attorney's representation only if this conflict will 'materially [limit]' the lawyer's representation of the insured. Because of the safeguards inherent in the HRPC, as well as alternate remedies existing in the case of misconduct, we disagree... that HRPC Rule 1.7 bars an attorney retained by the insurer from representing the insured under these circumstances without the informed consent of the insured." *Id.* at 1154.

**Idaho:** No instructive authority.

**Illinois:** The Appellate Court of Illinois refused to adopt a rule that a defense provided by an insurer, under a reservation of rights, creates a per se conflict that automatically entitles the insured to retain independent counsel at the insurer's expense. *Nandorf, Inc. v. CNA Ins. Cos.*, 479 N.E. 2d 988, 992 (Ill. App. Ct. 1985). The court explained its decision concerning the potential right to independent counsel as follows: "In determining whether a conflict of interest exists, Illinois courts have considered whether, in comparing the allegations of the complaint to the policy terms, the interest of the insurer would be furthered by providing a less-than-vigorous defense to those allegations. An insurer's interest in negating policy coverage does not, in and of itself, create sufficient conflict of interest to preclude the insurer from assuming the defense of its insured. However, a conflict of interest has been found where the underlying action asserts claims that are covered by the insurance policy and other causes which the insurer is required to defend but asserts are not covered by the policy." *Id.* at 992. (citations omitted); *see also Maryland Cas. Co. v. Peppers*, 355 N.E.2d 24, 31 (Ill. 1976) (recognizing that the insured is entitled to have independent counsel in a conflict situation and that the insurer is entitled to have an attorney of its choosing participate in all phases of the litigation subjection to the control of the case by the insured's attorney); *Stoneridge Dev. Co. v. Essex Ins. Co.*, 888 N.E.2d 633, 645 (Ill. App. Ct. 2008) (providing examples of cases in which Illinois courts have found the existence of a conflict of interest); *National Cas. Co. v. Forge Indus. Staffing Inc.*, 567 F.3d 871, 878 (7th Cir. 2009) (applying Illinois law) (holding that the requirements for the appointment of independent counsel were not met because the case did not present mutually exclusive theories of liability or factual allegations which, when resolved, would preclude coverage).

**Indiana:** An Indiana District Court declined to hold that a reservation of rights presents a per se conflict of interest for defense counsel. *Armstrong Cleaners, Inc. v. Erie Ins. Exch.*, 364 F. Supp. 2d 797, 816 (S.D. Ind. 2005). Instead, the court concluded that the determination must be made on a case-by-case basis and requires that some predictions be made about the course of the representation. *Id.* "If there is a reasonable possibility that the manner in which the insured is defended could affect the outcome of the insurer's coverage dispute, then the conflict may be sufficient to require the insurer to pay for counsel of the insured's choice. Evaluating that risk requires close attention to the details of the underlying litigation. The court must then make a reasonable judgment about whether there is a significant risk that the attorney selected by the insurance company will have the representation of the insureds significantly impaired by the attorney's relationship with the insurer." *Id.* at 808; *see also American Family Mut. Ins. Co. v. C.M.A. Mortg., Inc.*, 682 F. Supp. 2d 879, 890-91 (S.D. Ind. 2010) ("This position taken by [the insurer] created an immediate conflict of interest between it and [the insured] insofar as a finding of intentional conduct would benefit [the insurer] but not [the insured][.]... An insurer faced with such a conflict is required to reimburse its insured's independent counsel as part of its duty to defend.").

**Iowa:** The Court of Appeals for the Eighth Circuit, applying Iowa law, addressed whether an insurer that defended its insured for several months, without issuing a reservation of rights, was estopped to deny coverage. *City of Carter Lake v. Aetna Casualty & Surety Company*, 604 F.2d 1052, 1059 (8th Cir. 1979). The decision did not address the independent counsel issue. However, among the court's various reasons why the insured was prejudiced by the insurer's defense was the possibility of a conflict of interest. *Id.* at 1062. "During the time [insurer] had control of the city's defense against the [insureds'] claim, its attorneys could have simultaneously prepared a defense for [insurer] against the city on policy coverage." *Id.*

**Kansas:** The Supreme Court of Kansas held that if there is a conflict of interest between the insured and the insurer, the proper procedure to protect the rights of both parties is for the insurer to hire independent counsel to defend the insured and notify the insured that it is reserving all rights under the policy. *Patrons Mut. Ins. Ass'n v. Harmon*, 732 P.2d 741, 745 (Kan. 1987). Such procedure eliminates the necessity of multiple suits to determine the same issues. *Id.* The *Harmon* Court did not discuss what qualifies as a conflict. However, by way of the example, the underlying action involved liability that could have been based on either negligent or intentional conduct and the court concluded that, under such circumstances, the interest of the insurer and the insured were adverse. *Id.* The *Harmon* Court provided no guidance on how counsel qualifies as "independent."

**Kentucky:** No instructive authority. *But see Am. Ins. Ass'n v. Ky. Bar Ass'n*, 917 S.W.2d 568, 573 (Ky. 1996) (prohibiting a lawyer from defending an insured under a flat fee arrangement). The Supreme Court of Kentucky rejected the insurer's argument that the potential for conflict is very often lacking in a flat fee arrangement. *Id.* After examining some of the potential conflicts, the court held that the "mere appearance of impropriety is just as egregious as any actual or real conflict." *Id.* "Inherent in all of these potential conflicts is the fear that the entity paying the attorney, the insurer, and not the one to whom the attorney is obligated to defend, the insured, is controlling the legal representation." *Id.*

**Louisiana:** The Court of Appeal of Louisiana held that, because the insurer asserted at least six grounds of noncoverage, a conflict of interest existed that entitled the insured to select independent counsel at the insurer's expense. *Belanger v. Gabriel Chemicals, Inc.*, 787 So. 2d 559, 566 (La. Ct. App. 2001). The *Belanger* Court stated that, to determine whether the insurer and the insured have a conflict, the question is whether the interests of the insurer would be furthered by providing a less than vigorous defense to the allegations in the complaint. *Id.* However, the court provided no explanation why a conflict existed that was sufficient to justify the insured's retention of independent counsel at the insurer's expense.

**Maine:** The Supreme Judicial Court of Maine sought guidance from the Supreme Court of Arizona's decision in *United Services Auto Ass'n v. Morris*, 741 P.2d 246 (Ariz. 1987) and held that "an insured being defended under a reservation of rights is entitled to enter into a reasonable, noncollusive, nonfraudulent settlement with a claimant, after notice to, but without the consent of, the insurer. The insurer is not bound by any factual stipulations entered as part of the underlying settlement, and is free to litigate the facts of coverage in a declaratory judgment action brought after the settlement is entered. If the insurer prevails on the coverage issue, it is not liable on the settlement. If the insurer does not prevail as to coverage, it may be bound by the settlement, provided the settlement, including the amount of damages, is shown to be fair and reasonable, and free from fraud and collusion." *Patrons Oxford Insurance Company v. Harris*, 905 A.2d 819, 828 (Me. 2006).

**Maryland:** The Court of Appeals for the Fourth Circuit, applying Maryland law, relied on the Maryland high court's decision in *Broham v. Transamerica Insurance Co.*, 347 A.2d 842 (Md. 1975) to conclude that "Maryland has rejected a per se rule whereby the insurer is required to pay for the insured's independent counsel any time that the insured's objectives might differ from the objectives of the insurer. However, when an actual conflict of interest does exist, an insurer's duty to defend necessarily involves the duty to pay for the insured's independent counsel." *Driggs Corp. v. Pa. Mfrs.' Ass'n Ins. Co.*, No. 98–2140, 1999 WL 305044, at *5 (4th Cir. May 14, 1999) (citation omitted) (concluding that an actual conflict of interest did not exist when counsel retained by the insurer was specifically instructed to defend the insured without consideration of the insurer's interest and rejecting the insured's argument that appointed counsel could "steer" the case toward uncovered claims). "[U]nder the Canons of Professional Responsibility, the attorney selected by the insurer to represent the insured, although employed by the insurer, still has the duty to represent the insured with complete fidelity and may not advance the interests of the insurer to the prejudice of the rights of the insured." *Broham* at 852. "When such a conflict of interest arises, the insured must be informed of the nature of the conflict and given the right either to accept an independent attorney selected by the insurer or to select an attorney himself to conduct his defense. If the insured elects to choose his own attorney, the insurer must assume the reasonable costs of the defense provided." *Id.* at 854.

**Massachusetts:** The Supreme Judicial Court of Massachusetts held that a reservation of rights creates a per se conflict that allows the insured to choose its own counsel to be paid for by the insurer. *Sullivan, Inc. v. Utica Mut. Ins. Co.*, 788 N.E.2d 522, 539 (Mass. 2003). The *Sullivan* Court stated that "[w]hen an insurer seeks to defend its insured under a reservation of rights, and the insured is unwilling that the insurer do so, the insured may require the insurer either to relinquish its reservation of rights or relinquish its defense of the insured and reimburse the insured for its defense costs." *Id.*; *see also Watts Water Techs. v. Fireman's Fund Ins. Co.*, No. 05–2604-BLS2, 2007 WL 2083769, at *6 (Mass. Super. Ct. July 11, 2007) ("The insurer cannot reserve its rights to disclaim liability in a case and at the same time insist on retaining control of its defense.") (internal quotation and citation omitted).

**Michigan:** A Michigan District Court declined to hold that a conflict of interest is presumed because the insurer selects defense counsel. *Cent. Mich. Bd. of Trs. v. Employers Reinsurance Corp.*, 117 F. Supp. 2d 627, 636 (E.D. Mich. 2000). The court held that "under Michigan law an insurer complies with its duty to defend when, after it has reserved its rights to contest its obligation to indemnify, it fully informs the insured of the nature of the conflict and selects independent counsel to represent the insured in the underlying litigation. The insured has no absolute right to select the attorney himself, as long as the insurer exercises good faith in its selection and the attorney selected is truly independent." *Id.* at 634–35. The court based its decision on the attorney's fiduciary obligation owed to its client. "[F]or the very reason that the interest of the insured and the insurer are not always congruent, 'courts have consistently held that the defense attorney's primary duty of loyalty lies with the insured, and not the insurer.'" *Id.* at 636 (quoting *Atlanta Int'l Ins. Co. v. Bell*, 475 N.W.2d 294, 297 (Mich. 1991)).

**Minnesota:** The Court of Appeals of Minnesota declined to adopt the rule that a reservation of rights by itself creates a conflict of interest that justifies the insured retaining independent counsel. *Mut. Serv. Cas. Ins. Co. v. Luetmer*, 474 N.W.2d 365, 368 (Minn. Ct. App. 1991). "We believe the more reasoned approach to be that before an insured will be entitled to counsel of its own choice, an actual conflict of interest, rather than an appearance of a conflict of interest, must be established." *Id.*; *see also C.H. Robinson Co. v. Zurich Am. Ins. Co.*, No. 02–4794, 2004 WL 2538468, at *7 (D. Minn. Nov. 5, 2004) ("When an insurer reserves its right to deny coverage for punitive damages, a risk exists that the insurer will be less motivated to achieve the best possible result if it believes that the loss will result from punitive damages. Furthermore, it may be tempted to devote more effort into the non-coverage issue than into defending the insured.") (holding that conflict under *Luetmer* avoided because insurer tendered its limits, making its reservation of rights moot); *Hawkins, Inc. v. Am. Intl. Specialty Lines Ins. Co.*, No. A07–1529, 2008 WL 4552683, *7 (Minn. Ct. App. Oct. 14, 2008) (discussing *Luetmer* in the context of two insureds' right to separate counsel on account of conflicting interests).

**Mississippi:** The Supreme Court of Mississippi adopted a per se rule that a reservation of rights requires the insurer to pay for the insured's independent counsel. *Moeller v. Am. Guarantee & Liab. Ins. Co.*, 707 So. 2d 1062, 1071 (Miss. 1996). "A law firm which cannot be one hundred percent faithful to the interests of its clients offers no defense at all. 'There is no higher ethical duty in the legal profession than complete absolute fidelity to the interest of the client.'" *Id.* (quoting *State Farm. Mut. Auto. Ins. Co. v. Commercial Union Ins. Co.*, 394 So.2d 890, 894 (Miss. 1981)). The *Moeller* Court also concluded—while recognizing the inconvenience—that the insurer could have retained counsel to defend solely the one covered claim against the insured. *Id.* at 1070; *see also Liberty Mut. Ins. Co. v. Tedford*, 658 F. Supp. 2d 786,

797–98 (N.D. Miss. 2009) (insured presented genuine issues of material fact whether insurer should be equitably estopped from denying coverage, because of prejudice sustained by the insured, on account of the insurer failing to advise it of its rights under *Moeller*).

**Missouri:** The Eighth Circuit Court of Appeals, interpreting Missouri law, concluded that when a complaint alleged alternative grounds for relief, one covered by the policy and one not, the insurer "must either provide an independent attorney to represent the insured or pay the costs incurred by the insured in hiring counsel of its own choice." *Howard v. Russell Stover Candies, Inc.*, 649 F.2d 620, 625 (8th Cir. 1981) (quoting *U.S. Fidelity & Guar. Co. v. Louis A. Roser Co.*, 585 F.2d 932, 939 n.6 (8th Cir. 1978)).

**Montana:** A Montana trial court concluded that the Montana Supreme Court "would hold that when an insurer has a duty to defend but sends a reservation of rights letter to its insured on a coverage issue, the inherent conflict of interest between the insurer and the insured affords the insured the opportunity to choose counsel of his or her own choice at the insurer's expense." *Safeco Ins. Co. v. Liss*, No. DV 29–99–12, 2005 Mont. Dist. LEXIS 1073, at *40–41 (Mont. Dist. Ct. Mar. 11, 2005).

**Nebraska:** The Supreme Court of Nebraska addressed whether an insurer that defended its insured for over twelve months, without issuing a reservation of rights, was estopped to deny coverage. *First United Bank of Bellevue v. First Am. Title Ins. Co.*, 496 N.W.2d 474, 480–81 (Neb. 1993). The decision did not address the independent counsel issue. However, among the court's various reasons why the insurer was estopped was the possibility of a conflict of interest. *Id.* at 481. The court reasoned: "Moreover, the record indicates that, while American Title was controlling First United's defense, American Title was collecting data which would only be relevant in litigation against its insured… . Such conduct on the part of American Title at least raises the inference of divided loyalties." *Id.*

**Nevada:** A Nevada District Court, while not ruling on the independent counsel issue because it was not briefed by the parties, nonetheless observed that "[t]here is… respectable authority for the proposition that in a conflict of interest situation the right of the insurer to control the defense, investigation and settlement of the action includes the obligation to pay the reasonable value of the legal services and costs incurred for independent counsel for the insured." *Crystal Bay Gen. Improvement Dist. v. Aetna Cas. & Sur. Co.*, 713 F. Supp. 1371, 1379 (D. Nev. 1989) (citing *Executive Aviation, Inc. v. Nat'l Ins. Underwriters*, 16 Cal. App. 3d 799 (1971) and *Cay Divers, Inc. v. Raven*, 812 F.2d 866 (3d Cir. 1987)).

**New Hampshire:** The Supreme Court of New Hampshire, responding to an insurer's argument that a conflict precluded it from defending its insured, addressed the insured's right to independent counsel. *White Mountain Cable Constr. Corp. v. Transamerica Ins. Co.*, 631 A.2d 907, 912–13 (N.H. 1993).

While the court did not provide any analysis of the issue, it suggested that a conflict gives rise to an insured's right to independent counsel, stating "[t]his conflict, argues the [insurer], both prevented it from controlling the [insured's] defense and destroyed the privity between the [insured] and [insurer]. The [insurer] is correct to the extent that if there was a conflict of interest, it could not control the plaintiff's defense. Controlling the defense, however, is not synonymous with providing a defense. Having a duty to defend, and faced with a conflict of interest, the [insurer] could have hired independent counsel to defend the [insured] while intervening on its own behalf. In the alternative, the [insurer] could have provided the defense but reserved its right to later deny coverage." *Id.*

**New Jersey:** The Supreme Court of New Jersey held that an insurer that wishes to control its insured's defense, and simultaneously reserve the right to deny coverage, can do so only with the insured's consent. *Merchants Indem. Corp. v. Eggleston*, 179 A.2d 505, 512 (N.J. 1962). If the insured does not consent, it is free to defend itself, but the insurer's potential obligation to reimburse defense costs is subject to the applicability of *SL Indus. Inc. v. Am. Motorists Ins. Co.*, 607 A.2d 1266 (N.J. 1992) and its progeny (permitting allocation of defense costs between covered and uncovered claims when feasible). *Id.*; *see also Nazario v. Lobster House*, 2009 WL 1181620 (N.J. Super. Ct. App. Div. 2009) ("We find nothing in *Eggleston* or its progeny which suggests that the insured must prove actual prejudice to create coverage, or that the carrier may prove lack of prejudice to avoid coverage by estoppel, when a fully informed written consent is lacking. The control of the litigation without proper consent equates to creating the coverage without qualification under *Eggleston*.").

**New Mexico:** The Supreme Court of New Mexico cited the Supreme Court of Rhode Island's decision in *Employers' Fire Ins. Co. v. Beals*, 240 A.2d 397 (R.I. 1968), *overruled on other grounds by Peerless Ins. Co. v. Viegas*, 667 A.2d 785 (R.I. 1995), for its solution to a conflict of interest between the insurer and the insured. *Am. Employers' Ins. Co. v. Crawford*, 533 P.2d 1203, 1209 (N.M 1975). In *Beals*, the court held that the insurer could insist that the insured hire independent counsel or the insurer could hire two attorneys—one to represent the insured and the other to represent the insurer. *Id.*

**New York:** The Court of Appeals of New York held that, because the insurer was liable only for some, but not all, of the claims at issue, the insurer's interest in defending the lawsuit was in conflict with the insured's interest. Thus, the insured was entitled to a defense by an attorney of its own choosing, whose reasonable fee was to be paid by the insurer. *Pub. Serv. Mut. Ins. v. Goldfarb*, 425 N.E.2d 810, 815 (N.Y. 1981). But the New York high court was also clear to point out that independent counsel was not required in every case involving multiple claims, stating that "[i]ndependent counsel is only necessary in cases where the defense attorney's duty to the insured would require that he defeat liability on any ground and his duty to the insurer would require that he defeat liability only upon grounds which would render the insurer liable." *Id.* The Appellate Division of New York expanded upon *Goldfarb* in *Elacqua v. Physicians' Reciprocal Insurers,* 800 N.Y.S.2d 469 (A.D. 2005), holding that, in a situation in which *Goldfarb* applies, the insurer has an affirmative obligation to advise the insured of its right to independent counsel. Then, in a subsequent decision in *Elacqua,* the Appellate Division held that an insurer commits a deceptive business practice, under N.Y. Gen. Bus. Law § 349 (Consol.), if it fails to advise its insured that it is entitled to retain independent counsel. *Elacqua v. Physicians' Reciprocal Insurers,* 860 N.Y.S.2d 229, 231-32 (N.Y. App. Div. 2008); *see also N.Y. Marine & Gen. Ins. Co. v. Lafarge N. Am. Inc.,* 599 F.3d 102, 125 (2nd Cir. 2010) (applying N.Y. law) (rejecting insured's argument that a conflict is created under *Goldfarb* on the basis of a substantial difference between the amount at stake in the litigation and the limits of liability under the policy); *Executive Risk Indem. Inc. v. Icon Title Agency, LLC,* __ F. Supp. 2d __, No. 10 Civ. 2473, 2010 WL 3154558 *(S.D.N.Y. Aug. 3, 2010) (noting that New York's Appellate Departments are split on whether an insurer's* failure to inform its insured, of the insured's right to retain its own counsel, at the insurer's expense, can constitute a "deceptive act or practice" within N.Y. Gen. Bus. Law § 349).

**North Carolina:** No instructive authority.

**North Dakota:** No instructive authority.

**Ohio:** An Ohio Appeals Court declined to adopt a rule that a reservation of rights automatically requires the insurer to pay for the insured's private counsel. *Red Head Brass, Inc. v. Buckeye Union Ins.,* 735 N.E.2d 48, 55 (Ohio Ct. App. 1999). The *Red Head Brass* Court instead held that "an insurer in Ohio may proceed to defend the insured so long as the situation does not arise that the insurer's defense of the insured and its defense of its own interests are mutually exclusive. In such a case, the insurer, still bound in its duty to defend the insured, would have to pay the cost of the insured's private counsel." *Id.*

**Oklahoma:** The Court of Appeals of Oklahoma concluded, after examining cases nationally on the issue, that "not every perceived or potential conflict of interest automatically gives rise to a duty on the part of the insurer to pay for the insured's choice of independent counsel." *Nisson v. Am. Home Assurance Co.,* 917 P.2d 488, 490 (Okla. Civ. App. 1996). "Independent counsel is only necessary in cases where the defense attorney's duty to the insured would require that he defeat liability on any ground and his duty to the insurer would require that he defeat liability only upon grounds that would render the insurer liable." *Id.* (quoting *Pub. Serv. Mut. Ins. Co. v. Goldfarb,* 425 N.E.2d 810, 815 (N.Y. 1981).

**Oregon:** The Supreme Court of Oregon addressed the conflict issue by concluding that the judgment in the underlying action is not binding on the insurer or insured in a subsequent coverage action. *Ferguson v. Birmingham Fire Ins. Co.,* 460 P.2d 342, 349 (Or. 1969). As such, "there would be no conflict of interests between the insurer and the insured in the sense that the insurer could gain any advantage in the original action which would accrue to it in a subsequent action in which coverage is in issue." *Id.* The Oregon high court also declared minimal the risk of an insurer offering only a "token defense" in the action against its insured if it knows that it can later assert noncoverage. *Id.* "The insurer knows that when it is the defendant in a lawsuit brought by one of its policy holders the jury's sympathy for the insured frequently produces a plaintiff verdict even when the insurer's case is strong. Knowing this, the insurer is not likely to relax its efforts in defending the action against the insured." *Id.*

**Pennsylvania:** A Pennsylvania District Court stated that it is settled law that "where conflicts of interest between an insurer and its insured arise, such that a question as to the loyalty of the insurer's counsel to that insured is raised, the insured is entitled to select its counsel, whose reasonable fee is to be paid by the insurer." *Rector, Wardens & Vestryman of Saint Peter's Church v. Am. Nat'l Fire Ins. Co.*, No. 00–2806, 2002 WL 59333, at *10 (E.D. Pa. Jan. 14, 2002) (internal quotation marks and citations omitted). The *Rector* Court concluded that an actual conflict, and not merely a theoretical one, existed because the underlying liability could rest on either of two causes of action, one covered and one not. "In this situation, an insurer would be tempted to construct a defense which would place any damage award outside policy coverage." *Id.* at *29 (internal quotation marks and citations omitted). *See also PhotoMedex, Inc. v. St. Paul Fire & Marine Ins. Co.*, No. 09–00896, 2009 WL 2326750, at *11 (E.D. Pa. July 28, 2009) (same, quoting *Rector*); *St. Paul Fire & Marine Ins. Co. v. Roach Brothers*, 639 F. Supp. 134, 139 (E.D. Pa. 1986) ("With respect to the existence of both covered and uncovered claims or theories of liability, the potential for conflict is much greater, but actual conflict is not inevitable."); *Eckman v. Erie Ins. Exchange*, Court of Common Pleas of Montgomery County, Pennsylvania, No. 09-36724, at 9-10 (Aug. 6, 2010) ("The trial court is unwilling to accept the notion asserted by the Plaintiffs that any attorney selected by Erie will disregard the professional and ethical responsibilities which obligate him to represent only the interests of his client without qualification or reservation consistent with the time-honored tenets upon which there rests and relies the relationship between an attorney and his client.").

**Rhode Island:** The Supreme Court of Rhode Island held that, because of the existence of a conflict of interest (both negligent and intentional injuries were alleged), the insured should be entitled to select its own counsel at the expense of the insurer *or* the insurer and the insured should each be represented by separate counsel. *Employers' Fire Ins. Co. v. Beals*, 240 A.2d 397, 404 (R.I. 1968), *overruled on other grounds by Peerless Ins. Co. v. Viegas*, 667 A.2d 785 (R.I. 1995). The *Beals* Court expressed its belief that insurers should approve of either method "[b]ecause the insurer has a legitimate interest in seeing that any recovery based on finding of negligence on the part of its insured is kept within reasonable bounds[.]" *Id.*

**South Carolina:** The Fourth Circuit Court of Appeals, interpreting South Carolina law, declined to hold that a reservation of rights letter per se allowed an insured to hire counsel of its choosing at the insurer's expense. *Twin City Fire Ins. Co. v. Ben Arnold-Sunbelt Beverage Co. of S.C., LP*, 433 F.3d 365, 373 (4th Cir. 2005). Addressing whether a conclusive presumption exists that counsel hired by an insurer is unable to fully represent the insured without consciously or unconsciously compromising the insured's interests, the court stated that is was "unable to conclude that the Supreme Court of South Carolina would profess so little confidence in the integrity of the members of the South Carolina Bar." *Id.*

Instead, the Fourth Circuit looked to various provisions of the South Carolina Rules of Professional Conduct which provide rigorous ethical standards governing a lawyer's independence and duty of loyalty owed to its client, the insured, despite having been retained by the insurer. *Id.* The court concluded that these rules, various sanctions imposed for their violation and the threat of malpractice actions "provide strong external incentives for attorneys to comply with their ethical obligations." *Id.*

**South Dakota:** The Supreme Court of South Dakota concluded that a conflict of interest is avoided when an insurer defends its insured under a reservation of rights because the parties will not be estopped from litigating coverage issues in a later proceeding. *St. Paul Fire & Marine Ins. Co. v. Engelmann*, 639 N.W.2d 192, 200 (S.D. 2002). Under this arrangement, "the interests of the insured and the insurer in defending against the injured claimant will be identical." *Id.* Under *Engelmann*, because the insurer and insured will litigate in a subsequent coverage action whether the jury's verdict in the underlying action was based on uncovered intentional acts or covered negligence, no conflict was created by the insurer's choice of defense counsel. *Id.*

**Tennessee:** A Tennessee District Court concluded that the mere existence of a relationship between an insurer and defense counsel was not sufficient to create a conflict of interest. *Tyson v. Equity Title & Escrow Co. of Memphis, LLC*, 282 F. Supp. 2d 829, 832 (W.D. Tenn. 2003). The court seemed persuaded that the Tennessee Rules of Professional Conduct were sufficient to safeguard the insured, stating that "[t]ypically, the relationship between an insurance company and the attorney that it hires to defend an insured is that of principal and independent contractor. An insurance company clearly possesses no right to control the methods or means by which an attorney defends its insured. The employment of an attorney by an insurance company to represent its insured does not impose upon that attorney any duty or loyalty to the insurance company that could impair the attorney-client relationship between the attorney and the insured." *Id.* at 831–32 (citations omitted); *see also In re Petition of Youngblood*, 895 S.W.2d 322, 328–29 (Tenn. 1995) (rejecting a per se rule that an insurer cannot use staff counsel to defend its insureds and instead finding that whether there is a conflict in such arrangement must be determined on a case-by-case basis under the Tennessee Code of Professional Conduct.)

**Texas:** The Supreme Court of Texas held that, when defending an insured under a reservation of rights, if "the facts to be adjudicated in the liability lawsuit are the same facts upon which coverage depends, the conflict of interest will prevent the insurer from conducting the defense." *N. County Mut. Ins. Co. v. Davalos*, 140 S.W.3d 685, 689 (Tex. 2004). If so, the insurer loses the right to conduct the defense, but remains obligated to pay for it. *Id.* at 686. The *Davalos* court also listed other types of conflicts that may justify an insured's refusal of an offered defense: "(1) when the defense tendered 'is not a complete defense under circumstances in which it should have been,' (2) when 'the attorney hired by the carrier acts unethically and, at the insurer's direction, advances the insurer's interests at the expense of the insured's,' (3) when 'the defense would not, under the governing law, satisfy the insurer's duty to defend,' and (4) when, though the defense is otherwise proper, 'the insurer attempts to obtain some type of concession from the insured before it will defend.'" *Davalos*, 140 S.W.3d at 689 (quoting 1 ALLAN D. WINDT, INSURANCE CLAIMS & DISPUTES § 4.25 at 393 (4th ed. 2001)). *See also Rx. com, Inc. v. Hartford Fire Ins. Co.*, 426 F. Supp. 2d 546, 561 (S.D. Tex. 2006) ("Hartford's reservation of rights letter did not invoke a coverage exclusion that would be established by proof of the same facts to be decided in the underlying lawsuit.").

**Utah:** The Eight Circuit Court of Appeals, applying Utah law, left little doubt about what it thought of the risk for conflict when an insurer undertakes to defend its insured under a reservation of rights, stating "we cannot escape the conclusion that it is impossible for one attorney to adequately and fairly represent two parties in litigation in the face of the real conflict of interest which existed here. Even the most optimistic view of human nature requires us to realize that an attorney employed by an insurance company will slant his efforts, perhaps unconsciously, in the interests of his real client the one who is paying his fee and from whom he hopes to receive future business the insurance company." *U.S. Fidelity & Guar. Co. v. Louis A. Roser Co.*, 585 F.2d 932, 938 n.5 (8th Cir. 1978). Nonetheless, the court did not adopt the rule that a reservation of rights creates a per se conflict of interest. Rather, the court concluded that a conflict existed based on the specific facts at hand. *Id.* at 939. Among others, one of the three theories of recovery alleged in the underlying action was not covered by the policy. *Id.* at 938. In addition, the insurer filed a declaratory judgment action seeking a determination of no coverage. *Id.* at 940.

**Vermont:** The Supreme Court of Vermont held that a unilateral reservation of rights by an insurer is ineffective. *Am. Fidelity Co. v. Kerr*, 416 A.2d 163, 165 (Vt. 1980). "Control of the defense, with knowledge of the facts and without consent of the insured, constitutes an election to stand by the terms of the policy." *Id.*; *see also Beatty v. Employers' Liab. Assurance Corp., Ltd.*,

168 A. 919, 923 (Vt. 1933) (emphasis added) ("The insurer may, if it is in doubt as to its liability, refuse to assume the defense, and await the result, thus leaving the insured free to defend or compromise in his own way through his own counsel; *or it may obtain some agreement with the insured*, under which, by proceeding to defend, it shall not be considered to have enlarged its obligation under the policy, thus reserving its rights under that instrument.").

**Virginia:** The Supreme Court of Virginia addressed the conflict issue in the context of its decision that an insurer that defends its insured under a reservation of rights is not estopped from relitigating a fact issue that bears on coverage—specifically, whether its insured fired a gun negligently or intentionally. *State Farm Fire & Cas. Co. v. Mabry*, 497 S.E.2d 844 (Va. 1998). In *Mabry*, the court held that, in the underlying tort action, the insurer could not assert its position on the nature of the insured's conduct as the insurer was not a party. *Id.* at 846. The insurer also could not do so in conjunction with providing a defense to its insured because of the duty owed by the attorney retained by the insurer to the insured. *Id.* Thus, the court concluded that the declaratory judgment proceeding was the insurer's first opportunity to try its coverage defense on the merits. *Id.* at 847. By permitting the insurer to relitigate in a subsequent coverage forum an issue that was resolved in the underlying tort action, the Virginia high court's decision avoids the need for independent counsel. *Id.*

**Washington:** The Court of Appeals of Washington held that there is no presumption that a reservation of rights creates an automatic conflict of interest. *Johnson v. Cont'l Cas. Co.*, 788 P.2d 598, 601 (Wash. Ct. App. 1990). Instead, an insurer providing a defense under a reservation of rights must fulfill an "enhanced obligation of fairness." *Id.* at 600 (citing *Tank v. State Farm Fire & Cas. Co.*, 715 P.2d 1133, 1137 (Wash. 1986)). This enhanced obligation has been explained by the Supreme Court of Washington as follows: "First, the [insurer] must thoroughly investigate the cause of the insured's accident and the nature and severity of the plaintiff's injuries. Second, it must retain competent defense counsel for the insured. Both retained defense counsel and the insurer must understand that only the *insured* is the client. Third, the company has the responsibility for fully informing the insured not only of the reservation of rights defense itself, but of *all* developments relevant to his policy coverage and the progress of his lawsuit. Information regarding progress of the lawsuit includes disclosure of all settlement offers made by the company. Finally, an insurance company must refrain from engaging in any action which would demonstrate a greater concern for the insurer's monetary interest than for the insured's financial risk." *Tank*, 715 P.2d at 1137.

In addition to the criteria that must be satisfied by the insurer, the *Tank* Court also set out a list of obligations that must be satisfied by counsel who has been retained by the insurer to provide a defense under a reservation of rights. Counsel must understand that he or she represents only the insured, not the company. *Id.* at 1137. Defense counsel owes a duty of full and ongoing disclosure to the insured. *Id.* "This duty of disclosure has three aspects. First, potential conflicts of interest between insurer and insured must be fully disclosed and resolved in favor of the insured.... . Second, all information relevant to the insured's defense, including a realistic and periodic assessment of the insured's chances to win or lose the pending lawsuit, must be communicated to the insured. Finally, *all* offers of settlement must be disclosed to the insured as those offers are presented." *Id.* at 1137–38 (emphasis in original); *see also Carolina Cas. Ins. Co. v. Ott,* No. C09-5540, 2010 WL 1849230, at *6 (W.D. Wash. May 7, 2010) (discussing *Tank* factors); *Jaco Environmental, Inc. v. Am. Intern. Specialty Lines Ins. Co.,* No. 2:09-cv-0145, 2009 WL 1591340, at *7–8 (W.D. Wash. 2009) *(discussing Johnson and explaining why Washington's independent counsel rules differ from California's).*

**West Virginia:** The Supreme Court of Appeals of West Virginia addressed whether an insurer can be held liable under the West Virginia Unfair Trade Practices Act for the actions of a defense attorney retained to defend an insured (the simple answer is no). *Barefield v. DPIC Cos., Inc.,* 600 S.E.2d 256 (W. Va. 2004). The decision did not address the independent counsel issue. However, in arriving at its decision, the West Virginia high court addressed the tri-partite relationship in some detail, including citing to *U.S. Fidelity & Guar. Co. v. Louis A. Roser Co.,* 585 F.2d 932 (8th Cir. 1978). *Id.* at 557.

**Wisconsin:** A Wisconsin District Court held that the Wisconsin Supreme Court would not conclude that a mere reservation of rights automatically creates a conflict of interest between insured and insurer, which divests the insurer of control of the defense. *HK Systems, Inc. v. Admiral Ins. Co.,* No. 03 C 0795, 2005 WL 1563340, at *8 (D. Wis. June 27, 2005). Rather, for the insurer to be required to relinquish control of the defense, a real conflict of interest based on opposing defenses of insured and insurer must exist. *Id.* The *HK Systems* Court concluded that a real conflict of interest did exist because the insurer may benefit if HK Systems were found liable on certain claims, such as breach of contract or warranty, but not on others, such as negligence. *Id.* at 10.

**Wyoming:** No instructive authority.

# CHAPTER

# 6

# Insurer's Right to Reimbursement of Defense Costs

Many coverage issues develop over time, in response to new exposures for which insurance is sought. Such issues then sometimes fracture into various schools of thought as nuances emerge and more courts consider the issue. The duty to defend is not one of these issues. Rather, it is static and has been that way for a long time. Clearly no citation is needed for the principle that, in virtually all states, the duty to defend is broader than the duty to indemnify. And it has been that way for a very long time. *See Greer-Robbins Co. v. Pac. Sur. Co.*, 174 P. 110, 111 (Cal. Ct. App. 1918) (holding that the duty to defend is based on the allegations of the complaint and rejecting the insurer's argument that such duty depends upon the outcome of the action against the insured).

It is perhaps because the breadth of the duty to defend has achieved such taken-for-granted status that insureds do not take it lightly anytime they perceive an insurer straying from what they believe to be such a sacrosanct principle. One such circumstance is when an insurer, following a judicial determination that its duty to defend did not in fact exist, then attempts to recover the defense costs from the insured to whom it nonetheless provided a defense.

Insureds typically respond that reimbursement of defense costs must be impermissible because it would amount to the insurer achieving, at the conclusion of the case, that which it was not permitted to do at the inception of the case, namely, treating the duty to defend as other than broader than the duty to indemnify. *See Perdue Farms v. Travelers Cas. & Sur. Co.*, 448 F.3d 252, 258 (4th Cir. 2006) ("Under Maryland's comprehensive duty to defend, if an insurance policy potentially covers any claim in an underlying complaint, the insurer, as Travelers did here, must typically defend the entire suit, including non-covered claims. Properly considered, a partial right of reimbursement would thus serve only as a backdoor narrowing of the duty to defend, and would appreciably erode Maryland's long-held view that the duty to defend is broader than the duty to indemnify.") (citation omitted); *see also id.* at 259 ("In the absence of any contrary indication from the Maryland courts, we are unwilling to grant insurers a substantial rebate on their duty to defend.").

Nonetheless, despite this perceived challenge, litigation surrounding an insurer's right to reimbursement of defense costs has been active for the past fifteen years, with a significant spike in the past five. In general, insurers have won a few more of these cases than they've lost. But the score is close. And the minority view is gaining ground. *See American & Foreign Ins. Co. v. Jerry's Sport Center, Inc.,* 2 A.3d 526 (Pa. 2010).

Any discussion of an insurer's right to reimbursement of defense costs must begin with the best known case on the subject—*Jerry Buss v. Superior Court of Los Angeles County (Transamerica Ins. Co.),* 939 P.2d 766 (Cal. 1997). Buss owned the Los Angeles Lakers basketball team as well as other sports teams in Los Angeles, the Great Western Forum indoor arena, and various cable television broadcasting networks. *Id.* at 769. A dispute arose between Buss and H&H Sports over the provision of advertising for Buss. *Id.* H&H filed a twenty-seven-count complaint against Buss. *Id.* Buss sought coverage from Transamerica under commercial general liability policies. *Id.* Transamerica agreed to defend Buss on the basis of a defamation cause of action—the only cause of action out of twenty-seven that Transamerica believed was potentially covered. *Id.* at 770.

Transamerica reserved all of its rights, "including to deny that any cause of action was actually covered, and, '[w]ith respect to defense costs incurred or to be incurred in the future,… to be reimbursed and/or [to obtain] an allocation of attorney's fees and expenses in this action if it is determined that there is no coverage.'" *Buss,* 939 P.2d at 770 (alteration in original).

Buss paid H&H Sports $8.5 million to settle the dispute. *Id.* Transamerica paid Buss's defense counsel approximately $1 million, and a Transamerica expert concluded that the amount to defend the defamation cause of action was between $21,000 and $55,000. *Id.*

Addressing a dispute over coverage for defense costs, the Supreme Court of California held that, in a so-called "mixed" action, in which some claims are potentially covered and others are not—thereby triggering a duty to defend the action in its entirety—an insurer may thereafter seek reimbursement of defense costs for claims that are not potentially covered. *Id.* at 776–77. The *Buss* Court rested its decision on the following rationale:

> Under the policy, the insurer does not have a duty to defend the insured as to the claims that are not even potentially covered. With regard to defense costs for these claims, the insurer has not been paid premiums by the insured. It did not bargain to bear these costs. To attempt to shift them would not upset the arrangement. The insurer therefore has a right of reimbursement that is implied in law as quasi-contractual, whether or not it has one that is implied in fact in the

policy as contractual. As stated, under the law of restitution such a right runs against the person who benefits from "unjust enrichment" and in favor of the person who suffers loss thereby. The "enrichment" of the insured by the insurer through the insurer's bearing of unbargained-for defense costs is inconsistent with the insurer's freedom under the policy and therefore must be deemed "unjust."

*Id.* (citations omitted).

Other courts have permitted an insurer to recoup defense costs, but based on a rationale that differs from the one offered by *Buss*. Instead of concluding that the right to reimbursement is one that is implied in law to prevent unjust enrichment, as *Buss* did, some courts have reasoned that the insured's acceptance of the insurer's defense, with an express reservation of the insurer's right to recover defense costs, creates an implied in fact contract.

In *Colony Insurance Co. v. G & E Tires & Service, Inc.*, 777 So. 2d 1034 (Fla. Dist. Ct. App. 2000), the insurer was requested to provide a defense to its insured for claims by an employee for battery, sexual harassment, invasion of privacy, and intentional infliction of emotional distress. The insurer was adamant that no defense was owed because the claims were intentional torts and for injuries to employees in the workplace. *Id.* at 1035–36. Nonetheless, after initially sending three disclaimer letters, the insurer finally agreed to defend, but subject to a reservation of its right to be reimbursed for "defense costs incurred or to be incurred in the future." *Id.* at 1036. It was ultimately determined that the insurer was correct in its determination—the policy unequivocally excluded coverage for liability arising from the injuries. *Id.* at 1039. The insurer sought reimbursement of the defense costs incurred. *Id.* at 1038.

While the Florida appeals court in *G & E Tires* cited favorably to *Buss* in finding for the insurer, including quoting *Buss's* restitution analysis, the court did not expressly rely upon this rationale for its decision. *Id.* Instead, the *G & E Tires Court* rested its decision on contract principles—although not flowing from the insurance contract, but, rather, the reservation of rights. *G&E Tires*, 777 So. 2d at 1038. The *G & E Tires* Court held:

Colony timely and expressly reserved the right to seek reimbursement of the costs of defending clearly uncovered claims, which it consistently identified as such. Having accepted Colony's offer of a defense with a reservation of the right to seek reimbursement, G & E ought in fairness make Colony whole, now that it has been judicially determined that no duty to defend ever existed.

A party cannot accept tendered performance while unilaterally altering the material terms on which it is offered. See generally *Restatement (Second) of Contracts* § 69 (1981). * * * G & E's acceptance of the defense Colony offered to finance manifested acceptance of the terms on which Colony's offer to pay for the defense was tendered.

*Id.* at 1039; *see also Travelers Cas. & Sur. Co. v. Ribi Immunochem Research,* 108 P.3d 469, 480 (Mont. 2005) ("Travelers expressly reserved its right to recoup defense costs if a court determined that it had no duty to provide such costs. Travelers also provided specific and adequate notice of the possibility of reimbursement. Ribi implicitly accepted Traveler's defense under a reservation of rights when it posed no objections. Under these circumstances, the District Court appropriately concluded that Travelers may recoup its defense costs.")

But not all courts have been convinced that an insured's acceptance of a defense, with the insurer's express reservation of rights to recoup defense costs if it is determined that no duty to defend was owed, converts the reservation of rights letter into an implied in fact contract. Indeed, some courts see it the exact opposite.

In *Westchester Fire Insurance Co. v. Wallerich,* 563 F.3d 707, 719 (8th Cir. 2009), the Eighth Circuit Court of Appeals, interpreting Minnesota law, held that the insurer was not entitled to reimbursement of defense costs, despite asserting such right in its reservation of rights letter. Following an extensive survey of the law nationally on the issue, the court concluded that the insurer could have included a right to reimbursement in its policy. *Id.* As it did not, the insurer could not now unilaterally amend the policy through a reservation of rights letter. *Id.* Further, the court observed that the insureds explicitly rejected the terms of the reservation of rights, but accepted the defense nonetheless. *Id.* In this situation, because the insurer still tendered a defense, despite the insureds' rejection of the terms of the reservation of rights, the court concluded that the insurer was impliedly agreeing to proceed on the insureds' terms. *Id.*

Another rationale used by courts to reject an insurer's right to reimbursement of defense costs has its origin in *Terra Nova Insurance Company, Ltd. v. 900 Bar, Inc.,* 887 F.2d 1213 (3d Cir. 1989) (applying Pa. law). Decided at a time when there was very little law on the issue, as evidenced by the fact that the *Terra Nova* Court cited none (either controlling or persuasive), the court rested its decision on its view of certain practicalities of insurance and litigation. The *Terra Nova* Court stated:

> Faced with uncertainty as to its duty to indemnify, an insurer offers a defense under reservation of rights to avoid the risks that an inept or lackadaisical defense of the underlying action may expose it to if it turns out there is a duty to indemnify. At the same time, the insurer wishes to preserve its right to contest the duty to indemnify if the defense is unsuccessful. Thus, such an offer is made at least as much for the insurer's own benefit as for the insured's. If the insurer could recover defense costs, the insured would be required to pay for the insurer's action in protecting itself against the estoppel to deny coverage that would be implied if it undertook the defense without reservation.

*Terra Nova,* 887 F.2d at 1219–20. The *Terra Nova* Court's rationale for rejecting the insurer's right to reimbursement of defense costs was simple.

Since an insurer that is faced with uncertainty about its duty to indemnify receives a benefit from providing a defense, the insured is not unjustly enriched, even if it is ultimately determined that no duty to defend arose. *Id.*

It is not uncommon for courts that reject an insurer's right to reimbursement of defense costs to conclude that the insurer could have included such right in its policy. *See General Agents Ins. Co. of Am., Inc. v. Midwest Sporting Goods Co.*, 828 N.E.2d 1092, 1102 (Ill. 2005) ("Certainly, if an insurer wishes to retain its right to seek reimbursement of defense costs in the event it later is determined that the underlying claim is not covered by the policy, the insurer is free to include such a term in its insurance contract. Absent such a provision in the policy, however, an insurer cannot later attempt to amend the policy by including the right to reimbursement in its reservation of rights letter.").

While there is no shortage of states that allow an insurer to recover its defense costs following a determination that no duty to defend was owed, insurers sometimes find that practical problems associated with the implementation of this right diminish its actual value. As *Buss* itself noted: "An insurer is only entitled to recover those defense expenses which can be fairly and reasonably allocated *solely* to non-covered claims for which there never was any potential for coverage." *Buss*, 939 P.2d at 778 n.15 (quoting the Court of Appeal's decision in the case) (emphasis in original). Further, the court acknowledged that the task of allocating defense costs solely to claims that are not even potentially covered is at best extremely difficult and may never be feasible. *Id.* at 781 (discussing *Hogan v. Midland Nat'l Ins. Co.*, 476 P.2d 825 (Cal. 1970)). Thus, defense costs incurred to defend both actually or potentially covered claims, as well as noncovered claims, cannot be recovered. *Id.*

Since the majority of defense costs are incurred for claims that are both potentially covered and not covered, in many cases an insurer's right to reimbursement of defense costs has more bark than bite. This reality likely prevents some insurers from pursuing reimbursement of defense costs—either in an attempt to create the right or enforce it. For this reason, the real benefit for insurers when it comes to reimbursement of defense costs is likely limited to those cases that are not "mixed" actions, but, rather, where an insurer has undertaken a defense and can then establish that there were in fact no claims whatsoever that triggered such duty.

## 50-State Survey: Insurer's Right
## to Reimbursement of Defense Costs

**Alabama:** The Supreme Court of Alabama held that an insurer was not entitled to reimbursement of a payment made to settle a third-party claim against its insured if it was determined in a subsequent action that the policy did not provide coverage. *Mount Airy Ins. Co. v. The Doe Law Firm*, 668 So.

2d 534, 539 (Ala. 1995). Relying on the state's long history of disallowing recovery of voluntary payments, the court concluded, despite the insurer providing notice to the insured, that it would seek to recover the settlement payment, "such a protest by itself was insufficient to make the payment 'involuntary.'" *Id.* at 538. The court suggested that, to preserve a right to reimbursement of monies paid to settle a claim, an insurer must obtain a written nonwaiver agreement or a court order granting it the right to participate in a settlement without waiving the right to reimbursement. *Id.* (citations omitted). While the decision involved reimbursement of a settlement payment, the court's rationale would likely apply equally to defense costs.

**Alaska:** An Alaska District Court predicted that the Supreme Court of Alaska would hold that an insurer is entitled to seek reimbursement of defense costs, if it were determined that there was no duty to defend, provided that the insurer expressly reserved the right to do so. *Unionamerica Ins. Co., Ltd. v. Gen. Star Indem. Co.*, No. A01–0317-CV, 2005 WL 757386, at *8 (D. Alaska Mar. 7, 2005). "The law from other jurisdictions is clear that in order to be entitled to seek reimbursement, the insurer must expressly reserve that right." *Id.* (citing, among other authorities, *Grinnell Mut. Reinsurance Co. v. Shierk*, 996 F. Supp. 836 (S.D. Ill. 1998) in support of its decision). *But see Gen. Agents Ins. Co. of Am. v. Midwest Sporting Goods Co.*, 828 N.E.2d 1092, 1104 (Ill. 2005) (repudiating *Shierk*).

**Arizona:** No instructive authority.

**Arkansas:** The Supreme Court of Arkansas held that an insurer was not entitled to reimbursement of defense costs because attorney's fees are not recoverable except where expressly provided for by statute or rule—and none existed. *Med. Liab. Mut. Ins. Co. v. Curtis Enters. Inc.*, 285 S.W.3d 233, 235 (Ark. 2008). By relying on the so-called "American Rule," which provides that, absent a statute or agreement to the contrary, litigants bear their own attorney's fees, the court concluded that it did not need to consider the approaches taken by courts around the country that have addressed an insurer's right to reimbursement of defense costs. *Id.* A vigorous dissent maintained that the majority misapplied the American Rule, which applies to claims for attorney's fees by prevailing litigants. *Id.* at 238 (Brown, J., dissenting). "Whether an implied contract was formed to reimburse costs advanced in defense of a third-party claim is a far cry from the issue of payment of costs to a prevailing litigant, which is the subject of the American Rule. Simply put, that rule has no relevancy to the certified question before us." *Id.* "Our research has disclosed that no state court or federal court has based its reservation-of-rights [reimbursement of defense costs] decision on the American Rule, or even discussed it." *Id.* at 237.

**California:** The Supreme Court of California held that an insurer had a right to reimbursement of defense costs for claims that are not covered under the policy. *Jerry Buss v. Superior Court of Los Angeles County (Transamerica Ins. Co.)*, 939 P.2d 766, 775–78 (Cal. 1997). The court concluded that the insurer's right of reimbursement is one that is implied in law, to prevent unjust enrichment by the insured of defense costs for claims that were not covered by the policy, and, hence, for which the insured paid no premium. *Id.* at 776–77. Because such right is implied in law as quasi contractual, the insurer must specifically reserve it. *Id.* at 784 n.27. Further, the *Buss* court's decision applied to a so-called "mixed action," in which some claims were potentially covered and others were not. *Id.* at 775–77. However, the *Buss* court noted that, as a practical matter, the task of allocating defense costs solely to claims that are not potentially covered is at best extremely difficult and may never be feasible. *Id.* at 780 n.16; *see also Scottsdale Ins. Co. v. MV Trans.*, 115 P.3d 460, 471 (Cal. 2005) (holding that *Buss* also applies outside the context of a "mixed action," i.e., where no claim was potentially covered); *State Farm Gen. Ins. Co. v. Mintarsih*, 175 Cal. App.4th 274, 286 (2009) (applying *Buss* to hold that the insurer was not obligated to provide coverage for prevailing party attorney's fees, as costs, that could be allocated solely to claims that are not potentially covered); *Griffin Dewatering Corp. v. N. Ins. Co. of N.Y.*, 97 Cal. Rptr. 3d 568, 598–605 (Cal. Ct. App. 2009) (discussing *Buss* and related issues at length); *Burlington Ins. Co. v.* Devdhara, No. C 09-00421, 2010 WL 3749301 (N.D. Cal. Sept. 23, 2010) (applying principles of reimbursement of defense costs and a settlement to a multi-count complaint).

**Colorado:** The Supreme Court of Colorado held that "[t]he appropriate course of action for an insurer who believes that it is under no obligation to defend, is to provide a defense to the insured under a reservation of its rights to seek reimbursement should the facts at trial prove that the incident resulting in liability was not covered by the policy, or to file a declaratory judgment action after the underlying case has been adjudicated." *Hecla Mining Co. v. N.H. Ins. Co.*, 811 P.2d 1083, 1089 (Colo. 1991); *see also Valley Forge Ins. Co. v. Health Care Management Partners*, Nos. 09-1251, 09-1263, 09-1264, 09-1265, 09-1278, 09-1279, 2010 WL 3211170, __F.3d __ (10th Cir. Aug. 16, 2010) (applying Colorado law) (predicting, based on *Hecla Mining* and *Cotter Corp. v. Am. Empire Surplus Lines Ins. Co.*, 90 P.3d 814 (Colo. 2004), that the Colorado Supreme Court would allow an insurer to recover defense costs from its insured, where it reserved the right to do so by letter, regardless whether the insurer also reserved that right in the underlying insurance policy).

**Connecticut:** A Connecticut District Court described the Supreme Court of California's decision in *Buss* as "very logical and compelling" and predicted that, "given the right case and analogous set of facts," the Supreme Court of Connecticut would adopt a similar legal doctrine. *Ranger Ins. Co. v. Kovach*, No. 3:96CV02421, 1999 WL 1421657, at *3 (D. Conn. Dec. 3, 1999). Albeit in a different context, the Supreme Court of Connecticut also relied upon *Buss* in support of its conclusion that, for purposes of multiple-triggered policies, the appropriate method for allocation is pro rata and the insured must reimburse its insurer for defense costs attributed to periods of self-insurance. *Ins. Co.*

*of Hartford v. Lumbermens Mut. Cas. Co.*, 826 A.2d 107, 125 (Conn. 2003). "A cause of action for reimbursement is cognizable to the extent required to ensure that the insured not reap a benefit for which it has not paid and thus be unjustly enriched. Where the insurer defends the insured against an action that includes claims not even potentially covered by the insurance policy, a court will order reimbursement for the cost of defending the uncovered claims in order to prevent the insured from receiving a windfall." *Id.*

**Delaware:** No instructive authority.

**Florida:** The Court of Appeal of Florida, relying on *Buss*, held that an insurer is entitled to reimbursement of the costs of defending "clearly uncovered claims." *Colony Ins. Co. v. G & E Tries & Serv., Inc.*, 777 So. 2d 1034, 1039 (Fla. Dist. Ct. App. 2000). "[The insurer] timely and expressly reserved the right to seek reimbursement of the costs of defending clearly uncovered claims, which it consistently identified as such. Having accepted Colony's offer of a defense with a reservation of the right to seek reimbursement, [the insured] ought in fairness make [the insurer] whole, now that it has been judicially determined that no duty to defend ever existed." *Id.; accord Black & Assocs. v. Transcon. Ins. Co.*, 932 So. 2d 516, 518 (Fla. Dist. Ct. App. 2006) (relying on *Colony*). *But see Nationwide Mut. Fire Ins. Co. v. Hardin J. Royall, Jr.*, 588 F. Supp. 2d 1306, 1318 (M.D. Fla. 2008) (discussing *Colony* and *Black* and predicting that the Supreme Court of Florida would require that some reasonable time elapse before an insured's acquiescence of a defense constitutes acceptance) ("[T]he insurer should be required to give the insured a specific, reasonable time (*e.g.*, fifteen days) within which to accept or reject a written offer of a defense conditioned upon the reimbursement of fees and costs. Where this written offer clearly and expressly states that the failure to reject the offered defense within the stated period will constitute an acceptance, the insurer will be entitled to reimbursement in the event the insured fails to object and it is later determined that there is no coverage under the policy.").

**Georgia:** A Georgia District Court held that, in the absence of a provision in the reservation of rights letter requiring reimbursement of defense costs for uncovered claims, or case law instructing the court otherwise, the court was unwilling to allow reimbursement. *Transp. Ins. Co. v. Freedom Elecs., Inc.*, 264 F. Supp. 2d 1214, 1221 (N.D. Ga. 2003). The court reasoned that, since the bilateral reservation of rights and defense agreement did not specifically permit reimbursement, it would not recognize such right. *Id.* Moreover, the court concluded that, by its express terms, the reservation of rights precluded reimbursement. The agreement stated in pertinent part, "Carrier hereby agrees to assume defense of the claims presented by the underlying litigation from the date such claims were originally tendered... *unless and until such time* as it is established in a court of law that no duty to defend exists under the subject policy." *Id.* (emphasis added).

**Hawaii:** A Hawaii District Court, relying on the Supreme Court of California's decisions in *Buss* and *MV Transportation*, and other decisions nationally, held that an insurer that expressly reserved the right to seek reimbursement of defense costs was entitled to such recovery if the insured accepted the defense and it was determined that the insurer did not have a duty to defend. *Scottsdale Ins. Co. v. Sullivan Props., Inc.*, No. 04–00550 HG-BMK, 2007 WL 2247795, at *7 (D. Hawaii Feb. 27, 2006). *But see Executive Risk Indem. Inc. v. Pac. Educ. Servs., Inc.*, 451 F. Supp. 2d 1147, 1163–64 (D. Hawaii 2006) (expressing no opinion on whether Hawaii law recognizes a right to reimbursement of defense costs, the court was unwilling to decide the issue—which could "overhaul insurance litigation in Hawaii"—because it had not been the subject of adversarial briefing and the insurer provided no description of the costs and expenses it sought to recover).

**Idaho:** An Idaho District Court held that an insurer was not entitled to reimbursement of defense costs, despite the fact that it asserted such right in its reservation of rights letter. *St. Paul Fire & Marine Ins. Co. v. Holland Realty, Inc.*, No. CV07–390-S-EJL, 2008 WL 3255645, at *8 (D. Idaho Aug. 6, 2008). Relying on the Supreme Court of Illinois's decision in *General Agents Ins. Co. of Am., Inc. v. Midwest Sporting Goods Co.*, 828 N.E.2d 1092 (Ill. 2005), the court concluded that a reservation of rights letter can preserve only those rights that are listed in the policy. Since the policy did not include a provision for reimbursement of defense costs, the insurer had no such right. *Id.; see also Blue Cross of Idaho v. Atlantic Mut. Ins. Co.,* __ F. Supp. 2d __, No. 1:09-cv-246, 2010 WL 3326930 (D. Idaho Aug. 23, 2010) (addressing the reimbursement issue at length and following the "well reasoned" opinion in *Holland*).

**Illinois:** The Supreme Court of Illinois held that an insurer was not entitled to reimbursement of defense costs, despite the fact that it asserted such right in its reservation of rights letter. *General Agents Ins. Co. of Am., Inc. v. Midwest Sporting Goods Co.*, 828 N.E.2d 1092, 1104 (Ill. 2005). While the court acknowledged that other jurisdictions allow an insurer to recover defense costs from its insured, where the insurer provides a defense subject to this condition, the court declined to adopt such rule. *Id.* The court reasoned that the insured is not unjustly enriched when its insurer tenders a defense, even if it is later determined that the insurer did not owe such defense, because the insurer is protecting itself at least as much as it is protecting the insured. *Id.* at 1103. However, the court also stated that an insurer is free to include a provision in its policy that entitles it to seek reimbursement of defense costs if it were later determined that the underlying claim was not covered. *Id.* at 1104.

**Indiana:** No instructive authority.

**Iowa:** An Iowa District Court, following a comprehensive study of the issue, acknowledged that the majority of courts nationally permit an insurer to recover defense costs, based on an implied contract or unjust enrichment, but predicted that the Supreme Court of Iowa would not adopt such rule. *Pekin Ins. Co. v. TYSA, Inc.*, No. 3:05-cv-00030-JEG, 2006 WL 3827232, at *19 (S.D. Iowa Dec. 27, 2006). The court was persuaded to follow those courts nationally that have found "that using a reservation of rights to permit recovery of defense costs amounts to a unilateral modification of the policy terms and that, because the duty to defend is broader than the duty to indemnify, the insured is not unjustly enriched when the insurer provides a defense for claims that are at least possibly within the coverage terms, although such claims may later be found to be outside the policy." *Id.*

**Kansas:** No instructive authority.

**Kentucky:** The Sixth Circuit Court of Appeals, applying Kentucky law, held that, where the insurer asserted a timely reservation of rights, notified the insured of its intent to seek reimbursement and where the insured had meaningful control of the defense and settlement negotiations, Kentucky courts would permit an insurer to seek reimbursement of an amount paid in settlement. *Travelers Property Casualty Co. of America v. Hillerich & Bradsby Co.*, 598 F.3d 257, 268 (6th Cir. 2010). The court based its decision on an implied-in-law contract theory. *Id.* The court also relied on a fairness rationale in reaching its decision: "Here the insured was arguing that coverage was afforded for both defense and settlement costs, but refused to allow the insurer to seek reimbursement if a court later determined that the insured's position was incorrect. It would seem to be an unjust outcome for the insurer if this Court were to sanction that position." *Id.* at 269; *see also Employers Reinsurance Corp. v. Mut. Ins. Co.*, No. 3:05CV-556-S, 2007 WL 486715, at *2 (W.D. Ky. Feb. 9, 2007) (holding that an insurer was entitled to reimbursement of defense costs, if it were later determined that no coverage existed under the policy, as the insurer asserted such right in its reservation of rights letter) (insured could have declined to agree to the reservation of rights but it did not do so).

**Louisiana:** No instructive authority.

**Maine:** No instructive authority.

**Maryland:** The Court of Appeals for the Fourth Circuit, applying Maryland law, held that an insurer did not have a right to partial reimbursement of defense costs if it were later determined that there was no duty to defend certain claims. *Perdue Farms Inc. v. Travelers Cas. & Sur. Co.*, 448 F.3d 252, 254 (4th Cir. 2006). The court concluded that a partial right to reimbursement would be tantamount to a "backdoor narrowing" of the duty to defend and appreciably erode Maryland's long-held view that the duty to defend is broader than the duty to indemnify. *Id.* at 258. "In the absence of any contrary indication from the Maryland courts, we are unwilling to grant insurers a substantial rebate on their duty to defend." *Id.* at 259. The court also recognized that, even if Maryland looked favorably on a right of partial reimbursement, in this case the defense costs for covered and noncovered claims may have significantly overlapped. *Id.*

**Massachusetts:** The Supreme Judicial Court of Massachusetts held that "[w]here an insurer defends under a reservation of rights to later disclaim coverage... it may later seek reimbursement for an amount paid to settle the underlying tort action only if the insured has agreed that the insurer may commit the insured's own funds to a reasonable settlement with the right later to seek reimbursement from the insured, or if the insurer secures specific authority to reach a particular settlement which the insured agrees to pay. The insurer may also notify the insured of a reasonable settlement offer and give the insured an opportunity to accept the offer or assume its own defense." *Med. Malpractice Joint Underwriting Ass'n of Mass. v. Goldberg*, 680 N.E.2d 1121, 1129 (Mass. 1997); *see also Dash v. Chi. Ins. Co.*, No. 00–11911, 2004 WL 1932760, at \*8–9 (D. Mass. Aug. 23, 2004) (discussing *Buss* but declining to reach the issue because the insurer had breached its duty to defend).

**Michigan:** A Michigan District Court, looking to *Buss* for guidance, held that an insurer may recoup defense costs incurred for those claims which "clearly and unequivocally do not give rise to a duty to defend." *Travelers Prop. Cas. Co. v. R.L. Polk & Co.*, No. 06–12895, 2008 WL 786678 at \*2 (E.D. Mich. Mar. 24, 2008). "Under the policy, the insurer does not have a duty to defend the insured as to the claims that are not even potentially covered. With regard to defense costs for these claims, the insurer has not been paid premiums by the insured. It did not bargain to bear these costs. To attempt to shift them would not upset the arrangement." *Id.* (quoting *Buss*, 939 P.2d at 776) (internal quotations omitted); *see also Lumbermens Mut. Cas. Co. v. RGIS Inventory Specialists, LLC*, No. 08 Civ. 1316, 2010 WL 2017272, \*4 (S.D.N.Y. May 20, 2010) (applying Michigan law) ("Although the Michigan Supreme Court has not addressed this question, decisions of other courts in Michigan support a prediction that Michigan would allow an insurer to recoup a contribution to a settlement, where it is ultimately determined that the insured was not entitled to coverage under the insurance policy.") (finding instructive *Travelers Property Casualty Co. of America v. Hillerich & Bradsby Co.*, 598 F.3d 257 (6th Cir. 2010) (applying Ky. law)).

**Minnesota:** The Eighth Circuit Court of Appeals, applying Minnesota law, held that an insurer was not entitled to reimbursement of defense costs, despite asserting such right in its reservation of rights letter. *Westchester Fire Ins. Co. v. Wallerich*, 563 F.3d 707, 719 (8th Cir. 2009). Following an extensive survey of the law nationally on the issue, the court concluded that the insurer could have included a right to reimbursement in its policy. *Id.* As it did not, the insurer could not now unilaterally amend the policy through a reservation of rights letter. *Id.* Further, the court observed that the insureds explicitly rejected the terms of the reservation of rights, but accepted the defense nonetheless. In this situation, because the insurer still tendered a defense, despite the insureds' rejection of the terms of the reservation of rights, the court concluded that the insurer was impliedly agreeing to proceed on the insureds' terms. *Id.*

**Mississippi:** A Mississippi District Court held that the insurer was not entitled to reimbursement of defense costs incurred prior to the court's determination that the insurer had no duty to defend. *Certain Underwriters at*

*Lloyd's London v. Magnolia Mgmt. Corp.*, No. 04CV540TSL, 2009 WL 1873026, at *2 (S.D. Miss. June 26, 2009). The court's reasoning was minimal and related to the specifics of the case. However, addressing the right to reimbursement in general, the court set forth the test from *United Nat'l. Ins. Co. v. SST Fitness Corp.*, 309 F.3d 914, 921 (6th Cir. 2002) (applying Ohio law), and concluded that no right to reimbursement existed because the policy did not provide such a right and the reservation of rights letter was not specific or clear enough to have afforded notice of such right. *Id.* at *1; *see also Liberty Mut. Ins. Co. v. Tedford*, 658 F. Supp. 2d 786, 801 (N.D. Miss. 2009) ("Without holding that Mississippi recognizes or should recognize a right of reimbursement, under the facts of this case, namely Liberty Mutual's duty to defend the underlying complaint, even jurisdictions that authorize a right of reimbursement would not find reimbursement proper here.").

**Missouri:** The Eighth Circuit Court of Appeals, applying Missouri law, held that the insurer was not entitled to reimbursement of defense costs following a determination that it had no duty to defend. *Liberty Mut. Ins. Co. v. FAG Bearings Corp.*, 153 F.3d 919, 924 (8th Cir. 1998). The court did not address the various arguments often raised for and against the right to reimbursement. Instead, the court rested its decision on the insurer's obligation to defend its insured so long as there remained any question whether the underlying claims were covered by the policy. *Id.*

**Montana:** The Supreme Court of Montana held that an insurer was entitled to reimbursement of defense costs when it was determined that the insurer had no duty to defend. *Travelers Cas. and Sur. Co. v. Ribi Immunochem Research, Inc.*, 108 P.3d 469, 480 (Mont. 2005). The court concluded that reimbursement was permissible because the insurer had timely and explicitly reserved such right and the insured implicitly accepted the defense under the reservation of rights when it posed no objections. *Id.* at 479–80 (citing, among other authorities, *Grinnell Mut. Reinsurance Co. v. Shierk*, 996 F. Supp. 836 (S.D. Ill. 1998) in support of its decision). *But see Gen. Agents Ins. Co. of Am. v. Midwest Sporting Goods Co.*, 828 N.E.2d 1092, 1104 (Ill. 2005) (repudiating *Shierk*).

**Nebraska:** No instructive authority.

**Nevada:** The Ninth Circuit Court of Appeals, applying Nevada law, held that there was sufficient evidence of an "understanding" that the insurer reserved its right to seek reimbursement of defense costs for uncovered claims. *Forum Ins. Co. v. County of Nye*, No. 91–16724, 1994 WL 241384, at *3 (9th Cir. June 3, 1994). The court concluded that such right existed because the insurer unilaterally, but explicitly, reserved it. *Id.* at *2. The court was persuaded that, while the insured objected to this reservation, it continued to accept the defense—valued at hundreds of thousands of dollars. *Id.* The court further reasoned that, if the insurer were denied the ability to recoup defense costs, the insurer would be forced to withhold the defense to obtain the requisite agreement and reserve its right to seek a later adjudication. *Id.* at *3.

As a result the insured would be prejudiced in the underlying action and the insurer would potentially be subject to other liabilities. *Id.*; *see also Capitol Indem. Corp. v. Blazer*, 51 F. Supp. 2d 1080, 1090 (D. Nev. 1999) (citing *Nye* and holding that the insurer was not entitled to reimbursement of defense costs for claims not potentially covered under the policy because there was no clear understanding between the parties that the insurer had reserved such right).

**New Hampshire:** No instructive authority.

**New Jersey:** A New Jersey District Court, in granting a motion to stay a declaratory judgment action, held that, upon completion of the underlying litigation, the insurer may recommence the coverage action to recoup defense expenses. *Transcon. Ins. Co. v. Jocama Constr. Corp.*, No. 06-cv-03358, 2007 WL 2212367, at *6 (D.N.J. July 27, 2007). The court did not provide any analysis of the right of reimbursement of defense costs. However, the court reasoned that the insurer was not unduly prejudiced by defending its insured under a reservation of rights because the insurer could subsequently seek reimbursement for defense costs incurred. *Id.* Any consideration of an insurer's right to reimbursement of defense costs under New Jersey law would also likely be affected by the manner in which the defense is being handled vis-à-vis *Burd v. Sussex Mutual Insurance Co.*, 267 A.2d 7 (N.J. 1970). *See* Chapter 4.

**New Mexico:** A Louisiana District Court, applying New Mexico law, held that an insurer was entitled to reimbursement of defense costs for uncovered claims. *Resure, Inc. v. Chemical Distribs., Inc.*, 927 F. Supp. 190, 194 (M.D. La. 1996). Without citing another case, the court concluded that such right existed because the insurer issued a timely reservation of rights that specifically referred to the possibility that it might seek reimbursement for any and all costs of defense. *Id.* Further, there was nothing in the record to suggest that the insured objected to such reservation. *Id.*

**New York:** A New York District Court held that an insurer was entitled to reimbursement of defense costs. *Gotham Ins. Co. v. GLNX, Inc.*, No. 92 Civ. 6415, 1993 WL 312243, at *4 (S.D.N.Y. Aug. 6, 1993). The court reasoned that the insurer was so entitled because it explicitly reserved its right to seek reimbursement if it were determined that no duty to defend existed. *Id.* Further, the insured offered no evidence that it expressly refused to consent to the insurer's reservation of rights as to reimbursement or that the defense costs related to a certain claim that was in fact covered. *Id.*

**North Carolina:** No instructive authority.

**North Dakota:** No instructive authority.

**Ohio:** The Sixth Circuit Court of Appeals, applying Ohio law, following a review of decisions nationally, held that an insurer had a right to reimbursement of defense costs for uncovered claims. *United Nat'l Ins. Co. v. SST Fitness Corp.*, 309 F.3d 914, 921 (6th Cir. 2002). The court adopted the rationale that, by accepting the defense subject to the insurer's right to reimbursement, the insured entered into an implied in fact contract. *Id.* at 917–21 (citing, among other authorities, *Grinnell Mut. Reinsurance Co. v. Shierk*, 996 F. Supp. 836 (S.D. Ill. 1998) in support of its decision). *But see Gen. Agents Ins. Co. of Am. v. Midwest Sporting Goods Co.*, 828 N.E.2d 1092, 1104 (Ill. 2005) (repudiating *Shierk*).

**Oklahoma:** An Oklahoma District Court held that an insurer was entitled to reimbursement of a settlement payment if it were subsequently determined that no coverage was owed. *Melton Truck Lines, Inc. v. Indem. Ins. Co. of N. Am.*, No. 04-CV-263-JHP-SAJ, 2006 WL 1876528, at *3 (N.D. Okla. June 26, 2006). The court relied on the fact that, under Oklahoma law, an insurer who settles an underlying claim does not waive any coverage defenses vis-à-vis its insured. *Id.* at *2. Cautionary Note: The *Melton Truck* Court also relied on the Supreme Court of Texas's 2005 decision in *Excess Underwriters at Lloyd's v. Franks Casing Crew & Rental Tools*, No. 02–0730, 2005 WL 1252321 (Tex. May 27, 2005), and its reasoning that an insured is not prejudiced by a requirement that it reimburse its insurer for settlement payments if there is no coverage because, in such case, the insured is in the same position, or at least no worse position, than it would have been if there had been no insurance policy. *Id.* However, at the time of the Oklahoma District Court's decision in *Melton Truck*, *Franks Casing* had been withdrawn by the Supreme Court of Texas by a January 6, 2006 grant of rehearing and was substituted with a decision in 2008. *See* Texas.

**Oregon:** No instructive authority.

**Pennsylvania:** The Supreme Court of Pennsylvania held that an insurer was not entitled to reimbursement of defense costs when it was determined that the insurer had no duty to defend. *American & Foreign Ins. Co. v. Jerry's Sport Center, Inc.*, 2 A.3d 526, 546 (Pa. 2010). "[P]ermitting reimbursement by reservation of rights, absent an insurance policy provision authorizing the right in the first place, is tantamount to allowing the insurer to extract a unilateral amendment to the insurance contract." *Id.* at 544. "Insured was not unjustly enriched by [insurer's] payment of defense costs. [The insurer] had not only the duty to defend, but the right to defend under the insurance contract. This arrangement benefited both parties. The duty to defend benefited Insured to protect it from the cost of defense, while the right to defend allowed [the insurer] to control the defense to protect itself against potential indemnity exposure." *Id.* at 545.

**Rhode Island:** No instructive authority.

**South Carolina:** No instructive authority.

**South Dakota:** No instructive authority.

**Tennessee:** A Tennessee District Court, fully incorporating a magistrate judge's report and recommendation, predicted that the Supreme Court of Tennessee would recognize a right to reimbursement of defense costs. *Cincinnati Ins. Co. v. Grand Pointe, LLC*, 501 F. Supp. 2d 1145, 1168 (E.D. Tenn. 2007). The court examined case law nationally on both sides of the issue and concluded that an insurer has a right to reimbursement, even if the policy does not contain an express provision to such effect, so long as the insurer provided timely, specific, and adequate notice to the insured of the insurer's right to seek reimbursement if it were determined there was no duty to defend. *Id.*

**Texas:** The Supreme Court of Texas held that "when coverage is disputed and the insurer is presented with a reasonable settlement demand within policy limits, the insurer may fund the settlement and seek reimbursement only if it obtains the insured's clear and unequivocal consent to the settlement and the insurer's right to seek reimbursement." *Texas Ass'n of Counties County Government Risk Management Pool v. Matagorda County*, 52 S.W.3d 128, 135 (Tex. 2000). The court recognized that insurers faced with a reasonable settlement offer within policy limits, where coverage is in question, are in an untenable position. *Id.* at 135. However, the court concluded that an insurer in such a position can seek prompt resolution of the coverage dispute in a declaratory judgment action, a step that the court noted it has encouraged insurers to take. *Id.* The court was also persuaded that "[o]n balance, insurers are better positioned to handle this risk, either by drafting policies to specifically provide for reimbursement or by accounting for the possibility that they may occasionally pay uncovered claims in their rate structure." *Id.* at 136; *see also Excess Underwriters at Lloyd's London v. Frank's Casing Crew and Rental Tools, Inc.*, 246 S.W.3d 42, 43 (Tex. 2008) (refusing to recognize an exception to *Matagorda County* and a reimbursement obligation when the policy involves excess coverage, the insurer has no duty to defend under the policy, and the insured acknowledges that the claimant's settlement offer is reasonable and demands that the insurer accept it).

**Utah:** A Utah District Court denied an insurer's request for reimbursement of defense costs pending the Supreme Court of Utah's ruling on whether such request is permissible under Utah law. *Westport Ins. Corp. v. Ong*, No. 1:07CV10 DAK, 2008 WL 892941, at *6 (D. Utah Mar. 28, 2008). The court certified the question to the Utah high court because the issue had never been addressed by Utah courts, was controlling in the case and there was significant split among courts across the country. *Id.* However, the parties subsequently filed a stipulated dismissal with prejudice of all claims and counterclaims. *Westport Ins. Corp. v. Ong*, No. 1:07CV10 DAK, Docket Entry No. 47 (D. Utah Sept. 30, 2008).

**Vermont:** No instructive authority.

**Virginia:** The Fourth Circuit Court of Appeals, applying Virginia law, held that certain coverage issues were not ripe for appellate review. *Penn-America Ins. Co. v. Mapp*, 521 F.3d 290, 298 (4th Cir. 2008). However, the court also concluded, without analysis, that once the issues became ripe, the insurer, pursuant to its reservation of rights, could seek reimbursement of its defense costs if it were determined that the insurer did not have a duty to defend. *Id.*

**Washington:** No instructive authority.

**West Virginia:** No instructive authority.

**Wisconsin:** A Wisconsin District Court addressed the issue of reimbursement of defense costs for uncovered claims, following a reservation of such right by the insurer, in the context of deciding the insurer's motion to file an amended counterclaim seeking reimbursement. *Kreuger Int'l, Inc. v. Fed. Ins. Co.*, 637 F. Supp. 2d 604 (E.D. Wis. 2008). While the court did not resolve the question, it concluded, following a review of case law nationally on both sides of the issue, that the insurer's claim for reimbursement of defense costs was not frivolous. *Id.* at 624. As such, the court granted the motion to amend because it would not be futile to do so. *Id.* at 620.

**Wyoming:** The Supreme Court of Wyoming held that allocation of defense costs between covered and uncovered claims, followed by requiring reimbursement by the insured of defense costs for uncovered claims, was not permitted, even if such right is asserted by the insured in its reservation of rights letter. *Shoshone First Bank v. Pac. Employers Ins. Co.*, 2 P.3d 510, 515–16 (Wyo. 2000). The court based its decision on the recognition that an insurer is charged with the duty of defending the entire suit and the insurer could have included an allocation provision in its policy, but failed to do so. *Id.* Further, the court observed that "[t]he question as to whether there is a duty to defend an insured is a difficult one, but because that is the business of an insurance carrier, it is the insurance carrier's duty to make that decision. If an insurance carrier believes that no coverage exists, then it should deny its insured a defense at the beginning instead of defending and later attempting to recoup from its insured the costs of defending the underlying action." *Id.* at 516 (quoting *Am. States Ins. Co. v. Ridco, Inc.*, No. 95CV158D, 1996 WL 33401184, at *3 (D. Wyo. Feb. 8, 1996)).

# CHAPTER
# 7

# Prevailing Insured's Right to Recover Attorney's Fees in Coverage Litigation

When an insurance company is evaluating whether to file a declaratory judgment action or defend one filed against it, the principal issues under consideration are likely to be the insurer's chance of success and the amount of attorney's fees that will be incurred to achieve the desired result. Of course, those are the paramount considerations of *any* party that is contemplating litigation over *any* issue—not just insurance coverage.

On one hand, insurers are like all others parties that undertake the deliberative process when deciding to enter the litigation arena. On the other hand, insurers must often weigh an additional factor in the litigation equation that most others need not: If the insurer does not prevail, will it be obligated to pay its insured's attorney's fees? To be clear, these are attorney's fees that are *in addition to* any attorney's fees that the insurer may be obligated to pay to its insured, for the defense of an underlying action, if the insurer did not provide a defense and it was now determined in the coverage litigation that a defense was in fact owed.

As a general rule, in almost all litigation, the losing party is not obligated to pay the prevailing party's attorney's fees. This is often referred to as the "American Rule." *ACMAT Corp. v. Greater N.Y. Mut. Ins. Co.*, 923 A.2d 697, 702 (Conn. 2007) ("The general rule of law known as the American rule is that attorney's fees and ordinary expenses and burdens of litigation are not allowed to the successful party absent a contractual or statutory exception.") (citations and internal quotation omitted); *see also Barnes v. Okla. Farm Bureau Mut. Ins. Co.*, 11 P.3d 162, 185 n.11 (Okla. 2000) ("In contrast to the American Rule, the English Rule calls for an across-the-board *postdecisional* cost- and counsel-fee shifting in favor of the victorious party.") (emphasis in original).

Therefore, the possibility of an unsuccessful insurer in coverage litigation being obligated to pay its insured's attorney's fees hinges on the existence of an exception to the American Rule in the relevant state. And such exceptions are not granted lightly. *Monahan v. GMAC Mortgage Corp.*, 893 A.2d 298, 322 (Vt. 2005) ("We have recognized that courts may invoke their equity powers to deviate from [the American] rule, but only in exceptional cases and for dominating reasons of justice.") (citation and internal quotation omitted).

Notwithstanding this demanding standard, most states have carved out an exception of some type to the American Rule when it is judicially determined that an insurer is obligated to provide coverage to an insured. One commonly cited rationale for this exception is that, if the insured must bear the expense of obtaining coverage from its insurer, it may be no better off financially than if it did not have the insurance policy in the first place. *See Mountain W. Farm Bureau Mut. Ins. Co. v. Brewer*, 69 P.3d 652, 657–58 (Mont. 2003) (citing 7C John Alan Appleman et al., *Insurance Law and Practice* § 4691, at 282–83 (1979)); *see also Olympic Steamship Co., Inc. v. Centennial Ins. Co.*, 811 P.2d 673, 681 (Wash. 1991) ("When an insured purchases a contract of insurance, it seeks protection from expenses arising from litigation, not vexatious, time-consuming, expensive litigation with its insurer.") (citation and internal quotation omitted).

While an unsuccessful insurer in coverage litigation likely faces an exception to the American Rule, requiring it to pay for its insured's attorney's fees, the specific approaches vary widely and can have a significant impact on the likelihood of the insurer in fact incurring such obligation. *Crist v. Ins. Co. of N. Am.*, 529 F. Supp. 601, 606 (D. Utah 1982) ("There are innumerable cases dealing with this specific issue [recovery of attorney's fees in bringing a declaratory judgment action against an insurer], and the courts have resolved the issue in practically every conceivable way.").

In general, some states have enacted statutes that provide for a prevailing insured's recovery of attorney's fees in an action to secure coverage. Other states achieve similar results, but do so through common law. But whichever approach applies, the most important factor is the same: whether the prevailing insured's right to recover attorney's fees is automatic or must the insured prove that the insurer's conduct was unreasonable or egregious in some way.

For example, a Hawaii statute mandates an award of attorney's fees without regard to the insurer's conduct in denying the claim. In other words, it imposes strict liability for attorney's fees on an insurer that is ordered to pay a claim. HAW. REV. STAT. ANN. § 431:10–242 (LexisNexis 2009) ("Where an insurer has contested its liability under a policy and is ordered by the courts to pay benefits under the policy, the policyholder, the beneficiary under a policy, or the person who has acquired the rights of the policyholder or beneficiary under the policy shall be awarded reasonable attorney's fees and the costs of suit, in addition to the benefits under the policy.").

Maryland also takes a strict liability approach, but it is the result of a decision from its highest court. *Bausch & Lomb, Inc. v. Utica Mut. Ins. Co.*, 735 A.2d 1081, 1094–95 (Md. 1999) ("[I]n the absence of a statute, rule or contract expressly allowing the recovery of attorneys' fees, a prevailing party in a lawsuit may not ordinarily recover attorneys' fees. There is one nonstatutory exception to the American rule in actions involving insurance policies. Where an action is brought to enforce an insurer's obligations under the third party liability provisions of a policy, and it is determined that there is coverage under the policy, the insurer is liable for the prevailing party's attorneys' fees.") (citations and internal quotation omitted).

Alternatively, a Virginia statute departs from strict liability and permits an award of attorney's fees, but only if there was a finding that the insurer's denial of coverage was not in good faith. VA. CODE ANN. § 38.2-209 (Westlaw 2009) ("[I]n any civil case in which an insured individual [defined to include a company or organization] sues his insurer to determine what coverage, if any, exists under his present policy... or the extent to which his insurer is liable for compensating a covered loss, the individual insured shall be entitled to recover from the insurer costs and such reasonable attorney fees as the court may award. However, these costs and attorney's fees shall not be awarded unless the court determines that the insurer, not acting in good faith, has either denied coverage or failed or refused to make payment to the insured under the policy.").

Connecticut also rejects a strict liability rule, but it was established judicially and not legislatively. *ACMAT Corp.*, 923 A.2d at 708 ("[E]ven without an authorizing contractual or statutory provision, a trial court may award attorney's fees to a policyholder that has prevailed in a declaratory judgment action against its insurance company only if the policyholder can prove that the insurer has engaged in bad faith conduct prior to or in the course of the litigation.").

A handful of states use a combination of legislative and judicial avenues to address whether attorney's fees are to be awarded to a prevailing insured. Under this hybrid approach, consideration is first given to the state's general statute that allows for an award of attorney's fees in an action on a contract. The court then interprets this statute, covering contracts in general, to include an insurance contract dispute. For example, ARIZ. STAT. ANN. § 12-341.01(A) (LexisNexis 2009) provides that "[i]n any contested action arising out of a contract, express or implied, the court may award the successful party reasonable attorney fees."). The Arizona Court of Appeal in *Lennar Corp. v. Auto-Owners Ins. Co.*, 151 P.3d 538, 553 (Ariz. Ct. App. 2007) then held that "[w]e have the discretion to award reasonable attorneys' fees to a prevailing party in an insurance contract dispute pursuant to [ARIZ. STAT. ANN. § 12–341.01(A)].").

And some states address the issue by applying their general statutes permitting an award of attorney's fees against a party that engages in frivolous or vexatious litigation. For example, a Colorado statute provides that a court may award attorney's fees "when the bringing or defense of an action, or part thereof... is determined to have been substantially frivolous, substantially groundless, or substantially vexatious." COLO. REV. STAT. ANN. § 13–17–101 (Westlaw 2009).

While the vast majority of states provide a mechanism of some sort for a prevailing insured in a coverage action to recover its attorney's fees, a few states maintain strict adherence to the American Rule and do not allow such recovery. *See Clark v. Exch. Ins. Ass'n*, 161 So. 2d 817, 819–20 (Ala. 1964) (holding that the insurer was not liable for attorney's fees in a declaratory judgment action, regardless of who brings the action or whether it is successful or unsuccessful from the complainant's view); *see also AIK Selective Self-Insurance Fund v. Minton*, 192 S.W.3d 415, 420 (Ky. 2006) (quoting *Aetna Cas. & Sur. Co. v. Commonwealth*, 179 S.W.3d 830, 842 (Ky. 2005)) ("[W]ith the exception of a specific contractual provision allowing for recovery of attorneys' fees or a fee-shifting statute… each party assumes responsibility for his or her own attorneys' fees.").

While the mechanisms vary, in almost all cases an insurer that is unsuccessful in coverage litigation will either be automatically obligated to pay for its insured's attorney's fees or may be litigating post-trial whether such obligation exists. Whichever the case, the potential for being saddled with the attorney's fees incurred by its prevailing insured in a declaratory judgment action is a consideration that insurers will usually not be able to avoid.

## 50-State Survey: Prevailing Insured's Right to Recover Attorney's Fees in Coverage Litigation

**Alabama:** The Supreme Court of Alabama held that "Alabama has long recognized that, absent a pertinent statute or contractual provision, an insured may not recover from his insurer attorney fees incurred in a declaratory judgment action to determine the existence of coverage under a liability policy." *Alliance Ins. Co. v. Reynolds*, 504 So. 2d 1215, 1216 (Ala. Civ. App. 1987); *see also Clark v. Exch. Ins. Ass'n*, 161 So. 2d 817, 819–20 (Ala. 1964) (holding that the insurer was not liable for attorney's fees in a declaratory judgment action, regardless of who brings the action or whether it is successful or unsuccessful from the complainant's view).

**Alaska:** An Alaska statute provides that "[e]xcept as otherwise provided by law or agreed to by the parties, the prevailing party in a civil case shall be awarded attorney's fees as calculated under this rule." ALASKA R. CIV. P. 82 (2009) (stating that a percentage of attorney's fees is awarded and it varies depending on the amount of the judgment, whether the case was contested, and whether the case went to trial, with the maximum award being 20 percent); *see also State v. Native of Nunapitchuk*, 156 P.3d 389, 394 (Alaska 2007) (noting that "Alaska is the only state with a general "loser pays" rule for attorney's fees in most civil litigation"); *Ryan v. Sea Air, Inc.*, 902 F. Supp. 1064,

1070 (D. Alaska 1995) (noting that Alaska follows the English Rule in upholding an award of attorney's fees an insurer incurred in bringing a declaratory judgment action against its insured).

**Arizona:** An Arizona statute gives a court discretion to award attorney's fees in an action on a contract. ARIZ. STAT. ANN. § 12–341.01(A) (LexisNexis 2009). "In any contested action arising out of a contract, express or implied, the court may award the successful party reasonable attorney fees. If a written settlement offer is rejected and the judgment finally obtained is equal to or more favorable to the offeror than an offer made in writing to settle any contested action arising out of a contract, the offeror is deemed to be the successful party from the date of the offer and the court may award the successful party reasonable attorney fees." *Id.* This statute has been interpreted to apply to the prevailing party, including an insurer, in an insurance coverage dispute. *See Lennar Corp. v. Auto-Owners Ins. Co.*, 151 P.3d 538, 553 (Ariz. Ct. App. 2007) ("We have the discretion to award reasonable attorneys' fees to a prevailing party in an insurance contract dispute pursuant to [ARIZ. STAT. ANN. § 12-341.01(A)].").

**Arkansas:** An Arkansas statute permits the recovery of attorney's fees in an action for coverage under an insurance policy. ARK. CODE ANN. § 23-79-209 (2009). "In all suits in which the judgment or decree of a court is against a life, property, accident and health, or liability insurance company, either in a suit by it to cancel or lapse a policy or to change or alter the terms or conditions thereof in any way that may have the effect of depriving the holder of the policy of any of his or her rights thereunder, or in a suit for a declaratory judgment under the policy, or in a suit by the holder of the policy to require the company to reinstate the policy, the company shall also be liable to pay the holder of the policy all reasonable attorney's fees for the defense or prosecution of the suit, as the case may be." *Id.; see also* ARK. CODE ANN. § 23-79-208 (2009) (allowing attorney's fees and 12 percent penalty under certain circumstances); *Med. Liab. Mut. Ins. Co. v. Alan Curtis Enters.*, 285 S.W.3d 233 (Ark. 2008) (addressing statutes); *Shelter Mut. Ins. Co. v. Smith*, 779 S.W.2d 149 (Ark. 1989) (addressing statutes).

**California:** The Supreme Court of California held that "[w]hen an insurer's tortious conduct [failing to deal fairly and in good faith with its insured by refusing, without proper cause, to compensate its insured for a loss covered by the policy] reasonably compels the insured to retain an attorney to obtain the benefits due under a policy, it follows that the insurer should be liable in a tort action for that expense. The attorney's fees are an economic loss—damages—proximately caused by the tort. These fees must be distinguished from recovery of attorney's fees *qua* attorney's fees, such as those attributable to the bringing of the bad faith action itself." *Brandt v. Superior Court*, 693 P.2d 796, 798 (Cal. 1985) (citation omitted); *see also Essex Ins. Co. v. Five Star Dye House, Inc.*, 137 P.3d 192, 194 (Cal. 2006) (holding that an assignee of a bad faith claim has the right to recover *Brandt* fees).

**Colorado:** A Colorado statute provides that a court may award attorney's fees "when the bringing or defense of an action, or part thereof... is determined to have been substantially frivolous, substantially groundless, or substantially vexatious." COLO. REV. STAT. ANN. § 13-17-101 (Westlaw 2009). The statute further provides that "[a]ll courts shall liberally construe the provisions of this article to effectuate substantial justice." *Id.*; *see also Allstate Ins. Co. v. Huizar*, 52 P.3d 816, 821–22 (Colo. 2002) (citing Section 13-17-101 as providing for the award of attorney's fees incurred in a declaratory judgment action, but holding that the facts before it lacked substantial frivolity or vexatiousness to warrant such an award, despite an insured prevailing in an action to establish that an insurance policy was void as against public policy).

**Connecticut:** The Supreme Court of Connecticut held that "even without an authorizing contractual or statutory provision, a trial court may award attorney's fees to a policyholder that has prevailed in a declaratory judgment action against its insurance company only if the policyholder can prove that the insurer has engaged in bad faith conduct prior to or in the course of the litigation. This limited exception reflects an appropriate accommodation between the policy underlying the American rule of permitting parties, including insurance companies, to litigate claims in good faith, but still provides protection to those policyholders that might confront 'stubbornly litigious' insurance companies that take specious positions in order to attempt to avoid paying legitimate claims." *ACMAT Corp. v. Greater N.Y. Mut. Ins. Co.*, 923 A.2d 697, 708 (Conn. 2007). *But see* Middlesex Ins. Co. v. Mara, 699 F. Supp. 2d 439, 461 **(D. Conn. 2010)** ("Connecticut courts in insurance cases have declined to award attorney's fees when rendering declaratory judgment absent a showing of statutory or contractual entitlement.").

**Delaware:** A Delaware statute permits the recovery of attorney's fees in an action for coverage under a property insurance policy: "The court upon rendering judgment against any insurer upon any policy of property insurance, as 'property' insurance is defined in § 904 of this title, shall allow the plaintiff a reasonable sum as attorney's fees to be taxed as part of the costs." DEL. CODE ANN. tit. 18, § 4102 (2009); *see also Galiotti v. Travelers Indem. Co.*, 333 A.2d 176, 180 (Del. Super. Ct. 1975) ("Nothing in the statute indicates a legislative intent to confine such award to instances where an insurer has taken an unreasonable position."); *Nassau Gallery, Inc. v. Nationwide Mut. Fire Ins. Co.*, No. 00C-05–034, 2003 WL 22852242, at *3 (Del. Super. Ct. Nov. 18, 2003) (addressing what constitutes reasonable attorney's fees). It does not appear that attorney's fees are recoverable in an action for coverage under a liability insurance policy. *See Bellanca v. Ins. Co. of North America*, No. 80C-DE-122, 1983 Del. Super. LEXIS 738, at *9–10 (Del. Super. Ct. July 20, 1983) ("[P]laintiff's claim for attorney's fee would appear to hinge upon his success in establishing INA's duty to defend. In the absence of such success his entitlement cannot be recognized. In any event, recovery of attorney's fees is not permitted in the absence of a specific statutory authorization which is lacking here.");

*American General Life Ins. v. Goldstein*, __ F. Supp. 2d __, No. 09-369, 2010 WL 3833955, at *10 (D. Del. Sept. 30, 2010) ("Delaware follows the American rule where, absent a statute or contract to the contrary, "prevailing litigants are responsible for the payment of their own attorney fees.").

**Florida:** A Florida statute permits the recovery of attorney's fees in an action for coverage under an insurance policy. FLA. STAT. ANN. § 627.428(1) (LexisNexis 2009). "Upon the rendition of a judgment or decree by any of the courts of this state against an insurer and in favor of any named or omnibus insured or the named beneficiary under a policy or contract executed by the insurer, the trial court or, in the event of an appeal in which the insured or beneficiary prevails, the appellate court shall adjudge or decree against the insurer and in favor of the insured or beneficiary a reasonable sum as fees or compensation for the insured's or beneficiary's attorney prosecuting the suit in which the recovery is had." *Id.*; *see also Lewis v. Universal Prop. & Cas. Ins. Co.*, 13 So. 3d 1079, 1081 (Fla. Dist. Ct. App. 2009) ("The purpose behind section 627.428 is to place the insured in the place she would have been if the carrier had seasonably paid the claim or benefits without causing the payee to engage counsel and incur obligations for attorney's fees.") (citation and internal quotation marks omitted); *First Floridian Auto & Home Ins. Co. v. Myrick*, 969 So. 2d 1121, 1123–24 (Fla. Dist. Ct. App. 2007) ("The legislature enacted section 627.428 to discourage an insurer from contesting a valid claim and to level the playing field so that the insurer's economic power does not overwhelm the insured.").

**Georgia:** A Georgia statute permits the recovery of attorney's fees in an action for coverage under an insurance policy. GA. CODE ANN. § 33-7-15 (b.1) (Westlaw 2009). "In the event the insurer denies coverage and it is determined by declaratory judgment or other civil process that there is in fact coverage, the insurer shall be liable to the insured for legal cost and attorney's fees as may be awarded by the court." *Id.* However, the Court of Appeals of Georgia held that the statute is limited to those situations involving noncooperation by an insured with his insurance company. *Stedman v. Cotton States Ins. Co.*, 562 S.E.2d 256, 259 (Ga. Ct. App. 2002). "Although the language of subsection (b.1) does not expressly limit recovery of attorney fees only to situations of non-cooperation by the insured, placement of the subsection in the context of GA. CODE ANN. § 33-7-15 [titled "Cooperation by insured with insurer in connection with defense of action or threatened action under policy"] leads to the conclusion that the legislature did intend to so limit the application of the subsection." *Id.*

**Hawaii:** A Hawaii statute permits the recovery of attorney's fees in an action for coverage under an insurance policy: "Where an insurer has contested its liability under a policy and is ordered by the courts to pay benefits under the policy, the policyholder, the beneficiary under a policy, or the person who has acquired the rights of the policyholder or beneficiary under the policy shall be awarded reasonable attorney's fees and the costs of suit, in addition to the benefits under the policy." HAW. REV. STAT. ANN. § 431:10–242 (LexisNexis 2009); *see also Allstate Ins. Co. v. Pruett*, 186 P.3d 609, 621 (Haw. 2008) ("[T]he fundamental question with respect to the issue of awarding attorney's fees and the costs of suit is whether the insurer has in fact been ordered to pay benefits within the meaning of... § 431:10–242.") (citation and internal quotation omitted).

**Idaho:** An Idaho statute provides that "[a]ny insurer... [that] fail[s] for a period of thirty (30) days after proof of loss has been furnished as provided in [its] policy... to pay to the person entitled thereto the amount justly due under such policy... shall in any action thereafter brought against the insurer in any court in this state for recovery under the terms of the policy... pay such further amount as the court shall adjudge reasonable as attorney's fees in such action." IDAHO CODE ANN. § 41–1839 (Westlaw 2009). This section and Section 12–123 (allowing attorney's fees to be awarded to any party adversely affected by another party's frivolous conduct) "provide the exclusive remedy for the award of... statutory attorney's fees in all actions between insured and insurers involving disputes arising under policies of insurance. Provided, attorney's fees may be awarded... when... a case was brought, pursued or defended frivolously, unreasonably or without foundation." *Id.*; *see also Allstate Ins. Co. v. Mocaby*, 990 P.2d 1204, 1213 (Idaho 1999) (holding that the insured was not entitled to attorney's fees under Section 41–1839 because the insurer reasonably believed it had a basis for noncoverage and therefore could not be said to have acted unreasonably or frivolously); *Northland Ins. Co. v. Boise's Best Autos & Repairs*, 958 P.2d 589, 591 (Idaho 1998) (holding that the insured was not entitled to collect attorney's fees under Section 41–1839 because, having provided a defense to its insured, there was no evidence that the insurer failed to pay an amount "justly due" under the policy).

**Illinois:** An Illinois statute provides that when an insurer's denial of coverage is "vexatious and unreasonable," the imposition of attorney's fees is proper, subject to certain statutory maximums. 215 ILL. COMP. STAT. ANN. 5/155 (Westlaw 2009). Based on this statute, the Illinois Court of Appeal held that "[a]bsent vexatious behavior by the insurer, an insured cannot recover attorney fees incurred in bringing a declaratory judgment action against the insurer to establish coverage. Nor can an insured recover attorney fees and costs for defending a declaratory judgment action brought by an insurer absent vexatiousness." *Westchester Fire Ins. Co. v. G. Heileman Brewing Co.*, 747 N.E.2d 955, 968 (Ill. App. Ct. 2001); *see also Am. Alliance Ins. Co. v. 1212 Restaurant Group, L.L.C.*, 794 N.E.2d 892, 901 (Ill. App. Ct. 2003) (finding that, given the facts of the case, the insurer did not act vexatiously or unreasonably in denying coverage).

**Indiana:** The Court of Appeals of Indiana held that an insured's entitlement to attorney's fees incurred in a declaratory judgment action depends on "whether [the insurer] acted in bad faith in denying the coverage to [the insured]." *Learman v. Auto-Owners Ins. Co.*, 769 N.E.2d 1171, 1178 (Ind. Ct. App. 2002); *see also Mikel v. Am. Ambassador Cas. Co.*, 644 N.E.2d 168, 172 (Ind. Ct. App. 1994) ("We hold that when the insured brings an action for a declaration of coverage and prevails, absent a bad faith denial of coverage by the insurer, attorney's fees incurred by the insured in the prosecution of that action are not incurred at the 'request' of the insurer. Our holding is consistent with the long-standing rule in Indiana that the insurer may dispute claims in good faith.").

**Iowa:** The Supreme Court of Iowa held that, when an insurer seeks a declaratory judgment to determine its obligation to provide coverage, the insurer is liable for attorney's fees incurred by the insured to defend the lawsuit only where "there is a showing… that the insurance company… acted in 'bad faith or fraudulently or was stubbornly litigious.'" *Clark-Peterson Co. v. Indep. Ins. Assocs.*, 514 N.W.2d 914, 915–16 (Iowa 1994) (quoting *N.H. Ins. Co. v. Christy*, 200 N.W.2d 834, 845 (Iowa 1972)). The *Clark-Petersen* Court concluded that the insurer was not overly litigious, but merely believed that no coverage existed under the policy. *Id.* at 916. Further, the insurer did not act fraudulently in initially denying the claim because coverage was reasonably debatable. *Id.*

**Kansas:** A Kansas statute provides "[t]hat in all actions hereafter commenced, in which judgment is rendered against any insurance company as defined in *K.S.A.* 40–201, and including in addition thereto any fraternal benefit society and any reciprocal or interinsurance exchange on any policy or certificate of any type or kind of insurance, if it appear from the evidence that such company, society or exchange has refused without just cause or excuse to pay the full amount of such loss, the court in rendering such judgment shall allow the plaintiff a reasonable sum as an attorney's fee for services in such action, including proceeding upon appeal, to be recovered and collected as a part of the costs: Provided, however, That when a tender is made by such insurance company, society or exchange before the commencement of the action in which judgment is rendered and the amount recovered is not in excess of such tender no such costs shall be allowed." KAN. STAT. ANN. § 40–256 (LexisNexis 2008); *see also Farm Bureau Mut. Ins. Co. v. Kurtenbach by & Through Kurtenbach*, 961 P.2d 53, 64 (Kan. 1998) ("[W]here an insurer denies coverage and the duty to defend and brings a declaratory judgment action against the insured to determine that issue, the insured may recover his or her attorney fees incurred in the defense of the declaratory judgment action if it is determined as a result of that action that there is coverage. The same rule is applicable where an insurer agrees to assume the duty to defend under a reservation of rights, but before the underlying matter is resolved brings a declaratory judgment action seeking a determination that no duty to defend or coverage exists.") (citation omitted).

**Kentucky:** The Supreme Court of Kentucky held that, "with the exception of a specific contractual provision allowing for recovery of attorneys' fees or a fee-shifting statute... each party assumes responsibility for his or her own attorneys' fees." *AIK Selective Self-Insurance Fund v. Minton*, 192 S.W.3d 415, 420 (Ky. 2006) (quoting *Aetna Cas. & Sur. Co. v. Commonwealth*, 179 S.W.3d 830, 842 (Ky. 2005)).

**Louisiana:** The Supreme Court of Louisiana held that, because the insurance policy did not impose a duty on the insurer to pay attorney's fees in connection with the insured's pursuit of coverage, and nor was there any statute providing for such, the insured was not entitled to recover its attorney's fees. *Steptore v. Masco Construction Co.*, 643 So. 2d 1213, 1218 (La. 1994); *see also Shaffer v. Stewart Construction Co.*, 865 So. 2d 213 (La. Ct. App. 2004) (same); *Weaver v. CCA Industries, Inc.*, No. 01–2096, 2009 WL 1322290, at *5 (May 12, 2009 W.D. La.) ("Under Louisiana law, attorney's fees are recoverable only when authorized by contract or statute.").

**Maine:** A Maine statute provides that when an insurer seeks a declaratory judgment "to determine [its] contractual duty to defend an insured under an insurance policy, if the insured prevails on such action, the insurer shall pay court costs and reasonable attorney's fees." ME. REV. STAT. ANN. tit. 24, § 2436-B (Westlaw 2009). With this statute the Maine Legislature codified Maine common law which held an insurer liable for its insured's attorney's fees when an insured prevails in a declaratory judgment to establish the insurer's duty to defend. *See Foremost Ins. Co. v. Leversque*, 926 A.2d 1185, 1188 (Me. 2007) (addressing *Gibson v. Farm Family Mut. Ins. Co.*, 673 A.2d 1350 (Me. 1996)). In *Leversque,* the Supreme Judicial Court of Maine concluded that the statute was limited to the duty to defend and did not include the duty to indemnify. *Id.* Faced with that, the court determined to extend its common law rules, allowing for the recovery of attorney's fees to establish the duty to defend, to the duty to indemnify: "Unsuccessful litigation filed by an insurer against its insured subjects the insured to significant costs that may render victory for the insured on the indemnification issue meaningless. In that case, the insured will be in no better position than he would be without having purchased insurance." *Id.* at 1190.

**Maryland:** The Court of Appeals of Maryland held that "Maryland follows the American rule which stands as a barrier to the recovery, as consequential damages, of foreseeable counsel fees incurred in enforcing remedies for breach of contract. Therefore, in the absence of a statute, rule or contract expressly allowing the recovery of attorneys' fees, a prevailing party in a lawsuit may not ordinarily recover attorneys' fees. There is one nonstatutory exception to the American rule in actions involving insurance policies. Where an action is brought to enforce an insurer's obligations under the third party liability provisions of a policy, and it is determined that there is coverage under the policy, the insurer is liable for the prevailing party's attorneys' fees." *Bausch & Lomb, Inc. v. Utica Mut. Ins. Co.*, 735 A.2d 1081, 1094–95 (Md. 1999) (citations and internal quotation omitted).

**Massachusetts:** The Supreme Judicial Court of Massachusetts adopted an exception to its traditional rule disallowing attorney's fees and expenses and held that an insured is entitled to the reasonable attorney's fees and expenses incurred in successfully establishing the insurer's duty to defend. *Preferred Mut. Ins. Co. v. Gamache*, 686 N.E.2d 989, 993 (Mass. 1997); *see also John T. Callahan & Sons, Inc. v. Worcester Ins. Co.*, 902 N.E.2d 923, 926–27 (Mass. 2009) (declining to extend *Gamache* to allow one insurer to recovery attorney's fees incurred to establish another insurer's duty to defend); *Wilkinson v. Citation Ins. Co.*, 856 N.E.2d 829, 837 (Mass. 2006) (declining to extend *Gamache* to the duty to indemnify); *Global Investors Agent Corp. v. Nat. Fire Ins. Co. of Hartford*, 927 N.E.2d 480, 495–96 (Mass. Ct. App. 2010) (addressing *Gamache* and permitting the insured to recover attorney's fees and costs only for the time period necessary to establish the insurer's duty to defend, as well as significantly reducing the amount of recoverable fees based on an assessment of reasonableness factors).

**Michigan:** The Court of Appeals of Michigan held that "[a]lthough actual attorneys' fees for the insured's defense of an action by a third party are recoverable from the insurer which breaches its duty to defend, the established rule in Michigan is that the insured may not be allowed attorneys' fees in excess of taxable costs for the declaratory action to enforce insurance coverage." *Shepard Marine Constr. Co. v. Maryland Cas. Co.*, 250 N.W.2d 541, 543 (Mich. Ct. App. 1976); *accord Iacobelli Constr. Co. v. W. Cas. & Sur. Co.*, 343 N.W.2d 517, 523 (Mich. Ct. App. 1983); *see also Aladdin's Carpet Cleaning v. Farm Bureau Gen. Ins. Co.*, No. 278605, 2009 WL 499209, at *7 n.5 (Mich. Ct. App. Feb. 26, 2009) ("We note that while plaintiff is entitled to damages consisting of its costs, expenses, and fees incurred in defending the underlying Earns litigation, it is not entitled to attorney fees incurred in the present suit against defendant Farm Bureau."); *Auto-Owners Ins. Co. v. Ferwerda Enterprises, Inc.*, No. 277574, 2010 WL 322986 (Mich. App. Ct. Jan. 28, 2010) (holding that, because the insurer's declaratory judgment action was not frivolous, attorney's fees were not proper under MCR 2.625).

**Minnesota:** The Supreme Court of Minnesota held that "[t]he insured is not entitled to recover attorney fees incurred in maintaining or defending a declaratory action to determine the question of coverage unless the insurer has breached the insurance contract in some respect—usually by wrongfully refusing to defend the insured." *American Standard Ins. Co. v. Le*, 551 N.W.2d 923, 927 (Minn. 1996); *see also Jarvis & Sons, Inc. v. Int'l Marine Underwriters*, 768 N.W.2d 385, 371 (Minn. Ct. App. 2009) ("Where an insurer has breached a duty to defend an insured, the insured is entitled to recover reasonable attorney fees expended in maintaining a declaratory judgment action to determine coverage.").

**Mississippi:** The Supreme Court of Mississippi held that "[i]n the absence of a showing of gross negligence or willful wrong entitling the [m]ovant to punitive damages," a successful litigant is not entitled to attorney's fees.

*Miller v. Allstate Ins. Co.*, 631 So. 2d 789, 795 (Miss. 1994) (citing *Cent. Bank v. Butler*, 517 So. 2d 507, 512 (Miss. 1988) and *Aetna Cas. & Sur. Co. v. Steele*, 373 So. 2d 797, 801 (Miss. 1979)). *See also Barden Mississippi Gaming, LLC v. Great Northern Ins. Co.*, No. 3:07CV21, 2010 WL 2694983, at *6 (N.D. Miss. July 2, 2010) (holding that, although it was determined that the insurer's decision not to provide a defense was incorrect, there existed a legitimate, arguable reason for the decision and it was not wrongful or tortious, thereby precluding recovery of attorney's fees).

**Missouri:** A Missouri statute provides a court discretion to award attorney's fees in a declaratory judgment action. Mo. Rev. Stat. § 527.100 (LexisNexis 2008). "In any proceeding under sections 527.010 to 527.130 [declaratory judgments] the court may make such award of costs as may seem equitable and just." *Id.; see also Am. Econ. Ins. Co. v. Ledbetter*, 903 S.W.2d 272, 276 (Mo. Ct. App. 1995) ("While the absence of 'bad faith' in filing suit is a factor in arriving at equity and justice in assessing costs, such absence does not compel denial of attorney fees."); *Windsor Ins. Co. v. Lucas*, 24 S.W.3d 151, 156 (Mo. Ct. App. 2000) ("[C]osts under section 527.100 does not necessarily include attorney's fees. Rather, the American Rule applies to declaratory judgment actions. Under the American Rule, absent statutory authorization or contractual agreement, with few exceptions, each litigant must bear his own attorney's fee.") (citations and internal quotation omitted); *Westchester Surplus Lines Ins. Co. v. Maverick Tube Corp.*, __ F. Supp. 2d __, No. H-07–540, 2010 WL 2635623, at *6 (S.D. Tex. June 28, 2010) (applying Missouri law) ("Although Missouri courts have held that 'costs' may include attorneys' fees, subsequent cases have clarified that attorneys' fees may be awarded as costs under § 527.100 only under 'very unusual circumstances.'") (citation omitted).

**Montana:** The Supreme Court of Montana held that "an insured is entitled to recover attorney fees, pursuant to the insurance exception to the American Rule, when the insurer forces the insured to assume the burden of legal action to obtain the full benefit of the insurance contract, regardless of whether the insurer's duty to defend is at issue." *Mountain W. Farm Bureau Mut. Ins. Co. v. Brewer*, 69 P.3d 652, 660 (Mont. 2003); *see also Jacobsen v. Allstate Ins. Co.*, 215 P.3d 649, 656 (Mont. 2009) (discussing *Brewer* and declining to extend the insurance exception to a third-party claimant, even one that proves tortious conduct by the insurer, because the insurer did not owe a fiduciary duty to the claimant—a nonparty to the insurance contract).

**Nebraska:** A Nebraska statute permits the recovery of attorney's fees in an action for coverage under an insurance policy. Neb. Rev. Stat. Ann. § 44–359 (LexisNexis 2008). "In all cases when the beneficiary or other person entitled thereto brings an action upon any type of insurance policy, except workers' compensation insurance, or upon any certificate issued by a fraternal benefit society, against any company, person, or association doing business in this state, the court, upon rendering judgment against such company, person, or association, shall allow the plaintiff a reasonable sum as an attorney's fee in addition to the amount of his or her recovery, to be taxed as part of the costs. If such cause is appealed, the appellate court shall likewise allow a reasonable sum as an attorney's fee for the appellate proceedings, except that if the plaintiff fails to obtain judgment for more than may have been offered by such company, person, or association in accordance with section 25–901, then the plaintiff shall not recover the attorney's fee provided by this section." *Id.*; *see also Esch v. State Farm Mut. Auto. Ins. Co.*, No. A-08–199, 2009 WL 52176, at *5-6 (Neb. Ct. App. Jan. 6, 2009) (addressing § 44–359 and noting that attorney's fees and expenses may be recovered only where provided for by statute or pursuant to a recognized and accepted uniform course of procedure).

**Nevada:** A Nevada statute provides that "[i]n addition to the cases where an allowance is authorized by specific statute, the court may make an allowance of attorney's fees to a prevailing party: (a) When he has not recovered more than $20,000; or (b) Without regard to the recovery sought, when the court finds that the claim, counterclaim, cross-claim or third-party complaint or defense of the opposing party was brought or maintained without reasonable ground or to harass the prevailing party. The court shall liberally construe the provisions of this paragraph in favor of awarding attorney's fees in all appropriate situations." NEV. REV. STAT. ANN. § 18.010 (Westlaw 2008); *see also Am. Excess Ins. Co. v. MGM Grand Hotels, Inc.*, 729 P.2d 1352, 1355 (Nev. 1986) (holding that the district court improperly awarded attorney's fees to the insured under section 18.010 because there was no evidence that the insurer brought the declaratory judgment action "without reasonable ground or to harass" the insured given that the issue was one of first impression).

**New Hampshire:** A New Hampshire statute permits the recovery of attorney's fees in an action for coverage under an insurance policy. N.H. REV. STAT. ANN. §491:22-b (LexisNexis 2009). "In any action to determine coverage of an insurance policy pursuant to RSA 491:22 [regarding declaratory judgments], if the insured prevails in such action, he shall receive court costs and reasonable attorneys' fees from the insurer." *Id.*; *see also EnergyNorth Natural Gas, Inc. v. Certain Underwriters at Lloyd's*, 934 A.2d 517, 528 (N.H. 2007) ("Recovery of these fees and costs [under RSA 491:22-b] does not depend upon whether, after all is said and done, the excess insurer actually has to pay any indemnification. The insured becomes entitled to the fees and costs once it obtains rulings that demonstrate that there is coverage under the excess insurance policy.").

**New Jersey:** A New Jersey court rule permits the recovery of attorney's fees in an action for coverage under an insurance policy. N.J. CT. R. ANN. 4:42–9 (LexisNexis 2009). "No fee for legal services shall be allowed in the taxed costs or otherwise, except (6) In an action upon a liability or indemnity policy of insurance, in favor of a successful claimant." *Id.; see also Shore Orthopaedic Group, LLC v. Equitable Life Assur. Soc'y*, 938 A.2d 962

(N.J. Super. Ct. App. Div. 2008), *affirmed* 972 A.2d 381 (N.J. 2009) (addressing applicability of the rule to liability policies); Myron Corp. v. Atlantic Mut. Ins. Corp., 970 A.2d 1083 (N.J. Super. Ct. App. Div. 2009), *affirmed* __ A.3d __, 2010 WL 2898970 (N.J. July 27, 2010) (addressing applicability of the rule to coverage litigation taking place outside of New Jersey in conjunction with New Jersey-venued coverage litigation).

**New Mexico:** The Court of Appeals of New Mexico held that "[f]ees for counsel representing the insured in disputes with the insurer are ordinarily not recoverable in the absence of statute or contract." *Lujan v. Gonzales*, 501 P.2d 673, 682 (N.M. Ct. App. 1972) (citations omitted).

**New York:** The Court of Appeals of New York held that an insured who is "cast in a defensive posture by the legal steps an insurer takes in an effort to free itself from its policy obligations," and who prevails on the merits, may recover attorneys' fees incurred in defending against the insurer's action. *Mighty Midgets v. Centennial Ins. Co.*, 389 N.E.2d 1080, 1085 (N.Y. 1979). In other words, "such a recovery may not be had in an affirmative action brought by an assured to settle its rights." *Id.*; *see also U.S. Underwriters Ins. Co. v. City Club Hotel, LLC*, 822 N.E.2d 777, 780 (N.Y. 2004) ("We hold that under *Mighty Midgets,* an insured who prevails in an action brought by an insurance company seeking a declaratory judgment that it has no duty to defend or indemnify the insured may recover attorneys' fees regardless of whether the insurer provided a defense to the insured."); *RLI Ins. Co. v. Smiedala*, No. CA 09-02296, 2010 WL 3817114 (N.Y. App. Div. Oct. 1, 2010) (holding that insured may recover attorney's fees from an excess insurer, even if its duty to defend had not been triggered because primary insurance had not been exhausted, because insured was "cast in a defensive posture") (quoting *Mighty Midgets*).

**North Carolina:** The North Carolina Court of Appeals held that "attorney's fees incurred by the insured... are not recoverable as damages where those fees are incurred in the course of litigation to determine coverage and compel the insurer to perform its duties. Our decision today does not hold that an insured's attorney's fees can never be recovered in coverage litigation. Attorney's fees clearly can be recovered in situations, for example, where an insurer acts in bad faith in denying coverage or where recovery of fees is otherwise authorized by contract or statute." *Collins & Aikman Prods. Co. v. Hartford Accident & Indem. Co.*, 481 S.E.2d 96, 97–98 (N.C. Ct. App. 1997); *see also Hubbard Tel. Contractors Inc. v. Mich. Mut. Ins. Co.*, No. COA02–1090, 2003 WL 21030439, at \*2 (N.C. Ct. App. May 6, 2003) (citing *Collins* for the proposition that attorney's fees are recoverable in a declaratory action against an insurer where it is shown that the insurer acted in bad faith in denying coverage).

**North Dakota:** A North Dakota statute provides that "[f]urther relief based on a declaratory judgment or decree may be granted whenever necessary or proper." N.D. CENT. CODE § 32–23–08 (Westlaw 2008). North Dakota courts utilize this statute in awarding attorney's fees incurred by an insured in bringing or defending a declaratory judgment action. *See, e.g., State Farm Fire and Cas. Co. v. Sigman*, 508 N.W.2d 323, 326–27 (N.D. 1993) (awarding attorney's fees based on language of the insurance policy, by which the insurer agreed to pay "reasonable expenses an insured incurs at [the insurer's] request," and on Section 32–23–08, reasoning that "[w]hen the insured gets that policy protection only by court order after litigating coverage, it is both 'necessary' and 'proper' to award attorney fees and costs to give the insured the full benefit of his insurance contract... . If an insured is not awarded attorney fees as supplemental relief, he is effectively denied the benefit he bargained for in the insurance policy"); *see also R.D. Offutt Co. v. Lexington Ins. Co.*, 494 F.3d 668, 675–76 (8th Cir. 2007) (applying North Dakota law) (upholding an award of attorney's fees based on section 32–23–08 and *Sigman*, and establishing that an award of attorney's fees under section 32–23–08 is appropriate "even if an insurer denies coverage in good faith," regardless of which party initiates the litigation and even absent a contractual provision providing for the award of such fees).

**Ohio:** An Ohio statute provides that "[a] court of record shall not award attorney's fees to any party on a claim or proceeding for declaratory relief under this chapter unless: (a) A section of the Revised Code explicitly authorizes a court of record to award attorney's fees on a claim for declaratory relief under this chapter." OHIO REV. CODE ANN. § 2721.16 (Westlaw 2009). Notwithstanding that Ohio has expressed its adherence to the American Rule via statute, the Court of Appeals of Ohio has recognized certain exceptions. *See Westfield Cos. v. O.K.L. Can Line*, 804 N.E.2d 45, 53–54 (Ohio Ct. App. 2003) (attorney's fees awarded upon a finding that the "losing party has acted in bad faith, vexatiously, wantonly, obdurately, or for oppressive reasons") (quoting *Sorin v. Bd. of Educ. of Warrensville Heights Sch. Dist.*, 347 N.E.2d 527, 530 (Ohio 1976)); *see also id.* at 56 (upholding an award of attorney's fees due to the insurer's "stubborn propensity for needless litigation," and finding such propensity evidenced by the insurer "filing a declaratory-judgment action under an old insurance policy not at issue, using a reversed case as legal authority for an argument before the court, and blaming [the insured] for its confusion").

**Oklahoma:** An Oklahoma statute provides that "[i]t shall be the duty of the insurer, receiving a proof of loss, to submit a written offer of settlement or rejection of the claim to the insured within ninety (90) days of receipt of that proof of loss. Upon a judgment rendered to either party, costs and attorney fees shall be allowable to the prevailing party. For purposes of this section, the prevailing party is the insurer in those cases where judgment does not exceed written offer of settlement. In all other judgments the insured shall be the prevailing party." OKLA. ST. ANN. tit. 36, § 3629(B) (Westlaw 2009); *see also An-son Corp. v. Holland-America Ins. Co.*, 767 F.2d 700, 703–04 (10th Cir. 1985) (applying Oklahoma law) (rejecting the insurer's argument that Oklahoma courts only apply section 3629(B) to "first party" cases); *Stauth v. Nat'l Union Fire Ins. Co. of Pittsburgh*, 236 F.3d 1260, 1264 (10th Cir. 2001) (applying Oklahoma law) (holding that an insured was entitled to an award of attorney's fees under section 3629(B) when it prevailed in a declaratory judgment action against its insurer, whether such action is to determine the insurer's duty to defend or duty to indemnify).

**Oregon:** An Oregon statute provides that "[e]xcept as otherwise provided in subsections (2) and (3) of this section [relating to certain automobile claims], if settlement is not made within six months from the date proof of loss is filed with an insurer and an action is brought in any court of this state upon any policy of insurance of any kind or nature, and the plaintiff's recovery exceeds the amount of any tender made by the defendant in such action, a reasonable amount to be fixed by the court as attorney fees shall be taxed as part of the costs of the action and any appeal thereon." Or. Rev. Stat. Ann. § 742.061 (Westlaw 2009) (formerly cited as section 743.114); *see also McGraw v. Gwinner*, 578 P.2d 1250, 1253 (Or. 1978) ("We adhere to the proposition that in order to secure attorney fees pursuant to [section 742.061], the insured must recover a money judgment against the insurer; it is not sufficient that the insured establish coverage which may in turn lead to a subsequent recovery of money.").

**Pennsylvania:** A Pennsylvania statute provides that "[i]n an action arising under an insurance policy, if the court finds that the insurer has acted in bad faith toward the insured, the court may... (3) [a]ssess court costs and attorney fees against the insurer." 42 Pa. Cons. Stat. Ann. § 8371 (Westlaw 2009); *see also Regis Ins. Co. v. Wood*, 852 A.2d 347, 350–51 (Pa. Super. Ct. 2004) (noting that, in addition to being recoverable generally in any action arising under an insurance policy where the insurer acted in bad faith, attorney's fees are also recoverable under the Declaratory Judgment Act, 42 Pa. Cons. Stat. Ann. §§ 7531–7541 (Westlaw 2009)). Like attorney's fees awarded under Section 8371, attorney's fees awarded under the Declaratory Judgment Act require a showing that the "'insurance company has acted in bad faith or fraudulently or was stubbornly litigious,'" with this bad faith standard "being [no] less stringent than it [is] in the Section 8371 context." *Regis*, 852 A.2d at 350–51 (citing *Kelmo Enterprises, Inc. v. Commercial Union Ins. Co.*, 426 A.2d 680, 685 (Pa. Super. Ct. 1981)).

**Rhode Island:** A Rhode Island statute provides that "an insured... may bring an action against [its] insurer... when it is alleged the insurer wrongfully and in bad faith refused to pay or settle a claim made pursuant to the provisions of the policy, or otherwise wrongfully and in bad faith refused to timely perform its obligations under the contract of insurance. In any action brought pursuant to this section, an insured may also make claim for compensatory damages, punitive damages, and reasonable attorney fees." R.I. Gen. Laws § 9–1-33 (Westlaw 2008); *see also Skaling v. Aetna Ins. Co.*, 799 A.2d 997, 1010 (R.I. 2002) (holding that "bad faith is established when the proof demonstrates that the insurer denied coverage or refused payment without a reasonable basis in fact or law for the denial"); R.I. Gen. Laws

§ 9-1-45 (Westlaw 2008) ("The court may award a reasonable attorney's fee to the prevailing party in any civil action arising from a breach of contract in which the court: (1) Finds that there was a complete absence of a justiciable issue of either law or fact raised by the losing party[.]"); *Ins. Co. of N. Am. v. Kayser-Roth Corp.*, 770 A.2d 403, 419 (R.I. 2001) (noting that attorney's fees may only be awarded when there exists a contractual or statutory authorization and citing both Sections 9-1-33 and 9-1-45 as providing such statutory authorization).

**South Carolina:** The Supreme Court of South Carolina held that the legal fees incurred by an insured, in successfully asserting its rights against its insurer's attempt, by way of a declaratory judgment action, to avoid its obligation to defend, were recoverable as damages arising directly as a result of the breach of the contract. *Hegler v. Gulf Ins. Co.*, 243 S.E.2d 443, 444-45 (S.C. 1978). The South Carolina high court reasoned that "the insured has a contract right to have actions against him defended by the insurer, at its expense. If the insurer can force him into a declaratory judgment proceeding and, even though it loses in such action, compel him to bear the expense of such litigation, the insured is actually no better off financially than if he had never had the contract right mentioned above." *Id.* (internal citation and quotation omitted); *see also State Auto Prop. & Cas. Ins. Co. v. Raynolds*, 592 S.E.2d 633, 637 (S.C. 2004) ("It is well-settled in South Carolina that when a defendant insured prevails in a declaratory judgment action, the insured is entitled to recover attorney's fees.").

**South Dakota:** A South Dakota statute provides that "[i]n all actions or proceedings hereafter commenced against [an]… insurance company… on any policy… of insurance, if it appears from the evidence that such company… has refused to pay the full amount of such loss, and that such refusal is vexatious or without reasonable cause, the… court, shall, if judgment or an award is rendered for [the insured], allow the [insured] a reasonable sum as an attorney's fee to be recovered… provided, however, that when a tender is made by such insurance company… before the commencement of the action or proceeding in which judgment or an award is rendered and the amount recovered is not in excess of such tender, no such cost shall be allowed." S.D. CODIFIED LAWS § 58-12-3 (Westlaw 2009). Despite the express language of the statute ("in all actions… commenced *against* [an]… insurance company," *id.* (emphasis added)), the Supreme Court of South Dakota held that "whether the insurer is the named plaintiff and the insured named the defendant is not dispositive of attorney fee liability." *All Nation Ins. Co. v. Brown*, 344 N.W.2d 493, 494 (S.D. 1984) (holding that if the insurer's refusal to pay was vexatious or unreasonable the insured would be entitled to recover attorney's fees incurred when insurer brought declaratory judgment action against insured to determine liability).

**Tennessee:** The Supreme Court of Tennessee held that "[i]n the absence of contract, statute, or recognized ground of equity, there is no inherent right to have attorneys' fees paid by opposing side." *Carter v. Virginia Surety Co.*, 216 S.W.2d 324, 328 (Tenn. 1948); *see also State v. Thomas*, 585 S.W.2d 606, 607 (Tenn. 1979) ("The rule is well established in this state that in the absence of a contract, statute or recognized ground of equity so providing there is no right to have attorneys' fees paid by an opposing party in civil litigation.") (non-insurance context). *But see Forrest Construction, Inc. v. The Cincinnati Ins. Co.*, __ F. Supp. 2d. __, No. 3:09-1036, 2010 WL 3035759 (M.D. Tenn. Aug. 2, 2010) (interpreting *Carter* to be in accord with the rule of those jurisdictions that only award attorney's fees to the insured in the case of bad faith on the part of the insurer).

**Texas:** The Texas Declaratory Judgment Act provides that "[i]n any proceeding under this chapter, the court may award costs and reasonable and necessary attorney's fees as are equitable and just." TEX. CIV. PRAC. & REM. CODE § 37.009 (Vernon 2009). "[T]he Declaratory Judgments Act entrusts attorney fee awards to the trial court's sound discretion, subject to the requirements that any fees awarded be reasonable and necessary, which are matters of fact, and to the additional requirements that fees be equitable and just, which are matters of law." *Bocquet v. Herring*, 972 S.W.2d 19, 21 (Tex. 1998)); *see also Stevens Transport, Inc. v. Nat'l Cont'l Ins. Co.*, No. 05–98–00244-CV, 2000 WL 567225, at *5 (Tex. Ct. App. May 11, 2000) (overturning an award of attorney's fees under the Declaratory Judgment Act by reasoning that the insurer's counterclaim for declaratory relief "did not present any new disputes that were not already pending before the trial court").

**Utah:** The Supreme Court of Utah held that an insured may recover attorney's fees incurred in a declaratory judgment action. *Farmers Ins. Exch. v. Call*, 712 P.2d 231, 237 (Utah 1985). However, "'[b]efore an award of attorney's fees [can] be made in the declaratory judgment action, it must appear that the insurance company acted in bad faith or fraudulently or was stubbornly litigious.'" *Id.* (alteration in the original) (quoting *Am. States Ins. Co. v. Walker*, 486 P.2d 1042, 1044 (Utah 1971)). The *Farmers* Court observed that attorney's fees are not warranted where an insurer merely states its position and initiates an action of what appears to be a judiciable controversy. *Id.* at 237–38; *see also W. Am. Ins. Co. v. AV & S, Inc.*, 145 F.3d 1224, 1231 (10th Cir. 1998) (interpreting Utah law and citing *Farmers* in affirming the district court's award of attorney's fees).

**Vermont:** The Supreme Court of Vermont generally follows the American Rule, requiring litigants to bear their own attorney's fees and deviates from this rule "'only in exceptional cases and for dominating reasons of justice.'" *D.J. Painting, Inc. v. Baraw Enters.*, 776 A.2d 413, 419 (Vt. 2001) (quoting *Sprague v. Ticonic Nat'l Bank*, 307 U.S. 161, 167 (1939)). The Vermont Supreme Court suggested that bad faith may be one such "exceptional case." *See Concord Gen. Mut. Ins. Co. v. Woods*, 824 A.2d 572, 579 (Vt. 2003) ("In the absence of a finding of bad faith on the part of the insurance company, or outrageous conduct... [which] we have held to be necessary to justify a departure from the American Rule... [insureds] are not entitled to attorneys' fees incurred in defending against a declaratory judgment action."). However, the Vermont high court has since indicated that the language from *Woods* was merely *dicta*, the status of the rule in Vermont is in fact unclear and the court declined to settle the issue. *Monahan v. GMAC Mortgage Corp.*, 893 A.2d 298, 323–34 (Vt. 2005).

**Virginia:** A Virginia statute provides that "in any civil case in which an insured individual [defined to include a company or organization] sues his insurer to determine what coverage, if any, exists under his present policy... or the extent to which his insurer is liable for compensating a covered loss, the individual insured shall be entitled to recover from the insurer costs and such reasonable attorney fees as the court may award. However, these costs and attorney's fees shall not be awarded unless the court determines that the insurer, not acting in good faith, has either denied coverage or failed or refused to make payment to the insured under the policy." VA. CODE ANN. § 38.2–209 (Westlaw 2009). Whether an insurer acted in bad faith, so as to warrant the award of attorney's fees under this section, requires a determination of "whether reasonable minds could differ in the interpretation of policy provisions defining coverage and exclusions; whether the insurer had made a reasonable investigation of the facts and circumstances underlying the insured's claim; whether the evidence discovered reasonably supports a denial of liability; whether it appears that the insurer's refusal to pay was used merely as a tool in settlement negotiations; and whether the defense the insurer asserts at trial raises an issue of first impression or a reasonably debatable question of law or fact." *Nationwide Mut. Ins. Co. v. St. John*, 524 S.E.2d 649, 651 (Va. 2000) (citing *CUNA Mut. Ins. Soc'y v. Norman*, 375 S.E.2d 724, 727 (1989)).

**Washington:** The Supreme Court of Washington held that an insured may "recoup attorney fees that it incurs because an insurer refuses to defend or pay the justified action or claim of the insured, regardless of whether a lawsuit is filed against the insured... . When an insured purchases a contract of insurance, it seeks protection from expenses arising from litigation, not 'vexatious, time-consuming expensive litigation with its insurer.' Whether the insured must defend a suit filed by third parties, appear in a declaratory action, or... file a suit for damages to obtain the benefit of its insurance contract is irrelevant. In every case, the conduct of the insurer imposes upon the insured the cost of compelling the insurer to honor its commitment and, thus, is equally burdensome to the insured." *Olympic Steamship Co. v. Centennial Ins. Co.*, 811 P.2d 673, 681 (Wash. 1991) (internal citations omitted). The Supreme Court of Washington held that *Olympic Steamship* fees are not awarded when an insurer simply disputes the value of a claim. *Dayton v. Farmers Ins. Group*, 876 P.2d 896, 898 (Wash. 1994); *see also Colo. Structures, Inc. v. Ins. Co. of the W.*, 167 P.3d 1125, 1141 (Wash. 2007) (en banc) (stating that while "[g]enerally, when an insured must bring a suit against its own insurer to obtain a legal determination interpreting the meaning or application of an insurance policy, it is a coverage dispute," when the dispute involves a question of liability in tort or extent of the damages it is not a coverage dispute and the *Olympic Steamship* rule does not apply to allow the award of attorney's fees).

**West Virginia:** The Supreme Court of Appeals of West Virginia held that "where an insurer has violated its contractual obligation to defend its insured, the insured should be fully compensated for all expenses incurred as a result of the insurer's breach of contract, including those expenses incurred in a declaratory judgment action. To hold otherwise would be unfair to the insured, who originally purchased the insurance policy to be protected from incurring attorney's fees and expenses arising from litigation." *Aetna Cas. & Sur. Co. v. Pitrolo*, 342 S.E.2d 156, 160 (W. Va. 1986); *see also Hayseeds, Inc. v. State Farm Fire & Cas.*, 352 S.E.2d 73, 79–80 (W. Va. 1986) (quoting *Pitrolo* and holding "that whenever a policyholder must sue his own insurance company over any property damage claim, and the policyholder substantially prevails in the action, the company is liable for the payment of the policyholder's reasonable attorneys' fees").

**Wisconsin:** The Supreme Court of Wisconsin held that an insurer was not liable for its insured's attorney's fees when the insurer obtained a stay in the underlying liability case to have a "fairly debatable question of coverage determined." *Reid v. Benz*, 629 N.W.2d 262, 273–74 (Wis. 2001). The court distinguished the situation from *Elliott v. Donahue*, 485 N.W.2d 403 (Wis. 1992), where the insured was awarded its attorney's fees. *Benz*, 629 N.W.2d at 272–73. The *Benz* Court reasoned that equities compelled the award of attorney's fees in *Elliott* due to the insurer's indirect breach of its duty to defend in failing to comply with the dictates of *Mowry v. Badger State Mut. Cas. Co.*, 385 N.W.2d 171 (Wis. 1986), which required the insurer to bifurcate the coverage and liability issues and obtain a stay of the liability case until coverage has been decided. *Benz*, 629 N.W.2d at 272–73. In *Reid*, in contrast, "[t]here [was] no contention that [the insurer]... breached its duty to defend... nor... that [the insurer's] challenge to coverage was unfair or unreasonable, or in bad faith." *Id.* at 273.

**Wyoming:** A Wyoming statute provides that "[i]n any actions or proceedings commenced against any insurance company on any insurance policy or certificate of any type or kind of insurance, or in any case where an insurer is obligated by a liability insurance policy to defend any suit or claim or pay any judgment on behalf of a named insured, if it is determined that the company refuses to pay the full amount of a loss covered by the policy and that the refusal is unreasonable or without cause, any court in which judgment is rendered for a claimant may also award a reasonable sum as an attorney's fee and interest at ten percent (10%) per year." Wyo. Stat. Ann. § 26-15-124 (Westlaw 2009); *see also Stewart Title Guar. Co. v. Tilden*, 110 P.3d 865, 874 (Wyo. 2005) (upholding the award of attorney's fees under Section 26-15-124; finding the insurer's failure to cure a title defect in a timely manner unreasonable).

# CHAPTER
# 8

# Number of Occurrences

Most disputes under general liability policies center around the fundamental question whether an insurer is obligated to defend and/or indemnify its insured for certain "bodily injury" or "property damage." But, in some cases, after it is determined that indemnity is owed, a dispute ensues over the extent of the insurer's obligation. In particular, a significant issue bearing on the amount of the insurer's obligation may be the number of "occurrences" that caused the covered "bodily injury" or "property damage."

This issue arises because the Insuring Agreement of virtually all commercial general liability policies states that coverage is owed for "bodily injury" or "property damage" that is caused by an "occurrence." *See, e.g.,* INS. SERVS. OFFICE PROPS., INC., COMMERCIAL GENERAL LIABILITY COVERAGE FORM, No. CG 00011207, § I1b(1) (2007). In addition, the commercial general liability (CGL) policy's Limits of Liability section typically states that the policy's Each Occurrence Limit is the most that the insurer will pay for the sum of damages because of all "bodily injury" and "property damage" arising out of any one "occurrence." ISO FORM, CG 00011207 at § III5. Lastly, most policies define "occurrence" as "an accident, including continuous or repeated exposure to substantially the same general harmful conditions." ISO FORM, CG 00011207 at § V13. The combination of these policy provisions, when applied to certain facts, leads to what is commonly referred to the "number of occurrences" issue.

Consider a commercial general liability policy that is subject to a $1 million Each Occurrence Limit and a $2 million General Aggregate Limit (being the most that will be paid under the policy for *all* damages—perhaps with an exception for those damages included in the "products-completed operations hazard," which may have its own Aggregate Limit). Under this relatively common limits of liability scenario, if all "bodily injury" and "property damage," even if there are multiple persons injured and multiple properties damaged, arises out of one "occurrence," then the insurer's maximum liability for *all* such damage will be capped at the policy's $1 million Each

Occurrence Limit. On the other hand, if the same injury to persons and properties damaged is determined to have been caused by separate "occurrences," then *each* injured person or damaged property (or some combination of persons or property) will be covered up to the policy's $1 million Each Occurrence Limit. Because there is now more than one "occurrence," with each having a $1 million limit, the insured is in a position to collect up to the policy's $2 million General Aggregate Limit for all such damages.

As this simple, but not unrealistic, illustration demonstrates, the determination of "number of occurrences" can have a significant impact on the amount of an insured's recovery and, hence, an insurer's exposure for a claim. It can oftentimes double, or more, the limits of liability at issue. For this reason, it is not surprising that so much litigation has arisen over determining the number of occurrences.

One example of number of occurrences litigation with a lot at stake—and, because of that, it even drew the attention of the mainstream media—was over the amount payable by numerous insurers for the September 11, 2001, collapse of the World Trade Center. The property was collectively insured by multiple insurers for approximately $3.5 billion. However, the property owners sought to collect $7 billion on the basis that each plane attack qualified as a separate occurrence. Following protracted litigation, including a lengthy decision from the Second Circuit Court of Appeals, the court largely upheld a single occurrence determination. *World Trade Ctr. Props., LLC v. Hartford Fire Ins. Co.*, 345 F.3d 154, 190 (2d Cir. 2003). A subsequent jury trial led to certain insurers being obligated to pay based on two occurrences. In the end, the potential recovery under the policy was $4.6 billion. In essence, number of occurrences had the potential to be a $3.5 billion issue.

As with many coverage issues, courts confronted with a "number of occurrences" dispute usually examine the various tests that courts coming before them have adopted to resolve the issue and then decide which of the approaches to follow. In general, courts nationally have adopted two approaches for determining number of occurrences. Under the "effect" test, number of occurrences is determined by examining the effect that an event had, i.e., how many individual claims or injuries resulted from it. Conversely, under the "cause" test, number of occurrences is determined by examining the cause or causes of the damage. The "cause" test is the majority rule nationwide. *Liberty Mut. Ins. Co. v. Pella Corp.*, 631 F. Supp. 2d 1125, 1135 (S.D. Iowa 2009).

A typical example of a court adopting the "cause" test, and holding that, despite the existence of multiple injuries, all such injuries were caused by a single occurrence, and, hence subject to a single limit of liability, is *Donegal Mutual Insurance Co. v. Baumhammers*, 938 A.2d 286 (Pa. 2007). Here, the Supreme Court of Pennsylvania adopted the "cause" test and held that, where the insured's son, over a two-hour period, shot and killed a neighbor and then drove to three townships where he shot and killed four people and wounded another, all such "bodily injury" was caused by a single "occurrence." *Id.* at 295–96. Based on the "cause" approach, the court concluded that the insured-parents' negligence—failing to confiscate their son's weapon and/or notify law enforcement or his mental health providers of his unstable condition—constituted a single occurrence. *Id.* The court reasoned that "[s]ince the policy was intended to insure Parents for their liabilities, the occurrence should be an event over which Parents had some control." *Id.* at 296.

Compare *Baumhammers* to *Lombard v. Sewerage and Water Board of New Orleans*, 284 So. 2d 905 (La. 1973), where the Supreme Court of Louisiana applied the "effects" test and held that, where 119 plaintiffs were damaged as a consequence of the construction of an underground drainage canal, there were multiple occurrences. *Id.* at 915–16. The court concluded that the word "occurrence" must be construed from the point of view of the persons whose property was damaged and, therefore, the damage to each plaintiff was a separate occurrence. *Id.* at 915.

While most courts resolve number of occurrences disputes by deciding whether to adopt the "cause" test or the "effect" test, one court specifically declined to adopt a one-size-fits-all approach. In *Owners Insurance Co. v. Salmonsen*, 622 S.E.2d 525 (S.C. 2005), the Supreme Court of South Carolina addressed number of occurrences for multiple claims against a distributor for property damage allegedly caused by defective stucco. The court noted that "[t]he discussion of a majority-versus-minority view summarizes an amalgam of cases, including vehicle accidents, flooding, fist-fights, and so on, and is not limited to product liability cases. Notably, there is no prevailing view in the specific context of product liability cases involving the distribution of a defective product. In light of the diverse contexts in which the meaning of 'occurrence' may arise, we decline the district court's invitation to simply choose the majority or minority view and instead focus narrowly on the issue at hand." *Id.* at 526.

In general, a court's adoption of the "cause" test frequently leads to a single "occurrence" determination—on the basis that, despite multiple injuries or damaged properties, it all has a common cause. That the "cause" test frequently leads to a single "occurrence" determination, despite multiple injuries or damaged properties, is also tied to the fact that the definition of "occurrence" in many policies includes "continuous or repeated exposure to substantially the same general harmful conditions," or some language to that effect.

But despite the "cause" test frequently leading to a single "occurrence" determination, it would be unwise to reach a number of occurrences conclusion based solely on the label of the test that a state applies. For example, in *Koikos v. Travelers Insurance Co.*, 849 So. 2d 263 (Fla. 2003), the Supreme Court of Florida, despite specifically adopting the "cause" test, held that injuries sustained by two individuals who were shot in a restaurant lobby constituted separate occurrences. The policy defined "occurrence" as "an accident, including continuous or repeated exposure to substantially the same general harmful conditions." *Id.* at 266. The court concluded that, notwithstanding that the insured–restaurant owner was sued for negligent failure to provide security [akin to the single cause of the multiple injuries in *Baumhammers*, 938 A.2d 286], "occurrence" was defined by the immediate injury-producing act and not by the underlying tortious omission. *Id.* at 272. Florida's high court stated: "[I]n this case, the immediate causes of the injuries were the intervening intentional acts of the third-party—the intruder's gunshots." *Id.*

Another example of "don't judge number of occurrences solely on the applicable test" is the Supreme Court of Illinois's recent decisions on the issue. In both cases, the court applied the "cause" test, yet concluded that the injuries or damages were separate occurrences. *See Addison Ins. Co. v. Fay*, 905 N.E.2d 747, 756 (Ill. 2009) (holding that only "if cause and result are simultaneous or so closely linked in time and space as to be considered by the average person as one event, then the injuries will be deemed the result of one occurrence") and *Nicor Inc. v. Associated Elec. & Gas Ins. Servs., Ltd.*, 860 N.E.2d 280, 294 (Ill. 2006) (adopting the "cause" test, but concluding that "where each asserted loss is the result of a separate and intervening human act, whether negligent or intentional, or each act increased the insured's exposure to liability, Illinois law will deem each such loss to have arisen from a separate occurrence").

The Supreme Court of South Carolina would likely point to these Illinois decisions as an example of why, in *Salmonsen, supra*, it declined to be pigeon-holed into a majority or minority view on the "number of occurrences" issue and instead adopted an approach that requires resort to each case individually.

In addition to number of occurrences determinations having a direct affect on the limits of liability available for certain injuries or damages, the same analysis can also dictate the number of deductibles or self-insured retentions that must be satisfied by an insured. This is so because, just as with limits of liability, deductibles and self-insured retentions are often applicable on a "per occurrence" or similar basis.

When number of occurrences arises for purposes of determining the number of deductibles or self-insured retentions that an insured must satisfy, as opposed to the number of limits of liability than an insurer must pay, some insureds and insurers may sometimes find themselves making what appear to be atypical arguments.

For example, when a number of occurrences dispute is over the number of limits of liability that an insurer must pay, insureds can be expected to argue for a multiple occurrences determination. Here, more occurrences means more coverage under the policy for the insured. But when number of deductibles or self-insured retentions are at issue, some insureds may find themselves arguing for a single occurrence determination, so that they need only satisfy a single deductible or self-insured retention. Now, more occurrences means more personal exposure under the policy for the insured.

Likewise, insurers that argue for a single occurrence, when the issue arises in the context of determining its limits of liability, may argue for multiple occurrences, when number of deductibles or self-insured retentions are at issue. *See CSX Transp., Inc. v. Cont'l Ins. Co.*, 680 A.2d 1082 (Md. 1996) (involving the insurers' argument that each of 20,000-plus noise-induced hearing loss claims arose from a separate occurrence for purposes of policies that contained self-insured retentions that ranged from $100,000 to $3 million for each occurrence); *see also Washoe County v. Transcon. Ins. Co.*, 878 P.2d 306 (Nev. 1994) (involving the insurers' argument that each child sexually abused by a daycare center worker constituted a separate occurrence for purposes of settlements between $2,000 and $25,000 per child under policies that contained a $50,000 self-insured retention).

In a similar vein, a primary insurer that argues for a single occurrence may now advocate for multiple occurrences when it is operating in the capacity as an excess insurer. Excess insurers typically benefit from a multiple occurrence determination as it may serve to increase the amount of primary limits that must be exhausted before the excess policy attaches.

Nobody disputes that courts' number of occurrences determinations can have a dramatic impact on the amount of coverage owed for certain claims. As a result, for claims involving significant injuries or damages, a multiple occurrences determination can serve as a basis for providing the amount of coverage that, in hindsight, needed to be purchased by the insured. As a result, there may a temptation for some courts to make number of occurrences decisions that are outcome determinative. At least one court has recognized this possibility and cautioned against it. *Unigard Ins. Co. v. U.S. Fid. & Guar. Co.*, 728 P.2d 780, 782 (Idaho Ct. App. 1986) ("A determination of the number of occurrences cannot be result-oriented. It must rest on a principled analysis that is not predisposed to favor insureds or insurers.").

## 50-State Survey: Number of Occurrences

**Alabama:** The Supreme Court of Alabama adopted the "cause" test and held that, where a roofing crew failed to adequately cover the exposed portion of a roof under repair, causing additional damage, the two events, because they were easily distinguishable in time and space, and because one event did not cause the other, each constituted a separate occurrence. *U.S. Fire Ins. Co. v. Safeco Ins. Co.*, 444 So. 2d 844, 846–47 (Ala. 1983). The policy defined "one occurrence" "[f]or the purpose of determining the limit of the company's liability" as "all bodily injury and property damage arising out of continuous or repeated exposure to substantially the same general conditions shall be considered as arising out of one occurrence." *Id.* at 845–46. The court held that "[a]s long as the injuries stem from one proximate cause there is a single occurrence." *Id.* at 846 (quoting *Appalachian Ins. Co. v. Liberty Mut. Ins. Co.*, 676 F.2d 56, 61 (3rd Cir. 1982)). The court viewed the negligent act of the roofing crew as a separate, intervening cause and not a proximate cause. *Id.* at 847; *see also St. Paul Fire & Marine Ins. Co. v. Christiansen Marine, Inc.*, 893 So. 2d 1124, 1137 (Ala. 2004) (holding that, for purposes of calculating the deductible owed, in the absence of evidence of more than one proximate cause, the breakup of several barges constituted a single occurrence).

**Alaska:** No instructive authority.

**Arizona:** The Supreme Court of Arizona held that embezzlement, committed over a five-year period by an employee of the insured, by forging company checks, constituted a single occurrence under an employee fidelity policy. *Employers Mut. Cas. Co. v. DGG & CAR, Inc.*, 183 P.3d 513, 518–19 (Ariz. 2008). The policy defined "occurrence" as "all loss caused by, or involving, one or more 'employees,' whether the result of a single act or series of acts." *Id.* at 515. The court held that, based on this definition, the employee's embezzlement, although including a number of thefts, was a "series of acts," each one following the other. *Id.* "The policy plainly considers the loss resulting from the embezzlement of a single employee an occurrence, with an attendant $50,000 policy limit." *Id.* at 516. The Supreme Court of Arizona also concluded that its decision was consistent with the majority of courts interpreting similar policy language in corresponding factual situations. *Id.*

**Arkansas:** The Supreme Court of Arkansas applied the "cause" test and held that, where a man purchased a pistol and a shotgun at a sporting goods store, shot a policeman, killed and wounded several other persons, and then committed suicide, the insured's sale of the weapons constituted a single occurrence within the meaning of the policy. *Travelers Indem. Co. v. Olive's Sporting Goods, Inc.*, 764 S.W.2d 596, 599 (Ark. 1989). The policy defined "occurrence," in pertinent part as, "an accident including continuance [of] or repeated exposure to conditions." *Id.* (alteration in original). The policy also provided that "the limit stated in the declarations as applicable to 'each occurrence' is the total limit of liability… for all damages… arising out of bodily injury… sustained by one or more persons… as a result of any one occurrence." *Id.* The court based its decision on the terms of the policy and its conclusion that, following a review of decisions from other jurisdictions, the "cause" test, rather than the "effect" test, holds the better view. *Id.*; *see also Fireman's Fund Ins. Co. v. Scottsdale Ins. Co.*, 968 F. Supp. 444, 448 (E.D. Ark. 1997) (applying the cause test and predicting that the Supreme Court of Arkansas would hold that, in the absence of evidence of two or more independent events/causes, multiple sales of contaminated food at a restaurant to several customers constitute a single occurrence within the meaning of a commercial general liability policy).

**California:** The Court of Appeal of California adopted the "cause" test and held that damage to downhill property caused by a landslide constituted one "occurrence." *Safeco Ins. Co. of America v. Fireman's Fund Ins. Co.*, 148 Cal. App. 4th 620, 633–34 (Cal. Ct. App. 2007). The policies at issue defined "occurrence," in relevant part, as "[a]n accident, including continuous or repeated exposure to the same or similar harmful conditions, which results, during the policy period, in 'bodily injury' or 'property damage.'" *Id.* at 631 (alteration in original). "When all injuries emanate from a common source…, there is only a single occurrence for purposes of policy coverage. It is irrelevant that there are multiple injuries or injuries of different magnitudes, or that the injuries *extend over a period of time.* Conversely, when a cause is interrupted, or when there are several autonomous causes, there are multiple 'occurrences' for purposes of determining policy limits and assessing deductibles." *Id.* at 633–34 (quotation omitted) (emphasis and alteration in original). The court concluded that there was one uninterrupted cause or event, the landslide, that resulted in all of the damage. *Id.* at 634; *but see Evanston Ins. Co. v. Ghillie Suits.com, Inc.*, No. C 08–2099, 2009 WL 734691, at *11 (N.D. Cal. Mar. 19, 2009) (recognizing *Safeco* as the appropriate law but holding that two Marines injured by fire constituted separate occurrences because the proximate cause of the first Marine's injuries was the ignition of his camouflage suit, while the other Marine's suit ignited after he decided to rescue the first Marine and came into contact with the fire) ("Allowing the insurer to limit the number of occurrences to a particular remote cause would effectively eviscerate the purpose of having a per-occurrence limitation as opposed to an aggregate limit.").

**Colorado:** No instructive authority.

**Connecticut:** The Supreme Court of Connecticut held that hundreds of thousands of asbestos bodily injury claims, filed against an insurer of employee healthcare plans, alleging that the insurer failed to adequately publicize the health risks of exposure to asbestos, constituted multiple occurrences (but each claimant was not automatically a separate occurrence). *Metro. Life Ins. Co. v. Aetna Cas. & Sur. Co.*, 765 A.2d 891, 896 (Conn. 2001). The policies did not define the term "occurrence." *Id.* at 897. However, the policies contained "continuous exposure" language that combined claims arising from each claimant's exposure to asbestos at the same place, at approximately the same time, into one occurrence. *Id.* at 898. The court concluded that "the language of the defendants' insurance policies is not ambiguous. A plain reading of the policies indicates that the occurrence in this case was the exposure of the claimants to asbestos, not [the insurer's] alleged failure to warn. Moreover, the proper interpretation of the continuous exposure clause is that it combines exposures to asbestos that occurred at the same place, at approximately the same time, resulting *still*, in multiple occurrences under the policy. The clause cannot be read plausibly, as Metropolitan contends, to combine hundreds of thousands of exposures that occurred under different circumstances throughout the country over a period of sixty years, into one occurrence." *Id.* at 900 (emphasis in original).

**Delaware:** The Supreme Court of Delaware adopted the "cause" test and held that thousands of claims for property damage, on account of defective resin material used in polybutylene plumbing systems, constituted a single occurrence. *Stonewall Ins. Co. v. E.I. DuPont De Nemours & Co.*, 1254 A.2d 1257-58 (Del. 2010). The policies at issue defined "occurrence" as "an accident or a happening or event or a continuous or repeated exposure to conditions which unexpectedly and unintentionally results in personal injury, property damage or advertising liability during the policy period. All such exposure to substantially the same general conditions existing at or emanating from one premises location shall be deemed one occurrence." *Id.* at 1257. The supreme court concluded that the lower court correctly identified and applied the "cause" test and affirmed the court's decision that, when determining the number of occurrences in a products liability case, the proper focus is on production and dispersal—not on the location of injury or the specific means by which injury occurred. *Id.* at 1258. "Therefore, DuPont's production of an unsuitable product triggered only one single occurrence under the policies." *Id.* The court observed that, if the excess insurer's multiple occurrence position were adopted, DuPont would have to incur almost $24 trillion in damages before being entitled to reach its excess insurers. *Id.*

**Florida:** The Supreme Court of Florida held that injuries sustained by two individuals who were shot in a restaurant lobby constituted separate occurrences. *Koikos v. Travelers Ins. Co.*, 849 So. 2d 263, 273 (Fla. 2003). The policy defined "occurrence" as "an accident, including continuous or repeated exposure to substantially the same general harmful conditions." *Id.* at 266. The court concluded that, notwithstanding that the insured restaurant owner was sued for negligent failure to provide security, "occurrence" is defined by the immediate injury-producing act and not by the underlying tortious omission. *Id.* at 272. Despite this multiple occurrence holding, the court specifically emphasized that it was adopting the "cause," and not the "effect," test. *Id.* at 273. "[I]n this case, the immediate causes of the injuries were the intervening intentional acts of the third-party—the intruder's gunshots." *Id.* at 272; *see also Guideone Elite Ins. Co. v. Old Cutler Presbyterian Church, Inc.*, 420 F.3d 1317, 1332 (11th Cir. 2005) (applying *Koikos* and holding that the rape, robbery, kidnapping, and each act of assault and battery upon a victim, and each of her children, were each separate occurrences since the various acts committed by the perpetrator were separated by sufficient "time and space").

**Georgia:** The Supreme Court of Georgia adopted the "cause" test for purposes of determining how many accidents occurred when a motorist struck two bicyclists, perhaps just over one second apart. *State Auto Prop. & Cas. Co. v. Matty*, 690 S.E.2d 614, 618 (Ga. 2010). "[T]he term 'each accident' appears in the limitation of liability section of the State Auto policy, which clearly contemplates that there can be a single 'accident' in which there are multiple vehicles, injured parties, and claims and provides that for that type of single accident, there will be a liability limit of $100,000." *Id.* at 618–19.

The court rejected the "effect" theory (number of impacts), as it would mean that there would never be a single limit of liability in a multiple vehicle collision, because it is virtually impossible for multiple vehicles to collide simultaneously. *Id.* at 617. The supreme court remanded to the trial court to determine whether, applying the "cause" theory, there was "but one proximate, uninterrupted, and continuing cause which resulted in all of the injuries and damage." *Id.* at 619 (citation omitted).

**Hawaii:** A Hawaii District Court held that an employee's discharge, in retaliation for objecting to sexual harassment, constituted one "occurrence" under a liability policy. *CIM Ins. Corp. v. Masamitsu*, 74 F. Supp. 2d 975, 988 (D. Haw. 1999). The policy defined "occurrence" as "continuous or repeated exposure to substantially the same general harmful conditions." *Id.* at 979 n.2. The court noted that most courts determine number of occurrences by looking to the cause of the damage and not the number of claims or injuries. *Id.* The court concluded that the retaliation claim constituted a single occurrence—a pattern and practice of tolerating harassment. *Id.*

**Idaho:** The Court of Appeals of Idaho applied the "continuous process test" and held that a snow plow that damaged ninety-eight doors of a mini-storage rental facility, in a four-hour period, constituted one "occurrence," and, hence, only one deductible applied. *Unigard Ins. Co. v. U.S. Fid. & Guar. Co.*, 728 P.2d 780, 783 (Idaho Ct. App. 1986). The policy did not define the term "occurrence." *Id.* at 782. The court determined that the cause of the damage was the negligence of the snow plow operator, which was continuous and repetitive. *Id.* at 783.

**Illinois:** The Supreme Court of Illinois adopted the "cause" test and held that damage caused by mercury, which spilled from gas meters while being replaced in numerous residences, constituted multiple occurrences. *Nicor Inc. v. Associated Elec. & Gas Ins. Servs., Ltd.*, 860 N.E.2d 280, 299 (Ill. 2006). The policies at issue defined "occurrence" as "one happening or series of happenings arising out of or due to one event taking place during the term of this contract" and "(1) an accident, or (2) event or continuous or repeated exposure to conditions which result in bodily injury, personal injury, death or physical damage to or destruction of tangible property, including the loss of use. All damages arising out of such exposure to substantially the same general conditions shall be considered as arising out of one occurrence." *Id.* at 284. The supreme court adopted the appellate court's view that each mercury spill constituted a separate occurrence as each asserted loss was the result of a separate and intervening human act or each act increased the insured's exposure to liability. *Id.* at 295. As the spills had no common cause and occurred at different times over a seventeen-year period, "[t]o say that each of the 195 spills emanated from a single cause would, under these circumstances, be completely untenable." *Id.* In *Addison Insurance Co. v. Fay*, 905 N.E.2d 747 (Ill. 2009), the Supreme Court of Illinois expanded upon *Nicor's* "cause" test and adopted a "time and space" test—"if cause and result are simultaneous or so closely linked in time and space as to be considered by the average person as one event, then the injuries will be deemed the result of one occurrence." *Id.* at 756 (quoting *Doria v. Ins. Co. of N. Am.*, 509 A.2d 220, 224 (N.J. Super. App. Div. 1986)). Then, once the insured provides the necessary facts to establish coverage and the value of the loss, the burden shifts to the insurer to prove that the event or events giving rise to the damage constituted a single occurrence. *Id.* at 753; *see also Auto-Owners Ins. Co. v. Munroe*, 614 F.3d. 322 (7th Cir. 2010) (applying Illinois law) (discussing *Nicor* and *Fay* and holding that, even if causes could properly be called separate, none were intervening, but, rather, came together at the same time to produce a single set of circumstances that caused a single accident) (addressing an uninterrupted chain reaction involving several vehicles).

**Indiana:** An Indiana District Court held that property damage, caused by defective concrete supplied by the insured to contractors, constituted multiple occurrences. *Irving Materials, Inc. v. Zurich Am. Ins. Co.*, No. 1:03-CV-361, 2007 WL 1035098, at *21 (S.D. Ind. Mar. 30, 2007). The policy defined "occurrence" as "an accident including continuous or repeated exposure to substantially the same general harmful conditions." *Id.* at *20. The court held that each contract between the insured and a third party, requiring the insured to deliver a specific formulation of concrete, was a separate occurrence. *Id.* at *21. The court reasoned that the event for which the insured was liable under its contract was the distribution of defective concrete, and not some other event in the causal chain, such as its receipt of faulty aggregate from a supplier. *Id.* at *20.

**Iowa:** An Iowa District Court adopted the "cause" test and held that, defective windows manufactured and sold by the insured, that resulted in water damage, constituted a single "occurrence." *Liberty Mut. Ins. Co. v. Pella Corp.*, 631 F.Supp.2d 1125, 1135-36 (S.D. Iowa 2009). The policy defined "occurrence" as "an accident, including continuous or repeated exposure to substantially the same general harmful conditions." *Id.* at 1136. After acknowledging a lack of guidance under Iowa law, the court adopted the majority view—the "cause" test—and held that "the damages alleged by each of the plaintiffs in the Underlying Lawsuits arise from the 'the continuous or repeated exposure to the same general harmful conditions'—that is, to the design, manufacture, and allegedly fraudulent sale of a product containing the same latent defect." *Id.*

**Kansas:** The Supreme Court of Kansas adopted the "cause" test and held that, where the cause of a patient's injuries were a physician's failure to diagnose a malignant lesion, followed by continuing failure to diagnose, there was one proximate, uninterrupted, and continuing cause that resulted in all of the injuries and damages. *Wilson v. Ramirez*, 2 P.3d 778, 785 (Kan. 2000); *see also American Family Mutual Insurance Co. v. Wilkins*, 179 P.2d 1104, 1114 (Kan. 2008) (adopting the "cause" test and holding that number of occurrences, in the context of an automobile accident, was based on the time-space continuum between the collisions and the drivers' level of control over the vehicle) ("Collisions with multiple vehicles constitute one occurrence when the collisions are nearly simultaneous or separated by a very short period of time and the insured does not maintain or regain control over his or her vehicle between collisions. When collisions between multiple vehicles are separated by a period of time or the insured maintains or regains control of the vehicle before a subsequent collision, there are multiple occurrences.").

**Kentucky:** The Court of Appeals of Kentucky held that injuries sustained by three patrons of a nightclub, in an altercation with employees of the club, constituted one "occurrence." *Cont'l Ins. Cos. v. Hancock*, 507 S.W.2d 146, 152 (Ky. Ct. App. 1973). The court held, without explanation, that all of the injuries arose out of "continuous exposure to substantially the same general conditions." *Id.*

**Louisiana:** The Supreme Court of Louisiana held that damage to 119 properties, caused by the construction of an underground drainage canal, constituted multiple occurrences. *Lombard v. Sewerage & Water Bd. of New Orleans*, 284 So. 2d 905, 915–16 (La. 1973). The policy defined "occurrence" as "an accident or a continuous or repeated exposure to conditions which results during the policy period in injury to person or real or tangible property which is accidentally caused. All damages arising out of such exposure to substantially the same general conditions shall be considered as arising out of one occurrence." *Id.* at 915. The court reasoned that the word "occurrence" "must be construed from the point of view of the many persons whose property was damaged." *Id.* "As to each of these plaintiffs, the cumulated activities causing damage should be considered as one occurrence, though the circumstances causing damage consist of a continuous or repeated exposure to conditions resulting in damage arising out of such exposure." *Id.* at 915–16; *see also Liberty Mut. Ins. Co. v. Jotun Paints, Inc.*, 555 F. Supp. 2d 686, 695–96 (E.D. La. 2008) (surveying Louisiana case law addressing number of occurrences).

**Maine:** A Maine District Court adopted the "cause" test and held that damage to a large dryer, manufactured by the insured for use by paper manufacturers, constituted separate "occurrences." *Honeycomb Sys., Inc. v. Admiral Ins. Co.*, 567 F. Supp. 1400, 1406 (D. Me. 1983). The policy defined "occurrence" as "an accident, including continuous or repeated exposure to conditions." *Id.* at 1404. The court concluded that there was not one proximate, uninterrupted, and continuing cause which resulted in all of the injuries and damage. *Id.* at 1405–06. "The 1977 failure was not a recurrence of the 1975 failure, but rather a crack in the back head caused by a failure to follow the design in boring out the hub and affixing the hub plate. It had nothing to do with welding [1975 failure]. Thus in no meaningful sense can the failures be said to have the same proximate cause." *Id.* at 1406.

**Maryland:** The Court of Appeals of Maryland held that, for purposes of determining the number of applicable self-insured retentions, each of thousands of noise-induced hearing loss claims constituted a separate "occur-rence." *CSX Trans., Inc. v. Cont'l Ins. Co.*, 680 A.2d 1082, 1097 (Md. 1996). Many of the 246 excess liability policies at issue defined "occurrence," and most did so as "an accident, including continuous or repeated exposure to conditions, which result in personal injury or property damage neither expected or [*sic*] intended from the standpoint of the insured." *Id.* at 1086. The court rejected the insured's argument that each claim had a common cause—the insured's failure to prevent the exposure by mandating the use of hearing protection. *Id.* at 1097. The court concluded that, to have "arisen out of one occurrence, the exposure of each claimant must have some common-ality with the exposure of the other claimant; each exposure must have occurred at the same place or been caused by the same source." *Id.* at 1097; *see also Commercial Union Ins. Co. v. Porter Hayden Co.*, 698 A.2d 1167, 1211 (Md. 1997) (holding that each claimant's exposure to asbestos must be viewed as a separate "occurrence" because each individual claimant had a unique work history). *But see Board of County Commissioners of St. Mary's County v. Marcas, LLC*, __ A.3d __, 2010 WL 3619546 (Md. Sept. 20, 2010) (citing "number of "occurrences" decisions and holding that multiple injuries to property, resulting from migration of toxic substances from a county landfill, constituted the "same occurrence" for purposes of the monetary caps on the county's liability under the Maryland Local Government Tort Claims Act).

**Massachusetts:** The Appeals Court of Massachusetts applied the "cause" test and held that a shooting spree by a college student that lasted eighteen minutes, spanned approximately a quarter of a mile and resulted in two deaths and injuries to four people, arose from a single "occurrence." *RLI Ins. Co. v. Simon's Rock Early College*, 765 N.E.2d 247, 255 (Mass. App. Ct. 2002). The policy defined "occurrence" as an "accident, including continuous or repeated exposure to substantially the same general harmful conditions." *Id.* at 251. The court held that the insured college's negligent acts or omissions in failing to prevent the student from using his gun constituted the "occurrence" for purposes of determining general liability coverage. *Id. But see Worcester Ins. Co. v. Fells Acres Day Sch., Inc.*, 558 N.E.2d 958, 973–74 (Mass. 1990) ("The tort plaintiffs allege numerous discrete acts of abuse, negligence, and breach of duty by several different defendants, some individual and one corporate, at different locations. These allegations preclude the possibility that there was but a 'single, ongoing cause' of the injuries alleged. Further, we have rejected attempts by insurers to characterize seemingly discrete events as emanating from a single, ongoing cause."). *See also Keyspan New England, LLC v. Hanover Ins. Co.*, Nos. 93–01458, 04–01855, 2008 WL 4308310, at *10–11 (Mass. Super. Ct. Aug. 14, 2008) (reconciling *Fells Acres* and *Simon's Rock*).

**Michigan:** A Michigan District Court applied the "cause" test and held that pipe leaks, caused by defective resin manufactured by the insured, con-stituted a single occurrence. *Associated Indem. Corp. v. Dow Chem. Co.*, 814 F. Supp. 613, 623 (E.D. Mich. 1993). The policy defined "occurrence" as "an event, including continuous or repeated exposure to conditions which results, during the policy period, in personal injury or property damage not intended from the standpoint of the insured." *Id.* at 617. The court determined that the "production of defective resin was the sole, proximate, uninterrupted, and continuing cause of all of the property damage in the case for which Dow Canada could be responsible." *Id.* at 623. The court distinguished its decision from others involving Dow and its insurers which concluded that damage to building facades, caused by the use of Dow's mortar, constituted separate occurrences. *Id.* at 620.

**Minnesota:** The Supreme Court of Minnesota held that an employee's embezzlement scheme constituted two "occurrences" under an employee dishonesty policy. *Am. Commerce Ins. Brokers, Inc. v. Minn. Mut. Fire & Cas. Co.*, 551 N.W.2d 224, 231 (Minn. 1996). The court declined to adopt the "cause" test, but, rather, held that "a court may consider several factors in concluding whether dishonest acts are part of a 'series of related acts,' including whether the acts are connected by time, place, opportunity, pattern, and, most importantly, method or modus operandi." *Id.* The court examined the nature of the embezzlement scheme and concluded that it involved two distinct "series of related acts." *Id.; see also Farmers Ins. Exchange v. Hallaway*, 564 F. Supp. 2d 1047, 1053–54 (D. Minn. 2008) (following *Am. Commerce* and concluding that a defamatory e-mail campaign, occurring over a two-year period, constituted one "occurrence" under a homeowner's policy that provided "[r]epeated or continuous exposure to the same general conditions is considered to be one occurrence").

**Mississippi:** The Court of Appeals of Mississippi held that a claim against the perpetrator of an assault, for failure to seek medical assistance for his victim, constituted only one occurrence. *Cooper v. Missey*, 881 So. 2d 889, 895 (Miss. Ct. App. 2004). The policy defined "occurrence" as "continuous and repeated exposure to the same general conditions." *Id.* at 894. The court reasoned that "[e]ven if we assume that [the victim's] condition was such that [the insured-perpetrator] knew or should have known that [the victim] needed medical assistance, that knowledge and the resulting failure to seek medical assistance continued unbroken until the time that [the insured-perpetrator] ultimately called for an ambulance... . [T]here is no evidence that would break the chain of negligence once [the victim's] condition rose to a level that demanded medical assistance. If we follow [the victim's] argument, every minute could constitute a separate occurrence under the policy." *Id.* The *Cooper* Court addressed *Crum v. Johnson*, 809 So. 2d 663 (Miss. 2002) and *Universal Underwriters Insurance Co. v. Ford*, 734 So. 2d 173 (Miss. 1999), both Supreme Court of Mississippi decisions finding multiple occurrences because the policies at issue did not unambiguously state that multiple injuries may not result in multiple occurrences. *Id.* at 894.

**Missouri:** A Missouri District Court held that a claim for injuries sustained by two joggers that were attacked by the insured's dog constituted one occurrence.

*Allstate Prop. & Cas. Co. v. McBee*, No. 08–0534, 2009 WL 1124973, at *5 (W.D. Mo. Apr. 27, 2009). The policy defined "occurrence" as "an accident, including continuous or repeated exposure to substantially the same general harmful conditions during the policy period, resulting in bodily injury or property damage." *Id.* at *2. The court declined to follow the Supreme Court of Florida's decision in *Koikos v. Travelers Ins. Co.*, 849 So. 2d 263 (Fla. 2003). Instead, the court adopted the "cause" test and concluded that the injuries sustained by each of the McBees were the result of continuous exposure to substantially the same harmful condition—the insured's failure to prevent the dog's escape. *Id.* at *5; *see also Kansas Fire & Cas. Co. v. Koelling*, 729 S.W.2d 251, 252–53 (Mo. Ct. App. 1987) (adopting the "cause" test in the context of an automobile policy and concluding that a near simultaneous collision with two automobiles constituted only one accident); *Westchester Surplus Lines Ins. Co. v. Maverick Tube Corp.*, No. H-07–540, 2010 WL 2635623, at *6 (S.D. Tex. June 28, 2010) (applying Missouri law) (distinguishing *McBee* and *Koelling* but nonetheless adopting the cause test and finding a single occurrence) ("The liability-causing event was Maverick's defective manufacturing of the drill casing. All of the damage flowed proximately from the manufacturing defect. Neither the sale of the casing nor its installation, as Westchester suggests, were necessary to make Maverick liable. Nor did those later events interrupt the causal chain. The 'cause' analysis supports a conclusion that Maverick's defective manufacturing was a single 'occurrence.'").

**Montana:** The Supreme Court of Montana adopted the "cause" test and held that the death of a thirteen-month-old girl, from a toxic dose of diphenhydramine administered at a daycare facility, constituted one "occurrence." *Travis v. Capitol Indem Corp.*, 154 P.3d 1189, 1197 (Mont. 2007). The policy defined "occurrence" as "an accident, including continuous or repeated exposure to substantially the same general harmful conditions." *Id.* at 1193–94. The court determined that the only cause of the child's death was the lethal dose of diphenhydramine. *Id.* at 1197.

**Nebraska:** The Supreme Court of Nebraska adopted the "cause" test and held that contamination by an insured, at four different sites, over the course of several decades, constituted one occurrence. *See Dutton-Lainson Co. v. Continental Ins. Co.*, 778 N.W.2d 433, 443 (Neb. 2010). The policy defined "occurrence" as "an accident, including continuous or repeated exposure to conditions, which results in bodily injury or property damage neither expected nor intended from the standpoint of the insured." *Id.* "Contamination occurred at four different sites, but all of the contamination was caused by the actions of [the insured]. The underlying cause of the damage was the use of TCE and TCA in the manufacturing operation. This action was continuous and repeated over a number of years." *Id.*

**Nevada:** The Supreme Court of Nevada applied the "cause" test and held that, for purposes of determining the number of applicable self-insured retentions, the sexual abuse of numerous children at a daycare center, over a three-year period, constituted one "occurrence." *Washoe County v. Transcon. Ins.*

*Co.*, 878 P.2d 306, 310 (Nev. 1994). The policy defined "occurrence" as "an accident, or event, including injurious exposure to conditions, which results, during the policy period, in personal injury, property damage, or public officials errors and omissions." *Id.* at 307. The court concluded that the term "occurrence" should be defined in a way to give meaning to the insured's connection to liability. *Id.* at 310. On that basis, because the county "caused" the children's injuries, through its failure to act with the requisite care in the process of licensing the daycare center, such failure constituted a single "occurrence." *Id.*

**New Hampshire:** The Supreme Court of New Hampshire held that damage to several properties caused by a fire constituted one "accident" under a liability policy. *Travelers Indem. Co. v. New England Box Co.*, 157 A.2d 765, 768–69 (N.H. 1960). The policy provided that the "each accident" limit was the total limit for all damages for injury of all property of one or more persons as a result of any one accident. *Id.* at 768–69. The court held that such policy language was an indication that, in interpreting the limit of property damage liability for "each accident," the word "accident" was intended to be construed from the standpoint of cause rather than effect. *Id.* at 769.

**New Jersey:** The New Jersey Superior Court, Appellate Division, held that claims arising out of an insured's adult son firing a shotgun and hitting two police officers multiple times constituted a single occurrence. *Bomba v. State Farm Fire & Cas. Co.*, 879 A.2d 1252, 1256 (N.J. Super. Ct. App. Div. 2005). The policy defined "occurrence" as "an accident, including exposure to conditions, which results in: a. bodily injury." *Id.* at 1253. Relying on the court's adoption of the "cause" test in *Doria v. Insurance Co. of North Ame*rica, 509 A.2d 220, 221 (N.J. Super. Ct. App. Div. 1986), the court held that the cause of the injuries was the negligence of the gunman's parents in permitting him to have access to firearms in their home. *Id.* at 1255. In *Doria*, the Appellate Division of the New Jersey Superior Court held that injury to two boys that fell into a swimming pool were one occurrence because the cause of the injuries was the insured's failure to properly fence in and cover an abandoned pool. *Id.* at 224.

**New Mexico:** No instructive authority.

**New York:** The New York Court of Appeals applied the "unfortunate events" test and held that each individual exposed to asbestos insulation in turbines, at work sites across the country, constituted a separate occurrence. *Appalachian Ins. Co. v. Gen. Elec. Co.*, 863 N.E.2d 994, 1000 (N.Y. 2007). The policies defined occurrence as "an accident, event, happening or continuous or repeated exposure to conditions which unintentionally results in injury or damage during the policy period." *Id.* at 996. Relying on its prior decisions in *Arthur A. Johnson Corp. v. Indem. Ins. Co. of N. Am.*, 164 N.E.2d 704 (N.Y. 1959) and *Hartford Acc. & Indem. Co. v. Wesolowski*, 305 N.E.2d 907 (N.Y. 1973) for guidance, New York's highest court analyzed the policy language, the "temporal and spatial relationships between the incidents and the extent to which they were part of an undisputed continuum" and concluded that, since the policy language did not reflect an intent to group incidents, and there was no spatial or temporal relationship, "there were unquestionably multiple occurrences." *Id.* at 1000–01. The court concluded that each individual plaintiff's "continuous or repeated exposure" to asbestos gave rise to liability. *Id.* at 1000; *see also ExxonMobil Corp. v. Certain Underwriters at Lloyd's, London*, 855 N.Y.S. 2d 484, 485 (N.Y. App. Div. 2008) ("Each installation of ExxonMobil's polybutylene resin into a municipal utility water system, and each introduction of AV-1 lubricant into an aircraft engine, created 'exposure' to a condition that resulted in property damage, to multiple claimants on different dates over many years. Under the circumstances, the underlying product liability claims 'share few, if any, commonalities.'") (quoting *Appalachian*); *Bausch & Lomb Inc. v. Lexington Ins. Co.*, 679 F. Supp. 2d 345, 353–54 (W.D.N.Y. 2009) (addressing *Appalachian* in detail) ("[T]here is no dispute that the incidents giving rise to liability: i.e., exposure to the plaintiff's contact lens solutions, occurred in thousands of different locations, at thousands of different times, as a result of different solutions manufactured at different times and in different locations. The record reveals that claimants come from several different states and countries, allege different types of injuries, and allege that the exposure to the plaintiff's products took place in various locations at various times over the course of several years. As a result, there is no close temporal and spatial relationship between the incidents giving rise to the alleged injuries, and there is no basis for holding that the incidents can be viewed as part of the same causal continuum, without intervening agents or factors."); *Mt. McKinley Ins. Co. v. Corning Inc.*, 903 N.Y.S.2d 709 (N.Y. Sup. Ct. 2010) (lengthy discussion of New York law concerning number of occurrences).

**North Carolina:** The Supreme Court of North Carolina held that the leakage of a contaminant from pressure vessels into sixty tons of a dye product constituted a single "occurrence." *Gaston County Dyeing Machine Co. v. Northfield Ins. Co.*, 524 S.E.2d 558, 564 (N.C. 2000). The policy defined "occurrence" as "an accident, including continuous or repeated exposure to substantially the same general harmful conditions." *Id.* The court concluded that "all the damage occurred as a result of exposure to the same harmful condition—continued leakage of the contaminant into the dye product." *Id.; see also W. World Ins. Co. v. Wilkie*, No. 5:06-CV-64-H, 2007 WL 3256947, at *5 (E.D.N.C. Nov. 2, 2007) (following *Gaston County* and predicting that the Supreme Court of North Carolina would conclude that the contracting of *E. coli* by several minors during visits to a petting zoo constituted a single occurrence).

**North Dakota:** No instructive authority.

**Ohio:** The Court of Appeals of Ohio held that numerous asbestos bodily injury claims, caused by the manufacture and sale of defective protective masks, each constituted a separate occurrence. *Cincinnati Ins. Co. v. ACE INA Holdings, Inc.*, 886 N.E.2d 876, 887 (Ohio Ct. App. 2007). The policy defined "occurrence" as "an accident, including injurious exposure to conditions, which results, during the policy period, in bodily injury." *Id.* at 885. The court reasoned that "[the insured's] masks were not intrinsically harmful; they failed to protect, and that failure to protect led to a multitude of physically and temporally distinct injuries under a multitude of differing factual scenarios that did not constitute the 'same general conditions' contemplated under the plain language of the [policy]." *Id.* at 887. The court concluded with a cautionary note that "blanket judicial application of any one test could frustrate the contracting parties' intent." *Id.* at 888; *see also Libbey v. Factory Mut. Ins. Co.*, No. 3:06 CV-2412, 2007 U.S. Dist. LEXIS 45160, at *20–26 (N.D. Ohio June 21, 2007) (adopting the cause test and holding that multiple claims for misformulated oil that was injected into certain machines constituted a single occurrence); Dutch Maid Logistics, Inc. v. Acuity, Nos. 91932 and 92002, 2009 WL 1019857, at *4 (Ohio Ct. App. 2009) (adopting the cause test) ("A plain reading of the policy language establishes that the policy defines an 'accident' as one encompassing as many vehicles and injuries as caused by the same tortfeasor. The trial court, in rendering its decision, correctly concluded that there was but one continuous accident that caused all the bodily injury claims that flowed from it.").

**Oklahoma:** The Tenth Circuit Court of Appeals, applying Oklahoma law, held that embezzlement by an employee, who wrote forty fraudulent checks, constituted one loss under a property policy. *Bus. Interiors, Inc. v. Aetna Cas. & Sur. Co.*, 751 F.2d 361, 363 (10th Cir. 1984) The court adopted the "cause" test and held that the insured's loss was the continued dishonesty of one employee. *Id.*

**Oregon:** An Oregon District Court held that numerous claims against an insured, for damage caused by the failure of its siding product, constituted one occurrence. *Cal. Ins. Co. v. Or. Ins. Guar. Assoc.*, No. 01–514, 2005 WL 627624, at *7 (D. Or. Mar. 17, 2005). The policy defined "occurrence" as "an accident, including continuous or repeated exposure to substantially the same general harmful conditions." *Id.* The court held that the "occurrence" was the continuous exposure to the siding manufactured and sold by the insured, which allegedly resulted in similar kinds of property damage to the plaintiffs' homes and buildings. *Id.*

**Pennsylvania:** The Supreme Court of Pennsylvania adopted the "cause" test and held that there was a single "occurrence" where the insured's son, over a two-hour period, shot and killed a neighbor and then drove to three townships where he shot and killed four people and wounded another. *Donegal Mut. Ins. Co. v. Baumhammers*, 938 A.2d 286, 296 (Pa. 2007). The homeowner's policy at issue defined "occurrence" as an "accident, including continuous or repeated exposure to substantially the same general harmful conditions, which results during the policy period in… bodily injury or property damage." *Id.* at 289 (alteration in original). Adopting the "cause" test, the court held that the insured-parents' negligence—failing to confiscate their son's weapon and/or notify law enforcement or his mental health providers of his unstable condition—constituted a single occurrence. *Id.* at 295–96. "Determining the number of occurrences by looking to the underlying negligence of the insured recognizes that the question of the extent of coverage rests upon the contractual obligation of the insurer to the insured. Since the policy was intended to insure Parents for their liabilities, the occurrence should be an event over which Parents had some control." *Id.* at 298; *see also Liberty Mut. Ins. Co. v. Treesdale, Inc.*, 418 F.3d 330, 339 (3d Cir. 2005) (applying Pennsylvania law) (holding that several thousand asbestos products claims arose from a single occurrence).

**Rhode Island:** A Rhode Island District Court adopted the "cause" test and held that a claim against the manufacturer of car-washing equipment, whose defective equipment resulted in the shutdown of a carwash, constituted a single "occurrence." *Bartholomew v. Ins. Co. of N. Am.*, 502 F. Supp. 246, 252 (D.R.I. 1980). The policy defined "occurrence" as "an accident, including continuous or repeated exposure to conditions." *Id.* at 251. The court concluded that, while the damage sustained from the shutdown of the entire operation may have differed from the damage caused by the intermittent operation of the machine, the source of all of the injury was a single event—the sale of a defectively designed and constructed carwash unit. *Id.* at 252.; *see also Avco Corp. v. Aetna Cas. & Sur. Co.*, 679 A.2d 323, 328 (R.I. 1996) (stating in the context of a notice issue that "the dissemination of contaminants from [the insured's] Williamsport plant site into area ground water resulting in the contamination of the Williamsport municipal water supply and in the various claims made against [the insured] as a result thereof must be classified as *an* occurrence, and more specifically as one occurrence") (emphasis in original); *Allstate Ins. Co. v. Bonn*, No. 09–171ML, 2010 WL 1779929, *5 (D.R.I. May 3, 2010) (relying on *Bartholomew* and finding a single occurrence in the context of exposure to lead paint in a residential setting) ("[T]he allegations of the underlying complaint all point to the same uninterrupted cause for the injuries suffered by D. and B.: the continuing, unabated presence of lead in the residence throughout the Jessups' tenancy. Although the children may have ingested the lead at different times and their blood tests showed different levels of exposure, the injuries all flowed from the same conditions in their immediate environment.")

**South Carolina:** The Supreme Court of South Carolina declined to adopt either the majority or minority view on number of occurrences because it is based on a summary of numerous types of cases. *Owners Ins. Co. v. Salmonsen*, 622 S.E.2d 525, 526 (S.C. 2005). Instead, the court chose to focus narrowly on the issue at hand—distribution of a defective product. *Id.* The policy defined "occurrence" as "an accident, including continuous or repeated exposure to substantially the same general harmful conditions." *Id.* at 525. The court held that, because the distributor took no distinct action giving rise to liability for each sale—the case did not involve defective distribution—the placing of a defective product into the stream of commerce was one occurrence under the policy. *Id.*

**South Dakota:** No instructive authority.

**Tennessee:** A Tennessee District Court held that the sexual abuse of several minors at a childcare facility, by a facility employee, constituted a single "sexual abuse occurrence." *TIG Ins. Co. v. Merryland Childcare & Dev. Ctr., Inc.*, No. 04–2666, 2007 WL 316571, at *6 (W.D. Tenn. Jan. 31, 2007). The policy defined "sexual abuse occurrence," in pertinent part, as "[a] single act, or multiple, continuous, sporadic, or related acts of sexual abuse or molestation caused by one perpetrator, or by two or more perpetrators acting together.... All acts of 'sexual abuse occurrence' by an actual or alleged perpetrator or perpetrators, including 'negligent employment' of such perpetrator or perpetrators, shall be deemed and construed as one occurrence which takes place when the first act of sexual abuse or molestation occurs, regardless of the number of persons involved, or the number of incidents or locations involved, or the period of time during which the acts of sexual abuse or molestation took place." *Id.* at *3. The court concluded that the abuse perpetrated by the facility's employee upon the students constituted one occurrence. *Id.* at *6.

**Texas:** The Court of Appeals of Texas held that, under the "cause" test, each claim against a builder, for water damage to homes that it built using synthetic stucco (EIFS), constituted a separate "occurrence." *Lennar Corp. v. Great American Ins. Co.*, 200 S.W.3d 651, 683 (Tex. Ct. App. 2006). The policies defined "occurrence" as "an accident, including continuous or repeated exposure to substantially the same general harmful conditions." *Id.* at 663. "Lennar was not the designer or the manufacturer of EIFS. Rather, Lennar's liability stemmed from the fact that it built and sold homes with EIFS. Thus, Lennar's liability to a particular homeowner stemmed from the application of EIFS, and the resulting damage, if any, to his or her particular home. Further, there was not one entrapment of water that caused damage to all the homes. Instead, the EIFS's entrapment of water on a particular home caused the damage to that home only. Therefore, Lennar was exposed to a new and separate liability for each home on which EIFS was applied." *Id.* at 682–83; *see also National Union Fire Ins. Co. v. Puget Plastics Corp.*, 649 F. Supp. 2d 613, 627–29 (S.D. Tex. 2009) (surveying Texas case law addressing number of occurrences); Pennzoil-Quaker State Co. v. American Intern. Specialty Lines Ins. Co., 653 F. Supp. 2d 690, 707 (S.D. Tex. 2009) (rejecting insured's single occurrence argument) ("The petitions in the underlying suits allege distinct kinds of emissions and releases, with distinct causes.... The petitions also allege that releases of different types of contaminants into two distinct areas— air and subsurface water—have occurred continuously for years.").

**Utah:** No instructive authority.

**Vermont:** No instructive authority.

**Virginia:** The Supreme Court of Virginia held that the sexual assault of several minors, by the resident manager of an apartment complex owned by the insured, constituted separate occurrences. *S.F. v. W. Am. Ins. Co.*, 463 S.E.2d 450, 452 (Va. 1995). The policy defined "occurrence" as "an accident, including continuous or repeated exposure to conditions, which results in bodily injury or property damage neither expected nor intended from the standpoint of the insured." *Id.* The court concluded that, because the occurrence could have been one of several things, the term was ambiguous and must be construed against the insurer. *Id.* However, the policy also stated that "[f]or the purpose of determining the limit of the Company's liability, all bodily injury and property damage arising out of a continuous or repeated exposure to substantially the same general conditions shall be considered as arising out of one occurrence." *Id.* Based on this language, the court held that, even though each minor was subjected to several acts of sexual molestation, such acts constituted only one occurrence per minor. *Id.*; *see also Norfolk & W. Ry. Co. v. Accident & Cas. Ins. Co. of Winterthur*, 796 F. Supp. 929, 937 (W.D. Va. 1992) (finding multiple occurrences for hearing-loss claims).

**Washington:** The Supreme Court of Washington applied the "cause" test and held that, "if each accident, collision, or injury has its own proximate cause then each will be deemed a separate 'accident' for insurance policy purposes even if the two accidents occurred coincident, or nearly coincident, in time." *Greengo v. Pub. Employees Mut. Ins. Co.*, 959 P.2d 657, 664 (Wash. 1998); *see also Transcon. Ins. Co. v. Wash. Pub. Utils. Dists.' Util. Sys.*, 760 P.2d 337, 346 (Wash. 1988) (holding that claims against a public utility for bond defaults "may exist on the basis of the bondholders' allegations of multiple separate causes, continuing causes, or longstanding causes resulting in injury during the policy period"); *Spokane County v. Am. Re-Insurance Co.*, No. CS-90–256, 1993 WL 13579995, at *1 (E.D. Wash. May 12, 1993) (citing *Washington Public Utilities* for the proposition that Washington is a "cause" state and holding that, because there was only one cause of injury—pollutants leaking into groundwater—all injury resulting from the contamination of groundwater, on- and off-site, is one occurrence); *Certain Underwriters at Lloyd's London v. Valiant Ins. Co.*, No. 63692–8-I, 2010 WL 1427571, at *3 (Wash. Ct. App. Apr. 12, 2010) (characterizing *Transcon.* and other Washington decisions as providing a general rule that the number of occurrences equals the number of causes of liability).

**West Virginia:** The Supreme Court of Appeals of West Virginia held that a physician's failure to diagnose a patient with cancer, during several examinations over a lengthy period of time, constituted one "incident" under a physician's professional liability policy. *Auber v. Jellen*, 469 S.E.2d 104, 108 (W. Va. 1996). The court reached its conclusion on the basis that the policy language "'all injury resulting from a series of acts or omissions in providing medical services to one person' will be *considered one incident*" was clear and unambiguous and would be given its plain, ordinary meaning. *Id.* (emphasis in original); *see also Beckley Mech., Inc. v. Erie Ins. Co.*, No. 09–1549, 2010 WL 1452616, at *2 (4th Cir. Apr. 13, 2010) (applying W. Va. law) (holding that embezzlement by a bookkeeper, who drafted approximately 293 checks to herself, was a "series of acts" and therefore considered one occurrence); *Smallwood-Small Insurance, Inc. v. American Automobile Ins. Co.*, No. 3:06-CV-107, 2007 WL 4556662, at *4 (N.D. W.Va. Dec. 20, 2007) (holding that failure by an insurance agency to obtain insurance for three clients constituted separate occurrences).

**Wisconsin:** The Supreme Court of Wisconsin applied the "cause" test and held that, where individuals were exposed to asbestos at different times and different geographical locations, each individual's repeated and continuous exposure to asbestos-containing products constituted a separate "occurrence." *Plastics Eng'g Co. v. Liberty Mut. Ins. Co.*, 759 N.W.2d 613, 623 (Wis. 2009). The policies defined "occurrence" similarly, including as "an accident, including continuous or repeated exposure to conditions, which results in bodily injury or property damage neither expected nor intended form the standpoint of the insured." *Id.* at 617. The court rejected the insurer's argument that it was the sale of asbestos-containing products without warning that was the occurrence. "The exposure must, quite obviously, be exposure to the injured person and not exposure to [the insured–Plastics Engineering Company]." *Id.* at 623; *see also Basler Turbo Conversions, LLC v. HCC Ins. Co.*, 601 F. Supp. 2d 1082, 1091 (E.D. Wis. 2009) (holding that a series of thefts over a six-month period by the same individual did not constitute a single "occurrence" and the insured was subject to a separate deductible for each theft).

**Wyoming:** No instructive authority.

# Coverage for Innocent Co-Insureds: "Any" Insured vs. "The" Insured and the Severability of Interests Clause

It is routine for a court, setting out to resolve an insurance coverage dispute, to begin its opinion by laying out the rules that will determine its decision. And it is likely that somewhere in the court's recitation will be a statement that its most important consideration is to be the language of the policy. This is the case today. *See James River Ins. Co. v. Ground Down Engineering, Inc.*, 540 F.3d 1270, 1274 (11th Cir. 2008) (quoting *Taurus Holdings, Inc. v. U.S. Fid. & Guar. Co.*, 913 So.2d 528, 537 (Fla. 2005) ("In interpreting insurance contracts... 'the language of the policy is the most important factor.'"). And that was also the case when Teddy Roosevelt was president. *See White v. Standard Life & Accident Ins. Co.*, 103 N.W. 735, 736 (Minn. 1905) ("While the rule is thoroughly settled that policies of this and like character are to be construed liberally, and that ambiguous provisions or those capable of two constructions should be construed favorably to the insured and most strongly against the insurer, plain, explicit language cannot be disregarded, nor an interpretation given the policy at variance with the clearly disclosed intent of the parties.").

Then, at the conclusion of the opinion resolving the coverage dispute, it is likely that one party will believe that the court was true to its word and made its decision by applying solely the plain language of the policy. The other party is likely to see it otherwise.

But there is one situation where both parties can likely agree that the court's decision was, at least up to a point, completely faithful to the policy language. Consider a suit filed by the victim of an attack at the hands of a teenager neighbor living in his parents' home. The teenager, as an "insured" under his parents' homeowners policy, will likely seek coverage for the suit under the liability section of such policy. In many instances, the policy will contain an exclusion for, among other things, bodily injury which results from "the criminal acts of any [or an] insured." And not surprisingly, if the teenage perpetrator–insured was convicted of a crime, the criminal act exclusion will usually preclude coverage for him.

It is likely that the plaintiff's attorney in the underlying case is well aware that coverage for the perpetrator may be hard to come by because of the possible existence of a "criminal act" exclusion. For that reason, the plaintiff may allege that the teen's parents bear responsibility for the victim's injuries, by *failing to prevent* their son from causing them. What's at work here is, in all likelihood, an effort by the plaintiff to secure insurance dollars by arguing that, *because the parents did not themselves commit a criminal act*, they are not bound by the policy exclusion. *See L.C.S., Inc. v. Lexington Ins. Co.*, 853 A.2d 974, 980 (N.J. App. Div. 2004) (discussing the possibility that a "failure to prevent" claim against an employer, for assault and battery committed by an employee, is a "bogus or thinly veiled attempt by a plaintiff designed only to reach the pot of gold at the end of the rainbow of an employer general liability policy").

While it is true that the parents themselves did not commit a criminal act, insurers frequently argue that coverage nonetheless remains unavailable to them. The insurer's expected argument will be that the exclusion at issue applies to injury that results from the "criminal acts of *any insured*"—and "any insured" (the parents' son) in fact committed a criminal act. In other words, in such a situation, expect insurers to maintain that the applicability of the criminal act exclusion is not limited solely to *the insured* that actually committed the criminal act. Rather, so the argument goes, it applies to all insureds, including so-called "innocent co-insureds." Insurers frequently make this argument for good reason—because many courts accept it.

But despite concluding that no coverage is owed to the innocent co-insured, courts sometimes point out that their decision would have been different if the exclusion at issue had applied to "criminal acts of *the insured*." If so, the exclusion's applicability would have been limited solely to *the insured* that committed the criminal act (the teenage son) and coverage for his parents would have remained available. Likewise, when an exclusion uses the phrase "the insured," and, as a result, does not preclude coverage for an innocent co-insured, courts sometimes point out that the insurer could have used different policy language to achieve a different result. *See, e.g., Travelers Indem. Co. v. Bloomington Steel & Supply Co.*, 718 N.W.2d 888, 895 (Minn. 2006) ("Instead of excluding coverage for bodily injury expected or intended from the standpoint of '*the*' insured, the Travelers' policies could have excluded coverage for bodily injury expected or intended from the standpoint of '*an*' or '*any*' insured.") (emphasis in original).

Numerous decisions abound following this pattern when addressing the scope of various general liability, homeowners, and auto policy exclusions under a host of circumstances. *See, e.g., Am. Family Mut. Ins. Co. v. Corrigan*, 697 N.W.2d 108, 109 (Iowa 2005) (addressing coverage for a parent–insured, for abuse committed by his son, during the operation of a daycare business in the parent's home, in the context of a policy exclusion for bodily injury arising out of violation of any criminal law for which *any* insured is convicted); *Litz v. State Farm Fire & Cas. Co.*, 695 A.2d 566, 572 (Md. 1997) (addressing coverage under the liability section of a homeowner's policy for an insured-husband, for injury to a child being cared for by his insured-wife, in the context of a policy exclusion for bodily injury arising out of business pursuits of *an insured*); *Am. Family Mut. Ins. Co. v. Copeland-Williams*, 941 S.W.2d 625, 629–30 (Mo. Ct. App. 1997) (addressing coverage under the liability section of a homeowner's policy for an insured-wife, for failing to prevent her insured-husband from molesting his step-granddaughter, in the context of a policy exclusion for bodily injury which is either expected or intended from the standpoint of *any insured*); *Hayner Hoyt Corp. v. Utica First Ins. Co.*, 760 N.Y.S.2d 706, 706 (N.Y. App. Div. 2003) (addressing coverage under a commercial general liability policy for an additional insured, for bodily injury to employees of the named insured, in the context of a policy exclusion for bodily injury to an employee of *an insured* if it occurs in the course of employment); *BP Am. Inc. v. State Auto Prop. & Cas. Co.*, 148 P.3d 832, 836–42 (Okla. 2005) (addressing coverage under a commercial general liability policy for an additional insured, for bodily injury caused by a motor vehicle in which the named insured's employee was allegedly at fault, in the context of a policy exclusion for bodily injury arising out of the ownership, maintenance, use, or entrustment to others of any auto owned or operated by or rented or loaned to *any insured*).

Insureds that are denied coverage, and perhaps for a very significant claim, based on the difference between "any" or "an" and "the" may find themselves in disbelief that such seemingly innocuous words could have so much import. Their response may be that the insurer is simply hiding behind a technicality. But courts that uphold the distinction do not see it that way. *See, e.g., Vanguard Ins. Co. v. McKinney*, 459 N.W.2d 316, 319–20 (Mich. Ct. App. 1990) (dismissing the insured's argument that the distinction between "an" insured and "the" insured is "irrelevant semantics").

Perhaps the starkest evidence that a court determining the availability of coverage between the words "any" or "an" and "the" is not just hiding behind a technicality, comes from the highest court of Maine. In *Johnson v. Allstate*, 687 A.2d 642, 644 (Me. 1997), the Supreme Judicial Court of Maine held that no coverage was owed under the liability section of a homeowner's policy to a grandmother for failing to prevent her husband from sexually abusing their granddaughter. A policy exclusion applied to bodily injury intentionally caused by *an insured person*. *Id.* The court held that an exclusion for damages intentionally caused by "an insured person" excludes coverage for damages intentionally caused by *any* insured person. *Id.*

However, *less than one month later*, Maine's Supreme Judicial Court held in *Hanover Insurance Co. v. Crocker*, 688 A.2d 928, 932 (Me. 1997) that coverage was owed under the liability section of a homeowner's policy to an insured-mother for her failure to take steps to prevent an insured-father's sexual abuse of their daughter. A policy exclusion applied to "bodily injury... which is either expected or intended from the standpoint of *the insured.*" *Id.* at 931 (emphasis added). The court held that coverage was owed to the mother because the injury was not expected or intended from her standpoint. *Id.* "Our conclusion is consistent with the majority of other jurisdictions that have held that provisions excluding from coverage injuries intentionally caused by 'the insured' refer to a definite, specific insured, who is directly involved in the occurrence that causes the injury." *Id.*

It would appear that, when a court concludes that "any" means any, thereby precluding coverage for an innocent co-insured, it is being completely faithful to the policy language. But policyholders often say, not so fast. Even if forced to concede that, at least on its face, "any" does mean any, policyholders are likely to argue that coverage nonetheless remains available for innocent co-insureds, because any other outcome would be inconsistent with the policy's "Separation of Insureds" provision.

Most commercial general liability policies and, to a lesser extent, homeowners policies, contain a Separation of Insureds provision—sometimes referred to interchangeably as a "Severability of Interests" provision. A typical Separation of Insureds clause, contained in a commercial general liability policy, provides as follows:

> 7. Separation of Insureds
> Except with respect to the Limits of Insurance, and any rights or duties specifically assigned in this Coverage Part to the first Named Insured, this insurance applies:
> a. As if each Named Insured were the only Named Insured; and
> b. Separately to each insured against whom claim is made or "suit" is brought.

*See, e.g.*, Ins. Servs. Office Props., Inc., Commercial General Liability Coverage Form, No. CG 00011207, § IV7 (2007). "The intent of the severability clause is to provide each insured with separate coverage, as if each were separately insured with a distinct policy, subject to the liability limits of the policy." *Bituminous Cas. Corp. v. Maxey*, 110 S.W.3d 203, 210 (Tex. Ct. App. 2003) (citation omitted).

Not surprisingly, innocent co-insureds, facing the prospect of no coverage because of an exclusion that applies to the conduct of "any insured," point to the Separation of Insureds clause in an effort to prevent such outcome. Their argument is that, to determine the availability of coverage for one insured, based on the conduct of another insured, would not be treating each insured as if they were separately insured with a distinct policy.

There is certainly support for this position. *See Litz v. State Farm Fire & Cas. Co.*, 695 A.2d 566, 572 (Md. 1997) ("This provision [severability clause] is a clear reflection that the parties intended the insurance policy to provide coverage for each named insureds separately. In light of this express severability clause, we construe the business pursuits exception in the Litzes' policy to mean that the business pursuits of 'an' insured disqualify only that insured from coverage in the event of property damage or bodily injury resulting from the business pursuit; other insureds, i.e., those not engaging in a business pursuit, remain covered under the policy."); *see also Premier Ins. Co. v. Adams*, 632 So. 2d 1054, 1057 (Fla. Dist. Ct. App. 1994) ("In accordance with the rules of construction of a contract, the most plausible interpretation is that the exclusionary clause [intentional acts of any insured] is to exclude coverage for the separate insurable interest of that insured who intentionally causes the injury. With this interpretation, all provisions in the policy are given meaning and one provision is not rendered meaningless by the other.").

However, the majority of courts have concluded that the presence of a Separation of Insureds provision does not serve as a basis to afford coverage to an innocent co-insured when the exclusion at issue applies to the conduct of "any insured." *Minkler v. Safeco Ins. Co.*, 232 P.3d. 612, 623 (Cal. 2010); *Argent v. Brady*, 901 A.2d 419, 425 (N.J. Super. Ct. App. Div. 2006). Courts rely on various rationales for this conclusion.

For example, if a Separation of Insureds clause is given effect, then the language of an exclusion, as it relates to "an insured" or "any insured" is "robbed of any meaning." *Argent v. Brady*, 901 A.2d at 426. "[T]he purpose of a severability clause... is designed solely to render the coverage actually provided by the insuring provisions of the policy applicable to all insureds equally, up to coverage limits. The severability clause is not denominated a 'coverage provision,' and it would be unreasonable to find that it operated independently in that capacity to increase the insurance afforded under the insuring provisions of the policy, or to partially nullify existing coverage exclusions." *Id.* at 426–27.

On one hand, "any" meaning any, as used in a policy exclusion, may be one situation where both insurers and policyholders can agree that the court's interpretation was completely faithful to the policy language. On the other hand, any such agreement is likely to be short-lived. Expect a dispute to quickly ensue whether the existence of a Separation of Insureds provision means that "any" really means "the."

## 50-State Survey: Coverage for Innocent Co-Insureds: "Any" Insured vs. "The" Insured and the Severability of Interests Clause

**Alabama:** The Supreme Court of Alabama held that coverage was owed under a fleet policy, to insured-supervisors of an employee, who was fatally injured while driving a vehicle within the scope of his employment for a board of education. *Wilson v. State Farm Mut. Auto. Ins. Co.*, 540 So. 2d 749, 752 (Ala. 1989). The fleet policy, issued to the board of education, contained an exclusion that applied to "any bodily injury to:... any employee of *an insured* arising out of his or her employment." *Id.* at 751 (emphasis added). The court reasoned that the exclusion did not apply to the supervisors because they did not employ the victim. *Id.* at 752. The court also concluded that the addition of a severability of interests clause did "not eliminate the ambiguity that exits in the exclusion where there are multiple insureds and the injured party is an employee of one or some, but not all." *Id.*; *see also Essex Ins. Co. v. Avondale Mills, Inc.*, 639 So. 2d 1339, 1342 (Ala. 1994) (following *Wilson* and holding that the employee exclusion only applied if the insured were sued by its own employees, rather than by those of another insured).

**Alaska:** The Supreme Court of Alaska held that no coverage was owed to the Department of Transportation, as an additional insured on a liability policy issued to an airline, for the death of an airline employee who was struck and killed while driving a snow machine across a runway. *State Dep't of Transp. & Pub. Facilities v. Houston Cas. Co.*, 797 P.2d 1200, 1204 (Alaska 1990). The policy contained an exclusion for "bodily injury... caused by... Aircraft owned, chartered, used, or operated by or on account of *the Insured.*" *Id.* at 1203 (emphasis added). The court held that, "in the absence of a severability of interest clause or other 'clearly stated condition[]' excluding the named insured [airline] from the term 'insured,' we conclude that the parties intended DOT's coverage to be co-extensive with, rather than independent from, [the airline's]." *Id.* at 1204.

**Arizona:** The Court of Appeals of Arizona held that no coverage was owed under the liability section of a homeowner's policy to insured-parents, for negligent supervision of their insured-son, who struck a male in the head with a pipe and was later convicted of aggravated assault. *Am. Family Mut. Ins. Co. v. White*, 65 P.3d 449, 457 (Ariz. Ct. App. 2003). The policy contained a "violation of law" exclusion which stated that "[w]e will not cover bodily injury or property damage arising out of... violation of any criminal law for which *any insured* is convicted." *Id.* at 452 (emphasis added) (alteration in original). "Courts have consistently interpreted the language 'any insured' as expressing a contractual intent to prohibit recovery by innocent co-insureds. Thus, if any one of the insureds [violates the exclusion], no other insureds can recover." *Id.* (quotation omitted) (alteration in original). Of note, the court concluded that "the phrase 'any insured' in an exclusionary clause means something more than the phrase 'an insured,'" with the distinction being that "an" refers to one object and "any" refers to one or more objects of a certain type. *Id.* (quotation omitted). The presence of a severability clause in the policy did not dictate a different result.

**Arkansas:** The Supreme Court of Arkansas held that no coverage was owed under a homeowner's policy to an insured-spouse whose insured-wife committed arson. *Noland v. Farmers Ins. Co.*, 892 S.W.2d 271, 273 (Ark. 1995). The policy contained an exclusion that provided: "[i]f *any insured* directly causes or arranges for a loss of covered property in order to obtain insurance benefits, this policy is void. We will not pay you or *any other insured* for this loss." *Id.* (emphasis added); *see also Bryan v. Employers Nat'l Ins. Corp.*, 742 S.W.2d 557, 557–58 (Ark. 1988) (holding that no coverage was available under a property policy to an innocent business partner-insured whose co-partner-insured committed arson) (policy language excluded coverage for any criminal act by "any insured"); *Brawner v. Allstate Indem. Co.*, No. 4:07-CV-00482, 2008 WL 166951, at *3 (E.D. Ark. Jan. 11, 2008) (following *Noland*). In none of the cases did the court discuss a severability of interests clause.

**California:** The Supreme Court of California held that coverage was owed under the liability section of homeowner's policies to an insured-mother for failing to take reasonable steps to prevent her insured-son from sexually molesting a minor over the course of several years. *Minkler v. Safeco Ins. Co.*, 232 P.3d. 612, 624 (Cal. 2010). The policies contained exclusions for "Personal Liability [coverage]… do[es] not apply to bodily injury or property damage: (a) which is expected or intended by *an insured* or which is the foreseeable result of an act or omission intended by *an insured.*" *Id.* at 617 (emphasis added and alteration in original). The court held "that, in light of the severability clause, Betty would reasonably have expected Safeco's policies, whose general purpose was to provide coverage for each insured's 'legal[] liab[ility]' for 'injury or… damage' to others, to cover her *separately* for her *independent* acts or omissions causing such injury or damage, so long as *her* conduct did not fall within the policies' intentional acts exclusion, even if the acts of *another* insured contributing to the same injury or damage *were* intentional. Especially when informed by the policies that '[t]his insurance applies separately to each insured,' it is unlikely Betty understood that by allowing David to reside in her home, and thus to become an additional insured on her homeowners policies, [she was] *narrowing [her] own coverage* for claims arising from his [intentional] torts. In light of the severability provision, Safeco's intent to achieve that result was not clearly expressed, and the ambiguity must be resolved in the [insured's] favor." *Id.* at 618 (alteration and emphasis in original) (internal quotes omitted). In reaching its decision, the California high court observed that courts nationally are "split on the general issue whether a severability-of-interests provision in a policy covering multiple insureds alters the otherwise collective effect of an exclusion for the acts of 'an' or 'any' insured." *Id.* at 614. The court acknowledged that it was adopting the minority view. *Id.* at 623.

**Colorado:** The Supreme Court of Colorado held that no coverage was owed under the liability section of a homeowner's policy to insured-parents whose insured-son vandalized an elementary school. *Chacon v. Am. Family Mut. Ins.*, 788 P.2d 748, 752 (Colo. 1990). A policy exclusion stated that the insurer would "not pay for property damage… caused intentionally by *any* *insured* who has attained the age of 13." *Id.* at 750 (emphasis added). "The inclusion of a severability clause within the contract is not inconsistent with the creation of a blanket exclusion for intentional acts. Instead, the inquiry is whether the contract indicates that the parties intended such a result." *Id.* at 752 n.6; *see also Swentkowski By and Through Reed v. Dawson*, 881 P.2d 437, 439 (Colo. App. Ct. 1994) ("Dawson contends that *Chacon v. American Family Mutual Insurance Co., supra,* is distinguishable because there the parents were vicariously liable under a statute. This argument is without merit. The supreme court analysis did not turn on the statute's imposition of vicarious liability, but rather, on its interpretation of the phrase 'any insured' in the exclusionary clause to preclude coverage for all insureds when one insured had acted intentionally.").

**Connecticut:** The Appellate Court of Connecticut held that coverage was owed under a liability policy, to an additional insured property owner, for a bodily injury claim brought by an employee of a named insured restaurant tenant, alleging that the property owner failed to properly maintain the grounds. *Sacharko v. Ctr. Ltd. P'ship*, 479 A.2d 1219, 1223 (Conn. App. Ct. 1984). The policy contained an exclusion for "[p]ersonal injury to any employee of the Insured arising out of and in the course of his employment by the insured." *Id.* at 1222 n.4 (alteration in original). "Where a policy contains a severability of interests clause, it is a recognition by the insurer that it has a separate and distinct obligation to each insured under the policy, and that the exclusion under the policy as to employees of the insured is confined to the employee of the insured who seeks protection under the policy." *Id.* at 1222; *see also Nationwide Mut. v. Mazur*, No. CV98–0489231S, 1999 WL 417346, at *10 (Conn. Super. Ct. June 3, 1999) ("The policy's specific use of the words, 'each' and 'an,' as opposed to the determiner 'any,' demonstrates an intent to provide coverage to the insureds separately.").

**Delaware:** A Delaware trial court held that coverage was owed under the liability section of a homeowner's policy to an insured-husband, for claims arising out of the death of a child that drowned while in a home daycare provided by an insured-wife. *McIntosh v. Liberty Mutual Fire Ins. Co.*, No. Civ. A 01C-07–148CL, 2003 WL 22852133, at *2 (Del. Super. Ct. Nov. 19, 2003). A policy exclusion applied to bodily injury "arising out of or in connection with a 'business' engaged in by *an 'insured.'" Id.* at *1 (emphasis added). The court rejected the insurer's argument that there is no distinction between the use of "an" and "any" in the insurance policy and held that, because there was evidence that the husband took no part in the care of the child, there was a genuine issue of material fact as to whether the husband was engaged in the "business" of providing daycare services. *Id.* at *2. The opinion includes no discussion of a severability provision.

**Florida:** The Court of Appeal of Florida held that coverage was owed under the liability section of a homeowner's policy to insured-parents, for negligent supervision of their insured-son, who sexually assaulted a child.

*Premier Ins. Co. v. Adams*, 632 So. 2d 1054, 1057 (Fla. Dist. Ct. App. 1994). A policy exclusion applied to "bodily injury… which is expected or intended by *any* insured." *Id.* at 1055 (emphasis added). The court held that coverage was owed to the parents on account of the policy's severability clause. *Id.* at 1057. "In accordance with the rules of construction of a contract, the most plausible interpretation is that the exclusionary clause is to exclude coverage for the separate insurable interest of that insured who intentionally causes the injury. With this interpretation, all provisions in the policy are given meaning and one provision is not rendered meaningless by the other." *Id.*

**Georgia:** A Georgia District Court held that coverage was owed under a liability policy to an additional insured, for a claim by an employee of the named insured, who was injured in a motor vehicle accident. *Ryder Truck Rental, Inc. v. St. Paul Fire & Marine Ins. Co.*, 540 F. Supp. 66, 73 (N.D. Ga. 1982). A policy exclusion applied to "bodily injury to any employee of *the Insured* arising out of and in the course of his employment by the Insured or to any obligation of the Insured to indemnify another because of damages arising out of such injury." *Id.* at 71 n.1 (emphasis added). The Georgia District Court identified a conflict between various decisions from the Court of Appeals of Georgia concerning the interplay between, among other things, the employee exclusion and the severability of interests clause. *Id.* at 69–70. The court synthesized the decisions and determined that, on one hand, the term "the insured" can be read to mean *any insured*, thereby excluding coverage for all insureds when the injured person is an employee of any insured. *Id.* at 71. However, the court concluded that "when read in light of the severability of interests clause, 'the insured' can be interpreted to refer only to the party seeking coverage under the policy, excluding coverage only when the injured claimant is the employee of the party seeking coverage." *Id.* at 72.

**Hawaii:** A District of Hawaii court held that no coverage was owed under a comprehensive personal liability policy to insured-parents for failing to prevent their insured-son from committing an assault. *Allstate Ins. Co. v. Kim*, 121 F. Supp. 2d 1301, 1308 (D. Haw. 2000). A policy exclusion applied to "bodily injury… which may reasonably be expected to result from the intentional or criminal acts of *an insured person*." *Id.* at 1303 (emphasis added). The court sided with what it described as "the majority of courts" that have held that an exclusion that uses the terms "any insured" or "an insured" "expresses a contractual intent to create joint obligations and preclude coverage to innocent co-insureds, despite the presence of a severability clause." *Id.* at 1308. However, the court also suggested that its opinion may have been different if the severability clause had been specifically denominated as such, and not as a Limits of Liability clause (that contained a severability statement). *Id.* at 1308 n.5; *see also Allstate Ins. Co. v. Davis*, 430 F. Supp. 2d 1112, 1133–34 (D. Haw. 2006) (following *Kim*, but without any discussion of the potential affect of a severability clause); *Nautilus Ins. Co. v. K. Smith Builders, Inc.*, __ F. Supp. 2d __, No. 09–00509, 2010 WL 2541832, at *10 (D. Haw. June 22, 2010) (holding that a severability of insureds clause did not render meaningless an exclusion that used the term "any insured") (examining the history of the separation of insureds clause as support, in part, for its conclusion).

**Idaho:** The Supreme Court of Idaho held that, without regard to certain statutory considerations, no coverage was owed under the property section of a homeowner's policy to an insured-wife, for the destruction of the insured-residence, caused by a fire that was intentionally set by the insured-husband. *Trinity Universal Ins. Co. v. Kirsling*, 73 P.3d 102, 106–07 (Idaho 2003). A policy exclusion applied to "any loss arising out of any act committed: (1) by or at the direction of an *'insured'*; and (2) with the intent to cause a loss." *Id.* at 104 (emphasis added). The court held that, based on the plain and unambiguous language of the policy, the intentional acts exclusion precluded coverage for an innocent co-insured. *Id.* at 106–07. The opinion includes no discussion of a severability provision. As an aside, the court ultimately concluded that coverage was owed for the innocent co-insured, otherwise the policy would have provided less coverage than Idaho's statutory standard fire insurance policy. *Id.* at 106.

**Illinois:** The Appellate Court of Illinois held that coverage was owed under the liability section of a homeowner's policy to an insured-defendant, who co-owned a building along with her insured-brother, for injuries sustained by her brother's wife in a fire at the insured-building. *State Farm Fire & Cas. Co. v. Hooks*, 853 N.E.2d 1, 8–9 (Ill. Ct. App. 2006). A policy exclusion applied to "bodily injury to [named insured] or any insured within the meaning of part a. or b. of the definition of insured." *Id.* at 3. The relevant definition of "insured" provided: "'insured' means [named insured] and, if residents of your household: a. relatives." *Id.* at 2. The court held that coverage was owed to the insured-defendant, notwithstanding that the injured party was an insured under the policy, on account of her status as the resident spouse of a named insured. *Id.* at 6. The court concluded that, on account of the policy's severability clause, the injured party's status as an "insured" is not determined once for the entire policy, but, rather, separately vis-à-vis both named insureds. *Id.* at 9. "[T]he clear import of the term 'applies separately to each insured' contained in the severability clause of the instant policy must be construed to modify the exclusion so as to render the insurer liable for claims brought by a related household member of one named insured against another named insured residing in a separate household." *Id.*; *see also James McHugh Const. Co. v. Zurich American Ins. Co.*, No. 1–09–2135, 2010 WL 1542633, at *5 (Ill. Ct. App. Apr. 13, 2010) (interpreting "the insured," as used in an Employer's Liability exclusion, to mean "the insured seeking coverage," so that both the named insured and additional insured are equally subject to the exclusion) ("If 'the insured' referred only to the named insured... then the additional insured would receive more protection under the policy because the employer's liability exclusion could never apply to it.").

**Indiana:** The Court of Appeals of Indiana held that no coverage was owed under the liability section of a homeowner's policy to an insured-husband for molesting a child in his insured-wife's home daycare center. *T.B. v. Dobson*, 868 N.E.2d 831, 838 (Ind. Ct. App. 2007). A policy exclusion applied, in pertinent part, to "any claim made or suit brought against any insured by: (1) any person who is in the care of any insured because of child care services provided by or at the direction of: (a) *any insured*." *Id.* at 835 (emphasis added). An exception to the exclusion applied, in pertinent part, to "the occasional child care services provided by *any insured*." *Id.* at 836 (emphasis added). The court held that it was "undisputed that [the wife] provided non-occasional child care services to [the minor]. When [the minor] was molested, she was in [the husband's] care because of non-occasional child care services provided by [his wife]. As such, the coverage exclusion applies, and the exception to the exclusion does not." *Id.* at 838. The court rejected the argument that the policy's severability clause dictated a different result. *Id.* at 837.

**Iowa:** The Supreme Court of Iowa held that no coverage was owed to an insured-father, under what appears to be the liability section of a homeowner's policy, for failing to prevent his insured-son from physically injuring a child while in a daycare center located in the father's home. *Am. Family Mut. Ins. Co. v. Corrigan*, 697 N.W.2d 108, 109 (Iowa 2005). The son was convicted of child endangerment. *Id.* at 109–10. The policy contained an exclusion for "bodily injury or property damage arising out of... violation of any criminal law for which *any insured* is convicted." *Id.* at 110 (emphasis added) (alteration in original). "Because the language of the exclusion clearly contemplates its applicability to multiple insureds under the policy, it would be unreasonable to interpret the severability-of-interests clause as the Corrigans suggest: that the clause calls for application of the policy as if [the father] were the sole insured. To interpret the policy in this manner would require this court to conclude the term 'the insured' means the same as 'any insured,' a conclusion we have rejected in the past." *Id.* at 116; *see also IMT Ins. Co. v. Crestmoor Golf Club*, 702 N.W.2d 492, 496–98 (Iowa 2005) (following *Corrigan*).

**Kansas:** The Supreme Court of Kansas held that coverage was owed under the liability section of a homeowner's policy to an insured-husband for negligence that contributed to his insured-wife's killing of a child in their care. *Brumley v. Lee*, 963 P.2d 1224, 1233 (Kan. 1998). A policy exclusion applied to "bodily injury... which is expected or intended by *any* insured." *Id.* at 1227 (emphasis added). The court held that the policy's severability clause created an ambiguity that required a construction that favored the insured. *Id.* at 1230. Looking at various dictionary definitions, the Kansas high court held that "the word 'any' is not materially different from the word 'a' or 'an,' and, contrary to the district court's ruling, [the insurer's] use of 'any' instead of 'an' in its policy does not eliminate the ambiguity created by the policy's severability clause." *Id.* at 1227–28.

**Kentucky:** The Court of Appeals of Kentucky held that no coverage was owed under a homeowner's policy to an insured–paternal grandmother, for failing to prevent her husband, an insured–step-grandfather, from sexually abusing their granddaughter. *K.M.R. v. Foremost Ins. Group*, 171 S.W.3d 751, 755 (Ky. Ct. App. 2005). The policy at issue contained, among others, an exclusion for bodily injury "[r]esulting from any act or omission that is intended by any of you to cause any harm or that any of you could reasonably expect to cause harm." *Id.* at 753. The policy defined "you" as the named insureds and family members and both grandparents were named insureds. *Id.* The court held that a clearly worded exclusion is not treated as ambiguous by the existence of a severability provision. *Id.* at 755; *see also Cincinnati Ins. Co. v. T. & T.R.*, 3:05-CV-792H, 2007 WL 628135, at *2 (W.D. Ky. Feb. 23, 2007) (following *K.M.R.*) ("The exclusions unambiguously operate to preclude coverage to all insureds for liability attributable to the excludable acts of any one of the Insureds."); *see also Am. Nat. Prop. & Cas. Co. v. M. M.*, No. 4:09CV-00079, 2010 WL 3341501, at *5 (W.D. Ky. Aug. 24, 2010) ("[The insurer] carefully drafted its intentional act exclusion using the words 'any insured' which, despite the severability clause, unambiguously excludes coverage to any insured for liability based on the excludable actions of any other insured. Therefore, the Court does not find any ambiguity in [the insurer's] policy due to the severability clause included therein."); *Holzknecht v. Kentucky Farm Bureau Mut. Ins. Co.*, ___S.W.3d___, No. 2009-CA-001022, 2010 WL 3187645, at *7 (Ky. Ct. App. Aug. 13, 2010) (exclusion for "bodily injury" [a]rising out of or in connection with a 'business' engaged in by an 'insured'") ("John David May plainly falls within the scope of the policy's business-pursuits exclusion because it appears that he was involved in the enterprise. We agree that the policy exclusion is unambiguous and broad enough to encompass him. Since severability clauses are not drafted to negate policy exclusions, the existence of that clause in Farm Bureau's policy does not render the exclusion ambiguous.").

**Louisiana:** A Louisiana District Court held that coverage for employees of a title agent, under an errors and omissions policy, for negligence claims brought by a title insurer, alleging that the title agent's escrow accounts were deficient, was not precluded by a policy exclusion for "[a]ny damages arising out of any intentional, dishonest, fraudulent, criminal or malicious act, error or omission by or on behalf of or at the direction of (1) *the insured* or (2) any employee regardless of whether or not qualifying as an insured." *Stewart Title Guaranty Co. v. Kiefer*, 984 F. Supp. 988, 996–97 (E.D. La. 1997) (emphasis added). The court held that, because the exclusion at issue used the term "the insured," claims against an insured are not barred from coverage "solely on the basis of the [excludable] acts of other insureds." *Id.* at 996 (internal quotes omitted and alteration in original). However, the court also made clear that its decision would have been different if the exclusion at issue had used the term "any insured"—even with a separation of insureds provision in the policy. *Id.*;

*see also Kleisch v. R&B Falcon Drilling U.S.A., Inc.*, No. Civ. A. 01–880, 2002 WL 31427381, at *5 (E.D. La. Oct. 29, 2002) ("'severability of interests clause' does not nullify the effect of the employer's liability exclusion which employs the '*any* insured' policy language") (emphasis in original).

**Maine:** The Supreme Judicial Court of Maine held that coverage was owed under the liability section of a homeowner's policy to an insured-mother for failing to take steps to prevent an insured-father's sexual abuse of their daughter. *Hanover Ins. Co. v. Crocker*, 688 A.2d 928, 932 (Me. 1997). A policy exclusion applied to "bodily injury... which is either expected or intended from the standpoint of *the insured*." *Id.* at 931 (emphasis added). The court held that coverage was owed to the mother because the injury was not expected or intended from her standpoint. *Id.* "Our conclusion is consistent with the majority of other jurisdictions that have held that provisions excluding from coverage injuries intentionally caused by 'the insured' refer to a definite, specific insured, who is directly involved in the occurrence that causes the injury." *Id.* One month earlier in *Johnson v. Allstate*, 687 A.2d 642, 644 (Me. 1997) the Supreme Judicial Court of Maine held that no coverage was owed under the liability section of a homeowner's policy to a grandmother for failing to prevent her husband from sexually abusing their granddaughter. A policy exclusion applied to bodily injury intentionally caused by *an insured person*. *Id.* The court held that an exclusion for damages intentionally caused by "an insured person" excludes coverage for damages intentionally caused by any insured person. *Id.* The court rejected the argument that the policy's severability clause dictated a different result. *Id.*; *Huber Engineered Woods, LLC v. Canal Ins. Co.*, 690 S.E.2d 739, 748 (N.C. Ct. App. 2010) (applying Maine law) (discussing *Crocker* and *Johnson*) ("As the Supreme Judicial Court of Maine has determined that 'the insured' refers only to the person or entity seeking coverage, we must apply that definition to the facts of this case.").

**Maryland:** The Court of Appeals of Maryland held that coverage was owed under the liability section of a homeowner's policy to an insured-husband for injury to a child being babysat by his insured-wife. *Litz v. State Farm Fire & Cas. Co.*, 695 A.2d 566, 572 (Md. 1997). A policy exclusion applied to "bodily injury... arising out of business pursuits of *an insured*." *Id.* at 568 (emphasis added). The court held that "[i]n light of th[e] express severability clause, we construe the business pursuits exception in the Litzes' policy to mean that the business pursuits of 'an' insured disqualify only that insured from coverage in the event of property damage or bodily injury resulting from the business pursuit; other insureds, i.e., those not engaging in a business pursuit, remain covered under the policy." *Id.* at 572. In *Standard Fire Ins. Co. v. Proctor*, 286 F. Supp. 2d 567, 575 (D. Md. 2003), the court held that a homeowner's policy exclusion for bodily injury "which is expected or intended by any insured" precluded coverage for an innocent co-insured. The court distinguished *Litz* because it involved an exclusion for the business pursuits of *an* insured, while the exclusion in *Proctor* applied to bodily injury expected or intended by *any* insured. *Id.* at 574. The policy at issue in *Proctor* contained a severability provision. *Id.* at 574–75.

**Massachusetts:** The Appeals Court of Massachusetts held that no coverage was owed under a personal umbrella policy to insured-parents for failing to prevent their insured–minor son from sexually assaulting other minors. *Hingham Mut. Fire Ins. Co. v. Smith*, 865 N.E.2d 1168, 1171 (Mass. App. Ct. 2007). The policy precluded coverage for "bodily injury… arising out of sexual molestation, corporal punishment or physical or mental abuse." *Id.* at 1173. The court rejected the parents' argument that coverage existed for them on the basis that the policy's severability clause required that each insured be treated as having separate coverage. *Id.* "Because the complaint in the underlying action alleges injuries due to sexual molestation, the exclusionary language in the definition of 'bodily injur[ies]' precludes coverage for claims against any insured, even when considered separately, where the claims brought against them would have no basis but for the molestation." *Id.* The *Hingham* Court also distinguished the Supreme Judicial Court's decision in *Worcester Mut. Ins. Co. v. Marnell*, 496 N.E.2d 158 (Mass. 1986), which held that, notwithstanding a homeowner's policy's exclusion for bodily injury arising out of the use of a motor vehicle operated by *any insured*, the policy's severability clause gave rise to coverage for a negligent supervision claim against parents who had supervised a party in which their son became intoxicated, subsequently causing the death of another while operating his motor vehicle. *Id.* According to *Hingham*, "the result in *Marnell* turned on the allocation of risks between homeowner's coverage and automobile liability insurance." *Id.*; *Miles v. Great Northern Ins. Co.*, 656 F. Supp. 2d 218, 224 (D. Mass. 2009) (provision upheld that bars coverage for an innocent co-insured spouse, through the inclusion of the term "any covered person").

**Michigan:** The Supreme Court of Michigan held that no coverage was owed under the liability section of a homeowner's policy to an insured-husband for negligent entrustment of a firearm that led to his insured-wife shooting a neighbor. *Allstate Ins. Co. v. Freeman*, 443 N.W.2d 734, 754–55 (Mich. 1989). A policy exclusion applied to "bodily injury… which may reasonably be expected to result from the intentional or criminal acts of *an insured person* or which is in fact intended by *an insured person*." *Id.* at 739 (emphasis added). The Michigan high court rejected the insured-husband's argument that the exclusion was ambiguous because "an insured" could mean "that insured," "the insured" or "any insured." *Id.* at 737. Instead, the court held that "an insured" unambiguously refers to "any insured." *Id.* The opinion includes no discussion of a severability provision. *See also Gorzen v. Westfield Ins. Co.*, 526 N.W.2d 43, 44–45 (Mich. Ct. App. 1994) (concluding that, even though the policy in *Freeman* did not contain a severability clause, the substance of it was considered by the supreme court and found not to affect the operation of the exclusion); *Vanguard Ins. Co. v. McKinney*, 459 N.W.2d 316, 318–19 (Mich. Ct. App. 1990) (distinguishing *Freeman* and finding coverage for an innocent co-insured, because the exclusion at issue applied to conduct of "the insured," which only precluded coverage for the particular insured that engaged in the conduct).

**Minnesota:** The Court of Appeals of Minnesota held that no coverage was owed under the liability section of a homeowner's policy to insured-parents for their failure to prevent their insured-son from assaulting a neighbor. *SECURA Supreme Ins. Co. v. M.S.M.*, 755 N.W.2d 320, 329 (Minn. Ct. App. 2008). A policy exclusion applied to bodily injury which results "from the criminal acts of *any insured*." *Id.* at 322 (emphasis added). The court rejected the argument that the policy's severability clause dictated a different result. *Id.* at 328–29. The court relied on the Supreme Court of Minnesota's decision in *Travelers Indem. Co. v. Bloomington Steel & Supply Co.*, 718 N.W.2d 888 (Minn. 2006), which stated (admittedly, in *dicta*) that if an insurer wanted to preclude coverage for an innocent co-insured, it could have tied its intentional act exclusion to the conduct of "any insured" or "an insured" instead of "the insured," even with a severability clause contained in the policy. *Id.*

**Mississippi:** A Mississippi District Court held that coverage was owed under a homeowner's policy to an insured-wife for damage caused by her estranged insured-husband's attack on the insured-residence with a baseball bat. *McFarland v. Utica Fire Ins. Co.*, 814 F. Supp. 518, 526 (S.D. Miss. 1992). A policy exclusion applied to "loss which results from an act committed by or at the direction of *an insured* and with the intent to cause a loss." *Id.* at 522 (emphasis added). The court held that the exclusion could be read two ways— that both insureds are denied coverage when one insured causes an intentional loss or that coverage is only precluded for the wrongful insured. *Id.* at 525. In finding that coverage was owed to the innocent-spouse, the court held that "[t]he [insurer] could have cured this ambiguity through clearer or more precise language… or, alternatively, through the addition of a non-severability clause. But, [the insurer's] policy contains no non-severability clause. Instead, on page 1 of the policy, there is found language which states that all insureds under the policy are 'separate insureds.'" *Id.* at 526 (citation omitted).

**Missouri:** The Court of Appeals of Missouri held that no coverage was owed under the liability section of a homeowner's policy to an insured-wife for failing to prevent her insured-husband from molesting his step-grand-daughter. *Am. Family Mut. Ins. Co. v. Copeland-Williams*, 941 S.W.2d 625, 629–30 (Mo. Ct. App. 1997). A policy exclusion applied to "bodily injury… which is either expected or intended from the standpoint of *any insured*." *Id.* at 627 (emphasis added). The court held that, even in the face of a severability clause, the phrase "any insured" unambiguously established that the insureds' rights are jointly and not severally held when one insured intends or expects bodily injury to another. *Id.* at 629–30. *But see Shelter Mut. Ins. Co. v. Brooks*, 693 S.W.2d 810, 811–12 (Mo. 1985) (holding that, based on a severability of interest clause, an automobile policy's liability exclusion for bodily injury to *the insured* only excluded bodily injury of the insured seeking coverage).

**Montana:** The Supreme Court of Montana held that no coverage was owed under a farm and ranch liability policy to insured-parents for failing to prevent their insured-son from committing a rape. *Farmers Union Mut. Ins. v. Kienenberger*, 847 P.2d 1360, 1361 (Mont. 1993). A policy provision stated that the insurer would pay damages for bodily injury caused by an "occurrence," defined as "an accident… neither expected nor intended from the standpoint of *the insured*." *Id.* (emphasis added). Notwithstanding that the coverage applied to damages neither expected nor intended from the standpoint of "the insured," the court held that no coverage was owed to the parents because the injuries "were caused by *an insured person's* intentional act, and the insurance contract clearly and unambiguously excludes coverage for intentional torts." *Id.* The opinion includes no discussion of a severability provision. However, other decisions from the Supreme Court of Montana, involving policies that contain severability clauses, have concluded that policy provisions are interpreted from the standpoint of the insured seeking coverage. *E.g., Swank Enters., Inc. v. All Purpose Servs., Ltd.*, 154 P.3d 52, 56 (Mont. 2007); *Travelers Ins. Co. v. Am. Cas. Ins. Co.*, 441 P.2d 177, 180 (Mont. 1968).

**Nebraska:** The Supreme Court of Nebraska held that no coverage was owed under the property section of a homeowner's policy to an insured-wife, for the destruction of the insured-residence, caused by a fire that was intentionally set by an insured-husband. *Volquardson v. Hartford Ins. Co.*, 647 N.W.2d 599, 606 (Neb. 2002). A policy exclusion applied to "any loss arising out of any act committed: (1) By or at the direction of *an insured*; and (2) With the intent to cause a loss." *Id.* at 604 (emphasis added). The court rejected the argument that only the phrase "any insured" contained in an intentional acts exclusion, and not "an insured," could serve to preclude coverage to an innocent co-insured. *Id.* at 605. The opinion includes no discussion of a severability provision.

**Nevada:** A Nevada District Court held that no coverage was owed under the liability section of a mobilehome policy to an insured-wife for her failure to prevent her insured-husband from sexually assaulting a minor. *Allstate Ins. Co. v. Foster*, 693 F. Supp. 886, 889 (D. Nev. 1988). A policy exclusion applied to "any bodily injury… which may reasonably be expected to result from the intentional or criminal acts of *an insured person* or which is in fact intended by an insured person." *Id.* at 887 (emphasis added). Noting that "A" or "an" is used in the sense of "any" and applied to more than one individual object, whereas "the" applies to the subject spoken of, the court held that "[s]ince the Allstate Mobilehome Policy excludes coverage for harm resulting from the intentional or criminal 'acts of *an* insured person,' the insurance policy excludes coverage to any other insureds… for liability arising from the harm which is directly attributable to the intentional or criminal act." *Id.* at 887. The opinion includes no discussion of a severability provision.

**New Hampshire:** The Supreme Court of New Hampshire held that coverage was owed under the liability section of a homeowner's policy to insured-parents for failing to prevent their insured-son from assaulting a minor. *Pawtucket Mut. Ins. Co. v. Lebrecht*, 190 A.2d 420, 423 (N.H. 1963). A policy exclusion applied to "injury… caused intentionally by or at the direction of *the Insured*." *Id.* at 422 (emphasis added). Noting that the policy used the term "the Insured" in certain provisions and "any Insured" or "an Insured" in others, the court held that it was "of the opinion that the provisions excluding from liability coverage injuries intentionally caused by 'the Insured' was meant to refer to a definite, specific insured, namely the insured who is involved in the occurrence which caused the injury and who is seeking coverage under the policy." *Id.* at 423. The policy contained a severability of interest clause but the court did not address what impact it would have on an exclusion that applied to "any Insured" or "an Insured." *Id.* at 422.

**New Jersey:** The Supreme Court of New Jersey held that no coverage was owed under the liability section of a homeowner's policy to insured-grandparents for failing to prevent their insured-son from sexually assaulting his brother's daughter while in her grandparents' home. *Villa v. Short*, 947 A.2d 1217, 1224 (N.J. 2008). Policies at issue excluded coverage for "any bodily injury… which may reasonably be expected to result from the intentional or criminal acts of *an insured person* or which is in fact intended by an insured person." *Id.* at 1222 (emphasis added). The court held that the policy excluded coverage for all insureds for damages caused by the intentional or criminal acts of an insured. *Id.* at 1224. The court rejected the argument that the policy's severability clause dictated a different result. *Id.* at 1225.

**New Mexico:** No instructive authority.

**New York:** The Supreme Court of New York, Appellate Division, held that no coverage was owed under a commercial general liability policy to an additional insured for bodily injury to employees of the named insured. *Hayner Hoyt Corp. v. Utica First Ins. Co.*, 760 N.Y.S.2d 706, 706 (N.Y. App. Div. 2003). A policy exclusion applied to "bodily injury to an employee of *an insured* if it occurs in the course of employment." *Id.* (emphasis added). The court held that the term "an insured" is unambiguous and encompassed the named insured and the additional insured. *Id.* Thus, coverage was precluded for the additional insured for claims by employees of the named insured. *Id.* The dissent would have found coverage for the additional insured on the basis of the "separability of insureds doctrine" (although it did not cite to a severability provision in the policy). *Id.* at 707 (Piggott, Jr., P.J. and Pine, J., dissenting); *see also DRK, LLC v. Burlington Ins. Co.*, 2010 WL 2572561, at *1 (N.Y. App. Div. June 29, 2010) (upholding an exclusion for "bodily injury" to an employee of *any insured*) (specifically rejecting a separation of insureds provision as a basis to preclude the exclusion's applicability to a party that was not the underlying plaintiff's employer); *Howard & Norman Baker, Ltd. v. Am. Safety Cas. Ins. Co.*, 904 N.Y.S. 2d 770 (N.Y. App. Div. 2010) (same). *But see Shelby Realty, LLC v. National Surety Corp.*, No. 06 Civ. 3260, 2007 WL 1180651, at *4 (S.D.N.Y. Apr. 11, 2007) (reaching the opposite conclusion as *Hayner Hoyt* on the basis that the Employee Exclusion at issue must be read in conjunction with the policy's Separation of Insureds clause); *Ostrowski v. American Safety Indem. Co.,* No. 07-CV-3977, 2010 WL 3924679, at *6 (E.D.N.Y. Sept. 30, 2010) (following *Shelby*) ("The 'Separation of Insureds' Clause limits our reading of the Employee Exclusion to individual insureds, as though each is the only insured under the policy. Thus, the Employee Exclusion does not apply to [Hi-Tower] unless one of [Hi-Tower's] employees is injured during the course of his employment. Since [Ostrowski] worked for [ENY] and not for [Hi-Tower], his employment is not relevant to [Hi-Tower's] coverage.") (alteration in original).

**North Carolina:** A North Carolina District Court held that coverage was owed under a liability policy to an additional insured, for a claim by an employee of the named insured, who was injured when he fell from a tractor-trailer owned by the additional insured. *Penske Truck Leasing Co. v. Republic Western Ins. Co.,* 407 F. Supp. 2d 741, 752 (E.D.N.C. 2006). A policy exclusion applied to "'Bodily injury' to: a. An 'employee' of *the 'insured'* arising out of and in the course of: (1) Employment by the 'insured.'" *Id.* at 750. (emphasis added). The court based its decision on the inclusion of a severability of interests provision contained in the policy. *Id.* However, the court also noted that "[i]f the exclusion barred coverage for bodily injury to an employee of 'any' insured, a different analysis may be required." *Id.*

**North Dakota:** The Supreme Court of North Dakota held that no coverage was owed under the liability section of a homeowner's policy to an insured-wife for negligently failing to prevent her insured-husband from sexually assaulting a child in the wife's home daycare center. *Northwest G.F. Mut. Ins. Co. v. Norgard,* 518 N.W.2d 179, 183 (N.D. 1994). A policy exclusion applied to "bodily injury… arising out of sexual molestation… by or at the direction of *an insured,* an insured's employee or any other person involved in any capacity in the day care enterprise." (emphasis added). The court's decision rested on two rationales. First, the breadth of the sexual molestation exclusion—it applies when anyone connected to the operation of the daycare center commits an act of sexual molestation. *Id.* at 183. Second, North Dakota law allows a contract to be explained by reference to "the circumstances under which it was made and the matter to which it relates"—"the increase in legal actions involving sexual abuse of children by adults who are not strangers to the children, including caretakers, is dramatic." *Id.* However, it appears that, without these rationales, the court could have found otherwise, stating that "we believe Northwest rolls the dice by insisting that the policy is clear on its face and by not attempting in the policy itself to more carefully reconcile the severability clause and the exclusions." *Id.* at 183.

**Ohio:** The Supreme Court of Ohio held that coverage was not precluded under a homeowner's or umbrella policy issued to insured-parents for their alleged negligence in failing to prevent their insured-son from stabbing a neighbor. *See Safeco Ins. Co. of Am. v. White*, 913 N.E.2d 426 (Ohio 2009). The exclusions at issue applied, in part, to bodily injury "expected or intended by *an insured*" and "[a]ny injury caused by a violation of a penal law or ordinance committed by or with the knowledge or consent of *any insured*." *Id.* at 430. (emphasis added). The court concluded that its finding, that intentional-act and illegal-act exclusions are inapplicable to acts of negligence related to intentional torts, is a continuation of and consistent with its approach to "examine each act on its own merits." *Id.* at 436 (citation omitted). At least one of the policies at issue contained a severability of insurance clause, but it played no part in the court's analysis.

**Oklahoma:** The Supreme Court of Oklahoma held that no coverage was owed under a commercial general liability policy to an additional insured for bodily injury caused by a motor vehicle in which the named insured's employee was allegedly at fault. *BP America, Inc. v. State Auto Prop. & Cas. Co.*, 148 P.3d 832, 842 (Okla. 2005). The policy contained an exclusion for "'bodily injury'… arising out of the ownership, maintenance, use or entrustment to others of any… 'auto'… owned or operated by or rented or loaned to *any insured*." *Id.* at 833 (emphasis added). The court held that the term "any insured" in the Auto Exclusion precluded coverage for all automobile occurrences attributed to any of the insureds. *Id.* at 839. The court rejected the argument that the policy's separation of insureds clause dictated a different result. *Id.* at 841–42; *see also Farmers Alliance Mut. Ins. Co. v. Willingham*, No. 08-CV-0532, 2009 WL 3429768, at *6 (N.D. Okla. Oct. 20, 2009) (following *BP America* and holding that the term "one or more insureds," as used in an exclusion, means the same as "any insured").

**Oregon:** The Court of Appeals of Oregon held that no coverage was owed under the liability section of a homeowner's policy to an insured-wife, for negligently failing to prevent her insured-husband, a convicted sex offender, from being alone in the house with the wife's granddaughter. *Ristine v. Hartford Ins. Co.*, 97 P.3d 1206, 1209 (Or. Ct. App. 2004). The husband sexually abused his wife's granddaughter during a sleep-over. *Id.* at 1207. The policy contained an exclusion for "bodily injury… arising out of sexual molestation." *Id.* The court concluded that the policy contained no wording that limited the exclusion to claims that arose out of sexual molestation *by the insured*. *Id.* at 1208. To the contrary, the court observed that other policy exclusions were expressly predicated on the conduct of *the insured* or *an insured*. *Id.* at 1209. "The policy refers to claims arising out of sexual molestation without reference to any limitation as to who committed the act of molestation. Thus, the policy appears to state that the exclusion is based on the nature of the act, not the identity of the actor." *Id.* The court rejected the argument that the policy's severability clause dictated a different result. *Id.* at 1209–10.

**Pennsylvania:** The Superior Court of Pennsylvania held that coverage was precluded under a personal umbrella liability policy to insured-parents for allegedly failing to prevent their insured-son from going on a shooting spree in which he killed five people. *Donegal Mut. Ins. Co. v. Baumhammers*, 893 A.2d 797, 819 (Pa. Super. Ct. 2006), *aff'd in part, rev'd in part, on other grounds*, 938 A.2d 286 (Pa. 2007). Policy exclusions applied to bodily injury or damage "caused by the intentional or purposeful act of *any insured*" and bodily injury or damage arising out of a criminal act of "any insured" whether or not such insured is convicted of a crime. *Id.* at 805. The court held that "the criminal act exclusion clearly states that the insurance policy does not apply to bodily or personal injury arising out of a malicious or criminal act of any insured whether or not such insured is convicted of a crime. Similarly, coverage is excluded for bodily or personal injury caused by the intentional or purposeful act of any insured. The bodily and personal injuries suffered by Plaintiffs arose from the intentional, malicious, and criminal acts of an insured, Richard Baumhammers." *Id.* at 819. The opinion includes no discussion of a severability provision. *See also Strouss v. Fireman's Fund Ins. Co.*, No. Civ. A. 03–5718, 2005 WL 418036, at *6 (E.D. Pa. Feb. 22, 2005) (holding that a severability clause did not render ambiguous an exclusion that applied to "bodily injury… which is expected or intended by one or more 'insureds'") ("as a matter of law… the obligations in the intentional injury exclusion are joint, rather than several"); *Becker v. Farmington Cas. Co.*, 1:08-CV-2228, 2010 WL 2898810 (M.D. Pa. July 22, 2010) (following Pennsylvania law that the phrases "any insured" or "an insured" plainly and unambiguously bar coverage for all insureds based on the actions of one insured); *Pa. Manuf. Assoc. Ins. Co. v. Aetna Cas. & Sur. Ins. Co.*, 233 A.2d 548, 550 (Pa. 1967) (considering the affect of a severability clause and rejecting the argument that an exclusion for "bodily injury… of any employee of *the insured*" only operated to exclude coverage for injury to those employees that were employed by the insured seeking coverage) (emphasis added); *Scottsdale Ins. Co. v. The City of Easton*, No. 09–1815, 2010 WL 1857358, at *9 (3rd Cir. May 11, 2010) (applying Pennsylvania law) (following *PMA*).

**Rhode Island:** The Supreme Court of Rhode Island held that coverage was owed under a general liability policy to a real estate manager for damage to an owner's property under its management. *Metro Props. v. Nat'l Union Fire Ins. Co.*, 934 A.2d 204, 210 (R.I. 2007). The property owner, the named insured under the policy, sued the real estate manager, who also qualified as an insured. *Id.* at 206. The court held that a policy exclusion for "'Property damage' to: (1) Property you own, rent, or occupy" did not preclude coverage to the real estate manager because it did not own, rent, or occupy the property that experienced damage. *Id.* at 209. While the court was not required to interpret the scope of an exclusion that applied to "any insured" or "an insured," its decision was based on its observation that "[s]everal courts that have considered this issue extend coverage, despite exclusionary language, based upon either a cross-liability provision or a severability-of-interests clause." *Id.* at 209–10.

**South Carolina:** The Court of Appeals of South Carolina held that no coverage was owed under the liability section of a homeowner's policy to the estate of an insured-father for negligence that led to the drowning death of his insured-daughter (and himself). *Allstate Ins. Co. v. Mangum*, 383 S.E.2d 464, 466 (S.C. Ct. App. 1999). A policy exclusion applied to "bodily injury to *an insured person.*" *Id.* at 465 (emphasis added). The court rejected the argument that, based on the policy's separability clause, the term "insured person" means only such person who is at fault and against whom the action is brought for negligence. *Id.* at 466. "Th[e] [separability] doctrine is not applicable to the policy before us because the obligation set forth in the insuring clause limits coverage to 'damages because of bodily injury… *covered by this part of the policy.*' The policy then clearly states that it does not cover bodily injury to an insured person and, under the terms of the policy, Inglis Paige Peurifoy [the daughter] is clearly an insured person." *Id.*

**South Dakota:** The Supreme Court of South Dakota held that coverage was precluded under the liability section of a homeowner's policy to insured-parents for bodily injury that their insured-son caused in a motor vehicle accident. *Great Cent. Ins. Co. v. Roemmich*, 291 N.W.2d 772, 775 (S.D. 1980). It was alleged that the parents failed to prevent their insured-son from operating the motor vehicle, when they knew of his propensity to do so in a reckless and careless manner. *Id.* at 773. A policy exclusion applied to "bodily injury… arising out of the ownership, maintenance, operation, use, loading or unloading of: …any motor vehicle owned or operated by, or rented or loaned to *any Insured.*" *Id.* at 774 (emphasis added). The court rejected the argument that the policy's severability of insurance clause dictated a different result. *Id.*; *see also EMCASCO Ins. Co. v. Diedrich*, 394 F.3d 1091 (8th Cir. 2005) (applying South Dakota law) (holding that homeowner's policy exclusion for bodily injury or property damage "which is expected or intended by *one or more* 'insureds'" precluded liability coverage to insured-parents for sexual assault committed by their insured-son and rejecting the argument that the policy's severability of insurance clause dictated a different result.)

**Tennessee:** The Court of Appeals of Tennessee held that coverage was not precluded under the liability section of a homeowner's policy to an insured-husband for the loss of a substantial amount of money that was intentionally burned by his insured-wife. *Tenn. Farmers Mut. Ins. Co. v. Evans*, No. 1, 1990 WL 64532, at *4 (Tenn. Ct. App. May 18, 1990). The wife discovered the money in a safe deposit box, believed it to be illegally obtained and burned it. *Id.* at *2. It was determined that the money did not belong to her husband. *Id.* A policy exclusion applied to "bodily injury or property damage expected or intended by *an insured person.*" *Id.* at *3 (emphasis added). The court concluded that the exclusion was in "obvious conflict" with the policy's severability of insurance clause. *Id.* at *4. Therefore, coverage was owed for the husband, unless it was later determined that he expected or intended the damage in question. *Id.*; *see also Tuturea v. Tennessee Farmers Mut. Ins. Co.,*

No. W2009-01866-COA-R3-CV, 2010 WL 2593627, at *18 (Tenn. Ct. App. June 29, 2010) ("[A]n insurance company is generally not obligated to provide liability coverage to an innocent co-insured under an insurance policy that excludes coverage for losses resulting from the intentional act of 'an insured' or 'any insured' absent structural or textual ambiguity created by additional policy provisions.").

**Texas:** The Court of Appeals of Texas held that no coverage was owed under a commercial general liability policy to all insureds for bodily injury caused by a motor vehicle accident. *Bituminous Cas. Corp. v. Maxey*, 110 S.W.3d 203, 215 (Tex. App. 2003). Coverage was precluded on the basis of a policy exclusion for "'bodily injury'… arising out of the ownership, maintenance, use or entrustment to others of any… 'auto'… owned or operated by or rented or loaned to '*any insured*.'" *Id.* at 209. The court concluded that the exclusion precluded coverage for bodily injury arising out of any conduct within the scope of the exclusion, by any entity or person insured by the policy, regardless of which insured is seeking coverage. *Id.* at 214. The court rejected the argument that the policy's separation of insureds clause dictated a different result. *Id.*

**Utah:** The Supreme Court of Utah held that no property coverage was owed under a homeowner's policy to an insured-wife for the destruction of her home on account of a fire that was intentionally set by her insured-husband. *Utah Farm Bureau Ins. Co. v. Crook*, 980 P.2d 685, 688 (Utah 1999). Coverage was precluded on the basis of a policy exclusion for "Intentional loss, meaning any loss arising out of any act committed: (1) By or at the direction of *an* '*insured*'; and (2) With the intent to cause a loss." *Id.* at 687 (emphasis added). The court acknowledged that other courts have concluded that "an" is ambiguous, based on various dictionary definitions. *Id.* However, the Supreme Court of Utah concluded that, when reading the policy as a whole ("Insured" means you and residents of your household and "you" means the named insured and the spouse if a resident of the same household), "'an insured' in the… Policy may refer to multiple persons by definition, and intentional property damage by any insured is excluded under the Policy." *Id.* at 688. The opinion includes no discussion of a severability provision.

**Vermont:** The Supreme Court of Vermont held that coverage was not precluded under a homeowner's policy to insured-parents for their alleged negligence in failing to prevent their insured-son from sexually abusing minors in the parents' home daycare business. *N. Sec. Ins. Co. v. Perron*, 777 A.2d 151, 166 (Vt. 2001). A policy exclusion applied to bodily injury "expected or intended by *the insured*." *Id.* at 155 (emphasis added). The Vermont high court acknowledged that "[c]ourts construing similar policy language have concluded that, when a provision uses the article 'the,' the provision applies only to claims brought against the particular insured named in the claim. Conversely, when the exclusionary language refers to intentional acts of 'an insured,' courts have uniformly concluded that the exclusion applies to all claims which arise from the intentional acts of any one insured, even though the claims are stated against another insured." *Id.* at 163. Based on this pronouncement, the court concluded that, because the exclusion precluded coverage for intentional acts of *the insured*, and not *an insured*, it did not preclude coverage to the parents for their son's acts of sexual abuse. *Id.* at 163–64. Despite the inapplicability of the "expected or intended" exclusion, coverage for the parents was ultimately precluded on the basis of the policy's "business-pursuits" exclusion. *Id.* at 164–66.

**Virginia:** The Supreme Court of Virginia held that no coverage was owed under an umbrella policy to an insured-husband-passenger for bodily injuries sustained in an automobile accident in which his wife was the driver. *Gov't Employees Ins. Co. v. Moore*, 580 S.E.2d 823, 830 (Va. 2003). Coverage was precluded on the basis of a policy exclusion for "personal injury to *any insured*." *Id.* at 825 (emphasis added). The court rejected the argument that the policy's severability of interest clause dictated a different result, reasoning that "[t]o do so would contradict the obvious intention of the parties and… convert the umbrella policy from a third-party excess liability policy into a first-party personal injury policy. There is no authority for applying the severability clause in such a manner." *Id.* at 830. In *Montgomery Mutual Insurance Company v. Dyer*, 170 F. Supp. 2d 618, 625 (W.D. Va. 2001), the court held that property coverage was owed to one insured under a homeowner's policy for a fire that was intentionally set by another insured. The exclusion at issue was for "*an insured* who commits or directs an act with the intent to cause loss." *Id.* (emphasis added). The relevant section of the policy did not contain a severability clause. The court acknowledged that many courts have interpreted intentional loss exclusions to preclude coverage for innocent co-insureds. *Id.* at 624. However, the court held that, unlike exclusions in other cases, the exclusion before it placed emphasis on the person committing the act, not on the act itself. *Id.*

**Washington:** The Court of Appeals of Washington held that no coverage was owed under a homeowner's policy to an insured-wife, for failing to protect a foster child from physical abuse inflicted by her insured-husband. *Mutual of Enumclaw Ins. Co. v. Cross*, 10 P.3d 440, 445 (Wash. App. Ct. 2000). The policy contained an exclusion for bodily injury "which is expected or intended by *an insured*." *Id.* at 441–42 (emphasis added). The court held that it agreed with those cases that have concluded that an exclusion that is clear and specific prevails over a severability clause. *Id.* at 445; *see also Truck Ins. Exchange v. BRE Properties, Inc.*, 81 P.3d 929, 933 (Wash. App. Ct. 2003) (citing *Cross* with approval but holding that an exclusion for bodily injury to "an 'employee' of *the insured* arising out of and in the course of employment" only excluded coverage for employees of "the insured" and not "an insured") ("When an insurance policy contains an exclusion for 'the insured,' each insured is entitled to read the policy as if applying only to that insured."); *Pacific Ins. Co. v. Catholic Bishop of Spokane*, 450 F. Supp. 2d 1186, 1202 (E.D.

Wash. 2006) ("Washington courts seem to differentiate between exclusionary clauses written in terms of the '*the* insured' and similar clauses written in terms of '*an* insured.'") (emphasis in original).

**West Virginia:** The U.S. Court of Appeals for the Fourth Circuit, applying West Virginia law, held that coverage was not precluded under an automobile policy to an omnibus insured for bodily injury sustained by an employee of the named insured. *Pepsi-Cola Bottling Co. of Charleston v. Indem. Ins. Co. of N. Am.*, 318 F.2d 714, 716 (4th Cir. 1963) (applying West Virginia law). A policy exclusion applied to "bodily injury to or sickness, disease or death of any employee of *the insured*." *Id.* at 715 (emphasis added). The Court of Appeals concluded that the exclusion did not apply as no reason was shown why an insured should not be indemnified against a claim of one outside *that insured's employment. Id.* at 716. The court also found it "strongly persuasive, if not conclusive" that the policy's severability of interests clause "compels consideration of each insured separately, independently of every other insured." *Id.* The severability of interests clause does not allow employment "to be attributed to another insured who in truth is not the employer." *Id.*

**Wisconsin:** The Supreme Court of Wisconsin held that no coverage was owed under a homeowner's policy to an insured-wife for her alleged negligence in failing to prevent her insured-husband's intentional sexual contact with a minor. *J.G. & R.G. v. Wangard*, 753 N.W.2d 475, 491 (Wis. 2008). Coverage was precluded on the basis of a policy exclusion for damages "arising out of an act intended by *any covered person* to cause personal injury." *Id.* at 480 (emphasis added). The court rejected the argument that the policy's severability clause dictated a different result. *Id.* at 487.

**Wyoming:** The Supreme Court of Wyoming held that no coverage was owed under the liability section of a homeowner's policy to insured–cattle-handlers for accidentally shooting the named insured's minor son. *Page v. Mountain W. Farm Bureau Mut. Ins. Co.*, 2 P.3d 506, 509 (Wyo. 2000). A policy exclusion applied to "bodily injury... [s]ustained by you [named insureds] or any insured as defined in paragraphs (1) and (2) of the definition of insured ['Insured means you and if residents of your household: 1. Your relatives; and 2. Minors in the care of those named above.'] (household exclusion)." *Id.* The minor child was neither a relative of the cattle-handlers nor a minor in their care. *Id.* The court rejected the argument that the policy's severability of interest clause limited the household exclusion to the household of the individual insured seeking coverage. *Id.* "Because [the injured minor] is so defined as an insured, the household exclusion clause clearly excludes the injuries he suffered from coverage... regardless of who is responsible for them." *Id.*

# CHAPTER
# 10

## Is Emotional Injury "Bodily Injury"?

It is axiomatic that a general liability insurance policy provides coverage for "bodily injury" and "property damage." Under many such policies, "bodily injury" is defined as "bodily injury, sickness or disease sustained by a person, including death resulting from any of these at any time." *See, e.g.*, INS. SERVS. OFFICE PROPS., INC., COMMERCIAL GENERAL LIABILITY COVERAGE FORM, No. CG 00011207, § V3 (2007).

In most general liability claim scenarios it is obvious whether the underlying claimant has sustained "bodily injury"—the blood or broken bones are a give-away. As such, whether damages are being sought for "bodily injury" is a non-issue. There are, however, situations where it is not so obvious. Most notably, when the underlying claimant alleges that he or she has sustained emotional injury, an issue sometimes arises whether such injury is "bodily injury." The issue also arises in the context of claims under the liability coverage part of homeowner's policies—which also provide coverage for "bodily injury." The legal issue is the same under both policy types, has arisen under a multitude of factual scenarios and courts have adopted several rationales for resolving it.[1]

In addition, the emotional injury/bodily injury issue also arises with frequency under automobile policies (especially uninsured and underinsured motorist), since, like general liability and homeowner's liability policies, automobile policies also provide coverage for "bodily injury." Whether emotional injury constitutes "bodily injury" usually arises under automobile policies in the context of a claimant alleging that he or she sustained emotional injury on account of witnessing—either from within or outside the vehicle—a loved one killed or injured in an accident.[2]

---

1. As used herein, for convenience, the term "emotional injury" also includes such injuries as emotional distress, mental distress, humiliation, and the like.
2. As used herein, for convenience, such witnesses to the accident are referred to as "bystanders," regardless of their physical presence at the time of the accident.

Claims often arise under this scenario for the following reason. Most automobile policies contain a limit of liability for "bodily injury" sustained by "each person" (such as $100,000) and a higher limit for bodily injury in "each accident" (such as $300,000). When the claim by a person who unquestionably sustained "bodily injury" has exhausted the policy's "each person" limit of liability, the bystander will often seek to qualify as a person who *also* sustained bodily injury. This is so in an effort by the bystander to recover under a separate "each person" limit of liability available under the policy. Since the policy has a $300,000 "each accident" limit of liability, coverage remains available for other "persons" who also sustained "bodily injury." *See State Farm Mut. Auto. Ins. Co. v. Jakupto*, 881 N.E.2d 654, 656 (Ind. 2008) (describing the significance of this issue as "obvious").

Despite the obvious differences between general liability, homeowners, and automobile policies, they share a similarity concerning the fundamental question whether emotional injury qualifies as "bodily injury." For this reason, courts examining the issue under one policy type sometimes look for guidance from decisions that have addressed it under another policy type.

The majority of courts that have addressed whether emotional injury qualifies as "bodily injury," under a policy that defines such term as "bodily injury (or bodily harm), sickness or disease," have determined that it does not. *See Evans v. Farmers Ins. Exch.*, 34 P.3d 284, 286 (Wyo. 2001) (noting that the "overwhelming majority" of jurisdictions hold that bodily injury encompasses only physical harm) (citation omitted). A common rationale for this conclusion is that the term "bodily" suggest something physical and corporeal. *See Moore v. Cont'l Cas. Co.*, 746 A.2d 1252, 1254–55 (Conn. 2000). Other courts reach the conclusion on the basis that "bodily injury" is narrower than "personal injury," which covers an affront or insult to a person's reputation or sensibilities. *Smith v. Animal Urgent Care, Inc.*, 542 S.E.2d 827, 831 (W. Va. 2000).

A notable exception to the majority rule is the New York Court of Appeals, which held that emotional injury does qualify as "bodily injury." New York's highest court reasoned that the term bodily injury was ambiguous and declined to rewrite the definition to read *"bodily* sickness" and *"bodily* disease." *Lavanant v. Gen. Accident Ins. Co. of Am.*, 595 N.E.2d 819, 822 (N.Y. 1992).

While a substantial majority of courts have concluded that emotional injury does not qualify as "bodily injury," the issue is not always that simple nor is that general pronouncement always the last word. Rather, many of those same courts have also held that "bodily injury" encompasses emotional injuries that are accompanied by physical manifestation. *See Allstate Ins. Co. v. Wagner-Ellsworth*, 188 P.3d 1042, 1051 (Mont. 2008) ("Many courts have concluded in insurance interpretation cases like this one that the term 'bodily injury' is ambiguous when applied to physical problems arising from a mental injury.").

For example, in *Voorhees v. Preferred Mutual Insurance Co.*, 607 A.2d 1255, 1262 (N.J. 1992), the Supreme Court of New Jersey held that a claim under a homeowner's policy issued to parents, for emotional distress accompanied by physical manifestations suffered by their child's teacher, on account of disparaging comments made by the parents, qualified as "bodily injury." The policy defined "bodily injury" as "bodily harm, sickness or disease to a person, including required care, loss of services and death resulting therefrom." *Id.* at 1258. The court held that the teacher's headaches, stomach pains, nausea, depression and body pains qualified as "bodily injury," concluding that such term was ambiguous as it relates to emotional distress accompanied by physical manifestations, and, therefore, should be interpreted in favor of the insured. *Id.* at 1261–62.

In some jurisdictions that have held that "bodily injury" encompasses emotional injuries accompanied by physical manifestation, a subsequent concern arises—how to define what constitutes adequate physical manifestation. *See Pekin Ins. Co. v. Hugh*, 501 N.W.2d 508, 512 (Iowa 1993) (noting that "every emotional disturbance has a physical aspect and every physical disturbance has an emotional aspect") (citation omitted). One court described the reason for such concern as follows:

> We have not been anxious to expand the availability of damages for emotional distress… . This reluctance has arisen from the concern that claims of mental anguish may be speculative and so likely to lead to fictitious allegations that there is a potential for abuse of the judicial process… .Thus, we have been careful to limit the availability of such damages to "those plaintiffs who prove that emotional injury occurred under circumstances tending to guarantee its genuineness."

*Twin Cities Glaziers Architectural Metals & Glass Workers Local #1324 v. W. Nat'l Ins. Group*, No. C3-96-1741, 1997 WL 53033, at *2 (Minn. Ct. App. Feb. 11, 1997) (quoting *Lickteig v. Alderson, Ondov, Leonard & Sween, P.A.*, 556 N.W.2d 557, 560 (Minn. 1996)); *see also Voorhees*, 607 A.2d at 1262 ("[A]lthough a few plaintiffs may be tempted to assert emotional distress with accompanying physical manifestations more often, that will not necessarily obligate insurers to undertake unbounded duties to defend and indemnify. When an emotional distress claim is not supported factually, the insurer can and should move to dismiss the meritless claims.").

In *SL Industries, Inc. v. Am. Motorists Insurance Co.*, 607 A.2d 1266, 1274 (N.J. 1992), the Supreme Court of New Jersey acknowledged the difficulty in distinguishing between mental and physical injuries and concluded that the phrase "bodily injury" "should be analyzed on a case-by-case basis to determine whether the alleged [mental] injuries are sufficiently akin to physical injuries to render the term 'bodily injury' ambiguous." Here, the court held that sleeplessness was an emotional, and not physical, injury. *Id.* at 1273. The *SL Industries* Court distinguished this scenario from its companion case, *Voorhees*, *supra*, which concluded that headaches, stomach pains, nausea, depression, and body pains qualified as physical manifestation of emotional distress. *Voorhees*, 607 A.2d at 1262.

As *SL Industries* concluded, whether emotional injury rises to the level of physical injury should be, and, in fact is, analyzed on a case-by-case basis. *See Allstate Ins. Co. v. Wagner-Ellsworth*, 188 P.3d 1042, 1051 (Mont. 2008) ("Courts have struggled with these distinctions, focusing on the facts of each case.").

For example, in *Admiral Insurance Co. v. Hosler*, 626 F. Supp. 2d 1105, 1108 (D. Colo. 2009), the Colorado District Court addressed coverage for claims by condominium residents against the developer for construction defects that led to excessive noise on account of the residents' ability to hear sounds coming from other units. The court addressed whether the underlying plaintiffs had established physical manifestation of their alleged emotional harm to trigger coverage for "emotional harm." *Id.* at 1113.

Adopting *SL Industries*'s mandate, that the question whether emotional injury rises to the level of physical injury should be analyzed on a case-by-case basis, the *Hosler* Court concluded that none of the plaintiffs' injuries qualified as physical. *Id.* at 1114–19. The court rejected the following conditions as physical manifestation of emotional injury: frustration, embarrassment, and dissatisfaction, *id.* at 1115; sleeplessness, *id.* at 1116–17; feelings of paranoia, anxiety, dazed confusion, lack of safety, and embarrassment. *Id.* at 1118; *see also Economy Preferred Ins. Co. v. Quanxi Jia*, 92 P.3d 1280, 1284 (N.M. Ct. App. 2004) ("We do not resolve what would be sufficient to constitute bodily injury; we simply hold that crying, shaking, and sleep difficulties are not enough."). *But see Trinh v. Allstate Ins. Co.*, 37 P.3d 1259, 1264 (Wash. Ct. App. 2002) (finding that genuine issues of material fact were raised whether weight loss, hair loss, fragile fingernails, loss of sleep, headaches, stomach pains, and muscle aches are physical manifestations of emotional injury); *State Farm Fire & Cas. Co. v. Westchester Inv. Co.*, 721 F. Supp. 1165, 1167 (C.D. Cal. 1989) (finding that dry throat, rise in body temperature, and knot in stomach were sufficient physical manifestations of emotional injury to constitute bodily injury).

While many courts hold that emotional injury, when accompanied by physical manifestation, qualifies as "bodily injury," at least one state has not been willing to go so far. *See Babalola v. Donegal Group, Inc.*, No. 1:08-CV-621, 2008 WL 4006721, at *3 (M.D. Pa. Aug. 26, 2008) (holding that a claim under a homeowner's policy issued to a hospital employee, for emotional distress, including physical manifestation, sustained by a co-worker who was allegedly subjected to inappropriate sexual touching by and interaction with the insured, did not qualify as "bodily injury"); *id.* ("Pennsylvania courts have soundly rejected the contention that policy definitions of injury or bodily injury encompass mental or emotional harm.... Generally, a complaint alleging only physical manifestations of mental or emotional harm likewise fails to trigger coverage under a policy insuring against claims brought for 'bodily injury.'") (citation and internal quotation omitted).

Lastly, one consideration that may arise in the automobile context, that is not relevant when the issue arises in the general liability or homeowner's context, is that the bystander's claim may be viewed as derivative of, and not separate from, the injured party's claim. In other words, if bystanders are not considered separate *persons* who sustained "bodily injury," coverage for them would be precluded, even if emotional injury qualifies as "bodily injury." *See Farm Bureau Ins. Co. v. Martinsen*, 659 N.W.2d 823, 828 (Neb. 2003) ("There is no evidence or suggestion in the record that the [the parents] developed physical conditions causally related to the emotional distress they suffered as a result of the accident, and we do not consider whether this scenario, if established, could impose separate per-person liability on Farm Bureau whether or not the $300,000 per-person limit had been exhausted. Upon the record before us, we determine that the [parents'] emotional distress is a byproduct of and entirely dependent upon the bodily injury to [their son].")

## 50-State Survey: Is Emotional Injury "Bodily Injury"?

**Alabama:** An Alabama District Court held that a claim under a commercial general liability policy issued to a bank, for emotional injury suffered by an individual whose claim under a credit life policy was denied, on account of the bank's failure to ask certain questions on the policy's application, qualified as "bodily injury." *Am. Economy Ins. Co. v. Fort Deposit Bank*, 890 F. Supp. 1011, 1017 (M.D. Ala. 1995). The policy defined "bodily injury" as "bodily injury, sickness or disease sustained by a person, including death resulting from any of these at any time." *Id.* at 1015. The court concluded that "sickness" or "disease" encompassed mental anguish. *Id.* at 1017.

**Alaska:** An Alaska District Court held that a claim for emotional distress suffered by a mother, who did not witness her son's fatal collision, qualified as "bodily injury" for purposes of an automobile insurance policy. *Gov't Employees Ins. Co. v. Encelewski*, No. A94–0211, 1995 WL 25427 (D. Alaska Jan. 13, 1995). The policy defined "bodily injury" as "bodily injury to a person, including resulting sickness, disease or death." *Id.* at *1. The court found that the definition of "bodily injury" was unambiguous and rejected the insurer's argument that "sickness, disease, or death" is only that which "result[s]" from a bodily injury and that emotional distress is a sickness that results from a mental or non-bodily injury. *Id.* at *4. The court concluded that "[a]lthough 'painful study' of the insurance policy might lead to [the insurer's] conclusion, the objectively reasonable expectations of the insured are that this provision covers negligent infliction of emotional distress claims with physical manifestations." *Id.*

**Arkansas:** No instructive authority.

**Arizona:** The Court of Appeals of Arizona held that a claim under an underinsured motorist policy, for exposure to HIV-infected blood by trained medical professionals who were providing emergency medical care to automobile accident victims, did not qualify as "bodily injury." *Transamerica Ins. Co. v. Doe*, 840 P.2d 288, 291 (Ariz. Ct. App. 1992). While the policy did not define "bodily injury," the court found the term to be unambiguous and interpreted it according to its "ordinary meaning," namely, physical injuries, impairment of physical condition, sickness, disease, or substantial pain. *Id.* The court concluded that no "bodily injury" had been sustained within the meaning of the policy based on exposure to the blood because no physical injury, sickness, disease, or substantial pain resulted therefrom. *Id.* The court also rejected the argument that anxiety and emotional distress resulting from fear of contracting AIDS qualified as bodily injury. *Id.* at 292. "Appellant's failure to adduce evidence tending to establish the existence of any physical harm or medically identifiable effect from their exposure to a disease requires a finding that, as a matter of law, the necessary prerequisite for recovering damages for emotional distress is lacking." *Id.* (citation and internal quotation omitted).

**California:** The Court of Appeal of California held that a claim under a general liability policy issued to a restaurant, for emotional distress suffered by an employee who was injured in an automobile accident, but whose health insurance application had not been submitted by her employer to the insurer, did not qualify as "bodily injury." *Aim Ins. Co. v. Culcasi*, 229 Cal. App. 3d 209, 220 (Cal. Ct. App. 1991). The policy defined "bodily injury" as "bodily injury, sickness or disease" (although it was not considered by the court as there was no record reference to support it). *Id.* at 218. Following a lengthy review of dictionary definitions and case law nationally, the court held that "[g]iven the clear and ordinary meaning of the word 'bodily,' we find the term 'bodily injury' unambiguous. It means physical injury and its consequences. It does not include emotional distress in the absence of *physical* injury." *Id.* at 220 (emphasis in original); *see also Chatton v. Nat'l Union Fire Ins. Co.*, 13 Cal. App. 2d 318, 327 (Cal. Ct. App. 1992) (holding that "bodily injury" did not include "emotional distress"); *Waller v. Truck Ins. Exchange*, 900 P.2d 619, 632 (Cal. 1995) (holding that because the "occurrence" itself must directly cause any "bodily injury," emotional distress and attendant physical injury, caused by economic loss, did not qualify as "bodily injury").

**Colorado:** The Supreme Court of Colorado held that a claim under a comprehensive business liability policy issued to a city, for emotional distress suffered by a police officer on account of wrongful termination, did not qualify as "bodily injury." *Nat'l Cas. Co. v. Great Sw. Fire Ins. Co.*, 833 P.2d 741, 747 (Colo. 1992). The policy defined "bodily injury" as "bodily injury, sickness, or disease sustained by any person which occurs during the policy period, including death at any time resulting therefrom." *Id.* at 746. The Colorado high court declined to follow those few courts nationally that have determined that "bodily injury" includes emotional distress in the absence of physical impact, fear, or physical harm or physical manifestation of emotional distress. *Id.* at 747. Since no allegations of any physical injury, physical contact, or pain were made, the former police officer's claim for emotional distress was not within the bodily injury coverage provided by the policy. *Id.*; *see also Williams v. State Farm Mut. Auto. Ins. Co.*, 195 P.3d 1158, 1161 (Colo. App. 2008) (following *Great Sw.* and holding that emotional injury, without physical manifestation, did not qualify as "sickness" under Colorado's uninsured motorist statute).

**Connecticut:** The Supreme Court of Connecticut held that a claim under a homeowner's policy, for emotional distress suffered by the insured's sister, on account of the insured obtaining a line of credit secured by a home that was jointly owned by his sister, did not qualify as "bodily injury." *Moore v. Cont'l Cas. Co.*, 746 A.2d 1252, 1257 (Conn. 2000). The policy defined "bodily injury" as "bodily harm, sickness or disease… including required care, loss of services and death resulting therefrom." *Id.* at 1254. The court reached its decision on the following bases: (1) "bodily," as used in the English language, strongly suggests something physical and corporeal; (2) nonbodily or noncorporeal torts are contemplated by "Personal Injury" coverage; and (3) the majority rule nationally is that bodily injury does not include emotional distress unaccompanied by physical harm. *Id.* at 1254–56. The Connecticut high court acknowledged that emotional distress might ordinarily be accompanied by some physical manifestations. *Id.* at 1257. Nonetheless, "[t]he question in this case is the legal meaning of 'bodily injury' as defined in the policy. It is not the medical or scientific question of the degree to which the mind and the body affect each other." *Id.*; *see also Taylor v. Mucci*, 952 A.2d 776, 781–82 (Conn. 2008) (following *Moore* and holding that emotional distress, without accompanying physical harm, did not constitute "bodily injury" for purposes of a bystander claim under an automobile policy); *Allstate Inc. Co. v. Burnard*, No. 3:08cv603, 2010 WL 1332002 (D. Conn. Mar. 31, 2010) (discussing *Moore* and concluding that it acknowledged the possibility that an allegation of emotional distress, with accompanying symptoms, such as psoriasis, could qualify as "bodily injury").

**Delaware:** No instructive authority.

**Florida:** A Florida District Court held that a claim under a commercial general liability policy issued to a staffing company, for depression suffered by a client who was inappropriately touched by a temporary employee assigned by the staffing company, qualified as "bodily injury." *Prof'l Staffing v. Illinois Union Ins. Co.*, No. 8:04-cv-793-T-30EAJ, 2005 WL 2290243, at *1 (M.D. Fla. Sept. 19, 2005). The policy defined "bodily injury" as "bodily injury, sickness or disease sustained by a person, including death resulting from any of these at any time." *Id.* The court concluded that, notwithstanding that the victim never testified that she experienced any physical pain, the violation of one's person through sexual battery, which results in such debilitating conditions as depression and post-traumatic stress disorder, constitutes a "bodily injury." *Id.* The *Prof'l Staffing* Court distinguished *Allstate Insurance Co. v. Clohessy*, 32 F. Supp. 2d 1333 (M.D. Fla. 1998), question certified by 199 F.3d 1293 (11th. Cir. 2000), *rev. dism.* by 763 So. 2d 1042 (Table) (Fla. 2000), which held that, while emotional distress did not constitute "bodily injury" under an automobile policy, such emotional distress did not involve direct physical harm. Rather, it arose from witnessing an accident involving a relative. *Id.* n.2. By contrast, *Prof'l Staffing* involved physical harm, irrespective of whether it manifested into physical pain. *Id.*

**Georgia:** A Georgia District Court held that a claim under a commercial general liability policy issued to a real estate developer, for emotional injury suffered by potential buyers of a lot in a residential development, on account of race discrimination, did not qualify as "bodily injury." *Auto-Owners Ins. Co. v. Robinson*, No. 3:05-CV-109, 2006 WL 2583356, at *3 (M.D. Ga. Sept. 6, 2006). The policy defined "bodily injury" as "bodily injury, sickness or disease sustained by a person, including death resulting from any of these at one time." *Id.* at *2. The court held that no coverage was owed because the underlying plaintiffs did not allege that the humiliation, embarrassment, and emotional distress that they sustained were the result of a physical injury. *Id.* at *3. Further, the court rejected the argument that "bodily injury" includes physical manifestation of emotional distress. *Id.* at *3; *see also Nationwide Mut. Fire Ins. Co. v. Somers*, 591 S.E.2d 430, 435 (Ga. Ct. App. 2003) (holding that no coverage was owed under a general liability policy issued to a cemetery, for a claim brought by a mother, whose son's grave was not perpetually care for, because "bodily injury" is limited to physical injury to the body and does not include nonphysical, emotional, or mental harm).

**Hawaii:** The Supreme Court of Hawaii held that claims by immediate family members, for negligent infliction of emotional distress on account of the death of their son, husband, and father, qualified as "bodily injury" under an automobile policy. *First Ins. Co. of Haw. v. Lawrence*, 881 P.2d 489, 494 (Haw. 1994). As the policy did not define the term "bodily injury," the court substituted "accidental harm," as used in the statute governing required automobile coverage. "Accidental harm" was defined as "bodily injury, death, sickness, or disease caused by a motor vehicle accident to a person." Hawaii's top court was persuaded by the Court of Appeals of New York's decision in *Lavanant v. Gen. Acc. Ins. Co. of Am.*, 595 N.E.2d 819, 822 (N.Y. 1992), which held that the average person reading an insurance policy would not conclude that mental anguish was excluded from the ambit of sickness. *Id.* at 494; *see also Allstate Ins. Co. v. Gadiel*, No. 07–00565 DAE KSC, 2008 WL 4830847, at *6 (D. Haw. Nov. 7, 2008) (citing *Lawrence*) ("Plaintiff additionally contends that Argus does not allege sufficient facts demonstrating physical injury and, instead, merely asserts a claim for emotional distress. Even if true, this argument is irrelevant. For purposes of insurance coverage in Hawai'i, bodily injuries include emotional distress.").

**Idaho:** An Idaho District Court held that a claim under a truckers occupational accident policy issued to a truck driver, for psychological counseling necessitated by an accident, qualified as "bodily injury." *Reyerson v. Nat'l Union Fire Ins. Co.*, No. CV-06–493-E-BLW, 2008 WL 974922, at *5 (D. Idaho Apr. 8, 2008). The insured suffered nightmares, nausea, stomach pain, fatigue, and hypertension, among other ailments, on account of post-traumatic stress disorder brought on by the accident. *Id.* at *4. The policy did not define "bodily injury." *Id.* at *3. Noting that Idaho courts have not specifically addressed or defined "bodily injury," the court examined the split on the issue nationally. *Id.* at *3-4. The District Court followed the Supreme Court of New Jersey's decision in *SL Industries, Inc. v. Am. Motorists Ins. Co.*, 607 A.2d 1266 (N.J. 1992) and held that the term "bodily injury," as used in the policy, was ambiguous as it was unclear whether "bodily injury" applied to psychological and/or emotional injuries resulting in physical manifestations. *Id.* at *4.

**Illinois:** The Appellate Court of Illinois held that a claim under an automobile insurance policy issued to a medical transportation provider, for strong anxiety and fear suffered by a client that was sexually assaulted in the course of transport, did not qualify as "bodily injury." *SCR Med. Transp. Servs., Inc. v. Browne*, 781 N.E.2d 564, 571 (Ill. App. Ct. 2002). The policy defined "bodily injury" as "bodily injury, sickness or disease sustained by a person, including death that results from any of these." *Id.* at 570. Following a survey of Illinois decisions, the court concluded that, when a policy defines "bodily injury" as "bodily injury," and not "injury" alone, the definition is restricted to actual physical injury. *Id.* at 571; *see also Commercial Union Ins. Co. v. Image Control Prop. Mgmt.*, 918 F. Supp. 1165, 1171 n.8 (N.D. Ill. 1996) ("In light of the complaint's failure to allege physical injury, we need not decide whether emotional distress falls within the definition of bodily injury when the distress is manifested by physical injury.").

**Indiana:** The Supreme Court of Indiana held that the emotional distress sustained by a wife and children, on account of being passengers in an automobile in which their husband and father was severely injured, qualified as "bodily injury" under an underinsured motorist policy. *State Farm Mut. Auto. Ins. Co. v. Jakupto*, 881 N.E.2d 654, 658–59 (Ind. 2008). The policy defined "bodily injury" as "bodily injury to a person and sickness, disease or death which results from it." *Id.* at 656. The Indiana high court was persuaded by *Wayne Township Board of School Commissioners v. Indiana Insurance Co.*, 650 N.E.2d 1205 (Ind. Ct. App. 1995) and held that the average layperson would conclude that mental anguish comes within the ambit of "sickness." *Id.* at 658. However, the Supreme Court of Indiana also concluded that bodily injury does not include emotional injury unless it arises from a bodily touching—which was the case with the wife and children at issue as they were present in the automobile at the time of the accident. *Id.* at 658–59; *see also State Farm Mut. Auto. Ins. Co. v. D.L.B.*, 881 N.E.2d 665, 666 (Ind. 2008) (holding, on the same day as *Jakupto*, that emotional distress, even accompanied by physical manifestation, did not qualify as bodily injury under an automobile policy because the bystander seeking coverage did not suffer impact, force, or harm to his body).

**Iowa:** The Supreme Court of Iowa held that a bystander claim for emotional distress qualified as "bodily injury" for purposes of an underinsured motorist policy. *Pekin Ins. Co. v. Hugh*, 501 N.W.2d 508, 511 (Iowa 1993). The policy defined bodily injury as "bodily harm, sickness or disease, including death that results." *Id.* at 510. The court held that "[u]nlike the loss of consortium claim, an injury the bystander suffers is not one that results from an injury to another person. Rather, the injury is directly to the bystander as a result of the bystander seeing the accident and reasonably believing that the direct victim of the accident would be seriously injured or killed. In addition, the emotional distress must be serious. That is, emotional distress should ordinarily be accompanied with *physical* manifestations of the distress." *Id.* at 511 (internal quotation omitted). The bystander claim was therefore subject to a separate "per person" limit of liability. *Id.*

**Kansas:** The Tenth Circuit Court of Appeals, applying Kansas law, held that a claim under a commercial general liability policy, issued to a real estate agency/financial advisor, for anxiety, worry, and mental and emotional distress suffered by clients from whom investment funds were misappropriated, did not qualify as "bodily injury." *ERA Franchise Sys., Inc. v. N. Ins. Co.*, No. 99–3022, 2000 U.S. App. LEXIS 2493, *16 (10th Cir. Feb. 17, 2000). The policy defined "bodily injury" as "bodily injury, sickness or disease." *Id.* at *10. The court held that emotional injury did not qualify as "bodily injury." *Id.* at *16. "We agree with the majority of courts and conclude the phrase 'bodily injury' standing alone or defined as 'bodily injury, sickness or disease' is unambiguous and extends coverage to physical harm only. The majority view that the term 'bodily' modifies the terms 'sickness' and 'disease' is the more logical interpretation." *Id.* In *Travelers Casualty & Surety Co. v. Rage Administrative & Marketing Services, Inc.*, 42 F. Supp. 2d 1159, 1168 (D. Kan. 1999), the court held that humiliation, embarrassment, emotional distress, and mental anguish, sustained as a result of race discrimination, did not qualify as "bodily injury," defined under a commercial general liability policy as "bodily injury, sickness or disease." While the court did not formally address whether physical manifestation of emotional injury qualified as bodily injury, the court did state that there was no evidence that the insurer "failed to undertake a good faith analysis of all information known to it or reasonably ascertainable by inquiry and investigation in order to determine the possibility of coverage for physical manifestations of [emotional] injury." *Id.*

**Kentucky:** The Supreme Court of Kentucky held that no coverage was owed under a professional liability policy issued to a cemetery for claims that it interred bodies in already occupied graves. *Employers Ins. of Wausau v. Martinez*, 54 S.W.3d 142, 145 (Ky. 2001). The court based its decision on an exclusion for bodily injury caused by willful violation of a penal statute. *Id.* However, a dissenting opinion concluded that the majority erred by applying the exclusion. *Id.* at 146 (Johnstone, J., dissenting). Among other reasons, the dissent looked to the definition of "bodily injury"—"sickness or disease sustained by any person"—and noted that, under Kentucky law, the tort of infliction of intentional distress does not depend on the occurrence of bodily injury to be actionable. *Id.* Thus, the dissent concluded: "The exclusion in question applies only to 'bodily injury.' The exclusion does not, and cannot under Kentucky law, apply to the plaintiffs' claims for intentional infliction of emotional distress. A number of jurisdictions are in accord and hold that the term 'bodily injury' in insurance contracts does not encompass claims for mental injury." *Id.* at 147 (citations omitted).

**Louisiana:** The Supreme Court of Louisiana held that a claim by a wife and her children, for emotional distress sustained on account of the death of her husband and the children's father, did not qualify as "bodily injury" for purposes of an underinsured motorist policy. *Hebert v. Webre*, 982 So. 2d 770, 777 (La. 2008). The policy defined "bodily injury" as "physical bodily injury to a person and sickness, disease or death which results from it." *Id.* at 773. In reaching its conclusion, the Louisiana high court looked closely at its decision in *Crabtree v. State Farm Ins. Co.*, 632 So. 2d 736 (La. 1994). *Id.* at 774. In *Crabtree*, the court held that mental anguish constituted "bodily injury" under an automobile policy that defined the term as "bodily injury to a person, and sickness, disease or death which results from it." *Id.* (quoting *Crabtree*, 632 So. 2d at 739). The *Crabtree* Court concluded that such definition was circular as the term being defined was used in the definition. *Id.* at 775 (quoting *Crabtree*, 632 So. 2d at 744). The *Crabtree* Court also concluded that, if the definition of "bodily injury" were intended to cover only external, physical injuries, then it could have been drafted in a more restrictive manner. *Id.* The *Hebert* Court, distinguishing the policy language before it from that which was at issue in *Crabtree*, concluded "that the addition of the word 'physical' is sufficient under *Crabtree* to differentiate a 'bodily injury' sustained in a physical manner, which would be entitled to separate per person limits, from an injury which is emotional in nature and, though might have physical consequences, is not a 'physical' bodily injury." *Id.* at 777.

**Maine:** The Supreme Judicial Court of Maine held that a bystander claim for emotional distress may qualify as "bodily injury" for purposes of an underinsured motorist policy. *Ryder v. USAA Gen. Indem. Co.*, 938 A.2d 4, 9 (Me. 2007). The policy defined "bodily injury" as "bodily harm, sickness, disease or death." *Id.* at 6. Finding that the definition of "bodily injury" was ambiguous, the court concluded that the words "sickness" and "disease" were not modified by the word "bodily," but, rather, served to expand coverage beyond "bodily harm." *Id.* at 7. Turning to the terms "sickness" and "disease," the court held that a bystander claim for emotional distress will qualify as "bodily injury," and trigger a separate per-person limit, if the claimant can "show that [it] suffered emotional distress that was serious" and that "the distress constitutes a diagnosable sickness or disease." *Id.* at 9.

**Maryland:** The Court of Appeals of Maryland held that a parents' claim for emotional distress on account of the death of their son did not qualify as "bodily injury" for purposes of an automobile policy. *Daley v. United Servs. Auto. Ass'n,* 541 A.2d 632, 636 (Md. 1988). The policy defined "bodily injury," in pertinent part, as "bodily injury, sickness or disease, including death resulting therefrom." *Id.* at 633. Basing its decision entirely on the policy language, the court held that, since the parents suffered no separate and distinct bodily injuries of their own, the insurer's obligation for all damages suffered by the parents and their son was limited to the policy's "each person" limit. *Id.* at 636. The Maryland high court acknowledged that the Court of Special Appeals held in *Loewenthal v. Security Insurance Co. of Hartford,* 436 A.2d 493 (Md. Ct. Spec. App. 1991) that bodily injury encompasses a claim for pain, suffering, and mental anguish. *Id.* However, the court distinguished *Loewenthal* because it involved a broad duty to defend under a general liability policy and not the application of policy limits. *Id.*

**Massachusetts:** The Supreme Judicial Court of Massachusetts held that a claim under a homeowner's policy issued to parents, for mental pain and anguish suffered by their daughter's teacher, on account of being defamed by the parents, did not qualify as "bodily injury." *Allstate Ins. Co. v. Diamant,* 518 N.E.2d 1154, 1157 (Mass. 1988). The policy defined "bodily injury" as "bodily injury, sickness or disease, including resulting death, care and loss of services." *Id.* at 1155. The court held that the term "bodily injury" was "unambiguous and understood to mean hurt or harm to the human body, contemplating actual physical harm or damage to the human body." *Id.* at 1157 (citation omitted). In *McNeill v. Metro. Prop. & Liab. Ins. Co.,* 650 N.E.2d 793, 796 (Mass. 1995), the Supreme Judicial Court of Massachusetts held that a bystander claim under an automobile policy, for emotional distress that exacerbated a father's diabetic condition, and led to his development of an ulcer, did not qualify as bodily injury. *See also Richardson v. Liberty Mut. Fire Ins. Co.,* 716 N.E.2d 117, 121 (Mass. App. Ct. 1999) (citing *Diamant* and *McNeill* and holding that bodily injury as used in an insurance policy includes only actual physical injuries to the human body and the consequences thereof).

**Michigan:** The Court of Appeals of Michigan held that a claim under a homeowner's policy, for emotional injuries caused by the insured's defamatory statements, did not qualify as "bodily injury." *Fitch v. State Farm Fire and Cas. Co.,* 536 N.W.2d 273, 275 (Mich. Ct. App. 1995). The policy defined "bodily injury," in part, as "physical injury, sickness, or disease to a person." *Id.*

The policy also stated that "bodily injury" excluded emotional and mental disorder unless it arose out of actual physical injury. *Id.* The court held that "[u] nder Michigan law, when mental injury is alleged, at least some physical manifestation of the injury is required in order to bring it within the definition of 'bodily injury.'" *Id.* In *Meridian Mutual Insurance Co. v. Conti Development Corp.*, No. 1:97-CV-904, 1998 U.S. Dist. LEXIS 7133, at *9 (W.D. Mich. Apr. 22, 1998), the court followed *Fitch* and rejected the argument that the decision was based on the express exclusion from the definition of "bodily injury" for emotional distress unless it arose out of actual physical injury. "[T]he *Fitch* court only cited this portion of the policy [the emotional distress exclusion] as an alternative reason for finding in favor of the insurance company." *Id.*

**Minnesota:** The Supreme Court of Minnesota held that a claim under a general liability policy, issued to an insurance agent, for emotional distress suffered by a customer upon learning, after a serious automobile accident, that the agent had not procured automobile insurance for her, did not qualify as "bodily injury." *Garvis v. Employers Mut. Cas. Co.*, 497 N.W.2d 254, 257 (Minn. 1993). The policy defined "bodily injury" as "bodily injury, sickness, or disease sustained by a person." *Id.* The court held that "emotional distress with appreciable physical manifestations can qualify as 'bodily injury' within the meaning of the insurance policy." *Id.* However, the court also concluded that the plaintiff's complaint did not allege any physical manifestation of emotional distress. *Id.*; *see also Mattson v. CSC Ins. Agency, Inc.*, No. C6-01–1409, 2002 Minn. App. LEXIS 186, at *6–7 (Minn. Ct. App. Feb. 5, 2002) (finding that claims of depression, anxiety, and sleeping problems constituted only emotional problems and did not satisfy the physical manifestation test, designed to assure the genuineness of the alleged emotional distress).

**Mississippi:** A Mississippi District Court held that a claim under a homeowner's policy issued to the director of the Mississippi Bureau of Narcotics, for emotional distress sustained by individuals on account of the insured's dissemination of false information about them to the press, did not qualify as "bodily injury." *Allstate Ins. Co. v. Melton*, 482 F. Supp. 2d 775, 782 (S.D. Miss. 2007). The policy defined "bodily injury" as "bodily harm, sickness or disease." *Id.* at 781. The insured argued that, under Mississippi law, because emotional distress damages for negligent infliction of emotional distress are available only if the plaintiff proves physical manifestation of injury or demonstrable physical harm, then a charge of negligent infliction of emotional distress must imply physical "bodily" injury of some sort. *Id.* at 782. The court concluded that, even if the insured's premise were correct, "physical manifestations of emotional distress, as contrasted with physical harm inflicted from some outside source, do not constitute 'bodily injury' under [the insurer's] policy." *Id.*

**Missouri:** The Court of Appeals of Missouri held that a claim under a homeowner's policy, for emotional distress sustained by individuals, on account of the insureds' recommendation of a life insurance agent that ultimately committed fraud, did not qualify as "bodily injury." *Citizens Ins. Co. of Am. v. Leiendecker*, 962 S.W.2d 446, 452 (Mo. Ct. App. 1998). The policy defined "bodily injury" as "bodily harm, sickness or disease, including required care, loss of services and death that results." *Id.* at 451. The court cited a litany of cases nationally and followed the majority rule: "[T]he over-whelming majority of jurisdictions which have considered the issue hold that 'bodily injury' standing alone or defined in a policy as 'bodily injury [or harm], sickness or disease' is unambiguous and encompasses only physical harm." *Id.* at 452; *see also Am. Family Mut. Ins. Co. v. Wagner*, No. 05–4394-CV-C-NKL, 2007 WL 1029004, at *3 (W.D. Mo. Mar. 29, 2007) (rejecting the argument that emotional harm that includes a component of physical harm is "bodily injury," but decision based solely on the specific policy language).

**Montana:** The Supreme Court of Montana held that a bystander claim for emotional distress, accompanied by stress, migraine headaches, and a rapid heart beat upon hearing a siren, qualified as "bodily injury" for purposes of an automobile policy. *Allstate Ins. Co. v. Wagner-Ellsworth*, 188 P.3d 1042, 1051 (Mont. 2008). The policy defined "bodily injury" as "physical harm to the body, sickness, disease or death." The Montana high court overruled its decision in *Jacobsen v. Farmers Union Mutual Insurance. Co.*, 87 P.3d 995 (Mont. 2004), and held that "bodily injury" includes mental or psychological injury that is accompanied by physical manifestations. *Id.* at 1051. However, the court main-tained that, in the case of purely emotional injuries, without physical manifestation, "bodily injury" connotes solely a physical problem. *Id.*

**Nebraska:** The Supreme Court of Nebraska held that a bystander claim for emotional distress did not qualify as "bodily injury" for purposes of an auto-mobile policy. *Farm Bureau Ins. Co. v. Martinsen*, 659 N.W.2d 823, 827–28 (Neb. 2003). The policy defined "bodily injury" as "injury to a person's body and includes sickness, disease or death which results from it." *Id.* at 827. The court held that "a 'bodily injury' that could give rise to a separate per-person claim must be a physical, as opposed to a purely emotional, injury." *Id.* "There is no evidence or suggestion in the record that the [the parents] developed physical conditions causally related to the emotional distress they suffered as a result of the accident, and we do not consider whether this scenario, if established, could impose separate per-person liability on Farm Bureau whether or not the $300,000 per-person limit had been exhausted. Upon the record before us, we determine that the [parents'] emotional distress is a byproduct of and entirely dependent upon the bodily injury to [their son]." *Id.* at 828. The bystander claim was therefore not subject to a separate "per person" limit of liability. *Id.*

**Nevada:** The Ninth Circuit Court of Appeals, applying Nevada law, addressed, but did not answer, whether a claim under a homeowner's policy for emotional distress sustained by a minor, on account of sexual abuse com-mitted by her stepfather, qualified as "bodily injury." *State Farm Fire & Cas. Co. v. Pickard*, 849 F.2d 1220, 1222 (9th Cir. 1998). The policy defined "bodily injury" as "bodily harm, sickness or disease." *Id.* at 1221. The court acknowledged a split among courts nationally whether the term "bodily injury" includes emotional distress. *Id.* at 1222. However, the court concluded that it did not need to reach the issue because, even if "bodily injury" included emotional distress, coverage would be precluded by the policy's "household members" exclusion (denying coverage to relatives living in the same household as the named insured). *Id.*

**New Hampshire:** The Supreme Court of New Hampshire held that a claim under what appears to be a general liability policy, issued to a mobilehome seller, for physical discomfort, emotional pain and suffering, aggravation, and embarrassment, sustained by owners of a mobile home, on account of the negligent design or installation of its vapor barrier that produced cold, dampness, clamminess, and a musty smell, did not qualify as "bodily injury." *Artcraft of N.H., Inc. v. Lumberman's Mut. Cas. Co.*, 497 A.2d 1195, 1196 (N.H. 1985). The policy defined "bodily injury" as "bodily injury, sickness or disease." *Id.* at 1195. Concluding that "sickness" or "disease" are "more than a mere temporary indisposition," the court held: "The record before us indicates that the Burnses sought no medical treatment either for the physical discomfort alleged, or for the emotional pain and suffering claimed. They also acknowledged that they suffered no loss of sleep, appetite, or weight or other physical consequences. They lost no time from work and incurred no out-of-pocket expenses related to the effects on them of living in their mobile home. Lack of any such physical manifestations precludes a finding that the physical discomfort and emotional pain and suffering complained of here can rise to the level of 'bodily injury' as defined in the policy." *Id.* at 1196.

**New Jersey:** The Supreme Court of New Jersey held that a claim under a homeowner's policy issued to parents, for emotional distress accompanied by physical manifestations suffered by their child's teacher, on account of disparaging comments made by the parents, qualified as "bodily injury." *Voorhees v. Preferred Mut. Ins. Co.*, 607 A.2d 1255, 1262 (N.J. 1992). The policy defined "bodily injury" as "bodily harm, sickness or disease to a person, including required care, loss of services and death resulting therefrom." *Id.* at 1258. The court held that the teacher's headaches, stomach pains, nausea, depression, and body pains qualified as "bodily injury," concluding that such term is ambiguous as it relates to emotional distress accompanied by physical manifestations, and, therefore, should be interpreted in favor of the insured. *Id.* at 1261–62; *see also SL Indus., Inc. v. Am. Motorists Ins. Co.*, 607 A.2d 1266, 1274 (N.J. 1992) (concluding that sleeplessness is not a physical injury for purposes of "bodily injury" and that purely emotional injuries, without physical manifestations, do not qualify as "bodily injury").

**New Mexico:** The Court of Appeals of New Mexico held that a bystander claim for emotional distress did not qualify as "bodily injury" for purposes of an uninsured motorist policy. *Economy Preferred Ins. Co. v. Quanxi Jia*, 92 P.3d 1280, 1284 (N.M. Ct. App. 2004). The policy defined "bodily injury" as "bodily harm, sickness or disease, including death that results." *Id.* at 1282. The Court of Appeals noted that the Supreme Court of New Mexico, in *Gonzales v. Allstate Insurance Co.*, 921 P.2d 944 (N.M. 1996), held that, by its plain meaning, "bodily injury" constitutes injury to the physical body and not mental and emotional injuries. *Id.* at 1283. However, the court also stated that *Gonzales* left open the possibility that physical manifestation of emotional injury might constitute bodily injury. *Id.* The Court of Appeals concluded that physical manifestation of emotional injury qualified as bodily injury. *Id.* at 1284. However, the court held that the specific maladies before it did not qualify as the requisite physical manifestation. *Id.* "We do not resolve what would be sufficient to constitute bodily injury; we simply hold that crying, shaking, and sleep difficulties are not enough." *Id.* In *Hart v. State Farm Mutual Automobile Insurance Co.*, 193 P.3d 565, 568 (N.M. Ct. App. 2008), the Court of Appeals of New Mexico characterized its decision in *Economy Preferred* as holding that an uninsured motorist policy affords no coverage for emotional damages unless the injury is physical in nature. Noting a similarity to *Economy Preferred*, the *Hart* Court likewise concluded that a claim for the physical, cognitive, or emotional manifestations of the effects of a sexual touching of a child (taking place in an uninsured vehicle) did not qualify as "bodily injury" under her parents' uninsured motorist policy. *Id.*

**New York:** The Court of Appeals of New York held that a claim under a general liability policy issued to a landlord, for emotional distress sustained by tenants when a portion of the ceiling in their apartment collapsed, qualified as "bodily injury." *Lavanant v. Gen. Acc. Ins. Co. of Am.*, 595 N.E.2d 819, 822 (N.Y. 1992). The policy defined "bodily injury" as "bodily injury, sickness or disease." *Id.* at 820. The court concluded that the term "bodily injury" was ambiguous. *Id.* at 822. "We decline General Accident's invitation to rewrite the contract to add 'bodily sickness' and 'bodily disease,' and a requirement of prior physical contact for compensable mental injury. General Accident could itself have specified such limitations in drafting its policy, but it did not do so." *Id.*; *see also State Farm Mut. Auto. Ins. Co. v. Glinbizzi*, 780 N.Y.S. 2d 434 (N.Y. App. Div. 2004) (holding that a definition of "bodily injury" in an automobile policy that was seemingly specifically drafted to avoid coverage for bystander claims under *Lavanant*—"bodily injury to a person and sickness, disease or death which results from it"—was ambiguous and could mean that any sickness, disease, or death to any person is covered if it results from bodily injury to the same or a different person).

**North Carolina:** The Court of Appeals of North Carolina held that a claim under a general liability policy issued to an employer, for emotional distress sustained by an employee (which would allegedly decrease his life expectancy), on account of wrongful termination and discrimination, qualified as "bodily injury." *Fieldcrest Cannon, Inc. v. Fireman's Fund Ins. Co.*, 477 S.E.2d 59, 72 (N.C. App. Ct. 1996). The policy defined "bodily injury" as "bodily injury, sickness or disease sustained by any person which occurs during the policy period, including death at any time resulting therefrom." *Id.* at 66. The court held that the employee made a *prima facie* claim for negligent infliction of emotional distress, which is "bodily injury" under the policy. *Id.* at 72.

**North Dakota:** The Supreme Court of North Dakota held that a claim for post-traumatic stress disorder, resulting in vomiting, weight loss, severe headaches, loss of sleep, night sweats, and nightmares, qualified as "bodily injury" under an automobile policy. *Hartman v. Estate of Anthony J. Miller,* 656 N.W.2d 676, 685 (N.D. 2003). The policy defined "bodily injury" as "bodily injury to or sickness, disease or death of any person." *Id.* at 677. The court agreed with the rationale of *Trinh v. Allstate Ins. Co.,* 37 P.3d 1259 (Wash. Ct. App. 2002) and held that the term "bodily injury" within the meaning of the policy included "post-traumatic stress disorder accompanied by nontransitory physical manifestations." *Id.* at 685.

**Ohio:** The Court of Appeals of Ohio held that an insured's claim for mental anguish, on account of the death of his brother, did not qualify as "bodily injury" under an uninsured/underinsured motorist policy. *Gilkey v. Gibson,* No. 97APE11–1477, 1998 Ohio App. LEXIS 3807, at \*9 (Ohio Ct. App. Aug. 20, 1998). The policy defined "bodily injury," in pertinent part, as "physical injury to or sickness, disease, or death of any person." *Id.* at \*7. The court noted that, while the policy defined "bodily injury" broadly, to include in the terms "sickness" or "disease," the term under consideration was "bodily injury" not simply "injury." *Id.* at \*9. The court held that, because the word "bodily" must have some meaning in the context of the policy and cannot be ignored, "the injury, sickness, or disease under consideration must originate in the body as distinguished from the psyche. The definition does not encompass nonphysical, emotional, or mental harm originating in the mind, not the body." *Id.*; *see also Allstate Ins. Co. v. Oldham,* No. 2002-P-0008, 2003 Ohio App. LEXIS 861, at \*5 (Ohio Ct. App. Feb. 28, 2003) (holding that humiliation and embarrassment did not constitute "bodily injury" under a homeowner's policy).

**Oklahoma:** The Supreme Court of Oklahoma held that a husband's loss of consortium claim did not qualify as "bodily injury" under an underinsured motorist policy. *Littlefield v. State Farm Fire & Cas. Co.,* 857 P.2d 65, 70–71 (Okla. 1993). The policy defined "bodily injury" as "bodily injury to a person and sickness, disease or death which results from it." *Id.* at 67. The husband argued that his loss of consortium claim should be considered a separate "bodily injury," thereby invoking the policy's "per accident" limit. *Id.* at 68. The court held that, because the policy referred to "all damages due to bodily injury to one person," and because only the wife suffered "bodily injury," the "each person" limit applied. *Id.* at 70. Although the decision was based on the policy language, the Oklahoma high court also stated that "[w]hile the husband may have suffered emotionally, he has not incurred a bodily injury within the meaning of the policy." *Id.*

**Oregon:** An Oregon District Court held that a claim under a general liability policy issued to property owner-sellers, for physical manifestation of emotional distress sustained by homeowners who purchased the property and then seemingly learned of the historic release of asbestos on it, qualified as "bodily injury." *Am. States Ins. Co. v. Bercot*, No. 03–637-CO, 2004 WL 1490321, at *9 (D. Or. July 1, 2004). The policy defined "bodily injury" as "bodily injury, sickness or disease sustained by any person." *Id.* at *1. The court held that the physical manifestation of emotional distress, on account of the release of asbestos to the atmosphere and the environment which threatened the homeowners' health, qualified as "bodily injury." *Id.* at *9; *see also Klamath Pac. Corp. v. Reliance Ins. Co.*, 950 P.2d 909 (Or. Ct. App. 1997) (finding that, even if the insurer were correct, that emotional distress did not qualify as "bodily injury" unless it resulted from physical trauma to the body, the facts at issue—grabbing one's breasts and buttocks—could have caused the requisite trauma).

**Pennsylvania:** A Pennsylvania District Court held that a claim under a homeowner's policy issued to a hospital employee, for emotional distress, including physical manifestation, sustained by a co-worker who was allegedly subjected to inappropriate sexual touching by and interaction with the insured, did not qualify as "bodily injury." *Babalola v. Donegal Group, Inc.*, No. 1:08-CV-621, 2008 U.S. Dist. LEXIS 65207 at *14 (M.D. Pa. Aug. 26, 2008). The policy defined "bodily injury" as "bodily harm, sickness, or disease, including required care, loss of services and death that results." *Id.* at *9. The court summarized its review of several Pennsylvania decisions as follows: "Pennsylvania courts have soundly rejected the contention that policy definitions of injury or bodily injury encompass mental or emotional harm... . Generally, a complaint alleging only physical manifestations of mental or emotional harm likewise fails to trigger coverage under a policy insuring against claims brought for 'bodily injury.'" *Id.* at *9–10 (citation and internal quotation omitted).

**Rhode Island:** The Supreme Court of Rhode Island held that a claim under a homeowner's policy issued to a doctor, for humiliation, shame, emotional distress, and mental anguish sustained by a patient whose blood alcohol level became public, did not qualify as "bodily injury." *Mellow v. Medical Malpractice Joint Underwriting Ass'n of R.I.*, 567 A.2d 367, 368 (R.I. 1989). The policy defined "bodily injury" as "any physical harm, sickness, or disease and includes any care that is required or any services that are lost or death that results from bodily injury." *Id.* The court concluded that the complaint "allege[d] an invasion of privacy that led to emotional, rather than physical harm." *Id.*; *see also Aetna Cas. & Sur. Co. v. Wannamoisett County Club, Inc.*, 706 A.2d 1329, 1330 (R.I. 1998) (holding that a claim under the employer's liability section of a workers' compensation policy, for battery and nonconsensual touching, did not allege bodily injury).

**South Carolina:** A South Carolina District Court held that a claim under a general liability policy issued to a beer distributor, for loss of reputation, mental anguish, humiliation, and loss of enjoyment of life sustained by an employee for a racially motivated firing, did not qualify as "bodily injury." *Jefferson-Pilot Fire & Cas. Co. v. Sunbelt Beer Distribs., Inc.*, 839 F. Supp. 376, 379 (D.S.C. 1993). The policy defined "bodily injury" as "bodily injury, sickness, or disease sustained by a person, including death resulting from these at any time." *Id.* The court held that it was "not prepared to extend the interpretation of 'bodily injury' to include purely emotional damage absent some objective indication of physical symptoms." *Id.* In reaching its decision, the *Sunbelt* Court declined to follow the District of South Carolina's decision in *Allstate Ins. Co. v. Biggerstaff*, 703 F. Supp. 23 (D.S.C. 1989) or the Supreme Court of South Carolina's decision in *State Farm Mut. Ins. Co. v. Ramsey*, 374 S.E.2d 896 (S.C. 1988), which the *Sunbelt* Court characterized as recognizing that emotional trauma may constitute bodily injury for purposes of insurance coverage. *Id.* at 379. According to the *Sunbelt* Court, both *Biggerstaff* and *Ramsey* in fact involved physical manifestation of emotional injury, since they were addressing claims for negligent infliction of emotional distress, which has, as an essential element, "emotional distress [that] must both manifest itself by physical symptoms capable of objective diagnosis and be established by expert testimony." *Id.* at 379 n.3.

**South Dakota:** A South Dakota District Court held that a claim under a commercial general liability policy issued to a municipality, for high blood pressure sustained by the wife of a cancer-stricken municipal employee, on account of the municipality's group health insurance policy being cancelled, qualified as "bodily injury." *Western Cas. & Sur. Co. v. Waisanen*, 653 F. Supp. 825, 832 (D.S.D. 1987). The policy defined "bodily injury" as "bodily injury, sickness, or disease sustained by any person which occurs during the policy period, including death at any time resulting therefrom." *Id.* The court's opinion suggests that it may have ruled otherwise if the wife's injuries were solely emotional, which had been alleged in addition to high blood pressure. *Id.* (distinguishing *Rolette County v. Western Cas. & Sur. Co.*, 452 F. Supp. 125 (D.N.D. 1978), which held that coverage was denied because allegations were limited to mental anguish and emotional distress and there were no allegations of physical harm).

**Tennessee:** The Court of Appeals of Tennessee held that a claim under a commercial general liability policy issued to an employer, for emotional distress suffered by a female employee who was subjected to gender and racial discrimination, did not qualify as "bodily injury." *American Indem. Co. v. Foy Trailer Rentals, Inc.*, No. W2000–00397-COA-R3-CV, 2000 WL 1839131, at *4 (Tenn. Ct. App. Nov. 28, 2000). The policy defined "bodily injury" as "bodily injury, sickness or disease sustained by a person, including death resulting from these at any time." *Id.* at *3. The court relied on, among other cases *Guardian Life Ins. Co. of Am. v. Richardson*, 129 S.W.2d 1107 (Tenn. Ct. App. 1939), which held that, when "disease" is unrestricted by anything in context, it includes disease of the mind as well as the body. *Id.* at *4. However, when disease is restricted by the word "bodily," and when "bodily" grammatically modifies "disease" and "injury," it was inserted for the purpose of excluding mental disease. *Id.*

**Texas:** The Supreme Court of Texas held that a claim under a homeowner's policy issued to a clerk at a photo developing store, for severe mental pain, loss of privacy and humiliation, sustained by a customer whose revealing photos were disseminated to others, did not qualify as "bodily injury." *Trinity Universal Ins. Co. v. Cowan*, 945 S.W.2d 819, 820 (Tex. 1997). The policy defined "bodily injury" as "bodily harm, sickness or disease." *Id.* The court held that, "absent an allegation of physical manifestation of mental anguish, a claim of mental anguish is not a 'bodily injury' as defined in the policy for purposes of invoking the duty to defend." *Id.*; *see also Haralson v. State Farm Mut. Auto. Ins. Co.*, 564 F. Supp. 2d 616, 626–27 (N.D. Tex. 2008) (holding that extreme emotional distress accompanied by headaches, migraines, stomach aches, nausea, and sleeplessness, qualified as bodily injury for purposes of a bystander claim under an uninsured motorist policy).

**Utah:** No instructive authority. *But see Progressive Cas. Ins. Co. v. Ewart*, 167 P.3d 1011 (Utah 2007). The Supreme Court of Utah held that a Utah statute, requiring mandatory liability limits for bodily injury, did not require an insurer to pay a separate policy limit for a loss of consortium claim brought by the spouse of an insured driver. *Id.* at 1015. The court noted that the question whether claims for emotional or psychological injuries are claims for "bodily injury" was not before it. *Id.* at n.15. However, the court commented that "'bodily' is commonly understood to refer to, simply, the 'body,'" and the spouse's loss of consortium claim in no way involves a bodily injury to her. *Id.* at 1014.

**Vermont:** The Supreme Court of Vermont held that a claim for emotional distress, as a result of exposure to formaldehyde gas, qualified as "bodily injury" under a homeowner's policy that provided coverage for damages "because of" bodily injury. *American Protection Ins. Co. v. McMahan*, 562 A.2d 462, 466 (Vt. 1989). "We held above that 'bodily injury' includes exposure to a toxic product. It follows that American is under a duty to defend and indemnify the McMahans for any damages incurred *because of* exposure to such product. This duty includes the emotional distress damages claimed by the Livaks." *Id.* (emphasis in original).

**Virginia:** A Virginia District Court held that a claim under a general liability policy issued to a bank, for emotional distress sustained by an employee on account of wrongful termination, did not qualify as "bodily injury." *W. Am. Ins. Co. v. Bank of Isle of Wright*, 673 F. Supp. 760, 765 (E.D. Va. 1987). The court did not state whether the policy contained a definition of "bodily injury." Relying on a then recent Virginia District Court decision,

*American & Foreign Insurance Co. v. Church Schools*, 645 F. Supp. 628 (E.D. Va. 1986), and the prevailing rule in other jurisdictions, the court held that coverage for "bodily injury" was limited to physical injury to the body and did not include claims for emotional harm. *Id.* The opinion does not address whether physical manifestation of emotional injury can qualify as bodily injury. *See also Rockingham Mut. Ins. Co. v. Davis*, No. CL01–12576, 2002 WL 737474, at *3 (Va. Cir. Ct. Apr. 26, 2002) (distinguishing *Isle of Wright* because the underlying plaintiff's claim against the insured for inappropriate touching alleged, in addition to emotional injury, physical pain on account of the plaintiff's arm being grabbed, which constituted "bodily injury" under a homeowner's policy).

**Washington:** The Court of Appeals of Washington held that a bystander claim for emotional distress, accompanied by inability to eat, constant sickness to the stomach, vomiting, and hair loss, qualified as "bodily injury" for purposes of an uninsured motorist policy. *Trinh v. Allstate Ins. Co.*, 37 P.3d 1259, 1264 (Wash. Ct. App. 2002). The policy defined "bodily injury" as "bodily injury, sickness, disease or death." *Id.* at 1264. Following a review of a litany of cases nationally addressing the issue, and observing that the definition of "bodily injury" before it included sickness or disease, the court held that "bodily injury" includes emotional injuries that are accompanied by physical manifestations. *Id.* at 1264; *see also Daley v. Allstate Ins. Co.*, 958 P.2d 990, 998 (Wash. 1998) ("The term 'bodily injury' is unambiguous and does not include recovery for emotional distress unrelated to a physical injury.").

**West Virginia:** The Supreme Court of Appeals of West Virginia held that a claim under a general liability policy issued to a veterinary office, for emotional distress sustained by an employee on account of unwelcome sexual advances by a veterinarian, did not qualify as "bodily injury." *Smith v. Animal Urgent Care, Inc.*, 542 S.E.2d 827, 831 (W. Va. 2000). The policy defined "bodily injury" as "bodily injury, sickness or disease sustained by a person, including death resulting from any of these at any time." *Id.* at 829. The court examined case law nationally and concluded that the majority position—"bodily injury" is narrower than "personal injury," which covers an affront or insult to a person's reputation or sensibilities—was persuasive. *Id.* at 831. The West Virginia high court held that "in an insurance liability policy, purely mental or emotional harm that arises from a claim of sexual harassment and lacks physical manifestation does not fall within a definition of 'bodily injury' which is limited to 'bodily injury, sickness, or disease.'" *Id.*; *see also Tackett v. Am. Motorists Ins. Co.*, 584 S.E.2d 158, 166 (W. Va. 2004) (holding that "great embarrassment, consternation, mental pain and anguish, and emotional upset" did not constitute "bodily injury" under the insurance policy).

**Wisconsin:** The Supreme Court of Wisconsin held that a claim under a general liability policy issued to a radio station, for emotional injury sustained by a person against whom station employees filed a false security interest with the secretary of state, qualified as "bodily injury." *Doyle v. Ward Engelke*, 580 N.W.2d 245, 250 (Wis. 1998). The policy defined "bodily injury" as "any physical harm, including sickness or disease, to the physical health of other persons… includ[ing] any of the following that results at any time from such physical harm, sickness or disease[:] Mental anguish, injury or illness. Emotional distress. Care, loss of services, or death." *Id.* at 249. The insurer argued that emotional distress is insufficient to constitute "bodily injury" because of the "physical harm" requirement in the definition. *Id.* The Wisconsin high court disagreed, holding that "we are unable to separate a person's nerves and tensions from his [or her] body. It is common knowledge that worry and anxiety can and often do have a direct effect on other bodily functions." *Id.* at 250 (quoting *Levy v. Duclaux*, 324 So. 2d 1, 10 (La. Ct. App. 1975) (alteration in original and internal quotation omitted); *see also Washington v. Krahn*, 440 F. Supp. 2d 911, 913–14 (E.D. Wis. 2006) (relying on *Doyle* and holding that emotional distress qualified as "bodily injury" pursuant to a definition that defined the term as sickness or disease).

**Wyoming:** The Supreme Court of Wyoming held that a bystander claim for emotional distress qualified as "bodily injury" for purposes of an underinsured motorist policy. *Evans v. Farmers Ins. Exch.*, 34 P.3d 284, 287 (Wyo. 2001). The policy defined "bodily injury" as "bodily harm to or sickness, disease or death of any person." *Id.* at 287. The court first concluded that, given such grammatical structure, the term "bodily" did not modify the terms "sickness" and "disease," as in the majority of cases on the issue that define "bodily injury" as "bodily injury, sickness or disease." *Id.* at 287. After reviewing dictionary definitions of the terms "sickness" and "disease," the court concluded that emotional injuries are neither expressly included nor expressly excluded. *Id.* The court therefore concluded that the term "bodily injury" was ambiguous and construed it in favor of coverage. *Id.*

CHAPTER

# 11

# Is Faulty Workmanship an "Occurrence?"

When it comes to claims for latent injuries and damages, such as asbestos and hazardous waste, some would say that they were never contemplated under the historic policies that were later—sometimes decades later—called upon to respond. That being so, it is not surprising that questions such as trigger of coverage and allocation have been viewed by courts as particularly vexing, with the result being a lack of unanimity in their handling as different schools of thought developed in response to the issues.

But claims for coverage for construction defects, and the damage they cause, present a different situation. It is unquestionably contemplated that such claims will be made under commercial general liability policies— especially when the insured is in the construction business. For this reason, it is surprising that so much disparity has developing around the country in the case law over the treatment of such claims, especially those involving relatively similar facts and oftentimes identical policy language.

Many construction defect claims follow a typical pattern. A general contractor is hired to build a residential or commercial building. The general contractor employs various subcontractors to assist with the completion of the project, such as to pour the foundation, frame the building, or install the plumbing, windows, HVAC, etc. The house or building is completed. After taking possession, the owner discovers defects in the construction—such as defectively installed windows that are now leaking or an improperly poured foundation that is causing the building to shift. The owner and general contractor are unable to resolve the problem in a manner that is satisfactory to both parties. Left with no choice, the owner files suit against the general contractor. The general contractor then files a third-party complaint against the allegedly at-fault subcontractors. And all defendants turn to their commercial general liability policies seeking coverage for a defense and any liability that may be assessed against them.

As a general rule, courts have concluded that defects in the insured's work product are not covered—unless a certain exception applies, as discussed below. As another general rule, with a few exceptions, defective workmanship

221

that *causes* "property damage" to something *other than* the insured's work product, is covered. While these general rules accurately describe the outcome of most construction defect claims, there is a fracture among courts in the rationales used to get there. And the choice of rationale employed can have a dramatic effect on the extent of coverage owed.

While insurers' handling of claims for coverage for construction defects may vary widely, they generally all begin with the same initial questions: Are any of the damages being sought from the insured (1) for "property damage"; and (2) if so, was such "property damage" caused by an "occurrence"?

The source of such questions is the insuring agreement of the commercial general liability coverage form, which often provides that the insurer "will pay those sums that the insured becomes legally obligated to pay as damages because of… 'property damage' to which this insurance applies" (*See, e.g.*, Ins. Servs. Office Props., Inc., Commercial General Liability Coverage Form, No. CG 00011207, § I1a (2007)), provided that the "'property damage' is caused by an 'occurrence.'" ISO Form, CG 00011207 at § I1b1. "Occurrence" is typically defined as "an accident, including continuous or repeated exposure to substantially the same general harmful conditions." ISO Form, CG 00011207 at § V13. It is also a requirement that any "property damage" occur during the policy period. ISO Form, CG 00011207 at § I1b2. This "timing" issue is addressed separately. *See* Chapters 15 and 16.

The principal schools of thought that have emerged, in response to the question whether coverage for construction defects is available under a commercial general liability policy, are as follows.

The majority of courts have held that defective workmanship, standing alone, which results in damage solely to the insured's completed work product, is not an accident, and, hence, not an "occurrence." *Essex Ins. Co. v. Holder*, 261 S.W.3d 456, 459–60 (Ark. 2007). The Arkansas high court's rationale, which is not an uncommon one, was that its "case law has consistently defined an 'accident' as an event that takes place without one's foresight or expectation—an event that proceeds from an unknown cause, or is an unusual effect of a known cause, and therefore not expected. Faulty workmanship is not an accident; instead, it is a foreseeable occurrence, and performance bonds exist in the marketplace to insure the contractor against claims for the cost of repair or replacement of faulty work." *Id.* at 460 (citation omitted).

Other courts have likewise held that defective workmanship, which results in damage solely to the insured's completed work product, is not covered—but for a different reason. These courts initially conclude that defects in the insured's work product *do* constitute an "occurrence." *See Bituminous Cas. Corp. v. Kenway Contracting, Inc.*, 240 S.W.3d 633, 639–40 (Ky. 2007) (holding that a claim against a contractor, who was supposed to demolish a carport, but instead also demolished half of the attached residential structure, qualified as an "occurrence" because such outcome was not the plan, design, or intent of the insured). However, such courts then usually conclude that, despite the existence of an "occurrence," damage that is solely to the insured's completed work product is nonetheless excluded from coverage on account of the policy's so-called "your work" exclusion, which applies to "'property damage' to 'your [named insured's] work' arising out of it or any part of it and included in the 'products-completed operations hazard.'" ISO FORM, CG 00011207 at § 12l.

Whether it is because defective workmanship is not an "occurrence" or the operation of the "your work" exclusion, damage to the insured's completed work product is not covered. While these outcomes are the same, which rationale a court employs to reach it can make a world of difference. The reason being that the "your work" exclusion also contains what is commonly referred to as the "subcontractor exception," which provides: "This exclusion does not apply if the damaged work or the work out of which the damage arises was performed on your [named insured's] behalf by a subcontractor." *Id.*

The "subcontractor exception" restores coverage for "property damage" to the insured's own work, that would otherwise be excluded by the "your work" exclusion, if the cause of the damage to the insured's work was the operations of the insured's subcontractor. *See Am. Family Mut. Ins. Co. v. Am. Girl, Inc.*, 673 N.W.2d 65, 83–84 (Wis. 2004) ("There is coverage under the insuring agreement's initial coverage grant. Coverage would be excluded by the business risk exclusionary language, except that the subcontractor exception to the business risk exclusion applies, which operates to restore the otherwise excluded coverage.").

In *Travelers Indem. Co. of Am. v. Moore & Assocs., Inc.*, 216 S.W.3d 302, 309 (Tenn. 2007), the Supreme Court of Tennessee illustrated the significant impact that the "subcontractor exception" can have on the extent of coverage available for a construction defect claim. The insured was the building contractor for the construction of a hotel. *Id.* at 304. The insured hired a subcontractor to provide and install the windows. *Id.* The owner of the hotel alleged that the windows were negligently designed and installed, resulting in damage to other components of the interior and exterior of the building. *Id.*

The *Moore* Court concluded that the entire hotel qualified as the insured's work for purposes of the "your work" exclusion. *Id.* at 310. Therefore, *all* of the damages to the hotel were *initially* excluded by the "your work" exclusion. *Id.* However, because the policy at issue contained a "subcontractor exception" to the "your work" exclusion, the court's analysis did not end there: "It is alleged that the installation of the windows was performed by subcontractors hired by [the insured]. Therefore, damages resulting from the subcontractors' faulty installation of the windows are not excluded from coverage, even if those damages affected [the insured's] work." *Moore*, 216 S.W.3d at 301. On account of the "subcontractor exception," coverage was restored for the otherwise excluded damage to the hotel caused by the subcontractor's negligent design and installation of the windows. *Id.*

So while coverage is not owed for damage to an insured's defective workmanship, the "subcontractor exception" to the "your work" exclusion demonstrates, in stark terms, why it matters whether a court reaches that conclusion based on the absence of an "occurrence" or the operation of the "your work" exclusion. Many courts hold that, if damage to an insured's defective workmanship is not covered, because it does not qualify as an "occurrence," then the insured has not satisfied the requirements of the insuring agreement. As a result, coverage is excluded and the court's analysis ends there, without any need to address the potential applicability of policy exclusions. In other words, by resting its decision on the insured's failure to satisfy the insuring agreement, it is unnecessary for the court to reach the "your work" exclusion. Translation—policyholders are denied the opportunity to invoke the "subcontractor exception" to such exclusion to restore coverage for damage to their own work that was caused by the operations of a subcontractor. *See Amerisure, Inc. v. Wurster Constr. Co.*, 818 N.E.2d 998, 1005 (Ind. Ct. App. 2004) ("Because Wurster's claim fails the definitional requirements of the terms 'property damage' and 'occurrence' in order for coverage to apply, we do not reach the applicability of the various policy exclusions [including the 'your work' exclusion]."); *see also Nabholz Constr. Corp. v. St. Paul Fire & Marine Ins., Co.*, 354 F. Supp. 2d 917, 923 (E.D. Ark. 2005) ("The Court need not reach CONARK's argument that coverage exists based on the Policy's completed work exclusion, or more accurately, based upon an exception to this exclusion. Because the Court's finding is based upon its conclusion that coverage is lacking under the basic insuring clause, it is unnecessary to consider this exclusion. An exception to an exclusion cannot create or extend coverage where none exists under the terms the policy's basic insuring agreement.").

The availability of coverage, for damage to an insured's completed work product, depends upon certain legal and factual issues: Does defective workmanship qualify as an "occurrence" and did the insured use subcontractors that caused damage to the insured's work? Given these variables, courts vary in their answers.

On the other hand, most courts are uniform in their conclusion that, if faulty workmanship *caused* property damage, to something *other than* the insured's work product, such injury or damage was caused by an "occurrence" and coverage exists. *ACUITY v. Burd & Smith Constr., Inc.*, 721 N.W.2d 33, 39 (N.D. 2006) ("We agree with the rationale of those courts holding that faulty workmanship causing damage to property other than the work product is an accidental occurrence for purposes of a CGL policy."); *see also Auto-Owners Ins. Co. v. Home Pride Cos.*, 684 N.W.2d 571, 577–78 (Neb. 2004) ("[A]lthough faulty workmanship, *standing alone*, is not an occurrence under a CGL policy, an accident caused by faulty workmanship is a covered occurrence. Stated otherwise, although a standard CGL policy does not provide coverage for faulty workmanship that damages only the resulting work product, if faulty workmanship causes bodily injury or property damage to something other than the insured's work product, an unintended and unexpected event has occurred, and coverage exists.") (citations omitted and emphasis on original).

While it is almost universally held that coverage exists for such consequential damages caused by an insured's faulty workmanship, a few courts have deviated from this path. For example, Pennsylvania courts have rejected this principle adopted by the vast majority of courts. In *Kvaerner Metals Division of Kvaerner U.S., Inc. v. Commercial Union Insurance Co.*, 908 A.2d 888, 899 (Pa. 2006), the Supreme Court of Pennsylvania held that damage to the insured faulty workmanship did not constitute an "occurrence." Then in *Millers Capital Insurance Co. v. Gambone Brothers Development Co.*, 941 A.2d 706, 713 (Pa. Super. Ct. 2007), the Superior Court of Pennsylvania addressed coverage for damage caused by the insured's faulty workmanship. Despite confronted with a paradigm example of property damage caused by a contractor's faulty workmanship—water intrusion damage caused by defective residential windows and stucco—the Pennsylvania appellate court concluded that no coverage was owed for such consequential damages. *Id.* Addressing *Kvaerner Metals*, *Gambone Brothers* held that "natural and foreseeable acts, such as rainfall, which tend to exacerbate the damage, effect, or consequences caused *ab initio* by faulty workmanship also cannot be considered sufficiently fortuitous to constitute an 'occurrence' or 'accident' for the purposes of an occurrence based CGL policy." *Id.; see also Great Divide Ins. Co. v. Bitterroot Timberframes of Wyoming, LLC*, No. 06-CV-020, 2006 WL 3933078, at *8 (D. Wyo. Oct. 20, 2006) ("Defendant's inadequate preparation and installation of the siding on the resort was not an 'accident' since defendant intended to perform in compliance with the contract, but allegedly failed to do so. Defendant could foresee the natural consequences of any negligence or poor workmanship, thus, any resulting damage is not considered an 'accident' triggering an 'occurrence' under the Policy.").

In summary, and putting aside a few exceptions, the general rules concerning coverage for construction defects are as follows. No coverage is owed for damage solely to the insured's completed work product—either because it is not an "occurrence" or the applicability of the "your work" exclusion. However, if damage to the insured's completed work product qualifies as an "occurrence," then coverage is owed for such damage if its cause was the operations of an insured's subcontractor. And notwithstanding the varying rules and rationales concerning coverage for damage to the insured's work product, "property damage" to something other than the insured's work product is an "occurrence," and covered.

## 50-State Survey: Is Faulty Workmanship an "Occurrence?"

**Alabama:** The Supreme Court of Alabama held that defective grout, which led to the need for extensive repairing and remodeling of a waste-water treatment plant, qualified as an "occurrence." *U.S. Fid. & Guar. Co. v. Andalusia*

*Ready Mix, Inc.*, 436 So. 2d 868, 871 (Ala. 1983). The court relied, in part, on *Yakima Cement Prods. v. Great Am. Ins. Co.*, 608 P.2d 254 (Wash. 1980), which held that a product's failure to perform the function for which it was manufactured and sold, necessitating its removal, refabrication, and repair, constituted an "accident" and, thus, an "occurrence" within the terms of the policy. *Id.* at 870–71; *see also Liberty Mut. Ins. Co. v. Wheelwright Trucking Co.*, 851 So. 2d 466, 496 (Ala. 2002) (holding that coverage was owed for tractors that, although physically undamaged, were rendered less useful as a result of the failure of the insured's trailers to meet specifications); *Auto-Owners Ins. Co. v. L. Thomas Development, Inc.*, No. 2:07cv1041, 2010 WL 2308190, at *3 (M.D. Ala. June 9, 2010) ("[I]n determining whether an event is an 'occurrence,' Alabama courts have generally examined whether the challenged conduct was 'expected or intended' by the insured; in general, if the conduct at issue was 'expected or intended' then it was not an 'accident' and thus was not a covered 'occurrence.'") (construction defect).

**Alaska:** The Supreme Court of Alaska held that the failure of an improperly constructed curtain drain (device designed to prevent groundwater from penetrating a septic system's leach field), that caused a septic system to stop functioning, constituted an "occurrence." *Fejes v. Alaska Ins. Co.*, 984 P.2d 519, 523 (Alaska 1999). "The mere fact that a complaint against a contractor is based on a theory of misrepresentation or deceit does not mean that the facts underlying the claim did not arise from an accident." *Id.*; *see also Clear, LLC v. Am. & Foreign Ins. Co.*, No. 3:07-cv-00110, 2008 WL 818978, at *7 (D. Alaska Mar. 24, 2008) ("This court has no trouble extending the reach of *Fejes* to say that defective work by the general contractor which damages other property falls within the CGL coverage, because the same analysis by which the Alaska court concluded that the subcontractor's work was an accident supports the conclusion that the general contractor's own defective work damaging other property was an accident.").

**Arizona:** The Court of Appeals of Arizona held that the use of defective soil at a residential development, which resulted in expansion, leading to cracking of drywall and tile grout in completed homes, qualified as an "occurrence" for purposes of the resulting damage. *Lennar Corp. v. Auto-Owners Ins. Co.*, 151 P.3d 538, 545 (Ariz. Ct. App. 2007). "The Pinnacle Hill plaintiffs... do not claim faulty work alone; they also claim that property damage resulted from the faulty work. This is sufficient to allege an occurrence under the policies at issue." *Id.* (noting that, pursuant to *U.S. Fid. & Guar. Corp. v. Advance Roofing & Supply Co.*, 788 P.2d 1227 (Ariz. App. Ct. 1989), faulty workmanship, standing alone, cannot constitute an occurrence); *see also U.S. Home Corp. v. Maryland Cas. Co.*, No. 06–15092, 2007 WL 4467633, at *1 (9th Cir. Dec. 20, 2007) ("Appellant's complaint fails to allege any property damage other than the defective stucco and damage resulting from repair of that stucco. Under Arizona law, the faulty stucco, standing alone, does not constitute an 'occurrence' as defined in the insurance policy.") (citing *Advance Roofing* and *Lennar*).

**Arkansas:** The Supreme Court of Arkansas held that claims against a builder, for damages resulting from delays, defective construction, and employment of incompetent subcontractors, in the construction of a residence, did not qualify as an "occurrence." *Essex Ins. Co. v. Holder*, 261 S.W.3d 456, 460 (Ark. 2007). The court chose to side with what it viewed as the majority rule—that defective workmanship, standing alone, which results in damages only to the work product itself, is not an "accidental occurrence." *Id.* at 459–60. The court was persuaded that faulty workmanship is a foreseeable occurrence and performance bonds exist to insure a contractor against claims for the cost of repair or replacement of faulty work. *Id.* at 460. While one of the policies at issue defined "occurrence" to specifically exclude defective construction, the court's decision was based on the definition of "occurrence" without regard to the express exception. *Id.* at 457; *see also Cincinnati Ins. Cos. v. Collier Landholdings*, 614 F. Supp. 2d 960, 966 (W.D. Ark. 2009) ("[B]ecause the defective construction alleged by Collier is not an 'occurrence' under the CGL policy issued by Cincinnati, Benchmark is not entitled to recover the repair and remediation cost *arising from* its defective workmanship under the policy.") (emphasis added); *id.* at 967 ("The focus of the Arkansas approach is on the act or event that caused the underlying damage and not on the foreseeability of the resulting damage.").

**California:** The Supreme Court of California held that defects in aluminum doors sold to a building contractor were unexpected, undesigned, and unforeseen and constituted an "accident." *Geddes & Smith, Inc. v. St. Paul-Mercury Indem. Co.*, 334 P.2d 881, 884 (Cal. 1959). "Accident, as a source and cause of damage to property, within the terms of an accident policy, is an unexpected, unforeseen, or undesigned happening or consequence from either a known or an unknown cause." *Id.* (citation and internal quotes omitted). "They [door failures] were not the result of normal deterioration, but occurred long before any properly constructed door might be expected to wear out or collapse." *Id.*; *but see Fire Ins. Exchange v. Superior Court*, 181 Cal.App. 4th 388, 390 (2010) (holding that homeowners' action in building a house that encroached on a neighbor's property—even if the owners acted in the good faith but mistaken belief that they were legally entitled to build where they did—was not an "accident" under homeowner's policy).

**Colorado:** The Colorado Court of Appeals held that a claim for damages arising from defective workmanship, standing alone, does not qualify as an "occurrence," regardless of the underlying legal theory pled (tort, contract, or breach of warranty). *Gen. Sec. Indem. Co. of Ariz. v. Mountain States Mut. Cas. Co.*, 205 P.3d 529, 534 (Colo. Ct. App. 2009). However, the court also adopted a "corollary" to such rule—an "accident" and "occurrence" are present "when consequential property damage has been inflicted upon a third party as a result of the insured's activity." *Id.* at 535; *see also Greystone Constr., Inc. v. Nat'l Fire*

*& Marine Ins. Co.*, 649 F. Supp. 2d 1213, 1219 (D. Colo. 2009) ("It is clear from both the discussion in *General Security* and those cases it cites that the 'damage inflicted on a third party' necessary to invoke the corollary refers to faulty workmanship causing property damage to something *other than* the work product itself.") (emphasis in original); *id.* (explaining that poor workmanship that resulted in property damage only to a home itself would not be considered an "occurrence," but damage to personal property of the homeowner kept inside the house, or damage to neighbor's houses, could be considered an "occurrence"); *United Fire & Cas. Co. v. Boulder Plaza Residential, LLC*, No. 06-CV-00037, 2010 WL 420046, at *6 (D. Colo. Feb. 1, 2010) (addressing *General Sec.* in detail and rejecting the insured's effort to separate out "loss of use" of the work product, from the work product itself, as it would cause the consequential damage exception to swallow the rule). However, on May 21, 2010, the Colorado General Assembly enacted An Act Concerning Commercial Liability Insurance Policies Issued to Construction Professionals, H.B. 10–1394. *See* C.R.S.A. § 13-20-808. The Act specifically described the Court of Appeals' decision in *General Security* as not properly considering a construction professional's reasonable expectation that an insurer would defend the construction professional against a construction defect claim. *Id.* at § (1)(b) (III). The Act addresses several issues relevant to coverage for construction defects, most notably declaring that: "In interpreting a liability insurance policy issued to a construction professional, a court shall presume that the work of a construction professional that results in property damage, including damage to the work itself or other work, is an accident unless the property damage is intended and expected by the insured." *Id.* at § 3. However, nothing in the Act "[r]equires coverage for damage to an insured's own work unless otherwise provided in the insurance policy; or [c]reates insurance coverage that is not included in the insurance policy." *Id.* at § 3(a), (b). The impact of C.R.S.A. § 13-20-808 on *Greystone Constr.* is before the 10th Circuit (docket no. 09-1412). *See Crossen v. Am Family Mut. Ins. Co.*, No. 09-cv-02859, 2010 WL 2682103, at *5 (D. Colo. July 7, 2010) (concluding that, because the policy could cover the injury alleged, notwithstanding *General Security*, it was not necessary to address the impact of C.R.S.A. § 13-20-808).

**Connecticut:** A Connecticut trial court held that the loss of use of property, caused by the need to relocate tenants and lost rental revenue, on account of the insured's installation of unsuitable telephone cable in residential units, did not qualify as an "occurrence." *Times Fiber Commc'ns, Inc. v. Travelers Indem. Co. of Ill.*, No. CVX05CV030196619S, 2005 WL 589821, at *10 (Conn. Super. Ct. Feb. 2, 2005). "[T]he 'accident' is 'the event' causing the injury, not the cause of that event. In this case the alleged 'accident' would have to be the removal of the cable because this was and will be the event causing the injury to the [multi-dwelling units]. The alleged loss of use of property is therefore based entirely on harm which resulted from repair activities necessary to replace the nonconforming cable. The accident was therefore not the installation of the non-conforming cable as claimed by plaintiff." *Id.* (quotation omitted). A Connecticut District Court held that claims against a swimming pool builder, for defective construction of pools (cracking in the concrete walls and floors), did not qualify as an "occurrence." *Scottsdale Ins. Co. v. R.I. Pools, Inc.*, No. 3:09CV01319, 2010 WL 3827948 (D. Conn. Sept. 22, 2010). "[A]lthough an accident can be a consequence of faulty workmanship, faulty workmanship alone is not an accident." *Id.* at *7.

**Delaware:** A Delaware District Court held that a claim against a homebuilder for construction deficiencies, including missing flashing, fiberglass installation, and improper installation of a wrap system, did not qualify as an "occurrence." *Brosnahan Builders, Inc. v. Harleysville Mut. Ins. Co.*, 137 F. Supp. 2d 517, 526 (D. Del. 2001). "[T]he Pinkerts claim that plaintiffs were directed to install specific water proofing materials and failed to do so, and that the materials used were installed improperly... . The situation that led to the damage to the Pinkerts' home was clearly within the control of plaintiffs, as general contractor of the construction project, and not a fortuitous circumstance happening 'without human agency.'" *Id.*; *see also AE-Newark Associates, L.P. v. CNA Ins. Cos.*, No. Civ. A 00C-05–186JEB, 2001 WL 1198930, at *3 (Del. Super. Ct. Oct. 2, 2001) (holding that damage to apartment buildings and tenants' personal property, caused by faulty installation of a roof system, was "clearly" "property damage" that was caused by an "occurrence").

**Florida:** The Supreme Court of Florida held that faulty workmanship that is neither intended nor expected from the standpoint of the insured can constitute an "accident" and, thus, an "occurrence." *U.S. Fire Ins. Co. v. J.S.U.B., Inc.*, 979 So. 2d 871, 888 (Fla. 2007). "[W]e reject a definition of 'occurrence' that renders damage to the insured's own work as a result of a subcontractor's faulty workmanship expected, but renders damage to property of a third party caused by the same faulty workmanship unexpected." *Id.* at 885. The court next examined whether there was "property damage," holding that "faulty workmanship or defective work that has damaged the otherwise non-defective completed project has caused 'physical injury to tangible property' within the plain meaning of the definition in the policy. If there is no damage beyond the faulty workmanship or defective work, then there may be no resulting 'property damage.'" *Id.* at 889. In *Auto-Owners Insurance Co. v. Pozzi Window Co.*, 984 So. 2d 1241 (Fla. 2008), the Supreme Court of Florida held that a subcontractor's defective installation of defective windows was not itself "physical injury to tangible property," and, therefore, was not "property damage," thereby precluding coverage for the costs of repair or replacement of the defective windows. *Id.* at 1249. "Conversely, if the claim is for the repair or replacement of windows that were not initially defective but were damaged by the defective installation, then there is physical injury to tangible property. In other words, because the windows were purchased separately by the Homeowner, were not themselves defective, and were damaged as a result of the faulty installation, then there is physical injury to tangible property, i.e., windows damaged by defective installation." *Id.*; *see also Amerisure Mut. Ins. Co. v. Auchter Co.*, No. 3:08-cv-645, 2010 WL 457386, at *4–6 (M.D. Fla. Feb. 4, 2010) (addressing *J.S.U.B.* and *Pozzi Windows* at length).

**Georgia:** The Court of Appeals of Georgia addressed a general contractor's claim against a plumbing subcontractor for faulty workmanship and held that, "while construction defects constituting a breach of contract are not covered by CGL policies, negligently performed faulty workmanship that damages other property may constitute an 'occurrence' under a CGL policy." *Hathaway Dev. Co. v. Am. Empire Surplus Lines Ins. Co.*, 686 S.E.2d 855, 860 (Ga. Ct. App. 2009) (citing *SawHorse, Inc. v. S. Guar. Ins. Co. of Ga.*, 604 S.E.2d 541 (Ga. Ct. App. 2004)); *see also SawHorse, Inc.*, 604 S.E.2d at 546 ("Southern Guaranty has cited no Georgia authority supporting its apparent claim that faulty workmanship cannot constitute an 'occurrence' under a general commercial liability policy. And this claim runs counter to case law finding that policies with similar 'occurrence' language provide coverage for the risk that... defective or faulty workmanship will cause injury to people or damage to other property.") (citation and internal quotes omitted).

**Hawaii:** The Supreme Court of Hawaii held that "[w]ater damage to an exposed building is the foreseeable result of a contractor's abandonment of a roofing contract, such that this class of damages did not arise from an 'occurrence' as defined by the CGL policy." *Keneke Roofing, Inc. v. Island Ins. Co., Ltd.*, No. 24726, 2004 WL 2239233, at *1 (Hawaii Oct. 5, 2004); *see also Burlington Ins. Co. v. Oceanic Design & Constr., Inc.*, 383 F.3d 940, 948 (9th Cir. 2004) (applying Hawaii law) ("General liability policies... are not designed to provide contractors and developers with coverage against claims their work is inferior or defective. The risk of replacing and repairing defective materials or poor workmanship has generally been considered a commercial risk which is not passed on to the liability insurer. Rather liability coverage comes into play when the insured's defective materials or work cause injury to property other than the insured's own work or products.") (citation omitted); *Group Builders, Inc. v. Admiral Ins. Co.*, No. 29402, 231 P.3d 67, 73 (Hawaii Ct. App. 2010) (holding that construction defect claims do not constitute an "occurrence" under a CGL policy).

**Idaho:** No instructive authority. *See W. Heritage Ins. Co. v. Green*, 54 P.3d 948 (Idaho 2002) (addressing various business risk exclusions and acknowledging that the parties conceded that the nonapplication or insufficient application of fertilizer and weed control chemicals to farm ground, resulting in damage to potato crops, constituted an "occurrence" within the meaning of the policy).

**Illinois:** The Appellate Court of Illinois stated that "Illinois courts have held in numerous cases that construction defects that damage something other than the project itself will constitute an "occurrence" under a CGL policy." *CMK Dev. Corp. v. W. Bend Mut. Ins. Co.*, 917 N.E.2d 1155, 1164

(Ill. App. Ct. 2009) (citations and quotations omitted). The court examined several alleged construction defects and concluded that none qualified as damage to something other than the home itself. *Id.* at 1166–67; *see also Stoneridge Dev. Co., Inc. v. Essex Ins. Co.*, 888 N.E.2d 633, 656–57 (Ill. App. Ct. 2008) (holding that the "subcontractor exception" to the "your work" exclusion did not provide coverage for damage to a home, even though it was a subcontractor's defective soil compaction that caused the damage, because such damage was not "property damage" caused by an "occurrence" and an exception to an exclusion cannot create coverage).

**Indiana:** The Indiana Supreme Court held that claims against a general contractor, for defective construction of a home – lack of adequate flashing and quality caulking around the windows, lack of a weather resistant barrier behind the brick veneer, improperly installed roof shingles, among other things—constituted an "occurrence." *Sheehan Construction Company, Inc. v. Continental Casualty Co.*, __N.E.2d__ No. 49S02-1001-CV-32, 2010 WL 3823107 (Ind. Sept. 30, 2010). The court held that it was aligning itself "with those jurisdictions adopting the view that improper or faulty workmanship does constitute an accident so long as the resulting damage is an event that occurs without expectation or foresight." *Id.* at *6. "[I]f the faulty workmanship is 'unexpected' and 'without intention or design' and thus not foreseeable from the viewpoint of the insured, then it is an accident within the meaning of a CGL policy." *Id.* at *7. Among other reasons, the Indiana high court was persuaded that, if property damage to an insured's own work cannot be an "occurrence," then there would be no reason for the policy to contain a "your work" exclusion. *Id.* at *8 (discussing Clifford J. Shapiro, "The Good, the Bad, and the Ugly: New State Supreme Court Decisions Address Whether an Inadvertent Construction Defect is an 'Occurrence' Under CGL Policies," 25 *Constr. Law.*, Summer 2005, at 9, 12). The court distinguished *Indiana Ins. Co. v. DeZutti*, 408 N.E.2d 1275 (Ind. 1980) on the basis that it relied on exclusions to determine that no coverage existed and it was not the intent to suggest that faulty workmanship, that damages the contractor's own work, can never constitute a covered "occurrence." *Id.* at *5.

**Iowa:** The Supreme Court of Iowa held that claims against an insured who built basements and other portions of homes below the floodplain, in violation of a city ordinance, necessitating that the level of the homes be raised, did not qualify as an "occurrence." *Pursell Const., Inc. v. Hawkeye-Security Ins. Co.*, 596 N.W.2d 67, 71 (Iowa 1999). "If the policy is construed as protecting a contractor against mere faulty or defective workmanship, the insurer becomes a guarantor of the insured's performance of the contract, and the policy takes on the attributes of a performance bond." *Id.*; *see also W.C. Stewart Constr., Inc. v. Cincinnati Ins. Co.*, No. 08–0824, 2009 WL 928871, at *2–3 (Iowa Ct. App. Apr. 8, 2009) (holding that no coverage was owed for defective grading performed by insured, causing building movement and cracks in walls, because the damages sought were to the very property upon which the insured performed work and rejecting insured's argument that coverage was owed because its faulty workmanship required reconstruction of walls that it had not built).

**Kansas:** The Supreme Court of Kansas held that moisture leakage over time, caused by defective windows installed by the insured's subcontractor, which led to structural damage within a constructed home, qualified as an "occurrence." *Lee Builders, Inc. v. Farm Bureau Mut. Ins. Co.*, 137 P.3d 486, 495 (Kan. 2006). "The damage in the present case is an occurrence—an even more expansive coverage term than 'accident'—because faulty materials and workmanship provided by Lee's subcontractors caused continuous exposure of the Steinberger home to moisture. The moisture in turn caused damage that was both unforeseen and unintended." *Id.*

**Kentucky:** The Supreme Court of Kentucky held that a claim against a contractor, who was supposed to demolish a carport, but instead also demolished half of the attached residential structure, qualified as an "occurrence." *Bituminous Cas. Corp. v. Kenway Contracting, Inc.*, 240 S.W.3d 633, 640 (Ky. 2007). "The damage to the Turners' property was unexpected and unintended by the insured. It was not the plan, design, or intent of the insured. Therefore, the fortuity requirement in the definition of accident is satisfied." *Id.* at 639; *see also Cemex, Inc. v. LMS Contracting, Inc.*, No. 3:06-CV-124, 2008 WL 4682349, at *2 (W.D. Ky. Oct. 21, 2008) ("LMS did not intend or expect for explosives to be left on the job site, and as such the damage caused by leaving the explosives resulted from an accident.") (following *Kenway Contracting*). However, in *Cincinnati Ins. Co. v. Motorists Mut. Ins. Co.*, 306 S.W.3d 69 (Ky. 2010) the Supreme Court of Kentucky held, as a matter of first impression, that a claim against a builder, for defective construction of a home, did not qualify as an "occurrence". *Id.* at 76. Since the builder had control over the construction of the home, it could not be said that the allegedly substandard construction was a fortuitous, truly accidental event. *Id.* The court rejected any notion that its decision in *Bituminous Cas. Corp.* compelled a different result: "[T]he quick destruction of a residence is manifestly a completely different undertaking than the protracted improper construction of a residence. The home construction in the case at hand occurred over a period of weeks; the mistaken destruction of a carport in *Bituminous Cas. Corp.* occurred in a short flurry of activity on only one day. Because of this inescapable, material factual difference, *Bituminous Cas. Corp.* is not controlling on the narrow issue presented in this case: whether a claim of faulty construction may qualify as an 'occurrence' under a standard CGL policy." *Id.* at 77; *see also Acuity v. Krumpelman Builders, Inc.*, No. 09-9-DLB, 2010 WL 1434269, at *4 (E.D. Ky. Apr. 8, 2010) (following *Cincinnati*); *Global Gear & Machine Co., Inc. v. Capitol Indemnity Corp.*, No. 5:07-CV-00184, 2010 WL 3341464, at *3 (W.D. Ky. Aug. 23, 2010) (observing that the court in *Cincinnati* did not address whether property damage to something other than the insured's faulty workmanship is an "occurrence" and concluding that it is) (coverage precluded on other grounds).

**Louisiana:** The Court of Appeal of Louisiana held that a claim against a pile driving contractor, for damage to a newly constructed home, qualified as an "occurrence." *Rando v. Top Notch Props., L.L.C.*, 879 So. 2d 821, 833 (La. Ct. App. 2004). Following a comprehensive survey of Louisiana law, the court held that "the clear weight of authority in more recent cases considers defects in construction that result in damage subsequent to completion to be accidents and occurrences when they manifest themselves. However, a clear signal from the Supreme Court on this issue would surely do much to eliminate expensive future litigation." *Id.*; *see also Joe Banks Drywall & Acoustics, Inc. v. Transcon. Ins. Co.*, 753 So. 2d 980, 983 (La. Ct. App. 2000) (holding that a claim against a sheet vinyl flooring subcontractor, for staining of a floor that it installed, qualified as an "occurrence" because there was no allegation that the damage at issue was intentional); *Supreme Servs. & Specialty Co. v. Sonny Greer, Inc.*, 958 So. 2d 634, 643 (La. 2007) (holding that a CGL policy containing a "work product" exclusion did not insure any obligation of the policyholder to repair or replace his own defective product) (not addressing whether the damage was caused by an "occurrence").

**Maine:** The Supreme Judicial Court of Maine held that a claim against a contractor, for failure to frame two houses in accordance with the plans and specifications, did not qualify as an "occurrence." *Peerless Ins. Co. v. Brennon*, 564 A.2d 383, 386 (Me. 1989). "An 'occurrence of harm risk' is a risk that a person or property other than the product itself will be damaged through the fault of the contractor. A 'business risk' is a risk that the contractor will not do his job competently, and thus will be obligated to replace or repair his faulty work. The distinction between the two risks is critical to understanding a CGL policy. A CGL policy covers an occurrence of harm risk but specifically excludes a business risk." *Id.* (citation omitted); *see also Baywood Corp. v. Maine Bonding & Cas. Co.*, 628 A.2d 1029, 1031 (Me. 1993) ("[G]eneral comprehensive liability policy affords coverage when faulty work causes an accident resulting in physical damage to others, but not for contractor's product or complete work, which is a business expense.") (citing *Brennon*, 564 A.2d at 386).

**Maryland:** The Court of Special Appeals of Maryland held that an insured contractor's liability for the negligent installation of a façade on a building was not unexpected or unforeseen and, therefore, did not result from an accident. *Lerner Corp. v. Assurance Co. of Am.*, 707 A.2d 906, 911 (Md. Ct. Spec. App. 1998); *see also French v. Assurance Co. of Am.*, 448 F.3d 693, 706 (4th Cir. 2006) (holding that the CGL policy does not provide coverage to a general contractor for the cost to correct defective workmanship performed by a subcontractor, but coverage is owed for the cost to remedy unexpected and unintended property damage to the contractor's otherwise nondefective work-product caused by the subcontractor's defective workmanship); *Travelers Indem. Co. of Am. v. Tower-Dawson, LLC*, 299 Fed. App'x 277, 282 (4th Cir. 2008) (following *French*) ("[I]t is evident that the cost of installing the new retaining wall and the cost of repairing the damage to the federally-protected wetlands brought about by the installation of the new retaining wall are not covered losses under the Policies.").

**Massachusetts:** The Appeals Court of Massachusetts held that an insured's subcontractor's negligent installation of a concrete slab, in the course of construction of a school building, did not qualify as an "occurrence." *Mello Constr., Inc. v. Acadia Ins. Co.*, No. 06-P-100, 2007 WL 2908267, at *3 (Mass. App. Ct. Oct. 5, 2007); *see also Friel Luxury Home Constr., Inc. v. ProBuilders Specialty Ins. Co. RRG*, No. 09-cv-11036, 2009 WL 5227893, at *4–5. (D. Mass. Dec. 22, 2009) (holding that a claim against an insured contractor, for faulty construction and renovation work on a home, did not qualify as "property damage," nor caused by an "occurrence"); *Am. Home Assurance Co. v. AGM Marine Contractors, Inc.*, 467 F.3d 810, 813 (1st Cir. 2006) ("Whether Massachusetts would follow the 'occurrence' cases is not certain. In *Caplette* [*Commerce Ins. Co. v. Betty Caplette Builders, Inc.*, 647 N.E.2d 1211 (Mass. 1995)] the Supreme Judicial Court bypassed the issue in a case involving damage to the insured's product, going instead directly to the exclusions. This might suggest that the SJC thought that the occurrence and property damage requirements were satisfied, but the parties did not dispute the issue. In all events, one of the exclusions in this case bars coverage even if we assume *arguendo* that there was an occurrence and property damage within the meaning of the policy.").

**Michigan:** The Court of Appeals of Michigan held that an insured–mobilehome seller's provision of defective instructions to contractors hired by the home's purchaser, for the construction of a basement foundation and erection of the home on such foundation, qualified as an "occurrence." *Radenbaugh v. Farm Bureau Gen. Ins. Co. of Mich.*, 610 N.W.2d 272, 280 (Mich. Ct. App. 2000). "[I]t is clear that the underlying complaint alleged damages broader than mere diminution in value of the insured's product caused by alleged defective workmanship, breach of contract, or breach of warranty." *Id.* at 276; *see also Ahrens Constr., Inc. v. Amerisure Ins. Co.*, No. 288272, 2010 WL 446543, at *2 (Mich. Ct. App. Feb. 10, 2010) ("[T]here is little dispute that damages arising solely from faulty workmanship are not considered as resulting from an 'occurrence.'"); *Groom v. Home-Owners Ins. Co.*, No. 272840, 2007 WL 1166050, at *5 (Mich. Ct. App. Apr. 19, 2007) ("[W]here the 'damage arising out of the insured's defective workmanship is confined to the insured's own work product, the insured is the injured party, and the damage cannot be viewed as accidental within the meaning of the standard liability policy.'") (quoting *Radenbaugh*, 610 N.W.2d at 280) (citation omitted); *Houseman Construction Co. v. Cincinnati Ins. Co.*, No. 1:08-CV-719, 2010 WL 1658959, at *4 (W.D. Mich. Apr. 23, 2010) (holding that a sinking floor, which was the result of defective workmanship, was not an "occurrence").

**Minnesota:** The Supreme Court of Minnesota addressed the potential for coverage for construction defects without regard to whether the claim qualified as "property damage" caused by an "occurrence." *Thommes v. Milwaukee Ins. Co.*, 641 N.W.2d 877 (Minn. 2002). Instead, the court's analysis was based on the general principle that business risks arising from contractual liability for defective materials and workmanship are not covered, while risks arising from tort liability to third parties are covered. *Id.* at 881 (addressing *Bor-Son Bldg. Corp. v. Employers Commercial Union Ins. Co. of Am.*, 323 N.W.2d 58 (Minn. 1982) and *Knutson Constr. Co. v. St. Paul Fire & Marine Ins. Co.*, 396 N.W.2d 229 (Minn. 1986)). However, the analysis did not end with the business risk principles: "If parties to an insurance contract demonstrate their intent, using clear and unambiguous language, to exclude the risk of damage to the real property of third parties, then there is no need to look to business risk principles to ascertain whether the policy was intended to cover such risks." *Id.* at 882.

**Mississippi:** The Supreme Court of Mississippi held that a claim against a contractor, for damages caused by a subcontractor's failure to install rebar in the foundation of a building, qualified as an "occurrence." *Architex Ass'n, Inc. v. Scottsdale Ins. Co.*, 27 So. 3d 1148, 1162 (Miss. 2010). "While the alleged 'property damage' may have been 'set in motion' by Architex's intentional hiring of the subcontractors, the 'chain of events' may not have 'followed a course consciously devised and controlled by [Architex], without the unexpected intervention of any third person or extrinsic force.'" *Id.* at 1159 (citation omitted) (alteration in original). The opinion does not address the "occurrence" issue outside the subcontractor context.

**Missouri:** The Missouri Court of Appeals held that a claim against a contractor, for the cost to remove and replace a home's subfloor and framing, on account of defective concrete supplied by the insured's subcontractor and used for a foundation, qualified as an "occurrence." *Columbia Mut. Ins. Co. v. Epstein*, 239 S.W.3d 667, 673 (Mo. Ct. App. 2007). "Epstein sold and delivered to the Doerrs concrete for a basement foundation, that through no fault of Epstein, the concrete was defective, that the defective nature of the concrete damaged the sub-floor and framing of the home in that it all had to be torn down and replaced, and that neither the defect in the concrete nor the damage to the home was foreseeable to Epstein." *Id.* at 672–73. The court distinguished *American States Insurance Co. v. Mathis*, 974 S.W.2d 647 (Mo. Ct. App. 2007), which held that failure to construct ducts according to contract specifications did not qualify as an "occurrence" because it was within the insured's control and management and it did not cause damage to other property. *Id.* at 672.

**Montana:** The Supreme Court of Montana held that an insured's subcontractor's defective manufacturing of disposable sanitary bags, for use in another party's portable toilets, qualified as an "event," defined in the policy as an "accident." *Revelation Indus., Inc. v. St. Paul Fire & Marine Ins. Co.*, 206 P.3d 919, 929 (Mont. 2009). The court rested its decision, in part, on the following example contained in the policy of the operation of the "your work" exclusion and "subcontractor exception," which the court deemed to be indistinguishable from the situation before it: "You construct a building as a general contractor. Some of the work is done by you while the rest is done for you by subcontractors. The building is accepted by the owner. If it's damaged by a fire caused by electrical wiring installed by a subcontractor, we won't apply the exclusion. However, if the wiring was installed by you, we'll apply the exclusion to property damage to your completed work done by you." *Id.*; *see also King v. State Farm Fire & Cas. Co.*, No. CR 09–96-M-DWM, 2010 WL 1994708, at *4–5 (D. Mont. May 18, 2010) (holding that claims against the seller of a log home kit, for misrepresentations about the quality of the logs and refusal to correct deficiencies, did not allege an "occurrence").

**Nebraska:** The Supreme Court of Nebraska held that damage to roof structures and buildings, caused by an insured's subcontractor's negligent installation of shingles, qualified as an "occurrence." *Auto-Owners Ins. Co. v. Home Pride Cos.*, 684 N.W.2d 571, 579 (Neb. 2004). "[A]lthough a standard CGL policy does not provide coverage for faulty workmanship that damages only the resulting work product, if faulty workmanship causes bodily injury or property damage to something other than the insured's work product, an unintended and unexpected event has occurred, and coverage exists." *Id.* at 578. The court described the damage to the roof structures and buildings as "an unintended and unexpected consequence of the contractors' faulty workmanship" which went beyond damages to the contractors' own work product, and, therefore, qualified as an occurrence. *Id.* at 579.

**Nevada:** A Nevada District Court held that claims against an insured framing contractor, for water damage to homes allegedly caused by its defective work, qualified as an "occurrence." *Gary G. Day Constr. Co. v. Clarendon Am. Ins. Co.*, 459 F. Supp. 2d 1039, 1047 (D. Nev. 2006). The court noted that the Supreme Court of Nevada, interpreting similar "occurrence" language, defined "accident" as "a happening that is not expected, foreseen, or intended." *Id.* (quoting *Beckwith v. State Farm Fire & Cas. Co.*, 83 P.3d 275, 277 (Nev. 2004)). "The Court finds that water intrusion is a 'happening that is not expected, foreseen, or intended' and thus falls within the definition of 'occurrence.' Certainly, neither the Plaintiff nor the homeowners intended to have water intrude into the 20 homes. Nor can it be said that either the Plaintiff or the homeowners expected or foresaw the water intrusion." *Id.*

**New Hampshire:** The Supreme Court of New Hampshire held that a claim against a landscaper, for faulty workmanship in constructing a leach field and performing landscaping, did not qualify as an "occurrence." *McAllister v. Peerless Ins. Co.*, 474 A.2d 1033, 1036–37 (N.H. 1984) (Souter, J.). "The fortuity implied by reference to accident or exposure is not what is commonly meant by a failure of workmanship." *Id.* at 1036; *see also Webster v. Acadia Ins. Co.*, 934 A.2d 567, 573 (N.H. 2007) (distinguishing *McAllister* and holding that the "occurrence" requirement was satisfied because the claim alleged damage to property other than the work of the contractor-insured); *see also Concord Gen. Mut. Ins. Co. v. Green & Co. Building & Develop. Corp.*, __A.3d __, No. 2009-699, 2010 WL 3618713 (N.H. Sept. 17, 2010) (acknowledging that defective work, standing alone, does not constitute an "occurrence," but, rather, an "occurrence" is damage to property other than the work product and damage to the work product other than the defective workmanship) (holding that the entry of carbon monoxide into homes, caused by defective chimneys, was not an "occurrence" because the carbon monoxide caused no physical, tangible alteration of the property, homeowners continued to occupy their homes and no homeowners suffered bodily injury) ("The only effect caused by the faulty chimneys was their loss of use. The loss of use of the insured's work product, standing alone, is not sufficient to constitute an 'occurrence' under the policy.").

**New Jersey:** The Superior Court of New Jersey, Appellate Division, held that claims against a general contractor, for the cost of replacing substandard firewalls installed by subcontractors in condominiums, did not qualify as an "occurrence." *Firemen's Ins. Co. of Newark v. Nat'l Union Fire Ins. Co.*, 904 A.2d 754, 763 (N.J. Super. Ct. App. Div. 2006). The court's decision was based on the fact that the damage was limited to the cost of replacing the firewalls. *Id.* at 762–63; *see also S.N. Golden Estates, Inc. v. Cont'l Cas. Co.*, 680 A.2d 1114, 1117 (N.J. Super. Ct. App. Div. 1996) (holding that claims against a developer, for the failure of septic systems, causing effluent to seep onto lawns and into homes, qualified as an "occurrence"); *Pa. Nat'l Mut. Cas. Ins. Co. v. Parkshore Dev. Corp.*, No. 07–1331, 2008 WL 4276917, at *4 (D.N.J. Sept. 10, 2008) (holding that damage limited to an insured's work product did not qualify as an "occurrence") (comparing *Firemen's* and *S.N. Golden Estates*).

**New Mexico:** No instructive authority. *But see King v. Travelers Ins. Co.*, 505 P.2d 1226 (N.M. 1973). The Supreme Court of New Mexico addressed whether water damage had been caused by "accidental discharge, leakage or overflow," as required by a first-party property policy. *Id.* at 1228. In addressing the issue, the court cited with approval the holding of the Supreme Court of Minnesota in *Hauenstein v. Saint Paul-Mercury Indemnity Co.*, 65 N.W.2d 122 (Minn. 1954): "There is no doubt that the property damage to the building caused by the application of the defective plaster was 'caused by accident' within the meaning of the insurance contract, since the damage was a completely unexpected and unintended result. Accident, as a source and cause of damage to property, within the terms of an accident policy, is an unexpected, unforeseen, or undesigned happening or consequence from either a known or an unknown cause." *Travelers Ins. Co.*, 505 P.2d at 1229–30 (quoting *Hauenstein*, 65 N.W.2d at 126).

**New York:** The Supreme Court of New York, Appellate Division, held that a claim against a construction manager for failing to adequately and properly supervise the installation of (1) a building's wood flooring, leading to its buckling and cracking, and (2) a curtain wall and windows that caused widespread water infiltration, did not qualify as an "occurrence." *George A. Fuller Co. v. U.S. Fid. & Guar. Co.*, 613 N.Y.S.2d 152, 155 (N.Y. App. Div. 1994). The policy "does not insure against faulty workmanship in the work product itself but rather faulty workmanship in the work product which creates a legal liability by causing bodily injury or property damage to something other than the work product. The policy was never intended to provide contractual indemnification for economic loss to a contracting party because the work product contracted for is defectively produced." *Id.*; *see also Transp. Ins. Co. v. AARK Constr. Group, Ltd.*, 526 F. Supp. 2d 350, 357 (E.D.N.Y. 2007) (following *Fuller* and holding that the costs of repair of a garage, and loss of use of the building incident to the closure of the garage, did not qualify as an "occurrence" because the alleged negligence only affected the property owner's economic interest in the insured contractor's completed work product); *Saks v. Nicosia Contracting Corp.*, 625 N.Y.S.2d 758, 760 (N.Y. App. Div. 1995) (distinguishing *Fuller* and finding an "occurrence" because the claim against the contractor was not that the house it built was defective, but, rather, was for damage to real property on which the house encroached); *Continental Ins. Co. v. Huff Enterprises, Inc.*, No. 07-CV-3821, 2010 WL 2836343, at *4 (E.D.N.Y. June 21, 2010) ("[I]f the damage to be remedied is faulty work or the product itself, rather than an injury to a person or other property because of the faulty work product, the alleged act is not an 'occurrence' under standard insurance contracts.").

**North Carolina:** The Supreme Court of North Carolina held that a claim against a roofer, for water damage resulting from its failure to cover a partially removed roof, qualified as an "accident." *Iowa Mut. Ins. Co. v. Fred M. Simmons, Inc.*, 128 S.E.2d 19, 25 (N.C. 1962). "[W]e do not subscribe to the view that the term 'accident,' used in the liability policy here, considered in its usual, ordinary, and popular sense necessarily excludes human fault called negligence, because negligence would most probably be the predicate of any likely liability against appellant." *Id.* More recent decisions addressing North Carolina law have focused on the "property damage" requirement of the insuring agreement—and not the "occurrence" requirement—and have held that damage solely to an insured's work does not qualify as "property damage." *See Production Systems, Inc. v. Amerisure Ins. Co.*, 605 S.E.2d 663 (N.C. Ct. App. 2004); *see also Breezewood of Wilmington Condominiums Homeowners' Assn. Inc. v. Amerisure Mut. Ins. Co.*, 335 Fed. Appx. 268, 271 (4th Cir. 2009) ("North Carolina state courts and federal courts sitting in diversity have consistently held that 'property damage' in the context of commercial general liability policies means 'damage to property that was previously undamaged' and does not include 'the expense of repairing property or completing a project that was not done correctly or according to contract in the first instance' by the insured.") (citing cases).

**North Dakota:** The Supreme Court of North Dakota held that water damage to the interior of a building, caused by the insured's failure to protect it against rain during a roof replacement project, qualified as an "occurrence." *ACUITY v. Burd & Smith Constr., Inc.*, 721 N.W.2d 33, 39 (N.D. 2006). "We agree with the rationale of those courts holding that faulty workmanship causing damage to property other than the work product is an accidental occurrence for purposes of a CGL policy. That rationale is consistent with the coverage risks for a CGL policy and the plain and ordinary language of the policy. We conclude property damage caused by faulty workmanship is a covered occurrence to the extent the faulty workmanship causes bodily injury or property damage to property other than the insured's work product." *Id.*

**Ohio:** The Court of Appeals of Ohio held that claims against a condominium developer, for property damage caused by its negligence in constructing and designing a condominium complex, qualified as an "occurrence." *Erie Ins. Exch. v. Colony Dev. Corp.*, 736 N.E.2d 941, 947 (Ohio Ct. App. 1999). The court agreed with the general proposition that a liability policy is not a performance bond and does not cover claims for the repair or replacement of defective work. *Id.* However, "the rationale for the proposition is not that the allegations of negligent construction or design practices do not fall within the broad coverage for property damage caused by an occurrence, but that,… the damages resulting from such practices are usually excluded from coverage by the standard exclusions found in such policies." *Id.*; *see also Dublin Bldg. Sys. v. Selective Ins. Co. of S.*, 874 N.E.2d 788, 792 (Ohio Ct. App. 2007) (holding that a claim against a general contractor for property damage, including mold contamination, resulting from defective workmanship by its exterior stucco subcontractor, qualified as an "occurrence"); *Beaverdam Contracting v. Erie Ins. Co.*, No. 1–08–17, 2008 WL 4378153, at *3 n.5 (Ohio Ct. App. Sept. 29, 2008) ("We note that many courts in Ohio have reached different conclusions as to whether claims of negligence and/or failure to perform in a workmanlike manner constitute an accident for purposes of establishing an 'occurrence' under CGL insurance contracts."); *Westfield Ins. Co. v. R.L. Diorio Custom Homes, Inc.*, No. CA2009–09–125, 2010 WL 918030, at *3 (Ohio App. Ct. Mar. 15, 2010) (despite recognizing that some courts have concluded that an insured's defective workmanship on a construction project constitutes an "occurrence," including *Colony Dev. Corp.*, the court held, without analysis, that defective workmanship does not constitute an "occurrence").

**Oklahoma:** An Oklahoma District Court held that a claim for damages resulting from the insured's delivery of defective concrete to a bridge construction project qualified as an "occurrence." *Employers Mut. Cas. Co. v. Grayson*, No. CIV-07–917, 2008 WL 2278593, at *5 (W.D. Okla. May 30, 2008). "[I]t is undisputed that Ready Mix [the insured] did not knowingly deliver concrete containing fly ash. Nor is there any suggestion that a reasonable supplier in its position would have known the concrete contained fly ash or was otherwise non-conforming. Thus, the damage to the bridge deck and to its structural components during the required removal of the defective concrete was the unintended consequence of Ready Mix innocently supplying a non-conforming product." *Id.*

**Oregon:** The Supreme Court of Oregon held that a claim against a general contractor on a residential construction project, for the removal and replacement of a subcontractor's interior painting work that had failed to cure properly, did not qualify as an "occurrence." *Oak Crest Constr. Co. v. Austin Mut. Ins. Co.*, 998 P.2d 1254, 1258 (Or. 2000). "Had the facts demonstrated that the claimed problem with the cabinets and woodwork was the result of that kind of breach [of the duty to act with due care—as opposed to breach of contract], or that plaintiff might be liable to the owners in tort for other damage, that might have qualified as an 'accident' within the meaning of the commercial liability policy." *Id.*; *see also MW Builders, Inc. v. Safeco Ins. Co. of Am.*, 267 Fed. App'x 552, 554 (9th Cir. 2008) (applying Oregon law) (holding that damage to a hotel as a result of faulty installation of EIFS, as opposed to any damages associated with the actual replacement of the EIFS, qualified as an "occurrence").

**Pennsylvania:** The Supreme Court of Pennsylvania held that claims against the insured, for defective design and construction of a coke oven battery, did not qualify as an "occurrence." *Kvaerner Metals Div. of Kvaerner U.S., Inc. v. Commercial Union Ins. Co.*, 908 A.2d 888, 899 (Pa. 2006). "We hold that the definition of 'accident' required to establish an 'occurrence' under the policies cannot be satisfied by claims based upon faulty workmanship. Such claims simply do not present the degree of fortuity contemplated by the ordinary definition of 'accident' or its common judicial construction in this context." *Id.*; *see also Millers Capital Ins. Co. v. Gambone Bros. Dev. Co., Inc.*, 941 A.2d 706, 713 (Pa. Super. Ct. 2007) (addressing *Kvaerner*) ("[N]atural and foreseeable acts, such as rainfall, which tend to exacerbate the damage, effect, or consequences caused *ab initio* by faulty workmanship [of windows, roofs and stucco exteriors] also cannot be considered sufficiently fortuitous to constitute an 'occurrence' or 'accident' for the purposes of an occurrence based CGL policy."); *Specialty Surfaces International, Inc. v. Continental Cas. Co.*, 609 F.3d 223 (3rd Cir. 2010) (holding that, based on *Kvaerner* and *Gambone*, no coverage was owed to an insured for its faulty workmanship, nor for any damage to other property that was a reasonably foreseeable result of such faulty workmanship, on the basis that neither constituted an "occurrence"); *Nationwide Mut. Ins. Co. v. CPB International, Inc.*, 562 F.3d 591 (3rd Cir. 2009) (holding that no coverage was owed for the consequential damages caused by combining the insured's defective chondroitin, with glucosamine, to form nutritional tablets, because it was foreseeable that the product that the insured sold would be used for the purpose for which it was sold); *Erie Ins. Exchange v. Abbott Furnace Co.*, 972 A.2d 1232 (Pa. Super. Ct. 2009) (holding that no coverage was owed for damage to property caused by the insured's defective furnace); *Bomgardner Concrete v. State Farm Fire & Cas.*, No. 10-1287, 2010 WL 3657084 (E.D. Pa. Sept. 14, 2010) (holding that no coverage was owed to a cement installer, for a defective floor, notwithstanding that the spalling and delamination of the concrete was caused by the concrete itself (excess water and failing to properly cure) — that had been supplied by a party other than the insured).

**Rhode Island:** A Rhode Island trial court held that claims against an insured, for damages allegedly caused by its negligent preparation of specifications used by others on a sewer project, qualified as an "occurrence." *Aetna Cas. & Sur. Co. v. Consulting Envtl. Eng'rs, Inc.*, No. P.C. 88–2075, 1989 WL 1110231, at *4 (R.I. Super. Ct. June 20, 1989). "The installation of the manholes and pipes at the wrong level in one location and their settlement to the wrong level at another may well have been the foreseeable consequence of some negligence of the defendant [insured]... . But, one cannot say that the defendant expected the damaging consequences of its conduct unless one can say that the defendant knew that its conduct would result in the harmful consequence and pursued it anyway, taking what has been called a 'calculated risk.'" *Id.*

**South Carolina:** The Supreme Court of South Carolina held that the deterioration of roads, caused by a contractor's faulty workmanship, did not qualify as an "occurrence." *L-J, Inc. v. Bituminous Fire & Marine Ins. Co.*, 621 S.E.2d 33, 36 (S.C. 2005). The court concluded that the roadway contractor's faulty workmanship, which caused damaged to only the roadway system, was not something that is typically caused by an accident, and, therefore, did not constitute an "occurrence." *Id.*; *see also Auto Owners Ins. Co. v. Newman*, 684 S.E.2d 541, 546 (S.C. 2009) (holding that the "expected or intended" exclusion did not serve as a basis to preclude coverage for damage to a home's framing and exterior sheathing, caused by a subcontractor's negligent application of stucco that lead to water intrusion, because the insured did not expect or intend its subcontractor to perform negligently); *Builders Mut. Ins. Co. v. R. Design Construction Co.*, No. 2:07–1890, 2010 WL 2079741, at *6 (D.S.C. May 24, 2010) (discussing *L-J* and *Newman* and holding that, because numerous defects discovered early in the construction process could have been corrected before the project was completed, damage to other parts of the structure, caused by faulty workmanship, was not an accident, and, hence, not an "occurrence."); *Builders Mut. Ins. Co. v. Wingard Properties, Inc.*, No. 4-07-3183, 2010 WL 3699989 (D.S.C. Sept. 13, 2010) (discussing *L-J* and *Newman* and holding that, because some punch-list items may assert some minimal resulting damage to a residence, as a result of faulty workmanship, some "occurrence" could be present under the policy) (discussing a "your work" exclusion that had been amended to eliminate the "subcontractor exception").

**South Dakota:** The Supreme Court of South Dakota, addressing a policy that contained a Broad Form Property Damage Endorsement (BFPDE) (now the "your work" exclusion with "subcontractor exception") held that a subcontractor's faulty workmanship, that resulted in damage to the insured's work, was covered, provided that such damage was caused by an "occurrence." *Corner Constr. Co. v. U.S. Fid. & Guar. Co.*, 638 N.W.2d 887, 894 (S.D. 2002). "As required by the insuring clause, there was an accident or unintended event, resulting in property damage that was neither expected nor intended by the insured, at least in respect to the following: Cub [subcontractor], which was hired to do the insulation work, left voids in the insulation between the studs and failed to securely attach the vapor barrier. The vapor barrier fell, causing temperature fluctuations and other ventilation problems. As a result, Corner's [insured] own work was damaged by the faulty work of its subcontractor... . Such damage is covered by the insuring clause in connection with the BFPDE." *Id.* at 894–95.

**Tennessee:** The Supreme Court of Tennessee held that various types of damage to a hotel construction project, caused by the insured's subcontractor's negligent installation of windows, qualified as an "occurrence." *Travelers Indem. Co. of Am. v. Moore & Assocs., Inc.*, 216 S.W.3d 302, 309 (Tenn. 2007). The court concluded that, because it must be assumed that the windows would be installed properly, the insured could not have foreseen the water penetration, and, therefore, the damage qualified as an accident and an "occurrence." *Id.* The court also addressed the "subcontractor exception" to the "your work" exclusion: "It is alleged that the installation of the windows was performed by subcontractors hired by [the insured]. Therefore, damages resulting from the subcontractors' faulty installation of the windows are not excluded from coverage, even if those damages affected [the insured's] work." *Id.* at 310; *see also Cincinnati Ins. Co. v. Grand Pointe, LLC*, Nos. 105-CV-161, 105-CV-157, 2007 WL 1585542, at *3 (E.D. Tenn. May 30, 2007) (addressing *Moore & Associates* and holding that damage solely to a condominium building that the insureds were contracted to design and build did not qualify as "property damage") (declining to address the "subcontractor exception" to the "your work" exclusion because "it is futile to consider the exclusions to the policy since there is no initial coverage under the insuring agreement").

**Texas:** The Supreme Court of Texas held that a claim against a general contractor, for damage to a home's sheetrock and veneer, caused by the contractor's negligence in designing and constructing the home's foundation, qualified as an "occurrence." *Lamar Homes, Inc. v. Mid-Continent Cas. Co.*, 242 S.W.3d 1, 9 (Tex. 2007). The court concluded that there is no logical basis within the definition of "occurrence" for distinguishing between damage to the insured's work and damage to a third party's property. *Id.* "Both types of property damage are caused by the same thing—negligent or defective work." *Id.* (quoting *Erie Ins. Exch. v. Colony Dev. Corp.*, 736 N.E.2d 950, 952 n.1 (Ohio Ct. App. 2000)); *see also Century Sur. Co. v. Hardscape Constr.*

*Specialties Inc.*, 578 F.3d 262, 266 (5th Cir. 2009) (discussing *Lamar Homes*) (allegations of unintended construction defects may constitute an "accident" or "occurrence" under commercial general liability policies).

**Utah:** A Utah District Court held that a claim against a contractor, for inadequate preparation of a soil pad at a construction site, did not qualify as an "occurrence." *H.E. Davis & Sons, Inc. v. N. Pac. Ins. Co.*, 248 F. Supp. 2d 1079, 1084 (D. Utah 2002). The failure to adequately compact the soil led to its natural consequences—removal and replacement of the soil pad and the concrete footings. *Id.* "So long as the consequences of plaintiff's work were natural, expected, or intended, they cannot be considered an 'accident.'" *Id.* In *Great American Insurance Co. v. Woodside Homes Corp.*, 448 F. Supp. 2d 1275 (D. Utah 2006), the court distinguished *H.E. Davis* and held that a subcontractor's faulty work is an "occurrence" from the standpoint of the insured. *Id.* at 1283. "Given the Utah Supreme Court's focus on the acts of the insured when determining whether there has been an occurrence, it follows that the negligent acts of Woodside's subcontractors can be considered an occurrence from Woodside's 'point of view.'" *Id.* at 1281. "[T]he conclusion that defective subcontractor work can be considered an occurrence harmonizes other provisions contained in the policy that might otherwise be in tension." *Id.* at 1282 (analyzing the "occurrence" issue in conjunction with the "subcontractor exception" to the "your work" exclusion); *see also Cincinnati Ins. Co. v. Linford Bros. Glass Co.*, No. 2:08-CV-387, 2010 WL 520490, at *3 (D. Utah Feb. 9, 2010) ("Because the reasonably foreseeable consequences of negligently manufacturing windows and doors include damage to the property in which the defective products are installed, there can be no 'occurrence' here under Utah law.").

**Vermont:** A Vermont District Court held, without analysis, that claims against a construction company, for negligent construction or design of the dormers and heating system of a hotel, qualified as an "occurrence," because an accident is "an unexpected happening without intention or design." *Transcon. Ins. Co. v. Engelberth Constr., Inc.*, No. 1:06-CV-213, 2007 WL 3333465, at *3 (D. Vt. Nov. 8, 2007) (quoting *Commercial Union Ins. Co. v. City of Montpelier*, 353 A.2d 344, 346 (Vt. 1976)); *see also Fine Paints of Europe, Inc. v. Acadia Ins. Co.*, No. 2:08-CV-81, 2009 WL 819466, at *6 (D. Vt. Mar. 24, 2009) (finding that there being no dispute that the insured paint retailer did not intend the injury caused by its faulty paint (cracking, chipping, peeling, loss of adhesion, and separation from the primer), the paint failure constituted an "occurrence" under Vermont law).

**Virginia:** The Fourth Circuit Court of Appeals, applying Virginia law, held that clams against a general contractor, for damages to homes caused by mold contained in trusses supplied by a subcontractor, qualified as an "occurrence." *Stanley Martin Cos. v. Ohio Cas. Group*, 313 Fed. App'x 609, 614 (4th Cir. 2009). "Stanley Martin's obligation to repair or replace the defective trusses was not unexpected or unforeseen under the terms of its building contracts for the townhouses and does not trigger a duty to indemnify.

However, any mold damage that spread beyond the defective trusses and the gypsum fire walls to nondefective components of the townhouses was an unintended accident, or an occurrence that triggered coverage under the Ohio Casualty policy." *Id.* The court distanced itself from its seemingly opposite decision in *Travelers Indemnity Co. of America v. Miller Building Corp.*, 142 Fed. App'x 147 (4th Cir. 2005) (applying Virginia Law), on the basis that the holding in *Miller Building* rested on "case law that addressed damage that a general contractor's defective work caused to its own finished product, not damage that a subcontractor's defective work caused to the general contractor's nondefective work." *Id.* at 613.

**West Virginia:** The Supreme Court of Appeals of West Virginia held that claims against an insured engineering firm, for damages caused by its defective design and supervision of construction of a landfill, did not qualify as an "occurrence." *Webster County Solid Waste Auth. v. Brackenrich & Assocs., Inc.*, 617 S.E.2d 851, 856 (W. Va. 2005). The court concluded that all of the claims were for poor workmanship, which, standing alone, did not constitute an "occurrence." *Id.*; *see also N. Am. Precast, Inc. v. Gen. Cas. Co. of Wis.*, No. 3:04–1307, 2008 WL 906327, at *7 (S.D. W. Va. Mar. 31, 2008) ("The collapse of the [concrete] panel, though caused by North American's poor workmanship, may be considered an accident and thus possibly an occurrence under the policy to the limited extent that the panel is found to have damaged the floor and one or two of the walls of the jail structure under construction[.]"); *Simpson-Littman Construction, Inc. v. Erie Ins. Prop. & Cas. Ins. Co.*, No. 3:09-0240, 2010 WL 3702601 (S.D .W. Va. Sept 13, 2010) (examining West Virginia and other state case law in detail and concluding that faulty workmanship is not an "occurrence," but, rather, something more than the flawed performance is required to trigger coverage).

**Washington:** The Court of Appeals of Washington held that a claim against a construction company, for damage to a building, caused by dry rot which resulted from dirt having been piled against the box sills of the building by backfilling during construction, qualified as an "occurrence." *Gruol Constr. Co., Inc. v. Ins. Co. of N. Am.*, 524 P.2d 427, 429 (Wash. Ct. App. 1974). "We recognize that dry rot is the expected result when moisture is introduced to dirt which is too close to wood but the fact that the condition (defective backfilling) was not detected during construction supports the finding that the dry rot which resulted from the unknown condition was unexpected. It cannot be disputed that it was undesigned." *Id.* at 430; *see also Mid-Continent Cas. Co. v. Titan Constr. Corp.*, 281 Fed. App'x 766, 768 (9th Cir. 2008) (applying Washington law) ("Absent any allegation that the substandard construction in this case resulted from an intentional breach of contract by Titan, we conclude that the negligent construction of the Williamsburg project that resulted in breach of contract and breach of warranty claims constituted an 'occurrence.'").

**Wisconsin:** The Supreme Court of Wisconsin held that damage to a warehouse constructed by an insured–general contractor, caused by a soil engineering subcontractor's faulty site-preparation advice, qualified as an "occurrence." *Am. Family Mut. Ins. Co. v. Am. Girl, Inc.*, 673 N.W.2d 65, 76 (Wis. 2004). "The damage to the 94DC occurred as a result of the continuous, substantial, and harmful settlement of the soil underneath the building. Lawson's inadequate site-preparation advice was a cause of this exposure to harm. Neither the cause nor the harm was intended, anticipated, or expected." *Id.* The court also addressed the "subcontractor exception" to the "your work" exclusion and rejected the insurer's argument that it creates coverage where none existed: "There is coverage under the insuring agreement's initial coverage grant. Coverage would be excluded by the business risk exclusionary language, except that the subcontractor exception to the business risk exclusion applies, which operates to restore the otherwise excluded coverage." *Id.* at 83–84; *see also Toldt Woods Condominiums Owner's Ass'n, Inc. v. Madeline Square, LLC*, No. 2007AP1763, 2008 WL 3387532, at *7 (Wis. Ct. App. Aug. 13, 2008) (examining several Wisconsin decisions and concluding that faulty workmanship is not an "occurrence," but, rather, faulty workmanship that causes damage to other property is an "occurrence"); *Mantz Automation, Inc. v. Navigators Ins. Co.*, No. 2009AP1681, 2010 WL 1881941 (Wis. Ct. App. May 12, 2010) (holding that faulty workmanship in itself does not constitute an "occurrence" and there was no evidence of subsequent property damage).

**Wyoming:** A Wyoming District Court held that claims against a contractor for water damage to a resort, caused by improper installation and waterproofing of siding, did not qualify as an "occurrence." *Great Divide Ins. Co. v. Bitterroot Timberframes of Wyoming, LLC*, No. 06-CV-020, 2006 WL 3933078, at *8 (D. Wyo. Oct. 20, 2006). "[T]he allegations demonstrate losses resulting from breach of contract, as water damage is the natural and foreseeable result of improper installation and waterproofing of exterior siding, and therefore can not constitute an 'accident' for purposes of determining coverage." *Id.* "Defendant's inadequate preparation and installation of the siding on the resort was not an 'accident' since defendant intended to perform in compliance with the contract, but allegedly failed to do so. Defendant could foresee the natural consequences of any negligence or poor workmanship, thus, any resulting damage is not considered an 'accident' triggering an 'occurrence' under the Policy." *Id.*

CHAPTER

# 12

# Permissible Scope of Indemnification in Construction Contracts

Indemnification agreements are not "coverage" issues in the purest sense of the word. Yet the extent of an insurer's coverage obligation for a claim is sometimes tied—and inextricably so—to its insured's agreement to indemnify another party for loss.

An indemnification agreement is a "contract between two parties whereby the one undertakes and agrees to indemnify the other against loss or damage arising from some contemplated act on the part of the indemnitor, or from some responsibility assumed by the indemnitee, or from the claim or demand of a third person, that it, to make good to him such pecuniary damage as he may suffer." BLACK'S LAW DICTIONARY 393 (5th ed. 1979). *See also Walsh Const. Co. v. Mutual of Enumclaw*, 104 P.3d 1146, 1148 (Or. 2005) (defining "indemnify" to mean: "[t]o restore the victim of a loss, in whole or in part, by payment, repair, or replacement. To save harmless; to secure against loss or damage; to give security for the reimbursement of a person in case of an anticipated loss falling upon him. To make good; to compensate; to make reimbursement to one of a loss already incurred by him") (quoting BLACK'S LAW DICTIONARY 393 (5th ed. 1979)) (alteration in original).

Indemnification agreements, however, become insurance issues because commercial general liability policies typically provide coverage for an insured's obligation to "assume the tort liability of another party to pay for bodily injury or property damage to a third person or organization," i.e., an indemnification agreement. *See, e.g.*, INS. SERVS. OFFICE PROPS., INC., COMMERCIAL GENERAL LIABILITY COVERAGE FORM, NO. CG 00011207, §§ I2b, V9f (2007). In other words, notwithstanding that indemnification agreements are formed between two parties—neither of which is an insurance company—in certain circumstances the party that is taking on the indemnification obligation likely has insurance to satisfy such obligation.

A common indemnification scenario that gives rise to potential insurance coverage obligations is one that involves bodily injury that occurs in the course of construction. For example, take a worker that sustains bodily injuries on a construction project. He will very likely bring an action against the project's general contractor, alleging, among other things, that the general contractor breached an obligation to maintain a safe working environment. The general contractor likely retained subcontractors for some or all of the work being performed, including entering into written agreements with such subcontractors governing their work. If so, such agreements likely contain a provision that obligates the subcontractor to indemnify the general contractor for the general contractor's liability for bodily injuries sustained by third parties (here, the injured worker). Therefore, despite the general contractor's duty to maintain the premises in a safe condition, the general contractor will likely seek to be indemnified by its subcontractors for the general contractor's liability for breaching this obligation.

If the factual scenario contemplated under the indemnity agreement to trigger the indemnitor's obligation has been satisfied, and provided the indemnity agreement is enforceable, discussed below, the subcontractor will be required to indemnify the general contractor for the general contractor's liability (likely including defense) for the bodily injuries sustained by the third-party injured worker. In this situation, the subcontractor's contractual indemnification obligation is likely covered under its general liability policy as an "assum[ption] of the tort liability of another party [the general contractor] to pay for bodily injury or property damage to a third person or organization [the injured worker]." *Id.*

Therefore, not surprisingly, an insurer that stands to be required to provide coverage to its insured, for its insured's contractual indemnification obligation, is likely to have a lot of interest in whether its insured will in fact be liable for such obligation. It is for this reason that, despite indemnification agreements existing outside of the insurance relationship, those handling claims that arise out of such agreements often pay close attention to their scope and enforceability.

While indemnification agreements have long been a part of commercial transactions, so too have been concerns by courts and legislatures over their permissibility. *See Weckerly v. German Lutheran Congregation*, 3 Rawle 172 (Pa. 1831) (addressing public policy concerns in the context of the enforceability of an indemnification agreement). Virtually all states recognize the potential for problems caused by the use of indemnification agreements. Courts and legislatures have particular concern with indemnification contracts in which an indemnitee is seeking to be indemnified for its *own* negligence. Such agreements have been referred to as "hazardous" and "unusual and extraordinary." *Perry v. Payne*, 66 A. 553, 557 (Pa. 1907). It is for this reason that there can be no presumption that the indemnitor intended to assume the responsibility for the negligence of the indemnitee "unless the contract puts it beyond doubt by express stipulation." *Id.* But despite being in accord that, as a general matter, indemnification agreements that purport to indemnify a party for its own negligence are potentially problematic, and must be examined with a cautious eye, states differ in their response to the concern.

On one hand, the requirement that an indemnification agreement, that purports to indemnify the indemnitee for its own negligence, must be expressed in unequivocal terms, has survived to this day and become the clear majority rule. *See Bridston v. Dover Corp.*, 352 N.W.2d 194, 196 (N.D. 1984) ("It is almost universally held that an indemnity agreement will not be interpreted to indemnify a party against the consequences of his own negligence unless that construction is very clearly intended."); *see also Tateosian v. Statet*, 945 A.2d 833, 841 (Vt. 2007) ("[W]e adopt the general rule that an indemnity clause covers the sole negligence of the indemnitee only where it clearly expresses that intent."). *But see Brown Ins. Agency v. Star Ins. Co.*, 237 P.3d 92, 96-97 (Nev. 2010) (discussing, but declining to adopt the "modern minority view," which provides that, because indemnity contracts are "so common in the modern business world that courts should leave the parties with their bargain for 'any and all liability'") (citations omitted).

On the other hand, despite the fact that almost all courts are willing to allow a party to be indemnified for its own negligence, provided that the contractual language is expressed in unequivocal terms, many of the legislatures in those same states have adopted a different rule in the context of construction contracts. Here many states have enacted legislation that prohibit a party to a construction contract from being indemnified for its own negligence— no matter how unequivocal the terms of the agreement. *See* DEL. CODE ANN. tit. 6, § 2704 (Westlaw 2009) (stating that indemnification of a party to a construction contract for any aspect of its own negligence is void and unenforceable as against public policy "even where such covenant, promise, agreement or understanding is *crystal clear and unambiguous* in obligating the promisor or indemnitor to indemnify or hold harmless the promisee or indemnitee from liability resulting from such promisee's or indemnitee's own negligence") (emphasis added).

In general, there are two overarching reasons why construction contracts are often singled out for special treatment when it comes to the permissibility of indemnification for an indemnitee's own negligence. First is a concern that a party being indemnified for its own negligence will have less incentive to exercise due care in the performance of its work. *See Jankele v. Texas Co.*, 54 P.2d 425, 427 (Utah 1936) ("Undoubtedly contracts exempting persons from liability for negligence induce a want of care, for the highest incentive to the exercise of due care rests in a consciousness that a failure in this respect will fix liability to make full compensation for any injury resulting from the cause.").

The other rationale for treating indemnification in the construction arena differently from other contexts is a concern that general contractors, because of unequal bargaining power, can compel their subcontractors to accept such an onerous contractual term as one that requires a party to assume liability for the negligence of others. *See Brooks v. Judlau Contracting, Inc.*, 898 N.E.2d 549, 551 (N.Y. 2008) (quoting *Itri Brick & Concrete Corp. v. Aetna Cas. & Sur. Co.*, 680 N.E.2d 1200, 1204 (N.Y. 1997)) ("The Legislature concluded that such 'coercive' bidding requirements unnecessarily increased the cost of construction by limiting the number of contractors able to obtain the necessary hold harmless insurance, and unfairly imposed liability on subcontractors for the negligence of others over whom they had no control. The agreements also needlessly created expensive double coverage for hold harmless or general liability insurance.").

Statutes that limit indemnification in the context of a construction contract usually define what they mean by a "construction" contract. While each case must be examined individually, many of the definitions are similar and along the lines of the following: "contract or agreement relative to the construction, alteration, repair or maintenance of a building, structure, appurtenance and appliance, including moving, demolition and excavating connected therewith." Mich. Comp. Laws Ann. § 691.991 (Westlaw 2009); *see also* Miss. Code Ann. § 31-5-41 (Westlaw 2008) ("[C]ontracts or agreements, for the construction, alteration, repair or maintenance of buildings, structures, highway bridges, viaducts, water, sewer or gas distribution systems, or other work dealing with construction, or for any moving, demolition or excavation connected therewith.").

Despite all such statutes existing to address concerns with the concept of one party to a construction contract being obligated to indemnify another for that party's own negligence, some of these statutes specifically limit the prohibition to instances in which the indemnitee is solely negligent. Other states have adopted broader legislation that prohibits a party from being indemnified for any character of its own negligence—either in whole or in part. Needless to say, this is a very important distinction and one that is evidenced by the fifty-state survey of the issue that follows.

Lastly, it is not unusual that, when an insurer's exposure is tied to its insured's indemnification obligation, the insurer may face additional potential exposure on account of the indemnitee also being an "additional insured" under the indemnitor's general liability policy. While contractual indemnity and additional insured issues are separate, they nonetheless often arise in tandem. This is so because the contract that contains the indemnification obligation may also contain an obligation on the part of the indemnitor to have the indemnitee named as an additional insured under the indemnitor's general liability policy.

If a party is entitled to indemnity under an indemnification agreement, as well as to coverage as an additional insured under the indemnitor's liability policy, it generally should not serve to increase the exposure for the indemnitor's insurer. In general, the coverage afforded to an additional insured creates the same exposure for the insurer that it would have in providing coverage to its named insured for the named insured's contractual obligation to indemnify the additional insured. In other words, the indemnitee either recovers from the insurer *directly*—as an additional insured; or *indirectly*—as the beneficiary of the indemnitor's coverage for its contractual liability. One exception being that, if a defense is owed to an additional insured, the insurer's liability for such defense is likely supplemental to the policy's limits of liability. On the other hand, if an insurer is obligated to provide coverage to its named insured, for the named insured's contractual obligation to pay an indemnitee's defense costs, such defense costs will likely erode the limit of liability.

Where there is a significant difference for insurers, between the obligation to provide coverage to an additional insured, versus coverage to the named insured for its contractual indemnity obligation, is when only one of these two avenues to recovery is available. For example, consider a party who, despite being an indemnitee under an indemnification agreement, even for its own negligence, can not enforce such right because of a statutory prohibition. In such case, this same party is nonetheless likely entitled to coverage as an additional insured, under the indemnitor's general liability policy. There are few prohibitions against an additional insured being entitled to coverage for its own negligence. *But see* Oregon, *supra*.

Alternatively, a party may be named as an additional insured, but nonetheless denied coverage because its liability does not satisfy the scope of the additional insured endorsement, e.g., the additional insured coverage is limited to ongoing operations (as if often the case), and the liability at issue arises out of completed operations. However, such party may also be an indemnitee under an indemnification agreement—and the scope of such agreement is not limited to ongoing operations. Therefore, despite being denied coverage as an additional insured, the party is now the beneficiary of the indemnitor's general liability coverage for its contractual obligation.

What follows is a survey of the right of an indemnitee to be indemnified for its own negligence in the context of a construction project. Where a state does not have a specific statute addressing indemnification in the construction context, the law generally concerning an indemnitee's right to be indemnified for its own negligence is provided.

## 50-State Survey: Permissible Scope of Indemnification in Construction Contracts

**Alabama:** The Supreme Court of Alabama held that an indemnitee may be indemnified for its own negligence provided that the contractual obligation is sufficiently explicit. *Indus. Tile, Inc. v. Stewart*, 388 So. 2d 171, 176 (Ala. 1980) ("[I]f the parties knowingly, evenhandedly, and for valid consideration, intelligently enter into an agreement whereby one party agrees to indemnify the other, including indemnity against the indemnitee's own wrongs, if expressed in clear and unequivocal language, then such agreements will be upheld."). "This Court has stated that an indemnity contract purporting to indemnify for the consequences of the indemnitee's own negligence is unambiguous and, therefore, enforceable when its language specifically refers to the negligence of the indemnitee. This Court, however, has also stated and held that such 'talismanic' or thaumaturgic language is not necessary if the requisite intent is otherwise clear." *Nationwide Mut. Ins. Co. v. Hall*, 643 So. 2d 551, 555 (Ala. 1994).

**Alaska:** Alaska statute prohibits indemnification for an indemnitee's sole negligence: "A provision, clause, covenant, or agreement contained in, collateral to, or affecting a construction contract that purports to indemnify the promisee against liability for damages for (1) death or bodily injury to persons, (2) injury to property, (3) design defects, or (4) other loss, damage or expense arising under (1), (2), or (3) of this section from the sole negligence or willful misconduct of the promisee or the promisee's agents, servants, or independent contractors who are directly responsible to the promisee, is against public policy and is void and unenforceable[.]" ALASKA STAT. § 45.45.900 (2008). The statute does not affect the validity of certain insurance contracts or an indemnification agreement regarding the handling, containment, or cleanup of oil or hazardous substances as further defined by statute. *Id.*

**Arizona:** Arizona statute prohibits indemnification for an indemnitee's sole negligence: "A. A covenant, clause or understanding in, collateral to or affecting a construction contract or architect-engineer professional service contract that purports to indemnify, to hold harmless or to defend the promisee from or against liability for loss or damage resulting from the sole negligence of the promisee or the promisee's agents, employees or indemnitee is against the public policy of this state and is void." ARIZ. REV. STAT. § 32–1159 (LexisNexis 2009). The statute makes exceptions for: a person who, as an accommodation, enters into an agreement with a contractor that permits the contractor to enter on or adjacent to the person's property to perform the construction contract for others; and agreements to which the state or a political subdivision is a party. *Id.*

**Arkansas:** The Supreme Court of Arkansas held that an indemnitee may be indemnified for its own negligence provided that the contractual obligation is sufficiently explicit. *See Chevron U.S.A. Inc. v. Murphy Exploration & Prod. Co.*, 151 S.W.3d 306, 310 (Ark. 2004) ("When considering indemnification agreements entered into by prime or general contractors and subcontractors, this court has held that a subcontractor's intention to obligate itself to indemnify a prime contractor for the prime contractor's own negligence must be expressed in clear and unequivocal terms and to the extent that no other meaning can be ascribed. While no particular words are required, the liability of an indemnitor for the negligence of an indemnitee is an extraordinary obligation to assume, and we will not impose it unless the purpose to do so is spelled out in unmistakable terms.") (citation omitted).

**California:** A California statute prohibits indemnification for an indemnitee's sole negligence: "Except as provided in Sections 2782.1 [indemnity for adjacent property owners that permit access], 2782.2 [indemnity of professional engineers], 2782.5 [agreements as to allocation or limitation of liability for design defects], and 2782.6 [indemnity of professional engineers or geologists with respect to hazardous materials], provisions, clauses, covenants, or agreements contained in, collateral to, or affecting any construction contract and that purport to indemnify the promisee against liability for damages for death or bodily injury to persons, injury to property, or any other loss, damage or expense arising from the sole negligence or willful misconduct of the promisee or the promisee's agents, servants, or independent contractors who are directly responsible to the promisee, or for defects in design furnished by those persons, are against public policy and are void and unenforceable; provided, however, that this section shall not affect the validity of any insurance contract, workers' compensation, or agreement issued by an admitted insurer as defined by the Insurance Code." West's Ann. Cal. Civ. Code § 2782(a). *See also* West's Ann. Cal. Civ. Code § 2782(c), *et seq.* (placing limitations on indemnification of builders and general contractors, by subcontractors, for construction defects, under residential construction contracts, and amendments, entered into after January 1, 2009, as well as addressing numerous others issues related to claims in this context) (E.g., "unenforceable to the extent the claims arise out of, pertain to, or relate to the negligence of the builder or contractor or the builder's or contractor's other agents, other servants, or other independent contractors who are directly responsible to the builder, or for defects in design furnished by those persons, or to the extent the claims do not arise out of, pertain to, or relate to the scope of work in the written agreement between the parties").

**Colorado:** The Supreme Court of Colorado held that an indemnitee may be indemnified for its own negligence. *Pub. Serv. Co. v. United Cable Television of Jeffco, Inc.*, 829 P.2d 1280, 1284 (Colo. 1992). While acknowledging that indemnity agreements which purport to indemnify for the negligent conduct of an indemnitee must be strictly construed, the Colorado high court also recognized that there is a growing trend to relax the rule of strict construction in construing indemnity contracts in commercial settings. *Id.* at 1284–85. "The increasing prevalence of such [insurance] contracts, as well as the absence of any disparity of bargaining power, provides further support for the relaxation of the rule of strict construction. We see no reason why commercial contracts, entered into by two sophisticated parties following full negotiation, should be construed in a manner which frustrates the obvious intent of the parties." *Id.* at 1285.

**Connecticut:** Connecticut statute prohibits indemnification for any character of an indemnitee's own negligence: "Any covenant, promise, agreement or understanding entered into in connection with or collateral to a contract or agreement relative to the construction, alteration, repair or maintenance of any building, structure or appurtenances thereto including moving, demolition and excavating connected therewith, that purports to indemnify or hold harmless the promisee against liability for damage arising out of bodily injury to persons or damage to property caused by or resulting from the negligence of such promisee, such promisee's agents or employees, is against public policy and void, provided this section shall not affect the validity of any insurance contract, workers' compensation agreement or other agreement issued by a licensed insurer." CONN. GEN. STAT. ANN. § 52-572k(a) (Westlaw 2009).

**Delaware:** Delaware statute prohibits indemnification for any character of an indemnitee's own negligence: "(a) A covenant, promise, agreement or understanding in, or in connection with or collateral to, a contract or agreement… relative to the construction, alteration, repair or maintenance in the State of a road, highway, driveway, street, bridge or entrance or walkway of any type constructed thereon in the State, and building, structure, appurtenance or appliance in the State,… purporting to indemnify or hold harmless the promisee or indemnitee or others, or their agents, servants and employees, for damages arising from liability for bodily injury or death to persons or damage to property caused partially or solely by, or resulting partially or solely from, or arising partially or solely out of the negligence of such promisee or indemnitee or others than the promisor or indemnitor, or its subcontractors, agents, servants or employees, is against public policy and is void and unenforceable, even where such covenant, promise, agreement or understanding is crystal clear and unambiguous in obligating the promisor or indemnitor to indemnify or hold harmless the promisee or indemnitee from liability resulting from such promisee's or indemnitee's own negligence… . (b) Nothing in subsection (a) of this section shall be construed to void or render unenforceable policies of insurance issued by duly authorized insurance companies and insuring against losses or damages from any causes whatsoever." DEL. CODE ANN. tit. 6, § 2704 (2009); *see also Pac. Ins. Co. v. Liberty Mut. Ins. Co.*, 956 A.2d 1246, 1258–59 (Del. 2008) (enforcing the insurance "savings provision" of § 2704 (b)).

**Florida:** Florida statute prohibits indemnification for any character of an indemnitee's own negligence "unless the contract contains a monetary limitation on the extent of the indemnification that bears a reasonable commercial relationship to the contract and is part of the project specifications or bid documents, if any. Notwithstanding the foregoing, the monetary limitation on the extent of the indemnification provided to the owner of real property by any party in privity of contract with such owner shall not be less than $1 million per occurrence, unless otherwise agreed by the parties." FLA. STAT. ANN.

§ 725.06 (Westlaw 2009) (see complete text of statute for other provisions, such as those relating to public contracts and a prohibition against an indemnitor indemnifying the indemnitee for damages to persons or property caused in whole or in part by any act, omission, or default of a party other than, among others, the indemnitor and any of its contractors, subcontractors, sub-subcontractors, materialmen, or agents of any tier or their respective employees).

**Georgia:** Georgia statute prohibits indemnification for an indemnitee's sole negligence: "A covenant, promise, agreement, or understanding in or in connection with or collateral to a contract or agreement relative to the construction, alteration, repair, or maintenance of a building structure, appurtenances, and appliances, including moving, demolition, and excavating connected therewith, purporting to require that one party to such contract or agreement shall indemnify, hold harmless, insure, or defend the other party to the contract or other named indemnitee, including its, his, or her officers, agents, or employees, against liability or claims for damages, losses, or expenses, including attorney fees, arising out of bodily injury to persons, death, or damage to property caused by or resulting from the sole negligence of the indemnitee, or its, his, or her officers, agents, or employees, is against public policy and void and unenforceable." GA. CODE. ANN. § 13–8-2(b) (Westlaw 2009); *see also Lanier at McEver, L.P. v. Planners & Eng'rs Collaborative, Inc.*, 663 S.E.2d 240, 243 n.2 (Ga. 2008) ("Parties may avoid violating... § 13–8-2(b) if their agreement also includes an insurance clause which shifts the risk of loss to an insurer, no matter who is at fault.").

**Hawaii:** Hawaii statute prohibits indemnification for an indemnitee's sole negligence: "Any covenant, promise, agreement or understanding in, or in connection with or collateral to, a contract or agreement relative to the construction, alteration, repair or maintenance of a building, structure, appurtenance or appliance, including moving, demolition or excavation connected therewith, purporting to indemnify the promisee against liability for bodily injury to persons or damage to property caused by or resulting from the sole negligence or willful misconduct of the promisee, the promisee's agents or employees, or indemnitee, is invalid as against public policy, and is void and unenforceable; provided that this section shall not affect any valid workers' compensation claim under chapter 386 or any other insurance contract or agreement issued by an admitted insurer upon any insurable interest under this code." HAW. REV. STAT. ANN. § 431:10–222 (Westlaw 2009).

**Idaho:** Idaho statute prohibits indemnification for an indemnitee's sole negligence: "A covenant, promise, agreement or understanding in, or in connection with or collateral to, a contract or agreement relative to the construction, alteration, repair or maintenance of a building, structure, highway, appurtenance and appliance, including moving, demolition and excavating connected therewith, purporting to indemnify the promisee against liability for damages arising out of bodily injury to persons or damage to property caused by or resulting from the sole negligence of the promisee, his agents or employees, or indemnitees, is against public policy and is void and unenforceable." IDAHO CODE ANN. § 29–114 (2009).

**Illinois:** Illinois statute prohibits indemnification for any character of an indemnitee's own negligence: "With respect to contracts or agreements, either public or private, for the construction, alteration, repair or maintenance of a building, structure, highway bridge, viaducts or other work dealing with construction, or for any moving, demolition or excavation connected therewith, every covenant, promise or agreement to indemnify or hold harmless another person from that person's own negligence is void as against public policy and wholly unenforceable." 740 ILL. COMP. STAT. ANN. 35/1 (LexisNexis 2009).

**Indiana:** Indiana statute prohibits indemnification for an indemnitee's sole negligence: "All provisions, clauses, covenants, or agreements contained in, collateral to, or affecting any construction or design contract except those pertaining to highway contracts, which purport to indemnify the promisee against liability for: (1) Death or bodily injury to persons; (2) Injury to property; (3) Design defects; or (4) Any other loss, damage or expense arising under either (1), (2) or (3); from the sole negligence or willful misconduct of the promisee or the promisee's agents, servants or independent contractors who are directly responsible to the promisee, are against public policy and are void and unenforceable." IND. CODE ANN. § 26-2-5-1 (Westlaw 2009). An exception is provided for "a construction or design contract if liability insurance normally available within the United States at standard rates cannot be obtained for the facility being constructed or designed because it constitutes a dangerous instrumentality." *Id.* at § 26-2-5-2.

**Iowa:** The Supreme Court of Iowa held that an indemnitee may be indemnified for its own negligence provided that the contractual obligation is sufficiently explicit. *McNally & Nimergood v. Neumann-Kiewit Constructors, Inc.*, 648 N.W.2d 564, 571–72 (Iowa 2002) ("A contract for indemnification is generally subject to the same rules of formation, validity and construction as other contracts. However, we have crafted a special rule of construction for indemnification contracts when the contract is claimed to relieve the indemnitee from liability for its own negligence. This rule provides that indemnification contracts will not be construed to permit an indemnitee to recover for its own negligence unless the intention of the parties is clearly and unambiguously expressed.... [O]ur rule of construction does not actually require the contract to specifically mention the indemnitee's negligence or fault as long as this intention is otherwise clearly expressed by other words of the agreement.") (citations omitted).

**Kansas:** Kansas statute prohibits indemnification for any character of an indemnitee's own negligence: "An indemnification provision in a construction contract or other agreement, including, but not limited to, a right of entry, entered into in connection with a construction contract, which requires the indemnitor to indemnify the indemnitee for the indemnitee's negligence is against public policy and is void and unenforceable." KAN. STAT. ANN. § 16–121(b) (2009). The statute applies to indemnification provisions entered into after July 1, 2004 and it does not affect the contractual obligation of a contractor or owner to provide railroad protective insurance or general liability insurance. *Id.* at § 16–121(c), (d).

**Kentucky:** The Supreme Court of Kentucky held that an indemnitee may be indemnified for its own negligence provided that the contractual obligation is sufficiently explicit. *Fosson v. Ashland Oil & Ref. Co.*, 309 S.W.2d 176, 178 (Ky. 1957) ("[W]hen there is a doubt as to the meaning of an indemnity clause the construction should be against the contention that the contract was meant to indemnify against an indemnitee's own negligence. We have said that every presumption is against such intention. But such clauses are not against public policy and in cases where it is not improbable that a party would undertake such an indemnification of another party we reach a different result.") (citation omitted). More recently, however, the Court of Appeals of Kentucky addressed *Fosson*, and other related Kentucky cases, and held that indemnification provisions for an indemnitee's own negligence are "not against public policy generally, but they are when agreed to by a party in a clearly inferior bargaining position." *Speedway SuperAmerica, LLC v. Erwin*, 250 S.W.3d 339, 344 (Ky. Ct. App. 2008).

**Louisiana:** The Supreme Court of Louisiana held that an indemnitee may be indemnified for its own negligence provided that the contractual obligation is sufficiently explicit. *Berry v. Orleans Parish Sch. Bd.*, 830 So. 2d 283, 205 (La. 2002) ("[A] contract of indemnity whereby the indemnitee is indemnified against the consequences of his own negligence is strictly construed, and such a contract will not be construed to indemnify an indemnitee against losses resulting to him through his own negligent acts unless such an intention is expressed in unequivocal terms."); *see also* LA. REV. STAT. ANN. § 38:2216.G (2008) ("[A]ny provision contained in a public contract, other than a contract of insurance, providing for a hold harmless or indemnity agreement, or both, [f]rom the contractor to the public body [or other public contractors] for damages arising out of injuries or property damage to third parties caused by the negligence of the public body, its employees, or agents [or other public contractors]… is contrary to the public policy of the state, and any and all such provisions in any and all contracts are null and void.") .

**Maine:** The Supreme Judicial Court of Maine held that an indemnitee may be indemnified for its own negligence provided that the contractual obligation is sufficiently explicit. *Emery Waterhouse Co. v. Lea*, 467 A.2d 986, 993 (Me. 1983) ("Indemnity clauses to save a party harmless from damages due to negligence may lawfully be inserted in contracts… and such clauses are not against public policy. But, when purportedly requiring indemnification of a party for damage or injury caused by that party's own negligence, such contractual provisions, with virtual unanimity, are looked upon with disfavor by the courts, and are construed strictly against extending the indemnification to include recovery by the indemnitee for his own negligence. It is only where the contract on its face by its very terms clearly and unequivocally reflects a mutual intention on the part of the parties to provide indemnity for loss caused by negligence of the party to be indemnified that liability for such damages will be fastened on the indemnitor, and words of general import will not be read as expressing such an intent and establishing by inference such liability.") (citations omitted).

**Maryland:** Maryland statute prohibits indemnification for an indemnitee's sole negligence: "A covenant, promise, agreement or understanding in, or in connection with or collateral to, a contract or agreement relating to the construction, alteration, repair, or maintenance of a building, structure, appurtenance or appliance, including moving, demolition and excavating connected with it, purporting to indemnify the promisee against liability for damages arising out of bodily injury to any person or damage to property caused by or resulting from the sole negligence of the promisee or indemnitee, his agents or employees, is against public policy and is void and unenforceable. This section does not affect the validity of any insurance contract, workers' compensation, or any other agreement issued by an insurer." MD. CODE ANN., CTS. & JUD. PROC. § 5–401(a) (LexisNexis 2009).

**Massachusetts:** Massachusetts statute prohibits indemnification by a subcontractor for injury or damage not caused by the subcontractor: "Any provision for or in connection with a contract for construction, reconstruction, installation, alteration, remodeling, repair, demolition or maintenance work, including without limitation, excavation, backfilling or grading, on any building or structure, whether underground or above ground, or on any real property, including without limitation any road, bridge, tunnel, sewer, water or other utility line, which requires a subcontractor to indemnify any party for injury to persons or damage to property not caused by the subcontractor or its employees, agents or subcontractors, shall be void." MASS. GEN. LAWS ANN. ch. 149, § 29C (Westlaw 2009); *see also Spellman v. Shawmut Woodworking & Supply, Inc.*, 840 N.E.2d 47, 52 (Mass. 2006) ("[Section 29C] in no way prohibits contractual indemnity arrangements whereby the subcontractor agrees to assume indemnity obligations for the entire liability when both the subcontractor and the general contractor or owner are causally negligent.") (internal quotation and citations omitted).

**Michigan:** Michigan statute prohibits indemnification for an indemnitee's sole negligence: "A covenant, promise, agreement or understanding in, or in connection with or collateral to, a contract or agreement relative to the construction, alteration, repair or maintenance of a building, structure, appurtenance and appliance, including moving, demolition and excavating connected therewith, purporting to indemnify the promisee against liability for damages arising out of bodily injury to persons or damage to property caused by or resulting from the sole negligence of the promisee or indemnitee, his agents or employees, is against public policy and is void and unenforceable." MICH. COMP. LAWS SERV. § 691.991 (LexisNexis 2009).

**Minnesota:** Minnesota statute prohibits indemnification for any character of an indemnitee's own negligence: "An indemnification agreement contained in, or executed in connection with, a building and construction contract is unenforceable except to the extent that: (1) the underlying injury or damage is attributable to the negligent or otherwise wrongful act or omission, including breach of a specific contractual duty, of the promisor or the promisor's independent contractors, agents, employees, or delegatees; or (2) an owner, a responsible party, or a governmental entity agrees to indemnify a contractor directly or through another contractor with respect to strict liability under environmental laws." MINN. STAT. ANN. § 337.02 (Westlaw 2008); *see also Seward Hous. Corp. v. Conroy Bros. Co.*, 573 N.W.2d 364, 366 (Minn. 1998) ("[N]o party can be indemnified when its own negligent acts or omissions are the underlying cause of the injury or damages. This restriction ensures that each party remains responsible for its own negligent actions."). MINN. STAT. ANN. § 337.05 (Westlaw 2008) contains several provisions concerning insurance for indemnification obligations.

**Mississippi:** Mississippi statute prohibits indemnification for any character of an indemnitee's own negligence: "With respect to all public or private contracts or agreements, for the construction, alteration, repair or maintenance of buildings, structures, highway bridges, viaducts, water, sewer or gas distribution systems, or other work dealing with construction, or for any moving, demolition or excavation connected therewith, every covenant, promise and/or agreement contained therein to indemnify or hold harmless another person from that person's own negligence is void as against public policy and wholly unenforceable. This section does not apply to construction bonds or insurance contracts or agreements." MISS. CODE ANN. § 31–5-41 (2008).

**Missouri:** Missouri statute prohibits indemnification for any character of an indemnitee's own negligence, subject to exceptions: "1. Except as provided in subsection 2 of this section, in any contract or agreement for public or private construction work, a party's covenant, promise or agreement to indemnify or hold harmless another person from that person's own negligence or wrongdoing is void as against public policy and wholly unenforceable. 2. The provisions of subsection 1 of this section shall not apply to: (1) A party's covenant, promise or agreement to indemnify or hold harmless another person from the party's own negligence or wrongdoing or the negligence or wrongdoing of the party's subcontractors and suppliers of any tier; (2) A party's promise to cause another person or entity to be covered as an insured or additional insured in an insurance contract;... (8) An agreement containing a party's promise to indemnify, defend or hold harmless another person, if the agreement also requires the party to obtain specified limits of insurance to insure the indemnity obligation and the party had the opportunity to recover the cost of the required insurance in its contract price; provided, however, that in such case the party's liability under the indemnity obligation shall be limited to the coverage and limits of the required insurance." Mo. ANN. STAT. § 434.100 (Westlaw 2008).

**Montana:** Montana statute prohibits indemnification (or additional insured rights) for any character of an indemnitee's own negligence: "(1) Except as provided in subsections (2) and (3), a construction contract provision that requires one party to the contract to indemnify, hold harmless, insure, or defend the other party to the contract or the other party's officers, employees, or agents for liability, damages, losses, or costs that are caused by the negligence, recklessness, or intentional misconduct of the other party or the other party's officers, employees, or agents is void as against the public policy of this state. (2) A construction contract may contain a provision: (a) requiring one party to the contract to indemnify, hold harmless, or insure the other party to the contract or the other party's officers, employees, or agents for liability, damages, losses, or costs, including but not limited to reasonable attorney fees, only to the extent that the liability, damages, losses, or costs are caused by the negligence, recklessness, or intentional misconduct of a third party or of the indemnifying party or the indemnifying party's officers, employees, or agents; or (b) requiring a party to the contract to purchase a project-specific insurance policy, including but not limited to an owner's and contractor's protective insurance, a project management protective liability insurance, or a builder's risk insurance." MONT. CODE ANN. § 28-2-2111 (LexisNexis 2007).

**Nebraska:** Nebraska statute prohibits indemnification for any character of an indemnitee's own negligence: "In the event that a public or private contract or agreement for the construction, alteration, repair, or maintenance of a building, structure, highway bridge, viaduct, water, sewer, or gas distribution system, or other work dealing with construction or for any moving, demolition, or excavation connected with such construction contains a covenant, promise, agreement, or combination thereof to indemnify or hold harmless another person from such person's own negligence, then such covenant, promise, agreement, or combination thereof shall be void as against public policy and wholly unenforceable. This subsection shall not apply to construction bonds or insurance contracts or agreements." NEB. REV. STAT. ANN. § 25–21,187(1) (LexisNexis 2008). NEB. REV. STAT. ANN. § 25–21,187(2) (LexisNexis 2008) addresses protections for architects, engineers and surveyors.

**Nevada:** The Supreme Court of Nevada held that an indemnitee may be indemnified for its own negligence provided that the contractual obligation is sufficiently explicit. *Brown Ins. Agency v. Star Ins. Co.*, 237 P.3d 92, 96 (Nev. 2010) ("Where the indemnification clause does not specifically and expressly include indemnity for the indemnitee's own negligence, an indemnification clause 'for any and all liability' will not indemnify the indemnitee's own negligence."). The court rejected what it called the "modern minority rule," which provides that "an indemnity provision 'for any and all liability' means *all* lia-bility, including that arising from the indemnitee's concurrent negligence." *Id.* at 96-97 (citation omitted and emphasis in original). "The rationale behind the minority view is that such indemnity contracts are so common in the modern business world that courts should leave the parties with their bargain for 'any and all liability.'" *Id.* (citations omitted). The court concluded that the majority rule provides clarity and fairness to the parties, while the modern minority rule "allows for too much to be read into the terms of a contract that the parties may not have intended and could substantially benefit one party to the extreme detriment of the other." *Id.* at 97.

**New Hampshire:** The Supreme Court of New Hampshire held that an indemnitee may be indemnified for its own negligence provided that the con-tractual obligation is sufficiently explicit. *Merrimack Sch. Dist. v. Nat'l Sch. Bus Serv.*, 661 A.2d 1197, 1199 (N.H. 1995) ("[I]ndemnity agreements are strictly construed, particularly when they purport to shift responsibility for an individual's own negligence to another. The indemnity provision, however, need not state explicitly the parties' intent to provide indemnity for the negligence of another. Express language is not necessary where the parties' intention to afford protection for another's negligence is clearly evident.") (internal quotation and citation omitted).

**New Jersey:** New Jersey statute prohibits indemnification for an indemni-tee's sole negligence: "A covenant, promise, agreement or understanding in, or in connection with or collateral to a contract, agreement or purchase order, relative to the construction, alteration, repair, maintenance, servicing, or security of a building, structure, highway, railroad, appurtenance and appli-ance, including moving, demolition, excavating, grading, clearing, site prepa-ration or development of real property connected therewith, purporting to indemnify or hold harmless the promisee against liability for damages arising out of bodily injury to persons or damage to property caused by or resulting from the sole negligence of the promisee, his agents, or employees, is against public policy and is void and unenforceable; provided that this section shall not affect the validity of any insurance contract, workmen's compensation or agreement issued by an authorized insurer." N.J. STAT. ANN. § 2A:40A-1 (Westlaw 2009).

**New Mexico:** New Mexico statute prohibits indemnification for any character of an indemnitee's own negligence: "A provision in a construction contract that requires one party to the contract to indemnify, hold harmless, insure or defend the other party to the contract, including the other party's employees or agents, against liability, claims, damages, losses or expenses, including attorney fees, arising out of bodily injury to persons or damage to property caused by or resulting from, in whole or in part, the negligence, act or omission of the indemnitee, its officers, employees or agents, is void, unenforce-able and against the public policy of the state." N. M. S. A. 1978, § 56–7-1 A. An indemnification agreement in a construction contract will be enforced "only to the extent that the liability, damages, losses or costs are caused by, or arise out of, the acts or omissions of the indemnitor or its officers, employees or agents." N. M. S. A. 1978, § 56-7-1 B.

**New York:** New York statute prohibits indemnification for any character of an indemnitee's own negligence: "1. A covenant, promise, agreement or understanding in, or in connection with or collateral to a contract or agreement relative to the construction, alteration, repair or maintenance of a building, structure, appurtenances and appliances including moving, demolition and excavating connected therewith, purporting to indemnify or hold harmless the promisee against liability for damage arising out of bodily injury to persons or damage to property contributed to, caused by or resulting from the negligence of the promisee, his agents or employees, or indemnitee, whether such negligence be in whole or in part, is against public policy and is void and unenforceable; provided that this section shall not affect the validity of any insurance contract, workers' compensation agreement or other agreement issued by an admitted insurer. This subdivision shall not preclude a promisee requiring indemnification for damages arising out of bodily injury to persons or damage to property caused by or resulting from the negligence of a party other than the promisee, whether or not the promisor is partially negligent." N.Y. GEN. OBLIG. § 5-322.1 (LexisNexis 2009).

**North Carolina:** North Carolina statute prohibits indemnification for any character of an indemnitee's own negligence: "Any promise or agreement in, or in connection with, a contract or agreement relative to the design, planning, construction, alteration, repair or maintenance of a building, structure, highway, road, appurtenance or appliance, including moving, demolition and excavating connected therewith, purporting to indemnify or hold harmless the promisee, the promisee's independent contractors, agents, employees, or indemnitees against liability for damages arising out of bodily injury to persons or damage to property proximately caused by or resulting from the negligence, in whole or in part, of the promisee, its independent contractors, agents, employees, or indemnitees, is against public policy and is void and unenforceable. Nothing contained in this section shall prevent or prohibit a contract, promise or agreement whereby a promisor shall indemnify or hold harmless any promisee or the promisee's independent contractors, agents, employees or indemnitees against liability for damages resulting from the sole negligence of the promisor, its agents or employees. This section shall not affect an insurance contract, workers' compensation, or any other agreement issued by an insurer." N.C. GEN. STAT. § 22B-1 (2008).

**North Dakota:** The Supreme Court of North Dakota held that an indemnitee may be indemnified for its own negligence under certain circumstances. "It is almost universally held that an indemnity agreement will not be interpreted to indemnify a party against the consequences of his own negligence unless that construction is very clearly intended." *Bridston v. Dover Corp.*, 352 N.W.2d 194, 196 (N.D. 1984). Following a review of several Supreme

Court of North Dakota decisions, the Eighth Circuit Court of Appeals concluded that "the general rule emerges that when an indemnity agreement contains both hold harmless and insurance provisions, the parties clearly intend that the indemnitee will be indemnified against the consequences of its own negligence." *Myers v. ANR Pipeline Co.*, 959 F.2d 1443, 1448 (8th Cir. 1992) (internal quotation omitted); *see Bridston*, 352 N.W.2d at 196 ("The requirement that the YMCA obtain liability insurance in an amount satisfactory to UND is clearly meant to provide further assurance to UND of indemnity from the YMCA in the event an action is brought against the UND for the negligent acts of either or both UND and YMCA.") (internal quotation omitted).

**Ohio:** Ohio statute prohibits indemnification for any character of an indemnitee's own negligence: "A covenant, promise, agreement, or understanding in, or in connection with or collateral to, a contract or agreement relative to the design, planning, construction, alteration, repair, or maintenance of a building, structure, highway, road, appurtenance, and appliance, including moving, demolition, and excavating connected therewith, pursuant to which contract or agreement the promisee, or its independent contractors, agents or employees has hired the promisor to perform work, purporting to indemnify the promisee, its independent contractors, agents, employees, or indemnities against liability for damages arising out of bodily injury to persons or damage to property initiated or proximately caused by or resulting from the negligence of the promisee, its independent contractors, agents, employees, or indemnities is against public policy and is void. Nothing in this section shall prohibit any person from purchasing insurance from an insurance company authorized to do business in the state of Ohio for his own protection or from purchasing a construction bond." OHIO REV. CODE ANN. 2305.31 (LexisNexis 2009).

**Oklahoma:** The Supreme Court of Oklahoma held that an indemnitee may be indemnified for its own negligence provided that the contractual obligation is sufficiently explicit. *Fretwell v. Prot. Alarm Co.*, 764 P.2d 149, 152–53 (Okla. 1988) ("An indemnity agreement is a valid agreement in Oklahoma, and is governed by statute. [OKLA. STAT. ANN. tit. 15, §§ 421–430 (Westlaw 2009)]. This Court will strictly construe an agreement which would have the result of indemnifying one against his own negligence, but where the intention to do so is unequivocally clear from an examination of the contract, such an agreement is enforceable."). Oklahoma's indemnity statute (OKLA. STAT. ANN. tit. 15, §§ 421–430) does not contain any provisions that limit indemnity for an indemnitee's own negligence.

**Oregon:** Oregon statute prohibits indemnity for any character of an indemnitee's own negligence (as well as additional insured rights): "(1) Except to the extent provided under subsection (2) of this section, any provision in a construction agreement that requires a person or that person's surety or insurer to indemnify another against liability for damage arising out of death or bodily injury to persons or damage to property caused in whole or in part by the negligence of the indemnitee is void. (2) This section does not affect any provision in a construction agreement that requires a person or that person's surety or insurer to indemnify another against liability for damage arising out of death or bodily injury to persons or damage to property to the extent that the death or bodily injury to persons or damage to property arises out of the fault of the indemnitor, or the fault of the indemnitor's agents, representatives or subcontractors." O.R.S. § 30.140. *See also Walsh Const. Co. v. Mutual of Enumclaw*, 104 P.3d 1146, 1150 (Or. 2005) (agreeing with the decision of the Court of Appeals that "[w]hether the shifting allocation of risk is accomplished directly, *e.g.*, by requiring the subcontractor itself to indemnify the contractor for damages caused by the contractor's own negligence, or indirectly, *e.g.*, by requiring the subcontractor to purchase additional insurance covering the contractor for the contractor's own negligence, the ultimate—and [in this respect] statutorily forbidden—end is the same.").

**Pennsylvania:** The Supreme Court of Pennsylvania held that an indemnitee may be indemnified for its own negligence provided that the contractual obligation is sufficiently explicit. *See Bernotas v. Super Fresh Food Mkts., Inc.*, 863 A.2d 478, 482–83 (Pa. 2004) ("It is well-settled in Pennsylvania that provisions to indemnify for another party's negligence are to be narrowly construed, requiring a clear and unequivocal agreement before a party may transfer its liability to another party. *Ruzzi v. Butler Petroleum Co.*, 588 A.2d 1, 7 (Pa. 1991); *Perry v. Payne*, 66 A. 553 (Pa. 1907). Accordingly, indemnification provisions are given effect only when clearly and explicitly stated in the contract between two parties."). "No inference from words of general import can establish such indemnification." *Ruzzi*, 588 A.2d at 4. However, 68 PA. CONS. STAT. ANN. § 491 (Westlaw 2009) prohibits indemnification of an architect, engineer, surveyor, or his agents, servants, or employees arising out of: (1) the preparation or approval of maps, drawings, opinions, reports, surveys, change orders, designs, or specifications or (2) the giving of or the failure to give directions or instructions by the architect, engineer, surveyor, or his agents, servants, or employees provided such giving or failure to give is the primary cause of the damage, claim, loss or expense.

**Rhode Island:** Rhode Island statute prohibits indemnification for any character of an indemnitee's own negligence: "(a) A covenant, promise, agreement, or understanding in, or in connection with or collateral to, a contract or agreement relative to the design, planning, construction, alteration, repair, or maintenance of a building, structure, highway, road, appurtenance, and appliance... pursuant to which contract or agreement the promisee... has hired the promisor to perform work, purporting to indemnify the promisee... against liability for damages arising out of bodily injury to persons or damage to property proximately caused by or resulting from the negligence of the promisee... is against public policy and is void; provided that this section shall not affect the validity of any insurance contract, worker's compensation agreement, or an agreement issued by an insurer. (b) Nothing in this section shall prohibit any person from purchasing insurance for his or her own protection or from purchasing a construction bond." R.I. GEN. LAWS § 6–34–1 (LexisNexis 2008).

**South Carolina:** South Carolina statute prohibits indemnification for an indemnitee's sole negligence: "Notwithstanding any other provision of law, a promise or agreement in connection with the design, planning, construction, alteration, repair or maintenance of a building, structure, highway, road, appurtenance or appliance... purporting to indemnify the promisee... against liability for damages arising out of bodily injury or property damage proximately caused by or resulting from the sole negligence of the promisee... is against public policy and unenforceable. Nothing contained in this section shall affect a promise or agreement whereby the promisor shall indemnify or hold harmless the promisee... against liability for damages resulting from the negligence, in whole or in part, of the promisor, its agents or employees. The provisions of this section shall not affect any insurance contract or workers' compensation agreements; nor shall it apply to any electric utility, electric cooperative, common carriers by rail and their corporate affiliates or the South Carolina Public Service Authority." S.C. CODE ANN. § 32–2-10 (Westlaw 2008).

**South Dakota:** South Dakota statute prohibits indemnification for an indemnitee's sole negligence: "A covenant, promise, agreement or understanding in, or in connection with or collateral to, a contract or agreement relative to the construction, alteration, repair or maintenance of a building, structure, appurtenance and appliance, including moving, demolition and excavating connected therewith, purporting to indemnify the promisee against liability for damages arising out of bodily injury to persons or damage to property caused by or resulting from the sole negligence of the promisee, his agents or employees, or indemnitee, is against the policy of the law and is void and unenforceable." S.D. CODIFIED LAWS § 56–3-18 (Westlaw 2009); *see also id.* at §§ 56–3-16 and 56–3-17 (limiting the obligations of a contractor for the liability of an architect or engineer).

**Tennessee:** Tennessee statute prohibits indemnification for an indemnitee's sole negligence: "A covenant promise, agreement or understanding in or in connection with or collateral to a contract or agreement relative to the construction, alteration, repair or maintenance of a building, structure, appurtenance and appliance, including moving, demolition and excavating connected therewith, purporting to indemnify or hold harmless the promisee against liability for damages arising out of bodily injury to persons or damage to property caused by or resulting from the sole negligence of the promisee, the promisee's agents or employees, or indemnitee, is against public policy and is void and unenforceable." TENN. CODE ANN. § 62–6-123 (2008).

**Texas:** The Supreme Court of Texas held that an indemnitee may be indemnified for its own negligence provided that the contractual obligation is sufficiently explicit. *See Ethyl Corp. v. Daniel Constr. Co.*, 725 S.W.2d 705, 707–08 (Tex. 1987) (rejecting the clear and unequivocal test in favor of the express negligence doctrine, which provides that parties seeking to indemnify the indemnitee from the consequences of its own negligence must express that intent in specific terms within the four corners of the contract); *see also Cabo Const., Inc. v. R S Clark Const., Inc.*, 227 S.W.3d 314, 317 (Tex. Ct. App. 2007) (holding that, in addition to the express negligence doctrine, a party seeking to be indemnified for its own negligence must also satisfy the conspicuousness requirement, which mandates that the contract language appear in larger type or contrasting colors, or otherwise call attention to itself) (citing *Storage & Processors, Inc. v. Reyes*, 134 S.W.3d 190, 192 (Tex. 2004)) ("However, if both contracting parties have actual knowledge of the plan's terms, an agreement can be enforced even if the fair notice requirements were not satisfied."); *see also* Tex. Gov't Code Ann. § 2252.902 (LexisNexis 2009) (addressing the permissible scope of indemnification in a "contract or agreement made and entered into by a state governmental entity, contractor, construction manager, subcontractor, supplier, or equipment lessor, concerning the construction, alteration, or repair, of a state public building or carrying out or completing any state public work"); Tex. Civ. Prac. & Rem. Code Ann. § 130.002 (LexisNexis 2009) (precluding indemnification in various situations involving registered architects and licensed engineers).

**Utah:** Utah statute prohibits indemnification for any character of an indemnitee's own negligence, except for that of an owner in certain circumstances: "(2) Except as provided in Subsection (3), an indemnification provision in a construction contract is against public policy and is void and unenforceable. (3) When an indemnification provision is included in a contract related to a construction project between an owner and party listed in Subsection (1)(a) [construction manager; general contractor; subcontractor; sub-subcontractor; supplier; or any combination of the foregoing], in any action for damages described in Subsection (1)(b)(i) [bodily injury to a person; damage to property; or economic loss], the fault of the owner shall be apportioned among the parties listed in Subsection (1)(a) pro rata based on the proportional share of fault of each of the parties listed in Subsection (1)(a), if: (a) the damages are caused in part by the owner; and (b) the cause of the damages defined in Subsection (1)(b)(i) did not arise at the time and during the phase of the project when the owner was operating as a party defined in Subsection (1)(a)." Utah Code Ann. § 13–8–1 (2009).

**Vermont:** The Supreme Court of Vermont held that an indemnitee may be indemnified for its own negligence provided that the contractual obligation is sufficiently explicit. *See Tateosian v. State of Vermont*, 945 A.2d 833, 841 (Vt. 2007) ("[W]e adopt the general rule that an indemnity clause covers the sole negligence of the indemnitee only where it clearly expresses that intent."); *see also Hamelin v. Simpson Paper Co.*, 702 A.2d 86, 88 (Vt. 1997) (finding that the indemnitee could be indemnified because such arrangement was explicitly contemplated in the agreement).

**Virginia:** Virginia statute prohibits indemnification for an indemnitee's sole negligence: "Any provision contained in any contract relating to the construction, alteration, repair or maintenance of a building, structure or appurtenance thereto, including moving, demolition and excavation connected therewith, or any provision contained in any contract relating to the construction of projects other than buildings by which the contractor performing such work purports to indemnify or hold harmless another party to the contract against liability for damage arising out of bodily injury to persons or damage to property suffered in the course of performance of the contract, caused by or resulting solely from the negligence of such other party or his agents or employees, is against public policy and is void and unenforceable. This section applies to such contracts between contractors and any public body, as defined in § 2.2–4301. This section shall not affect the validity of any insurance contract, workers' compensation, or any agreement issued by an admitted insurer." VA. CODE ANN. § 11–4.1 (2009); *see also* VA. CODE ANN. § 11-4.4 (2009) (addressing the enforceability of indemnification provisions in private and public contracts with design professionals).

**Washington:** Washington statute prohibits indemnification for any character of an indemnitee's own negligence: "A covenant, promise, agreement or understanding in, or in connection with or collateral to, a contract or agreement relative to the construction, alteration, repair, addition to, subtraction from, improvement to, or maintenance of, any building, highway, road, railroad, excavation, or other structure, project, development, or improvement attached to real estate, including moving and demolition in connection therewith, purporting to indemnify against liability for damages arising out of bodily injury to persons or damage to property: (1) Caused by or resulting from the sole negligence of the indemnitee, his agents or employees is against public policy and is void and unenforceable; (2) Caused by or resulting from the concurrent negligence of (a) the indemnitee or the indemnitee's agents or employees, and (b) the indemnitor or the indemnitor's agents or employees, is valid and enforceable only to the extent of the indemnitor's negligence and only if the agreement specifically and expressly provides therefor, and may waive the indemnitor's immunity under industrial insurance, Title 51 RCW, only if the agreement specifically and expressly provides therefor and the waiver was mutually negotiated by the parties. This subsection applies to agreements entered into after June 11, 1986." WASH. REV. CODE ANN. § 4.24.115 (LexisNexis 2009).

**West Virginia:** West Virginia statute prohibits indemnification for an indemnitee's sole negligence: "A covenant, promise, agreement or understanding in or in connection with or collateral to a contract or agreement entered into on or after the effective date of this section, relative to the construction, alteration, repair, addition to, subtraction from, improvement to or maintenance of any building, highway, road, railroad, water, sewer, electrical or gas distribution system, excavation or other structure, project, development or improvement attached to real estate, including moving and demolition in connection therewith, purporting to indemnify against liability for damages arising out of bodily injury to persons or damage to property caused by or resulting from the sole negligence of the indemnitee, his agents or employees is against public policy and is void and unenforceable and no action shall be maintained thereon. This section does not apply to construction bonds or insurance contracts or agreements." W. Va. Code Ann. § 55-8-14 (LexisNexis 2009). However, indemnification for an indemnitee's sole negligence is permitted if it can be "inferred from the contract that there was a proper agreement to purchase insurance for the benefit of all concerned." *Dalton v. Childress Serv. Corp.*, 432 S.E.2d 98, 101 (W. Va. 1993).

**Wisconsin:** The Supreme Court of Wisconsin held that an indemnitee may be indemnified for its own negligence provided that the contractual obligation is sufficiently explicit. *See Deminsky v. Arlington Plastics Mach.*, 657 N.W.2d 411, 420–21 (Wis. 2003) ("[A]greements to indemnify a party against its own negligence must be strictly construed, but so long as that standard is met, such agreements are valid."). The *Deminsky* Court held that the agreement must satisfy the conspicuous standard set forth in Wis. Stat. Ann. § 401.201(10) (Westlaw 2009) (defining "conspicuous" as "[a] term or clause is conspicuous when it is so written that a reasonable person against whom it is to operate ought to have noticed it. A printed heading in capitals (as: NONNEGOTIABLE BILL OF LADING) is conspicuous. Language in the body of a form is 'conspicuous' if it is in larger or other contrasting type or color. But in a telegram any stated term is 'conspicuous.' Whether a term or clause is 'conspicuous' or not is for decision by the court").

**Wyoming:** The Supreme Court of Wyoming held that an indemnitee may be indemnified for its own negligence provided that the contractual obligation is sufficiently explicit. *Wyoming Johnson, Inc. v. Stag Indus.*, 662 P.2d 96, 99 (Wyo. 1983) ("Generally, contracts exculpating one from the consequences of his own acts are looked upon with disfavor by the courts. Therefore, an agreement for indemnity is construed strictly against the indemnitee, particularly when the indemnitee was the drafter of the instrument. If the indemnitee means to throw the loss upon the indemnitor for a fault in which he himself individually shares, he must express that purpose beyond any peradventure of doubt. The test is whether the contract language specifically focuses attention on the fact that by the agreement the indemnitor was assuming liability for indemnitee's own negligence.") (citations omitted). However, Wyo. Stat. Ann. § 30-1-131 (2009) prohibits indemnification for the sole or concurrent negligence of the indemnitee in any agreement pertaining to any well for oil, gas, or water, or mine for any mineral.

CHAPTER

# 13

# Qualified Pollution Exclusion

As Oliver Wendell Holmes famously observed, a page of history is worth a volume of logic, an aphorism worth remembering when dealing with claims that may (or may not) be classified as pollution claims and consequently may or may not be covered under the standard commercial general liability policy.

The commercial general liability (CGL) policy was the result of insurance industry efforts during the 1930s to improve the basic liability insurance product to make it more attractive to businesses seeking insurance protection as part of their approach to risk management and was formally established during the 1940s. There is a 1941 version of the CGL policy, but the 1943 version was the first to be widely sold. Other major revisions occurred in 1955, 1966, 1973, and 1986—with still further versions following, this time more frequently and with less significant changes. Prior to the CGL, businesses typically had to consider purchasing separate insurance for their various exposures.

The CGL was sold as one-stop shopping for general liability protection (and was even called the "comprehensive" general liability policy until the name was changed in 1986 to reduce the risk that courts would seize on this to broaden the coverage insurers thought they were selling) and contained the now famous insuring agreement that the insurer would pay "all sums that the insured becomes legally obligated to pay as damages" because of "bodily injury" or "property damage" covered by the insurance. *See generally* JEFFREY W. STEMPEL, STEMPEL ON INSURANCE CONTRACTS § 14.01 (3d ed. 2006 & Supp. 2009); BARRY R. OSTRAGER & THOMAS R. NEWMAN, HANDBOOK ON INSURANCE COVERAGE DISPUTES Ch. 7 (14th ed. 2008); EUGENE ANDERSON, JORDAN STANZLER, & LORELIE S. MASTERS, INSURANCE COVERAGE LITIGATION CH. 1 (2d ed. 2004).

Under the CGL as interpreted by most courts, anything for which the policyholder might be liable was covered (or at least potentially covered for purposes of triggering the duty to defend) unless it was specifically excluded.

In addition, most courts apply the general rule of contract law that exclusions are strictly construed against the insurer and that the insurer bears the burden of persuasion to show that an exclusion applies. The net effect was to require that claims against a policyholder involving pollution-related liability (e.g., an oil spill, toxic waste disposal, smokestack emissions) would likely be found to be covered.

Reacting to this, the Insurance Services Office (ISO) developed and issued in 1970 a pollution exclusion now generally referred to as the "qualified pollution exclusion," so named in retrospect because it was replaced in 1986 by today's "absolute" and "total" pollution exclusions. After its issuance in 1970, the qualified pollution exclusion was widely used and became part of the 1973 CGL form. During its roughly fifteen-year reign, the qualified exclusion became the focus of considerable coverage litigation, with courts dividing almost in half between the meaning proffered by policyholders and that proffered by insurers.[1]

The 1970 exclusion is qualified in that, while it bars coverage for pollution, coverage is reinstated by an exception to the exclusion if the discharge of the pollutant in question was "sudden and accidental"—words that have been at the heart of the coverage disputes involving the exclusion. It should also be noted that, under the ground rules of insurance contract interpretation, if the insurer demonstrates the applicability of an exclusion, a policyholder seeking to restore coverage bears the burden of persuasion as to the applicability of the exception it is trying to invoke. STEMPEL ON INSURANCE CONTRACTS §§ 2.06; 4.04. Consequently, litigation over the qualified pollution exclusion involved a process where typically the policyholder would tender defense of a liability claim, the insurer would argue that the claim involved the release of pollution, and the policyholder would in turn argue that the alleged pollution discharge was sudden and accidental. The qualified pollution exclusion contained in the 1973 CGL form stated that the insurance policy did not apply to "bodily injury" or "property damage" arising out of the discharge, dispersal, release or escape of smoke, vapors, soot, fumes, acids, alkalis, toxic chemicals, liquids or gases, waste materials or other irritants, contaminants or pollutants into or upon land, the atmosphere or any watercourse or body of water; but this exclusion does not apply if such discharge, dispersal, release or escape is sudden and accidental.

In most cases involving the exclusion, there was no dispute that a claim alleged liability stemming from the release of chemical pollutants. The battleground between insurers and policyholders was whether the pollution claim might nonetheless be covered because the discharge of the chemicals in

---

1. There were, of course, versions of the qualified pollution exclusion used in policies sold prior to 1970. But the ISO issuance of the widely used 1970 form made the qualified pollution exclusion effectively part of the standard CGL policy.

question had been "sudden and accidental." Insurers took the position that only an abrupt discharge met the language of the exception restoring coverage while policyholders argued that a discharge that had been gradual but unintended satisfied the exception and mandated coverage. In addition, policyholders argued that where they did not intentionally cause harmful pollution, they should be covered while insurers argued that the critical question was whether the discharge was intended even if bad consequences from the discharge were unforeseen.

Insurers focused on the voluntariness of the release of chemicals. Policyholders focused on whether there was intent to injure. Insurers argued that a "sudden" release must also be an abrupt or swift release—a so-called "temporal" element. Policyholders noted that the term "sudden" is in many dictionaries defined as merely "unexpected" rather than fast and that there should be coverage because of the standard axiom that ambiguous language is construed against the insurer/contract drafter, particularly if it is contained in an exclusion. Insurers argued that policyholders had the burden to prove the clarity of the term "sudden" since it was part of an exception to an exclusion and that the dictionary definition of sudden-as-unexpected was not the common understanding of the word. And on and on.

Faced with these arguments, some courts ruled for policyholders based on the ambiguity argument and the dictionary entry (sometimes listed as the first or preferred meaning) that "sudden" means "unexpected" as well as "abrupt." Other courts took the view that the common use of the word "sudden" implied speed or abruptness and was insufficiently ambiguous to invoke the *contra proferentem* rule that ambiguities be construed against the drafter of unclear or problematic language. STEMPEL ON INSURANCE CONTRACTS § 4.08. In addition, courts siding with insurers often noted that construing sudden to mean merely unexpected would make "sudden" a mere synonym for "accidental." This would make the words "sudden and accidental" redundant, violating the general rule that each term in a contract is to be given effect.

Typical of the pro-policyholder view of the qualified pollution exclusion is *Claussen v. Aetna Casualty & Surety Co.*, 380 S.E.2d 686 (Ga. 1989), in which the Supreme Court of Georgia viewed the word "sudden" as sufficiently ambiguous that it could reasonably mean that an unexpected discharge (or even unexpected harm) was not within the scope of the exclusion, which must be strictly construed to avoid unfairly depriving the policyholder of coverage. The court explained that, while it is difficult to think of "sudden" without a temporal connotation (such as, a sudden flash, a sudden burst of speed, or a sudden bang), "even in its popular usage, 'sudden' does not usually describe the duration of an event, but rather its unexpectedness: a sudden storm, a sudden turn in the road, sudden death... . Thus, it appears that 'sudden' has more than one reasonable meaning. And, under the pertinent rule of construction the meaning favoring the insured must be applied, that is, 'unexpected.'" *Id.* at 688.

In making this determination, the Supreme Court of Georgia was responding to a certified question from the Eleventh Circuit Court of Appeals, which was reviewing a federal trial court's determination that the unambiguous meaning of sudden meant abrupt or swift. Not only were different states dividing over the qualified pollution exclusion, but federal and state judges were disagreeing over the meaning of the words in the exclusion and their application.

Representative of the pro-insurer view of the qualified pollution exclusion is *Dimmitt Chevrolet, Inc. v. Southeastern Fidelity Insurance Corp.*, 636 So. 2d 700 (Fla. 1993), in which the Supreme Court of Florida read the language literally to focus on the nature of the discharge rather than the nature of the alleged injury or the policyholder's state of mind. Notwithstanding the dictionary definitions of "sudden" as "unexpected," *Dimmitt* held that the plain and ordinary meaning of "sudden" carried a temporal dimension and that any other view would needlessly make the word "accidental" redundant. The court concluded that, while the word "sudden" can connote a sense of the unexpected, it is not standing alone in the pollution exclusion, but, rather, is an integral part of the conjunctive phrase "sudden and accidental." *Id.* at 704. "The term accidental is generally understood to mean unexpected or unintended. Therefore, to construe sudden also to mean unintended and unexpected would render the words sudden *and* accidental entirely redundant.... . The very use of the words 'sudden *and* accidental' reveal [*sic*] a clear intent to define the words differently, stating two separate requirements. Reading 'sudden' in its context... the inescapable conclusion is that 'sudden,' even if including the concept of unexpectedness, also adds an additional element. .... . This additional element is the temporal meaning of sudden, i.e., abruptness or brevity." *Id.*

In so holding, the *Dimmitt* Court reversed its decision of six months earlier in the same case, ruling for the insurer in response to a motion for rehearing. Not only were state courts (even neighboring state courts) and federal courts disagreeing with each other over the meaning of the qualified pollution exclusion, here the same court was disagreeing with itself.

The division and uncertainty of this state of affairs, as well as the size of the claims that insurers were forced to cover in states rendering pro-policyholder construction of the qualified pollution exclusion, prompted insurers to revise the exclusion—adopting the "absolute pollution exclusion" in the 1986 CGL form, an exclusion that remains commonly in use in CGL forms (or, by endorsement, an even broader "total pollution exclusion").

Although the qualified pollution exclusion was in essence abolished close to twenty-five years ago, there remain potential claims involving pre-1986 policies or claims still in the litigation pipeline because of the nature of occurrence-based CGL policies, which can be triggered by injurious events afflicting claimants years in the past. In addition, some customized CGL policies or other types of liability policies such as environmental impairment may continue to use the sudden-and-accidental discharge language of the qualified pollution exclusion. The phrase is also used in the CGL form's "impaired property" exclusion and some first-party property policies. Consequently, the precedents established in the various states regarding the qualified pollution exclusion would logically continue to apply to any similarly worded pollution language or for purposes of interpreting the phrase "sudden and accidental" as used in other policy language.

For further discussion of the qualified pollution exclusion: STEMPEL ON INSURANCE CONTRACTS §14.11[B]; BARRY R. OSTRAGER & THOMAS R. NEWMAN, HANDBOOK ON INSURANCE COVERAGE DISPUTES §10.02 (14th ed. 2008); EUGENE R. ANDERSON, JORDAN S. STANZLER, & LORELIE S. MASTERS, INSURANCE COVERAGE LITIGATION §15.06 (2d ed. 2004); PETER KALIS, THOMAS M. REITER, & JAMES R. SEGERDAHL, POLICYHOLDER'S GUIDE TO THE LAW OF INSURANCE COVERAGE §10.04[B] (1997 & Supp. 2004).

## 50-State Survey: Qualified Pollution Exclusion

**Alabama:** The Supreme Court of Alabama stated that "[b]ecause the 'judicial construction placed upon particular words or phrases made prior to the issuance of a policy employing them will be presumed to have been the construction intended to be adopted by the parties,' we hold that the 'sudden and accidental' exception to the pollution exclusion clause provides coverage when the 'discharge, dispersal, release or escape' of contaminants into the environment was unexpected and unintended." *Ala. Plating Co. v. U.S. Fid. & Guar. Co.*, 690 So. 2d 331, 336 (Ala. 1996) (noting that courts had, prior to the decision, uniformly interpreted the term "sudden and accidental" to mean that the damage had to be unintended or unexpected for the provision to apply and therefore insurance contracts provided coverage for gradual events) (contamination from a plant that had permission to discharge treated water into a waterway not subject to exclusion). The court held that the term "sudden" was sufficiently ambiguous such that it could be construed to provide coverage where a policyholder gradually released material that allegedly caused injury to a third party's person or property. *Id.*; *see also Porterfield v. Audubon Indem. Co.*, 856 So. 2d 789, 800–01 (Ala. 2002) (restating the holding of *Alabama Plating* after engaging in a lengthy discussion of its reasoning, in a case involving coverage under an absolute pollution exclusion for lead paint exposures).

**Alaska:** No instructive authority. *See Whittier Props. Inc. v. Alaska Nat'l Ins. Co.*, 185 P.3d 84, 89 (Alaska 2008) (noting that courts interpreting Alaska law have declined to interpret the meaning of the phrase "sudden and accidental") (citing *Sauer v. Home Indem. Co.*, 841 P.2d 176 (Alaska 1992) and *MAPCO Alaska Petroleum, Inc. v. Cent. Nat'l Ins. Co. of Omaha*, 795 F. Supp. 941 (D. Alaska 1991)).

**Arizona:** The Ninth Circuit Court of Appeals held that, under Arizona law, "the 'sudden and accidental' exception 'unmistakably connotes a temporal quality.'" *Smith v. Hughes Aircraft Co.*, 22 F.3d 1432, 1437 (9th Cir. 1993) (applying Arizona law). The court reasoned that, otherwise, "sudden" would simply be a synonym for "accidental" and the temporal brevity furthered public policy by excluding deliberate indifference on the part of a polluting insured. *Id.* The Court of Appeals affirmed the District Court's decision to reject the insured's attempt to "break down its long-term waste practices into temporal components in order to find coverage," for claims resulting from the contamination of drinking water through the discharge of TCE into unlined ponds, as "the evidence unequivocally demonstrates that the pollution was gradual." *Id.* at 1438.

**Arkansas:** No instructive authority.

**California:** The Supreme Court of California held that "[t]he sudden and accidental exception to the pollution exclusion refers to the discharge of pollutants. 'Sudden' has a temporal element and does not mean a gradual or continuous discharge. 'Accidental' means an unexpected or unintended *discharge*, not unexpected or unintended *damage*." *Standun, Inc. v. Fireman's Fund Ins. Co.*, 73 Cal. Rptr. 2d 116, 120 (Cal. Ct. App. 1998). In *State v. Allstate Insurance Co.*, 201 P.3d 1147, 1156 (Cal. 2009), the Supreme Court of California cited *Standun* for the proposition that the sudden and accidental pollution exclusion means an unexpected discharge, not simply unexpected damage. The court held that, in a case like the one at hand, involving deposit of waste material into an evaporating pond, "the initial deposit of wastes [is] not a polluting event subject to the policy exclusion," rather the claim of liability is directed at "the subsequent escape of chemicals from the [insured's] ponds into the surrounding soils and groundwater, making that the relevant set of polluting events." *Id.* at 1157. "Our holding does not extend indemnity to situations where the policyholder can do no more than speculate that some polluting events may have occurred suddenly and accidentally, or where sudden and accidental events have contributed only trivially to the property damage from pollution.... . Only if the insured can identify particular sudden and accidental events and prove they contributed substantially to causing indivisible property damage for which the insured bore liability is the insurer obliged to indemnify its insured for the entirety of the damages." *Id.* at 1168.

**Colorado:** The Supreme Court of Colorado held that "[a]lthough 'sudden' can reasonably be defined to mean abrupt or immediate, it can also reasonably be defined to mean unexpected and unintended. Since the term 'sudden' is susceptible to more than one reasonable definition, the term is ambiguous, and we therefore construe the phrase 'sudden and accidental' against the insurer to mean unexpected and unintended." *Hecla Mining Co. v. N.H. Ins. Co.*, 811 P.2d 1083, 1092 (Colo. 1991) ("If we were to construe 'sudden and accidental' to have a solely temporal connotation, the result would be inconsistent definitions within the CGL policies. In the portion of the policies defining occurrence, accident is defined to include 'continuous or repeated exposure to conditions, which result in bodily injury or property damage, neither expected nor intended from the standpoint of the insured.' If 'sudden' were to be given a temporal connotation of abrupt or immediate, then the phrase 'sudden and accidental discharge' would mean: an abrupt or immediate, and continuous or repeated discharge. The phrase 'sudden and accidental' thus becomes inherently contradictory and meaningless.") (involving claims for environmental damaged caused by insured's mining operations); *see also Cotter Corp. v. Am. Empire Surplus Lines Ins. Co.*, 90 P.3d 814, 821 (Colo. 2004) (applying the definition of "sudden and accidental" from *Hecla* in the context of claims for bodily injury and property damage caused by seepage from insured's mill); *Pub. Serv. Co. of Colo. v. Wallis & Co.*, 986 P.2d 924, 933 (Colo. 1999) ("[W]e construe the phrase 'sudden, unintended and unexpected' in the London pollution exclusion clause to mean 'unprepared for, unintended and unexpected'").

**Connecticut:** The Supreme Court of Connecticut held that "the term 'sudden' requires that the release in question occurs abruptly or within a short amount of time." *Buell Indus., Inc. v. Greater N.Y. Mut. Ins. Co.*, 791 A.2d 489, 496 (Conn. 2002) (recognizing that the meaning of the sudden and accidental pollution exclusion was an issue of first impression in Connecticut, but acknowledging that lower courts in the state had interpreted "sudden" to embrace a temporal element). The court explained that its conclusion was dictated by the juxtaposition of the word "accidental" with the word "sudden": "The very use of the words sudden and accidental... reveal a clear intent to define the words differently, stating two separate requirements. Reading sudden in its context,... the inescapable conclusion is that sudden, even if including the concept of unexpectedness, also adds an additional element because unexpectedness is already expressed by accident[al]. This additional element is the temporal meaning of sudden, i.e., abruptness or brevity. To define sudden as meaning only unexpected or unintended, and therefore as a mere restatement of accidental, would render the suddenness requirement mere surplusage." *Id.* (citation and quotation omitted) (finding that the leak of toxins into groundwater occurring over a period of years could not be considered "sudden"); *see also R.T. Vanderbilt Co. v. Cont'l Cas. Co.*, 870 A.2d 1048, 1060 (Conn. 2005) (recognizing *Buell Industries'* holding in defining "sudden" in a sudden and accidental pollution exclusion as containing a temporal meaning); *Schilberg Integrated Metals Corp. v. Cont'l Cas. Co.*, 819 A.2d 773, 781–82 (Conn. 2003) (applying the definition of "sudden and accidental" from *Buell Industries'* in the context of pollution caused by insured's recycling of metal wires).

**Delaware:** The Supreme Court of Delaware held "that the term 'sudden,' as used in [a sudden and accidental] provision, clearly and unambiguously includes a temporal element synonymous with 'abrupt.'" *E.I du Pont de Nemours & Co. v. Allstate Ins. Co.*, 693 A.2d 1059, 1061 (Del. 1997); *see also*

*Hercules, Inc. v. AIU Ins. Co.*, 784 A.2d 481, 496 (Del. 2001) (holding that the qualified pollution exclusion at issue barred "coverage for pollution unless" caused by a 'sudden, unexpected and unintended' happening and that "[b]ecause the jury did not find that the property damage for which [insured] was found liable was the result of a 'sudden' or 'abrupt' event, coverage was barred") (applying the exclusion in the context of soil and groundwater contamination caused by the leakage of dioxin).

**Florida:** The Supreme Court of Florida held that "[t]he use of the word 'sudden' can connote a sense of the unexpected. However, rather than standing alone in the pollution exclusion clause, it is an integral part of the conjunctive phrase 'sudden and accidental.' The term accidental is generally understood to mean unexpected or unintended. Therefore, to construe sudden also to mean unintended and unexpected would render the words sudden *and* accidental entirely redundant. ... The very use of the words 'sudden *and* accidental' reveal [*sic*] a clear intent to define the words differently, stating two separate requirements. Reading 'sudden' in its context... the inescapable conclusion is that 'sudden,' even if including the concept of unexpectedness, also adds an additional element. ... This additional element is the temporal meaning of sudden, i.e., abruptness or brevity." *Dimmitt Chevrolet, Inc. v. S.E. Fid. Ins. Corp.*, 636 So. 2d 700, 704 (Fla. 1993) (emphasis in original) (involving leakage from a petroleum tank); *see also Liberty Mut. Ins. Co. v. Lone Star Indus., Inc.*, 661 So. 2d 1218, 1220 (Fla. Dist. Ct. App. 1995) (holding that an expected and intentional release of contaminants over a period of years could not be "sudden and accidental" under *Dimmitt*).

**Georgia:** The Supreme Court of Georgia held that "the [sudden and accidental] pollution exclusion clause is capable of more than one reasonable interpretation [and therefore]... must... be construed in favor of the insured to mean 'unexpected and unintended.'" *Claussen v. Aetna Cas. & Sur. Co.*, 380 S.E.2d 686, 690 (Ga. 1989) (involving contamination caused by the release of hazardous substances into a landfill owned by the insured). The court explained that, while it is difficult to think of "sudden" without a temporal connotation (such as, a sudden flash, a sudden burst of speed or a sudden bang), "even in its popular usage, 'sudden' does not usually describe the duration of an event, but rather its unexpectedness: a sudden storm, a sudden turn in the road, sudden death. ... Thus, it appears that 'sudden' has more than one reasonable meaning. And, under the pertinent rule of construction the meaning favoring the insured must be applied, that is, 'unexpected.'" *Id.* at 688.

**Hawaii:** No instructive authority. *See Pac. Employers Ins. Co. v. Servco Pac., Inc.*, 273 F. Supp. 2d 1149, 1157–58 (D. Hawaii 2003) (recognizing that the meaning of the "sudden and accidental" pollution exclusion was an open issue under Hawaii law) (holding that, on account of such legal ambiguity regarding the meaning of the exclusion, there was a potential for coverage under Hawaii law and the insurer was obligated to defend); *see also Sentinel*

*Ins. Co. v. Fire Ins. Co. of Haw.*, 875 P.2d 894, 916 (Haw. 1994) (addressing the evolution of the CGL policy for purposes of resolving trigger of coverage and noting that, while "accident" suggested an intent to cover only sudden, unexpected, but identifiable events, the "occurrence" approach expressly provided that an occurrence included any injury or damage that resulted, not only from an accident, but also from injurious exposure over an extended period).

**Idaho:** The Supreme Court of Idaho concluded that the phrase "sudden and accidental" in a qualified pollution exclusion was not ambiguous and refers to an unexpected, unintentional incident that occurs over a short period of time. *N. Pac. Ins. Co. v. Mai*, 939 P.2d 570, 572 (Idaho 1997) (involving environmental contamination of a landfill caused by automobile oil waste). The court explained: "'Sudden' is defined as 'happening or coming unexpectedly... changing angle or character all at once... marked by or manifesting abruptness or haste... made or brought about in a short time.' It is not reasonable to interpret 'sudden' to include an event that occurs over anything other than a short period of time. Therefore, it is not ambiguous. 'Accidental' is a derivative of 'accident,' which this Court has said has a settled legal meaning in the context of other insurance policies.... an unintentional happening, an event that is unusual and not expected." *Id.* (citations omitted) (alteration in original). "The trial court interpreted the exclusion as excluding only those occurrences that are neither expected nor intended from the viewpoint of the insured. Although this may be an appropriate interpretation of 'accidental,' we conclude it does not create ambiguity in the exception." *Id.* at 573.

**Illinois:** The Supreme Court of Illinois held "that the term 'sudden' in the pollution exclusion exception... is ambiguous and... construe[d] it in favor of the insured to mean unexpected or unintended." *Outboard Marine Corp. v. Liberty Mut. Ins. Co.*, 607 N.E.2d 1204, 1220 (Ill. 1992) (finding that the insurer was required to defend its insured for claim involving the gradual discharge of pollutants into Lake Michigan). The court explained: "The pollution exclusion exception retriggers coverage for toxic releases which are 'sudden and accidental.' The policies define 'accident' to include 'continuous or repeated exposure to conditions.'... [A]n accidental release or discharge would include, according to the policy, a gradual release or a 'continuous or repeated' release. To construe 'sudden' to mean 'abrupt' results in a contradiction if one accepts the insurers' own definition of the term 'accident.' Such a construction would result in the pollution exclusion exception clause retriggering coverage for toxic releases which are 'abrupt' *and* gradual or 'continuous or repeated' releases. Clearly, under such a construction this clause would be rendered absurd. However, if 'sudden' means unexpected or unintended, as it is defined by numerous dictionaries, the clause retriggers coverage for unexpected or unintended releases which are exactly the type of uncertainties or risks that an insured would want to insure against." *Id.* at 1219 (citations omitted and emphasis in original); *see also Keystone Consol. Indus., Inc. v. Employers Ins. Co. of Wausau*, 470 F. Supp. 2d 873, 887 (C.D. Ill. 2007) (citing *Outboard Marine* for the proposition that, under Illinois law, "sudden" means "unexpected or unintended," and addressing the exclusion in the context of environmental contamination from the operation of insured's wire mill).

**Indiana:** The Supreme Court of Indiana held that the interpretation of "sudden" in the qualified pollution exclusion was ambiguous and therefore would be interpreted in favor of the insured. *Am. States Ins. Co. v. Kiger*, 662 N.E.2d 945, 948 (Ind. 1996) (addressing contamination from an underground storage tank at a gas station). The court held that "sudden" could be understood to mean "unexpected." *Id.* "When the insurance industry itself has offered differing interpretations of the same language, [a court] must assume that the insured understood the coverage in the more expansive way." *Id.* (examining the drafting history of the exclusion).

**Iowa:** The Supreme Court of Iowa held that the phrase "sudden and accidental," in the context of the qualified pollution exclusion, is comprised of two parts: "sudden," which constitutes a "temporal element," and "accidental" which is "an unexpected and unintended event." *Iowa Comprehensive Petroleum Underground Storage Tank Fund Bd. v. Farmland Mut. Ins. Co.*, 568 N.W.2d 815, 818 (Iowa 1997). The court rejected the argument that "sudden" meant only unforeseen or unexpected, reasoning that such an interpretation "would render either the term 'accidental' or 'sudden' redundant; they would mean virtually the same." *Id.* at 819 (contamination caused by leaks from an underground storage tank, taking place over at least a ten-year period, could not be considered "sudden" under the policy); *see also Hydrite Chem. Co. v. Aetna Cas. & Sur. Co.*, No. 02–0111, 2005 WL 839403, at *4 (Iowa Ct. App. Apr. 13, 2005) (finding there existed a genuine issue of material fact "whether the contamination was sudden, or was a result of leakage over a long period of time").

**Kansas:** The Court of Appeals of Kansas held "that the term 'sudden and accidental' should be given a temporal meaning, that it is unambiguous, and that the meaning of the word 'sudden' combines both the elements of without notice or warning and quick or brief in time." *Farm Bureau Mut. Ins. Co., Inc. v. Laudick*, 859 P.2d 410, 412 (Kan. Ct. App. 1993) (involving a leak over a long period of time from a gas station's underground storage tank). "[W]e are persuaded that 'sudden' possesses a temporal element, generally connoting an event that begins abruptly or without prior notice or warning, but the duration of the event—whether it lasts an instant, a week, or a month—is not necessarily relevant to whether the inception of the event is sudden." *Id.* at 414 (quotation omitted); *see also Coffeyville Resources Refining & Marketing, LLC v. Liberty Surplus Ins. Corp.*, ___ F. Supp. 2d ___, No. 08–1204-WEB-KMH, 2010 WL 1740887, at *48 (D. Kan. Apr. 28, 2010) (addressing the release of a large amount of crude oil from policyholder's oil refinery where discharge occasioned by consequences of flooding, carrying oil residue into neighboring city) (reviewing Kansas precedent requiring that discharge and duration of pollution be abrupt to fall within exception to qualified pollution exclusion and finding that coverage was owed given that the "uncontroverted facts show[ed] that the release of crude oil from the [Insured's] refinery was 'abrupt and neither expected nor intended by the Insured' within the meaning" of the policy).

**Kentucky:** The Sixth Circuit Court of Appeals, applying Kentucky law, held that it was not "possible to define 'sudden' without reference to a temporal element that joins together conceptually the immediate and the unexpected." *U.S. Fid. & Guar. Co. v. Star Fire Coals, Inc.*, 856 F.2d 31, 34 (6th Cir. 1988) (applying Kentucky law). "We believe that the phrase 'sudden and accidental' is not a synonym for 'unexpected and unintended,' and that it should not be defined by reference to whether the accident or damages were expected.... 'Sudden' in its common usage, means 'happening without previous notice or with very brief notice,' while 'accidental' means 'occurring sometimes with unfortunate results by chance alone.' The meaning of these terms is clear and should not be twisted simply to provide insurance coverage when the courts deem it desirable." *Id.* at 34–35 (citations omitted) (holding that it was impossible to characterize the discharge of coal dust, on a regular ongoing basis over a seven- to eight-year period, as "sudden"); *see also Transamerica Ins. Co. v. Duro Bag Mfg. Co.*, 50 F.3d 370, 373 (6th Cir. 1995) (declining to certify the question to the Supreme Court of Kentucky given that, in the court's opinion, settled issues of contract interpretation resolved the issue of the exclusion's meaning) ("We see no meaningful distinction between *Star Fire Coals* and the present case. In both cases, the insured had deliberately discharged waste over a period of years. Accordingly, defendant cannot claim the protection of the 'sudden and accidental' language, and the District Court correctly concluded that the pollution exclusion clause bars coverage in this case.").

**Louisiana:** The Louisiana Court of Appeal stated that "the [sudden and accidental] exception is not implicated merely because the damages may have been accidental, in the sense that they were unexpected or unintended. What is relevant is whether the insured expected or intended the discharge or release." *Grefer v. Travelers Ins. Co.*, 919 So. 2d 758, 772 (La. Ct. App. 2005) (discussing the qualified pollution exclusion in the course of addressing the applicability of a total pollution exclusion to claims for property damage caused by naturally occurring radioactive material from a pipe-cleaning process).

**Maine:** The First Circuit Court of Appeals predicted that Maine would likely join the jurisdictions that accord "sudden" its unambiguous, plain, and commonly accepted meaning of temporally abrupt. *A. Johnson & Co. v. Aetna Cas. & Sur. Co.*, 933 F.2d 66, 72 (1st Cir. 1991) (applying Maine law) (addressing the exclusion in the context of the disposal of waste at a hazardous waste site). The court reached its decision based on *Travelers Indem. Co. v. Dingwell*,

414 A.2d 220 (Me. 1980), in which the Maine Supreme Judicial Court concluded that only the initial release—and not the behavior of the pollutants in the environment after the initial release—is "relevant to the 'sudden and accidental' inquiry." *Id.*; *see also Barrett Paving Materials, Inc. v. Cont'l Ins. Co.*, 488 F.3d 59, 63–64 (1st Cir. 2007) (failing to clarifying the meaning or application of the qualified pollution exclusion, but distinguishing *A. Johnson*, relying on *Dingwell*, 414 A.2d at 224–27, to find that the "sudden and accidental" pollution exclusion did not preclude a duty to defend) (concluding that, unlike in *A. Johnson*, where the allegations involved an alleged polluter's regular business activity over an extended period of time, the allegations at issue did not specify how the pollutants may have been released from the facility into the soil or the sewers, i.e., suddenly and accidentally, or through routine operations) (involving the discharge of pollutants from a manufactured gas plant).

**Maryland:** The Court of Appeals of Maryland held that "the language of [the qualified pollution] exclusion provides coverage only for pollution which is both sudden *and* accidental. It does not apply to gradual pollution carried out on an ongoing basis during the course of business. The notion of giving a temporal aspect to the terms 'sudden and accidental' and excluding coverage for gradual pollution has been embraced by numerous other jurisdictions.... . We agree with the numerous cases holding that allegations of longstanding business activities resulting in pollution do not constitute allegations of 'sudden and accidental' pollution." *Am. Motorists Ins. Co. v. ARTRA Group, Inc.*, 659 A.2d 1295, 1308–10 (Md. 1995) (emphasis in original). The court embraced those decisions that rejected the insured's attempt to break down its long-term waste practices into temporal components in order to find coverage where the evidence unequivocally demonstrated that the pollution was gradual. *Id.* (holding that the exclusion applied to claims involving the release of hazardous chemicals over a long period of time from an insured's paint manufacturing facility); *see also Indus. Enters., Inc. v. Penn Am. Ins. Co.*, No. RDB-07-2239, 2008 WL 4120221, at *4 (D. Md. Sept. 2, 2008) ("[U]nder Maryland law, pollution that is both temporally isolated and unintended is covered because it meets the 'sudden and accidental' exception to the pollution exclusion. Pollution that accumulates gradually, even if unintended, is not covered.").

**Massachusetts:** The Supreme Judicial Court of Massachusetts held that "[f]or the word 'sudden' to have any significant purpose, and not to be surplusage when used generally in conjunction with the word 'accidental,' it must have a temporal aspect to its meaning, and not just the sense of something unexpected. We hold, therefore, that when used in describing a release of pollutants, 'sudden' in conjunction with 'accidental' has a temporal element." *Lumberman's Mut. Cas. Co. v. Belleville Indus., Inc.*, 555 N.E.2d 568, 572 (Mass. 1990) (addressing the exclusion in the context of PCB pollution of a harbor arising out of the manufacture of electrical capacitors); *see also*

*House of Clean, Inc. v. St. Paul Fire & Marine Ins. Co., Inc.*, No. 07–10839, 2010 WL 1372474, at *4 (D. Mass. Apr. 2, 2010) ("Under Massachusetts law, 'sudden' carries a temporal element requiring an abrupt, non-gradual release. As a result, there is no duty to defend where the complaints arise out of routine business practices or activities.") (citing *Belleville Indus.*); *Century Indem. Co. v. Liberty Mut. Ins. Co.*, No. 09–285 S, 2010 WL 1704381, at *7–9 (D.R.I. Apr. 27, 2010) (applying Massachusetts law) (addressing whether there were sufficient allegations of a "sudden and accidental" release to trigger a duty to defend).

**Michigan:** The Supreme Court of Michigan "conclude[d] that when considered in its plain and easily understood sense, 'sudden' is defined with a 'temporal element that joins together conceptually the immediate and the unexpected.' The common, everyday understanding of the term 'sudden' is 'happening, coming, made or done quickly, without warning or unexpectedly; abrupt.' 'Accidental' means '[o]ccurring unexpectedly and unintentionally; by chance.'... [W]e find that the terms 'sudden' and 'accidental' used in the pollution-exclusion clause are unambiguous." *Upjohn Co. v. N.H. Ins. Co.*, 476 N.W.2d 392, 397–98 (Mich. 1991) ("[W]e conclude that the release of material from tank FA-129 could not possibly be considered 'sudden' because the release of by-product from tank FA-129 was not unexpected by [the insured].") (citation and quotation omitted) (addressing applicability of the exclusion to releases of chemical by-products from a pharmaceutical company's underground storage tank); *see also S. Macomb Disposal Auth. v. Nat'l Sur. Corp.*, 608 N.W.2d 814, 818 (Mich. Ct. App. 2000) (finding that the initial leakage from underneath a landfill site, not the secondary migration which contaminated surrounding groundwater, was the relevant event for the purpose of determining whether the qualified pollution exclusion applied); *Arco Indus. Corp. v. Am. Motorists Ins. Co.*, 594 N.W.2d 61, 66 (Mich. Ct. App. 1998) (finding that incidents of discharge, such as a bucket tipping or a drum being punctured, possessed the temporal element that "sudden" requires); *City of Bronson v. American States Ins. Co.*, 546 N.W.2d 702, 706 (Mich. Ct. App. 1996) (involving the release of contaminants at an industrial area, occurring over decades during which an insured intentionally and continuously collected toxic wastes in lagoons, while on notice that the lagoons were the source of groundwater pollution, was not unexpected and could not be "sudden and accidental.").

**Minnesota:** The Supreme Court of Minnesota held that, in the context of the qualified pollution exclusion "'sudden and accidental' modifies 'discharge [etc.].' It refers not to the placement of waste in a particular place but to the discharge or escape of the waste from that place. The word 'sudden' is used in tandem with the word 'accidental,' and 'accidental' in liability insurance parlance means unexpected or unintended; thus to construe 'sudden' to mean 'unexpected' is to create a redundancy. It seems incongruous, too, to think of a leakage or seepage that occurs over many years as happening suddenly.... .

[H]ere... the term 'sudden' is used to indicate the opposite of gradual. Consequently, we hold that the 'sudden and accidental' exception to the pollution exclusion does not apply to asbestos fibers released gradually over time from the insured's product." *Bd. of Regents of Univ. of Minn. v. Royal Ins. Co. of Am.*, 517 N.W.2d 888, 892 (Minn. 1994); *accord. Tinucci v. Allstate Ins. Co.*, 487 F. Supp. 2d 1058 (D. Minn. 2007); *see also Anderson v. Minn. Ins. Guar. Ass'n*, 534 N.W.2d 706, 709 (Minn. 1995) ("[A] CGL policy with a pollution exclusion clause affords no coverage for a waste disposal site which gradually over time pollutes an area. On the other hand, if an explosion sends chemical fumes over a residential area, or an oil truck overturns and spills oil into a marsh, these would be sudden and accidental happenings, so that the exclusion would not apply and there would be insurance coverage."); *Westling Mfg. Co. v. W. Nat'l Mut. Ins. Co.*, 581 N.W.2d 39, 46 (Minn. Ct. App. 1998) (concluding that it was reasonable for the jury to find that abrupt spill of contaminants that eventually leaked into the groundwater was sufficiently "sudden" for the exclusion exception to apply).

**Mississippi:** A Mississippi District Court held that "sudden and accidental as used in the language of the pollution exclusion should be accorded its plain and ordinary meaning, i.e., without notice and by chance, so as to exclude routine and repeated discharges." *U.S. Fid. & Gaur. Co. v. T.K. Stanley, Inc.*, 764 F. Supp. 81, 84–85 (S.D. Miss. 1991) (addressing the exclusion in the context of the emission of hydrogen sulfide gas from a salt water disposal facility); *see also U.S. Fidelity and Guar. Co. v. B & B Oil Well Service, Inc.*, 910 F. Supp. 1172, 1182 (S.D. Miss. 1995) ("[T]he exception is not implicated merely because the damages may have been accidental, in the sense that they were unexpected or unintended. What is relevant is whether the insured expected or intended the discharge or release.").

**Missouri:** The Eighth Circuit Court of Appeals, applying Missouri law, held that "[t]he term 'sudden,'... 'when considered in its plain and easily understood sense,... is defined with a temporal element that joins together conceptually the immediate and the unexpected.' Indeed, assigning meaning to both 'sudden' and 'accidental' eliminates any perceived ambiguity... . Because 'accidental' includes the unexpected, however, 'sudden' must mean abrupt. To hold otherwise would render the word 'sudden' superfluous." *Aetna Cas. & Sur. Co. v. Gen. Dynamics Corp.*, 968 F.2d 707, 710 (8th Cir. 1992) (applying Missouri law) (addressing the exclusion in the context of claims against the insured for environmental contamination at several sites); *see also Trans World Airlines, Inc. v. Associated Aviation Underwriters*, 58 S.W.3d 609, 622–23 (Mo. Ct. App. 2001) (citing *Aetna* for the proposition that "sudden" must include a temporal element such that it is abrupt, immediate, and unexpected, but concluding it was a moot point since the discharge at issue—deliberate disposal of waste—could not be considered "accidental").

**Montana:** The Supreme Court of Montana "h[e]ld that in the context of the phrase 'sudden and accidental,' the word 'sudden,' even if it includes the concept of unexpectedness, also encompasses a temporal element, because unexpectedness is already expressed by the word 'accidental.'" *Sokoloski v. Am. W. Ins. Co.*, 980 P.2d 1043, 1045 (Mont. 1999) (addressing coverage under a homeowner's policy for damage to walls and other property caused by soot from the prolonged burning of candles during the holiday season) ("While time is relative and a geologist might speak of sudden events occurring over hundreds or even thousands of years and an astrophysicist may speak in terms of millions of years, most people and institutions measure time in much more finite terms. So must the courts. In the context of the coverage of smoke damage by a homeowner's insurance policy, the Court determines that 'sudden' connotes a sense of immediacy, which is measured in seconds, minutes and might be stretched to hours, but not weeks. Therefore, the Court rules the gradual accumulation of soot and smoke over a 4–5 week period is not 'sudden and accidental' for purposes of policy coverage."); *see also Travelers Cas. & Sur. Co. v. RibiImmunochem Research, Inc.*, 108 P.3d 469, 476 (Mont. 2005) ("[I]n order for the word 'sudden' to have significant purpose, and not to be surplusage when used generally in conjunction with the word 'accidental,' it must have a temporal aspect to its meaning, and not merely a sense of something unexpected.") (specifically extending *Sokoloski*'s holding to the qualified pollution exclusion in a general liability policy).

**Nebraska:** The Supreme Court of Nebraska concluded, following a comprehensive survey of the issue nationally, that "[s]ince the 'sudden and accidental' exception to the pollution exclusion clause is expressed in the conjunctive, both requirements must be met for the exception to become operative." *Dutton-Lainson Co. v. Cont'l Ins. Co.*, 716 N.W.2d 87, 97 (Neb. 2006). "[U]under the terms of the policy at issue, an event occurring over a period of time is not sudden. The language of an insurance policy should be considered in accordance with what a reasonable person in the position of the insured would have understood it to mean." *Id.* at 99. The court concluded that this means that "the term 'sudden,' as found in the context of the qualified pollution exclusion,… refer[s] to the objectively temporally abrupt release of pollutants into the environment." *Id.* (addressing the applicability of the exclusion to property damage caused by the deposit of drums containing degreaser solvent into a landfill over a course of years); *see also Bituminous Cas. Corp. v. Aaron Ferer & Sons Co.*, No. 4:06CV3128, 2007 WL 2066452, at *2 (D. Neb. July 16, 2007) (relying on *Dutton-Lainson* and holding that "[b]ecause the [insureds] have presented no evidence tending to show that the release of hazardous substances at the Site was sudden and accidental, [the insurer] is entitled to the entry of summary judgment").

**Nevada:** No instructive authority.

**New Hampshire:** The Supreme Court of New Hampshire addressed a policy provision that afforded coverage when an insured suffered loss or damage to livestock that was caused by sudden and accidental damage from artificially generated electrical current and held, following an examination of qualified pollution exclusion decisions, that "defining 'sudden' to include unexpected events does not strip the word of its independent meaning and significance. While it is certainly possible to read the term 'accidental' to include unexpected events, the joint use of the words 'sudden and accidental' serves distinct purposes not accomplished by either word standing alone... . '[S]udden' is not to be construed as synonymous with 'instantaneous.'... [S]uch an interpretation suggests that the term 'sudden and accidental' is at least reasonably susceptible to an interpretation consistent with 'unexpected and unintended.'... [E]ven if the word 'sudden' is given the temporal connotation the defendant advances, in this policy it is not clear if in order to be covered the *onset* of damages must occur 'suddenly' or if the *aggregate* damage must occur 'suddenly.' [T]he term 'sudden and accidental' is, at the very least, not 'so clear as to create no ambiguity which might affect the insured's reasonable expectations.'... We... construe 'sudden and accidental' in such a way as to provide coverage to the insured on the basis that the phrase includes events that are 'unexpected and unintended.'" *Hudson v. Farm Family Mut. Ins. Co.*, 697 A.2d 501, 504 (N.H. 1997) (emphasis in original); *see also EnergyNorth Nat. Gas, Inc. v. Am. Home Assur. Co.*, No. 99–502-JD, 2003 WL 21663646, at *8–9 (D.N.H. July 17, 2003) (following *Hudson* and holding that the pollution exclusion did not apply to claims for the discharge of manufactured gas plant waste over a long period of time because the exclusion's exception for "seepage, pollution or contamination... caused by a sudden, unintended and unexpected happening during the period of this Insurance" was satisfied).

**New Jersey:** The Supreme Court of New Jersey stated that "[a]lthough the word 'sudden' is hardly susceptible of precise definition, and is undefined in those CGL policies that include the standard pollution-exclusion clause, we are persuaded that 'sudden' possesses a temporal element, generally connoting an event that begins abruptly or without prior notice or warning, but the duration of the event—whether it lasts an instant, a week, or a month—is not necessarily relevant to whether the inception of the event is sudden." *Morton Int'l, Inc. v. Gen. Accident Ins. Co.*, 629 A.2d 831, 847 (N.J. 1993) (addressing the exclusion in the context of claims for property damage at a mercury processing plant). However, the court went on to hold that, on account of misrepresentations made by insurers to state regulators, concerning the scope of the qualified pollution exclusion, it would be "construed to provide coverage identical with that provided under the prior occurrence-based policy, except that the clause will be interpreted to preclude coverage in cases in which the *insured* intentionally discharges a known pollutant, irrespective of whether the resulting property damage was intended or expected." *Id.* at 875.

**New Mexico:** The Tenth Circuit Court of Appeals, applying New Mexico law, and recognizing that New Mexico courts had not addressed the issue, predicted that a New Mexico court would likely honor the plain meaning of the word "sudden" and conclude that the term encompasses a temporal component, and, thus, pollution must occur quickly or abruptly before the exception will apply. *Mesa Oil Co. v. Ins. Co. of N. Am.*, 123 F.3d 1333, 1340 (10th Cir. 1997) (applying New Mexico law). "The word 'sudden' clearly expresses a meaning of quickness or abruptness, particularly in light of the fact that it would be entirely redundant when paired with the word 'accidental' if it merely meant 'unexpected.'" *Id.* (addressing the exclusion in the context of claims for damage caused by the mishandling of oil over many years).

**New York:** The Court of Appeals of New York held that "eliminating the temporal aspect from the meaning of sudden in the exception to the pollution coverage exclusion would render the sudden and accidental contingencies of the exception unavoidably redundant for unintended pollutant discharges. This redundancy is removed by including within the meaning of *sudden* in the pollution exclusion exception its temporal quality, as a discharge of the pollutant *abruptly, precipitantly or brought about in a short time*.... The focus in determining whether the temporally sudden *discharge* requirement is met, for the purpose of nullifying the pollution coverage exclusion, is on the initial release of the pollutant, not on the length of time the discharge remains undiscovered, nor the length of time that damage to the environment continued as a result of the discharge, nor on the timespan of the eventual dispersal of the discharged pollutant in the environment." *Northville Indus. Corp. v. Nat'l Union Fire Ins. Co. of Pittsburg*, 679 N.E.2d 1044, 1047–48 (N.Y. 1997) (emphasis in original) (quotations and citations omitted) (addressing the exclusion in the context of the release of gasoline from storage tanks over a period of years); *see also Flynn v. Allstate Indem. Co.*, No. 08–30417, 2009 WL 782520, at *6 (N.Y. City Ct. Mar. 24, 2009) ("[T]here can be little doubt that the initial discharge of waste oil was 'sudden and accidental.'... The fact that the discharge was not readily discoverable and, thus, continued for a period of time, through no fault of the insured, should not move an otherwise covered occurrence within the rather shadowy perimeter of the exclusion.").

**North Carolina:** The Supreme Court of North Carolina held that "sudden" has a temporal element. *Waste Mgmt. of Carolinas, Inc. v. Peerless Ins. Co.*, 340 S.E.2d 374, 383 (N.C. 1986). "[T]he focus of the 'pollution exclusion' is *not* upon intention, expectation, or even foresight. Rather, the exclusion clause is concerned less with the accidental nature of the occurrence than with the nature of the damage. The exclusion limits the insurer's liability for accidental events by excluding damage caused by the gradual release, escape, discharge, or dispersal of irritants, contaminants, or pollutants. The focus of the exclusion is not upon the release but upon the fact that it pollutes or contaminates. When courts consider the release alone to be the key to the pollution exclusion clause, the sudden and accidental exception can be bootstrapped onto almost any allegations that do not specify a gradual release or emission." *Id.* at 380–81 (emphasis in original) (addressing exclusion in the context of claims for contamination caused by dumping hazardous materials at a landfill over the course of several years); *see also Home Indem. Co. v. Hoechst Celanese Corp.*, 494 S.E.2d 774, 783 (N.C. Ct. App. 1998) (following *Waste*

*Management* and holding that leaks and spills that occurred on regular or sporadic basis during day-to-day operations at manufacturing plant were not sudden).

**North Dakota:** No instructive authority. *But see Indiana Lumbermens Ins. Co. v. PrimeWood, Inc.*, No. A3–97–23, 1999 WL 33283343, at * 5–6 (D.N.D Jan. 8, 1999) (addressing the exception to the "impaired property" exclusion for damages that result from the loss of use of other property not physically damaged that is caused by *sudden and accidental* physical damage to the insured's products after they have been put to their intended use) (interpreting "sudden and accidental" to mean "unexpected and unintended" and holding that the exception to the "impaired property" exclusion applied to claims against a cabinet manufacturer for the premature yellowing of cabinet doors).

**Ohio:** The Supreme Court of Ohio "h[e]ld that the word 'sudden' in the exception is *not* synonymous with the word 'unexpected' in the typical definition of 'occurrence'; instead, the word also has a *temporal* aspect." *Hybud Equip. Corp. v. Sphere Drake Ins. Co.*, 597 N.E.2d 1096, 1102 (Ohio 1992) (emphasis in original). The court gave three reasons for its conclusion: "First,... the word 'sudden,'... is not ambiguous.... As it is most commonly used, 'sudden' means happening quickly, abruptly, or without prior notice. ... Second,... unless 'sudden' is interpreted to have a temporal aspect, the word does not add anything to the phrase 'sudden and accidental.'... Third, if 'sudden' were interpreted to be synonymous with 'unexpected,' then the entire pollution exclusion would not serve the purpose for which it was clearly included.... [T]he pollution exclusion would exclude only bodily injury or property damage that was already excluded by the common definition of 'occurrence.'" *Id.* (addressing the pollution exclusion in the context of environmental damage caused by the disposal of waste); *see also Goodrich Corp. v. Commercial Union Ins. Co.*, Nos. 23585, 23586, 2008 WL 2581579, at *23 (Ohio Ct. App. June 30, 2008) (finding that the insured had "established to the jury that it had sustained damages due to sudden and accidental releases of [contaminants] into the groundwater").

**Oklahoma:** The Supreme Court of Oklahoma held that "[t]he ordinary and popular meaning of 'sudden' necessarily includes an element of time. Decisions finding ambiguity have focused on technical distinctions crafted by lawyers rather than the ordinary understanding of the word. A finding of ambiguity requires that the term 'sudden' be lifted from its context in the policy and scrutinized so closely that any plain meaning is no longer discernable." *Kerr-McGee Corp. v. Admiral Ins. Co.*, 905 P.2d 760, 763 (Okla. 1995). The court reasoned that defining "sudden" to mean "unexpected or unintended" would make the term "mere surplusage" as the word "accidental" embraces this meaning. *Id.* at 764. "Clearly, the ordinary meaning of 'sudden' cannot describe the gradual routine disposal of industrial waste that occurred over a number of years." *Id.*; *see also Macklanburg-Duncan Co. v. Aetna Cas. & Sur. Co.*, 71 F.3d 1526, 1537 (10th Cir. 1995) (applying Oklahoma law) (disposal of hazardous waste pursuant to long-term, routine, disposal practices were clearly not "sudden" within the meaning ascribed by *Kerr-McGee*); *Stanley v. Farmers Ins. Co.*, No. 05–622-M, 2006 WL 3300461, at *4 (W.D. Okla. Oct. 25, 2006) (citing *Kerr-McGee* as dictating the meaning of the sudden and accidental discharge of water exception to a faulty workmanship exclusion in a homeowner's policy).

**Oregon:** The Supreme Court of Oregon held that "the phrase 'sudden and accidental' could be synonymous with the phrase 'unintended and unexpected.'" *St. Paul Fire & Marine Ins. Co. v. McCormick & Baxter Creosoting*, 923 P.2d 1200, 1217 (Or. 1996). The court rejected the insurers' argument that such a reading of the phrase "sudden and accidental" renders it redundant. *Id.* (rejecting the insurers' argument that an unintended event is always an unexpected event and concluding that not every unintended event (or result) necessarily is unexpected). The court was also persuaded by the fact that, before the phrase "sudden and accidental" was incorporated into pollution exclusions, it had been used in numerous "machinery and boiler" policies where it had been routinely interpreted to mean "unintended and unexpected." *Id.* (finding that environmental contamination caused by the leaching of chemicals from wood treatment plants was sudden and accidental within the meaning of the exclusion). *But see Precision Castparts Corp. v. Hartford Acc. & Indem. Co.*, 04–1699, 2008 WL 2446124, at *5 (D. Or. June 12, 2008) (distinguishing *McCormick & Baxter* and holding that the discharge of thorium into the city sewer was expected and intended and, thus, not "sudden and accidental"); *see also Employers Ins. of Wausau, A Mut. Co. v. Tektronix, Inc.*, 156 P.3d 105, 119 (Or. Ct. App. 2007) (engaging in lengthy discussion of which party bears the burden of providing the "sudden and accidental" exception before concluding that it rests with the insured).

**Pennsylvania:** The Supreme Court of Pennsylvania, addressing the issue at the state court equivalent stage of a Rule 12(b)(6) motion, held that, because of the special usage of the term "sudden and accidental" in the insurance industry, an insured can establish coverage under a general liability policy, which includes a qualified pollution exclusion, whether the contamination be gradual or abrupt "so long as it was unexpected and unintended." *Sunbeam Corp. v. Liberty Mut. Ins. Co.*, 781 A.2d 1189, 1195 (Pa. 2001). The court also endorsed the so-called regulatory estoppel argument: "[H]aving represented to the insurance department, a regulatory agency, that the new language in the 1970 policies—'sudden and accidental'—did not involve a significant decrease in coverage from the prior language, the insurance industry will not be heard to assert the opposite position when claims are made by the insured policyholders." *Id.* at 1192–93 (addressing the exclusion in the context of environmental pollution caused by manufacturers); *see also Bituminous Cas. Corp. v. Hems*, No. 06–1047, 2007 WL 1545641, at *6 (E.D. Pa. May 3, 2007) ("In *Sunbeam Corp*... . the Supreme Court of Pennsylvania held that the meaning of the 'sudden and accidental' exception to the standard pollution exclusion clause included in insurance liability policies should be interpreted based on the custom and usage of terms in the industry. The *Sunbeam* court concluded that the exception applies to both gradual and abrupt pollution or contamination as long as it is unexpected and unintended.").

**Rhode Island:** The Supreme Court of Rhode Island held that the word "sudden" "bars coverage for the intentional or reckless polluter but provides coverage to the insured that makes a good-faith effort to contain and to neutralize toxic waste but, nonetheless, still experiences unexpected and unintended releases of toxic chemicals that cause damage. Thus, coverage will be provided when the contamination was unexpected from the insured's standpoint: that is, when the insured reasonably believed that the waste-disposal methods in question were safe. The insured must show that it had no reason to expect the unintended damage and that it undertook reasonable efforts to contain the waste safely. In other words, a manufacturer that uses state-of-the-art technology, adheres to state and federal environmental regulations, and regularly inspects, evaluates, and upgrades its waste-containment system in accordance with advances in available technology should reap the benefits of coverage under our construction of this type of pollution-exclusion clause. But one that knowingly or recklessly disposes of waste without the necessary and advisable precautions will forfeit coverage under this clause." *Textron, Inc. v. Aetna Cas. & Sur. Co.*, 754 A.2d 742, 750 (R.I. 2000) (addressing hazardous waste generated during the insured's long-term use of a manufacturing facility in the context of exceptions to pollution exclusions for "sudden and accidental" discharges and "seepage, pollution or contamination… caused by a sudden, unintended and unexpected happening during the period of this Insurance").

**South Carolina:** The Supreme Court of South Carolina held that the term "sudden" is ambiguous and susceptible of more than one reasonable interpretation, and, therefore, construing the ambiguity, as it must, in favor of the insured, "sudden" is to be interpreted as "unexpected." *Greenville County v. Ins. Reserve Fund, a Div. of S.C. Budget & Control Bd.*, 443 S.E.2d 552, 553 (S.C. 1994) (addressing the exclusion in the context of claims by landowners, against a county, for inverse condemnation of their property caused by the county's maintenance of a landfill over the course of many years); *see also Helena Chem. Co. v. Allianz Underwriters Ins. Co.*, 594 S.E.2d 455, 460 (S.C. 2004) ("[T]his Court [in *Greenville*] specifically held that the term 'sudden' is to be interpreted as 'unexpected.' Consequently, we must determine whether the discharge, release, or escape of the pesticide was unexpected and accidental.") (holding that contamination at various sites was caused by the insured's routine business operations and was, therefore, not unexpected and accidental and did not fall within the exception to the pollution exclusion); *see also Graf v. Allstate Ins. Co.*, No. 2:06-cv-1045-CWH, 2007 WL 221244, at *2 (D.S.C. Jan. 25, 2007) (citing *Greenville* for the proposition that "sudden" means "unexpected") ("The record does not show that the plaintiffs expected or intended their home to suffer from moisture intrusion. Nor does the record show that the plaintiffs expected or intended that the builder would defectively install the stucco exterior on their home. Therefore, the damage to the plaintiffs' house was sudden [within the context of a homeowner's policy providing coverage for "sudden and accidental physical loss to the property"].").

**South Dakota:** A South Dakota District Court held that the discharge of toxic chemicals from frozen pipes at an insured's chemical treatment plant was sudden and accidental, thereby triggering the exception to the pollution exclusion. *American Universal Ins. Co. v. Whitewood Custom Treaters, Inc.*, 707 F. Supp. 1140, 1147 (D.S.D. 1989) (applying *Benedictine Sisters of St. Mary's Hospital v. St. Paul Fire & Marine Ins. Co.*, 815 F.2d 1209, 1211 (8th Cir. 1987)) (applying South Dakota law). "[The Insured] did not knowingly create the harm caused when frozen pipes burst. There is no evidence that [the Insured] was aware of any problem with the design of the pipes that would cause them to freeze. Because [the Insured] did not expect or intend the harm at the time it occurred, the Court holds that the discharge was sudden and accidental." *Id.*; *see also Headley v. St. Paul Fire & Marine Ins. Co.*, 712 F. Supp. 745, 748–49 (D.S.D 1989) ("sudden and accidental" exception did not apply to property damage which occurred gradually and over an extended period of time and which was anticipated and predictable) (applying *Benedictine Sisters*).

**Tennessee:** The Court of Appeals of Tennessee held "that the proper interpretation of the term 'sudden' necessarily includes a temporal element... . We find that the usual, natural, and ordinary meaning of 'sudden' is 'abrupt'— the opposite of 'gradual,' 'routine,' or 'continuous.'" *Drexel Chem. Co. v. Bituminous Ins. Co.*, 933 S.W.2d 471, 477 (Tenn. Ct. App. 1996). "When discharges of pollution occur on a regular, ongoing basis over a lengthy period of time as a normal part of an operation, such discharges are not 'sudden' within the meaning of the pollution exclusion clause. However, where the damage is caused by a 'few discrete polluting events, each of which was short in duration and accidental in nature,' the discharge will fall within the 'sudden and accidental' exception to the pollution exclusion and, therefore, the insurer will be liable for coverage under the policy." *Id.* (addressing contamination from numerous spills and leaks that occurred in the regular operation of a chemical mixing company's facility over course of several years); *see also Sulphuric Acid Trading Co., Inc. v. Greenwich Ins. Co.*, 211 S.W.3d 243, 250 n.3 (Tenn. Ct. App. 2006) (explaining *Drexel* in the context of addressing the absolute pollution exclusion).

**Texas:** The Court of Appeals of Texas, after noting that only Texas federal courts had addressed the issue (and holding that "sudden" has a temporal element), held that "[t]he term 'sudden' has several recognized meanings, among which are 'unexpected' and 'unintended.' To determine its meaning in this case, the term must be read within the context of the policy. To read the word 'sudden' in the pollution exclusion to mean only unexpected and unintended would make it redundant of the word 'accidental.' The term 'accidental' already encompasses the concepts of being unexpected and unintended. In contrast, common usage of the term 'sudden' includes a temporal aspect." *Mesa Operating Co. v. Cal. Union Ins. Co.*, 986 S.W.2d 749, 755 (Tex. Ct. App. 1999) (addressing the exclusion in the context of claims for damages caused by salt water that leaked from a well into an aquifer over the course of several years); *see also Saint Paul Surplus Lines Ins. Co. v. Geo Pipe Co.*, 25 S.W.3d 900, 904 (Tex. Ct. App. 2000) (following *Mesa* and holding that the sudden and accidental physical damage exception to the "impaired property" exclusion did not apply to a hole in oil well tubing, which was caused by corrosion of a weld, because corrosion is physical damage that is incremental or gradual); *Gulf Metals Indus., Inc. v. Chi. Ins. Co.*, 993 S.W.2d 800, 807 (Tex. Ct. App. 1999) ("[T]he word 'sudden' clearly and unambiguously imparts a sense of temporal urgency.").

**Utah:** The Supreme Court of Utah held "that the language [of the qualified pollution exclusion] is unambiguous and that the term 'sudden' contains a temporal element, such as being abrupt or quick, and the term 'accidental' means something akin to unintended or unexpected. … The courts adopting this view have reasoned that the term 'sudden' includes an element of 'immediacy,' 'quickness,' or 'abruptness,' because the contrary reading would render the word 'accidental' (which clearly means unexpected) redundant." *Sharon Steel Corp. v. Aetna Cas. & Sur. Co.*, 931 P.2d 127, 135 (Utah 1997). "[I]f the releases were part of the overall business operations, then even if some of the releases viewed individually may have been 'sudden,' this does not alter the conclusion that the overall pattern of discharges was not 'sudden and accidental.'" *Id.* at 136 (citation and internal quotes omitted) (finding that the "sudden and accidental" exception did not restore coverage for the release of toxic material from tailings from the insured's ore milling operations).

**Vermont:** No instructive authority. *But see Maska U.S., Inc. v. Kansa Gen. Ins. Co.*, 198 F.3d 74 (2nd Cir. 1999) (applying Vermont law) (addressing evidence that since 1970, when liability insurers began including pollution exclusions in their policies, the Vermont Department of Banking Insurance disapproved such policies based on its determination that the exclusions were unfair and discriminatory and inconsistent with the public's expectation of coverage under a general liability policy).

**Virginia:** A Virginia District Court, after noting the absence of a Supreme Court of Virginia decision interpreting the "sudden and accidental" pollution exclusion, predicted that a Virginia court would find that "[t]he sounder interpretation of the phrase 'sudden and accidental,' and the one adopted by the majority of jurisdictions, is that the phrase means both unexpected and unintended *and* quick or abrupt. This interpretation is the most accurate because it gives effect to both words in the phrase." *Morrow Corp. v. Harleysville Mut. Ins. Co.*, 101 F. Supp. 2d 422, 431 (E.D. Va. 2000) (emphasis in original) (addressing the pollution exclusion in the context of environmental property damage caused by the release of perchloroethylene in the insured's dry-cleaning business); *see also Guyton v. U. S. Fid. & Guar. Co.*, No. LD986, 1981 WL 180513, *1 (Va. Cir. Ct. Mar. 30, 1981) (finding no duty to defend because the face of the complaint showed a slow, gradual leak, which could not be considered "sudden and accidental") (citing no case law, from any jurisdiction, in support of the interpretation of "sudden and accidental").

**Washington:** The Supreme Court of Washington, after finding the qualified pollution exclusion language to be ambiguous, held that "'sudden and accidental' means 'unexpected and unintended.' That is, for injury or damage to be covered under the occurrence clause, it must be neither expected nor intended. Gradual polluting events may fall within the occurrence clause provided they result in unexpected and unintended damage." *Queen City Farms, Inc. v. Aetna Cas. & Sur. Co.*, 882 P.2d 703, 723 (Wash. 1994) (noting that, because insurance policies often use words with similar meanings (i.e., "discharge, dispersal, release or escape"), "sudden and accidental" could mean unexpected and unintended) (discussing at length that representations were made by insurers to state insurance regulators that the pollution exclusion was intended to exclude coverage for intentional polluters and clarify the "occurrence" clause) (holding that toxic chemicals leaking out of a waste pit was "sudden and accidental"); *see also Am. Nat'l Fire Ins. Co. v. B & L Trucking & Constr. Co.*, 951 P.2d 250, 255 (Wash. 1998) (citing *Queen City* for the meaning of "sudden and accidental").

**West Virginia:** The Supreme Court of Appeals of West Virginia held that "the policies issued by [the insurer] covered pollution damage, even if it resulted over a period of time and was gradual, so long as it was not expected or intended." *Joy Techs., Inc. v. Liberty Mut. Ins.*, 421 S.E.2d 493, 500 (W. Va. 1992). The court's decision was based, in part, on the fact that "the insurance group representing [the insurer] unambiguously and officially represented to the West Virginia Insurance Commission that the exclusion in question did not alter coverage under the policies involved, coverage which included the injuries in the present case." *Id.* at 499–500 (addressing the qualified pollution exclusion in the context of contamination caused by PCBs used to clean mining equipment).

**Wisconsin:** The Supreme Court of Wisconsin concluded "that the phrase 'sudden and accidental' is susceptible to more than one reasonable meaning, including abrupt and immediate as [the insurer] claims as well as unexpected and unintended as the property owners claim. Thus the phrase 'sudden and accidental' contained in the pollution exclusion clause is ambiguous." *Just v. Land Reclamation, Ltd.*, 456 N.W.2d 570, 573 (Wis. 1990). "This conclusion comports with substantial evidence indicating that the insurance industry itself originally intended the phrase to be construed as 'unexpected and unintended.' This court may examine extrinsic evidence as an aid to determining the meaning of contract language when an insurance contract is ambiguous." *Id.* (addressing the exclusion in the context of environmental damage caused by discharges from a landfill); *see also Sharp v. Vick*, No. 21544114, 2003 WL 02–1575, at *6–7 (Wis. Ct. App. 2003) (citing *Just* for the meaning of "sudden and accidental" in a homeowner's policy and concluding that the exception to the pollution exclusion applied because the insureds did not expect or intend the bodily injuries caused by their improper maintenance of a water well).

**Wyoming:** The Supreme Court of Wyoming held the "the words 'sudden and accidental' encompass a temporal aspect that requires the occurrence of an event to happen abruptly, without any significant notice and unexpectedly." *Sinclair Oil Corp. v. Republic Ins. Co.*, 929 P.2d 535, 543 (Wyo. 1996). "The exception to the exclusion clauses does not preserve coverage for gradual and unintentional discharges of pollutants unless such discharge is caused by a 'sudden and accidental' event as we have defined that phrase." *Id.* (addressing the exclusion in the context of damages from the insured's refinery operations); *see also Gainsco Ins. Co. v. Amoco Prod. Co.*, 53 P.3d 1051, 1062 (Wyo. 2002) (citing *Sinclair* in the context of addressing the total pollution exclusion).

# CHAPTER

# 14

# "Absolute" Pollution Exclusion

As discussed in the previous chapter, commercial general liability insurance policies have for some time sought to exclude coverage for pollution. The 1973 commercial general liability (CGL) form contained the qualified pollution exclusion addressed in the prior chapter. Under this exclusion, pollution-related claims were generally not covered unless the discharge of the pollutant was "sudden and accidental." Insurers interpreted this language to mean that the discharge must be both unintentional and abrupt if there was to be coverage. However, approximately half the states disagreed and found it sufficient to establish coverage if the discharge (or sometimes even the damage from the discharge) was unintentional, no matter how extended or ongoing the time period of the discharge. As the previous chapter illustrates, litigation over the meaning of "sudden and accidental" was abundant.

Reacting to this situation, the insurance industry replaced the qualified pollution exclusion with an "absolute" pollution exclusion that became part of the 1986 CGL form. Under the absolute pollution exclusion, the CGL policy clearly provides that it does not cover Superfund-style government-mandated cleanup and also states, more generally, that the policy does not cover bodily injury or property damage "arising out of the actual, alleged or threatened discharge, dispersal, seepage, migration, release or escape of 'pollutants,'" provided that such discharge, dispersal, etc. was of waste or from various specifically described premises, subject to certain exceptions. See INS. SERVS. OFFICE INC., COMMERCIAL GENERAL LIABILITY COVERAGE FORM, No. CG 00011185, § I2f (1984).

"Pollutants" is defined as

> any solid, liquid, gaseous or thermal irritant or contaminant, including smoke, vapor, soot, fumes, acids, alkalis, chemicals and waste. Waste includes materials to be recycled, reconditioned or reclaimed.

*Id.*

While the absolute pollution exclusion has undergone changes between the 1986 and 2007 CGL forms, its general purpose has remained the same—eliminate the "sudden and accidental" exception that had generated so much litigation over the scope of the qualified pollution exclusion.

Despite the breadth of the absolute pollution exclusion that is contained in the Insurance Services Office (ISO) CGL form, it is not unusual for insurers to replace it with an endorsement that is even broader in scope. This modified version is often referred to as the "total" pollution exclusion. While the absolute pollution exclusion requires that the discharge, dispersal, etc. of "pollutants" be of waste or from certain specifically described premises, the total pollution exclusion, as its name implies, does not contain this qualification. One commonly used total pollution exclusion provides as follows:

> This insurance does not apply to:
> f. Pollution
>
> (1) "Bodily injury" or "property damage" which would not have occurred in whole or part but for the actual, alleged or threatened discharge, dispersal, seepage, migration, release or escape of "pollutants" at any time.
> (2) Any loss, cost or expense arising out of any:
>     (a) Request, demand, order or statutory or regulatory requirement that any insured or others test for, monitor, clean up, remove, contain, treat, detoxify or neutralize, or in any way respond to, or assess the effects of "pollutants"; or
>     (b) Claim or suit by or on behalf of a governmental authority for damages because of testing for, monitoring, cleaning up, removing, containing, treating, detoxifying or neutralizing, or in any way responding to, or assessing the effects of, "pollutants".

Ins. Servs. Office Props., Inc., Total Pollution Exclusion Endorsement, No. CG 21 49 09 99 (1998).

For purposes of the issue discussed in this chapter, the absolute and total pollution exclusions are considered equivalent and are sometimes referred to herein as simply the pollution exclusion.

Although adoption of the absolute pollution exclusion was supposed to end the split in the states that had surrounded the qualified pollution exclusion, this proved not to be the case. While all courts have consistently applied the pollution exclusion to bar coverage for suits against a CGL policyholder involving traditional "smokestack" or "dumping" pollution, courts have divided over whether the exclusion, despite its broad language, applies to any claim involving a chemical or irritant—in other words, any hazardous substance.

Liability insurers have been aggressive and rather successful in some states invoking the exclusion to deny claims involving any hazardous substance, such as carbon monoxide poisoning due to faulty furnace repair, injuries from paint or adhesive fumes, bug or lawn spraying, and even to drifting smoke—all claims that many policyholders contend do not meet the commonsense definition of a pollution claim. In other states, courts have refused to give the absolute exclusion such a broad and literal (policyholders would say "hyperliteral") reading if this results in no coverage for liability claims that were noncontroversially viewed as within the scope of general liability policy coverage prior to 1986. Where the claim is one ordinarily arising out of the appropriate everyday activity of a commercial policyholder (faulty repair, negligent maintenance of a job site, poor performance) rather than due to polluting conduct per se, these courts tend to find the claim outside the scope of the pollution exclusion. *See W. Alliance Ins. Co. v. Gill*, 686 N.E.2d 997, 1000 (Mass. 1997) ("A reasonable policyholder might well understand carbon monoxide is a pollutant when it is emitted in an industrial or environmental setting, but would not reasonably characterize carbon monoxide emitted from a malfunctioning or improperly operated restaurant oven as pollution.") (citation and quotation omitted).

As the following survey of the issue demonstrates, in some states there are precedents that are inconsistent or at least in tension, requiring counsel and claims professionals to make distinctions that place a claim within one or another line of cases (see, for example, in Washington (discussed below) a claim involving chemical fumes from waterproofing was excluded but a spurting gasoline claim was not).

The basic divide is one of whether the pollution exclusion clause is interpreted in a highly textual, broad, literal manner to apply to liability arising out of or related to the discharge of any hazardous substance (the pro-insurer position, at least in the most common factual scenarios leading to dispute) or whether the exclusion is construed in a more functional manner focusing on the intent, purpose, and goal of the exclusion (the pro-policy-holder position in most cases).[1] The divide between the courts regarding

---

1. Insurer counsel will, of course, contend that the purpose of the pollution exclusion was indeed to bar coverage for any case that involved the discharge of a chemical. The available drafting history of the exclusion and the background of its adoption, however, appears to be to the contrary—at least to one of the authors. Jeffrey W. Stempel, *Reason and Pollution: Correctly Construing the "Absolute" Exclusion in Context and in Accord with Its Purpose and Party Expectation*, 34 Tort & Ins. L.J. 1 (1998); Jeffrey W. Stempel, *Unreason in Action: A Case Study in the Wrong Approach to Construing the Liability Insurance Pollution Exclusion*, 50 Fla. L. Rev. 463 (1998). *But see* William P. Shelley & Richard C. Mason, *Application of the Absolute Pollution Exclusion to Toxic Tort Claims: Will Courts Choose Policy Construction or Deconstruction?*, 33 Tort & Ins. L.J. 749 (1998) (taking opposite view and supporting insurer position on breadth of pollution exclusion). *See also Apana v. TIG Ins. Co.*, 574 F.3d 679 (9th Cir. 2009) (characterizing divide in judicial decisions as between those looking at the literal text of the exclusion versus those that consider the reasonable expectations of the policyholder); *MacKinnon v. Truck Ins. Exch.*, 73 P.3d 1205, 1208-09 (Cal. 2003) (explaining division of authority).

application of the pollution exclusion is also frequently described as a difference over whether the exclusion applies only to what is historically regarded as a pollution claim, such as hazardous waste or industrial pollution, often referred to as "traditional environmental pollution," or whether the exclusion, based on a broad linguistic reading, makes it applicable to claims involving any hazardous substance. *Compare Reed v. Auto-Owners Ins. Co.*, 667 S.E.2d 90, 92 (Ga. 2008) (holding that the pollution exclusion precluded coverage for a carbon monoxide claim as nothing in the text of the exclusion supported a reading that it was "limited to what is commonly or traditionally considered environmental pollution") *with Am. States Ins. Co. v. Koloms*, 687 N.E.2d 72, 79 (Ill. 1997) (holding that the pollution exclusion did not preclude coverage for a carbon monoxide claim) ("[W]e agree with those courts which have restricted the exclusion's otherwise potentially limitless application to only those hazards traditionally associated with environmental pollution. We find support for our decision in the drafting history of the exclusion, which reveals an intent on the part of the insurance industry to so limit the clause.").

Pro-policyholder courts on this issue are also more likely to emphasize that the pollution exclusion is an exclusion, which under the ground rules of insurance policy construction requires the insurer to shoulder the burden of persuasion to demonstrate that the exclusion clearly applies to the claim at issue. In addition, the general rule of contract construction in most states is that exclusions are to be narrowly construed and that policy language operating in the nature of an exclusion (e.g., narrow definitional language) should be strictly construed. Further, all states subscribe in some form to the *contra proferentem* principle in which ambiguous contract language is construed against the drafter, which is usually the insurer in most coverage disputes. *See Am. States Ins. Co. v. Kiger*, 662 N.E.2d 945, 949 (Ind. 1996) ("[S]ince the term 'pollutant' does not obviously include gasoline and, accordingly, is ambiguous, we once again must construe the language against the insurer who drafted it.").

Policyholder counsel also contend that the exclusion was not designed to read out from historical CGL coverage claims that do not involve widespread injury impacting the underwriting and risk pooling attending the CGL. Under this view, a carbon monoxide poisoning claim involving a house or parts of an apartment building would not be excluded although a tanker truck explosion blanketing an entire neighborhood would fall within the exclusion because the nature and magnitude of the injury and claim are different.

As one court described the litigation over the pollution exclusion: "[T]here exists not just a split of authority, but an absolute fragmentation of authority." *Porterfield v. Audubon Indem. Co.*, 856 So. 2d 789, 800 (Ala. 2002). Another put it this way: "[T]here is a smorgasbord of authority offering a varying range of views and analyses [of the traditional versus non-traditional issue]." *TerraMatrix, Inc. v. U.S. Fire Ins. Co.*, 939 P.2d 483, 488 (Colo. App. 1997). Speaking of smorgasbords, see *Greengrass v. Lumbermans Mut. Cas. Co.*, No. 09 Civ. 7697, 2010 WL 3069560, at *9 (S.D.N.Y. July 27, 2010) (holding that the absolute pollution exclusion did not preclude coverage for odors emanating from the "Sturgeon King's" delicatessen) (noting that, according to Zagat's restaurant guide, "The smells alone are worth the price of admission.").

For more extensive discussion of the pollution exclusion and liability coverage for environmental claims generally, including CERCLA or other regulatory costs: JEFFREY W. STEMPEL, STEMPEL ON INSURANCE CONTRACTS §§ 14.11, 14.12 (3d ed. 2006 & Supp. 2009); BARRY R. OSTRAGER & THOMAS R. NEWMAN, HANDBOOK ON INSURANCE COVERAGE DISPUTES Ch. 10 (14th ed. 2008); EUGENE ANDERSON, JORDAN STANZLER, & LORELIE S. MASTERS, INSURANCE COVERAGE LITIGATION CH. 15 (2d ed. 2004); PETER KALIS, THOMAS M. REITER, & JAMES R. SEGERDAHL, POLICYHOLDER'S GUIDE TO INSURANCE COVERAGE §10.04 (1997 & Supp. 2004).

Following is a state-by-state listing of each state's dominant approach and key precedents. As always, some care is involved in reviewing the survey. Some precedents have obvious pro-insurer or pro-policyholder consequences but may be quite fact-specific. For example, a court may declare that the pollution exclusion is unambiguous in applying it to a clear case of traditional pollution. If a different case arises involving a less traditional pollution claim, the court may not be so confident in the exclusion's clarity. Similarly, a court may refuse to apply the exclusion to something like carbon monoxide poisoning of a camping family due to a malfunctioning space heater but be more willing to bar coverage if the carbon monoxide drifts to an adjoining campsite and causes injury there. Simply put, when it comes to the applicability of the pollution exclusion, facts can matter as much as the court's position on the fundamental divide between insurers and policyholder over the scope of the exclusion.

## 50-State Survey: "Absolute" Pollution Exclusion

**Alabama:** The Supreme Court of Alabama, despite concluding that lead paint qualifies as a "pollutant" under the terms of the pollution exclusion, went on to hold that the exclusion did not apply to preclude coverage because "a reasonably prudent insured might have concluded in 1991 that the presence of lead-paint flakes, chips, and/or dust in a residential apartment would not qualify as a discharge, dispersal, release, or escape of a pollutant." *Porterfield v. Audubon Indem. Co.*, 856 So. 2d 789, 805 (Ala. 2002) (noting also that more than sixty pollution exclusion cases were decided by courts during nine months case was pending); *see also Essex Ins. Co. v. Avondale Mills, Inc.*, 639

So. 2d 1339, 1342 (Ala. 1994) (finding a worker's exposure to asbestos released into "the environs of the building" during its dismantling was not a sufficient release into atmosphere to make exclusion applicable). *But see Federated Mut. Ins. Co. v. Abston Petroleum, Inc.*, 967 So. 2d 705, 713 (Ala. 2007) (finding the pollution exclusion precluded coverage for gas that leaked from underground lines of aboveground tanks) ("We hold that gasoline, although not a pollutant when properly used for the purposes for which it is intended, is clearly a pollutant when it leaks into the soil from underground lines or tanks or when fumes from such a leak are so dangerous that a business must be closed, as was the case here... . Because we conclude that gasoline is clearly a pollutant as that term is used in the policy, any argument that the pollution-exclusion clause is ambiguous cannot be supported.").

**Alaska:** The Supreme Court of Alaska held that the language of the pollution exclusion was unambiguous and applied it to preclude coverage for gasoline that leaked from a broken fill pipe connected to an underground storage tank. *Whittier Props., Inc. v. Ala. Nat'l Ins. Co.*, 185 P.3d 84, 89–92 (Alaska 2008). In this case of first impression the court "conclude[d] that the better-reasoned approach is the one advocated by [the insurer] and adopted by the majority of courts that have reviewed a pollution exclusion identical or markedly similar to the clause [here]. We hold that there is no ambiguity because, even though gasoline that is in the UST is a 'product' for purposes of other parts of the insurance policy, when the gasoline escapes or reaches a location where it is no longer a useful product it is fairly considered a pollutant." *Id.* at 90–91.

**Arizona:** The Court of Appeals of Arizona held that the pollution exclusion did not bar coverage for a claim for injury to a professional golfer, who ingested bacteria-contaminated drinking water at the policyholder's golf course, because the plain meaning of "pollutant does not include bacteria." *Keggi v. Northbrook Prop. & Cas. Ins. Co.*, 13 P.3d 785, 790 (Ariz. Ct. App. 2000). The court "decline[d] to interpret the term 'pollutants' so broadly as to include 'bacteria,' and thereby to negate coverage in this case, especially where there was no evidence that the contamination of the water with the bacteria was caused by traditional environmental pollution [which the court determined was the insurance industry's purpose in creating the absolute pollution exclusion]." *Id.* at 792.

**Arkansas:** The Supreme Court of Arkansas held that the pollution exclusion did not apply to a claim arising out of a sewer system backup in a mobilehome park. *Minerva Enter., Inc. v. Bituminous Cas. Corp.*, 851 S.W.2d 403, 406 (Ark. 1993). The court found that "the pollution exclusion in the case before us is, at least, ambiguous. It is not clear from the language of the policy that the single back-up of a septic tank in a mobile home park is necessarily the kind of damage the clause was intended to exclude." *Id.* "[T]he term 'waste' must be considered within the context of the entire list, all of which are pollutants related to industrial waste." *Id.; see also State Auto Prop. & Cas. Ins. Co. v. Ark. Dept. of Envtl. Quality*, 258 S.W.3d 736, 742–43 (Ark. 2007) (rejecting the insurer's argument that *Minerva* was wrongly decided, but reversing summary judgment granted to insured because fact finder failed to consider extrinsic evidence to decide whether release of gasoline from storage tanks was "persistent industrial pollution" that exclusion was meant to preclude); *Universal Cas. Co. v. Triple Transport, Inc.*, No. 4:08CV01822BSM, 2009 WL 2136175, at *5 (E.D. Ark. July 13, 2009) (finding fact question whether water containing hydrocarbons, reserve pit water, and drilling mud or oil were "pollutants").

**California:** The Supreme Court of California, seeking to avoid "absurd results," refused to apply the language of the absolute pollution exclusion literally and broadly, holding that the scope of the pollution exclusion would be limited "to injuries arising from events commonly thought of as pollution, i.e., environmental pollution." *MacKinnon v. Truck Ins. Exch.*, 73 P.3d 1205, 1216 (Cal. 2003) (holding that the pollution exclusion did not apply to preclude from coverage claims resulting from exposure to insecticide). The court recognized that "terms such as 'commonly thought of as pollution,' or 'environmental pollution,' are not paragons of precision, and further clarification may be required." *Id.* at 1217; *see also Griffin Dewatering Corp. v. N. Ins. Co. of N.Y.*, 97 Cal. Rptr. 3d 568, 589–90 (Cal. Ct. App. 2009) (finding that the "*MacKinnon* decision [was] the appropriate way to determine the reasonableness of the insurer's coverage determination" under the absolute pollution exclusion where the injury-causing event was the flow of raw sewage flowing from a sewer line under construction by the insured); *Johnson v. Clarendon Nat. Ins. Co.*, No. G039659, 2009 WL 252619 (Cal. Ct. App. Feb. 4, 2009) (analyzing *MacKinnon* and holding that the pollution exclusion did not preclude coverage for mold). *Compare SEMX Corp. v. Fed. Ins. Co.*, 398 F. Supp. 2d 1103 (S.D. Cal. 2005) (concluding that, because the injury-causing event [the release of ammonia gases into the air] was a one-time release, and not the result of the insured's normal operations, the pollution exclusion did not apply to preclude coverage) *with Garamendi v. Golden Eagle Ins. Co.*, 25 Cal. Rptr. 3d 642 (Cal. Ct. App. 2005) (holding that the pollution exclusion applied to preclude coverage for claims for injuries caused by the repeated long-term exposure to silica dust). *See also Am. Cas. Co. of Reading, PA v. Miller*, 71 Cal. Rptr. 3d 571, 582 (Cal. Ct. App. 2008) (holding that release of chemicals into sewer by furniture-stripping business was environmental pollution and therefore within absolute pollution exclusion).

**Colorado:** The Colorado Court of Appeals, noting that there is a "smorgasbord of authority" offering a varying range of views and analyses of the traditional versus non-traditional issue, aligned itself with the jurisdictions that have concluded that the plain language of the pollution exclusion is not limited solely to environmental or industrial contexts and held that "the pollution exclusion clause is unambiguous when applied to ammonia vapors, that ammonia constitutes a pollutant under the pollution exclusion clause, and that movement of the ammonia vapors within the office building air duct or ventilation system constituted a 'discharge, dispersal... release, or escape' within the meaning of the pollution exclusion." *TerraMatrix, Inc. v. U.S. Fire Ins. Co.*, 939 P.2d 483, 488 (Colo. App. 1997) (alteration in original); *see also New Salida Ditch Co., Inc. v. United Fire & Cas. Co.*, No. 08-cv-00391, 2009 WL 5126498, at *10 (D. Colo. Dec. 18, 2009) (finding claims arising out of the discharge of soil, sand, dirt, rocks, and sediment into a river precluded by the pollution exclusion).

**Connecticut:** The Supreme Court of Connecticut held that the leakage of contaminants and hazardous substances into soil and water, at a site where the insured removed insulation from copper wire, fell squarely within the pollution exclusion. *Schilberg Integrated Metals Corp. v. Continental Cas. Co.*, 819 A.2d 773, 785 (Conn. 2003) (holding that *Heyman Assocs. No. 1 v. Ins. Co. of the State of Pa.*, 653 A.2d 122 (Conn. 1995) did not adopt the approach that the exclusion does not apply when pollution occurs in the course of the insured's central business activity); *see also Heyman Assocs.*, 653 A.2d at 122 (holding that exclusion precluded coverage for fuel oil released into a harbor). *But see Danbury Ins. Co. v. Novella*, 727 A.2d 279, 285 (Conn. Super. Ct. 1998) (distinguishing *Heyman Assocs.* and finding exclusion inapplicable, as ambiguous, in case involving lead paint chipping and flaking off interior and exterior walls of insured's rental unit) ("Although *Heyman* did not expressly adopt an 'environmental' reading of pollution exclusion clauses, its underlying facts, where fuel oil spilled or released into a waterway caused environmental damage, present a classic case of environmental pollution."); *Nat'l Grange Mut. Ins. Co. v. Caraker*, No. CV030070715, 2006 WL 853153, at *7 (Conn. Super. Ct. Feb. 28 2006) ("The exclusion clause is... ambiguous with respect to whether asbestos released as described in the complaint can be properly classified as a pollutant.").

**Delaware:** No instructive authority. Delaware courts that have addressed the pollution exclusion have done so applying the law of another state.

**Florida:** The Supreme Court of Florida held that the pollution exclusion precluded coverage for claims for bodily injury and loss of income arising out of a blueprint machine that was knocked over in an office and emitted ammonia fumes. *Deni Assocs. of Fla., Inc. v. State Farm Fire & Cas. Ins. Co.*, 711 So. 2d 1135, 1141 (Fla. 1998). The court rejected various arguments that the pollution exclusion was ambiguous and only excluded environmental or industrial pollution. *Id.* at 1138–39; *see also Fogg v. Fla. Farm Bureau Mut. Ins. Co.*, 711 So. 2d 1135, 1141 (Fla. 1998) (companion case to *Deni*) (holding that the pollution exclusion precluded coverage for bodily injury claims by bystanders who were negligently sprayed with a chemical by a crop-dusting plane); *First Specialty Ins. v. GRS Mgmt.*, No. 08-81356, 2009 WL 2524613, at *5 (S.D. Fla. Aug. 17, 2009) (involving a claim arising out of ingestion of swimming pool water tainted by viral contaminants subject to pollution exclusion); *Nova Cas. Co. v. Waserstein*, 424 F. Supp. 2d 1325, 1334 (S.D. Fla. 2006) (holding that the pollution exclusion applied to preclude coverage for personal injury claims filed by workers in a building who alleged that they were harmed when the building owner/insured failed to keep the air and surfaces in the building free of various organisms and allergens); *Phila. Indem. Ins. Co. v. Yachtsman's Inn Condominium Assoc., Inc.*, 595 F. Supp. 2d 1319, 1325 (S.D. Fla. 2009) (finding pollution exclusion unambiguously applied to claims for exposure to battery acid, raw sewage, and feces). *But see WPC Indus. Contractors Ltd. v. Amerisure Mut. Ins. Co.*, 660 F. Supp. 2d 1341, 1348 (D. Fla. 2009) (holding that the pollution exclusion did not apply—but on the basis that the exclusion's specific terms were not satisfied).

**Georgia:** The Supreme Court of Georgia held that the pollution exclusion unambiguously precluded coverage for a carbon monoxide leak in an insured landlord's rental property because it qualified as a "pollutant." *Reed v. Auto-Owners Ins. Co.*, 667 S.E.2d 90, 92 (Ga. 2008). "As all parties recognize, the question thus narrows to whether carbon monoxide gas is a 'pollutant'—i.e., matter, in any state, acting as an 'irritant or contaminant,' including 'fumes.' We need not consult a plethora of dictionaries and statutes to conclude that it is." *Id.* The court concluded that nothing in the text of the pollution exclusion supported a reading that it was "limited to what is commonly or traditionally considered environmental pollution." *Id.*; *see also Truitt Oil & Gas Co. v. Ranger Ins. Co.*, 498 S.E.2d 572, 574 (Ga. Ct. App. 1998) (holding pollution exclusion applicable to claim arising out of gasoline leak from storage container, rendering neighbor's real property inaccessible, because of road closure due to cleanup). *But see Barrett v. Nat'l Union Fire Ins. Co. of Pittsburgh*, 626 S.E.2d 326, 330 (Ga. Ct. App. 2010) (declining to follow *Reed* because the allegations of the complaint indicated that the release of natural gas, standing alone, did not cause the underlying plaintiff's injuries) (distinguishing cases where the presence of the pollutant, following its release, dispersal, or seepage was the "but-for" cause of the plaintiff's injury).

**Hawaii:** A Hawaii District Court held that the pollution exclusion precluded coverage to a plumbing company, for claims arising out of its use of an extremely strong drain cleaner at a Wal-Mart store, which generated "noxious fumes" injuring a store employee. *Apana v. TIG Ins. Co.*, 504 F. Supp. 2d 998, 1006 (D. Haw. 2007). "Nothing in the language of the Total Pollution Exclusion Endorsement references or even impliedly limits the clause to instances of traditional environmental pollution or requires that the pollution cover an extended area." *Id.* On appeal, the Ninth Circuit certified the "traditional" versus "non-traditional" issue to the Supreme Court of Hawaii. *Apana v. TIG Ins. Co.*, 574 F.3d 679 (9th Cir. 2009). The case was subsequently dismissed by the parties. *Apana v. TIG Ins. Co.*, No. 29942, 2010 WL 1434763 (Haw. April 7, 2010); *see also Allstate Ins. Co. v. Leong*, No. 09–00217, 2010 WL 1904978, at *5 (D. Haw. May 11, 2010) (finding pollution exclusion not applicable to sewage flow that damaged a neighbor's retaining wall) ("Even if the court assumes that the sewer pipe leaked 'waste materials or other irritants, contaminants or pollutants,' it is unclear whether the damage to the retaining wall was *caused* by 'waste materials or other irritants, contaminants or pollutants.'").

**Idaho:** An Idaho District Court held that the pollution exclusion precluded coverage for claims for damages caused by tailings (an unwanted by-product of a manufacturing process) from mining operations. *Monarch Greenback, LLC v. Monticello Ins. Co.*, 118 F. Supp. 2d 1068, 1080 (D. Idaho 1999). "[N]ot only are mine tailings within the pollution exclusion's definition of 'pollutant,' but also the 'hazardous substances' found within the tailings clearly constitute an 'irritant' or 'contaminant' and are 'pollutants.'" *Id.*; *see also Esterovich v. City of Kellogg*, 80 P.3d 1040, 1042 (Idaho 2003) (addressing a procedural issue, unrelated to the pollution exclusion, Supreme Court of Idaho noted that the trial court had found that the exclusion did not preclude coverage for injury caused by exposure to smoke used to test a city's sewer system).

**Illinois:** The Supreme Court of Illinois held that the pollution exclusion did not preclude coverage for claims arising out of carbon monoxide emitted from a building's furnace. *Am. States Ins. Co. v. Koloms*, 687 N.E.2d 72, 79 (Ill. 1997). "[W]e agree with those courts which have restricted the exclusion's otherwise potentially limitless application to only those hazards traditionally associated with environmental pollution. We find support for our decision in the drafting history of the exclusion, which reveals an intent on the part of the insurance industry to so limit the clause." *Id.*; *see also Conn. Specialty Ins. Co. v. Loop Paper Recycling, Inc.*, 824 N.E.2d 1125, 1138 (Ill. App. Ct. 2005) (holding that the exclusion focuses on traditional environmental pollution and for it to apply "the pollutant must actually spill beyond the insured's premises and into the environment"); *Kim v. State Farm Fire & Cas. Co.*, 728 N.E.2d 530, 536 (Ill. App. Ct. 2000) (holding that, under *Koloms*, since the release of "perc" [dry cleaning chemical] did constitute traditional environmental pollution, the pollution exclusion applied to bar coverage). *But see Pacific Employers Ins. Co. v. Clean Harbors Environmental Services, Inc.*, No. 08 C 2180, 2010 WL 438372, at *5 (N.D. Ill. Feb. 4, 2010) ("That a personal injury was caused by chemicals does not remove it from the intended scope of the policy based on the pollution exclusion language before this Court. This is so even if the chemicals are classified as contaminant or irritants and the accident was caused by their escape or release[.]... In the context of the facts of this case, [Plaintiff] Lopez sustained injuries during his day-to-day duties. That those injuries were sustained from the chemicals in drums he was hauling does not place the claim within the pollution exclusion.").

**Indiana:** The Supreme Court of Indiana held that the pollution exclusion did not preclude coverage for claims for damages caused by the discharge of petroleum from an underground storage tank at a gas station. *Am. States Ins. Co. v. Kiger*, 662 N.E.2d 945, 949 (Ind. 1996). "[S]ince the term 'pollutant' does not obviously include gasoline and, accordingly, is ambiguous, we once again must construe the language against the insurer who drafted it." *Id.* The court also described it as an "oddity" and "strange" that an insurance company would sell a "garage policy" to a gas station "when that policy specifically excluded the major source of potential liability." *Id.* at 948; *see also Freidline v. Shelby Ins. Co.*, 774 N.E.2d 37, 42 (Ind. 2002) (pollution exclusion not applicable to bodily injury claims arising from fumes inhaled during carpet installation); *Great Lakes Chem. Corp. v. Int'l Surplus Lines Ins. Co.*, 638 N.E.2d 847, 851 (Ind. Ct. App. 1994) (concluding that, while damages were environmental, the pollution exclusion was not applicable because claims were in the nature of products liability); *Nat'l Union Fire Ins. Co of Pittsburgh v. Standard Fusee Corp.*, 917 N.E.2d 170, 185 (Ind. Ct. App. 2009) (finding the pollution exclusion ambiguous and unenforceable for claims for perchlorate that leaked from a flare production facility). *But see W. Bend Mut. Ins. Co. v. U.S. Fid. & Guar. Co.*, 598 F.3d 918, 922–23 (7th Cir. 2010) (applying Indiana law) (finding the pollution exclusion precluded coverage for claims arising from leaks in gasoline storage tanks and noting that the pollution exclusion, as drafted, specifically eradicate the ambiguities on which *Kiger* rested).

**Iowa:** The Supreme Court of Iowa held that the pollution exclusion barred coverage for a claim involving the death of a worker at a hog confinement facility due to carbon monoxide that was released from a propane power washer in a restroom. *Bituminous Cas. Corp. v. Sand Livestock Systems, Inc.*, 728 N.W.2d 216, 222 (Iowa 2007). "We agree with Bituminous that carbon monoxide falls within the extremely broad language of the policies' definition of 'pollutants.' It is difficult to say the exclusions are 'fairly susceptible to two interpretations,' which is required for us to find the exclusions ambiguous." *Id.* at 221. "The plain language in the exclusions encompasses the injury at issue here because carbon monoxide is a gaseous irritant or contaminant, which was released from the propane power washer." *Id.* at 222.

**Kansas:** The Tenth Circuit Court of Appeals certified the following question to the Supreme Court of Kansas: "If the definition of a 'pollutant' in the exclusion clause is ambiguous [first Certified Question], and must, therefore, be construed in a light most favorable to the insured, is a mist of anhydrous ammonia fertilizer released from a plow during farm fertilizing operations nonetheless a 'pollutant' under the exclusion clause, such that the liability claim for injuries caused by exposure to that mist is not covered?" *Union Ins. Co. v. Mendoza*, No. 09–3159, 2010 WL 1260130, at *1 (10th Cir. Mar. 29, 2010) (noting that, while the interpretation of the pollution exclusion has been considered by two Kansas Court of Appeals decisions, they differ from earlier interpretations of Kansas law by two federal district courts).

**Kentucky:** The Court of Appeals of Kentucky held that the pollution exclusion did not apply to claims for bodily injury arising out of a carbon monoxide leak from a boiler used by a dry cleaner. *Motorists Mut. Ins. Co. v.*

*RSJ, Inc.*, 926 S.W.2d 679, 681–82 (Ky. Ct. App. 1996) (examining drafting history of the exclusion and continued use of environmental law terminology). "[W]e are convinced that an ordinary business person would not apprehend the provision as excluding coverage for the type of damage incurred through an unexpected leak in a vent pipe." *Id.* at 682. *But see Sunny Ridge Enters., Inc. v. Fireman's Fund Ins. Co.*, 132 F. Supp. 2d 525, 527 (E.D. Ky. 2001) (holding that pollution exclusion precluded coverage for damage caused by nuclear material that was released by a monitoring gauge that was destroyed during the melting of scrap metal); *Grizzly Processing LLC v. Wausau Underwriters Ins. Co.*, No. 7:08–226, 2010 WL 934250, at *5 (E.D. Ky. Mar. 11, 2010) (holding that coal dust is a pollutant and no coverage for claims alleging bodily injury caused by contamination of homes in the vicinity of a coal mine).

**Louisiana:** The Supreme Court of Louisiana held that the pollution exclusion did not preclude coverage for claims for hydrocarbons in a parish water system. *Doerr v. Mobil Oil Corp.*, 774 So. 2d 119, 136 (La. 2000). "[W]e find that the proper interpretation of the pollution exclusion in this case is that the exclusion was designed to exclude coverage for environmental pollution only and not for all interactions with irritants or contaminants of any kind." *Id.* "The applicability of a total pollution exclusion in any given case must necessarily turn on several considerations: (1) Whether the insured is a 'polluter' within the meaning of the exclusion; (2) Whether the injury-causing substance is a 'pollutant' within the meaning of the exclusion; and (3) Whether there was a 'discharge, dispersal, seepage, migration, release or escape' of a pollutant by the insured within the meaning of the policy." *Id.* at 135. The *Doerr* Court set out numerous factors to be examined for purposes of determining if these criteria have been met. *Id.* at 135–36; *see also State Farm Fire & Cas. Co. v. M.L.T. Constr. Co., Inc.*, 849 So. 2d 762, 771 (La. Ct. App. 2003) (finding that workplace exposure to mold and mildew from ongoing roof work not subject to pollution exclusion); *Finger v. Audubon Ins. Co.*, No. 09–8071, 2010 WL 1222273 (La. Civ. Dist. Ct., Orleans Parish, Mar. 23, 2010) (order granting motions) (finding pollution exclusion inapplicable in Chinese drywall litigation because, based on *Doerr* and a 1997 advisory letter from the Louisiana Department of Insurance, the exclusion was never intended to apply to residential homeowner's claims for damage caused by substandard building materials).

**Maine:** The First Circuit Court of Appeals, applying Maine law, held that the pollution exclusion did not preclude coverage for claims arising out of exposure to fumes from roofing products at a job site. *Nautilus, Inc. v. Jabar*, 188 F.3d 27, 31 (1st Cir. 1999). "[T]he total pollution exclusion clause is ambiguous as applied to the… claims because an ordinarily intelligent insured could reasonably interpret the pollution exclusion clause as applying only to environmental pollution." *Id.* at 30; *see also Boise Cascade Corp. v. Reliance Nat'l Indem. Co.*, 99 F. Supp. 2d 87, 102 (D. Me. 2000) (following *Jabar* and holding that the pollution exclusion did not preclude coverage for claims for bodily injury caused by exposure to chlorine gas).

**Maryland:** The Court of Appeals of Maryland held that the pollution exclusion did not preclude coverage for claims for bodily injuries caused by exposure to manganese welding fumes. *Clendenin Bros., Inc., v. U.S. Fire Ins. Co.*, 889 A.2d 387, 395 (Md. 2006). "Without some limiting principle, the pollution exclusion clause would extend far beyond its intended scope, and lead to some absurd results." *Id.* at 396; *see also Sullins v. Allstate Ins. Co.*, 667 A.2d 617, 624 (Md. 1995) (holding that the pollution exclusion was ambiguous and did not apply in the context of lead paint). "We conclude that an insured could reasonably have understood the provision at issue to exclude coverage for injury caused by certain forms of industrial pollution, but not coverage for injury allegedly caused by the presence of leaded materials in a private residence. There simply is no language in the exclusion provision from which to infer that the provision was drafted with a view toward limiting liability for lead paint-related injury." *Id.* at 620. *But see Bernhardt v. Hartford Fire Ins. Co.*, 648 A.2d 1047, 1052 (Md. Ct. Spec. App. 1994) (finding no coverage for carbon monoxide claim brought by tenants against landlord for faulty ventilation system that caused chimney flue buildup to block free air passage).

**Massachusetts:** The Supreme Judicial Court of Massachusetts held that the pollution exclusion did not preclude coverage for a claim by a restaurant patron for carbon monoxide poisoning arising out of a tandoori oven located in the restaurant's poorly ventilated kitchen. *W. Alliance Ins. Co. v. Gill*, 686 N.E.2d 997, 1000 (Mass. 1997). The pollution exclusion "should not reflexively be applied to accidents arising during the course of normal business activities simply because they involve a 'discharge, dispersal, release or escape' of an 'irritant or contaminant.'" *Id.* at 999. "A reasonable policyholder might well understand carbon monoxide is a pollutant when it is emitted in an industrial or environmental setting, but would not reasonably characterize carbon monoxide emitted from a malfunctioning or improperly operated restaurant oven as pollution." *Id.* at 1000 (citation and quotation omitted). The *Gill* Court rested its decision, in part, on *Atlantic Mutual Insurance Co. v. McFadden*, 595 N.E.2d 762, 764 (Mass. 1992), which held that the pollution exclusion did not apply to claims for exposure to lead paint in a residential setting. *But see McGregor v. Allamerica Ins. Co.*, 868 N.E.2d 1225, 1228 (Mass. 2007) (finding pollution exclusion precluded coverage for home heating oil spill) (distinguishing *Gill* and *McFadden* because they "rested primarily on the observation that the harm at issue was not caused by the kind of release that an ordinary insured would understand as pollution. By contrast, spilled oil is a classic example of pollution, and a reasonable insured would understand oil leaking into the ground to be a pollutant.") ("The location of an oil spill at a residence, rather than an industrial or manufacturing site, does not automatically alter the classification of spilled oil as a pollutant.").

**Michigan:** The Court of Appeals of Michigan held that there was a genuine issue of material fact whether the pollution exclusion precluded coverage for claims for injuries caused by exposure to a sanitizing agent used by an air-duct cleaning service. *Hastings Mut. Ins. Co. v. Safety King, Inc.*, 778 N.W.2d 275, 282 (Mich. Ct. App. 2009). "[The insurer] did not prove that triclosan is an irritant or contaminant. Rather, the evidence set forth by [the insured] showed that triclosan was supposed to be where it was located, i.e., in duct-work, and that it is *not* generally expected to cause injurious or harmful effects to people." *Id.* at 280. *But see McKusick v. Travelers Indem. Co.*, 632 N.W.2d 525, 531 (Mich. Ct. App. 2001) (concluding that the pollution exclusion precluded coverage for injuries caused by release of chemicals from a high-pressure hose delivery system) ("There are no exceptions to the exclusion and no limitations regarding its scope, including the location or other character-istics of the discharge. Although we recognize that other jurisdictions have considered the terms 'discharge,' 'dispersal,' 'release,' and 'escape' to be envi-ronmental terms of art, thus requiring the pollutant to cause traditional envi-ronmental pollution before the exclusion is applicable, we cannot judicially engraft such limitation."); *McGuirk Sand & Gravel, Inc. v. Meridian Mut. Ins. Co.*, 559 N.W.2d 93, 98 (Mich. Ct. App. 1996) (concluding that the pollution exclusion precluded coverage for claims for damage caused by noncombus-tible water contaminated with petroleum, even though it was determined to be safe enough for disposal in city's wastewater system).

**Minnesota:** The Court of Appeals of Minnesota held that the pollution exclusion precluded coverage for claims brought by homeowners against neighboring hog farm for emitting manure odors. *Wakefield Pork, Inc. v. RAM Mut. Ins. Co.*, 731 N.W.2d 154, 160 (Minn. Ct. App. 2007). The court concluded that the plain language of the exclusion precluded coverage for harm from the gases, hydrogen sulfide, and noxious and offensive odors that emanated from the insured's pig farm. *Id.* The court distinguished the Supreme Court of Minnesota's decision in *Board of Regents v. Royal Insurance Co.*, 517 N.W.2d 888 (Minn. 1994), which held that the pollution exclusion did not preclude coverage for the release of asbestos that originated from inside a building and "did not address a situation where contaminants were released 'into the atmosphere' from neighboring land and then contaminated or polluted air inside a building." *Id.* at 161; *see also Cont'l Cas. Co v. Advance Terrazzo & Tile Co., Ins.*, 462 F.3d 1002, 1009 (8th Cir. 2006) (applying Minnesota law and finding pollution exclusion precluded coverage for claims arising out of exposure to carbon monoxide); *Auto-Owners Inc. Co. v. Hanson*, 588 N.W.2d 777, 779–81 (Minn. Ct. App. 1999) (concluding that lead paint was a "pollutant" within the terms of the pollution exclusion and chipping and flaking of paint was a "discharge, dispersal or release"); *League of Minn. Cities Ins. Trust v. City of Coon Rapids*, 446 N.W.2d 419, 422 (Minn. Ct. App.

1989) (finding that the pollution exclusion precluded coverage for claims by ice rink patrons exposed to nitrogen dioxide, a toxic by-product of a Zamboni ice-cleaning machine, that had built up in an arena).

**Mississippi:** The Fifth Circuit Court of Appeals held that the pollution exclusion precluded coverage for claims for injuries arising out of a hyper-sensitive plaintiff's exposure to paint and glue fumes released during the painting of a residence. *Am. States Ins. Co. v. Nethery*, 79 F.3d 473, 478 (5th Cir. 1996) (applying Mississippi law). "An irritant is a substance that produces a *particular* effect, not one that generally or probably causes such effects. The paint and glue fumes that irritated Nethery satisfy both the dictionary definition and the policy exclusion of irritants." *Id.* at 476 (emphasis in original); *see also Am. States Ins. Co., v. F.H.S., Inc.*, 843 F. Supp. 187, 189 (S.D. Miss. 1994) (concluding that the pollution exclusion precluded coverage for injuries caused by an ammonia leak from a pressure relief valve of a refrigeration system); *Eott Energy Pipeline, L.P. v. Hattiesburg Speedway, Inc.*, 303 F. Supp. 2d 819, 825 (S.D. Miss. 2004) (concluding that the pollution exclusion precluded coverage for costs of cleaning up oil spill, complying with regulatory authorities and oil lost in spill, but that the exclusion did not preclude coverage for the repair of a pipeline or lost profits because they were not caused by the release of a pollutant, but, rather, a motor grader blade striking a pipeline).

**Missouri:** The Missouri Court of Appeals held that the pollution exclusion did not preclude coverage for property damage claims arising from the release of 2,000 gallons of gasoline from a storage tank at a service station. *Hocker Oil Co., Inc. v Barker-Phillips-Jackson, Inc.*, 997 S.W.2d 510 (Mo. Ct. App. 1999). "Hocker is in the business of transporting, selling and storing gasoline on a daily basis. Gasoline is not a pollutant in its eyes. Gasoline is the product it sells. Gasoline belongs in the environment in which Hocker routinely works.... . [I]n that environment, gasoline is not a pollutant. Hocker was entitled to characterize gasoline in a manner consistent with its daily activities absent specific policy language to the contrary. [The insurer's] failure to identify 'gasoline' as a pollutant in its pollution exclusion resulted in uncertainty and indistinctness. The policy was, therefore, ambiguous as to whether gasoline was a pollutant for purposes of the exclusion." *Id.* at 518 (citing to *Kiger's* observation [*see* Indiana] that it would be an oddity for an insurance company to sell a liability policy to a gas station that would specifically exclude that insured's major source of liability); *see also Heringer v. Am. Family Mut. Ins. Co.*, 140 S.W.3d 100, 104–06 (Mo. Ct. App. 2004) (pollution exclusion precluded coverage for claim for exposure to lead paint) (distinguishing *Hocker* because lead was specifically and unambiguously defined in the policy as a pollutant) (rejecting insured's argument that the pollution exclusion is only applicable to traditional environmental pollution); *Hartford Accident & Indem. Co. v. Doe Run Resources Corp.*, No. 4:08-CV-1687, 2010 WL 1687623, at *6 (E.D. Mo. Apr. 26, 2010) (concluding that it could not state, as a matter of law, that lead was a pollutant within the meaning of the pollution exclusion, as insured's lead claims went beyond smelter emissions); *American Western Home Ins. Co. v. Utopia Acquisition L.P.*, No. 08-0419, 2009 WL 792483, at *2 (W.D. Mo. Mar. 24, 2009) (pollution exclusion applied to "airborne contaminants and/or irritants") ("[*Hocker Oil*] rested on the unique facts of that particular case; particularly, the oddity of having a policy issued to a gas station exclude coverage for spilled gasoline on the basis that gasoline was a pollutant. Under Missouri law, the term 'pollutant' is not limited to traditional environmental pollutants or situations, and the pollution exclusion is not limited to so-called 'environmental pollution.'").

**Montana:** The Supreme Court of Montana held that the pollution exclusion precluded coverage for diesel fuel that leaked from an underground tank at a gas station. *Mont. Petroleum Tank Release Compensation Bd. v. Crumleys, Inc.*, 174 P.3d 948, 959 (Mont. 2008). "[W]e conclude that most consumers would consider diesel a pollutant when it leaks into the ground and contaminates soil and groundwater. As the Supreme Court recognized, even a valuable and useful product can become a pollutant when it contaminates a natural resource." *Id.* (referring to *U.S. v. Standard Oil Co.*, 384 U.S. 224 (1966)). That diesel is a pollutant "is evidenced by both the clear language of the policy, and by the obvious hazards diesel fuel poses to community health and safety once it has leaked into the soil." *Id.*

**Nebraska:** The Supreme Court of Nebraska held that the pollution exclusion precluded coverage for claims for contamination of food stored in a warehouse due to fumes from a floor sealant. *Cincinnati Ins. Co. v. Becker Warehouse, Inc.*, 635 N.W.2d 112, 120 (Neb. 2001). "We conclude that as a matter of law, [the insurer's] pollution exclusion, though quite broad, is unambiguous. The language of the policy does not specifically limit excluded claims to traditional environmental damage; nor does the pollution exclusion purport to limit materials that qualify as pollutants to those that cause traditional environmental damage." *Id.; see also Harleysville Ins. Group v. Omaha Gas Appliance Co.*, 772 N.W.2d 88, 95–96 (Neb. 2009) (involving claims for carbon monoxide poisoning, due to faulty repair of a gas boiler, which the parties agreed were precluded from coverage by the pollution exclusion) (rejecting argument that an umbrella policy's pollution exclusion only precluded coverage for strict liability pollution claims, but not pollution-related injuries caused by negligence); *Ferrell v. State Farm Ins. Co.*, No. A-01–637, 2003 WL 21058165, at *5 (Neb. Ct. App. May 13, 2003) (following *Becker Warehouse* and holding that coverage for injuries caused by exposure to mercury in an apartment was precluded by the pollution exclusion).

**Nevada:** A Nevada District Court held that the pollution exclusion did not preclude coverage for claims arising out of carbon monoxide poisoning of guests in a policyholder's motel. *Century Sur. Co. v. Casino W., Inc.*, No. 3:07-CV-00636, 2010 WL 762188, at *4 (D. Nev. Mar. 4, 2010). "While a reasonable person of ordinary intelligence might understand carbon monoxide is a pollutant when emitted in some settings, an ordinary policyholder may not reasonably characterize carbon monoxide emitted from a motel pool heater as pollution. Additionally, a reasonable policyholder might not view the exception regarding fumes from the building's heater as an indication that all other possible types of indoor fumes would be excluded as 'pollutants.' Because the pollution exclusion in this case is subject to more than one reasonable interpretation, the Court finds that the exclusion creates an ambiguity." *Id.*; *see also Connolly Dev. Inc. v. Northbrook Prop. & Cas. Ins. Co.*, No. CV-N-91-363, 1992 WL 12073422, at *3 (D. Nev. July 31, 1992) ("Clearly dust is considered to be a form of air pollution under both the County and State Regulations. Dust is a solid irritant or contaminant under the ordinary meaning of the language contained in [the pollution exclusion].").

**New Hampshire:** The Supreme Court of New Hampshire held that the pollution exclusion did not preclude coverage for claims for injury to a child for lead poisoning on account of exposure to paint carried on his father's clothing from his workplace. *Weaver v. Royal Ins. Co.*, 674 A.2d 975, 978 (N.H. 1996). "Because there are two reasonable interpretations of the policy language, we conclude that the pollution exclusion is ambiguous." *Id.* at 978; *see also Titan Holdings Syndicate v. City of Keene*, 898 F.2d 265, 268 (1st Cir. 1990) (applying New Hampshire law) ("Excessive noise and light may be 'irritants,' but they are not *solid, liquid, gaseous or thermal* irritants. Nor are they generally thought of as similar to smoke, vapor, soot, fumes, acids, alkalis, chemicals or waste, the illustrative terms used in the policy definition."); *EnergyNorth Nat. Gas, Inc. v. Am. Home Assurance Co.*, No. Civ. 99–502-JD, 2003 WL 21663646, at *10 (D.N.H. July 16, 2003) (concluding that *Weaver* was not controlling because the pollution at issue (manufactured gas plant waste) was clearly environmental).

**New Jersey:** The Supreme Court of New Jersey held that the pollution exclusion should be read to apply "to injury or property damage arising from activity commonly thought of as traditional environmental pollution," or more specifically pollution resulting from "environmental catastrophe related to intentional industrial pollution." *Nav-Its, Inc. v. Selective Ins. Co. of Am.*, 869 A.2d 929, 937 (N.J. 2005) (addressing the exclusion in the context of exposure to toxic fumes in a floor coating/sealant operation). "[W]e are confident that the history of the pollution-exclusion clause in its various forms demonstrates that its purpose was to have a broad exclusion for traditional environmentally related damages." *Id.* at 936–37; *see also Baughman v. U.S. Liab. Ins. Co.*, 662 F. Supp. 2d 386, 399 (D.N.J. 2009) (holding that exposure to mercury, at a former thermometer manufacturing facility, because it was indoors, was not traditional environmental pollution and therefore not excluded by the pollution exclusion); *Merchants Ins. Co. of N.H., Inc. v. Hessler*, No. COV/03–5857, 2005 WL 2009902, at *2–3 (D.N.J. Aug. 18, 2005) (holding that the pollution exclusion did not apply to bodily injury and property damage resulting from exposure to lead paint).

**New Mexico:** No instructive authority.

**New York:** The Court of Appeals of New York held that the pollution exclusion did not preclude coverage for a bodily injury claim arising out of paint or solvent fumes discharged during painting and stripping work performed by the insured. *Belt Painting Corp. v. TIG Ins. Co.*, 795 N.E.2d 15, 21 (N.Y. 2003). "Were we to adopt [the insurer's] interpretation, under the language of this exclusion any 'chemical,' or indeed, any 'material to be recycled,' that could 'irritate' person or property would be a 'pollutant.' We are reluctant to adopt an interpretation that would infinitely enlarge the scope of the term 'pollutants,' and seemingly contradict both a 'common speech' understanding of the relevant terms and the reasonable expectations of a businessperson." *Id.* at 20. "Even if the paint or solvent fumes are within the definition of 'pollutant,' the exclusion applies only if the underlying injury is caused by 'discharge, dispersal, seepage, migration, release or escape' of the fumes. It cannot be said that this language unambiguously applies to ordinary paint or solvent fumes that drifted a short distance from the area of the insured's intended use and allegedly caused inhalation injuries to a bystander." *Id.*

**North Carolina:** The Court of Appeals of North Carolina held that the pollution exclusion did not preclude coverage for claims for damage to chicken that was contaminated by the insured's resurfacing of the floors in a chicken processing facility. *W. Am. Ins. Co. v. Tufco Flooring East, Inc.*, 409 S.E.2d 692, 699 (N.C. Ct. App. 1991) (overruled on other grounds in *Gaston County Dyeing Mach. Co. v. Northfield Ins. Co.*, 524 S.E.2d 558 (N.C. 2000)). "In light of the language of the [insurer's] policy and [insured's] reasonable belief that damages accidentally arising from its normal business activities would not be excluded, we agree that the pollution exclusion clause in the [insured's] policy applies only to discharges into the environment and not to the non-environmental damage that led to [plaintiff's] claim against [insured]." *Id.* at 700; *see also Auto-Owners Ins. Co. v. Potter*, 105 Fed. App'x 484, 497 (4th Cir. 2004) (applying North Carolina law) (following *Tufco* and holding that, to the extent claims were for traditional environmental damage, the pollution exclusion precluded coverage for injury and damage arising out of a housing developer's provision of contaminated well water).

**North Dakota:** No instructive authority.

**Ohio:** The Supreme Court of Ohio held that the pollution exclusion was not applicable to a claim for bodily injury caused by exposure to carbon monoxide from a faulty heater in an apartment. *Andersen v. Highland House Co.*, 757 N.E.2d 329, 334 (Ohio 2001). "Based on the history and original purposes for the pollution exclusion, it was reasonable for [the insureds] to believe that the policies purchased for their multiunit complex would not exclude claims for injuries due to carbon monoxide leaks." *Id.* at 333; *see also Bosserman Aviation Equip., Inc. v. U.S. Liab. Ins. Co.*, 915 N.E.2d 687, 696 (Ohio Ct. App. 2009) (following *Andersen* and holding that pollution exclusion did not preclude coverage for exposure to harmful chemical agents contained in aircraft fuel while reconditioning and repairing aircraft-refueling equipment) ("[A] pollution-exclusion clause of this nature does not apply to an exposure to toxic chemicals confined within an employee's work area, as there is no discharge, dispersal, release, or escape of pollutants."); *Citizens Ins. v. Lanly Co.,* Nos. 1:07 CV 241, 1:07 CV 467, 1:07 CV 469, 2007 WL 3129783 (N.D. Ohio Oct. 23, 2007) (addressing confusion over the pollution exclusion created by *Andersen*).

**Oklahoma:** The Supreme Court of Oklahoma held that the pollution exclusion precluded coverage for claims for injuries caused by exposure to lead paint by patients in a hospital's dialysis unit. *Bituminous Cas. Corp. v. Cowen Constr., Inc.,* 55 P.3d 1030, 1035 (Okla. 2002). "Nowhere in the policy's lexicon is there language employed which would sustain finding—as suggested by the insured—the pollution exclusion clause only excluded from coverage that bodily injury and/or property damage which occurred when the general 'environment' was damaged by the insured's acts." *Id.* at 1034. However, the court noted that the pollution exclusion at issue was an endorsement that applied, in part, to "Bodily injury or property damage arising out of the actual, alleged or threatened discharge, dispersal, release or escape of pollutants." *Id.* at 1031 n.1. The Oklahoma high court stated that the policy's original pollution exclusion, couched in geographic terms, could be read to support a finding that an "environmental" limitation exists as to its scope. *Id.* at 1034.

**Oregon:** The Court of Appeals of Oregon held that the pollution exclusion precluded coverage—but in the context of claims for property damage that was clearly caused by traditional environmental pollution. *Martin v. State Farm Fire & Cas. Co.,* 932 P.2d 1207, 1212 (Or. Ct. App. 1997) (involving petroleum contamination from underground petroleum tanks); *see also Larsen Oil Co. v. Federated Serv. Ins. Co.,* 859 F. Supp. 434, 438 (D. Or. 1994) (holding that the pollution exclusion unambiguously applied to claims for damage caused by the discharge of heating oil into a home, notwithstanding that the insured did not cause the discharge), *aff'd* 70 F.3d 1279 (9th Cir. 1995) ("The pollution exclusion contains no condition or qualification; it simply does not require that the insured discharge the pollutant.").

**Pennsylvania:** The Supreme Court of Pennsylvania held that the pollution exclusion precluded coverage for a bodily injury claim arising out of fumes emitted from a concrete sealer. *Madison Constr. Co. v. Harleysville Mut. Ins. Co.,* 735 A.2d 100, 110 (Pa. 1999). The court concluded that the definition of "pollutant" clearly and unambiguously encompassed the cement sealing agent and rejected the argument that the policy's definition of "pollutant" is so broad that virtually any substance, including many useful and necessary products, could be said to come within its scope. *Id.* at 606–07. "[G]uided by the principle that ambiguity (or the lack thereof) is to be determined by reference to a particular set of facts, we focus on the specific product at issue." *Id.* at 607;

*see also Wagner v. Erie Ins. Co.*, 801 A.2d 1226, 1232–33 (Pa. Super. Ct. 2002), *affirmed* 847 A.2d 1274 (Pa. 2004) (holding that the pollution exclusion precluded coverage for a claim for damages caused by gasoline that leaked into soil from an underground line at a gas station); *Jaskula v. Essex Ins. Co.*, 900 A.2d 931, 934 (Pa. Super. Ct. 2006) (finding that the pollution exclusion precluded coverage for response costs when an insured cut an oil line in the course of waterproofing a basement); *Matcon Diamond, Inc. v. Penn Nat'l Ins. Co.*, 815 A.2d 1109, 1114 (Pa. Super. Ct. 2003) (pollution exclusion precluded coverage for claims arising out of the release of carbon monoxide). *But see Lititz Mut. Ins. Co. v. Steeley*, 785 A.2d 975, 981–82 (Pa. 2001) (holding that lead paint is a "pollutant," but exclusion not applicable because the process by which it degrades and became available for ingestion and inhalation does not involve a "discharge," "dispersal," "release," or "escape"); *Whitmore v. Liberty Mut. Fire Ins. Co.*, No. 07–5162, 2008 WL 4425227, at *6 (E.D. Pa. Sept. 30, 2008) (finding that the pollution exclusion, under first-party policy, did not preclude coverage for claim for property damage caused by heating oil that spilled during delivery to an above-ground storage tank because it remained in the basement and did not contaminate the environment); *Westchester Fire Ins. Co. v. Treesdale, Inc.*, No. 2:05cv1523, 2008 WL 1943471, at *15 (W.D. Pa. May 2, 2008) (following *Lititz*) ("[T]he state of the law on the question of whether asbestos is a pollutant is unresolved. However, the Court need not resolve that difficult issue in this case because, as Defendants note, both policies require that the pollutant be dispersed in one of several defined ways to fall within the exclusion. Plaintiffs have not argued, much less demonstrated, that the manner in which the asbestos 'moved' in the Underlying Claims meets any of these defined ways.").

**Rhode Island:** No instructive authority. *But see Picerne-Military Housing, LLC v. Am. Int'l Specialty Lines Ins. Co.*, 650 F. Supp. 2d 135, 139–40 (D.R.I. 2009) (addressing whether buried construction and demolition debris was a "Pollution Condition" under a Pollution Legal Liability policy and noting that it was a twist on an oft-litigated issue: "[I]n the usual course the question of what constitutes a pollutant arises out of a general liability insurer's attempt to enforce a pollution exclusion. In that context, the insurer urges a broad reading of the exclusion while the insured presses for a narrow interpretation to afford greater coverage. Here, things are backwards. [The insurer's] pollution liability policy insures (in language mirroring the standard definition used by virtually all carriers in this context) that which most commercial general liability policies seek to exclude."). Despite being "backwards," the court's analysis—which cites to pollution exclusion decisions nationally for guidance—may be useful in the pollution exclusion context.

**South Carolina:** A South Carolina District Court held that the pollution exclusion did not apply to preclude coverage for claims for bodily injury caused by exposure to paint fumes, vapor, dust, and other residue from the insured's painting operations. *NGM Ins. Co. v. Carolina's Power Wash & Painting, LLC*,

No. 2:08-CV-3378, 2010 WL 146482, at *6 (D.S.C. Jan. 12, 2010) (noting that the scope and applicability of the absolute pollution exclusion had never been addressed by a South Carolina court). The court discussed the nationwide split of authority and concluded that, because the pollution exclusion is subject to more than one reasonable interpretation, it creates an ambiguity, and, therefore, must be construed liberally in favor of the insured and strictly against the insurer. *Id.*

**South Dakota:** The Supreme Court of South Dakota held that the pollution exclusion applied to preclude coverage for claims arising out of excessive dust emissions from a cement plant. *S.D. State Cement Plant Comm'n v. Wausau Underwriters Ins. Co.*, 616 N.W.2d 397, 406 (S.D. 2000). "Because the causes of action in the complaint are based upon alleged 'contamination,' assuming that the allegations that [the insured] caused contamination are true, no coverage would apply and [the insurer] would not have a duty to defend because the causes of action in the complaint all clearly fall within the definition of pollution in the pollution exclusion clause." *Id.* at 407. The court rejected the trial court's determination that a broad construction of the pollution exclusion would render it meaningless on the basis that any substance could conceivably irritate or contaminate. *Id.* at 406.

**Tennessee:** The Court of Appeals of Tennessee held that the pollution exclusion precluded coverage for a claim for injury caused when a tanker truck spewed 1,800 gallons of sulphuric acid on an employee of a loading company's subcontractor. *Sulphuric Acid Trading Co., Inc. v. Greenwich Ins. Co.*, 211 S.W.3d 243, 254 (Tenn. Ct. App. 2006). After addressing the split of authority nationally on the "traditional" versus "non-traditional" issue, the court concluded that "the facts of this case are such that we do not need to decide with which side Tennessee should be aligned…. It would defy logic to hold that the discharge of 1,800 gallons of sulphuric acid into the environment was anything other than environmental pollution. We hold that these facts demonstrate the type of 'classic environmental pollution' that would trigger the Absolute Pollution Exclusion under *either* of the two lines of reasoning adopted by the various states. While the facts before us do involve an employee injured in the course and scope of his employment, we must look at the big picture and cannot ignore the fact that the injury occurred during an event resulting in substantial environmental pollution. As applied to the facts of the instant case, we agree with the trial court that the Absolute Pollution Exclusion is not ambiguous. As to which of the two diverse lines of cases should be adopted in Tennessee, that decision must await another day and another case." *Id.* at 253–54; *see also State Auto. Mut. Ins. Co. v. Frazier's Flooring, Inc.*, No. 3:08-CV-178, 2009 WL 693142, at *6 (E.D. Tenn. March 13, 2009) (declining to exercise jurisdiction in a declaratory judgment action because the pollution exclusion is an unsettled question under Tennessee law) (discussing *Sulphuric Acid Trading* and federal decisions) ("Though there are two federal courts that have considered the interpretation of pollution exclusion clauses under Tennessee law, they are of little help to the Court here. Both cases, after stating that the issue is unsettled in Tennessee, apply the standard rules of contract interpretation under Tennessee law but, nevertheless, they reach opposite conclusions.").

**Texas:** The Supreme Court of Texas held that the pollution exclusion precluded coverage for claims arising out of a large cloud of hydrofluoric acid caused by an accident at an oil refinery. *Nat'l Union Fire Ins. Co. v. CBI Indus.*, 907 S.W.2d 517, 521–22 (Tex. 1995). The court held that, because "the contract language is not fairly susceptible of more than one legal meaning or construction, however, extrinsic evidence is inadmissible to contradict or vary the meaning of the explicit language of the parties' written agreement. In this case, the policies unequivocally deny coverage for damage resulting from pollutants, however the damage is caused." *Id.* (citations omitted); *see also Nautilus Ins. Co. v. Country Oaks Apartments Ltd.*, 566 F.3d 452, 458 (5th Cir. 2009) (applying Texas law) (concluding that the pollution exclusion precluded coverage for claims for emission of carbon monoxide from a furnace into an apartment). *But see Clarendon America Ins. Co. v. Bay, Inc.*, 10 F. Supp. 2d 736, 744 (S.D. Tex. 1998) (concluding that bodily injury caused when plaintiffs' skin touched wet cement and concrete, while the cement and its ingredients were in the cement's intended container or location, did not satisfy the "discharge, dispersal, seepage, migration, release or escape" requirement of the pollution exclusion).

**Utah:** A Utah District Court held that the pollution exclusion did not preclude coverage for injuries caused by the release of a hydrocarbon vapor cloud that led to an explosion and fire during the unloading of waste. *United Nat'l Ins. Co. v. Int'l Petroleum & Exploration*, No. 2:04-CV-00631, 2007 WL 4561460, at *11 (D. Utah Dec. 20, 2007). The court examined the "traditional" versus "non-traditional" debate and concluded that, because of two possible interpretations, the exclusion is ambiguous. *Id.* "Under [the insurer's] literal construction of the pollution exclusion, the exclusion would apply to potentially limitless circumstances and would, accordingly, severely limit [the insured's] coverage under the Policy." *Id.*

**Vermont:** No instructive authority. *But see Maska U.S., Inc. v. Kansa Gen. Ins. Co.*, 198 F.3d 74 (2nd Cir. 1999) (applying Vermont law) (addressing evidence that since 1970, when liability insurers began including pollution exclusions in their policies, the Vermont Department of Banking Insurance disapproved such policies based on its determination that the exclusions were unfair and discriminatory and inconsistent with the public's expectation of coverage under a general liability policy). *See also Vt. Mut. Ins. Co. v. Parson's Hill Partnership*, 1 A.3d 1016 (Vt. 2010) (finding that it did not need to reach the issue whether water adulterated with perchloroethylene, in an apartment complex's water system, was a pollutant within a pollution endorsement providing coverage under a landlord's general liability policy).

**Virginia:** The Supreme Court of Virginia held that the pollution exclusion precluded coverage for claims by 214 women for miscarriages arising out of contamination by trihalomethanes of a city's water supply. *City of Chesapeake v. States Self-Insurers Risk Retention Group, Inc.*, 628 S.E.2d 539, 541 (Va. 2006). The court declined the parties' request to examine how other jurisdictions have resolved similar disputes because the plain language of the policy provided the answer. *Id.* at 541–42; *see also Firemen's Ins. Co. of Wash., D.C. v. Kline & Son Cement Repair, Inc.*, 474 F. Supp. 2d 779, 798–99 (E.D. Va. 2007) (holding, following a comprehensive review of the issue, that the pollution exclusion precluded coverage for personal injury claim arising from inhalation of vapors following the insured's application of epoxy sealant to a concrete warehouse floor); *TRAVCO Ins. Co. v. Ward*, __ F. Supp. 2d. __, No 2:10cv14, 2010 WL 2222255, at *16 (E.D. Va. 2010) (following *City of Chesapeake* and *Kline* and holding that the pollution exclusion precluded coverage, under a homeowner's policy, for damage to the insured's residence caused by toxic gases released by Chinese drywall). *But see Nationwide Mut. Ins. Co. v. Boyd Corp.*, No. 3:09-CV-211, 2010 WL 331757, at *3 (E.D. Va. Jan. 25, 2010) ("[A] reasonable person would not classify flood waters alone as pollutants.").

**Washington:** The Supreme Court of Washington held that the pollution exclusion precluded coverage for claims for injuries suffered by a tenant when fumes from a waterproofing material being applied to her apartment building entered her unit. *Quadrant Corp. v. Am. States Ins. Co.*, 110 P.3d 733, 743 (Wash. 2005). The *Quadrant* Court distinguished *Kent Farms, Inc. v. Zurich Insurance Co.*, 998 P.2d 292 (Wash. 2000) on the basis that the "*Kent Farms* court distinguished between cases in which the substance at issue was polluting at the time of the injury and cases in which the offending substance's toxic character was not central to the injury." *Id.* at 742. The *Kent Farms* Court had held that the underlying plaintiff "was not polluted by diesel fuel. It struck him; it engulfed him; it choked him. It did not pollute him. Most importantly, the fuel was not acting as a 'pollutant' when it struck him any more than it would have been acting as a 'pollutant' if it had been in a barrel that rolled over him, or if it had been lying quietly on the steps waiting to trip him." *Kent Farms*, 998 P.2d at 295. The *Quadrant* court concluded that *Kent Farms*'s discussion of traditional environmental harms was limited by the facts of that case. *Quadrant*, 110 P.3d at 743; *see also Oregon Mut. Ins. Co. v. Seattle Collision Center, Inc.*, No. C08-1670JLR, 2009 WL 3067036 (W.D. Wash. Sept. 18, 2009) (addressing *Quadrant* and *Kent Farm's*).

**West Virginia:** A West Virginia District Court held that the pollution exclusion precluded coverage for claims for property damage caused by coal tar left by a coal fuel generation plant. *Supertane Gas Corp. v. Aetna Cas & Sur. Co.*, No. 92CV14, 1994 WL 1715345, at *5 (N.D. W.Va. 1994). "Although the Court did not find a West Virginia case on the absolute pollution exclusion, the Court is persuaded that West Virginia would find such an exclusion, as presented here, to be unambiguous." *Id.* at *3.

316 Chapter 14 *"Absolute" Pollution Exclusion*

**Wisconsin:** The Supreme Court of Wisconsin held that the pollution exclusion did not preclude coverage for claims arising out of inadequately ventilated carbon dioxide from breathing. *Donaldson v. Urban Land Interests, Inc.*, 564 N.W.2d 728, 732 (Wis. 1997). The court held that "the pollution exclusion clause does not plainly and clearly alert a reasonable insured that coverage is denied for personal injury claims that have their genesis in activities as fundamental as human respiration." *Id. But see Peace v. Nw. Nat'l Ins. Co.*, 596 N.W.2d 429, 440 (Wis. 1999) ("[W]e conclude that the pollution exclusion clause... excludes bodily injury from the ingestion of lead in paint that chips, flakes, or breaks down into dust or fumes. When the 'pollutant' lead—once contained—begins to disperse, discharge, or escape from the containment of the painted surface, it falls within the plain language of the pollution exclusion clause."); *Lagone v. Am. Family Mut. Ins. Co.*, 731 N.W.2d 334, 339 (Wis. Ct. App. 2007) ("Because the *Peace* and *Donaldson* courts applied a reasonable expectations test to the same policy language but reached different conclusions, it is important to consider the facts in each case.") (holding carbon monoxide more analogous to *Donaldson* and not a pollutant).

**Wyoming:** The Supreme Court of Wyoming aligned itself with those jurisdictions that have held that the pollution exclusion is limited to the concept of environmental pollution. *Gainsco Ins. Co. v. Amoco Prod. Co.*, 53 P.3d 1051, 1066 (Wyo. 2002) (holding that the pollution exclusion did not preclude coverage for bodily injury caused by exposure to poisonous hydrogen sulfide gas while emptying a vacuum truck in an oil field). Responding to the conflict in authority, the court considered the original purpose of the pollution exclusion—response to federal and state legislation mandating responsibility for the cleanup costs of environmental pollution—and concluded that the current version of the exclusion has the same purpose. *Id.* at 1066.

# 15

# Trigger of Coverage for Latent Injury and Damage Claims

The insuring agreement of Part A of the commercial general liability policy affords coverage for "bodily injury" and "property damage" (*see, e.g.,* INS. SERVS. OFFICE PROPS., INC., COMMERCIAL GENERAL LIABILITY COVERAGE FORM, NO. CG 00011207, § I1a (2007)), *provided* such injury or damage occurs "during the policy period." ISO FORM, CG 00011207 at § I1b2.

In most general liability claim scenarios it is obvious whether the "bodily injury" or "property damage" was sustained by the underlying claimant *during the policy period.* For example, if a customer slips on a banana peel and suffers a broken arm while on the premises of an insured-supermarket, it is quite easy to determine if this injury, occurring on a date certain, was during the policy period. The same goes for "property damage" in most cases. Take an insured–boiler manufacturer whose product explodes and causes fire damage. There is little chance of a dispute over the date of such damage and whether it was during the policy period.

While this "timing" issue will be a non-issue in most claims, there exists a category of claims where the answer to the question whether "bodily injury" or "property damage" occurred "during the policy period" is as challenging and contentious as a wayward banana peel claim is simple.

These vexing claims are ones in which bodily injury or property damage is caused by exposure to hazardous substances—most often bodily injury on account of exposure to asbestos and property damage on account of exposure to hazardous waste or other industrial pollution. In these situations, the injuries often evolve slowly. It could be years between the time that a person is exposed to asbestos and a disease is diagnosed. Likewise, it could be a long time between a property's exposure to hazardous waste and the day that its damaged condition is discovered.

These types of claims are known by various names, such as latent injury or damage, delayed manifestation, continuous injury or damage, or long-tail (referred to collectively as latent injury or damage claims). The message that all of these labels convey is that the claim involves injury or damage that may have been taking place for years—before anyone knew it. In other words, the injury or damage was latent.

What's at issue in the latent claims context is whether each policy on the risk during this lengthy period when unknown injury or damage was taking place is obligated to provide coverage for the loss that is eventually discovered.

Coverage for latent injury and damage claims has been aggressively and abundantly litigated for the past three decades. And no wonder. Considering the massive financial exposure faced by insureds targeted in asbestos bodily injury and environmental property damage claims, their ability to potentially tap multiple years of policies to respond to these behemoth losses was critical to their fiscal well-being (not to mention for creating adequate funds to compensate the underlying claimants for their injuries). It also served as a means to obtain coverage under policies that were on the risk prior to insurers' adoption of pollution and asbestos exclusions.

For example, an insured sued in the 1990s, by thousands of claimants that were exposed to its asbestos-containing product that was placed in the stream of commerce in 1950, stood to receive coverage under forty-plus years of insurance for some of these claims. This is a far cry from the potential alternative—coverage being limited to the one policy on the risk at the time that each claimant was diagnosed with an asbestos-caused injury. Tens of millions, and sometimes hundreds of millions, of dollars were at stake.

While the bulk of the litigation concerning coverage for latent injuries and damages involved asbestos and hazardous waste, it was not always so limited. Disputes also arose over which, and how many, policies were obligated to provide coverage for latent injuries caused by exposure to pharmaceuticals, medical devices, noise that resulted in hearing loss, Agent Orange, and others.

In addition to coverage litigation over latent injuries and damages being aggressive and abundant it was also frequently multi-party. By definition, if a policyholder is pursuing coverage under policies that were on the risk for twenty, thirty, or forty years, not to mention excess policies, there is likely a need to name numerous insurers (perhaps a dozen and sometimes many more) as defendants. With so much at stake and so many parties involved, litigation over latent injury and damage claims often proceeded at a glacial pace.

As is often the case with burgeoning insurance coverage issues, courts responded to the novelty of latent injury and damage claims by identifying various schools of though that provided answers and then determined which of these options to adopt for themselves. These schools of thought become known as "trigger of coverage" theories. While the term "trigger of coverage," or just "trigger" for short, is almost universally used in the latent claims context, the term appears nowhere in a commercial general liability policy. This is a point that was not lost on many courts. *See Atchison, Topeka & Santa Fe Ry. Co. v. Stonewall Ins. Co.*, 71 P.3d 1097, 1125 (Kan. 2003) ("Insurance policies do not refer to a trigger or trigger of coverage. Those terms are labels for the event or events that under the terms of the insurance policy determines whether a policy must respond to a claim in a given set of circumstances." (citation omitted). Perhaps courts felt the need to clarify this point lest parties would be reading *and re-reading* their commercial general liability (CGL) policies in search of a term that they would never find.

In general, five trigger theories emerged. Numerous courts, including state high courts, have spilled a lot of ink describing these methods in detail before announcing which one they adopt. These various trigger methods are as follows.

1. Manifestation Trigger: "[T]he date of loss is assigned to the policy period when property damage or actual damage [or bodily injury] is discovered, becomes known to the insured or a third party, or should have reasonably been discovered." *EnergyNorth Natural Gas, Inc. v. Certain Underwriters at Lloyd's*, 848 A.2d 715, 718 (N.H. 2004) (citation and internal quotes omitted). The manifestation trigger, which, by definition, limits coverage to a single policy year, was often advocated by insurers. However, it is the clear minority view. *See Associated Aviation Underwriters v. Wood*, 98 P.3d 572, 599 (Ariz. Ct. App. 2004).

One common reason for judicial rejection of the manifestation trigger was that "[in] most cases... a manifestation rule would reduce coverage: insurers would refuse to write new insurance for the insured when it became apparent that the period of manifestations, and hence a flood of claims, was approaching. The insured would be left without coverage for victims whose diseases were not yet manifested." *Owens Illinois, Inc. v. United Ins. Co.*, 650 A.2d 974, 981 (N.J. 1994). It has also been observed that "[n]othing in the language of the policies requires that the claimed property damage be discovered or manifested during the policy period. The inquiry instead, is whether the property damage, as defined in the policies, 'occurred' within the policy period and within the meaning of the word 'occurrence.'" *Trustees of Tufts Univ. v. Commercial Union Ins. Co.*, 616 N.E.2d 68, 74 (Mass. 1993).

2. Exposure Trigger: "[T]he exposure theory provides that coverage is triggered by the mere exposure to the harmful conditions during the policy period." *Cole v. Celotex Corp.*, 599 So. 2d 1058, 1076 (La. 1992). The exposure trigger has been justified on the basis that "each inhalation of asbestos fibers [does not] result[] in bodily injury, but rather every asbestos-related injury results from inhalation of asbestos fibers. Because such inhalation can occur only upon exposure to asbestos, and because it is impossible practically to determine the point at which the fibers actually imbed themselves in the victim's lungs, to equate exposure to asbestos with 'bodily injury' caused by the inhalation of the asbestos is the 'superior interpretation of the contract provisions.'" *Commercial Union Ins. Co. v. Sepco Corp.*, 765 F.2d 1543, 1546 (11th Cir. 1985) (applying Alabama law) (quoting *Ins. Co. of N. Am v. Forty-Eight Insulations, Inc.*, 633 F.2d 1212, 1223 (6th Cir. 1980)).

The exposure theory has also been adopted on the basis that it "honors the contracting parties' intent by providing for consistency between the insured's tort liability and the insurer's coverage: 'The contracting parties would expect coverage to parallel the theory of liability.'" *Cole*, 599 So. 2d at 1077 (La. 1992) (quoting *Forty-Eight Insulations*, 633 F.2d at 1219 (6th Cir. 1980)).

3. Injury-in-Fact Trigger: "[C]overage is first triggered at that point in time at which an actual injury can be shown, retrospectively, to have been first suffered. This rationale places the injury-in-fact somewhere between the exposure, which is considered the initiating cause of the disease or bodily injury, and the manifestation of symptoms, which, logically, is only possible when an injury already exists." *Montrose Chem. Corp. v. Admiral Ins. Co.*, 913 P.2d 878, 894 (Cal. 1995). The injury-in-fact trigger is sometimes referred to as an "actual injury" trigger. Adoption of the injury-in-fact trigger is often justified on the basis that it is truest to the policy language. *See Gelman Sciences, Inc. v. Fid. & Cas. Co. of N.Y.*, 572 N.W.2d 617, 623 (Mich. 1998), *overruled on other grounds by Wilkie v. Auto-Owners Ins. Co.*, 664 N.W.2d 776, 786 (Mich. 2003) ("[A]ccording to the policies' explicit terms, actual injury must occur during the time the policy is in effect in order to be indemnifiable, i.e., the policies dictate an injury-in-fact approach"). As discussed below, injury-in-fact can often be synonymous with a continuous trigger.

4. Continuous Trigger: "[T]he injury occurs continuously from exposure until manifestation." *Gelman Sciences, Inc. v. Fid. & Cas. Co. of N.Y.*, 572 N.W.2d 617, 621 (Mich. 1998), *overruled on other grounds by Wilkie v. Auto-Owners Ins. Co.*, 664 N.W.2d 776, 786 (Mich. 2003). The continuous trigger (also sometimes called the "multiple" or "triple" trigger) is premised on the notion that, even after a claimant (or property) is no longer *directly* exposed to a hazardous substance, the injury sustained upon initial exposure remains ongoing. In other words, the claimant is sustaining so-called "exposure in residence" (of their body). *See J.H. France Refractories Co. v. Allstate Ins. Co.*, 626 A.2d 502, 507 (Pa. 1993) ("The medical evidence in this case unequivocally establishes that injuries occur during the development of asbestosis immediately upon exposure, and that the injuries continue to occur even after exposure ends during the progression of the disease right up until the time that increasing incapacitation results in manifestation as a recognizable disease. If any of these phases of the pathogenesis occurs during the policy period, the insurer is obligated to indemnify [the insured] under the terms of the policy.")

The continuous trigger traces its origin to *Keene Corp. v. Ins. Co. of N. Am.*, 667 F.2d 1034 (D.C. Cir. 1981). The District of Columbia Court of Appeals examined the exposure and manifestation trigger theories and concluded that each one was appropriate, but not exclusive, for purposes of determining which policies were obligated to provide coverage for asbestos bodily injuries: "[I]nhalation exposure, exposure in residence, and manifestation all trigger coverage under the policies. We interpret 'bodily injury' to mean any part of the single injurious process that asbestos-related diseases entail." *Id.* at 1047.

In addition to the medical etiology of asbestos bodily injury, the *Keene* Court also rested its decision on Keene's reasonable expectations:

> When Keene purchased the policies, it could have reasonably expected that it was free of the risk of becoming liable for injuries of which it could not have been aware prior to its purchase of insurance. There is no doubt that these losses would be covered if the diseases at issue developed spontaneously upon inhalation. Inhalation of asbestos is an "occurrence" that causes injury for which Keene may be held liable. The possibility that the insurers may not be liable arises solely because there is a period of time between the point at which the injurious process began and the point at which injury manifests itself.

*Id.* at 1046.

Support for the continuous trigger has also been found in the drafting history of the commercial general liability (CGL) policy:

> [T]he drafters of the standard occurrence-based CGL policy, and the experts advising the industry regarding its interpretation when formulated in 1966, contemplated that the policy would afford liability coverage for all property damage or injury occurring during the policy period resulting from an accident, or from injurious exposure to conditions. Nothing in the policy language purports to exclude damage or injury of a continuous or progressively deteriorating nature, as long as it occurs during the policy period.

*Montrose*, 913 P.2d at 892 (Cal. 1995).

At least one court has concluded that "the continuous trigger theory is a legal fiction permitting the law to posit that many repeated small events occurring over a period of decades are actually only one ongoing occurrence. In cases where property damage is continuous and gradual and results from many events happening over a long period of time, it makes sense to adopt this legal fiction for the purposes of determining what policies have been triggered." *Pub. Serv. Co. of Colo. v. Wallis & Cos.*, 986 P.2d 924, 939 (Colo. 1999).

Given the significant difficulty of determining when an injury-in-fact or actual injury occurred in the context of asbestos bodily injury and environmental property damage, it is likely to be the case that, as a practical matter, an injury-in-fact trigger and continuous trigger are one and the same. For example, in *N. States Power Co. v. Fid. & Cas. Co. of N.Y.*, 523 N.W.2d 657 (Minn. 1994), the Supreme Court of Minnesota adopted a presumption that, where damages occurred over multiple policy periods, such damages were continuous from the point of the first damage to the point of discovery. Then "[a] party wishing to show that no appreciable damage occurred during a triggered policy period bears the burden of proving that fact." *Id.* at 664.

5. Double Trigger: While not discussed in many of the decisions that review the various trigger schools of thought, another method, sometimes called the "double" trigger, has been employed, albeit not frequently. Under this method, injury occurs at the time of exposure and manifestation but not necessarily during the period in between. *See Zurich Ins. Co. v. Raymark Indus., Inc.*, 514 N.E.2d 150, 160–61 (Ill. 1987). The theory behind the double trigger is a rejection of the continuous trigger's concept that, even after a claimant (or property) is no longer *directly* exposed to a hazardous substance, the injury sustained upon initial exposure remains ongoing "in residence." "The [*Raymark*] Court explicitly rejected the notion that 'those who ultimately manifest an asbestos-related disease necessarily sustained bodily injury between the time when they were no longer exposed to asbestos and the time when their disease manifested itself.'" *John Crane, Inc. v. Admiral Ins. Co.*, No. 04CH8266, 2006 WL 1010495, at *12 (Ill. Cir. Ct. Apr. 12, 2006) (quoting *Raymark* at 161).

Much has been written by courts over the various trigger of coverage options that exist for deciding which policies are obligated to provide coverage for latent injury and damage claims. Most judges authoring these opinions are quick to discuss the various named trigger theories and then select one to apply. Other courts have proceeded more cautiously, concluding that the trigger of coverage labels may not be as neat and tidy as they seem. *See Plantation Pipe Line Co. v. Cont'l Cas. Co.*, No. 1:03-CV-2811-WBH, 2006 WL 6106248, at *7 n.13 (N.D. Ga. Sept. 25, 2006) ("In its present analysis, the Court consciously avoids using a particular label in resolving the present trigger issue, instead focusing on the actual language and analysis in these cases. Neither the district courts nor the parties can agree about the appropriate verbiage for the different trigger theories, however, it is the substance, not the name that controls.").

Courts have also declined to immediately adopt a prenamed trigger theory on the basis that, while convenient, it may come at the expense of the facts and policy language:

> In reviewing several trigger cases from other jurisdictions, we think it apparent that some courts too quickly label the "trigger theory" they are supposedly applying without carefully considering the factual distinctions, or lack thereof, between exposure, injury in fact, and manifestation. Even more troubling, some courts are too hasty in applying a particular trigger without carefully considering the relevant policy language. We must not forget that the issue presented today is fundamentally a question of insurance contract interpretation.

*Gelman Sciences*, 572 N.W.2d at 622 (Mich. 1998), *overruled on other grounds by Wilkie v. Auto-Owners Ins. Co.*, 664 N.W.2d 776, 786 (Mich. 2003).

Despite their differences, the various trigger theories that have been debated and adopted over the years share a common trait: they generally result in multiple policies (in some manner) being obligated to provide coverage for latent injury and damage claims. The one theory that would have prevented this—manifestation—was resoundingly rejected. Needless to say, the adoption of trigger theories that resulted in more than a single policy year being obligated to provide coverage caused a significant increase in insurers' liability for asbestos and environmental claims. Indeed, the continuous trigger has been justified on the basis of its ability to maximize coverage. *See Owens Illinois*, 650 A.2d at 981 (N.J. 1994).

Once a court determines that multiple policy years are obligated to provide coverage for latent injury or damage, the focus often shifts to determining how much of such total damage must be borne by each insurer that issued one or more of the triggered policies. Like trigger, this issue, usually called "allocation," has been the subject of contentious, abundant, and slow-moving multi-party litigation over the past three decades. Allocation is the subject of Chapter 17.

## 50-State Survey: Trigger of Coverage for Latent Injury and Damage Claims

**Alabama:** The Court of Appeals for the Eleventh Circuit held that an exposure trigger applied to claims for bodily injury resulting from exposure to asbestos. *Commercial Union Ins. Co. v. Sepco Corp.*, 765 F.2d 1543, 1545–46 (11th Cir. 1985) (applying Alabama law). "[E]very asbestos-related injury results from inhalation of asbestos fibers. Because such inhalation can occur only upon exposure to asbestos, and because it is impossible practically to determine the point at which the fibers actually imbed themselves in the victim's lungs, to equate exposure to asbestos with 'bodily injury' caused by the inhalation of the asbestos is the 'superior interpretation of the contract provisions.'" *Id.* at 1546 (quoting *Ins. Co. of N. Am v. Forty-Eight Insulations, Inc.*, 633 F.2d 1212, 1223 (6th Cir. 1980)).

**Alaska:** An Alaska District Court held that an exposure trigger applied to claims for environmental property damage and that coverage was triggered when groundwater was exposed to contaminants. *Mapco Alaska Petroleum, Inc. v. Cent. Nat'l Ins. Co. of Omaha*, 795 F. Supp. 941, 948 (D. Alaska 1991). "In light of the Alaska Supreme Court's general concurrence with California insurance law, coverage should be triggered by exposure to contaminants rather than by manifestation of the damage." *Id.*

**Arizona:** The Court of Appeals of Arizona held that a continuous trigger applied to claims for bodily injury caused by exposure to water from an aquifer that was contaminated by TCE used at an aircraft-cleaning facility.

*Associated Aviation Underwriters v. Wood*, 98 P.3d 572, 602 (Ariz. Ct. App. 2004). "Under the particular facts of this case, we interpret 'bodily injury' to include the cellular damage caused by TCE exposure *and*, even after exposure has ceased, the continuing injurious process initiated thereby. In other words, both exposure and exposure-in-residence occurring during the policy period will trigger insurance coverage. In addition, the policy clearly is also triggered if 'disease' manifests itself during the policy period." *Id.* (emphasis in original).

**Arkansas:** No instructive authority.

**California:** The Supreme Court of California held that a continuous trigger applied to claims for bodily injury and property damage resulting from the insured's disposal of hazardous waste. *Montrose Chem. Corp. v. Admiral Ins. Co.*, 913 P.2d 878, 904 (Cal. 1995). "Under this trigger of coverage theory, bodily injuries and property damage that are continuous or progressively deteriorating throughout successive policy periods are covered by all policies in effect during those periods." *Id.* at 894; *see also Armstrong World Indus., Inc. v. Atena Cas. & Sur. Co.*, 45 Cal. App. 4th 1, 47 (Cal. Ct. App. 1996) (applying the continuous trigger theory in the context of asbestos-related bodily injury) ("[T]he trial court's factual findings here, made after consideration of extensive medical testimony, amply support the conclusion that injury actually occurs upon exposure and continues until death."); *Employers Ins. Co. of Wausau v. Pacific Employers Ins. Co.*, No. B204712, 2009 WL 1363475 (Calif. Ct. App. May 18, 2009) (addressing California's continuous trigger).

**Colorado:** The Supreme Court of Colorado held that a continuous trigger applied to claims for environmental property damage at waste sites. *Pub. Serv. Co. of Colo. v. Wallis & Cos.*, 986 P.2d 924, 939 (Colo. 1999). "We note that the continuous trigger theory is a legal fiction permitting the law to posit that many repeated small events occurring over a period of decades are actually only one ongoing occurrence. In cases where property damage is continuous and gradual and results from many events happening over a long period of time, it makes sense to adopt this legal fiction for the purposes of determining what policies have been triggered." *Id.*

**Connecticut:** In *Security Ins. Co. of Hartford v. Lumbermens Mut. Cas. Co.*, 826 A.2d 107 (Conn. 2003), the Supreme Court of Connecticut noted that the trial court had applied a continuous trigger and pro rata allocation to claims for bodily injury resulting from exposure to asbestos. *Id.* at 113–14. While the *Security Ins.* Court did not rule on the appropriate trigger mechanism, it discussed the various trigger theories and upheld the trial court's decision that pro rata was the appropriate allocation method. *Id.* at 115; *see also Steadfast Ins. Co. v. Purdue Frederick Co.*, No. X08CV020191697S, 2006 WL 2004984, at *7 (Conn. Super. Ct. May 18, 2006) (associating *Security Ins.*'s allocation methodology with the triggering of multiple insurance policies) (declining to adopt a continuous trigger in the context of claims for bodily injury resulting from the ingestion of the insured's pharmaceutical product OxyContin). "Injuries... [in environmental contamination cases] usually evolve slowly, and thus it is difficult to define the date on which an occurrence triggers liability for insurance purposes. Many years may pass from the time a toxin enters the body until the time the toxin's presence manifests itself in the form of a disease." *Id.* at *5 (citation and quotation omitted). "There is no contention that this case involves 'long latency loss claims' or a 'continuous trigger' situation." *Id.* at *6.

**Delaware:** The Delaware Superior Court held that "Delaware law supports the imposition of a continuous trigger." *E. I. du Pont de Nemours & Co. v. Admiral Ins. Co.*, No. 89C-AU-99, 1995 WL 654020, at *8 (Del. Super. Ct. Oct. 27, 1995). Following a review of the various trigger theories, the court explained: "The policy reasoning underlying continuous trigger fits logically within the context of contamination of soil and groundwater over a period of years. Since... the process of contamination had indisputably been ongoing for decades, the continuous trigger should apply." *Id.* at 9; *see also Hercules, Inc. v. AIU Ins. Co.*, 784 A.2d 481, 492 (Del. Super. Ct. 2001) (citing *du Pont* for the proposition that Delaware has adopted the continuous trigger theory and applying it for purposes of addressing allocation for environmental property damage).

**Florida:** A Florida District Court applied an injury-in-fact trigger to claims for environmental property damage. *CSX Transportation, Inc. v. Admiral Ins. Co.*, No. 93–132, 1996 WL 33569825, at *5 (M.D. Fla. Nov. 6, 1996). The parties agreed that the "injury in fact" trigger should be applied, despite the court's observation that there was substantial authority suggesting that the multiple or continuous trigger theory would be applied in the circumstances of this case. *Id.* Nonetheless, "in view of the parties' substantial agreement upon application of the injury in fact theory, coupled with the fact that, as a practical matter, the two theories appear to be functionally equivalent in these circumstances, the Court will adopt the injury in fact trigger of coverage." *Id.*

**Georgia:** A Georgia District Court, following a survey of several prior Georgia federal court decisions, held that coverage was triggered for environmental property damage that occurred within the effective dates of the policy periods, regardless of when the damage was discovered. *Plantation Pipe Line Co. v. Cont'l Cas. Co.*, No. 1:03-CV-2811-WBH, 2006 WL 6106248, at *7 (N.D. Ga. Sept. 25, 2006); *see also Briggs & Stratton Corp. v. Royal Globe Ins. Co.*, 64 F. Supp. 2d 1346, 1350 (M.D. Ga. 1999) (holding that an exposure trigger applied to environmental property damage resulting from the discharge of untreated waste water) ("It is not disputed that during the Transcontinental policy period PMI used the chemical materials it purchased from B & S in its electroplating operations, and that as a result of those electroplating operations waste waters containing chemical substances originating with B & S were discharged onto the property, damaging it."); *Boardman Petroleum, Inc. v. Federated Mut. Ins. Co.*, 498 S.E.2d 492, 493–94 (Ga. 1998) (failing to answer a certified question from the Eleventh Circuit Court of

Appeals asking which trigger of coverage theory applies in Georgia due to the court's resolution of another issue as dispositive).

**Hawaii:** In *Sentinel Ins. Co., Ltd. v. First Ins. Co. of Haw., Ltd.*, 875 P.2d 894, 915 (Haw. 1994) the Supreme Court of Hawaii adopted an injury-in-fact trigger in the context of a claim for construction defects. While the case involved construction defects, the court reached its decision based upon a review of cases nationally involving environmental property damage and toxic torts. *Id.* at 914–17. Further, the court noted that "[t]he injury-in-fact trigger is... true to the terms of the CGL policy and suitable for any type of injury." *Id.* at 917.

**Idaho:** No instructive authority. *But see State of Idaho v. Bunker Hill Co.*, 647 F. Supp. 1064, 1070 (D. Idaho 1986) (addressing the various trigger-of-coverage theories and holding that, under the circumstances of the case, the court did not need to adopt a trigger method because the language of the policies was clear and unambiguous that the environmental property damage for which insurance was provided must occur during the policy period).

**Illinois:** The Supreme Court of Illinois held that, for purposes of claims for bodily injury caused by exposure to asbestos, coverage is trigger under the policies on the risk when the person is exposed to asbestos, on the date of manifestation of a disease and at the time of a disordered, weakened, or unsound condition before the clinical manifestation of a disease. *Zurich Ins. Co. v. Raymark Indus., Inc.*, 514 N.E.2d 150, 160–61 (Ill. 1987). "The [*Raymark*] Court explicitly rejected the notion that 'those who ultimately manifest an asbestos-related disease necessarily sustained bodily injury between the time when they were no longer exposed to asbestos and the time when their disease manifested itself.'" *John Crane, Inc. v. Admiral Ins. Co.*, No. 04CH8266, 2006 WL 1010495, at *12 (Ill. Cir. Ct. Apr. 12, 2006) (quoting *Raymark* at 161); *see also Outboard Marine Corp. v. Liberty Mut. Ins. Co.*, 670 N.E.2d 740, 748 (Ill. Ct. App. 1996) (adopting a continuous trigger for purposes of environmental property damage).

**Indiana:** The Supreme Court of Indiana held that a multiple trigger theory applied to claims for bodily injury caused by the ingestion of DES and that "each insurer on the risk between the ingestion of DES and the manifestation of a DES-related illness is liable to the insured for indemnification." *Eli Lilly and Co. v. Home Ins. Co.*, 482 N.E.2d 467, 471 (Ind. 1985); *see also Travelers Cas. & Surety Co. v. U. S. Filter Corp.*, 895 N.E.2d 1172, 1179 (Ind. 2008) (favorably citing *Eli Lilly* for its adoption of the multiple trigger interpretation of occurrence-based policies in the delayed manifestation context); *PSI Energy, Inc. v. Home Ins. Co.*, 801 N.E.2d 705, 733 (Ind. Ct. App. 2004) ("We agree with the Insurers that our courts are required to apply the 'injury-in-fact' trigger of coverage approach.") (citing *Allstate Ins. Co. v. Dana Corp.*, 759 N.E.2d 1049, 1060–61 (Ind. 2001) (considering coverage for cleanup costs associated with environmental contamination from insured's manufactured gas plants); *Wolf Lake Terminals, Inc. v. Mutual Marine Ins. Co.*, 433 F. Supp. 2d 933, 948 (N.D. Ind. 2005) (holding that an "injury in fact" trigger applies in the context of coverage for environmental property damage).

**Iowa:** No instructive authority.

**Kansas:** The Supreme Court of Kansas held that a continuous trigger applied to claims for bodily injury caused by noise-induced hearing loss. *Atchison, Topeka & Santa Fe Ry. Co. v. Stonewall Ins. Co.*, 71 P.3d 1097, 1125–26 (Kan. 2003). "The unprotected employees have been subjected to excessive noise levels for a continuous period of time. It is part of the single injurious process which resulted in hearing impairment. Santa Fe's failure to protect the claimants is the occurrence which gives rise to the injury." *Id.* at 1126; *see also Cessna Aircraft Co. v. Hartford Acc. & Indem. Co.*, 900 F. Supp. 1489, 1503 (D. Kan. 1995) ("[A]pplication of the 'injury-in-fact' trigger is more consistent with the language of the... policies, especially where, as here, the contamination is alleged to have occurred in particular policy periods and to have continued through many policy periods.").

**Kentucky:** A Kentucky District Court, noting that no Kentucky court had ever adopted a specific trigger theory, declined to do so as such task was better left to the Supreme Court of Kentucky. *Eckstein v. Cincinnati Ins. Co.*, No. 505CV043M, 2005 WL 3050469, at *2–3 (W.D. Ky. Nov. 14, 2005) (addressing coverage for a residence damaged by mold); *see also Acuity Ins. Co. v. Higdon's Sheet Metal & Supply Co.*, No. 3:06-CV-162-H, 2007 WL 1034986, at *3 (W.D. Ky. 2007) ("Although some states have adopted a coverage trigger theory to establish the date of loss for determining when coverage is triggered... Kentucky has not done so. Instead, coverage is determined by examining the terms of the policies at issue.").

**Louisiana:** The Supreme Court of Louisiana held that an exposure trigger applied to claims for bodily injury caused by exposure to asbestos. *Cole v. Celotex Corp.*, 599 So. 2d 1058, 1076 (La. 1992). The court rested its decision on the fact that the exposure theory comports with a literal construction of the policy language, maximizes coverage, and honors the contracting parties' intent by providing consistency between the insured's tort liability and the insurer's coverage. *Id.* at 1076–77; *see also Grefer v. Travelers Ins. Co.*, 919 So. 2d 758, 765–66 (La. Ct. App. 2005) (citing *Cole* for the proposition that an exposure trigger applies to claims for environmental property damage) (court rejected a manifestation trigger and the argument that the exposure trigger only applies to bodily injury/latent disease cases); *Am. Guarantee & Liability Ins. Co. v. Anco Insulation, Inc.*, No. Civ.A.02–987A1, 2005 WL 1865552, at *5 (M.D. La. July 29, 2005) ("*Cole* and its progeny demonstrate that Louisiana law has expressly rejected the application of the triple-trigger theory and consistently applied the exposure theory when determining the date of accrual of a claim resulting from long-term exposure to latent, disease-producing substances such as asbestos.").

**Maine:** No instructive authority. *But see Citizens Communications Co. v. American Home Assur. Co.*, No. Civ. A. CV-02–237, 2004 WL 423059, at *2, n.3 (Me. Super. Ct. Feb. 19, 2004) (not addressing the issue, but noting, in the context of a claim involving environmental property damage, that "[m]ost courts now employ the 'continuous trigger,' by triggering any policy on the risk at any time the continuing loss occurred, and requiring the insurers of those triggered policies to either prepare to defend or to prepare to pay up to its policy limits").

**Maryland:** The Court of Appeals of Maryland held that "*at a minimum*, coverage under the policy to provide a defense and indemnification of the insured is triggered upon exposure to the insured's asbestos products during the policy period by a person who suffers bodily injury as a result of that exposure." *Lloyd E. Mitchell, Inc. v. Md. Cas. Co.*, 595 A.2d 469, 478 (Md. 1991) (emphasis added); *see also National Union Fire Ins. Co. of Pittsburgh, PA v. Porter Hayden Co.*, 331 B.R. 652, 661 (D. Md. 2005) (noting that the *Mitchell* Court cited with approval cases adopting not only an exposure trigger, but also injury-in-fact and continuous triggers, thereby precluding the court from concluding that *Mitchell* compels, or even supports, the argument that it adopted an "exposure-only" trigger); *Md. Cas. Co. v. Hanson*, 902 A.2d 152, 170 (Md. Ct. App. 2006) ("[T]he law in Maryland is that, in cases such as [those involving] proof of repeated exposure to lead, which, in turn, results in lead-based poisoning injuries that continue for several years with continuous exposure, the continuous injury or injury-in-fact trigger is applicable and thus triggers insurance coverage during all applicable policy periods.") (relying on *Riley v. United Services Auto. Ass'n*, 871 A.2d 599 (Md. Ct. App. 2005); *Harford County v. Harford Mut. Ins. Co.*, 610 A.2d 286, 294–95 (Md. 1992) (holding that, for purposes of environmental property damage, policies on the risk earlier than discovery or manifestation of damage can be triggered); *Mayor & City Council of Balt. v. Utica Mut. Ins. Co.*, 802 A.2d 1070, 1100 (Md. Ct. App. 2002) (holding that a continuous trigger applied to claims for asbestos in buildings).

**Massachusetts:** The Supreme Judicial Court of Massachusetts held that, under policies that provided coverage for an occurrence during the policy period, an exposure trigger applied to claims for bodily injury caused by exposure to asbestos. *A.W. Chesterton Co. v. Mass. Insurers Insolvency Fund*, 838 N.E.2d 1237, 1251–52 (Mass. 2005). It was stipulated that, under policies that did not require an occurrence during the policy period, a continuous trigger applied. *Id.* at 1251; *see also Rubenstein v. Royal Ins. Co. of Am.*, 694 N.E.2d 381, 387 (Mass. Ct. App. 1998) (addressing trigger of coverage for environmental property damage and noting that the language of the particular policy controlled and the focus of inquiry was whether property damage occurred within the policy period); *Keyspan New England, LLC v. Hanover Ins. Co.*, Nos. 93–01458, 04–01855, 2008 WL 4308310, at *6 (Mass. Super. Ct. Aug. 14, 2008) (holding that coverage for environmental property damage was triggered if damage happened within the policy period); *Boston Gas Co. v. Century Indem. Co.*, 910 N.E.2d 290, 301 (Mass. 2009) (noting that, in *Trustees of Tufts Univ. v. Commercial Union Ins. Co.*, 616 N.E.2d 68 (Mass. 1993), the Massachusetts high court rejected the manifestation trigger, for purposes of environmental contamination, and the court has not yet had occasion to adopt one of the other trigger theories in such context) (not addressing the issue because it was not before the court).

**Michigan:** The Supreme Court of Michigan held that an injury-in-fact trigger applied to claims for environmental property damage caused by seepage from a wastewater pond. *Gelman Sciences, Inc. v. Fid. & Cas. Co. of N.Y.*, 572 N.W.2d 617, 623 (Mich. 1998), *overruled on other grounds by Wilkie v. Auto-Owners Ins. Co.*, 664 N.W.2d 776, 786 (Mich. 2003). "[A]ccording to the policies' explicit terms, actual injury must occur during the time the policy is in effect in order to be indemnifiable, i.e., the policies dictate an injury-in-fact approach. The manifestation trigger simply is not supported by the policy language." *Id.*; *see also Wolverine World Wide, Inc. v. Liberty Mut. Ins. Co.*, No. 260330, 2007 WL 705981, at *3 (Mich. Ct. App. Mar. 8, 2007) (citing *Gelman* as establishing that Michigan uses an injury-in-fact trigger and applying it in the context of contamination related to the insured's disposal of toxic sludge from its tannery operations).

**Minnesota:** The Supreme Court of Minnesota applied an injury-in-fact trigger to claims for property damage resulting from the insured's coal-tar gasification plant operations. *N. States Power Co. v. Fid. & Cas. Co. of N.Y.*, 523 N.W.2d 657, 662–63 (Minn. 1994). "Where, as in this case, the damages occurred over multiple policy periods, the trial court should presume that the damages were continuous from the point of the first damage to the point of discovery or cleanup. A party wishing to show that no appreciable damage occurred during a triggered policy period bears the burden of proving that fact." *Id.* at 664; *see also In re Silicone Implant Ins. Coverage Litigation*, 667 N.W.2d 405, 417 (Minn. 2003) (holding that an injury-in-fact trigger applied to claims for bodily injury caused by silicone-gel breast implants) ("[B]ecause damage occurred at or about the time of implantation, we conclude that the policies were triggered at or about the time of implantation."); *Tony Eiden Co. v. State Auto Property and Cas. Ins. Co.*, No. A07–2222, 2009 WL 233883, at *2–3 (addressing Minnesota case law applying an injury-in-fact trigger).

**Mississippi:** No instructive authority.

**Missouri:** Missouri law appears unsettled concerning which trigger theory applies. *See United States v. Conservation Chem. Co.*, 653 F. Supp. 152, 197 (W.D. Mo. 1986) ("[T]he Special Master finds that Missouri tends to follow the injury in fact analysis to actually determine or discover when an injury occurred. But there may be circumstances where the Missouri courts will look to the exposure and manifestation theories to determine when the injury occurred.") (addressing coverage for environmental damage resulting from the operation of the insured's chemical waste disposal facility); *see also Nationwide Ins. Co. v. Central Missouri Elec. Cooperative, Inc.*, 278 F.3d 742, 747 (8th Cir. 2001) ("It is not entirely clear which of these [trigger] approaches is appropriate under Missouri law. Although we have previously predicted that Missouri would apply an exposure theory of damages, *Continental Ins. Co. v. Northeastern Pharm. & Chem. Co., Inc.*, 842 F.2d 977, 984 (8th Cir. 1988) (en banc), an argument can be made that an injury in fact approach is more appropriate. *Shaver*, 817 S.W.2d at 657 (coverage triggered 'when the complaining party was actually damaged.')"); *Independent Petrochem. Corp. v. Aetna Cas. Insur. Co.*, 672 F. Supp. 1, 3 (D.D.C. 1986) (applying Missouri law) ("Because we conclude that the obligations of both insurers are triggered under either theory of liability, we need not determine which method is required under Missouri law.").

**Montana:** No instructive authority.

**Nebraska:** No instructive authority. For guidance, *see Kaapa Ethanol, L.L.C. v. Affiliated FM Ins. Co.*, No. 7:05CV5010, 2008 WL 2986277 (D. Neb. July 29, 2008) addressed in Chapter 16. *See also Dutton-Lainson Co. v. Continental Ins. Co.*, 778 N.W.2d 433, 445 (Neb. 2010) (while not specifically addressing trigger of coverage, the court's analysis of allocation was undertaken based on a continuous trigger) ("[T]he total amount of the property damage should be allocated to the various policies in proportion to the period of time each was on the risk. If, for example, contamination occurred over a period of 10 years, 1/10th of the damage would be allocable to the period of time that a policy in force for 1 year was on the risk and 3/10ths of the damage would be allocable to the period of time a 3-year policy was in force.") (quoting *Northern States Power Co. v. Fidelity & Cas. Co. of N.Y.*, 523 N.W.2d 657, 664 (Minn. 1994)).

**Nevada:** No instructive authority. For guidance, *see* discussion in Chapter 16.

**New Hampshire:** The Supreme Court of New Hampshire held that, under policies that required property damage during the policy period, an injury-in-fact trigger applied to claims for property damage caused by the insured's manufactured gas plant operations. *EnergyNorth Natural Gas, Inc. v. Certain Underwriters at Lloyd's*, 848 A.2d 715, 721–22 (N.H. 2004) (*EnergyNorth I*). "The language of these three policies unambiguously distinguishes between the causative event—an accident or continuous or repeated exposure to conditions—and the resulting property damage. It is the property damage that must occur during the policy period, and 'which results' from the accident or 'continuous or repeated exposure to conditions.'" *Id.* at 721. With respect to policies that covered liability for accidents occurring during the policy period and those that applied to occurrences happening during the policy period, the court adopted an exposure trigger. *Id.* at 724–25; *see also EnergyNorth Natural Gas, Inc. v. Certain Underwriters at Lloyd's*, 934 A.2d 517 (N.H. 2007) (summarizing *EnergyNorth I*).

**New Jersey:** The Supreme Court of New Jersey held that a continuous trigger applied to claims for bodily injury and property damage caused by exposure to asbestos. *Owens Illinois, Inc. v. United Ins. Co.*, 650 A.2d 974, 995 (N.J. 1994). "[T]hat when progressive indivisible injury or damage results from exposure to injurious conditions for which civil liability may be imposed, courts may reasonably treat the progressive injury or damage as an occurrence within each of the years of a CGL policy." *Id.*; *see also Quincy Mut. Fire Ins. Co. v. Borough of Bellmawr*, 799 A.2d 499, 514 (N.J. 2002) (applying the continuous trigger to claims for environmental property damage) ("exposure relating to the Borough's initial depositing of toxic waste into the Landfill is the first trigger of coverage under the continuous trigger theory and constitutes an 'occurrence.'"); *Polarome Intern., Inc. v. Greenwich Ins. Co.*, 961 A.2d 29, 44–45 (N.J. Super. Ct. App. Div. 2008) (holding that policies issued after manifestation of injury were not obligated to provide coverage) ("[T]he last pull of the trigger occurs with the initial manifestation of a toxic-tort personal injury. Upon initial manifestation, the 'scientific uncertainties' that led to adoption of the continuous-trigger approach no longer exist.") (citation omitted).

**New Mexico:** No instructive authority. *But see Leafland Group-II, Montgomery Towers Ltd. Partnership v. Ins. Co. of N. Am.*, 881 P.2d 26, 28–29 (N.M. 1994) (involving diminution in the value of an apartment building resulting from the presence of asbestos and holding that first-party insurer did not owe coverage because its policy was not triggered). The court reasoned that "the underlying problem causing the diminution in property value—the use of asbestos in constructing the buildings—was present long before [the insured] acquired the property. The presence of asbestos had, in effect, already diminished the value of the property before [the insured] purchased the property and bought insurance from [the insurer], even though the presence of asbestos remained undetected for some time after [the insured] bought the property. In other words, the diminution in property value was discovered, but not caused, during the time the policy was in effect. Because the claimed loss occurred prior to the time the insurance was purchased, 'the concept of risk that is inherent in all policies of insurance is lacking.'" *Id.* at 29 (citation omitted).

**New York:** The New York Appellate Division observed that "[t]he issue of what constitutes the trigger point for coverage in cases involving long-term exposure to asbestos is not settled under New York law. The only Court of Appeals decision addressing the issue [*Cont'l Cas. Co. v. Rapid-American Corp.*, 609 N.E.2d 506 (N.Y. 1993)] has done so tangentially." *In re Liquidation of Midland Ins. Co.*, 709 N.Y.S.2d 24, 30 (N.Y. App. Div. 2000). "The trigger event in the policy at issue is *an occurrence which results in injury,* not the injury itself. In our view such policy language requires only an occurrence (inhalation) during the coverage period, and not the injury itself (the actual onset of asbestosis).... [I]t is more consistent with the 'occurrence' language of the policy to find that the injury first occurred when the individual was actually exposed to asbestos fibers by inhalation, than to conclude that an insurer coming upon the risk after actual exposure by inhalation has terminated should be bound to indemnify the insured. Thus, given the 'round hole, square peg' category of an asbestos claim, and the 'occurrence' language of the policy, the IAS court correctly found that coverage is triggered by exposure, whether first or continued, but not by exposure in residence." *Id.* at 32–33 (emphasis in original); *see also Cont'l Cas. Co. v. Employers Ins. Co. of Wausau*, 871 N.Y.S.2d 48, 62 (N.Y. App. Div. 2008) (noting that, in *Rapid-American*, the Court of Appeals of New York "declined to subscribe to an exposure theory… and instead appeared to approve of injury-in-fact as a trigger for coverage") (addressing asbestos bodily injury claims).

**North Carolina:** No instructive authority. For guidance, *see Gaston County Dyeing Mach. Co. v. Northfield Ins. Co.*, 524 S.E.2d 558 (N.C. 2000) and *Hutchinson v. Nationwide Mut. Fire Ins. Co.*, 594 S.E.2d 61 (N.C. Ct. App. 2004) addressed in Chapter 16.

**North Dakota:** No instructive authority. For guidance, *see Grinnell Mut. Reinsurance Co. v. Thies*, 755 N.W.2d 852 (N.D. 2008) addressed in Chapter 16.

**Ohio:** An Ohio trial court held that a continuous trigger applied to claims for bodily injury caused by exposure to asbestos. *Owens-Corning Fiberglas Corp. v. Am. Centennial Ins. Co.*, 660 N.E.2d 770, 788 (Ohio Com. Pl. 1995) ("This court, therefore, is not concerned with the distinction that all persons exposed to asbestos do not experience malignant diseases as a result of such exposure. This information does not change the fact that in every instance of asbestos exposure there is immediate injury which continues, with some degree of severity, throughout a person's life."); *see also Goodyear Tire & Rubber Co. v. Aetna Cas. & Sur. Co.*, 769 N.E.2d 835, 841 (Ohio 2002) (discussing continuous trigger principles in the context of adopting an allocation methodology) ("When a continuous occurrence of environmental pollution triggers claims under multiple primary insurance policies, the insured is entitled to secure coverage from a single policy of its choice that covers 'all sums' incurred as damages 'during the policy period,' subject to that policy's limit of coverage."); *Lincoln Elec. Co. v. St. Paul Fire and Marine Ins. Co.*, 210 F.3d 672, 690, n.24 (6th Cir. 2000) (applying Ohio law) (adopting a "flexible continuing trigger," for purposes of asbestos bodily injury claims, which presumes a continuous trigger but allows evidence of injury-in-fact to rebut such presumption and constrict the trigger period).

**Oklahoma:** No instructive authority. For guidance, *see* Chapter 16.

**Oregon:** The Supreme Court of Oregon held that an injury-in-fact trigger applied to claims for environmental property damage caused by the insured's wood-treatment operations. *St. Paul Fire & Marine Ins. Co., Inc. v. McCormick & Baxter Creosoting Co.*, 923 P.2d 1200, 1210 (Or. 1996). "The policies do not make coverage contingent on the time when the property damage was discovered or on the time when the insured's liability became fixed." *Id.* at 1211;

*see also Sierra Pac. Inv. Co. Unigard Sec. Ins. Co.*, No. 03–366-AS, 2003 WL 23962278, at *7 (D. Or. Nov. 17, 2003) (addressing *McCormick & Baxter* in the context of claims for environmental property damage).

**Pennsylvania:** The Supreme Court of Pennsylvania held that a continuous trigger applied to claims for bodily injury caused by exposure to asbestos. *J.H. France Refractories Co. v. Allstate Ins. Co.*, 626 A.2d 502, 506 (Pa. 1993). The court held that "[t]he medical evidence in this case unequivocally establishes that injuries occur during the development of asbestosis immediately upon exposure, and that the injuries continue to occur even after exposure ends during the progression of the disease right up until the time that increasing incapacitation results in manifestation as a recognizable disease. If any of these phases of the pathogenesis occurs during the policy period, the insurer is obligated to indemnify [the insured] under the terms of the policy." *Id.* at 507. The court determined that all phases of the disease process independently meet the policy definition of "bodily injury." *Id.*; *see also Koppers Co., Inc. v. Aetna Cas. and Sur. Co.*, 98 F.3d 1440, 1445–46 (3rd Cir. 1996) (applying Pa. law) (not adopting a trigger theory but holding that a jury instruction that allowed for a continuous trigger, even if erroneous, was harmless error because the insured introduced uncontroverted evidence that the property damage (mostly groundwater contamination through leaching) was continuous, progressive, and indivisible throughout the relevant policy periods, as well as evidence that the causes of the contamination (e.g., leaks, drips, spills, or disposals) existed at each site during each policy period).

**Rhode Island:** The Supreme Court of Rhode Island held that a manifestation trigger applied to claims for property damage resulting from groundwater contamination at the insured's aerospace equipment manufacturing facility. *Textron, Inc. v. Aetna Cas. & Sur. Co.*, 754 A.2d 742, 746 (R.I. 2000). "Property damage triggers coverage under this type of comprehensive general-liability-insurance policy when the damage (1) manifests itself, (2) is discovered or, (3) in the exercise of reasonable diligence is discoverable." *Id.* "The third trigger of [this] test does not force a manufacturer to 'go around looking to find out if he's contaminating anything.'… it simply addresses the problem of latent injury (such as asbestos poisoning) or latent damage (such as groundwater contamination), when the injury or damage, although covered by the policy, is not immediately discernible or occurs after an unexpected event sets in motion a series of incidents that eventually results in the manifestation of the damage." *Id.* (citation omitted); *see also CPC Int'l, Inc., v. Northbrook Excess & Surplus Ins. Co.*, 668 A.2d 647, 649 (R.I. 1995) (same); *Truk-Away of R.I., Inc. v. Aetna Cas. & Sur. Co.*, 723 A.2d 309, 313 (R.I. 1999) (same).

**South Carolina:** The Fourth Circuit Court of Appeals held that an injury-in-fact trigger applied to claims for property damage caused by the insured's leaking underground gasoline storage system. *Spartan Petroleum Co., Inc. v. Federated Mut. Ins. Co.*, 162 F.3d 805, 810–11 (4th Cir. 1998) (applying South Carolina law). "[T]he injury-in-fact trigger requires an insured to demonstrate that during the policy period an injury, caused by the underlying 'occurrence,' occurred to the property that is the subject of the underlying third-party action. Once an injury-in-fact has triggered coverage as to *that* property, coverage is triggered continuously thereafter to allow coverage under all policies in effect from the time of injury-in-fact during the progressive damage to that property." *Id.* at 811 (citation and internal quotes omitted) (emphasis in original). For additional guidance, *see* discussion in Chapter 16.

**South Dakota:** No instructive authority. For guidance, *see* discussion in Chapter 16.

**Tennessee:** No instructive authority. *But see In re Edge*, 60 B.R. 690 (M.D. Tenn. 1986). The Bankruptcy Court for the Middle District of Tennessee addressed whether a claim against a debtor-dentist, for pre-petition malpractice, arose post-petition as the injuries were discovered at that time. *Id.* at 691. In reaching its decision, the court looked for guidance to cases addressing trigger of coverage for asbestos bodily injury. *Id.* at 700–02. The court was persuaded by the Sixth Circuit's decision in *Ins. Co. of N. Am v. Forty-Eight Insulations, Inc.*, 633 F.2d 1212 (6th Cir. 1980), adopting an exposure trigger. *Id.* at 700–01. "Though we are not here interpreting the language of a contract, the analysis in *Forty-Eight Insulations* is compelling: The policies that guide interpretation of the Bankruptcy Code are served by the conclusion that a claim arises at the time of the negligent act, notwithstanding that access to other courts or the running of a statute of limitation may be timed from some other point in the relationship between tortfeasor and victim. This same logic forms the Sixth Circuit's holding in *Forty-Eight Insulations*." *Id.* at 701.

**Texas:** In *Don's Bldg. Supply, Inc. v. OneBeacon Ins. Co.*, 267 S.W.3d 20 (Tex. 2008), discussed in Chapter 16, the Supreme Court of Texas adopted an actual injury or injury-in-fact trigger for purposes of construction defect claims. The nature of the court's opinion, however, suggests that it is likely to be closely examined by future courts addressing trigger of coverage for environmental claims. The *Don's Bldg.* Court also concluded: "[W]e stress that we do not attempt to fashion a universally applicable 'rule' for determining when an insurer's duty to defend a claim is triggered under an insurance policy, as such determinations should be driven by the contract language—language that obviously may vary from policy to policy." *Id.* at 30; *see also Allstate Ins. Co. v. Hunter*, 242 S.W.3d 137 (Tx. Ct. App. 2007) (noting that Texas courts have adopted various trigger theories for different types of claims).

**Utah:** A Utah District Court held that an injury-in-fact trigger applied to claims for environmental pollution caused by the insured's waste oil disposal. *Quaker State Minit-Lube, Inc. v. Fireman's Fund Ins. Co.*, 868 F. Supp. 1278, 1304 (D. Utah 1994). "Using an actual injury trigger, an 'occurrence' for purposes of CGL insurance policy coverage took place each time hazardous waste such as drain oil was discharged onto the Ekotek Site property and, by definition, inflicted 'property damage' at that site.... . Where releases resulting in contamination are continuing, 'injuries-in-fact' triggering coverage are also continuing."

*Id.* (citations omitted). However, the court also noted that the "manifestation" trigger "may provide a meaningful starting point in a case of hidden, gradual, and probably underground hazardous waste contamination," but the site at issue did not present such a case. *Id.*

**Vermont:** The Supreme Court of Vermont held that a continuous trigger applied to claims for environmental property damage caused by the depositing of debris from a waste hauling business. *Towns v. N. Sec. Ins. Co.*, 964 A.2d 1150, 1165 (Vt. 2008). The court observed that a condition of coverage was that it applied only to bodily injury or property damage "which occur[ed] during the policy period" and the policy contained no other conditions or language stating that such damage must also be discovered or manifested during the policy period. *Id.* at 1163. "[T]o [apply a manifestation trigger] would in effect transform the typically more expensive occurrence-based policy into a cheaper claims-made policy, a form of coverage specifically designed to limit the insurer's risk by restricting coverage to claims made during the policy period '*without regard to the timing of the damage or injury.*'" *Id.* at 1164 (emphasis in original and citation omitted).

**Virginia:** No instructive authority. *See Morrow Corp. v. Harleysville Mut. Ins. Co.*, 110 F. Supp. 2d 441, 448 (E.D. Va. 2000) (recognizing that "[t]he Supreme Court of Virginia has not yet signaled which of these [trigger of coverage] approaches it will adopt, or, indeed, whether it will adopt some other approach to determining what triggers pollution coverage under occurrence-based CGL policies") (not selecting a trigger theory because the policy at issue specifically stated that it provided coverage for a "pollution occurrence at the time the property damage first manifests itself").

**Washington:** Trigger of coverage for latent injury claims has been limited to decisions from Washington District Courts. *See Skinner Corp. v. Fireman's Fund Ins. Co.*, No. C95–995WD, 1996 WL 376657, at *1 (W.D. Wash. Apr. 3, 1996) ("Washington has adopted the 'continuous trigger rule' for insurance coverage in cases involving undiscovered, progressively worsening conditions causing injury or damage. Under the continuous trigger rule, every policy in force throughout the injury-causing process is triggered.") (involving claims for bodily injury caused by exposure to asbestos); *Weyerhaeuser Co. v. Fireman's Fund Ins. Co.*, No. C06–1189MJP, 2007 WL 4420938, at *3 (W.D. Wash. Dec. 17, 2007) ("Washington has adopted the continuous trigger rule for insurance coverage in cases involving undiscovered, progressively worsening conditions causing injury or damage.") (involving claims for bodily injury caused by exposure to asbestos); *Time Oil Co. v. Cigna Prop. & Cas. Ins. Co.*, 743 F. Supp. 1400, 1417 (W.D. Wash. 1990) (parties agreed that Washington has adopted a continuous trigger) (involving claims for contamination of groundwater); *Cadet Mfg. Co. v. American Ins. Co.*, No. C04–5411, 2006 WL 2105065, at *4 (W.D. Wash. July 26, 2006) (noting that Washington has adopted the continuous trigger or continuous damage trigger for determining insurance coverage for ongoing environmental contamination).

**West Virginia:** A West Virginia Circuit Court held that a continuous trigger applied to claims for property damage resulting from contamination of soil and groundwater arising out of the insured's operations. *Wheeling Pittsburgh Corp. v. Am. Ins. Co.*, No. 93-C-340, 2003 WL 23652106, at *16 (W.Va. Cir. Ct. Oct. 18, 2003). "It is undisputed that the issue presented [to] the Court is one of first impression within this jurisdiction inasmuch as the West Virginia Supreme Court of Appeals has never addressed the issue of when insurance coverage is triggered within the context of environmental claims." *Id.* at *14. The court went on to examine case law from other jurisdictions addressing trigger theories and ultimately adopted the continuous trigger. *Id.* at *15–16. Applying a similar rationale as the Supreme Court of California in *Montrose Chem. Corp. v. Admiral Ins. Co.*, 913 P.2d 878 (Cal. 1995), the court concluded that "the present action involves allegations of a continuous, indivisible injurious process resulting from Wheeling Pittsburgh's operations and culminating in environmental property damage." *Id.* at *16.

**Wisconsin:** The Court of Appeals of Wisconsin held that a continuous trigger applied to claims for environmental property damage caused by contamination at the insured's dump. *Society Ins. Co. v. Town of Franklin*, 607 N.W.2d 342, 348 (Wis. Ct. App. 2000) (citing *Wis. Elec. Power Co. v. Cal. Union Ins. Co.*, 419 N.W.2d 255 (Wis. Ct. App. 1987)). "[P]olicies in effect from the time the contamination began up until its remediation are all triggered." *Id.*; *see also Plastics Eng'g Co. v. Liberty Mut. Ins. Co.*, 759 N.W.2d 613, 623 (Wis. 2009) (acknowledging *Society*'s holding that the continuous trigger theory applies in Wisconsin).

**Wyoming:** No instructive authority.

# CHAPTER
# 16

# Trigger of Coverage for Construction Defects and Non-Latent Injury and Damage Claims

Claims for coverage for latent bodily injury and property damage caused by exposure to hazardous substances—most notably asbestos and hazardous waste—have been the subject of contentious litigation over the past three decades. In general, at the center of these disputes is the fact that such injuries often evolve slowly. It could be years between the time that a person is exposed to asbestos and a disease is diagnosed. Likewise, it could be a long time between a property's exposure to hazardous waste and the day that its damaged condition is discovered. In other words, the claim involves injury or damage that may have been taking place for years—before anyone knew it.

This scenario gave rise to questions whether such latent injury or damage satisfied the requirement of the insuring agreement for Part A of the commercial general liability policy that, while coverage is available for "bodily injury" and "property damage" (*see, e.g.*, INS. SERVS. OFFICE PROPS., INC., COMMERCIAL GENERAL LIABILITY COVERAGE FORM, NO. CG 00011207, § I1a (2007)), such injury or damage must occur "during the policy period." ISO FORM, CG 00011207 at § I1b2. If so, coverage would be owed under multiple years of policies for latent injury and damage claims. In general, policyholders succeeded in this area by convincing courts to adopt one of several theories that allowed for the triggering of multiple years of coverage.

This issue—commonly referred to as "trigger of coverage"—is discussed in Chapter 15. Readers that are new to the trigger issue are recommended to review the introduction to Chapter 15 as the concepts discussed therein are the building blocks for this chapter.

Trigger of coverage disputes, however, are no longer limited to the asbestos and hazardous waste arenas. The adoption of various theories that obligated multiple years of policies to provide coverage for asbestos bodily injury and environmental property damage had an enormous impact on the amount of coverage available for such claims. So it should come as no surprise that efforts have been made by policyholders to apply these limits-increasing theories to claims outside the rubric of traditional toxic tort and hazardous waste. Most notably, policyholders have sought to apply the continuous or injury in fact trigger to the surfeit of construction defect claims. Just as they did with asbestos bodily injury and environmental property damage claims, insurers have been arguing for the adoption of the manifestation trigger.

While insurers fared poorly in their efforts to have courts apply a manifestation trigger to claims for asbestos bodily injury and environmental property damage, they have had a slightly better showing when the subject at hand has been construction defects. *See Korossy v. Sunrise Homes, Inc.*, 653 So. 2d 1215, 1226 (La. Ct. App. 1995) ("We find the manifestation theory should be applied in this case. The differential settlement resulted from each home's continuous or repeated exposure to the injurious conditions over a course of time, but the effects of the excessive settlement did not become 'damage' until it was discovered by the homeowners.").

But just as in the case of asbestos bodily injury and environmental property damage, the continuous and injury in fact triggers have enjoyed much success in coverage litigation for construction defects. *See Don's Bldg. Supply, Inc. v. OneBeacon Ins. Co.*, 267 S.W.3d 20, 24 (Tex. 2008). "[P]roperty damage occurred when a home that is the subject of an underlying suit suffered wood rot or other physical damage. The date that the physical damage is or could have been discovered is irrelevant under the policy." *Id.* "This policy links coverage to damage, not damage detection." *Id.* at 29. "The policy asks when damage happened, not whether it was manifest, patent, visible, apparent, obvious, perceptible, discovered, discoverable, capable of detection, or anything similar." *Id.* at 30; *see also Sentinel Ins. Co., Ltd. v. First Ins. Co. of Hawaii, Ltd.*, 875 P.2d 894, 917–18 (Hawaii 1994). "The injury-in-fact trigger is... true to the terms of the CGL policy and suitable for any type of injury." *Id.* at 917. The court concluded that all policies issued to a contractor, that were on the risk from shortly after completion of an apartment complex in 1981, to settlement of the underlying action in 1988, were potentially obligated to provide coverage. *Id.* at 918. The court also held that, if an insurer cannot establish with reasonable certainty which damages occurred during its policy period, then the continuous trigger would apply. *Id.*

In addition to construction defects, efforts have been made by policyholders, in a host of other claim scenarios, to obtain coverage under multiple policies on the basis that injury or damage was continuous. The issue also arises in the context of policyholders attempting to advocate for bodily injury or property damage taking place at a certain time—on account of a lack of coverage during the period when the insurer maintains that such injury or damage took place. As the following fifty-state survey of the issue demonstrates, the facts of these claims differ widely. For this reason there is no consensus that can describe the results of these efforts.

Chapter 15 addressed trigger of coverage for claims involving toxic torts and environmental property damage. This chapter addresses trigger of coverage for claims for (1) construction defects; (2) random scenarios in which efforts have been made by policyholders to establish that more than one general liability policy is obligated to provide coverage for ongoing, but unknown, bodily injury or property damage; and (3) bodily injury or property damage taking place at a time that the insurer maintains there was no policy in place. When reviewing this issue, reference should be made to Chapter 15 and the manner in which the relevant state responded to trigger arguments in the toxic tort and environmental property damage arenas. It is possible that the court, confronted with a trigger argument in a less traditional context, will look for guidance from traditional claims.

## 50-State Survey: Trigger of Coverage for Construction Defects and Non-Latent Injury and Damage Claims

**Alabama:** The Supreme Court of Alabama held that "as a general rule the time of an 'occurrence' of an accident within the meaning of an indemnity policy is not the time the wrongful act is committed but the time the complaining party was actually damaged." *Am. States Ins. Co. v. Martin*, 662 So. 2d 245, 250 (Ala. 1995) (citation and quotation omitted). The court concluded that mental anguish sustained by investors that lost money in a real estate business was not covered because such "bodily injury" was not experienced until after the policies expired. *Id.* The court observed that, under the terms of the policy, "an injury, and not an occurrence that causes injury, must fall within the policy period for it to be covered." *Id.* The court rejected the argument that the policies should be triggered because the incidents that led to the mental anguish occurred during the policy periods. *Id.*

**Alaska:** The Supreme Court of Alaska held that no coverage was owed under a liability policy issued to a garage where such policy was no longer on the risk at the time that a truck—on which the garage had previously performed brake service—was involved in an accident that killed and injured several people. *Makarka v. Great Am. Ins. Co.*, 14 P.3d 964, 969 (Alaska 2000). The court noted that the policy limited coverage to bodily injury occurring during the policy period. *Id.* at 968. "This language cannot reasonably be read as a reference to negligent acts that predate the occurrence of injury." *Id.* Therefore, the policy on the risk at the time that the garage performed the faulty brake servicing was not obligated to provide coverage. *Id.* at 968–69.

**Arizona:** The Court of Appeals of Arizona held that, in the context of a construction defect claim, coverage is owed for ongoing property damage that occurs during the policy period even if other similar damage preceded that damage. *Lennar Corp. v. Auto-Owners Ins. Co.*, 151 P.3d 538, 549 (Ariz. Ct. App. 2007). At issue were policies on the risk *after* the property damage manifested. *Id.* at 548. The court rejected the insurers' argument that all of the property damage should be deemed to have occurred when the first property damage manifested itself. *Id.* at 548. The appeals court declined to address the insurers' "known loss" argument because, since the issue was not raised in the trial court, there were insufficient facts for the court to evaluate. *Id.* at 549.

**Arkansas:** An Arkansas District Court held that "[t]he generally accepted rule is that the time of the occurrence of an accident within the meaning of an indemnity policy is not the time when the wrongful act was committed, but the time when the complaining party was actually damaged.... It is immaterial when the event which caused the injury took place; the deciding factor is when the injury occurred." *Valiant Ins. Co. v. Hamilton Funeral Serv. Ctrs.*, 926 F. Supp. 127, 129 (W.D. Ark. 1996) (citations omitted). Accordingly, no coverage was owed to a funeral home under a policy that was off the risk at the time that relatives discovered the condition of an exhumed body due to leakage of the casket and vault. *Id.*

**California:** The Court of Appeal of California discussed *Montrose Chemical Corp. v. Admiral Ins. Co.*, 913 P.2d 878 (Cal. 1995) at length and held that, because a tile manufacturer's injury from dust, emitted by a recycler, was continuous over multiple liability policy periods, all such policies were triggered, even though one insurer specifically covered the recycler's "tub grinding" which allegedly caused different type of damage by generating dust. *Stonelight Tile, Inc. v. California Ins. Guarantee Assn.*, 150 Cal. App. 4th 19, 35 (2007); *see also Garriott Crop Dusting Company v. Superior Court*, 270 Cal. Rptr. 678, 682 (Cal. Ct. App. 1990) (policy can be triggered even if the claimant did not yet own the damaged property during the policy period) ("Nowhere do the policies say to whom that property must belong, save that it must not belong to the insured. In other words, the policies themselves do not expressly require that the eventual claimant own the property at the time the property is damaged for coverage to ensue; they merely require that the damage, the 'physical injury to... tangible property,' take place during the policy period."); *Standard Fire Ins. Co. v. Spectrum Community Ass'n*, 46 Cal. Rptr.3d 804 (Cal. Ct. App. 2006) (following *Garriott*).

**Colorado:** The Court of Appeals of Colorado rejected a manifestation trigger and adopted an exposure trigger in the context of a claim for corrosion of a roof constructed by the insured. *Am. Employer's Ins. Co. v. Pinkard Constr. Co.*, 806 P.2d 954, 956 (Colo. Ct. App. 1990). "Although predominantly applied in asbestos cases involving progressive bodily injury, the exposure theory has been applied to cases dealing with property damage of the continuous and progressive type." *Id.* "Here, the damage slowly progressed.

And, although not immediately apparent, the evidence shows that progressive and continuous deterioration of the roof infected the integrity of the structure causing actual property damage during the respective policy periods." *Id.; see also Hoang v. Assurance Co. of Am.*, 149 P.3d 798 (Colo. 2007) (following *Garriott, see* California).

**Connecticut:** An Iowa District Court, applying Connecticut law, expressly rejected a manifestation trigger and adopted an injury-in-fact trigger for purposes of damage caused by construction defects. *Weitz Co., LLC v. Travelers Cas. & Sur. Co. of Am.*, 266 F. Supp. 2d 984, 1000 (D. Iowa 2003) (applying Connecticut law) (relying on *Aetna Cas. & Sur. Co. v. Abbott Laboratories, Inc.*, 636 F. Supp. 546 (D. Conn. 1986) which discussed *American Home Products Corp. v. Liberty Mut. Ins. Co.*, 748 F.2d 760 (2nd Cir. 1984) and concluded that "injury" did not mean "manifestation of injury").

**Delaware:** A Delaware trial court held that an injury-in-fact trigger applied to a claim under a homeowners policy for progressive damage to an insured's home. *See Carlozzi v. Fid. & Cas. Co.*, No. 99C-03–083JRS, 2001 WL 755385, at \*5 (Del. Sup. Ct. May 3, 2001). "Regardless of the cause of the water saturation, it is undisputed in the record that water saturation caused the foundation of the home to settle which resulted in damage to the home over an extended period of time. This extended period of time reached into the 1997 Policy period. Thus, the ongoing water damage was part of 'a series of related events… [which]… cause[d]… property damage during the policy period…' In other words, since progressive damage occurred during the 1997 Policy period, the 1997 Policy provides coverage unless the loss is otherwise excluded." *Id.* at \*6 (alteration in original). While *Carlozzi* involved coverage under a homeowner's policy, the policy language at issue, as well as the court's rationale for its decision, suggests that it would apply in the context of determining trigger of coverage for a construction defect claim under a general liability policy.

**Florida:** The Eleventh Circuit Court of Appeals rejected a manifestation trigger and adopted an injury-in-fact trigger for purposes of damage caused by construction defects. *Trizec Props., Inc. v. Biltmore Constr. Co.*, 767 F.2d 810, 813 (11th Cir. 1985) (applying Florida law). "It is the damage itself which must occur during the policy period for coverage to be effective. Here, the actual date that the damage occurred is not expressly alleged, but the language of the complaint, 'at least marginally and by reasonable implication,' could be construed to allege that the damage (cracking and leaking of roof deck with resultant rusting) may have begun to occur immediately after installation, 1971 to 1975, and continued gradually thereafter over a period of time." *Id.* (citation and quotation admitted). *But see Harris Specialty Chems., Inc. v. U.S. Fire Ins. Co.*, No. 3:98-CV-351-J-20B, 2000 WL 34533982, at \*12 (M.D. Fla. July 7, 2000) (court applied a manifestation trigger to claims for discoloration of the exterior of buildings that took place about three to five years after a water sealant was applied); *Mid-Continent Cas. Co. v. Frank*

*Casserino Construction, Inc.*, No. 6:09-cv-1065, 2010 WL 2431900, at *5 (M.D. Fla. June 16, 2010) (construction defect) ("In Florida... coverage under a CGL policy is triggered when property damage manifests itself, not when the negligent act or omission giving rise to the damage occurs.") (citing cases, including *Harris Specialty*, and noting that *Trizec* involved duty to defend and that the *Trizec* Court concluded that it did not need to address whether damage must manifest itself before coverage is triggered); *Arnett v. Mid-Continent Cas. Co.*, No. 8:08-CV-2373-T-27EAJ, 2010 WL 2821981, at *7-8 (M.D. Fla. July 16, 2010) (addressing fact issues over the time that property damage caused by faulty construction manifested). In *N. River Ins. Co. v. Broward County Sheriff's Office*, 428 F. Supp. 2d 1284, 1290 (S.D. Fla. 2006), the court concluded that the policy on the risk at the time of arrest and incarceration—being when the underlying plaintiff was actually harmed—is triggered for purposes of malicious prosecution. *Id.* However, the court was clear in distinguishing its decision from *Trizec Prop.* on the basis of the different factual underpinnings: "[T]he multiple trigger theory has been adopted in very limited circumstances, such as asbestosis, where the injuries caused by exposure do not manifest themselves until a substantial time after the exposure causing the injury." *Id.* at 1291 (citation omitted).

**Georgia:** A Georgia District Court held that a continuous trigger applied to a claims against an exterminator for property damage caused by termites. *Arrow Exterminators, Inc. v. Zurich Am. Ins. Co.*, 136 F. Supp. 2d 1340, 1349 (N.D. Ga. 2001). By so concluding, policies off the risk before the damage was discovered were nonetheless obligated to provide coverage because the damage occurred before the policies expired. *Id.*; *see also Ameristeel Corp. v. Employers Mut. Cas. Co.*, No. 7:96-CV-85 HL, 2005 WL 1785283, at *3 (M.D. Ga. July 26, 2005) ("Although Georgia courts have not ruled on the question, federal district courts in all three of Georgia's districts have applied Georgia law to 'occurrence' policies with similar terms to hold that exposure during dates of coverage to conditions that result in property damage constitutes an 'occurrence' within the meaning of these insurance contracts.") (citations and quotation omitted).

**Hawaii:** The Supreme Court of Hawaii held that an injury-in-fact trigger applied to a claim for property damage caused by construction defects. *Sentinel Ins. Co., Ltd. v. First Ins. Co. of Hawaii, Ltd.*, 875 P.2d 894, 917–18 (Hawaii 1994). "The injury-in-fact trigger is... true to the terms of the CGL policy and suitable for any type of injury." *Id.* at 917. The court concluded that all policies issued to a contractor, that were on the risk from shortly after completion of an apartment complex in 1981, to settlement of the underlying action in 1988, were potentially obligated to provide coverage. *Id.* at 918. The court also held that, if an insurer cannot establish with reasonable certainty which damages occurred during its policy period, then the continuous trigger would apply. *Id.*

**Idaho:** The Supreme Court of Idaho held that, for purposes of various claims arising out of a wrongful conviction, the occurrence took place when the resulting injury first manifested itself, which was at the time of arrest, charging, or prosecution (depending on the claim). *Idaho Counties Risk Mgmt. Program Underwriters v. Northland Ins. Cos.*, 205 P.3d 1220, 1225–26 (Idaho 2009). Thus, no coverage was owed to a municipality under policies issued to it several years after these events took place. *Id.* at 1228. Notwithstanding that the underlying plaintiff alleged "continuing torts," the court observed that "[r]eliance on the commencement of the statute of limitation is not dispositive in determining when a tort occurs for insurance purposes. Statutes of limitation and triggering dates for insurance purposes serve distinct functions and reflect different policy concerns." *Id.* at 1226. While the court used the term "manifestation," at issue was the availability of coverage for injury that allegedly took place *after* such manifestation.

**Illinois:** The Appellate Court of Illinois rejected a discovery trigger and adopted a continuous trigger for purposes of claims involving asbestos in buildings. *U.S. Gypsum Co. v. Admiral Ins. Co.*, 643 N.E.2d 1226, 1255–56 (Ill. App. Ct. 1994). "Our decision is consistent with the basic principles announced in *Zurich* [*Ins. Co. v. Raymark Indus., Inc.*, 514 N.E.2d 150 (Ill. 1987)] and *Wilkin* [*U.S. Fidelity & Guar. Co. v. Wilkin Insulation Co.*, 578 N.E.2d 926 (Ill. 1991)]. The supreme court's use of a triple trigger in *Zurich* recognizes that multiple policy periods can be triggered by the evolving nature of an illness resulting from the exposure to asbestos. Similarly, our application of a continuous trigger recognizes that the property damage that results from the release of asbestos fibers and the reentrainment of asbestos fibers is a continuing process which necessarily occurs over multiple policy periods. The *Zurich* decision looks beyond the discreet event of the manifestation of the disease as the sole trigger. Similarly, the seductive appeal of a single discovery trigger must bow to the policy language as well as to the empirical realities and other general equitable considerations of reasonableness and fairness." *Id.* at 1257.

**Indiana:** An Indiana District Court held that property damage took place from the time that defective concrete was poured through the time at which a third party discovered or was notified of the damage to its property and had an opportunity to prevent further damage from the defective concrete. *Irving Materials, Inc. v. Zurich Am. Ins. Co.*, No. 1:03-CV-361, 2007 WL 1035098, at *16 (S.D. Ind. Mar. 30, 2007). "[Insured's] expert determined that the distress produced by the alkali carbonate reactivity in the coarse aggregate provided... resulted in the property damage that occurred and was occurring during the September 1999 to September 2001 time period. This damage was not limited to the concrete itself but collaterally as well from the shoving, buckling, or crushing of adjacent materials, structures, and joints." *Id.* (citation omitted).

**Iowa:** An Iowa District Court applied an actual injury trigger in the context of claims for property damage caused by the insured's defective windows.

*Liberty Mut. Ins. Co. v. Pella Corp.*, 631 F. Supp. 2d 1134, 1135 (S.D. Iowa 2009). "Under Iowa law, property damage is deemed to occur at the time that the underlying claimant sustained or allegedly sustained any injury or damage. Successive policies may be triggered as long as the factual allegations contained in the underlying complaint permit a finding of continuing damage." *Id.* at 1134–35 (citation omitted).

**Kansas:** No instructive authority.

**Kentucky:** A Kentucky District Court suggested that an actual injury trigger may apply in the context of coverage for a construction defect claim. *Generali U.S. Branch v. Nat'l Trust Ins. Co.*, No. 5:07-CV-139, 2009 WL 2762273, at *5 (W.D. Ky. Aug. 27, 2009). For purposes of allocation, the court observed that there was some evidence that damage to a house was "ongoing and continuous through several policy periods." *Id.* While the court did not undertake allocation, it was because it was not convinced that the damage was not divisible or allocable between the policy periods. *Id.*; *see also Acuity Ins. Co. v. Higdon's Sheet Metal & Supply Co.*, No. 3:06-CV-162-H, 2007 WL 1034986, at *3 (W.D. Ky. 2007) ("Although some states have adopted a coverage trigger theory to establish the date of loss for determining when coverage is triggered… Kentucky has not done so. Instead, coverage is determined by examining the terms of the policies at issue.").

**Louisiana:** The Court of Appeal of Louisiana held that a manifestation trigger applied to termite infestation because the effects of such infestation "did not become 'damage' until it was discovered by the homeowners." *James Pest Control, Inc. v. Scottsdale Ins. Co.*, 765 So. 2d 485, 491 (La. Ct. App. 2000) (following *Korossy v. Sunrise Homes, Inc.*, 653 So. 2d 1215 (La. Ct. App. 1995) which adopted a manifestation trigger for property damage caused by construction defect). "[T]he application of manifestation theory eliminates the difficult factual issue of determining when a hidden property damage actually occurs, a proof problem that is not as difficult in asbestos cases when the dates of injurious exposure to a substance can usually be determined." *Id.*; *see also Oxner v. Montgomery*, 794 So. 2d 86, 93 (La. Ct. App. 2001) (following *Korossy* and *James Pest Control* and holding that a manifestation trigger applied to property damage caused by construction defect).

**Maine:** A Maine District Court held that a manifestation trigger applied to damage to a large industrial paper dryer designed and built by the insured. *Honeycomb Sys., Inc. v. Admiral Ins. Co.*, 567 F. Supp. 1400, 1405 (D. Me. 1983). "The general rule is that an occurrence happens when the injurious effects of the occurrence become 'apparent,' or 'manifest themselves.'" *Id.* However, more recently, a Vermont District Court, applying Maine law, held that Maine would adopt an injury-in-fact and continuous trigger standard to determine when property damage caused by construction defect occurred. *Travelers Indem. Co. v. Acadia Ins. Co.*, No. 1:08-CV-92, 2009 WL 1320965, at *7 (D. Vt. May 8, 2009). "[U]nder Maine law, coverage for progressive property damage is triggered under a standard occurrence-based CGL policy when property damage occurs (without regard to when it becomes manifest), and continuously thereafter while the damage is ongoing." *Id.* The court distinguished *Honeycomb Systems* on the basis that, unlike construction defect, that case "did not present a factual situation in which property suffered an injury that went unnoticed until the injury progressed to an advanced stage over time." *Id.*

**Maryland:** No instructive authority.

**Massachusetts:** A Massachusetts trial court held that an injury-in-fact trigger applied to a claim against a gun manufacturer, whose employee stole handgun components, assembled the guns, and sold them on the black market, one of which ended up in the hands of a drug-dealer who used it to injure one person and kill another. *Hernandez v. Scottsdale Ins. Co.*, No. 050758D, 2009 WL 2603361, at *7 (Mass. Super. Ct. Aug. 6, 2009). After examining various trigger theories, the court held that "[i]n this case, a jury could find that the occurrence comprised a host of negligent acts taking place over the course of nine months. Yet the appropriate trigger of coverage in these circumstances is the injury-in-fact theory, which implicates only the policy period during which injuries or damages can be proven." *Id.* Therefore, only the policy on the risk at the time that the underlying plaintiffs were shot was obligated to provide coverage. *Id.; see also Certain Interested Underwriters at Lloyds of London v. Boston Group Dev., Inc.*, No. 011885, 2002 WL 799710, at *3 (Mass. Super. Ct. Feb. 26, 2002) (addressing differences in trigger of coverage between environmental and nonenvironmental claims).

**Michigan:** The Sixth Circuit Court of Appeals, applying Michigan law, adopted an injury-in-fact trigger for purposes of property damage caused by the insured's defective wood chips used at playgrounds. *Newby Intern., Inc. v. Nautilus Ins. Co.*, 112 Fed. App'x 397, 402 (6th Cir. 2004) (applying Michigan law). "Under the injury-in-fact approach, the operative date is the date upon which the wood chips supplied by PMI damaged the property of another, and not the date upon which the School District discovered the damage." *Id.* (relying on *Gelman Scis., Inc. v. Fid. & Cas. Co. of N.Y.*, 572 N.W.2d 617 (Mich. 1998), *overruled on other grounds by Wilkie v. Auto-Owners Ins. Co.*, 664 N.W.2d 776 (Mich. 2003)).

**Minnesota:** The Supreme Court of Minnesota held that an "actual injury" or "injury-in-fact" trigger applied for purposes of damage caused by construction defects. *Wooddale Builders, Inc. v. Md. Cas. Co.*, 722 N.W.2d 283, 292 (Minn. 2006). "Under this rule, a liability policy is 'triggered' if the complaining party (here, the homeowner) is actually damaged during the policy period, regardless of when the underlying negligent act occurred. Thus, an insurer is on the risk with respect to a particular home if, during the period of one of its policies, there is property damage to that home—provided the damage results from a covered occurrence." *Id.* (citation omitted); *see also Donnelly Bros. Constr. Co., Inc. v. State Auto Prop. & Cas. Co.*, 759 N.W.2d 651, 656 (Minn. Ct. App. 2009) ("Minnesota applies an 'actual-injury' rule to determine whether insurance coverage has been triggered by an occurrence. To trigger a policy, the insured must show that some damage occurred during the policy period.") (citation and quotation omitted) (involving construction defects).

**Mississippi:** A Mississippi District Court, after reviewing various trigger theories, predicted that the Supreme Court of Mississippi would apply the continuous trigger to a claim for construction defects. *Essex Ins. Co. v. Massey Land & Timber, LLC*, No. 5:04 CV 102, 2006 WL 1454767, at *3 (S.D. Miss. 2006). The court concluded that, notwithstanding that certain dirt work performed by the insured, at a residential subdivision, was completed in August or September 1999, a policy on the risk in December 2000, when damage was reported, was obligated to provide coverage. *Id.* at *4.

**Missouri:** The Supreme Court of Missouri held that an occurrence policy "covers cases of progressive injury where the cause of the damage is present during the policy period but the damage is not apparent until after the policy period." *D.R. Sherry Construction, Ltd. v. Am. Family Mut. Ins. Co.*, 316 S.W.3d 899, 905 (Mo. 2010) (coverage owed to a general contractor under a policy on the risk at the time of construction notwithstanding that foundation and drywall cracking did not manifest until after the policy period had expired). The insured-contractor succeeded in arguing that coverage was owed because "the damage began during the policy period and was progressive from that point forward. [The insured's] progressive damage theory was premised on allegations that unanticipated and repeated exposure to poor soil conditions under the house, beginning during the policy period, caused the house to settle out of level, which caused property damage to the house's foundation." *Id.* at 904-05. A Missouri District Court held that, for purposes of a claim for conspiracy to deprive a person of a fair trial, the triggering date for coverage is that on which the conspiring first took place. *Am. States Preferred Ins. Co. v. McKinley*, No. 07–0584CV, 2009 WL 1139122, at *8 (W.D. Mo. Apr. 28, 2009). The court based its decision on *Hampton v. Carter Enterprises, Inc.*, 238 S.W.3d 170 (Mo. Ct. App. 2007), where the Missouri Court of Appeals, while noting the continuing nature of conduct constituting malicious prosecution, concluded that the "triggering date for coverage should be limited to the date on which the party first continued the malicious prosecution." *Id.* (quoting *Hampton*, 238 S.W.3d at 177). "The *Hampton* court noted that the offense of malicious prosecution is committed with the institution of the underlying prosecution—the point at which the judicial process is maliciously invoked without probable cause, causing the victim's injury." *Id.*

**Montana:** The Supreme Court of Montana adopted an actual injury trigger for purposes of damage caused by construction defect. *Swank Enters., Inc. v. All Purpose Servs., Ltd.*, 154 P.3d 52, 56 (Mont. 2007). The court concluded that the improper application of paint to tanks at a water treatment plant constituted physical injury at the time of such application. *Id.* Accordingly, the policy on the risk at the time of application was triggered. In so holding, however, the court noted that "the fact that the discovery or diagnosis of the problem did not occur until after the 1997 policy period is of no consequence. A 'physical injury' can occur even though the injury is not 'diagnosable,' 'compensable,' or manifest during the policy period as long as it can be determined, even retroactively, that some injury did occur during the policy period." *Id.* (citing *In re Silicone Implant Litig.*, 667 N.W.2d 405, 415 (Minn. 2003)) (quotations omitted).

**Nebraska:** A Nebraska District Court rejected a manifestation trigger and adopted an injury-in-fact trigger for a claim under a first-party property policy for process liquid tanks that were damaged due to ongoing settlement of unstable soil beneath the tanks. *Kaapa Ethanol, L.L.C. v. Affiliated FM Ins., Co.*, No. 7:05CV5010, 2008 WL 2986277, at *33 (D. Neb. July 29, 2008). "[T]he rule in the vast majority of the courts to have addressed the issue, is that coverage is triggered from the date of the first latent injury/damage and continues to be triggered at least until the date the injury/damage first becomes manifest. Since coverage is triggered in the event of an injury/damage during the policy period, the foregoing rule merely comports with the express terms of the policy. The same rule should be applied in interpreting similar policy language, whether the claim is for first party or third party coverage." *Id.* "[I]f faced with the question, Nebraska would adhere to the 'injury-in-fact' trigger and hold that in first party property insurance cases, coverage for property loss or damage that has progressed over time occurs when the damage commenced, not merely when it was discovered." *Id.*

**Nevada:** The Supreme Court of Nevada held that a manifestation trigger applied to a first-party property policy for purposes of cracks in the walls of a residence that occurred during several policy periods but were not discovered until a later policy was in effect. *Jackson v. State Farm Fire & Cas. Co.*, 835 P.2d 786, 789 (Nev. 1992). The court distinguished progressive property damage from asbestos cases and adopted the reasoning of *Prudential-LMI Com. Insurance v. Superior Court*, 798 P.2d 1230 (Cal. 1990) that, "[b]efore the manifestation, the loss is a mere contingency whereby the insured has not yet suffered a compensable loss." *Id.*; *see also United National Ins. Co. v. Frontier Ins. Co., Inc.*, 99 P.3d 1153, 1157 (Nev. 2004) (holding that policy on the risk at the time that a hotel marquee sign was negligently installed was not obligated to provide coverage for its collapse that occurred after the policy expired) ("[R]eading the word 'occurrence' and the phrase 'property damage' together, we conclude that the policy language is unambiguous and requires that tangible, physical injury must occur during the CGL policy period for coverage to be triggered under either prong of the definition."). In *Day Construction Co. v. Clarendon American Ins. Co.*, 459 F. Supp. 2d 1039, 1045–46 (D. Nev. 2006), the court noted that the Supreme Court of Nevada had never squarely addressed which trigger of coverage theory applied to liability policies. The court discussed *Jackson* and ultimately concluded that it need not predict which theory the Nevada high court might adopt because the policy at issue required "both the 'property damage' and an 'occurrence' giving rise to the property damage to occur within the Policy period. In addition, the Policy explicitly contracts out of the continuous exposure theory by way of the 'deemer' provision, wherein Clarendon avoids liability for property damage arising prior to the inception of, but continuing into, its Policy term." *Id.* at 1046.

**New Hampshire:** A New Hampshire District Court applied an injury-in-fact trigger to a claim for damages caused by the negligent construction of extraction and injection wells at a Superfund site. *MACTEC Eng'g & Consulting, Inc. v. OneBeacon Ins. Co.*, No. 06-CV-466, 2007 WL 2300706, at *3 (D.N.H. Aug. 8, 2007) (citing *EnergyNorth Natural Gas, Inc. v. Underwriters at Lloyd's, London*, 150 N.H. 828, 836 (2004)). Nonetheless, the court concluded that only a single policy was triggered because it was the only one on the risk at the time that the property damage was occurring. *Id.*

**New Jersey:** The Superior Court of New Jersey, Appellate Division, declined to automatically apply a continuous trigger to claims for damages caused by the incorporation of defective fire-retardant plywood into roofing systems of residential construction. *Aetna Cas. & Sur. Co. v. Ply Gem Indus., Inc.*, 778 A.2d 1132, 1146 (N.J. Super. Ct. App. Div. 2001). "[A]ll that is evident from the pleadings and documents in this record with respect to the Maryland complaints is that the FRTP which Hoover manufactured, and upon which these suits against Hoover are based, was installed within the policy periods and caused damage to other property at some point in time. There is no allegation as to when the property damage occurred and thus, no way to determine, without more, whether the allegations of property damage caused by the insured's product were covered claims because they occurred during the policy periods." *Id.* "At least in the absence of more proofs, we reject the theory that the 'continuous trigger' or 'progressive damage' theory requires us to conclude there was 'property damage' upon installation." *Id.*; *see also Crivelli v. Selective Ins. Co. of Am.*, No. 4358–02, 2005 WL 2649314, at *3 (N.J. Super. Ct. App. Div. Sept. 27, 2005) (holding that no coverage was owed under a policy on the risk after negligent installation of a roof because there was no evidence of ongoing or progressive injury or damage commencing at the time of installation).

**New Mexico:** No instructive authority.

**New York:** The Supreme Court of New York, Appellate Division, held that an insurer that issued a policy that was on the risk on the date that a criminal prosecution was terminated in favor of the accused was not obligated to provide coverage for a malicious prosecution claim. *Newfane v. General Star Nat. Ins. Co.*, 784 N.Y.S.2d 787, 791 (N.Y. App. Div. 2004). The court held that malicious prosecution was deemed to have occurred on the date that the criminal prosecution was instituted without probable cause (here, more than a decade before the relevant policy was issued). *Id.* at 793; *see also MRI*

*Broadway Rental, Inc. v. U.S. Mineral Products Co.*, 704 N.E.2d 550, 553 (N.Y. 1998) (characterizing its decision in *Sturges Mfg. Co. v. Utica Mut. Ins. Co.*, 332 N.E.2d 319 (N.Y. 1975) as adopting the installation date as the time of injury-in-fact when a defective component product is integrated into a larger product) (defective ski straps used in the manufacture of ski bindings); *Maryland Cas. Co. v. W.R. Grace and Co.*, 23 F.3d 617, 627 (2nd Cir. 1992) (applying New York law) (applying the injury-in-fact trigger from *Cont'l Cas. Co. v. Rapid-American Corp.*, 609 N.E.2d 506 (N.Y. 1993) and holding that claims for asbestos in buildings trigger the policy on the risk at the time of installation of asbestos—regardless of whether it had been discovered by the building owner).

**North Carolina:** The Supreme Court of North Carolina held that "where the date of the injury-in-fact can be known with certainty, the insurance policy or policies on the risk on that date are triggered." *Gaston County Dyeing Mach. Co. v. Northfield Ins. Co.*, 524 S.E.2d 558, 564 (N.C. 2000) (overruling *W. Am. Ins. Co. v. Tufco Flooring East, Inc.*, 409 S.E.2d 692 (N.C. Ct. App. 1991) to the extent that it purported to establish a bright-line rule that property damage occurs "for insurance purposes" at the time of manifestation or on the date of discovery). The court specifically declined to adopt the "continuous" or "multiple trigger" theory and concluded that, notwithstanding that the rupture of a pressure vessel caused ensuing property damage that continued over time, contaminating multiple dye lots and extending over two policy periods, because the injury-in-fact occurred on a date certain, only the policies on the risk on the date of the injury-causing event were triggered. *Id.* at 565; *see also Hutchinson v. Nationwide Mut. Fire Ins. Co.*, 594 S.E.2d 61, 64 (N.C. Ct. App. 2004) ("Assuming *arguendo* that the damage was caused by the continual entry of water, if it can be determined with certainty that the entry of water was caused by faulty construction pre-dating insurance coverage, defendants are not liable for plaintiffs' damages.").

**North Dakota:** The Supreme Court of North Dakota held that the liability policy on the risk at the time that the complaining party was "actually damaged" is obligated to provide coverage. *Grinnell Mut. Reinsurance Co. v. Thies*, 755 N.W.2d 852, 859 (N.D. 2008). The court concluded that homeowner's (liability) policies issued to the seller of a home were not obligated to provide coverage for a claim brought by the purchaser for mold damage that had existed prior to the sale but was not discovered until after the sale and the seller's policies had expired. *Id.* at 854. The policy's definition of "occurrence" required "property damage" "during the policy period." *Id.* at 856. The court concluded that such language supported a conclusion that the occurrence happened when the complaining party was actually damaged, rather than when any mold may have accumulated. *Id.* at 859. The *Grinnell* Court followed its decision in *Friendship Homes, Inc. v. Am. States Ins. Cos.*, 450 N.W.2d 778 (N.D. 1990), which held that, in the context of a third-party claim, policy language that requires damage to "occur during the policy period" means when the complaining party was actually injured. *Id.* at 859 (citing *Friendship Homes* at 779–80).

**Ohio:** The Court of Appeals of Ohio held that a continuous trigger applied to property damage caused by construction defect. *Westfield Ins. Co. v. Milwaukee Ins. Co.*, No. CA2004–12–298, 2005 WL 2179312, at *3 (Ohio Ct. App. Sept. 12, 2005). "[T]here is no requirement that the damage 'manifest' itself during the policy period. Rather, it is the damage itself which must occur during the policy period for coverage to be effective." *Id.* (citation and quotation omitted); *accord Plum v. W. Am. Ins. Co.*, No. C-050115, 2006 WL 256881 (Ohio Ct. App. Feb. 3, 2006). However, in *Fidelity & Guaranty Ins. Underwriters, Inc. v. Nationwide Tanks, Inc.*, No. C-1-03–843, 2006 WL 462443, at *4 (S.D. Ohio Feb. 22, 2006), the court declined to apply a continuous trigger to damage caused when an above-ground storage tank ruptured. "While damage to the tank itself from corrosion may have occurred continuously, including during the policy period, the injuries… alleged in the underlying case did not involve long-term exposure or delayed manifestation injuries. The injuries here occurred in one fell swoop, well outside the policy period, when the tank burst on March 3, 2000." *Id.*

**Oklahoma:** No instructive authority. *See Bituminous Cas. Corp. v. Cowen Constr., Inc.*, 55 P.3d 1030, 1032 (Okla. 2002) (concluding that there was no need to reach a certified question that sought the appropriate trigger of coverage for claims against a contractor, for negligent construction of a venting system in a dialysis unit of a hospital, that caused lead poisoning of patients); *see also Ball v. Wilshire Ins. Co.*, 184 P.3d 463, 465 n.8 (Okla. 2007) (recognizing that, in *Cowen*, the Supreme Court of Oklahoma declined to answer one of two certified questions where response to one disposed of the case).

**Oregon:** An Oregon District Court held that an injury-in-fact trigger applied to property damage caused by construction defect. *MW Builders, Inc. v. Safeco Ins. Co. of Am.*, No. CV 02–1578, 2009 WL 995050, at *11 (D. Or. Jan. 28, 2009). "Based on the uncontroverted evidence in the record, the court finds that the property damage to the Hotel began after its substantial completion in June 1997, and continued through 2000… . Oregon law finds coverage under a CGL policy for property damage that occurs during a policy period. Accordingly, coverage under each… policy in effect from June 1997, until September 2000, has been triggered." *Id.* at *13; *see also California Ins. Co. v. Stimson Lumber Co.*, No. 01–514, 2004 WL 1173185, at *13 (D. Or. May 26, 2004) (applying injury-in-fact trigger in the context of claims for property damage caused by the insured's defective siding).

**Pennsylvania:** The Superior Court of Pennsylvania adopted a manifestation trigger for purposes of a medical malpractice claim. *D'Auria v. Zurich Ins. Co.*, 507 A.2d 857, 862 (Pa. Super. Ct. 1986) (holding that the policy on the risk at the time that renal failure manifested was triggered and not policies on the risk while the patient was negligently treated by the physician); *see also Peerless Ins. Co. v. Brooks Sys. Corp.*, 617 F. Supp. 2d 348, 357–58

(E.D. Pa. 2008) (following *D'Auria* and predicting that the Supreme Court of Pennsylvania would adopt a manifestation trigger for purposes of a construction defect claim); *Consulting Eng'rs, Inc. v. Ins. Co. of N. Am.*, 710 A.2d 82, 88 (Pa. Super. Ct. 1998) (adopting a manifestation trigger for purposes of Wrongful Use of Civil Proceedings). "Here, we are not faced with a situation where the injuries, occasioned by the tort, lay dormant for extended periods. When the allegedly wrongful suit is filed, the injuries caused by the tort-humiliation, damage to reputation, suspense, physical hardship and legal expenses-manifest themselves and become evident to a reasonable defendant and, by implication, to the initiator of the wrongful proceedings." *Id.* at 87–88; *Coregis Ins. Co. v. City of Harrisburg*, No. 1:03-CV-920, 2006 WL 860710, at *10–11 (M.D. Pa. Mar. 30, 2006) (following *Consulting Engineers* and adopting a manifestation trigger for purposes of malicious prosecution).

**Rhode Island:** A Rhode Island trial court adopted an actual injury trigger for purposes of "bodily injury" (and mental injury) claims by adoptive parents, against an adoption agency, for withholding medical and family history information from them concerning an adopted child. *Travelers Indem. Co. v. Children's Friend & Serv., Inc.*, No. PC98–2187, 2005 WL 3276224, at *13 (R.I. Super. Ct. Dec. 1, 2005). The court concluded that "bodily injury" may have been sustained during the period of six policies issued to the adoption agency that were on the risk subsequent to the date of the adoption. *Id.* The court rejected the insurer's argument that the injury could not have been sustained later than the date of adoption because that was when "the parents were denied the opportunity to make a meaningful decision about whether to adopt a child and as a result have taken on an economic (and emotional) obligation to rear a child whom they might not have adopted had they been fully informed." *Id.* at *12.

**South Carolina:** The Supreme Court of South Carolina held that "a modified continuous trigger theory [applied] for determining when coverage is triggered under a standard occurrence policy. 'Under this theory, coverage is triggered whenever the damage can be shown in fact to have first occurred, even if it is before the damage became apparent, and the policy in effect at the time of the injury-in-fact covers all the ensuing damages.' Coverage is also triggered under every policy applicable thereafter." *Century Indem. Co. v. Golden Hills Builders, Inc.*, 561 S.E.2d 355, 357 (S.C. 2002) (quoting *Joe Harden Builders, Inc. v. Aetna Cas. & Sur. Co.*, 486 S.E.2d 89, 91 (S.C. 1997)). "This theory covers instances where an insured may be able to prove in retrospect that damage occurred during the policy period even though damage was not yet manifested at the time." *Joe Harden Builders*, 486 S.E.2d at 91 (addressing coverage for cracks to a brick wall); *see also Pharmacists Mut. Ins. Co. v. Scyster*, 232 Fed. App'x 217, 226 (4th Cir. 2007) (following *Joe Harden Builders* and holding that coverage was owed under a pharmacist's professional liability policy for patients who received injections of a drug compounded by a pharmacist prior to the policy's effective date but who suffered symptoms and were diagnosed with meningitis during the policy period); *Liberty Mutual Fire Ins. Co. v. J.T. Walker Indus., Inc.*, No. 2:08–2043, 2010 WL 1345287, at *4–5 (D.S.C. Mar. 30, 2010) (following *Century Indem. Co.* and *Joe Harden Builders*).

**South Dakota:** A South Dakota District Court held that a complaint filed by a city, against an architectural firm, for negligence in the performance of services related to the construction of a waste treatment facility, did not cause damage to the city until the facility was turned over to it. *Kirkham, Michael & Assocs., Inc. v. Travelers Indem. Co.*, 361 F. Supp. 189, 193 (D.S.D. 1973), *aff'd* 493 F.2d 475 (8th Cir. 1974). While the court noted that the architect's conduct may have constituted a continuous course of wrongful acts of negligence, it held that "[i]t is the damage incurred by 'accident' that triggers the policies' coverage, not the preceding wrongful acts." *Id.* "Prior to the facility being turned over to the City for possession and operation the City never sustained any *actual* damages." *Id.* (emphasis in original).

**Tennessee:** The Court of Appeals of Tennessee held that no coverage was owed under policies that were on the risk at the time when an insured negligently constructed a tennis court that subsequently caused a retaining wall on the perimeter of the court to collapse. *State Auto Mut. Ins. Co. v. Shelby Mut. Ins. Co.*, No. C.A. 1162, 1988 WL 67155, at *3 (Tenn. Ct. App. June 30, 1988). "We hold that coverage of property damage caused by an occurrence as defined in the policy is limited to damage occurring during the policy period. The negligence of Playrite in constructing the tennis court was not an 'occurrence'; rather, it was the collapse of the wall that constituted an 'occurrence' under appellant's policy." *Id.* Therefore, no coverage was owed under a policy that expired two years prior to the collapse of the wall. *Id.*

**Texas:** The Supreme Court of Texas rejected a manifestation trigger and adopted an actual injury or injury-in-fact trigger for purposes of construction defect claims. *Don's Bldg. Supply, Inc. v. OneBeacon Ins. Co.*, 267 S.W.3d 20, 24 (Tex. 2008). "[P]roperty damage occurred when a home that is the subject of an underlying suit suffered wood rot or other physical damage. The date that the physical damage is or could have been discovered is irrelevant under the policy." *Id.* "This policy links coverage to damage, not damage detection." *Id.* at 29. "The policy asks when damage happened, not whether it was manifest, patent, visible, apparent, obvious, perceptible, discovered, discoverable, capable of detection, or anything similar." *Id.* at 30; *see also Pine Oak Builders, Inc. v. Great Am. Lloyds Ins. Co.*, 279 S.W.3d 650, 653 (Tex. 2009) ("'[T]he key date is when injury happens, not when someone happens upon it'—that is, the focus should be on 'when damage comes to pass, not when damage comes to light.'") (quoting *Don's Bldg. Supply*, 267 S.W.3d at 22); *Mid-Continent Cas. Co. v. Academy Development, Inc.*, No. H-08-21, 2010 WL 3489355 (S.D. Tex. Aug. 24, 2010) (applying the "actual injury" rule adopted in *Don's Building* to damage to lake-front homes caused by defectively constructed lake walls).

**Utah:** No instructive authority.

**Vermont:** No instructive authority. *See City of Burlington v. Hartford Steam Boiler Inspection & Ins. Co.*, 190 F. Supp. 2d 663, 679 n.13 (D. Vt. 2002) ("In finding that no 'accident' occurred during the policy period, the Court does not adopt or endorse any particular insurance coverage 'trigger theory,' but instead follows what the HIC Boiler Policy itself defines as the trigger.") (addressing first-party property coverage for defective welds in a boiler).

**Virginia:** No instructive authority. *See Sting Sec., Inc. v. First Mercury Syndicate, Inc.*, 791 F. Supp. 555 (D. Md. 1992) (applying Virginia law) ("[W]here the substance of the complaint concerns economic damage arising from a contractual relationship, the occurrence takes place when the injuries first manifest themselves.") (citation and quotation omitted). Despite the court's adoption of the "manifestation" label, the decision addressed an insurer's obligation to provide coverage under policies issued *after* the date that defects in a security guard scheduling system became evident.

**Washington:** The Court of Appeals of Washington adopted a continuous trigger for purposes of property damage caused by negligent construction. *Gruol Constr. Co., Inc. v. Ins. Co. of N. Am.*, 524 P.2d 427, 430 (Wash. Ct. App. 1974). At issue was coverage for damage to a building caused by dry rot which resulted from dirt having been piled against the box sills of the building by backfilling during construction. *Id.* at 429. "Here, the resulting damage was continuous; coverage was properly imposed under the language of the policy on INA and Northwestern Mutual even though the initial negligent act (the defective backfilling) took place within the period of Safeco's policy coverage." *Id.* at 430; *see also Walla Walla College v. Ohio Cas. Ins. Co.*, 204 P.3d 961, 965 (Wash. Ct. App. 2009) (distinguishing *Gruol* and holding that property damage resulted when an improperly installed underground gasoline storage tank ruptured and not at the time of installation, since insured sought coverage for property damage for contamination from the leak, not for damage to the tank itself).

**West Virginia:** A West Virginia District Court adopted a manifestation trigger for purposes of property damage caused by negligent construction. *Simpson-Littman Construction, Inc. v. Erie Ins. Prop. & Cas. Ins. Co.*, No. 3:09-0240, 2010 WL 3702601, at *13 (S.D.W.Va. Sept. 13, 2010). At issue was coverage for structural defects to a home caused by faulty construction of its foundation. The court adopted a manifestation trigger: "According to the plain language of the policy, property damage that occurs as a result of physical injury or destruction is deemed to have occurred at the time of the physical injury that caused the damage. In other words, the date on which the property damage is deemed to have occurred is the date of the actual injury (i.e., the date the cracks appeared in the interior walls of the home, in the brick exterior, or in the block and foundation). This finding is consistent with the language of [the] Policy[.]" *Id.*

**Wisconsin:** The Supreme Court of Wisconsin held that a continuous trigger applied to property damage caused by construction defect. *Am. Family Mut. Ins. Co. v. Am. Girl, Inc.*, 673 N.W.2d 65, 84 (Wis. 2004). "Settlement had reached eight inches by the spring of 1995, when the first policy was still in force, and continued throughout 1996 and into 1997, by which time it was approaching one foot. Accordingly, under the continuous trigger holdings of *Society Insurance* [*Co. v. Town of Franklin*, 607 N.W.2d 342 (Wis. Ct. App. 2000) (environmental property damage)] and *Wisconsin Electric* [*Power Co. v. Cal. Union Ins. Co.*, 419 N.W.2d 255 (Wis. Ct. App. 1987) (stray voltage from power supply causing injury to cows)] the policies for the years 1994–95, 1995–96, and 1996–97 cover this loss." *Id.*

**Wyoming:** No instructive authority.

# CHAPTER

# 17

# Allocation of Latent Injury and Damage Claims

Guy A. Cellucci and Shane R. Heskin[1]

The method of allocating damages for claims for latent bodily injury and property damage, sometimes called long-tail or continuous injury or damage, is a critical and determinative question of law that may substantially impact the amount of an insurance company's liability under a commercial general liability (CGL) policy. The two most common types of claims presenting this allocation question are asbestos bodily injury and environmental property damage.

Two principal approaches have been developed over the years by courts confronting the question. The clear majority of jurisdictions has adopted the pro rata method, where, in its purest form, damages are allocated evenly among all years in which bodily injury or property damage has occurred. To take a simple example, if bodily injury or property damage spanned ten years, a policyholder electing to purchase insurance only for one of those years, and consciously deciding to "go bare" for the remaining nine years, would be able to recover only 10 percent of the loss.

---

1. Messrs. Cellucci and Heskin are partners in the Commercial Litigation Department of White and Williams LLP in Philadelphia, where they specialize in the representation of insurance clients involved in national, complex commercial coverage disputes. They have a combination of over forty years of experience in representing and advising insurance, reinsurance, and business clients in the resolution of complex, multi-party disputes. Messrs. Cellucci and Heskin both served as lead trial counsel in *Boston Gas Co. v. Century Indem. Co.*, 910 N.E.2d. 290 (Mass. 2009), and successfully argued the insurer's position on allocation before the Massachusetts Supreme Judicial Court.

A minority of jurisdictions, however, has adopted the joint-and-several, sometimes called "all sums," method, whereby any one policy year is answerable up to its full policy limits for all losses resulting from all years in which bodily injury or property damage has occurred. Under this approach, it does not matter how many years the policyholder chose to "go bare" or how few years the insurer assumed risk. Returning to the ten-year hypothetical, the policyholder can collapse all ten years of continuous bodily injury or property damage into a single year of its choosing. In other words, the policyholder purchasing only one year of coverage is treated the same as the policyholder purchasing ten years of continuous coverage.

Advocates of pro rata allocation argue that proration of damages is required by the policy language limiting coverage to property damage occurring *during* the policy period. Pro rata allocation honors this plain limitation of coverage by *approximating* the "quantum of bodily injury or property damage" occurring during the policy period when the facts do not permit a more precise determination of the *actual* "quantum of bodily injury or property damage" occurring during each policy period. It is also consistent with the widely followed maxim that an insurance policy must be read as a whole without placing undue emphasis on one provision (all sums) over another (during the policy period limitation). This interpretation is further supported by the reasonable expectations of the parties as many courts have observed that "[n]o reasonable policyholder could have expected that a single one-year policy would cover all losses caused by [bodily injury] or toxic industrial wastes released into the environment over the course of several decades."[2] Public policy considerations also dictate proration. Among other things, "the pro rata method promotes judicial efficiency, engenders stability in the insurance market, provides incentive for responsible commercial behavior, and produces an equitable result."[3]

Conversely, proponents of the "all sums" method argue that the insurer's promise to pay "all sums" trumps the policy language limiting coverage to the bodily injury or property damage that occurs during the policy period. In addition, "all sums" proponents argue that the "other insurance" and number of occurrence clauses contemplate coverage for occurrences that continue both before and after the policy period.

Advocates for pro rata would counter that this interpretation confuses the concepts of concurrent coverage with successive coverage and the number of limits with scope of coverage. Pro rata advocates would also be quick to note that those decisions adopting "all sums" frequently solicit passionate dissents, while no state high court decision adopting pro rata has ever invoked a single dissent.

---

2. *Boston Gas Co. v. Century Indem. Co.*, 910 N.E.2d 290, 309 (Mass. 2009).
3. *Id.* at 311.

As discussed in the fifty-state survey that follows, the majority of state high courts expressly rejecting the "all sums" method, in favor of pro rata allocation, include Colorado, Connecticut, Kansas, Kentucky, Louisiana, Massachusetts, Minnesota, Nebraska, New Jersey, New Hampshire, New York, Utah, and Vermont. Numerous other appellate courts nationwide— including the Second, Third, Fourth, Fifth, Sixth, Seventh, Eighth, and Eleventh Circuit Courts of Appeals—also have rejected the joint-and-several, "all sums" method, in favor of pro rata allocation. The minority of state high courts applying the joint-and-several, "all sums" approach, in some form or another, include California, Delaware, Illinois, Ohio, Pennsylvania, Washington, Wisconsin, and arguably, Indiana. Many of these decisions, however, are limited based on the case specific facts or policy language at issue.

Even those states within the same general allocation camp, however, may vary on the application of that method. The three prevailing pro rata approaches are (1) pro rata, time-on-the risk, (2) pro rata, available coverage block, and (3) pro rata, by limits and years. Under the "time-on-the risk" method, loss is assigned in proportion to the amount of time that a carrier's policies were in effect (the numerator) as a percentage of the total period of time in which injury occurred (the denominator). Thus, in the ten-year scenario discussed earlier, if total damages are $100 million, each year is allocated $10 million. A primary insurer in any one of those years with limits of $1 million, for example, is thus responsible for its full limits; the next $9 million then flows to the excess layer in that same year. And if no excess insurance is available above the primary layer of $1 million, the policyholder is responsible for the remaining $9 million.

Significantly, under a pure time-on-the risk approach, it makes no difference if insurance was "unavailable" in certain years. As the Massachusetts Supreme Judicial Court explained:

> [T]he unavailability exception "effectively provides insurance where insurers made the calculated decision not to assume risk and not to accept premiums. In effect, because the policyholder could not buy insurance, it is treated as though it did by passing those uninsurable losses to insured periods." This would not be equitable to insurers if the insured purchased coverage for only a few years where there was protracted damage.[4]

In order to maximize insurance recovery for the policyholder, however, some courts limit the allocation period to the available coverage block.[5] This exception often leads to the question of whether insurance was in fact available

---

4. *Boston Gas*, 910 N.E.2d at 297, n.11.
5. *See, e.g., Stonewall Ins. Co. v. Asbestos Claims Mgmt. Corp.*, 73 F.3d 1178, 1203 (2d. Cir. 1995).

for the covered risk at issue or whether the policyholder consciously elected to "go bare." It also raises the question of who has the burden of proving availability or unavailability.[6] Again, using the ten-year hypothetical, if it is established that insurance was available for only five years, and damages remain at $100 million, each policy year would be allocated $20 million based on the coverage block approach to "unavailability." Those endorsing pro rata allocation view this judicially created exception—to pro rata in its pure form—as unfair because the policyholder collects $50 million stemming from property damage for which it paid no premiums, and the insurers collectively pay an additional $50 million for property damage occurring in years they did not insure and for which they received no premium.

The most complicated of the pro rata approaches, however, commingles available coverage years and limits. The purported intent is to reflect the "risk transfer" assumed by the policyholder and its insurers in each insurable year of the loss. This approach was first recognized by the New Jersey Supreme Court in *Owens-Illinois, Inc. v. United Ins. Co.*, 650 A.2d 974 (N.J. 1994) and was most recently adopted by the New Hampshire Supreme Court in *Energy North Natural Gas, Inc. v. Certain Underwriters at Lloyd's*, 934 A.2d 518 (N.H. 2007). Again using the ten-year scenario for illustration, if the insured purchased $10 million of insurance in each of the first nine years for a total of $90 million, and $110 million of insurance in the very last year, the insured in the last year of coverage is responsible for 55 percent of the total loss based on its weighted share of the overall coverage block ($110 million out of a total $200 million). The remaining 45 percent of the total loss is spread evenly (5 percent in each year) among years one through nine based on the remaining weighted share of the overall coverage block (cumulatively $90 million out of a total $200 million). Thus, if total damages were $100 million, $55 million would be allocated to the last year, and $5 million would be allocated each of the remaining nine years for a cumulative total of $45 million.

Of course, the simplistic example used here does not often occur in practice, where there are frequently many other considerations in play. In addition to dealing with potentially overlapping and incongruous coverage layers resulting from stub policies, insolvencies, prior impairments, exhaustion, self-insured retentions, aggregates, or term limits, application of this method requires the additional consideration of whether the policyholder purchased sufficient insurance in each year. In other words, the policyholder can also "go bare" for a certain portion of the risk by under insuring in any particular year or years. Given these innumerable complexities, courts often appoint special "allocation" masters to assist them with determining each party's appropriate allocation.

---

6. *See, e.g., St. Paul Mercury Ins. Co. v. Northern Power Co.*, No. A07-1775, 2009 WL 2596074 (Minn. Ct. App. Aug. 25, 2009).

The "all sums" approach also presents similar variations that can greatly impact a targeted insurer's exposure. The principal point of distinction is how to deal with so called "reallocation." The issue of reallocation arises when a targeted insurer pays more than its equitable share of a loss in relation to the policyholder's other available coverage. In this situation, the targeted insurer is often forced to seek contribution from the policyholder's other available insurers or is left to obtain a judgment credit or setoff due to the settlement of other carriers on the same risk. Those who believe that the "all sums" approach to allocation is inherently inequitable to begin with usually view reallocation as a cause for further inequity.

The most equitable approach to reallocation is the "apportioned share setoff" method recognized by the Third Circuit Court of Appeals in applying Pennsylvania law.[7] Under this method, a targeted insurer may receive a judgment setoff based on the proportionate share of risk assumed by all settling insurers covering the same loss. The end result of this approach is similar to the pro rata, coverage block approach discussed above, but with some potential further inequities. Using the most basic ten-year example, if the targeted insurer covered five years of the $100 million loss and the settling carriers covered the remaining five years of the loss, the targeted insurer would receive a $50 million setoff for the settlement payments received by these carriers—regardless of the *actual* amount paid. Proponents of this approach say that it discourages collusion among parties while appropriately shifting the risk of settling too low on the policyholder. Of course, opponents of the approach argue it discourages settlement for the very same reason.

Theoretically, under this basic example, the targeted insurer is no better off or no worse off than under a pure pro rata, time-on-the risk approach. But more often than not, the realities of long-tail, continuous injury cases present coverage blocks and coverage questions that are far from basic. The above scenario may lead to further inequity, for example, if the policyholder purchased insurance from a low-rated insurer that later becomes insolvent. The question then arises whether to shift an equitable portion of these insolvent shares to the settled carriers through a setoff or whether to force the remaining carriers to bear the full burden of all insolvent shares. The same question arises if the insured consciously decided to "go bare" for a portion of the risk. Because the principles of setoff and contribution are rooted in equity, the answer is often fact dependent and may vary based on the unique equities of the case.

An alternative to the "apportioned share setoff" method is the *pro tanto* method, which provides a dollar-for-dollar credit based on the *actual* settlement amount paid. Detractors of this more common approach, however, see it as being riddled with even more inequities. Among its many flaws, they

---

7. See *Koppers Co., Inc. v. Aetna Cas. & Sur. Co.*, 98 F.3d 1440 (3d. Cir.1996).

would say, is that it places the risk of settling too low on the nonsettling insurer, a nonparticipant to the transaction. It further places the burden of proving the actual settlement amount on the nonsettling insurer, which was not privy to settlement discussions. Disclosure of those settlement details is also hindered by the public policy considerations of encouraging settlement and safeguarding settlement negotiations. This method also encourages collusion by allowing the policyholder to disguise the actual consideration or actual sum given in settlement. The most common mechanism of disguising the actual settlement amount is by including a release for other claims or by providing a broader release than the claim really at issue. In environmental cases, this is easily accomplished by including other sites not at issue or by including a release for potential future bodily injury or natural resource claims that have not been (and never expect to be) asserted. As one court put it in criticizing this approach: "Of course, quantifying the unquantifiable and allocating what is not yet able to be allocated is an impossible task, but it is one the Supreme Court has assigned to insurers... as an incentive for them to settle their claims. The Supreme Court has stated the law, and we are obliged to follow it."[8]

Another approach is horizontal exhaustion. This approach is unique to California and Illinois.[9] Under this approach, the policyholder must exhaust all applicable primary coverage before it taps an excess carrier for defense or indemnity. The rationale behind this approach is that excess coverage is fundamentally different from primary insurance both with respect to the risk assumed and the premiums accepted. As recognized by the Illinois Supreme Court, permitting "vertical exhaustion" would allow the policyholder to

> effectively manipulate the source of its recovery, avoiding the difficulties encountered as the result of its purchase of fronting insurance and the liquidation of some of its insurers. This would permit [the policyholder] to pursue coverage from certain excess insurers at the exclusion of others. Such a practice would blur the distinction between primary and excess insurance, and would allow certain primary insurers to escape unscathed when they would otherwise bear the initial burden of providing indemnification.[10]

A similar approach has been recognized under Ohio law, but with greater implications. In *GenCorp*, the Sixth Circuit affirmed the district court's holding that the policyholder had elected pro rata allocation by its own to decision to

---

8. *Puget Sound Energy v. Certain Underwriters at Lloyd's, London*, 138 P.3d 1068, 1077 (Wash. App. 2006).

9. *See, e.g., Kajima Constr. Services, Inc. v. St. Paul Fire and Marine Ins. Co.*, 879 N.E.2d 305 (Ill. 2007); *Community Redevelopment Agency of the City of Los Angeles v. Aetna Cas. & Sur. Co.*, 57 Cal. Rptr.2d 755 (2d Dist. 1996).

10. *Kajima*, 879 N.E.2d at 106–07.

settle with all of its primary insurers.[11] While the district court recognized the policyholder's right to seek indemnity from any one of its insurers under Ohio law, its decision to settle with *all* of its primary insurers eliminated each of the excess carriers' right to seek contribution. Having elected to allocate its liability over the broadest allocation period possible and having eliminated the only protection afforded to an overpaying insurer, the district court therefore did not permit the policyholder to subsequently "allocate its liability to one policy or to one policy year because this would be contrary to the settlements reached."[12]

A policyholder's recovery may also be limited under "all sums" when antistacking principles or noncumulation clauses of certain policies are strictly applied. Antistacking is the principle that a policyholder may select a single year in which to recover its loss but no more. This prohibition against stacking of limits was first recognized by the seminal "all sums" decision of *Keene*, reasoning that the "principle of indemnity implicit in the policies requires that successive policies cover single asbestos-related injuries.[13] That principle, however, does not require that [the policyholder] be entitled to 'stack' applicable policies' limits of liability."[14] Certain noncumulation clauses, however, may permit stacking but limit the order in which the policyholder may recover.[15]

In the unpublished decision of *Ashland Inc. v. Aetna Casualty*, Civ. A. No. 5:98–00340-JMH, Slip Op. (E.D. Ky. May 2, 2006), the District Court for the Eastern District of Kentucky required the policyholder to exhaust all *prior* coverage before tapping excess coverage in subsequent years based on the noncumulation clause of the policies at issue. The "Prior Insurance and Non-Cumulation of Liability" clause of those policies provided:

> It is agreed that if any loss covered hereunder is also covered in whole or in part under any other excess policy issued to the Assured prior to the inception date hereof the limit of liability hereon as stated in Item 2 of the Declarations shall be reduced by any amounts due to the Assured on account of such loss under prior insurance.

In construing this provision, the court held that this "condition applies broadly to 'any other excess policy' that covers the same loss... prior to the

---

11. *GenCorp. v. AIU*, 297 F. Supp. 2d 995 (N.D. Ohio 2003), *aff'd per curium*, 2005 U.S. App. LEXIS (6th Cir. 2005).

12. *Id.* at 1007–08.

13. *Keene Corp. v. Insurance Co. of N. Am.*, 667 F.2d 1034 (D.C. Cir. 1981).

14. *Id.* at 1049.

15. *See, e.g., Liberty Mutual v. Treesdale*, 418 F.3d 330 (3d Cir. 2005); *but see Spaulding Composites v. Aetna*, 819 A.2d 410 (N.J. 2003) (finding noncumulation clause an unenforceable escape clause), *Greene Tweed v. Hartford*, Civ. A. No. 03-3637, 2006 WL 1050110 (E.D. Pa. April 21, 2006) (same).

inception date of the… Policies." Thus, because the amount available under the policyholder's prior available insurance exceeded the limits of the excess policies at issue, the court concluded that "liability appears to be reduced to zero." *Id.* at 12. The court further reasoned that "[t]he all sums approach does not override such a provision, which appears to have been written specifically to address the type of situation at issue here, namely, the allocation of long-term exposure over multiple policy periods. [The Policyholder] is indeed entitled to select any applicable policy, but that selection cannot be made to grant coverage where none exists, any more than the *pro rata* approach can be used to limit the coverage that an insured has bargained for." *Id.* at 13.

## 50-State Survey: Allocation of Latent Injury and Damage Claims

**Alabama:** No instructive authority. *But see Commercial Union Ins. Co. v. Sepco Corp.*, 918 F.2d 920, 924 (11th Cir. 1990) (applying Alabama law and affirming the district court's decision to apply the pro rata approach to allocate liability among insurers for bodily injury from exposure to asbestos); *see also Liberty Mut. Ins. Co. v. Wheelwright Trucking Co., Inc.*, 851 So.2d 466, 487 (Ala. 2002) (citing with approval *Olin Corp. v. Insurance Co. of North America*, 221 F.3d 307 (2d Cir. 2000)) and holding that policyholder responsible for separate SIR under each triggered policy under Georgia law).

**Alaska:** No instructive authority.

**Arizona:** No instructive authority.

**Arkansas:** In an unpublished decision, an Arkansas trial court applied "all sums" to an environmental property damage claim involving three separate oils spills. *Murphy Oil USA, Inc. v. United States Fid. & Guar. Co.*, No. 91–439–2 (Ark. Cir. Ct. Feb. 21, 1995), reprinted in 9 Mealey's Ins. Litig. Rep. No. 19, Section I (Mar. 21, 1995).

**California:** The Supreme Court of California adopted the "all sums" method of allocation, with respect to defense costs, in the context of claims for environmental property damage. *Aerojet-Gen. Corp. v. Transport Indem. Co.*, 948 P.2d 909 (Cal. 1998). Relying on *Aerojet*, the California Court of Appeals held that indemnity costs incurred in the environmental property damage context also are allocable jointly and severally, and that the policyholder is permitted to stack the limits of all triggered policies across all policy periods. *State v. Cont'l Ins. Co.*, 88 Cal. Rptr. 3d 288, 311–13 (Cal. Ct. App. 2009), *appeal granted by* 91 Cal. Rptr. 3d 106 (Cal. 2009) (also known as *Stringfellow*).

**Colorado:** The Supreme Court of Colorado adopted the pro rata, time-on-the-risk method of allocation for the environmental cleanup costs of remediating soil and groundwater contamination. *Pub. Serv. Co. of Colo. v. Wallis & Cos.*, 986 P.2d 924, 939 (Colo. 1999). In expressly rejecting the "all sums" approach with respect to indemnity, the court reasoned: "We do not believe that these policy provisions can reasonably be read to mean that one single-year policy out of dozens of triggered policies must indemnify the insured's liability for the total amount of pollution caused by events over a period of decades, including events that happened both before and after the policy period." *Id.* at 939. Accordingly, the court held that "where property damage is gradual, long-term, and indivisible, the trial court should make a reasonable estimate of the portion of the 'occurrence' that is fairly attributable to each year by dividing the total amount of liability by the number of years at issue." *Id.* at 940. The *Public Service* Court explained further, however, that the "trial court should then allocate liability according to each policy-year, taking into account primary and excess coverage, SIRs, policy limits, and other insurance on the risk." *Id.* The consideration of policy limits should not confused with the *Owens-Illinois* approach (*see* New Jersey) where allocation is weighted toward years with higher policy limits. Rather, the consideration of policy limits comes into play only where there is concurrent coverage in the same year and coverage layer. *Id.* at 941–42; *see also Hoang v. Monterra Homes (Powderhorn) LLC*, (Colo. App. 2005), *rev'd on other grounds*, 149 P.3d 748 (Colo. 2007) (applying pro rata allocation approach in the context of claims for environmental property damage); *Globe Indem. Co. v. Travelers Indem. Co. of Ill.*, 98 P.3d 971, 974 (Colo. App. 2004) (holding pro rata not appropriate where damages can be traced to a single clear event, in this case, a landslide).

**Connecticut:** The Supreme Court of Connecticut adopted the pro rata time-on-the risk method of allocation, with respect to both defense and indemnity, in the context of claims for bodily injury resulting from inhalation of asbestos. *Sec. Ins. Co. of Hartford v. Lumbermen's Mut. Cas. Co.*, 826 A.2d 107 (2003). In applying this approach, the court held that the policyholder must bear its own equitable share for uninsured periods "not only because [the policyholder]... *chose* to forgo insurance, but also because [the insurer] never contracted to pay for defense [or indemnity] costs arising outside of its policy period." *Id.* at 126. The court further held that equity dictates that the policyholder bear the burden of establishing coverage during missing policy periods as the policyholder "is the party which could have prevented the loss or destruction of the policies" and thus "through its own actions or inactions... has put itself in the position of being, in essence, uninsured for a substantial period of time." *Id.*

**Delaware:** Delaware is widely assumed to be an "all sums" jurisdiction based on the Delaware Supreme Court's decision in *Hercules Inc. v. AIU Ins. Co.*, 784 A.2d 481 (Del. 2001), which involved environmental property damage. This assumption, however, is arguably incorrect. Most notably, the policy in *Hercules* included a nonstandard continuation of coverage clause extending coverage beyond the policy period in the case of continuing damage. In combination with the "all sums" language, the court did not reach any equitable considerations, concluding simply that the two clauses could not be reconciled with pro rata allocation. *Id.* at 494 n.46. In an earlier case, involving different policy language, continuous property damage, and substantial SIRs, the Delaware Superior Court applied a modified pro rata, time-on-the-risk method in *E.I. DuPont de Nemours & Co. v. Admiral Insurance Co.*, No. 89C-AU-99, 1995 WL 654020, at *15 (Del. Super. Ct. Oct. 27, 1995). The court concluded that "all sums" is inconsistent with the presumption that damage occurred at a constant, continuous rate from the inception of the environmental damage. *Id.* Other allocation cases decided under Delaware law have sided with "all sums" allocation, distinguishing their facts from those of *DuPont. See, e.g., Hercules*, 784 A.2d 481, 492–94 (rejecting equitable considerations based on continuation clause); *Am. Guarantee & Liab. Ins. Co. v. Intel Corp.*, No. No. 09C-01–170-JOH, 2009 WL 2589597, at *19 (Del. Super. Ct. July 24, 2009) ("[T]he Supreme Court in Hercules, adopted an 'all-sums' liability approach, it seemed to criticize such a modified pro rate allocation. But it did so, in part, based on a particular provision in the policy at issue in that case."); *E.I. DuPont de Nemours & Co. v. Allstate Ins. Co.*, 879 A.2d 929, 939–41 (Del. Super. Ct. 2004) (rejecting equitable considerations because property damage was divisible).

**Florida:** No instructive authority.

**Georgia:** A Georgia trial court adopted the pro rata, time-on-the-risk approach in an asbestos case in *National Serv. Indus., Inc. v. St. Paul Guardian Ins. Co.*, No. 2004 CV 83960 (Ga. Super. 2005, reprinted in 19 Mealey's Ins. Litig. Rep. No. 30, Section E (June 14, 2005). *But see Ameristeel Corp. v. Employers Mut. Cas. Co.*, No. 7:96-CV-85-HL, 2005 WL 1785283, *8 (M.D. Ga. July 26, 2005) (recognizing that Georgia courts have failed to address the allocation issue); *see also Liberty Mut. Ins. Co. v. Wheelwright Trucking Co., Inc.*, 851 So.2d 466, 487 (Ala. 2002) (applying Georgia law and holding that policyholder would be responsible for separate SIR under each triggered policy).

**Hawaii:** The Supreme Court of Hawaii's decision in *Sentinel Insurance Co. v. First Insurance. Co. of Hawaii*, 875 P.2d 894 (Haw. 1994) is often cited by both policyholders and insurers as supporting both the pro rata time on the risk and "all sums" methods of allocation. The decision, in fact, adopts neither approach. While a contribution case, the decision is instructive because the court adopted an injury-in-fact trigger and held that where the amount of damages cannot be accurately attributed to any particular year, damages should be shared by successive insurers on a time-on-the-risk basis. *Id.* at 915. The decision, however, did not answer the threshold question whether the policyholder may first seek "all sums" from any one of its available insurers as this issue was not before the court.

**Idaho:** No instructive authority.

**Illinois:** The Supreme Court of Illinois applied "all sums" allocation in *Zurich Insurance Co. v. Raymark Industries, Inc.*, 514 N.E.2d 150 (Ill. 1987) in the context of an asbestos claim. Although this "all sums" holding is still applied in asbestos cases, *see Caterpillar, Inc. v. Century Indemn. Co.*, No. 3–06–0161 (Ill. App. Ct. Feb. 2, 2007), it has been distinguished by numerous Illinois appellate courts in other types of cases based on the specific policy language at issue and the unique "triple trigger" applied in asbestos cases. This distinction was most recently recognized in *Federal Insurance Co. v. Binney & Smith, Inc.*, 913 NE.2d 43, 54 (Ill. App. Ct. 2009), holding that advertising injury claims should be allocated on a pro rata, time-on-the-risk basis in the absence of evidence showing actual extent of damages in each year. *See also AAA Disposal Sys., Inc. v. Aetna Cas. & Sur. Co.*, 821 N.E.2d 1278, 1289 (Ill. App. Ct. 2005) (allocating on a pro rata, coverage block basis); *Ill. Cent. R.R. Co. v. Accident & Cas. Co. of Winterthur*, 739 N.E.2d 1049, 1062 (2000) (allocating employment discrimination claims on a pro rata, time-on-the-risk basis); *Mo. Pac. R.R. Co. v. Int'l. Ins. Co.*, 679 N.E.2d 801, 806 (Ill. App. Ct. 1997) (allocating hearing loss claims on a pro rata, time-on-the-risk basis); *Outboard Marine Corp. v. Liberty Mut. Ins. Co.*, 670 N.E.2d 740, 750 (Ill. App. Ct. 1996) (allocating environmental property damage claim on pro rata, time-on-the-risk basis). A distinction must also be noted with respect to the Massachusetts Appeals Court decision in *Chicago Bridge & Iron Co. v. Certain Underwriters at Lloyd's, London*, 797 N.E.2d 434 (Mass. App. Ct. 2003), which was decided under Illinois law. As recognized by the Massachusetts high court in *Boston Gas, infra*, the unique policy language involved expressly provided that the policy would provide coverage for *continuing* bodily injury or property damage *after* "termination of this policy… without payment of additional premium." *Id.* at 304, n.30. *But see Benoy Motor Sales, Inc. v. Universal Underwriters Ins. Co.*, 679 N.E.2d 414 (Ill. App. Ct. 1997) (applying "all sums" based on deemer clause of policies).

**Indiana:** The Indiana Supreme Court's decision in *Allstate Insurance Co. v. Dana Corp.*, 759 N.E.2d 1049 (Ind. 2001), is often cited by policyholders as adopting the "all sums" method of allocation. But in *Federated Rural Elec. Ins. Exch. v. Nat'l Farmers Union Prop. & Cas. Co.*, 805 N.E.2d 456, 466 (Ind. Ct. App. 2004), *vacated on procedural grounds*, 816 N.E.2d 1157 (Ind. 2004), the court stated that "the determination… that Allstate was liable for 'all sums' up to policy limits under the language of its policies was not a final adjudication of the amount Allstate had to pay Dana. The parties err when they attempt to extract from *Dana I* and *Dana II* an 'all sums' rule and apply it out of context." Accordingly, the Indiana Court of Appeals concluded that the *Dana* decision "did not establish an 'all sums' rule to be applied in other contexts… [and] that other coverage and equitable principles may affect the ultimate amount payable in that case." *Id.; accord Irving Materials, Inc. v. Zurich Am. Ins. Co.*, No. 1:03-CV-361-SEB-JPG, 2007 WL 1035098 (S.D. Ind. Mar. 30, 2007).

**Iowa:** No instructive authority.

**Kansas:** The Supreme Court of Kansas held that, in the context of claims for noise-induced hearing loss, where damages cannot be measured and allocated to particular policy periods, a pro rata, time-on-the-risk method of allocation should be used. *Atchison, Topeka & Santa Fe Ry. Co. v. Stonewall Ins. Co.*, 71 P.3d 1097, 1133 (Kan. 2003). The court concluded that an allocation based on joint and several liability would contradict the fundamental insurance agreement to indemnify the insured for injuries during a specified policy period. *Id.* at 1134; *see also ACE Prop. & Cas. Ins. Co. v. Superior Boiler Works, Inc.*, 504 F. Supp. 2d 1154, 1159 (D. Kan. 2007) (following *Atchison* and holding that summary judgment on allocation was precluded because the key issue to be resolved was whether there existed a single continuous occurrence resulting in unallocable loss implicating successive policy periods).

**Kentucky:** The Supreme Court of Kentucky adopted the pro rata time-on-the-risk method of allocation in the context of claims for damage from nuclear waste disposal where damage is not divisible or allocable during and between policy periods. *Aetna Cas. & Sur. Co. v. Commonwealth*, 179 S.W.3d 830 (Ky. 2005); *see also Liberty Mut. Fire Ins. Co. v. Harpe Indus., Inc.*, No. 5:05-cv-243-R, 2007 WL 528523, at *4 (holding that the "insurers shall be responsible for their individual and proportionate share of defense costs… based on a pro rata basis" in the context of claims resulting from construction defects); *Aetna Cas. & Sur. Co.*, 179 S.W.3d at 842 (holding that liability for costs associated with cleanup of contamination from nuclear waste was properly prorated by the Kentucky appellate court in *Aetna Cas. & Sur. Co. v. Nuclear Eng'g Co.*, No. 2002 WL 363373, at *29–30 (Ky. Ct. App. Mar. 8, 2002)).

**Louisiana:** The Supreme Court of Louisiana endorsed pro rata allocation by holding that solvent insurers were not required to "fill the gap" left by an insolvent carrier and thereby pay more than their pro rata share of damages incurred in connection with silicosis-related bodily injuries. *S. Silica of La., Inc. v. La. Ins. Guar. Ass'n*, 979 So. 2d 460, 466 (La. 2008). In affirming the appellate court on different grounds, the Supreme Court expressly noted that the trial court's finding that solvent insurer's were required to "fill the gap" was "contrary to the proration of insurance coverage that is a component of the significant exposure test in long latency disease cases." *Id.* at 468; *see also Cole v. Celotex Corp.*, 599 So.2d 1058, 1080 (La. 1992) (allocating damages over all triggered policies in asbestos case); *Norfolk Southern Corp. v. California Union Ins. Co.*, 859 So.2d 201, 208, (La. App. 1st Cir. 2003) (allocating "by the total number of years that contaminating activities took place to obtain a judgment amount per year"); *Porter v. Am. Optical Corp.*, 641 F.2d 1128, 1145 (5th Cir. 1981) (recognizing that, under Louisiana law, insurance coverage is prorated among all carriers for cumulative injuries, like that in the case at hand involving exposure to asbestos).

**Maine:** No instructive authority.

**Maryland:** The Court of Special Appeals of Maryland adopted the pro rata time-on-the-risk method of allocation in the context of claims for bodily injury and property damage resulting from long-term and continuous exposure to asbestos. *Mayor & City Council of Balt. v. Utica Mut. Ins. Co.*, 802

A.2d 1070, 1104 (Md. Ct. Spec. App. 2002). In rejecting the all sums approach adopted in *Keene Corp. v. Insurance Co. of North America*, 667 F.2d 1034 (D.C. Cir. 1981), the Maryland court concluded that the "all sums" language of the general liability policy must be read in concert with other language that limits a policy's liability for damage or loss that occurs during the policy period. *Id.* at 1102–03. The court concluded that the pro rata approach is more consistent with the "injury-in-fact/continuous trigger" employed by Maryland courts. *Id* at 1104. Notably, under the Maryland approach, losses are prorated to the insured when there is a gap in coverage, unless that gap is due to the insured's "inability to obtain insurance." *Id.*; *see also Riley v. United Servs. Auto. Assoc.*, 871 A.2d 599 (Md. Ct. Spec. App. 2005), *aff'd on different grounds*, 899 A.2d 819 (Md. 2006) (endorsing pro rata, time-on-the risk to lead bodily injury claims where damages could not be determined in any particular year); *In re Wallace & Gale Co.*, 385 F.3d 820 (4th Cir. 2004) (applying pro rata allocation in the asbestos context).

**Massachusetts**: The Supreme Judicial Court of Massachusetts adopted the pro rata, time-on-the-risk method of allocation in the context of claims for costs of cleanup of oil and tar contamination. *Boston Gas Co. v. Century Indem. Co.*, 910 N.E.2d. 290, 306 (Mass. 2009). In holding that damages should be allocated over all years in which property damage occurred, the Massachusetts high court recognized that the pro rata approach addresses a problem of proof where "it is both scientifically and administratively impossible to allocate to each policy the liability for injuries occurring only within its policy period." *Id.* at 301. The court, therefore, did not foreclose the application of an "injury-in-fact" allocation where the evidence permits a more accurate "estimation of the quantum of property damage" occurring during the policy period. *Id.* at 316. The court also rejected the "unavailability" exception—noting that it "effectively provides insurance where insurers made the calculated decision not to assume risk and not to accept premiums." *Id.* at 315. The court, however, permitted the policyholder to prorate the amount of its self-insured retention on the same basis as the liability apportioned to each policy period. Thus, if pollution occurred "over the course of a decade, then one-tenth of the total cleanup cost would be apportioned to each policy year, and the [policyholder] would be responsible for one-tenth of the applicable self-insured retention for each year." *Id.* at 316. *But see Benjamin Moore v. Aetna*, 843 A.2d 1094 (N.J. 2004) (rejecting proration of SIRs). *See also New England Insulation Co. v. Liberty Mut. Ins. Co.*, 2010 WL 3219436, No. 10-2784-BLS2 (Mass. Super. Ct. July 28, 2010) (applying pro rata, time-on-the-risk allocation in the asbestos context); *Peabody Essex Museum, Inc. v. United States Fire Ins. Co.*, No. 06cv11209, 2010 WL 3895172 (D. Mass. Sept. 30, 2010) (applying injury-in-fact trigger to determine allocation period but declining to extend pro rata allocation to duty to defend).

**Michigan**: The Supreme Court of Michigan has not taken a definitive position on allocation in continuous injury cases, however, the Sixth Circuit along with numerous appellate courts and district courts, all applying Michigan law, have applied the pro rata, time-on-the-risk approach. In *Gelman Science, Inc. v. Fidelity & Cas. Co. of NY*, the Michigan Supreme Court commented on allocation in dicta, reinforcing consideration of the particular language of the policy at issue, and the availability of equitable means where the policyholder cannot meet its burden of showing how much damage occurred in each year. 572 N.W.2d 617, 622–25 (Mich. 1998). Two cases decided by the Michigan court of appeals have reached different results on different facts. In *Arco Industries Corp. v. American Motorists Insurance Co.*, the time-on-the-risk method was adopted to apportion pollution remediation costs among successive insurers for continuous property damage to which an injury-in-fact trigger of coverage had been applied. 594 N.W.2d 61, 69–70 (Mich. Ct. App. 1998) (emphasizing the policy language stating that coverage applies to damage and injury taking place "during the policy period.") Conversely, in an unpublished opinion, the Court of Appeals adopted the "all sums" approach based on distinctions in policy language in *Dow Corning Corp. v. Continental Cas. Co.*, Nos. 200143–200154, 1999 WL 33435067, *7 (Mich. Ct. App. Oct. 12, 1999). Most significantly, the *Dow Corning* Court highlighted unique language contained in the continuation clause of the policy, like in *Chicago Bridge* and *Hercules*, *supra*, extending coverage beyond the policy period in the case of continuing damage. *Id.* at *8. Numerous courts have since distinguished *Dow Corning* or held that the Michigan Supreme Court would instead adopt the pro rata time-on-the-risk method of allocation, as applied in *Arco Indus. See, e.g., Stryker Corp. v. Nat'l Union Fire Ins. Co.*, No. 4:01-CV-157, 2005 WL 1610663, *6 (W.D. Mich. July 1, 2005); *see also Cont'l Cas. Co. v. Indian Head Indus., Inc.*, No. 05–73918, 2010 WL 188083, *5 (E.D. Mich. Jan. 15, 2010) (highlighting that *Dow Corning* has limited precedential value, as an unpublished opinion, and because the Michigan Supreme Court affirmed *Arco* eight months *after* the *Dow Corning* opinion was issued); *Wolverine World Wide, Inc. v. Liberty Mut. Ins. Co.*, 2007 WL 70581, *3 (Mich. Ct. App. Mar. 8, 2007); *Century Indem. Co. v. Aero-Motive Co.*, 318 F. Supp. 2d 530, 544–45 (W.D. Mich. 2003) (allocating defense costs according to time-on-the-risk method); *City of Sterling Heights, Mich. v. United Nat'l Ins. Co.*, 319 Fed. App'x 357, 361–62 (6th Cir. 2009); *Continental Cas.*, 2010 WL 188083 at *5–6. Other distinctions made are that the insurer agreed to cover "those sums" not "all sums"; coverage was provided during the policy period only, not before or after; pro rata, time-on-the-risk is consistent with the "injury-in-fact" trigger of coverage adopted in *Gelman*; and also, there is an inherent simplicity and predictability with the pro rata, time-on-the-risk allocation method. *See, e.g., Stryker*, 2005 WL 1610663 at *6; *Continental Casualty*, 2010 WL 188083 at *6.

**Minnesota:** The Supreme Court of Minnesota was the first state high court to adopt the pro rata time-on-the-risk method of allocation. *See N. States Power Co. v. Fid. & Cas. Co. of N.Y.*, 523 N.W.2d 657, 664 (Minn. 1994) (addressing claims for proper damage due to soil and groundwater contamination) and *Domtar, Inc. v. Niagara Fire Ins. Co.*, 563 N.W.2d 724, 733–34 (Minn. 1997) (involving claims for costs associated with cleanup of environmental pollution). The Supreme Court of Minnesota later adopted an "unavailability" exception in *Wooddale Builders, Inc. v. Maryland Cas. Co.*, 722 N.W.2d 283, 297–98 (Minn. 2006). The court reasoned that this exception holds the insured responsible for only those risks that it elected to assume, while eliminating any windfall that would result if the insured received a benefit of insurance coverage that it had deliberately declined to purchase. *Id.* at 297. The insured has the burden of demonstrating "unavailability." *Id.*; *see also St. Paul Mercury Ins. Co. v. N. States Power Co.*, No. A07–1775, 2009 WL 2596074, *8 (Minn. Ct. App. Aug. 25, 2009) (holding insured failed to demonstrate that insurance was unavailable simply because claim may not be covered under earlier accident-based policies; rather the issue is "whether the coverage for the particular risk was generally available in the market place"). The Minnesota Supreme Court held in *Cargill, Inc. v. ACE Am. Ins. Co.*, 784 N.W.2d 341 (Minn. 2010) that an insurer honoring its duty to defend is entitled to contribution from other insurers on the risk on an "equal shares" basis, expressly overruling its prior decision in *Iowa National Mutual Ins. Co. v. Universal Underwriters Ins. Co.*, 150 N.W.2d 233 (Minn. 1967).

**Mississippi:** No instructive authority.

**Missouri:** Although Missouri law is unsettled on the issue of allocation, at least two intermediate appellate decisions support pro rata allocation. *See Cont'l Cas. Co. v. Med. Protective Co.*, 859 S.W.2d 789, 792 (Mo. Ct. App. 1993) ("Where the loss is caused not by a single event but by a series of cumulative acts or omissions, we believe the fair method of apportioning the loss among consecutive insurers is by application of the 'exposure theory' utilized in cases of progressive disease such as asbestosis.") (citing *Ins. Co. of N. Am. v. Forty-Eight Insulations, Inc.*, 633 F.2d 1212 (6th Cir. 1980)); *Nationwide Ins. Co. v. Cent. Mo. Elec. Co-op., Inc.*, 278 F.3d 742, 748 (8th Cir. 2001) (applying Missouri law and holding "time on the risk analysis was appropriate."). *But see Viacom, Inc., v. Transit Cas. Co.*, No. WD-62854, 2004 WL 414157 (Mo. Ct. App. 2004) (applying Pennsylvania law but noting that Missouri law would reach the same result); *Monsanto Co. v C.E. Heath Comp. & Liab. Ins. Co.*, 652 A.2d 30 (Del. 1995) (applying Missouri law and holding that Missouri is an "all sums" state based on *Tinsley v Aetna Ins. Co. of Hartford*, 205 S.W. 78 (Mo. Ct. App. 1918)).

**Montana:** A trial court in South Dakota applied the "all sums" method of allocation under Montana law in *NorthWestern Corp. v. AEGIS*, No. 07-1174 (S.D. Cir. Ct. July 29, 2010), *reprinted in* 24-37 Mealey's Litigation Report: Insurance (Aug. 4, 2010).

**Nebraska:** The Supreme Court of Nebraska adopted the pro rata time-on-the-risk method of allocation in the context of claims for environmental property damage. *Dutton-Lainson Co. v. Cont'l Ins. Co.*, 778 N.W.2d 433

(Neb. 2010). The court concluded that, based on the policy language, the insured could not assert joint-and-several liability without proving the amount of damages that occurred during the period of coverage provided by each insurer. *Id.* at 444–45.

**Nevada:** No instructive authority.

**New Hampshire**: The Supreme Court of New Hampshire adopted the pro rata, by limits and years approach in *EnergyNorth Natural Gas, Inc. v. Certain Underwriters at Lloyd's*, 934 A.2d 518 (N.H. 2007). In deciding whether to apply pro rata or "all sums" to the allocation question, the *EnergyNorth* Court made the salient point that the problem presented by long-term damage cases presents an atypical question. The court explained "[t]he typical occurrence covered by a liability policy is something akin to a car accident. Losses of this nature are relatively easy to identify because damages are both immediate and finite." *Public Service Company of Colorado v. Wallis and Companies*, 986 P.2d 924, 935 (Colo. 1999). By contrast, in long-term environmental pollution cases, "correlating degrees of damage to particular points along the loss timeline may be virtually impossible [,] [which] has led to substantial uncertainty as to how responsibility for such losses should be allocated where multiple insurers have issued successive policies to the insured over the period of time the damage was developing." *Id.* (quotation omitted). *EnergyNorth Natural Gas*, 934 A.2d at 521. After considering the various methods of allocation, the *EnergyNorth* Court followed the New Jersey Supreme Court by adopting the pro rata, by limits and years method announced in *Owens-Illinois, Inc. v. United Insurance Co.*, 650 A.2d 974, 993–94 (N.J. 1994). Again, under this approach, loss is allocated among all triggered policies based on both the number of years a policy was on the risk as well as that policy's limits. *EnergyNorth Natural Gas*, 934 A.2d at 523. In support of its decision, the court explained that joint and several liability is inconsistent with the injury in fact trigger approach adopted in New Hampshire because it allows the policyholder to determine which policy will pay and therefore is triggered. *Id.* at 526 (citing *EnergyNorth I*, 848 A.2d 715 (N.H. 2004) (adopting the injury-in-fact trigger). The court also criticized the joint-and-several approach, noting that it "rests on an assumption not in accordance with the development of the law: that at every point in the progression, the probable damages due to injury... from exposure to manifestation will be substantially the same," "creates a false equivalence between an insured who has purchased insurance coverage continuously for many years and an insured who has purchased only one year of insurance," it "does not solve the allocation problem; it merely postpones it." *Id.*

**New Jersey:** The New Jersey Supreme Court adopted the pro rata, by limits and years method of allocation in the context of claims for bodily injury and property damage from exposure to asbestos. *Owens-Illinois, Inc. v. United Ins. Co.*, 650 A.2d 974 (N.J. 1994). In rejecting an "all sums" approach to "occurrence" based policies, the court concluded that "to convert the 'all sums' or 'ultimate net loss' language into the answer to apportionment when injury occurs over a period of years is like trying to place one's hat on a rack that was never designed to hold it. It does not work. The language was never intended to cover apportionment when continuous injury occurs over multiple years." *Id.* at 989. To spread the risk, the court followed *Armstrong World Industries, Inc. v. Aetna Casualty & Surety Co.*, 26 Cal. Rptr. 2d 35, 57 (Cal. Ct. App. 1993), and allocated damages on the basis of the extent of risk assumed, i.e., proration on the basis of policy limits, multiplied by years of coverage. *Id.* at 993; *see also Carter-Wallace, Inc. v. Admiral Ins. Co.*, 712 A.2d 1116 (N.J. 1998) (adopting a pro rata method of allocation, accounting for the time-on-the-risk and the degree of the risk assumed, in the context of claims for property damage caused by environmental contamination); *Franklin Mut. Ins. Co. v. Metro. Prop. & Cas. Ins. Co.*, 968 A.2d 1191, 1192 (N.J. Super. Ct. App. Div. 2009) (holding that a separate *Owens-Illinois* allocation must be conducted separately for each policyholder in the context of continuous property damage involving multiple policyholders); *Quincy Mut. Fire Ins. v. Borough of Bellmawr*, 799 A.2d 499 (N.J. 2002) (holding that allocation must be reflected by actual days on the risk rather than rounding up by the year).

**New Mexico:** No instructive authority.

**New York:** New York is a pro rata jurisdiction. But contrary to common belief, it has not adopted any particular pro rata method over another. Rather, the Court of Appeals has allowed trial courts wide latitude to mold its allocation methodology to the unique facts and equities of the case. That is not to say that the court did not provide substantial guidance through its decision in *Consolidated Edison Co. of New York v. Allstate Insurance Co.*, 774 N.E.2d 687 (N.Y. 2002). Above all, the New York high court made abundantly clear that the one overriding maxim to be followed—in all instances—is that occurrence-based CGL policies provide coverage only for bodily injury or property damage that occurs *during the policy period*. Based on this fundamental principle, the court affirmed the trial court's decision to allocate damages "based on the amount of the time the policy was in effect in comparison to the overall duration of the damage." *Id.* at 224, 774 N.E.2d at 695, 746 N.Y.S.2d at 630. Some view New York law as providing that a policyholder is not responsible for periods where insurance became "unavailable" based on the Second Circuit decisions in *Stonewall Insurance Co. v. Asbestos Claims Management Corp.*, 73 F.3d 1178 (2d Cir. 1995) and *Olin Corp. v. Insurance Co. of N. Am.*, 221 F.3d 307, 324 (2d Cir. 2000). This belief is misplaced because, among other things, these decisions predate the New York high court's decision in *Con Edison*. Significantly, in reaching its decision in *Con Edison*, the New York Court of Appeals relied, in part, on the Seventh Circuit's decision in *Sybron Transition Corp. v. Security Insurance of Hartford*, 258 F.3d 595 (7th Cir. 2001), which expressly rejected the "unavailability" exception. *Id.* at 600; *see also Consolidated Edison Co. of New York v. Fyn Paint & Lacquer Co.*, No. CV-00-3764-DGT-MDG, 2005 WL 139170, *4 (E.D.N.Y. 2005) (rejecting "unavailability" exception and citing *In re Prudential Lines, Inc.*, 158 F. 3d 65, 84–85 (2d Cir. 1998)).

Applying New York law, the Second Circuit in *Olin* later confirmed that the trigger period extends so long as damage is continuing or progressing. *Olin Corp. v. Certain Underwriters at Lloyd's*, 468 F.3d 120 (2d Cir. 2006). As for the Court of Appeal's holding on allocation of defense costs in *Continental Casualty Co. v. Rapid-American Corp.*, 80 N.Y.2d 640, 655–56 (1993), the court did not endorse "all sums"; it simply held that the trial court did not err in failing to allocate defense costs where the factual record did not permit. Indeed, numerous courts have since held that allocation of defense costs is required under New York law. *See, e.g., Generali-U.S. Branch v. Caribe Realty Corp.*, No. 25499/91, 1994 WL 903279, *2 (N.Y. Sup. Ct. 1994); *NL Indus., Inc. v. Commercial Union Ins. Co.*, 926 F. Supp. 446, 463, *reconsideration granted in part*, 935 F. Supp. 513 (D.N.J. 1996). Confusion also lies whether New York law favors allocation of defense costs on an equal shares basis. *See, e.g., Cont'l Cas. Co. v. Employers Ins. Co. of Wausau*, 865 N.Y.S. 2d 855, 861 (N.Y. App. Div. 2008); *State of New York Ins. Dept. v. Generali*, 844 N.Y.S.2d 13, 15 (N.Y. App. Div. 2007). But these are fact-specific decisions where the trial court did not afford an insurer that had shirked its obligation to defend the protection of pro rata allocation. *See id.*

**North Carolina:** No instructive authority.

**North Dakota:** No instructive authority.

**Ohio:** Ohio courts presently take an "all sums" approach to allocation. In *Goodyear Tire & Rubber Co. v. Aetna Casualty & Surety Co.*, 769 N.E.2d 835 (Ohio 2002), the Supreme Court of Ohio overturned the Ohio Court of Appeals' adoption of pro rata allocation. In adopting the "all sums" approach, the Ohio Supreme Court focused on the clause in the policies which required the insurers to "pay on behalf of the insured *all sums* which the insured shall become legally obligated to pay as damages." *Goodyear*, 769 N.E.2d at 840. Assuming that this term was clear and unambiguous, the *Goodyear* Court explained that "th[is] plain language of this provision is inclusive of all damages resulting from a qualifying occurrence. Therefore, we find that the 'all sums' allocation approach is the correct method." *Id.* at 841. Supporting this decision, the Ohio Supreme Court turned to *Keene Corp. v. Ins. Co. of N. Am.*, 667 F.2d 1034 (D.C. Cir. 1981), and agreed that "Goodyear [like the insureds in *Keene*] expected complete security from each policy that it purchased." *Goodyear*, 769 N.E.2d at 841. The "all sums" approach, according to the *Goodyear* Court, struck the correct balance between providing this expected security to the insured, while still allowing the insurers to seek contribution from one another. *Id.* The "all sums" approach was recently affirmed by the Supreme Court of Ohio in *Pennsylvania Gen. Ins. Co. v. Park-Ohio Industries, Inc.*, 930 N.E.2d 800 (Ohio 2010).

**Oklahoma:** No instructive authority.

**Oregon:** The state legislature of Oregon has adopted "joint-and-several" allocation by statute with respect to environmental remediation claims. Or. Rev. Stat. § 465.480 (2003) ("An insurer with a duty to pay defense or indemnity costs, or both, to an insured for an environmental claim under a general liability insurance policy that provides that the insurer has a duty to pay all sums arising out of a risk covered by the policy, must pay all defense or indemnity costs, or both, proximately arising out of the risk pursuant to the applicable terms of its policy, including its limit of liability, independent and unaffected by other insurance that may provide coverage for the same claim."); *see also Fireman's Fund v. Ed Niemi*, 436 F.Supp. 2d 1174 (D. Or. 2006), *rev'd by, Fireman's Fund Ins. Co. v. Oregon Auto Ins. Co.*, 2008 WL 4946279 (9th Cir. Nov. 6, 2008) (discussing rights of contribution under Oregon statute); *Certain Underwriters v. Massachusetts Bonding & Ins.*, 230 P.3d 103 (Or. Ct. App. 2010); *Fireman's Fund v. Oregon Auto. Ins. Co.*, No. CV 03-0025-MO, 2010 WL 1542552 (D. Or. Apr. 15, 2010).

**Pennsylvania:** The Supreme Court of Pennsylvania adopted the "all sums" method of allocation for purposes of claims involving asbestos bodily injuries. *J.H. France Refractories Co. v. Allstate Ins. Co.*, 626 A.2d 502 (Pa. 1993). The Pennsylvania Supreme Court held that each insurer on the risk was jointly-and-severally liable for defense and indemnity costs, and the insured could select the policy or policies under which it would be indemnified. *Id.* at 507–09. The court further held that, when a particular insurer's limits are exhausted, the insured may seek indemnification from any other insurer on the risk. *Id.* at 509; *see also AstenJohnson, Inc. v. Columbia Cas. Co.*, 562 F.3d 213, 226–27 (3d Cir. 2009) (citing *J.H. France* for the proposition that the joint-and-several approach to allocation applies in Pennsylvania).

**Rhode Island:** The issue of allocation does not present itself under Rhode Island law because the Supreme Court of Rhode Island has adopted a manifestation trigger of coverage. *CPC Intern., Inc. v. Northbrook Excess & Surplus Ins. Co.*, 668 A.2d 647, 649 (R.I. 1995). Under a manifestation trigger, damages are allocated only to the year in which the property damage "(1) manifests itself, (2) is discovered or, (3) in the exercise of reasonable diligence is discoverable." *Textron, Inc. v. Aetna Cas. and Sur. Co.*, 754 A.2d 742, 746 (R.I. 2000). Because only one year is triggered under a manifestation trigger, only those policies in effect during the year of manifestation may be called upon to pay "all sums." *Emhart Indus., Inc. v. Century Indem. Co.*, 559 F.2d 57 (1st Cir. 2009). The duty to defend is the same yet different. Although the duty to defend exists only in the year of manifestation, all carriers on the risk have a duty to defend unless the year of manifestation can be readily ascertained by the complaint, or until the year of manifestation is established by the fact finder. *Id.*

**South Carolina:** No instructive authority. *But see Spartan Petroleum Co., Inc. v. Federated Mut. Ins., Co.*, 162 F.3d 805 (4th Cir. 1998) (predicting that South Carolina high court would adopt pro rata, time-on-the-risk allocation and that policyholder would be responsible for "uninsured" periods.)

**South Dakota:** No instructive authority. *But see NorthWestern Corp. v. AEGIS*, No. 07-1174 (S.D. Cir. Ct. July 29, 2010), *reprinted in* 24-37 Mealey's

Litigation Report: Insurance (Aug. 4, 2010) (applying the "all sums" method of allocation under Montana law).

**Tennessee:** No instructive authority.

**Texas:** The allocation of loss across multiple triggered policy periods is unsettled under Texas law. Federal courts in Texas (as well as out-of-state courts interpreting Texas law) have generally applied the pro rata, by time-on-the-risk method. *See, e.g., LaFarge Corp. v. Hartford Cas. Ins. Co.*, 61 F.3d 389, 403 (5th Cir. 1995) (applying pro rata, by time-on-the-risk in environmental coverage action); *Stonewall Ins. Co. v. Asbestos Claims Mgmt.*, 73 F.3d 1178, 1204 (2d Cir. 1995) (applying the pro rata, by time-on-the-risk approach in the context of claims for bodily injury caused by exposure to asbestos under both New York and Texas law); *Gulf Chem. & Metallurgical Corp. v. Associated Metals & Minerals Corp.*, 1 F.3d 365, 372 (5th Cir. 1993) (apportioning defense costs by time-on-the-risk in a latent—injury/toxic tort exposure case). However, while the Texas Supreme Court has not yet ruled on the issue, lower state courts in Texas have applied a joint-and-several approach to allocation. *See, e.g., Tex. Prop. & Cas. Ins. Guar. Ass'n v. Sw. Aggregates, Inc.*, 982 S.W.2d 600, 605 (Tex. App. 1998) (involving silicosis claims); *CNA Lloyds of Tex. v. St. Paul Ins. Co.*, 902 S.W.2d 657, 661 (Tex. App. 1995) (involving medical malpractice). Relying on these state court decisions, a federal district court applied the "all sums" method to the duty to defend. *See Mid-Continent Cas. v. Academy Dev.*, 2010 WL 3489355 (S.D. Tex. Aug. 24, 2010).

**Utah:** The Supreme Court of Utah adopted the pro rata, by limits and years method of allocation in the context of environmental property damage. *Sharon Steel Corp. v. Aetna Cas. & Sur. Co.*, 931 P.2d 127, 140 (Utah 1997). The court concluded that, in continuing injury cases, where multiple policies are triggered for consecutive injuries, multiplying the policy limits by the years of coverage results in a more equitable allocation than proration based on policy limits alone. *Id.* As for defense costs, the Utah Supreme Court applied the time-on-the-risk method, dividing costs by the relative percentage of time that each insurer, and insured, bore the risk of loss. *Id.* at 141; *see also Ohio Cas. Ins. Co. v. Unigard Ins. Co.*, 564 F.3d 1192, 1197 (10th Cir. 2009) (recognizing the holding from *Sharon Steel*).

**Vermont:** The Supreme Court of Vermont adopted the pro rata, time-on-the-risk method of allocation in the context of claims for environmental property damage. *Towns v. Northern Security Insurance Co.*, 964 A.2d 1150 (Vt. 2008) In *Towns*, the court held that, where the insured sought coverage for continuous environmental damage, spanning successive policy periods, including one in which the insured "went bare," the insured's defense and indemnity expenses were allocable pro rata by time. *Id.* at 1167. The Vermont Supreme Court also has applied a fact-based approach to allocation where the precise amount of property damage could accurately be determined in each year. *Agency of Nat'l Res. v. Glens Falls Ins. Co.*, 736 A.2d 768 (Vt. 1999) (allocating damages based on volumes released in each year).

**Virginia:** No instructive authority.

**Washington:** The Supreme Court of Washington adopted the "all sums" method of allocation for purposes of claims involving environmental property damage. *Am. Nat'l Fire Ins. Co. v. B & L Trucking & Constr. Co.*, 951 P.2d 250 (Wash. 1998). The jury had found that the insured expected environmental property damage for more than five of the seven years in which property damage occurred. *Id.* at 259. Over a vigorous dissent, the insured was permitted to collect 100 percent of all damages by collapsing all property damage, expected or not, into any policy period of its choosing. *Id.* at 260; *see also Polygon Nw. Co. v. Am. Nat'l Fire Ins. Co.*, 189 P.3d 777, 789 (Wash. Ct. App. 2008) (citing *B&L Trucking* for the proposition that the "all sums" method of allocation applies in Washington).

**West Virginia:** A West Virginia trial court adopted a modified version of "all sums" allocation with respect to an environmental property damage claim in *Wheeling Pittsburgh Corp. American Ins. Co.*, 2003 WL 23652106 (W. Va. Cir. Ct. 2003). Significantly, although the court held that the policy language at issue did not limit coverage to property damage occurring during the policy period, the court found that equitable principles dictated that the policyholder be responsible for periods when it consciously decided to "go bare." *Id.* at *11 ("[T]he Court finds and concludes that, in seeking contribution, the Defendants' are not precluded from seeking to allocate liability to the Plaintiffs for those periods of time wherein the Plaintiffs either elected not to obtain insurance or chose to self insure."); *but see Norfolk S. Corp. v. Cal. Union Ins. Co.*, 859 So. 2d 167, 195 (La. Ct. App. 2003) (applying Virginia law and adopting the pro rata, by limits and years method of allocation for claims involving environmental property damage).

**Wisconsin:** The Supreme Court of Wisconsin adopted the "all sums" method of allocation for purposes of claims involving bodily injury and property damage from exposure to asbestos. *Plastics Eng'g Co. v. Liberty Mut. Ins. Co.*, 759 N.W.2d 613 (Wis. 2009). The court stressed that its decision applying the "all sums" method of allocation was driven by the specific policy language at issue. *Id.* at 628. In particular, the majority rooted its decision on policy language that it found contemplated coverage "if an occurrence gives rise to Bodily Injury or Property Damage which occurs *partly before and partly within* the policy period." *Id.* at 618 (emphasis added). This language is in contrast to most standard commercial general liability policies that expressly limit coverage to "bodily injury or property damage, which occurs during the policy period" or expressly define bodily injury and property damage as that which occurs *during the policy period. See also Westport Ins. Corp. v. Appleton Papers*, No. 2009AP286, 2010 WL 2265638 (Wis. Ct. App. June 8, 2010) (rejecting horizontal exhaustion).

**Wyoming:** No instructive authority.

# CHAPTER 18

# Invasion of Privacy: Guidance from "Junk Fax" Claims

Technology sometimes creates new legal disputes. Social networking, camera phones, blogging, tweeting, texting, web cams, and other advances in technology are certain to result in an increase in suits brought for invasion of privacy. And just as day follows night, the targets of such suits are sure to look for coverage from their insurance policies, such as the liability sections of their homeowner's policies and commercial general liability policies.

Whether coverage is available for such new-technology claims will turn on several issues—with the principal one being whether the defendant-policy-holder invaded the right of privacy of the plaintiff (at least for purposes of how that term is defined in their insurance policy).

When insurers are confronted with novel issues, their first response is usually to look for guidance from prior claims that raised similar or at least related issues. So it is inevitable that insurers required to determine whether coverage is owed for invasion of privacy, caused by new communications technology, will turn for help to the large body of case law that developed the last time that a new communications technology led to claims for coverage for invasion of privacy–"junk faxes."

For reasons discussed below, junk fax litigation and related coverage disputes are riding into the sunset. However, the body of case law that they leave behind, over the insurance meaning of right of privacy, will not soon be forgotten. These decisions are likely to be turned to for guidance as coverage disputes for right of privacy claims increase in frequency. And this is likely to be the case even if there are fundamental differences between the nature of junk faxes and the other new technologies.

For this reason, this book includes a chapter that addresses coverage for junk fax claims, notwithstanding that the issue's days seem numbered. Although, judging from the several junk fax decisions handed down in 2010, it is not going away without a fight.

Although waning in use because of improvements in .pdf and scanning technology, the fax machine was a big breakthrough when it arrived in force during the 1980s, allowing businesses to send letters, reports, and other communications over the telephone line rather than mailing or shipping a hard copy to recipients. One dark side of the fax machine, however, was that it was always open to receiving material over the phone, allowing unsolicited marketers to deluge fax owners with flyers for all manner of wares.

In effect, many faxes sent were "junk" faxes akin to junk mail—but with a difference. When a vendor sends junk mail (e.g., a limited-time offer to obtain a picture of Maniloff with Mr. Redlegs, the Cincinnati Reds mascot—sure to be a classic), it inflicts some external injury on the U.S. Postal Service, which must carry the material at artificially low, subsidized rates and more tangentially inflicts environmental harm by helping to deforest the Amazon. It also distracts the recipient—for about a nanosecond—while he or she sorts through the mail and discards the unwanted overtures. But most of the cost of junk mail is borne by the sender, who pays for the paper, other materials, postage, and the labor of assembly and dispatch. By contrast, junk faxes consume little of the sender's physical resources but do consume the recipient's paper and ink, as well as putting wear-and-tear on its fax machine and tying up the line so that wanted deliveries are delayed and sometimes frustrated altogether.

Understandably, recipients of junk faxes were not happy. Indeed, Maniloff was distracted by a junk fax offering him low rates on life insurance at the same time that he was editing this chapter (we kid you not). And, unlike junk mail recipients, who are usually unorganized consumers, the coalition opposing junk faxes was largely composed of businesses with some political clout and savvy. In response to complaints, Congress in 1991 enacted the Telephone Consumer Protection Act (TCPA), 47 U.S.C. § 227. The TCPA prohibits the use of fax machines, computers, or other devices to send unsolicited advertisements to a fax machine. It has been viewed by most courts addressing the issue as creating a private right of action for anyone receiving an unwanted fax advertisement, permitting the recovery of $500 for each violation. When massive "blast" faxes (thousands at a time) violate the law, it can expose the sender to huge damage awards, which in turn attracts lawyers and can encourage litigation, particularly with the availability of the class action for this type of situation.

Sure enough, passage of the TCPA, combined with the continued incorrigibility or negligence of fax advertisers,[1] led to junk fax lawsuits, which

---

1. One common means of avoiding TCPA junk fax liability is for the advertising vendor to obtain the consent of the intended targets of the fax advertisements. For example, when joining an organization, making a purchase, applying for a credit account, or otherwise shopping, vendors often solicit consent to receive fax and e-mail advertisements. Failure to obtain consent or inadequately documented consent can lead to junk fax liability even for the vender that was not intentionally violating the law.

in turn led the defendants to look to their commercial general liability insurers for coverage. Commercial general liability (CGL) carriers resisted, producing a coverage litigation boom of sorts that began in earnest in the late 1990s, slowed because of the deterrent effect of the TCPA and exclusionary language now added to many CGL policies, but continues to unfold in a more halting, episodic pace.

Because the majority of TCPA statutory claims have been filed in federal court and because insurer-policyholder disputes often satisfy federal diversity jurisdiction requirements, the vast bulk of junk fax coverage decisions have been in federal court,[2] creating some continuing uncertainty in that relatively few state supreme courts have issued definitive coverage decisions. The lack of certainty is magnified somewhat in that, despite the general consistent standardization of CGL policies, the operative policy language at issue (usually portions of the personal and advertising injury coverage provisions) often differs, at least slightly. However, the basic arguments for and against coverage are now well-defined and some rough consensus or majority rule has emerged.

Policyholders seeking to obtain coverage under Part A of the CGL form (bodily injury and property damage) typically argue that, when sued under the TCPA, they are being accused of negligently inflicting "property damage" upon the recipients of junk faxes by using their paper and ink. In response, insurers commonly argue that the injurious sending of a junk fax by the policyholder was not an "accident" or "occurrence" and that the injuries inflicted were expected or intended from the standpoint of the policyholder. In response, policyholders contend that although the sending of the fax was volitional, its harm to the recipient was unexpected, unintended, and sufficiently accidental in that the policyholder assumed the fax would be appreciated as conveying useful information about the policyholder's products or services. Policyholders have generally not succeeded with this argument but there are some cases to the contrary. *See generally Universal Underwriters Ins. Co. v. Lou Fusz Automotive Network, Inc.*, 401 F.3d 876 (8th Cir. 2005) (applying Missouri law) (where junk faxes sent accidentally or under misimpression that there was consent of recipient, blast-faxing may qualify as an accident or occurrence with no intent or expectation of injury, but rejecting argument in instant case). For the most part, however, insurers have prevailed, with most courts rejecting claims for coverage for claims of property damage under Part A of the CGL form.

---

2. However, it appears clear that the TCPA creates concurrent jurisdiction and that junk fax claims may be brought in either federal or state court. *See MLC Mortgage Corp. v. Sun America Mortgage Co.*, 212 P.3d 1199, 1201 (Okla. 2009) ("[w]e join the almost unanimous pronouncements of extant federal and state courts having decided the issue and determine that private parties may pursue violation of the TCPA in [state] courts.") (also noting that statute creates private right of action).

More precisely, courts in junk fax coverage cases have usually been addressing whether the insurer must defend the junk fax claim rather than whether a successful junk fax judgment falls within coverage. As noted above, many junk fax claims have been brought as class actions, which tend to result in settlement rather than trial at even a higher rate than litigation overall, which only results in full-fledged trial in fewer than 5 percent of cases filed.

Where a matter settles, it is generally subject to insurance coverage if the claim had triggered the insurer's duty to defend. Indeed, where the duty to defend obtains, insurers are usually managing the litigation, perhaps defending under a reservation of rights, and agreeing to the settlement. Alternatively, where the insurer has refused to defend, it often does so at its peril. If the claim has a potential for coverage, the duty to defend attaches, which in most states permits the policyholder to make a good faith, reasonable settlement of the matter and obtain coverage in cases where the insurer has failed to defend. And in some states, the policyholder in certain circumstances is free to settle the potentially covered claim without the insurer's consent even though the insurer is defending the claim so long as the settlement is substantively reasonable and not collusive.

Although insurers have had substantial success avoiding even the duty to defend under Part A of the CGL standard form, policyholders have often been successful in obtaining a defense of junk fax claims under Part B of the CGL policy, which provides coverage for personal injury and advertising injury. Typically, Part B of the CGL policy provides coverage where the plaintiff claims injury by the policyholder for, among other things, "oral or written publication, in any manner, of material that violates a person's right of privacy," with some modest variance in policy language. As discussed below, it is under this provision of the CGL policy that policyholders usually succeed in obtaining coverage for junk fax claims.

A common Part B insuring agreement provides that the insurer

> will pay those sums that the insured becomes legally obligated to pay as damages because of "personal and advertising injury" to which this insurance applies. We will have the right and duty to defend the insured against any "suit" seeking those damages. However, we will have no duty to defend the insured against any "suit" seeking damages for "personal and advertising injury" to which this insurance does not apply. We may, at our discretion, investigate any offense and settle any claim or "suit" that may result.

*See, e.g.,* Ins. Servs. Office Props., Inc., Commercial General Liability Coverage Form, No. CG 00011207, § IB1 (2007).

Personal injury is commonly defined, within a dual-definition for "personal and advertising injury," as follows:

[I]njury, including consequential "bodily injury", arising out of one or more of the following offenses:

False arrest, detention or imprisonment;

Malicious prosecution;

The wrongful eviction from, wrongful entry into, or invasion of the right of private occupancy of a room, dwelling or premises that a person occupies, committed by or on behalf of its owner, landlord or lessor;

Oral or written publication, in any manner, of material that slanders or libels a person or organization or disparages a person's or organization's goods, products or services;

Oral or written publication, in any manner, of material that violates a person's right of privacy;

The use of another's advertising idea in your "advertisement"; or

Infringing upon another's copyright, trade dress or slogan in your "advertisement."

ISO FORM, CG 00011207 at § V14.

Part B then lists various exclusions from coverage claims for personal injury or advertising injury.

Boiled down to its essence, the debate in most junk fax coverage disputes is whether that aspect of the definition of "personal and advertising injury" for "[o]ral or written publication, in any manner, of material that violates a person's right to privacy," has been satisfied, thereby triggering the CGL insurer's duty to defend.

Insurers commonly argue that, while the unwanted fax may be annoying, it does not invade the plaintiff's privacy in that it reveals no sensitive or embarrassing information about the plaintiff. Conversely, policyholders argue that the right of privacy is one of seclusion—a right not to be bothered—and that his right is violated by junk faxes even where the materials faxed contain no revelations about the claimant.

The majority of courts deciding the issue have agreed with policyholders on this point and found that there is at least the potential for coverage of junk fax claims under the CGL policy, requiring the insurer to defend a claim that unwanted sending of junk faxes constituted an invasion of privacy within the meaning of Part B of the policy. *See, e.g., Penzer v. Transportation Ins. Co.*, 29 So. 3d 1000 (Fla. 2010) (answering in the affirmative certified question: "Does a [CGL] policy which provides coverage for 'oral or written publication of material that violates a person's right of privacy' . . . provide coverage for damages for violation of a law prohibiting using any [fax] machine to send unsolicited advertisement to a [fax] machine... when no private information is revealed in the facsimile?"). *Id.* at 1002 (large capitalization in certified question eliminated). *But see Penzer* at 1005 n.5 (Fla. 2010) (noting that "courts applying diverse reasoning have come down on both sides of the ledger") (citing cases).

These cases set forth extensive analysis of the issues and review several insurance policies with slightly different language but consistently reflect what appears to be the majority rule: no Part A bodily injury/property damage coverage because the sending of junk faxes is sufficiently intentional and likely to inflict injury; but a potential for Part B personal and advertising injury coverage (and likely indemnity coverage if the allegations of the complaint are correct) because receipt of unwanted faxes is invasion of privacy—right to be left alone—even if the faxes themselves contained no revealing or negative material about the recipient. *See also Terra Nova Ins. Co. v. Fray-Witzer*, 869 N.E.2d 565, 574–76 (Mass. 2007) (applying New Jersey law) (finding that TCPA is a remedial rather than penal statute and that coverage is not precluded by language excluding payment of penalties and that statutory damages provision does not constitute punitive damages for purposes of CGL provision excluding coverage for punitive damage liability); *Valley Forge Ins. Co. v. Swiderski Electronics, Inc.*, 860 N.E.2d 307, 315 (Ill. 2006) ("The essence of a TCPA fax-ad claim is that one party sends another an unsolicited fax advertisement. The receipt of an unsolicited fax advertisement implicates a person's right of privacy insofar as it violates a person's seclusion, and such violation is one of the injuries that a TCPA fax-ad claim is intended to vindicate.") (citation omitted).

As the *Swiderski Electronics* Court further observed:

> By faxing advertisements to the proposed class of fax recipients as alleged in [plaintiff] Rizzo's complaint, [defendant] Swiderski engaged in the "written *** publication" of the advertisements. Furthermore, the "material" that Swiderski allegedly published, advertisements, qualifies as "material that violates a person's right of privacy," because, according to the complaint, the advertisements were sent without first obtaining the recipients' permission, and therefore violated their privacy interest in seclusion. The language of the "advertising injury" provision is sufficiently broad to encompass the conduct alleged in the complaint. To adopt the insurers' proposed interpretation of it—i.e., that it is only applicable where the content of the published material reveals private information about a person that violates the person's right of privacy—would essentially require us to rewrite the phrase "material that violates a person's right of privacy" to read "material *the content of which* violates a person *other than the recipient's* right of privacy." This we will not do.

860 N.E.2d at 317–18 (italics in original).

An opposing perspective is reflected in *American States Ins. Co. v. Capital Associates of Jackson County, Inc.*, 392 F.3d 939 (7th Cir. 2004), where a federal appeals court applying Illinois law rejected any potential for coverage (and hence any duty to defend) for junk fax claims. Although *American States v. Capital Associates* has subsequently been replaced by *Swiderski Electronics* as the authoritative word on Illinois law, it remains an influential case and one that may be invoked by insurers resisting coverage in jurisdictions where the state's supreme court has not yet addressed the issue. *See also Resource Bankshares Corp. v. St. Paul Mercury Ins. Co.*, 407 F.3d 631, 641 (4th Cir. 2005) (applying Virginia law) (finding no potential for coverage and no duty to defend) (accepting insurer argument that right to privacy violation must involve more than mere intrusion but also reveal information).

One rationale employed by courts to conclude that an insurer does not owe coverage to its insured, for a TCPA violation, is that the "right of privacy" coverage in the policy must be interpreted with a view toward the words that surround it:

> Looking at the relevant definition of advertising injury in context persuades us that advertising injury coverage applies only to content-based claims. The provision at issue falls in the middle of four definitions of "advertising injury": (1) "oral or written publication of material that slanders or libels a person or organization or disparages a person's or organization's goods, products or services"; (2) *"oral or written publication of material that violates a person's right of privacy"*; (3) "misappropriation of advertising ideas or style of doing business"; or (4) "infringement of copyright, title or slogan." Definitions 1, 3 and 4 all involve injury caused by the information contained in the advertisement. In each of these cases, the victim is injured by the content of the advertisement, not its mere sending and receipt. Viewed in this context, definition 3 (sic) may most reasonably be interpreted as referring to advertising material whose content violates a persons right of privacy.

*State Farm General Ins. Co. v. JT's Frames, Inc.*, 104 Cal. Rptr. 3d 573, 587 (Cal. Ct. App. 2010) (emphasis in original).

Another rational used by courts to justify a lack of TCPA coverage is that "[t]he structure of the policy strongly implies that coverage is limited to secrecy interests. It covers a 'publication' that violates a right of privacy. In a secrecy situation, publication matters; otherwise secrecy is maintained. In a seclusion situation, publication is irrelevant." *American States Ins. Co.*, 392 F.3d at 942 (7th Cir. 2004).

As with many areas of insurance law, the ultimate resolution of a coverage dispute over junk fax claims varies from state to state and requires examination of each jurisdiction. In the absence of authoritative state supreme court guidance, both insurers and policyholders can marshal supporting authority from various courts, perhaps even federal courts or other state courts purporting to apply the instant state's law on the issue. But as the divergence between the Seventh Circuit in *American States* and the Illinois Supreme Court in *Swiderski Electronics* reveals, care must be taken not to rely too rigidly on federal court cases that under the *Erie* doctrine have power only to "predict" controlling state law. It is for the states' respective supreme courts to authoritatively announce state law on junk fax and other insurance matters.

For additional discussion of personal and advertising injury issues and junk fax coverage issues, *see* JEFFREY W. STEMPEL, STEMPEL ON INSURANCE CONTRACTS §§14.05, 14.06 (3d ed. 2006 & Supp. 2009); BARRY R. OSTRAGER & THOMAS R. NEWMAN, HANDBOOK ON INSURANCE COVERAGE DISPUTES §7.04(b) (7) (15th ed. 2009); PETER KALIS, THOMAS M. REITER, & JAMES R. SEGERDAHL, POLICYHOLDER'S GUIDE TO INSURANCE COVERAGE § 8.04 (1997 & Supp. 2004).

## 50-State Survey: Invasion of Privacy: Guidance from "Junk Fax" Claims

**Alabama:** No instructive authority.

**Alaska:** No instructive authority.

**Arizona:** No instructive authority. *But see National Union Fire Ins. Co. of Pittsburg, Pennsylvania v. ESI Ergonomic Solutions, LLC,* 342 F. Supp. 2d 853 (D. Ariz. 2004) (insurer failed to prove a justiciable controversy because the insured had not disputed the denial of coverage for TCPA junk fax violations).

**Arkansas:** No instructive authority.

**California:** The California Court of Appeal held that a duty to defend was not created by policy language covering damages for an advertising injury caused by "making known to any person or organization written or spoken material that violates an individual's right of privacy" because "making known" implies divulging information regarding a third party. *ACS Systems Inc. v. St. Paul Fire & Marine Ins. Co.,* 53 Cal. Rptr. 3d 786 (Cal. Ct. App. 2007). In other words, the content of the "material," when divulged, must violate a third party's right to privacy; not that the fax violates the receiver's sense of seclusion. Examining the duty to defend under the property damage clause, the court held that the duty to defend was not triggered because the faxes were intentional, and therefore not an "accident," which would trigger coverage. "[F]axes did not violate the recipients' right of privacy so as to constitute an 'advertising injury offense.'" *Id.* at 796. Similarly, "property damage was not caused by an 'event' because the fax transmissions were not an 'accident.'" *Id.* at 799; *see also State Farm General Ins. Co. v. JT's Frames, Inc.,* 104 Cal. Rptr. 3d 573 (Cal. Ct. App. 2010) (following *ACS*).

**Colorado:** No instructive authority.

**Connecticut:** No instructive authority.

**Delaware:** No instructive authority. *See New Century Mortgage Corp. v. Great Northern Ins. Co.,* No. 07-640, 2009 WL 3444759, at *5 (D. Del. Oct. 26, 2009) (applying Illinois law) (following *Valley Forge Ins. Co. v. Swiderski Electronics, Inc.,* 860 N.E.2d 307 (Ill. 2006) and holding that the right of privacy connotes both an interest in seclusion and secrecy of personal information, and, therefore, because an unsolicited fax violates an individual's seclusion, TCPA claims fall within the policy's advertising injury provision).

**Florida:** The Supreme Court of Florida held that the insurer had a duty to defend a TCPA action involving 24,000 junk faxes. *Penzer v. Transportation Ins. Co.*, 29 So. 3d 1000 (Fla. 2010). The court placed importance on "right" in "right of privacy" because "the plain meaning of 'right of privacy' is the legal claim one may make for privacy, which is to be gleaned from federal or Florida law, rather than defined by a dictionary." *Id.* at 1006. The court held that the TCPA was enacted to protect the privacy right to seclusion, and the plain language of the advertising injury provision provided coverage for the claim. "Based on our plain meaning analysis, we hold that an advertising injury provision in a commercial liability policy that provides coverage for an 'oral or written publication of material that violates a person's right of privacy' provides coverage for blast-faxing in violation of the TCPA." *Id.* at 1008.

**Georgia:** The Eleventh Circuit, applying Georgia law, held that an insurer was obligated to satisfy a final judgment after the policyholder lost a TCPA case. *Hooters of Augusta, Inc. v. American Global Ins. Co.*, 157 Fed. Appx. 201 (11th Cir. 2005). The insurance policy contained "no language explicitly limiting the scope of the term 'privacy' or, for that matter, alerting non-expert policyholders that coverage depends on the source of law underlying the relevant policy right." The court then followed Georgia law on contract interpretation and construed the ambiguous term in favor of greater coverage, and found a duty to defend. "The text of the policy and the language of the TCPA resolve these issues in favor of coverage when read in light of controlling Georgia law." *Id.* at 205. *See also Hooters of Augusta, Inc. v. American Global Ins. Co.*, 272 F. Supp. 2d 1365 (S.D. Ga. 2003) (lower court decision).

**Hawaii:** No instructive authority.

**Idaho:** No instructive authority.

**Illinois:** The Supreme Court of Illinois held that the TCPA protects the fax-receiver's "right to privacy," which includes the right to seclusion. *Valley Forge Ins. Co. v. Swiderski Electronics, Inc.*, 860 N.E.2d 307 (Ill. 2006). The Court reasoned that because the policies in question did not specifically define "right to privacy" violations (which are covered under the policies) to mean an interest in seclusion or an interest in secrecy, the court must use both meanings. Therefore, the advertising injury clause created a duty to defend. "The receipt of an unsolicited fax advertisement implicates a person's right of privacy insofar as it violates a person's seclusion, and such a violation is one of the injuries that a TCPA fax-ad claim is intended to vindicate." *Id.* at 315. The court noted that its decision was in line with the majority of federal courts that already decided the issue. *Id.* at 319. The court declined to reach whether the policy's Part A provision for property damage coverage would also trigger a duty to defend. *Id.* at 323.

**Indiana:** Indiana federal District Courts appear split on the availability of coverage for a TCPA violation. In *American Family Mutual Ins. Co. v. C.M.A. Mortgage, Inc.*, 682 F. Supp. 2d 879 (S.D. Ind. 2010), the court looked to *Swiderski* (*see* Illinois, *supra*) for its decision that there was a duty to defend under the advertising injury clause. *Id.* at 885. The court also compared injuries that arise under the TCPA with the Fair Credit Reporting Act: "The relevant question is not whether a tort has occurred; rather, the controlling issue is whether an insured would reasonably understand the policy language at issue to provide coverage." *Id. But see Ace Mortgage Funding, Inc. v. Travelers Indemnity Co. of Am.*, No. 1:05-cv-1631, 2008 WL 686953 (S.D. Ind. Mar. 10, 2008) and *Erie Ins. Exchange v. Kevin T. Watts, Inc.*, No. 1:05-cv-867, 2006 WL 3755329 (S.D. Ind. Dec. 19, 2006) (both concluding that there was no duty to defend under the advertising injury clause).

**Iowa:** The Seventh Circuit Court of Appeals held that no duty to defend a TCPA claim was owed. *Auto-Owners Ins. Co. v. Websolv Computing, Inc.*, 580 F.3d 543 (7th Cir. 2009) (applying Iowa law). The court decided to "stand by [the] analysis in *American States* [392 F.3d 939 (7th Cir. 2004)], even though Illinois has since adopted a different approach." *Id.* at 550. The "most natural reading of ['oral or written publication of material that violates a person's right of privacy'] is that it covers claims arising when the insured publicizes some secret or personal information—not claims arising when the insured disrupts another's seclusion." *Id.* Although Iowa courts had not addressed the issue, the court declined to certify the question because the insurance industry had begun to issue an endorsement specifically excluding TCPA claims from coverage, making the issue not worthy of certification. *Id.* at 549 n.3.

**Kansas:** The Tenth Circuit Court of Appeals held that a duty to defend a TCPA claim existed under the advertising injury provision of the policy because "privacy," as used in the policy, was ambiguous and, therefore, construed against the drafter. *Park University Enterprise, Inc. v. American Casualty Co. of Reading, Pa.*, 442 F.3d 1239 (10th Cir. 2006). "[W]hen the policy is strictly construed against American and in favor of Park University, a TCPA invasion of seclusion claim might be covered by the policy's advertising injury provisions." *Id.* at 1251.

**Kentucky:** No instructive authority.

**Louisiana:** No instructive authority. *Starnet Ins. Co. v. Fueltrac, Inc.*, Slip Copy, 2009 WL 1210508 (W.D. La. May 1, 2009) (insurance coverage for TCPA claims at issue, but court transferred case to the Middle District of Louisiana when insured failed to establish venue within the Western District).

**Maine:** No instructive authority.

**Maryland:** No instructive authority.

**Massachusetts:** A Massachusetts District Court held that the language in the policy was ambiguous because it did not define the term "right to privacy," and any ambiguity must be construed in favor of coverage. *Cynosure, Inc. v. St. Paul Fire & Marine Ins. Co.*, Slip Copy, No. 08-11210-PBS, 2009 WL 949077, at *2 (D. Mass. Apr. 8, 2009). The court relied upon *Terra Nova Ins. Co. v. Fray-Witzer*, 869 N.E.2d 565 (Mass. 2007) (*see* New Jersey, *infra*) as binding authority, even though the Massachusetts high court in that case was applying New Jersey law.

**Michigan:** No instructive authority. *See Farm Bureau Mut. Ins. Co. v. Graphics House Sports*, No. 277659, 2008 WL 2439997, at *4 (Mich. Ct. App. June 17, 2008) (declining to address whether coverage was owed for junk faxes because the claims had been threatened but not yet filed) ("[The insurer] asked the court to issue a declaratory judgment with regard to whether its policy provides [the insured] insurance coverage against claims that may never be brought. This is not a case where a declaratory judgment is necessary to guide [the insurer's] future conduct in order to preserve its legal rights.").

**Minnesota:** No instructive authority.

**Mississippi:** No instructive authority.

**Missouri:** The Eighth Circuit Court of Appeals held that unsolicited faxes constituted "injury" under the liability insurance policy defining injury to include private nuisance and invasion of rights of privacy/possession of personal property. *Universal Underwriters Ins. Co. v. Lou Fusz Automotive Network, Inc.*, 401 F.3d 876 (8th Cir. 2005) (applying Missouri law). The court noted that, although intent was not relevant to interpreting the TCPA, it was relevant to determining if the policy at issue provided coverage. If a finder of fact found that the faxes were sent with the intent to cause harm, the policy would not provide any coverage. The court distinguished its holding from *American States Ins. Co. v. Capital Associates of Jackson County, Inc.*, 392 F.3d 939, 940 (7th Cir. 2004), which found no duty to defend, because "the intentional nature of the violations [in *American*] appeared undisputed, and the policy specifically excluded... losses that were 'expected or intended from the standpoint of the insured.'" *Id.* at 882–83.

**Montana:** No instructive authority.

**Nebraska:** No instructive authority.

**Nevada:** No instructive authority.

**New Hampshire:** No instructive authority.

**New Jersey:** The Supreme Judicial Court of Massachusetts, applying New Jersey law, held that a duty to defend a TCPA action existed under the advertising injury provision because "right to privacy" was susceptible to two meanings and if the insurer intended to only cover right to secrecy claims, rather than those and right to seclusion claims, the policy language should have clarified as much. *Terra Nova Ins. Co. v. Fray-Witzer*, 869 N.E.2d 565 (Mass. 2007) (applying New Jersey law although stating that there was no relevant difference between New Jersey and Massachusetts law). "Although we conclude that the facsimile transmissions at issue were not 'accidents,' for purposes of insurance coverage, we hold that these advertisements violated their recipients' right of privacy, such that insurance coverage is triggered." *Id.* at 567. However, in *St. Paul Fire & Marine Ins. Co. v. Brother International Corp.*, 319 Fed. Appx. 121 (3rd Cir. 2009) (applying New Jersey law), the Third Circuit held that the policy's advertising injury provision did not apply to junk faxes. *Id.* at 125. The court reasoned that the phrase "making known" suggests a focus on secrecy and implies a disclosure to a third party. *Id.* at 125–26. The federal appeals court also concluded that no coverage was owed under the "property damage" portion of the policy: "Because the property damage here is the depletion of paper and toner, and because [the insured] knew that this damage would occur as a result of its unsolicited advertisements, we hold that [the insured] expected or intended to cause the injury." *Id.* at 127.

**New Mexico:** No instructive authority.

**New York:** A New York trial court held that coverage was owed for a TCPA claim. *Merchants and Businessmen's Mutual Ins. Co. v. A.P.O. Health Co.,* 28 N.Y.L.J. 1 (Aug. 29, 2002) (Supreme Court Nassau County). "Applying the test of common speech and focusing on the reasonable expectations of the insured, the Court concludes that the dissemination and receipt of unsolicited facsimile transmissions qualifies as a violation of the right of privacy, thereby triggering the coverage provision of the subject policies."); *see also Rudgayzer & Gratt v. Enine, Inc.,* 749 N.Y.S.2d 855, 450 n.5 (N.Y. City Civ. Ct. 2002), *rev'd on other grounds,* 779 N.Y.S.2d 882 (App. Div. 2004) (holding that insurer required to defend and indemnify a TCPA claim).

**North Carolina:** A North Carolina District Court found a duty to defend TCPA claims under the property damage portion of the policy because, although the policy defined the word occurrence as "an accident," the policy did not define "accident" and therefore it "include[d] injury resulting from an intentional act, if the injury is not intentional or substantially certain to be the result of the intentional act." *Prime TV, LLC v. Travelers Ins. Co.,* 223 F. Supp. 2d 744 (M.D.N.C. 2002). The court concluded that the insured believed that its faxes were sent to individuals that had requested the faxed information, and the insured had a duty to defend. *Id.* at 751–52. The court also held that the TCPA claims would be covered under the advertising injury clause because the faxes violated a right to privacy and the insured did not "have knowledge of [the faxes'] falsity," which would trigger an exception to the advertising injury coverage of right to privacy violations. *Id.* at 752–53.

**North Dakota:** No instructive authority.

**Ohio:** The Ohio Court of Appeals held that an insurer had an obligation to defend a TCPA action. *Motorists Mutual Ins. Co. v. Dandy-Jim, Inc.,* 912 N.E.2d 659 (Ohio Ct. App. 2009). The insurer argued that there should be no coverage for TCPA violations under the advertising injury provision because the TCPA was enacted to protect the seclusionary aspect of the right of privacy while the insurance policy intended to cover only the secrecy aspect of the right to privacy. The court rejected this view, stating that "'in determining the coverage issue… as opposed to TCPA-based claims in general, it matters not what kind of privacy interest the TCPA is meant to protect; rather, what matters is whether *the policy in question* provides coverage for TCPA-based claims that allege invasion of one's right of privacy in terms of seclusion.'" *Id.* at 665 (quoting *Schuetz v. State Farm Fire & Casualty Co.*, 890 N.E.2d 374 (Ohio Com. Pl. 2007)). The court also found that insurance coverage of treble damages was not against public policy because the TCPA was not punitive in nature.

**Oklahoma:** No instructive authority.

**Oregon:** No instructive authority.

**Pennsylvania:** The Superior Court of Pennsylvania, after noting the split in authority nationally over the issue, determined to follow the Eastern District of Pennsylvania's decision in *Melrose Hotel, infra,* and held that coverage was not owed under the advertising injury provision of the policy for junk faxes. *Telecommunications Network Design and Paradise Distributing Inc. v. Brethren Mutual Ins. Co.*, __ A.2d __, 2010 Pa. Super. 155, *11 (Pa. Super. Ct. Aug. 23, 2010). The court reasoned that the TCPA was enacted to protect one's right to be let alone. *Id.* at *11. However, the covered offenses listed in the policy "refer to the content of the material covered by the policies. Libel, slander, misuse of another's ideas or style, and copyright infringement, specifically focus on the message contained in the covered materials. None of these provisions address the intrusive nature of the method used to convey the message. Rather, the focus is on the content of the message itself." *Id.* at *13 (citations omitted). *See also Melrose Hotel Co. v. St. Paul Fire & Marine Ins. Co.*, 432 F. Supp. 2d 488 (E.D. Pa. 2006), *aff'd by* 503 F.3d 339 (3rd Cir. 2007) (predicting that a Pennsylvania state court would rule that the term "accident" in the property damage provision would not trigger a duty to defend based on Pennsylvania's interpretation of "accident," and, regarding the advertising injury provision, "privacy" refers to interests in secrecy).

**Rhode Island:** No instructive authority.

**South Carolina:** No instructive authority.

**South Dakota:** No instructive authority.

**Tennessee:** No instructive authority.

**Texas:** The Court of Appeals of Texas held that the plaintiff's right to privacy was sufficiently violated by written material so as to trigger a duty to defend a TCPA action under the advertising injury clause. *TIG Ins. Co. v. Dallas Basketball, Ltd.*, 129 S.W.3d 232 (Tex. Ct. App. 2004). "The [TCPA] presumes all advertising, so long as it is unsolicited, is an offensive intrusion into the recipient's solitude." *Id.* at 238 (citing *W. Rim Inv. Advisors v. Gulf Ins. Co.*, 269 F. Supp. 836 (N.D. Tex. 2003)); *see also Nutmeg Ins. Co. v. Employers Ins. Co. of Wausau*, No. Civ. A. 3:04-CV-1762B, 2006 WL 453235, at *10 (N.D. Tex. Feb. 24, 2006) (concluding that the Supreme Court of Texas would adopt the reasoning in *TIG* and held that a duty to defend a TCPA action was triggered under the advertising injury clause).

**Utah:** No instructive authority.

**Vermont:** No instructive authority.

**Virginia:** The Fourth Circuit Court of Appeals held that an insurer did not have a duty to defend an insured-bank that "accidentally" sent mass fax advertisements. *Resource Bankshares Corp. v. St. Paul Mercury Ins. Co.*, 407 F.3d 631 (4th Cir. 2005) (applying Virginia law). The court identified two meanings for "the right of privacy": "secrecy" and "seclusion." *Id.* at 640. The court determined that there was no duty to defend under the property damage provision because sending unsolicited faxes in violation of the TCPA are not "accidents" as required by the insurance policy. *Id.* at 638. The court also held the insurer had no duty to defend under the advertising injury coverage part because, although some "privacy" violations were involved, the "right to privacy" clause in the insurance policy, read in conjunction with surrounding clauses (discussing libel, slander, and unauthorized use of ideas), indicated that the advertising injury clause was intended to cover "the sharing of the *content* of the ad, not the mere *receipt* of the advertisement." *Id.* at 641 (emphasis in original).

**Washington:** The Ninth Circuit Court of Appeals held that the insurer did not have a duty to defend TCPA claims under the advertising injury provision of the policy. The court stated that the policy only covered a right to secrecy and the claim involved a right to seclusion. *St. Paul Fire & Marine Ins. Co. v. Onvia Inc.*, 301 Fed. Appx. 707 (9th Cir. 2008) (applying Washington law).

**West Virginia:** No instructive authority.

**Wisconsin:** No instructive authority.

**Wyoming:** No instructive authority.

CHAPTER

# 19

# Insurability of Punitive Damages

It is a question that is uttered by claims professionals and coverage counsel on a regular basis: Are punitive damages insurable in such and such state? In essence, what the questioner is often asking is whether the particular state's public policy permits a tortfeasor to insure against punitive damages that he or she may be legally obligated to pay. The answer provided is often one word: yes or no. While one of those two may be the right one generally, the issue is oftentimes much more complex than can be adequately answered with a single word. In fact, when all of the variations of the issue are considered, there may be as many as a dozen possible answers to the question.

The Supreme Court of Texas recognized the wide variation that exists over the insurability of punitive damages:

> The cases defy easy categorization, but it appears that: 19 states generally permit coverage of punitive damages; 8 states would permit coverage of punitive damages for grossly negligent conduct, but not for more serious conduct; 11 states would permit coverage of punitive damages for vicariously-assessed liability, but not directly-assessed liability; 7 states generally prohibit an insured from indemnifying himself against punitive damages; and the remainder have silent, unclear, or otherwise inapplicable law. States may fall into more than one category.

*Fairfield Ins. Co. v. Stephens Martin Paving, L.P.*, 246 S.W.3d 653, 688 (Tex. 2008) (Hecht, J., concurring).[1]

---

1. The Texas Supreme Court categorized the states as follows: The nineteen states that generally **permit** coverage of punitive damages are Alabama, Alaska, Arizona, Delaware, Georgia, Hawaii, Idaho, Maryland, Mississippi, Montana, New Hampshire, New Mexico, North Carolina, South Carolina, Tennessee, Vermont, Washington, Wisconsin, and Wyoming. The eight states that would permit coverage of punitive damages for **grossly negligent** conduct, but not for more serious conduct are Arkansas, Iowa, Kentucky, Louisiana, Nevada, Oregon, Virginia,

As the Texas high court demonstrated, the question of the insurability of punitive damages does not want for case law. The issue has been considered in every state, including, most of the time, by its highest court. Coverage for punitive damages has also been addressed in a few instances by state legislatures. The issue is a mature one and has well-defined battle lines. And as is often the case when an issue may turn on public policy considerations, judges are not shy about their feelings. Authors of opinions are frequently passionate in their views and dissenting opinions are not uncommon.

An award of punitive damages requires egregious conduct. *See State Farm Mut. Auto. Ins. Co. v. Campbell*, 538 U.S. 408, 419 (2003) ("[P]unitive damages should only be awarded if the defendant's culpability, after having paid compensatory damages, is so reprehensible as to warrant the imposition of further sanctions to achieve punishment or deterrence."). Therefore, even before reaching the public policy considerations, it is not unreasonable to ask why coverage would exist in the first place, under the terms of an insurance policy, for conduct that was "so reprehensible." For example, coverage under a commercial general liability policy requires an "occurrence," defined as an accident. Surely any conduct that can support an award of punitive damages could not have been accidental. But consider that the issue also arises outside of "occurrence" based commercial general liability policies that provide coverage for "bodily injury" or "property damage." The availability of coverage for punitive damages arises in such contexts as the "personal injury" section of a commercial general liability (CGL) policy, which covers some intentional torts, as well as CGL policies that have nonstandard language, automobile policies, and professional liability policies. And sometimes this issue is simply not addressed at all.

In addition, while an award of punitive damages requires egregious conduct, there are many different levels of such conduct. This can have an important affect on the availability of insurance for both compensatory and punitive damages. For example, West Virginia's highest court held that where "the liability policy of an insurance company provides that it will pay on behalf of the insured all sums which the insured shall become legally obligated to pay as damages because of bodily injury and the policy only excludes damages caused intentionally by or at the direction of the insured, such policy

---

and West Virginia. The eleven states that would permit coverage of punitive damages for **vicariously-assessed** liability, but not directly-assessed liability are California, Connecticut, Florida, Illinois, Indiana, Kansas, Kentucky, Minnesota, New Jersey, Oklahoma, and Pennsylvania. The seven states that generally **prohibit** an insured from indemnifying himself against punitive damages are Colorado, New York, North Dakota, Ohio, Rhode Island, South Dakota, and Utah. The states that have **silent, unclear, or otherwise inapplicable** law are Maine, Massachusetts, Michigan, Missouri, and Nebraska. *Stephens Martin Paving*, 246 S.W.3d at 688, nn.92–96. For further discussion, *see* the fifty-state survey of the insurability of punitive damages, *infra*.

will be deemed to cover punitive damages arising from bodily injury occasioned by gross, reckless or wanton negligence on the part of the insured." *Hensley v. Erie Ins. Co.*, 283 S.E.2d 227, 230 (W. Va. 1981). The court drew this distinction on the basis of its belief that gross, reckless, or wanton negligence does not carry the same degree of culpability as a purposeful or intentional tort, and, therefore, the right to insurance coverage should not be foreclosed. *Id.* at 233. In general, it is important to be mindful that the degree of culpability that gave rise to the award of punitive damages in the first place can have an impact on the insurance coverage issue.

The overarching public policy debate concerning insurance coverage for punitive damages is well-illustrated by the competing arguments made in the two most frequently cited decisions on the issue—*Northwestern National Casualty Co. v. McNulty*, 307 F.2d 432 (5th Cir. 1962) (applying Florida law) and *Lazenby v. Universal Underwriters Insurance Co.*, 383 S.W.2d 1 (Tenn. 1964).

In *McNulty*, the Fifth Circuit Court of Appeals held that public policy precluded a tortfeasor from securing insurance coverage for punitive damages that were awarded against him for bodily injury that he caused while driving drunk. *McNulty*, 307 F.2d at 440. In the eyes of the *McNulty* Court, to allow insurance for punitive damages would frustrate their purpose. *Id.* Since punitive damages are awarded for punishment and deterrence, it would serve no useful purpose if the party responsible for the wrong could shift the burden to its insurance company. *Id.* The court also described a global impact on the insurance market that it predicted would result if coverage for punitive damages were permitted:

> [Punitive] damages do not compensate the plaintiff for his injury, since compensatory damages already have made the plaintiff whole. And there is no point in punishing the insurance company; it has done no wrong. In actual fact, of course, and considering the extent to which the public is insured, the burden would ultimately come to rest not on the insurance companies but on the public, since the added liability to the insurance companies would be passed along to the premium payers. Society would then be punishing itself for the wrong committed by the insured.

*Id.*

The other side of the coin is *Lazenby*, where the Supreme Court of Tennessee was not convinced by the *McNulty* rationale for disallowing insurance coverage for punitive damages. *Lazenby*, 383 S.W.2d at 5. The Tennessee high court concluded that it was speculative that socially irresponsible drivers would be deterred from their wrongful conduct if coverage for punitive damages were not allowed. *Id.* "This State, in regard to the proper operation of motor vehicles, has a great many detailed criminal sanctions, which apparently have not deterred this slaughter on our highways and streets." *Id.*

The argument that there is a lack of any correlation between the insurability of punitive damages and irresponsible conduct was addressed with vigor by the Supreme Court of Wyoming in *Sinclair Oil Corp. v. Columbia Casualty Co.*, 682 P.2d 975 (Wyo. 1984). In holding that it was not against Wyoming public policy to insure against punitive damages, the court stated:

> We know of no studies, statistics or proofs which indicate that contracts of insurance to protect against liability for punitive damages have a tendency to make willful or wanton misconduct more probable, nor do we know of any substantial relationship between the insurance coverage and such misconduct. Neither is there any indication that to invalidate insurance contracts that protect against liability for punitive damages on grounds of public policy would have any tendency to deter willful and wanton misconduct.

*Sinclair Oil*, 682 P.2d at 981.

The competing rationales surrounding the insurability of punitive damages were also identified by the Supreme Court of Wisconsin in *Brown v. Maxey*, 369 N.W.2d 677 (Wis. 1985). On one hand, insurance for punitive damages would undermine their purpose and shift liability to the public in the form of higher insurance premiums. *Id.* at 687. On the other hand, the court observed that allowing insurance coverage for punitive damages is appropriate because public policy favors compelling an insurer to perform those obligations for which it contracted and received premium, the insurer could have excluded such coverage, there are alternative sanctions that can be imposed on an offender and it is questionable whether punitive damages have a deterrent effect. *Id.*

While "public policy" is often the starting point, and most frequently debated aspect of the insurability of punitive damages, the analysis does not always end there. There are in fact many other facets and nuances surrounding the issue that must be considered.

Simply because coverage for punitive damages is not precluded by public policy does not per se create such coverage. The availability of coverage for punitive damages is still dependent upon the existence of policy language that includes it. Many courts resolve this issue by concluding that the policy language "all sums which the insured shall become legally obligated to pay as damages because of bodily injury" is broad enough to encompass punitive damages. *United Servs. Auto. Ass'n v. Webb*, 369 S.E.2d 196, 199 (Va. 1988). However, a specific exclusion for punitive damages has been given effect even if public policy does not prohibit such coverage. *See State Farm Mut. Auto. Ins. Co. v. Wilson*, 782 P.2d 727, 733–34 (Ariz. 1989). And the flip-side— policy language that specifically covers punitive damages has been enforced, notwithstanding a general public policy prohibition against their insurability. *See Cont'l Cas/Co. v. Kinsey*, 499 N.W.2d 574, 580–81 (N.D. 1993). *But see Public Serv. Mut. Ins. Co. v. Goldfarb*, 425 N.E.2d 810, 814 (N.Y. 1981) (holding that coverage for punitive damages was impermissible even if an insurer agreed to provide such coverage and charged a premium for it).

It is also not uncommon for courts to preclude coverage for punitive damages on a public policy rationale, but make an exception for punitive damages that were awarded on the basis of vicarious liability. *Dayton Hudson Corp. v. Am. Mut. Liab. Ins. Co.*, 621 P.2d 1155, 1160 (Okla. 1980). ("In almost all jurisdictions which disallow insurance coverage for punitive damages, an exception is recognized for those torts in which liability is vicariously imposed on the employer for a wrong of his servant."). *See also Butterfield v. Giuntoli*, 670 A.2d 646, 655 (Pa. Super. Ct. 1995) ("[w]here corporate management commits an outrageous act, punishment is appropriate. Where the act is committed by... an agent, not pursuant to corporate policy or plan, the corporation, though vicariously liable for punitive damages, is entitled to insure against such damages") (alteration in original).

However, there are also situations where directly assessed punitive damages are uninsurable as a matter of law, vicariously assessed punitive damages are not, and a court nonetheless finds coverage for the directly assessed punitive damages. This can occur when the instructions given to the jury in the underlying action allowed for an award of punitive damages on the basis of both direct and vicarious liability—but the insurer did not request additional instructions or use special verdicts to have the jury's determination clarified. *E.g., U.S. Concrete Pipe Co. v. Bould*, 437 So. 2d 1061, 1065 (Fla. 1983).

The availability of insurance coverage for punitive damages also arises with frequency in the context of uninsured and underinsured motorist policies. It is not unusual for states to reach a different conclusion concerning coverage for punitive damages under such automobile policies than it does liability policies. The Supreme Court of Kentucky's decision in *Ky. Cent. Ins. Co. v. Schneider*, 15 S.W.3d 373 (Ky. 2000) provides a representative demonstration of how this issue is addressed nationally. A Kentucky statute provided "that every motor vehicle liability insurance policy shall provide coverage 'for the protection of persons insured thereunder who are legally entitled to recover damages from owners or operators of uninsured motor vehicles because of bodily injury, sickness or disease, including death.'" *Id.* at 374 (quoting KRS 304.20-020(1)).

The court held (and noted that its decision was consistent with the overwhelming majority of jurisdictions nationally) that *damages because of bodily injury* are regarded as compensatory damages, while punitive damages are not compensatory, but, rather, are damages awarded against a person to punish and to discourage him and others from similar conduct in the future. *Id.* at 374–75. The *Schneider* Court also addressed a public policy component surrounding the issue: "In addition to the definitional distinction between compensatory and punitive damages... most jurisdictions holding that punitive damages are not recoverable under the injured party's UM coverage also note that it would be antithetical to require the UM carrier to pay a penalty assessed against the wrongdoer, because the burden of payment would fall not upon the wrongdoer, or even the insurer of the wrongdoer, but upon the insurer of the innocent party." *Id.* at 375–76.

The following fifty-state survey of the insurability of punitive damages makes some references to the issue in the context of uninsured and underinsured motorist policies. However, as the focus of this book is liability insurance, this is not intended to be an exhaustive list.

## 50-State Survey: Insurability of Punitive Damages

**Alabama:** The Supreme Court of Alabama, without discussion of any public policy considerations, held that punitive damages were a "liability imposed by law," and, as such, within the coverage afforded by an automobile policy's insuring agreement, which provided: "To indemnify the assured… against loss from the liability imposed by law upon the assured arising or resulting from claims upon the assured for damages by reason of the ownership, maintenance or use of any [automobile]… if such claims are made on account of injury to persons." *Am. Fid. & Cas. Co. v. Werfel*, 164 So. 383, 383 (Ala. 1935).

**Alaska:** The Supreme Court of Alaska acknowledged a general prohibition against coverage for punitive damages. *Providence Wash. Ins. Co. of Alaska v. City of Valdez*, 684 P.2d 861, 863 (Alaska 1984). However, the court also stated, assuming, without deciding, that public policy prohibited insurance coverage for punitive damages, such prohibition would not apply to vicarious liability or governmental entity defendants. *Id.* The court held that the relevant policy language provided coverage for punitive damages (a sum that the insured is legally obligated to pay as damages) and that punitive damages were not specifically excluded under the policy. *Id.*; *see also State Farm Mut. Auto. Ins. Co. v. Lawrence*, 26 P.3d 1074, 1079–80 (Alaska 2001) (concluding that a liability policy that does not specifically exclude punitive damages and provides that the insurer will "pay damages which an insured becomes legally liable to pay because of… bodily injury to others" affords coverage for punitive damages). The Supreme Court of Alaska held that punitive damages were insurable under an uninsured and underinsured motorist policy. *See Lawrence*, 26 P.3d at 180–81. Neither the policy language nor public policy precluded such result. *Id.*

**Arizona:** The Supreme Court of Arizona held that "any public policy considerations militating against an insurer providing coverage for punitive damages were outweighed by the public policy that an insurance company which admittedly took a premium for indemnifying against all liability for damages, should honor its obligation… . [T]herefore,… an express exclusion was required to eliminate coverage for punitive damages from general liability insurance because the insured was personally at risk if his liability insurance did not cover those damages. The essence of the transaction was the insured's purchase of indemnification against all damages for which he might be held liable." *State Farm Mut. Auto. Ins. Co. v. Wilson*, 782 P.2d 727, 733–34 (Ariz. 1989) (characterizing *Price v. Hartford Accident & Indem. Co.*, 502 P.2d 522 (Ariz. 1972)). But uninsured and underinsured insurers are not obligated to pay for punitive damages unless they specifically agreed to do so. *Wilson*, 782 P.2d at 736; *see also Irvin v. Lexington Ins. Co.*, No. 1 CA-CV 09-0270, 2010 WL 3450986 (Ariz. App. Ct. Sept. 2, 2010) (examining various policy provisions and concluding that they were not sufficient to preclude coverage for punitive damages).

**Arkansas:** The Supreme Court of Arkansas held that punitive damages satisfied the policy's insuring agreement as they constituted a sum that the insured was legally obligated to pay as damages because of bodily injury. *S. Farm Bureau Cas. Ins. Co. v. Daniel*, 440 S.W.2d 582, 584 (Ark. 1969). The court also noted that it could not "find anything in the state's public policy that prevents an insurer from indemnifying its insured against punitive damages arising out of an accident, as distinguished from intentional torts." *Id.*; *see also Cal. Union Ins. Co. v. Ark. La. Gas Co.*, 572 S.W.2d 393, 394 (Ark. 1978) (reaffirming *Daniel*); *Med. Liab. Mut. Ins. Co. v. Curtis Enters., Inc.*, No. 4:05-CV-01317 GTE, 2006 U.S. Dist. LEXIS 89180, at * 11 (E.D. Ark. Dec. 8, 2006) (concluding that the phrase from *Daniel*—"as distinguished from intentional torts"—was *dicta*, and, therefore, leaving open the possibility that Arkansas public policy permits coverage for punitive damages for intentional torts).

**California:** The Supreme Court of California held, based on a public policy rationale, that "an insured may not shift to its insurance company, and ultimately to the public, the payment of punitive damages awarded in the third party lawsuit against the insured as a result of the insured's intentional, morally blameworthy behavior against the third party." *PPG Inds., Inc. v. Transamerica Ins. Co.*, 975 P.2d 652, 658 (Cal. 1999); *see also* CAL. INS. CODE § 533 (Deering 2008) ("An insurer is not liable for a loss caused by the willful act of the insured; but he is not exonerated by the negligence of the insured, or of the insured's agents or others."). A California District Court stated that, in vicarious liability cases, where an employer is required to pay punitive damages as a result of the actions of one of his employees, courts have held that § 533 does not apply and the employer can be indemnified. *Certain Underwriters at Lloyd's of London v. Pac. Sw. Airlines*, 786 F. Supp. 867, 869 (C.D. Cal. 1996). No coverage existed for punitive damages under the state's uninsured motorist statute. *See Cal. State Auto. Ass'n Inter-Ins. Bureau v. Carter*, 164 Cal. App. 3d 257, 263 (Cal. Ct. App. 1985) (noting that while an insurance policy may provide broader coverage than that required under law, the policy at issue was virtually identical to the statute).

**Colorado:** The Supreme Court of Colorado held that both Colorado public policy and the insurance policy at issue prohibited an insurer from providing coverage for punitive damages. *Lira v. Shelter Ins. Co.*, 913 P.2d 514, 517 (Colo. 1996); *see also Universal Indem. Ins. Co. v. Tenery*, 39 P.2d 776, 779 (Colo. 1934) ("The injured will not be allowed to collect from a nonparticipating party [the tortfeasor's insurer], for a wrong against the public.").

**Connecticut:** The Supreme Court of Connecticut held that an award of statutory double damages for violating certain motor vehicle statutes was uninsurable. *Tedesco v. Md. Cas. Co.*, 18 A.2d 357, 359 (Conn. 1941). The court acknowledged a public policy rationale, but instead rested its decision on the construction of policy language that enabled it to avoid reaching a determination on such basis. *Id.* at 359. ("[T]he additional sum representing the doubling of the compensatory damages is, in its essence, a liability imposed, not for damages because of bodily injury, but as a reward for securing the punishment of one who has committed a wrong of a public nature."). In *Avis Rent A Car System v. Liberty Mutual Insurance Co.*, 526 A.2d 522 (Conn. 1987), the Supreme Court of Connecticut declined to follow *Tedesco* and held that, because Avis was only vicariously liable for statutory damages, and was not being punished for its own wrongdoing, coverage was available. *Id.* at 525–26. In *Bodner v. United States Automobile Ass'n*, 610 A.2d 1212 (Conn. 1992), the Supreme Court of Connecticut concluded that common law punitive damages were not insurable under an uninsured motorist policy. *Id.* at 1222; *see also Caufield v. Amica Mut. Ins. Co.*, 627 A.2d 466, 467–69 (Conn. App. Ct. 1993) (following *Bodner* and holding that double or treble statutory damages awarded for deliberately or with reckless disregard operating a motor vehicle in violation of certain statutes were not insurable under an uninsured motorist policy).

**Delaware:** The Supreme Court of Delaware held that there was no evidence in the state of a public policy against insurance for punitive damages. *Whalen v. On-Deck, Inc.*, 514 A.2d 1072, 1074 (Del. 1986). "While the Superior Court and General Accident believe the purposes of punitive damages would be frustrated if such damages were insurable, we cannot infer from that concern a policy against such insurance. A wrongdoer who is insured against punitive damages may still be punished through higher insurance premiums or the loss of insurance altogether. More importantly, in light of the importance of the right of parties to contract as they wish, we will not partially void what might otherwise be a valid insurance contract as contrary to public policy in the absence of clear indicia that such a policy actually exists." *Id.* at 1074. The Supreme Court remanded the case to the trial court for a determination whether the policy language insured against punitive damages. The Supreme Court of Delaware held that both the policy language and public policy permitted coverage for punitive damages under an uninsured/underinsured motorist policy. *Jones v. State Farm Mut. Auto. Ins. Co.*, 610 A.2d 1352, 1353–54 (Del. 1992).

**Florida:** The Supreme Court of Florida held that the rationale for allowing punitive damages—punishment and deterrence—would be frustrated if such damages were covered by insurance. Thus, public policy precluded coverage for directly assessed punitive damages. *U.S. Concrete Pipe Co. v. Bould*, 437 So. 2d 1061, 1064 (Fla. 1983). However, the court also held that Florida public policy did not preclude coverage for punitive damages that were awarded when the insured is vicariously liable for another's wrong. *Id.* Nonetheless, coverage was permitted for directly assessed punitive damages because the instructions given to the jury in the underlying action allowed for an award of punitive damages on the basis of both direct and vicarious liability and the insurer did not request additional instructions or use special verdicts to have the jury's determination clarified. *Id.; see also First Specialty Ins. Co. v. Caliber One Indem. Co.*, 988 So. 2d 708, 713 (Fla. Dist. Ct. App. 2008) (no coverage for punitive damages under policy that defined "damages" as "compensatory amount" and that included an exclusion for "civil fines or penalties").

**Georgia:** The Supreme Court of Georgia held that the policy language at issue—all sums which the insured shall become legally obligated to pay as damages (1) *for*... mental anguish—included coverage for punitive damages. *Greenwood Cemetery, Inc. v. Travelers Indem. Co.*, 232 S.E.2d 910, 913 (Ga. 1977). The insurer argued that "for" meant "equivalent to" or "to the amount, value or extent of." *Id.* The insured argued that "for" meant "by reason of" or "because of or account of." *Id.* The Georgia high court concluded that the policy language was ambiguous and applied the interpretation that favored the insured. *Id.* The *Greenwood Cemetery* Court also rejected the insurer's argument that public policy precluded the insurability of punitive damages. *Id.* at 913–14; *see also Lunceford v. Peachtree Cas. Ins. Co.*, 495 S.E.2d 88, 89 (Ga. Ct. App. 1997) (concluding that because the phrase "because of bodily injury or property damage" was comparable to that which was construed in *Greenwood Cemetery*, the policy provided coverage for punitive damages). An insurer is relieved from its obligation to pay punitive damages if the policy explicitly excludes coverage for punitive damages. *Nationwide Mut. Fire Ins. Co. v. Kim*, 669 S.E.2d 517, 519–20 (Ga. Ct. App. 2008). In the uninsured motorist context, the Court of Appeals of Georgia held that "the legislative intention was to permit recovery of compensatory, and not punitive damages." *Bonamico v. Kisella*, 659 S.E.2d 666, 667 (Ga. Ct. App. 2008) (citation omitted).

**Hawaii:** "Coverage under any policy of insurance issued in this state shall not be construed to provide coverage for punitive or exemplary damages unless specifically included." HAW. REV. STAT. § 431:10–240 (LexisNexis 2009); *see Allstate Ins. Co. v. Takeda*, 243 F. Supp. 2d 1100, 1104 (D. Haw. 2003) (applying HAW. REV. STAT. § 431:10–240 and concluding that, because the policy did not specifically include coverage for punitive damages, the insurer was not responsible for them).

**Idaho:** The Supreme Court of Idaho held that punitive damages were covered under an automobile liability policy. *Abbie Uriguen Oldsmobile Buick, Inc. v. U.S. Fire Ins. Co.*, 511 P.2d 783, 789 (Idaho 1973). The court held that punitive damages were not specifically excluded by the terms of the policy. *Id.* The insurer promised "to pay on behalf of the insured *all* sums which the insured shall be legally obligated to pay as *damages* caused by the use of any automobile." *Id.* (emphasis added). On the subject of public policy, the *Uriguen Oldsmobile* Court concluded that it was not a prohibition against coverage for punitive damages. *Id.* The court adopted the oft-cited position of the Supreme Court of Tennessee in *Lazenby v. Universal Underwriters Insurance Co.*, 383 S.W.2d 1 (Tenn. 1964), which concluded that it is speculative that socially irresponsible drivers would be deterred from their wrongful conduct if coverage for punitive damages were not allowed. *Id.*

**Illinois:** The Appellate Court of Illinois adopted the rationale of *Northwestern National Casualty Co. v. McNulty*, 307 F.2d 432 (5th Cir. 1962), discussed in the introduction, and held that public policy prohibited insurance for liability for punitive damages that arose out of one's own misconduct. *Beaver v. Country Mut. Ins. Co.*, 420 N.E.2d 1058, 1060 (Ill. App. Ct. 1981). However, the *Beaver* Court did not disturb the rule set forth in *Scott v. Instant Parking, Inc.*, 245 N.E.2d 124 (Ill. App. 1969), that an employer may insure for punitive damages that are assessed on the basis of vicarious liability on account of the wrongful conduct of his employee. *Beaver*, 400 N.E.2d at 1061. *But see Nutmeg Ins. Co. v. E. Lake Mgmt. & Dev. Corp.*, No. 05 C 1328, 2006 U.S. Dist. LEXIS 85665, at *5–6 (N.D. Ill. 2006), *aff'd on other grounds* 260 Fed. App'x 914 (7th Cir. 2008) (distinguishing *Beaver* and holding that a landlord's liability for two times damages for violating a municipal ordinance, concerning the handling of security deposits, were not uninsurable as a matter of public policy because such damages are recoverable whether a landlord's failure to comply with the ordinance was inadvertent or intentional).

**Indiana:** An Indiana District Court held that "it would contravene public policy to allow [a] corporation to shift to an insurer the deterrent award imposed on account of the corporation's own wrongful acts; [but] it would not be inconsistent with public policy to allow the corporation to shift to an insurer the punitive damage award when that award is placed upon the corporation solely as a matter of vicarious liability." *Norfolk & W. Ry. Co. v. Hartford Accident & Indem. Co.*, 420 F. Supp. 92, 97 (N.D. Ind. 1976); *see also Executive Builders, Inc. v. Motorists Ins. Cos.*, No. IP00–0018-C-T/G, 2001 U.S. Dist. LEXIS 6775, at *5 (S.D. Ind. Mar. 30, 2001) (citing Norfolk in discussing public policy concerning the insurability of punitive damages). In *Commercial Union Insurance Co. v. Ramada Hotel Operating Co.*, 852 F.2d 298, 306 (7th Cir. 1988), the Seventh Circuit Court of Appeals, applying Indiana law, remanded the case to the District Court for the insurer to attempt to meet its burden that punitive damages were awarded based on the insured's direct liability and not vicarious.

**Iowa:** The Supreme Court of Iowa held that public policy did not preclude coverage for punitive damages. *Skyline Harvestore Sys., Inc. v. Centennial Ins. Co.*, 331 N.W.2d 106 (Iowa 1983). The court concluded that "[i]f the parties wish to contract for coverage of punitive damages, they may. If the insurance companies do not wish to provide such coverage, then they must exclude coverage of punitive damages specifically." *Id.* at 109. The court recognized that, by its decision, it was "elevat[ing] the public policy of freedom of contract for insurance coverage above the public policy purposes of punitive damages." *Id.*; *see also Grinnell Mut. Reinsurance Co. v. Jungling*, 654 N.W. 2d 530, 540–41 (Iowa 2002) (following *Skyline Harvestore* and concluding that the public policy of freedom of contract for insurance coverage should prevail over the public policy reasons for barring coverage for the intentional act of fraud).

**Kansas:** The Supreme Court of Kansas held that punitive damages are uninsurable under Kansas law and public policy. *Koch v. Merchants Mut. Bonding Co.*, 507 P.2d 189, 195–96 (Kan. 1973). In 1984, the Kansas Legislature adopted KAN. STAT. ANN. § 40–2115, which states that it does not violate public policy to provide coverage for punitive damages that are assessed against an insured on the basis of vicarious liability, without the actual prior knowledge of such insured. However, in 1987, the Kansas Legislature adopted KAN. STAT. ANN. § 60–3701(d)(1), which states: "In no case shall exemplary or punitive damages be assessed pursuant to this section against: a principal or employer for the acts of an agent or employee unless the questioned conduct was authorized or ratified by a person expressly empowered to do so on behalf of the principal or employer." This is sometimes referred to as the "complicity rule." In *Hartford Accident and Indem. Co. v. Am. Red Ball Transit Co.*, 938 P.2d 1281 (Kan. 1997), the Supreme Court of Kansas held that section 40–2115 has no effect in cases where punitive damages are awarded on the basis of the complicity rule set in section 60–3701(d)(1). *Id.* at 1292.

**Kentucky:** The Court of Appeals of Kentucky held that it was not against public policy to permit insurance for punitive damages that were imposed for a grossly negligent act of the insured rather than an intentional one. *Cont'l Ins. Cos. v. Hancock*, 507 S.W.2d 146, 151–52 (Ky. 1973). However, it was impossible to determine from the jury instructions what the basis was for authorizing compensatory and punitive damages. *Id.* Thus, the court "indulge[d] the presumption" that the punitive damages were awarded as a punishment for grossly negligent conduct and were therefore covered by the policy obligation to pay all sums which the insured shall be legally obligated to pay. *Id.* at 152. The court also held that punitive damages awarded on the basis of vicarious liability were insurable, whether the servant's act was intentional or grossly negligent. *Id.* at 151. The Supreme Court of Kentucky held that punitive damages were not insurable under an uninsured motorists policy that provided coverage for "damages... because of bodily injury." *Ky. Cent. Ins. Co. v. Schneider*, 15 S.W.3d 373, 374 (Ky. 2000).

**Louisiana:** The Court of Appeal of Louisiana held that the language of two policies at issue—"(1) all sums the insured legally must pay as damages *because of* bodily injury or property damage... [and] (2) indemnify the insured for ultimate net loss… which the insured shall become legally obligated to pay as damages *because of…* [p]ersonal injury"—included coverage for punitive damages. *Creech v. Aetna Cas. & Sur. Co.*, 516 So. 2d 1168, 1171 (La. Ct. App. 1987) (emphasis added). The *Creech* Court also held that Louisiana public policy did not preclude coverage for punitive damages, stating that "[p]ublic policy is better served by giving effect to the insurance contract rather than by creating an exclusion based on a judicial perception of public policy not expressed by the legislature." *Id.* at 1174. In the uninsured motorist context, LA. REV. STAT. § 22:1406(D)(1)(a)(i) allows an insurance policy to include an exclusion for punitive damages. *Pike v. Nat'l Union Fire Ins. Co.*, 796 So. 2d 696, 699–700 (La. Ct. App. 2001).

**Maine:** The Supreme Judicial Court of Maine held that insurers providing coverage under the provisions mandated by the uninsured motorist statute are not liable for punitive damages. *Braley v. Berkshire Mut. Ins. Co.*, 440 A.2d 359, 361–62 (Me. 1982). While the court did not address the issue in the liability insurance context, it did state that "[u]nder Maine law deterrence of the tortfeasor is 'the proper justification' for an award of punitive damages. Allowing punitive damages to be awarded against an insurance company can serve no deterrent function because the wrongdoer is not the person paying the damages. This has been recognized by many courts in the context of liability insurance." *Id.* at 362 (citations omitted) (quoting *Foss v. Me. Turnpike Auth.*, 309 A.2d 339, 345 (Me. 1973)). However, the *Braley* Court also noted that, in the liability context, the ability to raise the insured's premiums may achieve some small deterrent effect. *Id.* at 363.

**Maryland:** The Court of Appeals of Maryland held that it was not against public policy to permit coverage for punitive damages awarded for malicious prosecution. *First Nat'l Bank of Saint Mary's v. Fid. & Deposit Co.*, 389 A.2d 359, 362 (Md. 1978). Indeed, the court suggested that Maryland's public policy may be the exact opposite. *Id.* at 366. "[W]e strongly suspect that the common sense of the community as a whole would expect a judgment including exemplary damages to be satisfied through the insurance policies for which such small business people had paid. It would be outraged and have substantial difficulty in comprehending reasons for a holding to the contrary." *Id.; see also Bailer v. Erie Ins. Exch.*, 687 A.2d 1375, 1385 (Md. 1997) ("[W]e held [in *St. Mary's*] that it was not contrary to public policy to insure against liability for punitive damages awarded in a civil action for malicious prosecution, even though the punitive damages in legal theory are predicated upon malice.").

**Massachusetts:** The Supreme Judicial Court of Massachusetts held that punitive damages were not recoverable under an uninsured motorist policy. *Santos v. Lumbermens Mut. Cas. Co.*, 556 N.E.2d 983, 989 (Mass. 1990). "Requiring an insurance company to pay punitive damages to the insured would not serve to deter wrongdoing or punish the wrongdoer; rather it would result in payment of punitive damages by a party who was not a wrongdoer. In the underinsurance context, where the wrongdoer is not in a contractual relationship with the insurance company, there is not even the possible deterrent effect of higher premium rates." *Id.* at 990 (citations omitted).

**Michigan:** A Michigan District Court held that coverage was available for punitive damages under a liability policy that provided coverage for damages because of bodily injury and that did not contain an explicit exclusion for punitive damages. *Meijer, Inc. v. Gen. Star Indem. Co.*, 826 F. Supp. 241, 246–47 (W.D. Mich. 1993), *aff'd* No. 94–1152, 1995 U.S. App. LEXIS 19951 (6th Cir. July 21, 1995). The court concluded that "[t]o hold that punitive damages are not recoverable would create, in effect, an exclusion for which the parties did not negotiate and allow insurance companies to collect premiums for coverage of a risk that they voluntarily assumed and then escape their obligation to pay on a claim by a mere judicial declaration that the contract is void by reason of public policy." *Id.* at 247.

**Minnesota:** The Supreme Court of Minnesota held that "in most instances public policy should prohibit a person from insuring himself against misconduct of a character serious enough to warrant punitive damages." *Wojciak v. N. Package Corp.*, 310 N.W.2d 675, 680 (Minn. 1981). However, the *Wojciak* Court did not apply the rule because the punitive damages were awarded under a statute prohibiting retaliatory discharge of an employee that seeks workers' compensation benefits. *Id.* The court concluded that the punitive damages were awarded not only to punish employers and deter such conduct, but also to afford redress to employees who are victimized by retaliatory dismissal. *Id.* Punitive and exemplary damages awarded on the basis of vicarious liability are insurable. *See* MINN. STAT. § 60A.06, subd. 4 (Westlaw 2009). *But see Seren Innovations, Inc. v. Transcon. Ins. Co.*, No. A05–917, 2006 Minn. App. Unpub. LEXIS 535, *12–13 (Minn. Ct. App. May 23, 2006) ("Absent policy language providing coverage for punitive damages, we will not create coverage where coverage does not exist, even if such coverage would fall within the vicarious-liability exception to the punitive-damages-coverage prohibition.").

**Mississippi:** The Supreme Court of Mississippi reaffirmed its holding in *Anthony v. Frith*, 394 So. 2d 867 (Miss. 1981) that an "insurance company's liability 'for all damages arising from bodily injury' includes punitive damages. However, the extent or limit of that liability for punitive damage is governed by the agreement of the parties as reflected by the actual language in the policy of insurance." *Old Security Cas. Ins. Co. v. Clemmer*, 455 So. 2d 781, 783 (Miss. 1984); *see also Shelter Mut. Ins. Co. v. Dale*, 914 So. 2d 698, 703 (Miss. 2005) (holding that Mississippi law did not prevent an insurer from excluding coverage for punitive damages by amendatory endorsement to its automobile liability policy); *State Farm Mut. Auto. Ins. Co. v. Daughdrill*, 474 So. 2d 1048, 1054 (Miss. 1985) (finding that Mississippi Uninsured Motorist Act did not require an uninsured motorist provision in an automobile policy to cover punitive damages that the insured is legally entitled to collect from the uninsured motorist).

**Missouri:** The Supreme Court of Missouri has not addressed the availability of insurance coverage for punitive damages. Several Missouri appellate court decisions have addressed the issue and the results vary depending upon the policy language under consideration. *See DeShong v. Mid-States Adjustment, Inc.*, 876 S.W.2d 5 (Mo. Ct. App. 1994) (stating that punitive damages not covered under policy stating that the insurer will pay amounts the insured is "legally required to pay to compensate others for loss" because punitive damages are not compensatory in nature); *Heartland Stores, Inc. v. Royal Ins. Co.*, 815 S.W.2d 39, 40 (Mo. Ct. App. 1991) (finding that punitive damages were not covered under policy stating that the insurer will pay "all sums which the insured shall become legally obligated to pay as damages because of personal injury" because the policy was limited to compensation for personal injury and not sums awarded as punishment); *Schnuck Markets, Inc. v. Transamerica Ins. Co.*, 652 S.W.2d 206, 209 (Mo. Ct. App. 1983) ("Since punitive damages are never awarded merely because of a 'bodily injury' or 'personal injury' but only when the actor's conduct displays the requisite malice, we find they are not in the category of damages for 'bodily injury' or 'personal injury.'"); *Crull v. Gleb*, 382 S.W.2d 17, 22, 23 (Mo. Ct. App. 1964) (finding that policy language and public policy precluded coverage for punitive damages). *But see Colson v. Lloyd's of London*, 435 S.W.2d 42, 43, 46–47 (Mo. Ct. App. 1968) (finding that coverage for punitive damages permitted by the language of a False Arrest Insurance policy ("loss by reason of liability imposed by law upon the insured by reason of any false arrest") and public policy did not preclude coverage).

**Montana:** "Insurance coverage does not extend to punitive or exemplary damages unless expressly included by the contract of insurance." MONT. CODE ANN. § 33–15–317 (Westlaw 2007). The statute followed the Supreme Court of Montana's decision in *First Bank Billings v. Transamerica Ins. Co.*, 679 P.2d 1217 (Mont. 1984), which held that insurance coverage of punitive damages is not contrary to public policy. The court concluded that "[i]insurance companies are more than capable of evaluating risks and deciding whether they will offer policies to indemnify all or some conduct determined by judges or juries to be malicious, fraudulent or oppressive." *Id.* at 1222. The court was also persuaded that it was necessary for punitive damages to be insurable given the lack of consistency surrounding their award. *Id.* Because judges and juries may award punitive damages for a broad range of conduct (willful, wanton, reckless, or unjustified) and different fact finders in similar fact situations may reach different conclusions concerning the availability of punitive damages, the court concluded that the argument for the denial of coverage was difficult to sustain. *Id.*

**Nebraska:** Punitive damages are themselves not recoverable under Nebraska law. *See Abel v. Conover*, 104 N.W.2d 684, 688 (Neb. 1960) ("It has been a fundamental rule of law in this state that punitive, vindictive, or exemplary damages will not be allowed, and that the measure of recovery is all civil cases is compensation for the injury sustained. This rule is so well settled that we dispose of it merely by citation of cases so holding."); *Distinctive Printing & Packaging Co. v. Cox*, 443 N.W.2d 566, 574 (Neb. 1989) ("[P]unitive, vindictive, or exemplary damages contravene NEB. CONST. art. VII, § 5, and thus are not allowed in this jurisdiction.") *But see Cherry v. Burns*, 602 N.W.2d 477, 484 (Neb. 1999) (recognizing that punitive damages are recoverable in a civil rights action filed in Nebraska state court pursuant to 42 U.S.C. § 1983).

**Nevada:** "An insurer may insure against legal liability for exemplary or punitive damages that do not arise from a wrongful act of the insured committed with the intent to cause injury to another." NEV. REV. STAT. ANN. §681A.095 (LexisNexis 2008). The Supreme Court of Nevada held that punitive damages are not recoverable under an uninsured motorist policy. *Siggelkow v. Phoenix Ins. Co.*, 846 P.2d 303, 305 (Nev. 1993). The court based its decision on an unwillingness to distort the purpose of punitive damages, as well as the policy language reasoning that "[u]nder no construction can the language 'for bodily injury' be read to include punitive damages. Punitive damages are not awarded for bodily injury." *Id.* (internal quotations omitted) (quoting *State Farm Mut. Ins. Co. v. Blevins*, 551 N.E.2d 955, 959 (Ohio 1990)).

**New Hampshire:** The Supreme Court of New Hampshire held that "public policy sanctions rather than opposes insuring for liability arising directly against the insured from intentional torts such as false arrest, slander or § 1983 actions." *Am. Home Assurance Co. v. Fish*, 451 A.2d 358, 360 (N.H. 1982). However, the specific policy at issue excluded "fines and penalties imposed by law" from the definition of "loss." *Id.* The *Fish* Court held that, because punitive damages are fines and penalties, no coverage was owed for such damages. *Id.*; *see also Weeks v. St. Paul Fire & Marine Ins. Co.*, 673 A.2d 772, 775 (N.H. 1996) ("Even assuming, without deciding, that the claims are penal, we have held an insurance company liable [in *Fish*] for exemplary or punitive damages where fines and penalties are not expressly excluded by the policy language."); *MacKinnon v. Hanover Ins. Co.*, 471 A.2d 1166, 1168–69 (N.H. 1984) (rejecting the insurer's argument that public policy precludes coverage for all consequences of intentional acts of harm).

**New Jersey:** The New Jersey Appellate Division noted that "New Jersey sides with those jurisdictions which proscribe coverage for punitive damage liability because such a result offends public policy and frustrates the purpose of punitive damage awards." *Johnson & Johnson v. Aetna Cas. & Sur. Co.*, 667 A.2d 1087, 1091 (N.J. Super. App. Div. 1995). The *Johnson & Johnson* Court also declined to decide whether an exception existed to allow coverage for punitive damages that are awarded on the basis of vicarious liability because there was no finding that the insureds were found to be vicariously liable. *Id. But see Chubb Custom Ins. Co. v. Prudential Ins. Co. of Am.*, 948 A.2d 1285, 1293 n.3 (N.J. 2008) (noting parenthetically that there has never been a declaration by itself or the legislature that punitive damages are uninsurable and observing that the legislature (N.J. Stat. § 17:30A-5) has at least implicitly recognized that it does not violate public policy to insure punitive damages).

**New Mexico:** The Supreme Court of New Mexico held that punitive damages are insurable so long as they are not excluded by the language of the policy. *Baker v. Armstrong*, 744 P.2d 170, 173–74 (N.M. 1987). "Citizens and their insurers should have the right to contract for insurance against the possibility of a judicial decision finding that a person's conduct rises above ordinary negligence and justifies punitive damages. If insurance companies market policies which consumers reasonably expect cover all damages, then the insurer should honor that contract. Contracts should be held invalid against public policy only if there is an evil tendency connected with the contract itself, and insurance coverage of punitive damages has not been related in any substantial way to the commission of wrongful acts." *Id.; see also Rummel v. St. Paul Surplus Lines Ins. Co.*, 945 P.2d 985, 989 (N.M. 1997) (discussing *Baker* and addressing whether excess follow form policies provide or exclude coverage for punitive damages).

**New York:** The highest court of New York held that punitive damages are uninsurable because, to allow coverage for them, would defeat their purpose. *Pub. Serv. Mut. Ins. Co. v. Goldfarb*, 425 N.E.2d 810, 814 (N.Y. 1981). Indeed, the New York Court of Appeals went so far as to say that coverage for punitive damages was impermissible even if an insurer agreed to provide such coverage and charged a premium for it. *Id.* However, the *Goldfarb* Court also stated that "if punitive damages are awarded on any ground other than intentional causation of *injury*—for example, gross negligence, recklessness or wantonness—indemnity for compensatory damages would be allowable even though indemnity for the punitive or exemplary component of the damage award would be barred as violative of public policy." *Id.* at 815. The policy articulated in *Goldfarb* applies equally to cases involving conduct that is less culpable than intentional, such as grossly negligent, wanton or so reckless as to amount to a conscious disregard of the rights of others. *Home Ins. Co. v. Am. Home Prods. Corp.*, 550 N.E.2d 930, 932–33 (N.Y. 1990). New York's highest court has also held that punitive damages awarded on the basis of vicarious corporate liability are not insurable. *Zurich Insurance Co. v. Shearson Lehman Hutton, Inc.*, 642 N.E.2d 1065, 1070 (N.Y. 1994).

**North Carolina:** The Supreme Court of North Carolina held that it was not against the state's public policy to insure against punitive damages that are awarded for other than intentional conduct, such as for wanton or gross acts. *Mazza v. Med. Mut. Ins. Co. of N.C.*, 319 S.E.2d 217, 221–23 (N.C. 1984). The court emphasized that it was not deciding whether public policy prohibits insurance for intentional acts. *Id.* at 220. Turning to the policy language, the court rejected the insurer's argument that the term "damages" includes only those damages attributable to a particular injury, reasoning that "[t]he plain and ordinary meaning of the language used in the policy, particularly from the viewpoint of a layman, covers 'all damages' and contains no exclusion for punitive damages." *Id.* at 223; *see also New S. Ins. Co. v. Kidd,* 443 S.E.2d 85, 88 (N.C. Ct. App. 1994) (examining North Carolina cases addressing coverage for punitive damages and noting that they all reached the same conclusion—the policy must explicitly state that it does not provide such coverage).

**North Dakota:** The Supreme Court of North Dakota held that, in general, public policy precludes coverage for punitive damages. *Cont'l Cas/Co. v. Kinsey,* 499 N.W.2d 574, 580–81 (N.D. 1993). Specifically, N.D. CENT. CODE § 9–08–02 (Westlaw 2008) prohibits contracts that would exempt a person from being held responsible for the consequences of his wrongful intentional conduct and N.D. CENT. CODE § 26.1–32–04 (Westlaw 2008) precludes insurers from indemnifying insureds for losses caused by the insured's willful acts. *Id.* However, the specific insurance policy before the *Kinsey* Court expressly provided coverage for punitive damages. *Id.* at 577. Therefore, the court concluded that the insurer was obligated to pay for the punitive damages awarded. *Id.* at 581. But, in order to give effect to the legislature's objectives, the court held that the insurer was entitled to seek indemnity from its insured, who was prohibited by statute from being indemnified for injury caused by his own fraud or deceit. *Id.*

**Ohio:** Punitive or exemplary damages against an insured are precluded under uninsured and underinsured motorist policies, as well as any other policy of casualty or liability insurance that is covered by sections 3937.01 to 3937.17 of Ohio's Revised Code. OHIO REV. CODE § 3937.182 (LexisNexis 2009); *see also State Farm Mut. Ins. Co. v. Blevins,* 551 N.E.2d 955, 959 (Ohio 1990) (permitting coverage for punitive damages under an uninsured motorist policy if provided by the specific contractual language); *The Corinthian v. Hartford Fire Ins. Co.,* 758 N.E.2d 218, 221 (Ohio Ct. App. 2001) (addressing the history of section 3937.182 and holding that it does not preclude coverage for statutory punitive damages awarded without any finding of malice, intent, or ill will); *Neal-Pettit v. Lahman,* 928 N.E.2d 421 (Ohio 2010) (holding that attorney's fees awarded as a result of punitive damages were covered because (1) they could qualify as "damages which an insured person is legally obligated to pay" because of "bodily injury"; (2) they were not clearly and unambiguously within a policy exclusion for "punitive or exemplary damages, fines or penalties"; and (3) public policy did not serve as a prohibition); *Motorists Mut. Ins. Co. v. Dandy-Jim, Inc.,* 912 N.E.2d 659, 667 (Ohio Ct. App. 2009) (As a willful or knowing violation of the Telephone Consumer Protection Act is different from an intentionally malicious act that could give rise to punitive damages, the treble damages provision of the TCPA is not punitive in nature, and, therefore, public policy did not prohibit insurance coverage for treble damages under the TCPA); *Foster v. D.B.S. Collection Agency,* No. 01-CV-514, 2008 WL 755082, at *10 (S.D. Ohio Mar. 20, 2008) (following *Corinthian*) ("[T]o the extent that Plaintiffs are awarded punitive damages pursuant to a statute without any finding of malice, ill will, or other similar culpability, Northland must indemnify Dickerson/D.B.S. against those damages. If punitive damages are awarded after a finding of malice, ill will, or other similar culpability, or are awarded other than pursuant to a statute, Ohio public policy forbids their indemnification.").

**Oklahoma:** The Supreme Court of Oklahoma adopted the rationale of *Nw. Nat'l Cas. Co. v. McNulty,* 307 F.2d 432 (5th Cir. 1962), discussed in the introduction, and held that public policy prohibited insurance for liability for punitive damages that arose out of one's own misconduct. *Dayton Hudson Corp. v. Am. Mut. Liab. Ins. Co.,* 621 P.2d 1155, 1160 (Okla. 1980). However, the *Dayton Hudson* Court held that the public policy prohibition against coverage for punitive damages did not apply to such damages that are assessed on the basis of vicarious liability. *Id.* In reaching its decision, the Supreme Court of Oklahoma made much of the fact that the employer itself may be guilty of reckless disregard in not discharging an unfit employee. *Id.* at 1161. If so, public policy would prohibit coverage for punitive damages assessed against the employer. *Id.; see also Magnus Foods, Inc. v. Cont'l Cas. Co.,* 36 F.3d 1491, 1499 (10th Cir. 1994) (applying Oklahoma law) (finding that the insurer bears the burden of requesting a special verdict or special interrogatories to determine if punitive damages were awarded based on direct or vicarious liability and if it is impossible to determine such basis, the punitive damages are presumed to be covered.). The Supreme Court of Oklahoma held that public policy precludes coverage for punitive damages under an uninsured motorist policy. *Aetna Cas. & Sur. Co. v. Craig,* 771 P.2d 212. 214–15 (Okla. 1989).

**Oregon:** The Supreme Court of Oregon held that it is not against public policy for an insurer to provide coverage for punitive damages. *Harrell v. Travelers Indem. Co.,* 567 P.2d 1013, 1021 (Or. 1977). Instead, the *Harrell* Court concluded that the insurability of punitive damages is based on a decision by the insurer whether it wishes to take on such risk, reasoning that "as long as insurance companies are willing, for a price, to contract for insurance to provide protection against liability for punitive damages to persons or corporations deemed by them to be 'good risks' for such coverage, and as long as liability for punitive damages continues to be extended to 'gross negligence,' 'recklessness,' and for other conduct, 'contrary to societal interests,' we are in agreement with those authorities which hold that insurance contracts providing protection against such liability should not be held by courts to be void as against public policy." *Id.* Thus, punitive damages were covered under an automobile liability policy that insured for "all sums which the insured shall become legally obligated to pay as damages because of… bodily injury." *Id.* at 1014.

**Pennsylvania:** The Pennsylvania Superior Court held that punitive damages are uninsurable as a matter of law. *Esmond v. Liscio*, 224 A.2d 793, 800 (Pa. Super. Ct. 1966). "To permit insurance against the sanction of punitive damages would be to permit such offenders to purchase a freedom of misconduct altogether inconsistent with the theory of civil punishment which such damages represent." *Id.* at 799. The Pennsylvania Superior Court has also held that public policy does not preclude the insurability of punitive damages that are awarded against an insured on the basis of vicarious liability. *Butterfield v. Giuntoli*, 670 A.2d 646, 655 (Pa. Super. Ct. 1995). However, in *Butterfield*, because the insurer did not seek special jury interrogatories or intervene in the underlying action, for purposes of securing a determination whether any punitive damages that may be awarded were on the basis of vicarious or direct liability, it could not sustain its burden to prove that the punitive damages that were awarded were excluded from coverage. *Id.*

**Rhode Island:** The Supreme Court of Rhode Island discussed the competing public policy arguments concerning the insurability of punitive damages. *Allen v. Simmons*, 533 A.2d 541, 543 (R.I. 1987). While the court concluded that punitive damages were uninsurable, it did not do so on the basis of a public policy rationale. *Id.* The *Allen* Court explained "[the insurer's] obligation in this dispute is set forth in simple and direct language that tells the insured and those claiming under the terms of the policy that the insurer will pay for the damages arising from bodily injuries or damages to one's property arising out of an automotive mishap. The damages for which [the insurer] is obligated to respond are set forth in the provisions to which we have just alluded. Punitive or exemplary damages are awarded, not to enrich or reward a plaintiff, but rather to serve as an object lesson both to the wrongdoer and to others who might be tempted to follow in his or her path." *Id.*; *see also Town of Cumberland v. R.I. Interlocal Risk Mgmt. Trust, Inc.*, 860 A.2d 1210, 1218–19 (R.I. 2004) (rejecting an interpretation of *Allen* that insurers cannot insure for actions that are contrary to public policy and held that Rhode Island public policy did not bar an insured from indemnification for intentional torts where the policy explicitly provided such coverage).

**South Carolina:** The Supreme Court of South Carolina held that punitive damages were covered under an automobile liability policy. *Carroway v. Johnson*, 139 S.E.2d 908, 910 (S.C. 1965). The court concluded that "[i]nsurers have the right to limit their liabilities and to impose whatever conditions they please on their obligations, provided they are not in contravention of some statutory inhibition or public policy." *Id.* The court did not address the public policy issue any further. However, it was presumably not a prohibition to coverage because the *Carroway* Court held that coverage was owed. *Id.* at 910. "The policy under consideration did not limit recovery to actual or compensatory damages. The language of the policy here is sufficiently broad enough to cover liability for punitive damages as such damages are included in the 'sums' which the insured is legally obligated to pay as damages because of bodily injury within the meaning of the policy." *Id.* In *South Carolina State Budget & Control Board v. Prince*, 403 S.E.2d 643 (S.C. 1991), the Supreme Court of South Carolina relied upon *Carroway* and held that the policy language at issue encompassed punitive damages. *Prince*, 403 S.E.2d at 648. The court also rejected the insurer's public policy argument against providing coverage for intentional and malicious defamation reasoning that "[t]he [insurer] should not be permitted to deny coverage in the name of public policy when the language of its own policy specifically provides such coverage." *Id.*

**South Dakota:** The Supreme Court of South Dakota held that civil penalties awarded for an intentional violation of the Clean Water Act were punitive in nature and it would violate public policy to insure against them. *City of Fort Pierre v. United Fire & Cas. Co.*, 463 N.W. 2d 845, 848–49 (S.D. 1990); *see also St. Paul Fire & Marine Ins. Co. v. Engelmann*, 639 N.W.2d 192, 203 (S.D. 2002) (Dobberpuhl, J., concurring) (writing that a legislative expression of South Dakota's public policy that one may not insure against an intentional act is found at S.D. CODIFIED LAWS § 53-9-3, which provides that "[a]ll contracts which have for their object, directly or indirectly, to exempt anyone from responsibility for his own fraud or willful injury to the person or property of another or from violation of law whether willful or negligent, are against the policy of the law").

**Tennessee:** The Supreme Court of Tennessee held that the policy language at issue ("all sums which the insured shall become legally obligated to pay as damages because of bodily injury") included punitive damages, that it was speculative that socially irresponsible drivers would be deterred from their wrongful conduct if coverage for punitive damages were not allowed, and that coverage for punitive damages was not precluded on the basis of public policy. *See Lazenby v. Universal Underwriters Ins. Co.*, 383 S.W.2d 1, 5 (Tenn. 1964). The Supreme Court of Tennessee held that punitive damages are precluded from the statutory requirement that all motor vehicle insurers provide uninsured motorist coverage. *Carr v. Ford*, 833 S.W.2d 68, 71 (Tenn. 1992). However, insurers are free to voluntarily offer uninsured motorist coverage for punitive damages. *Id.*

**Texas:** The Supreme Court of Texas held that "the public policy of Texas does not prohibit insurance coverage of exemplary damages for gross negligence in the workers' compensation context." *Fairfield Ins. Co. v. Stephens Martin Paving, LP*, 246 S.W.3d 653, 670 (Tex. 2008). While the *Fairfield* Court's holding was limited to workers' compensation, the court also discussed the issue in other contexts. *Id.* at 668. For example, the court observed that Texas appellate courts have relied on public policy grounds to uniformly reject the insurability of exemplary damages under uninsured and underinsured motorists policies. *Id.* The *Fairfield* Court also stated that courts should consider valid arguments that businesses be permitted to insure against exemplary damages that are awarded on the basis of vicarious liability. *Id.* at 670. Looking outside the workers' compensation arena, the *Fairfield* Court left the door open to a public policy prohibition against the insurability of exemplary damages by noting that "extreme circumstances," involving extreme and avoidable conduct that causes injury, may justify such a conclusion. *Id.*; *see also Am. Int'l Specialty Lines Ins. Co. v. Res-Care, Inc.*, 529 F.3d 649, 663 (5th Cir. 2008) (applying Texas law) (citing *Fairfield* and holding that the circumstances before it (group-home neglect for mentally disabled individuals) demonstrated the kind of "avoidable conduct that causes injury" to justify a prohibition against coverage for punitive damages on public policy grounds); *Minter v. Great Am. Ins. Co. of N.Y.*, No. 09-10734, 2010 WL 3377639 (5th Cir. Aug. 27, 2010) (applying Texas law) (addressing *Fairfield*) (Texas public policy prohibited insurance coverage for an intoxicated insured, with two prior DWI convictions, who caused bodily injury).

**Utah:** "No insurer may insure or attempt to insure against: (1) a wager or gaming risk; (2) loss of an election; (3) the penal consequences of a crime; or (4) punitive damages." UTAH CODE ANN. § 31A-20–101 (Westlaw 2009).

**Vermont:** The Supreme Court of Vermont held that the policy language "all sums as damages" means the whole amount due a plaintiff as damages, regardless of how characterized. *State v. Glens Falls Ins. Co.*, 404 A.2d 101, 105 (Vt. 1979). "The insurer drafts the contract and can easily include exclusions for punitive damages, or can bargain a higher premium. Where it does neither and uses the language involved here, coverage ought to be had." *Id.* The *Glens Falls* Court also rejected the insurer's argument that public policy precludes coverage for punitive damages. *Id.* Even with coverage for punitive damages, a deterrent effect still exists as such damages could exceed the insured's limit of liability and also subject the insured to an increase in premium. *Id.* Indeed, the *Glens Falls* Court concluded that VT. STAT. ANN. tit. 8, § 4203 (Westlaw 2009) [requiring that liability policies provide as follows: "The company shall pay and satisfy *any* judgment that may be recovered against the insured upon any claim covered by this policy to the extent and within the limits of liability assumed thereby… ." (emphasis added)] was a legislative declaration of a public policy favoring complete coverage. *Id.*

**Virginia:** "It is not against the public policy of the Commonwealth for any person to purchase insurance providing coverage for punitive damages arising out of the death or injury of any person as the result of negligence, including willful and wanton negligence, but excluding intentional acts. This section is declaratory of existing policy." VA. CODE ANN. §38.2–227 (Westlaw 2009). The Supreme Court of Virginia held that punitive damages were covered under a policy that included an agreement to pay "'all sums which the insured shall become legally obligated to pay as damages because of bodily injury… including death resulting therefrom.' The insurance company could have inserted the word 'compensatory' before the word 'damages,' or specifically excluded liability for punitive damages elsewhere in the policy, and resolved the ambiguity, but it did not." *United Sers. Auto. Ass'n v. Webb*, 369 S.E.2d 196, 199 (Va. 1988).

**Washington:** The Supreme Court of Washington held that it does not violate the state's public policy to provide coverage for punitive damages. *Fluke Corp. v. Hartford Accident & Indem. Company*, 34 P.3d 809, 812 (Wash. 2001). Turning to the policy language to determine if it provides coverage for punitive damages awarded for malicious prosecution, the *Fluke* Court observed that "[b]ecause the policy uses the general term 'damages,' makes no distinction between compensatory and punitive damages, and contains no exclusion for the payment of punitive damages, the insuring agreement appears to be a straightforward promise to indemnify Fluke for all damages, compensatory or punitive, that Fluke becomes legally bound to pay." *Id.* at 814.

**West Virginia:** The Supreme Court of Appeals of West Virginia held that where "the liability policy of an insurance company provides that it will pay on behalf of the insured all sums which the insured shall become legally obligated to pay as damages because of bodily injury and the policy only excludes damages caused intentionally by or at the direction of the insured, such policy will be deemed to cover punitive damages arising from bodily injury occasioned by gross, reckless or wanton negligence on the part of the insured." *Hensley v. Erie Ins. Co.*, 283 S.E.2d 227, 230 (W. Va. 1981). The *Hensley* Court also held that public policy did not preclude coverage for punitive damages arising from gross, reckless, or wanton negligence. *Id.* at 233. Only a purposeful or intention tort carries the degree of culpability that should foreclose the right to insurance coverage. *Id.* The *Hensley* Court acknowledged that an insurer can decline to insure against punitive damages by way of an express policy exclusion. *Id.*

**Wisconsin:** The Supreme Court of Wisconsin held that the liability policy at issue provided coverage for punitive damages and that such coverage was not contrary to public policy. *Brown v. Maxey*, 369 N.W.2d 677, 688 (Wis. 1985). On the issue of policy language, the *Maxey* Court held that "[f]irst the punitive damage award in this case was a 'sum' that Maxey '[became] legally obligated to pay as damages.' The term 'damages' is sufficiently broad to cover liability for both compensatory and punitive damages. Punitive damages are not specifically excluded from the policy language. Second, it is clear that these punitive damages were awarded 'because of bodily injury.'" *Id.* at 686. Turning to the public policy question, the Wisconsin high court held that it was not a prohibition to coverage. *Id.* at 688. The court rejected the argument that allowing coverage for such awards will alleviate the deterrent effect of such awards. *Id.* Deterrence still exists because the insured's insurance premiums may rise, he may be unable to obtain insurance, the punitive damages may exceed the policy limits and his reputation in the community may be injured. *Id.*

**Wyoming:** The Supreme Court of Wyoming held that it is not against public policy "to insure against either liability for punitive damages imposed vicariously based on willful and wanton misconduct or personal liability for punitive damages imposed on the basis of willful and wanton misconduct." *Sinclair Oil Corp. v. Columbia Cas. Co.*, 682 P.2d 975, 981 (Wyo. 1984).

CHAPTER

20

# First- and Third-Party Bad Faith Standards

Most insurance coverage issues involve just that—whether a particular claim is *covered* under the terms and conditions of a certain insurance policy. But sometimes there is an additional aspect to an otherwise "is it covered" scenario. In certain instances the insurance company's conduct in handling the insured's claim, or the process by which the insurer arrived at a determination that a claim is not covered, becomes the subject of a separate claim for damages. This additional aspect of the claims process is usually referred to under the general heading called "bad faith."

Bad faith—or breach of the duty of good faith, as it is also sometimes called—is one of, if not the most, complex aspects of insurance coverage. The question whether a particular claim is covered is usually a narrow one, largely tied to the application of certain facts to the language of the insurance policy and perhaps with resort to case law for guidance. In most cases there are only two possible answers to the question whether a claim is covered: yes or no. But bad faith is many times more faceted. Moreover, oftentimes one of the most important issues surrounding bad faith is determining the insurance company's mindset in handling the insured's claim or arriving at its coverage determination. The need for the insured to get inside the insurance company's head, so to speak, brings a significant subjective element into play. That subjective determinations are never ones to lend themselves to cut-and-dried answers, in any context, is an important source of the complexity of bad faith.[1]

---

1. *But see Georgetown Realty, Inc. v. Home Ins. Co.*, 831 P.2d 7, 13 (Or. 1992) ("The insurer is negligent in failing to settle, where an opportunity to settle exists, if in choosing not to settle it would be taking an unreasonable risk—that is, a risk that would involve chances of unfavorable results out of reasonable proportion to the chances of favorable results. Stating the rule in terms of 'good faith' or 'bad faith' tends to inject an inappropriate subjective element—the insurer's state of mind—into the formula. The insurer's duty is best expressed by an objective

Any discussion of bad faith must begin with an explanation of the two general types—first-party and third-party. In its most common form—and the subject of this chapter—third-party bad faith arises in the context of an insured being sued by a third-party and the insured's liability insurer takes over its defense. *Braesch v. Union Ins. Co.*, 464 N.W.2d 769, 773 (Neb. 1991). In this situation, "[a] conflict of interest is inherent in the insurer's control of settlement when... there is potential exposure in excess of the policy limits. A settlement demand within the policy limits highlights that conflict, inasmuch as it will be in the insured's interest for that demand to be met. Such a settlement is not necessarily in the insurer's best interest, however, for by going to trial the insurer might be able to avoid liability altogether, or obtain a judgment for an amount less than the demand." *Myers v. Ambassador Ins. Co.*, 508 A.2d 689 (Vt. 1986).

"It is this control of the litigation by the insurer coupled with differing levels of exposure to economic loss which gives rise to the 'fiduciary' nature of the insurer's duty." *Id.* If an insurance company fails to settle a claim, when there was an opportunity to do so within the policy limits, and such a settlement was reasonable, the insurer subjects the insured to the risk of a judgment in excess of the policy limits—for which the insured would be liable but the insurer would not. To put it another way, "[b]y taking such an unreasonable risk, the insurer would be gambling with the insured's money to the latter's prejudice." *Shuster v. South Broward Hosp. Dist. Physicians' Prof. Liability Ins. Trust*, 570 So. 2d 1362, 1367 (Fla. Ct. App. 1990).

The typical consequence for an insurer that, in bad faith, fails to settle a claim, when there was an opportunity to do so within policy limits, is liability for the full amount of the judgment—even the amount in excess of the policy limit. This is sometimes referred to as the "judgment rule" and the majority of states have adopted it. *See Economy Fire & Cas. Co. v. Collins*, 643 N.E.2d 382, 385 (Ind. App. Ct. 1994) (rejecting the alternative "pre-payment rule"— which holds an insurer liable for a judgment in excess of policy limits only if part or all of the judgment has been paid by the insured—and instead adopting the "judgment rule" because it eliminates the insurer's ability to hide behind the financial status of its insured and it recognizes that the entry of judgment itself against an insured constitutes actual damage—such as impairing the insured's credit and damaging the insured's reputation).

Another type of third-party bad faith—although not nearly as common as third-party bad faith in the "failure to settle within limits context" (and not the subject of this chapter)—involves a claim by an injured party brought directly against the tortfeasor's insurer. The most well-known source of third-party bad faith is the Supreme Court of California's adoption of it in *Royal*

---

test: Did the insurer exercise due care under the circumstances?") (quoting *Me. Bonding & Cas. Co. v. Centennial Ins. Co.*, 693 P.2d 1296, 1299 (Or. 1985)).

*Globe Ins. Co. v. Superior Court,* 23 Cal.3d 880 (Cal. 1979). The court held that the Unfair Practices Act of the state's Insurance Code afforded a private party, *including a third party claimant,* the right to sue an insurer for violation of the Act—addressing various unfair claims settlement practices. *Id.* at 891. The court further held that "it is inconceivable that the Legislature intended that such a litigant would be required to show that the insurer committed the acts prohibited by that provision 'with such frequency as to indicate a general business practice.'" *Id.*

However, just nine years later *Royal Globe* was overruled by *Moradi-Shalal v. Fireman's Fund Ins. Companies,* 46 Cal.3d 287 (Cal. 1988). The *Moradi-Shalal* Court concluded that "developments occurring subsequent to our *Royal Globe* decision convince us that it was incorrectly decided, and that it has generated and will continue to produce inequitable results, costly multiple litigation, and unnecessary confusion unless we overrule it." *Moradi-Shalal* at 297 (also noting that courts in eight states had expressly acknowledged, but declined to follow, *Royal Globe*; courts in nine states had implicitly rejected its holding; and only two states other than California recognized a statutory cause of action for private litigants—with the courts in those states rejecting *Royal Globe's* conclusion that a single violation of their Unfair Practices Act is a sufficient basis for a suit for damages). While the *Moradi-Shalal* Court gave many reasons for its decision to overrule *Royal Globe,* a principal driver of its decision was a recognition of the adverse consequences that third-party bad faith would have on the general public vis-à-vis increased insurance premiums.

In contrast to coverage for insureds for injuries caused to third-parties, first-party bad faith involves claims by insureds for policy benefits for their *own* damages. *Universal Life Ins. Co. v. Giles,* 950 S.W.2d 48, 60 (Tex. 1997). While third-party bad faith dates back nearly a hundred years (*see Brassil v. Maryland Cas. Co.,* 104 N.E. 622 (N.Y. 1914)), first-party bad faith is of more recent vintage—with many courts giving credit for its origin to the Supreme Court of California in *Gruenberg v. Aetna Ins. Co.,* 510 P.2d 1032 (Cal. 1973), where the court held:

> [I]n the case before us we consider the duty of an insurer to act in good faith and fairly in handling the claim of an insured, namely a duty not to withhold unreasonably payments due under a policy.... . That responsibility is not the requirement mandated by the terms of the policy itself—to defend, settle, or pay. It is the obligation, deemed to be imposed by the law, under which the insurer must act fairly and in good faith in discharging its contractual responsibilities. Where in so doing, it fails to deal fairly and in good faith with its insured by refusing, without proper cause, to compensate its insured for a loss covered by the policy, such conduct may give rise to a cause of action in tort for breach of an implied covenant of good faith and fair dealing.

*Id.* at 1037; *see also Nichols v. State Farm Mutual Auto. Ins. Co.*, 306 S.E.2d 616, 618 (S.C. 1983) ("The *Gruenberg* decision is premised on an implied covenant of good faith and fair dealing that neither party will do anything to impair the other's rights to receive benefits under the contract.").

Courts have used various rationales for adopting a cause of action in tort for first-party bad faith:

> An insurance policy is not obtained for commercial advantage; it is obtained as protection against calamity. In securing the reasonable expectations of the insured under the insurance policy there is usually an unequal bargaining position between the insured and the insurance company.... . Often the insured is in an especially vulnerable economic position when such a casualty loss occurs. The whole purpose of insurance is defeated if an insurance company can refuse or fail, without justification, to pay a valid claim. We have determined that it is reasonable to conclude that there is a legal duty implied in an insurance contract that the insurance company must act in good faith in dealing with its insured on a claim, and a violation of that duty of good faith is a tort.

*Nicholson*, 777 P.2d at 1155 (Alaska 1989) (quoting *Noble v. National American Life Ins. Co.*, 624 P.2d 866, 867–68 (Ariz. 1981)); *see also Spencer v. Aetna Life & Cas. Ins. Co.*, 611 P.2d 149, 158 (Kan. 1980) (despite declining to adopt the bad faith tort, the court examined the rationales of many decisions that have and concluded that all of the arguments pertain to the unequal bargaining position between the insurer and insured and the public interest nature of the insurance industry); *Arnold v. National County Mut. Fire Ins. Co.*, 725 S.W.2d 165, 167 (Tex. 1987) (noting that, without a cause of action for first-party bad faith, insurers could arbitrarily deny coverage and delay payment of a claim with the penalty being limited to interest on the amount owed).

Some states have chosen to address bad faith by statute. *See Rose ex rel. Rose v. St. Paul Fire and Marine Ins. Co.*, 599 S.E.2d 673, 679, n.6 (W. Va. 2004) ("At least sixteen states, including West Virginia, also use statutes to impose various duties upon insurance companies to use 'good faith' toward a claimant throughout the settlement of a claim. These statutes—which, like West Virginia's, are usually patterned after the National Association of Insurance Commissioners' 'Model Unfair Trade Practices Act' or 'Model Unfair Claims Settlement Practices Act'—have been construed by courts to allow a claimant to bring an action against an insurance company for damages caused by a violation of the statute.")

While many do, not all states recognize a cause of action for first-party bad faith. Some states have declined to adopt such cause of action on the basis that adequate alternative remedies already exist to address insurer's improper behavior. *See Marquis v. Farm Family Mut. Ins. Co.*, 628 A.2d 644, 652 (Me. 1993) ("[i]n view of the broad range of compensatory damages available in a contract action and in view of the statutorily provided remedies of interest on the judgment and attorney fees, we believe sufficient motivation presently exists to stifle an insurer's bad faith tendencies without the further imposition of the specter of punitive damages under an independent tort cause of action") (quotation omitted) (alteration in original). Other states have refused to recognize the tort on the basis that the relationship between the insurer and insured, in the first-party context, is not a fiduciary one. *See Best Place, Inc. v. Penn. Am. Ins. Co.*, 920 P.2d 334, 343 (Hawaii 1996) (adopting tort cause of action but citing decisions from several states that have refused to do so).

In general, the significance of a court's adoption of a cause of action for first-party bad faith is the opening of the door to an insured's recovery of damages in tort, rather than its recovery being limited to damages for breach of contract:

> [T]he requirement that contract damages be foreseeable at the time of contracting in some cases would bar recovery for damages proximately caused by the insurer's bad faith. The measurement of recoverable damages in tort is not limited to those foreseeable at the time of the tortious act; rather they include "[a] reasonable amount which will compensate plaintiff for *all* actual detriment proximately caused by the defendant's wrongful conduct."

*White v. Unigard Mut. Ins. Co.*, 730 P.2d 1014, 1017–18 (Idaho 1986) (citations omitted and emphasis in original); *see also Tackett v. State Farm Fire & Cas. Ins. Co.*, 653 A.2d 254, 264 (Del. 1995) ("If the bad faith claim is viewed as an independent tort, the insured's recovery may include damages for emotional distress, as well as for economic loss. By contrast, if the bad faith claim is viewed as arising *ex contractu*, the damages generally are confined to the payment of money due, with interest for delay.").

Because first- and third-party bad faith address different risks for the insured, they are typically subject to different standards. In the third-party context, the insurer has the responsibility of defending the claim, usually has exclusive authority to accept or reject settlements and could subject the insured to liability in excess of the policy limits because of its refusal to settle within those limits. *Clearwater v. State Farm Mut. Auto. Ins. Co.*, 792 P.2d 719, 723 (Ariz. 1990). In third-party situations, the insurance policy creates a fiduciary relationship—on account of the insured being wholly dependent upon the insurer to see that the insured's best interests are protected. *Beck v. Farmers Ins. Exchange*, 701 P.2d 795, 799 (Utah 1985).

This same risk, however, is generally seen as lacking in the context of first-party claims, where "[t]he insurer is not in a position to expose the insured to a judgment in excess of the policy limits through its unreasonable refusal to settle a case, nor is it in a position to otherwise injure the insured by virtue of its exclusive control over the defense of the case." *Lawton v. Great Southwest Fire Ins. Co.*, 392 A.2d 576, 581 (N.H. 1978).

On account of the potential harm to the insured being greater in the third-party context, the applicable standards for establishing first- and third-party bad faith often differ. *See Clearwater v. State Farm Mut. Auto. Ins. Co.*, 792 P.2d 719, 722 (Ariz. 1990). And those differences can be substantial. For example, the Supreme Court of Colorado adopted a much higher standard for an insured to prove first-party versus third-party bad faith. *See Goodson v. Am. Standard Ins. Co. of Wis.*, 89 P.3d 409, 415 (Colo. 2004) (first-party claimant must prove that the insurer either knowingly or recklessly disregarded the validity of the insured's claim; for third-party bad faith, the insured need only show that a reasonable insurer under the circumstances would have paid or otherwise settled the third-party claim, i.e., negligence standard).

Therefore, because of the different purposes between first-party and third-party bad faith, any comparison between the applicable standards for establishing each is apples to oranges. But even when only one type of bad faith is examined, i.e., the comparison is apples to apples, the standards also vary widely between states. For example, in the third-party bad faith context, compare *Asermely v. Allstate Ins. Co.*, 728 A.2d 461, 464 (R.I. 1999) (adopting a standard that resembles strict liability for an insurer that fails to settle within policy limits) with *Helmbolt v. LeMars Mut. Ins. Co., Inc.*, 404 N.W.2d 55, 57 (S.D. 1987) (recognizing that there are an array of factors—at least seven—to consider in determining whether an insurer's refusal to settle was bad faith).

The standard for third-party bad faith can also vary widely within the *same* state—a fact that did not go unnoticed by New York's highest court:

> [C]ourts have had some difficulty selecting a standard for actionable "bad faith" because of the need to balance the insured's rightful expectation of "good faith" against the insurer's equally legitimate contract expectations. Consequently, a divergence of authority has arisen concerning whether a bad-faith finding may be predicated on a showing of the insurer's recklessness or "gross disregard" for the insured's interests… or whether a heightened showing of intentionally harmful, dishonest or disingenuous motive is required.

*Pavia v. State Farm Mut. Auto. Ins. Co.*, 626 N.E.2d 24, 27 (N.Y. 1993) (citations omitted) (rejecting the insurer's proposed "sinister motive" standard and instead holding that "in order to establish a prima facie case of bad faith, the plaintiff must establish that the insurer's conduct constituted a 'gross disregard' of the insured's interests—that is, a deliberate or reckless failure to place on equal footing the interests of its insured with its own interests when considering a settlement offer").

Decisions addressing bad faith often contain neat and tidy rules describing the standard that an insured must satisfy to establish its insurer's bad faith in handling a claim. Such rules are usually expressed by a litany of adjectives describing various forms of inappropriate behavior by an insurer. These standards make for convenient sound bites. However, the question whether an insurer actually committed such conduct—given the highly factual nature of the inquiry—is oftentimes easier said than done. For this reason, knowing the bad faith standard is only the first step—an important, yet small one—in attempting to establish that an insurer committed bad faith in its handling of an insured's claim.

In addition to the core issues concerning bad faith, such as the extent to which the causes of action are recognized and the varying standards for establishing them, bad faith has also given rise to various collateral issues. For example, numerous courts have addressed whether bad faith sounds in tort or contract—as the first step to determining the appropriate statute of limitations for such action. *See Noland v. Virginia Ins. Reciprocal*, 686 S.E.2d 23, 34, n.30 (W. Va. 2009) (noting that a majority of the courts that have addressed the issue have held that a common law bad faith action sounds in tort) (holding that a common law bad faith action sounds in tort and a one-year statute of limitations applies); *see also Ash v. Continental Ins. Co.*, 932 A.2d 877, 885 (Pa. 2007) (holding that the duty of good faith is a statutorily-created tort and subject to a two-year statute of limitations) (rejecting the argument that an action for bad faith sounds in contract and is subject to a six-year statute of limitations).

Another collateral issue that arrives with regularity in the bad faith context is whether an excess insurer can maintain an action for bad faith against a primary insurer on account of the primary insurer's failure to settle a claim within its policy limits—resulting in a verdict that exceeds the primary policy's limits and reaches the excess policy. The majority of states allow an excess insurer to sue a primary insurer for bad faith refusal to settle within the primary policy limits. The rationale often adopted for permitting such cause of action is equitable subrogation. In other words, because the insured, if it did not have excess coverage, would have a cause of action against the primary insurer for bad faith refusal to settle, this right is transferred to the excess insurer. *See Fireman's Fund v. Ins. Co. v. Continental Ins. Co.*, 519 A.2d 202 (Md. 1987); *but see Federal Ins. Co. v. Travelers Cas. & Sur. Co.*, 843 So. 2d 140, 143 (Ala. 2002) (holding that, in the absence of contrary contractual obligations, a primary insurer does not owe a duty of good faith to an excess insurer regarding settlement of a claim) (rejecting equitable subrogation as a basis for an excess insurer to maintain a bad faith action because the insured is not subject to a judgment that he would personally have to pay).

Lastly, any discussion of bad faith is likely to turn to the potential damages recoverable. Like the standards to establish bad faith, the potentially recoverable damages are also subject to wide variation between states—with the question of the availability of punitive damages often coming into play. While this issue is beyond the scope of this chapter, the cases cited in the following fifty-state survey frequently address the nature of damages that can be awarded to an insured for its insurer's bad faith.

## 50-State Survey: First- and Third-Party
## Bad Faith Standards

**Alabama:** The Supreme Court of Alabama recognized an intentional tort of bad faith in first-party insurance claims. *Chavers v. Nat'l Sec. Fire & Cas. Co.*, 405 So. 2d 1, 6 (Ala. 1981). Under Alabama law there are two types of bad faith: "normal" and "abnormal." *Jones v. Alfa Mut. Ins. Co.*, 1 So. 3d 23, 31 (Ala. 2008). "In the 'normal' bad-faith case, the plaintiff must show the absence of any reasonably legitimate or arguable reason for denial of a claim. In the 'abnormal' case, bad faith can consist of: 1) intentional or reckless failure to investigate a claim, 2) intentional or reckless failure to properly subject a claim to a cognitive evaluation or review, 3) the manufacture of a debatable reason to deny a claim, or 4) reliance on an ambiguous portion of a policy as a lawful basis for denying a claim." *Id.* at 32; *see also State Farm Fire & Cas. Co. v. Slade*, 747 So. 2d 293, 303–07 (Ala. 1999) (setting forth a lengthy discussion of the history of the state's bad faith law).

For purposes of establishing third-party bad faith, Alabama permits recovery against an insurer in situations where such wrongful refusal was either negligent or intentional. *Chavers* at 5. "In the third party context, therefore, counts based upon either negligence or bad faith are actionable. Furthermore, both counts may be joined in a single action with recovery proceeding from either. This is not to say, however, that a test for bad faith includes a negligence standard of conduct. In this jurisdiction negligence is not an element of bad faith." *Id.*

**Alaska:** The Supreme Court of Alaska stated that "while the tort of bad faith in first-party insurance cases may or may not require conduct which is fraudulent or deceptive, it necessarily requires that the insurance company's refusal to honor a claim be made without a reasonable basis." *Hillman v. Nationwide Mut. Fire Ins. Co.*, 855 P.2d 1321, 1324 (Alaska 1993). "[W]here the insurer establishes that no reasonable jury could regard its conduct as unreasonable, the question of bad faith need not and should not be submitted to the jury." *Id.* at 1325.

In the third-party bad faith context, the Supreme Court of Alaska held that "[w]hen a plaintiff makes a policy limits demand, the covenant of good faith and fair dealing places a duty on an insurer to tender maximum policy limits to settle a plaintiff's demand when there is a substantial likelihood of an excess verdict against the insured." *Jackson v. Am. Equity Ins. Co.*, 90 P.3d 136, 142 (Alaska 2004).

**Arizona:** The Supreme Court of Arizona stated that "the insurer breaches the implied duty of good faith and fair dealing if it (1) acts unreasonably towards its insured, and (2) acts knowingly or with reckless disregard as to the reasonableness of its actions. We have stated that this standard permits an insurer to challenge a claim that is 'fairly debatable.'" *Clearwater v. State Farm Mut. Auto. Ins. Co.*, 792 P.2d 719, 723 (Ariz. 1990).

In the third-party context, the Supreme Court of Arizona stated that "th[e] duty of good faith requires an insurer to give equal consideration to the protection of the insured's as well as its own interests. If an insurance company fails to settle, and does so in bad faith, it is liable to the insured for the full amount of the judgment." *Hartford Accident & Indem. Co. v. Aetna Cas. & Sur. Co.*, 792 P.2d 749, 752 (Ariz. 1990); *see also Acosta v. Phoenix Indem. Ins. Co.*, 153 P.3d 401, 404 (Ariz. Ct. App. 2007) ("An insurer must weigh a number of factors, including the strength of the third party's claim and the financial risk to the insured in the event of a judgment in excess of the policy limits. In determining whether an insurer has given consideration to the interests of the insured, the test is whether a prudent insurer without policy limits would have accepted the settlement offer.") (citations and internal quotation omitted).

**Arkansas:** The Supreme Court of Arkansas stated: "We have defined 'bad faith' as dishonest, malicious, or oppressive conduct carried out with a state of mind characterized by hatred, ill will, or a spirit of revenge. Mere negligence or bad judgment is insufficient so long as the insurer is acting in good faith. Moreover, the tort of bad faith does not arise from the mere denial of a claim; rather, there must be affirmative misconduct on the part of the insurer." *Switzer v. Shelter Mut. Ins. Co.*, 208 S.W.3d 792, 801 (Ark. 2005) (citations omitted).

In the third-party bad faith context, the Court of Appeals of Arkansas stated that "an insurer is liable to its insured for a judgment in excess of the policy limits if the insurer's failure to settle the claim was due to fraud, bad faith, or negligence." *Kirkwood v. State Farm Mut. Auto. Ins. Co.*, No. CA 95-359, 1996 WL 288888, at *2 (Ark. Ct. App. May 29, 1996) (citations omitted).

**California:** The Supreme Court of California stated that a cause of action exists in tort for breach of an implied covenant of good faith and fair dealing where an insurer "fails to deal fairly and in good faith with its insured by refusing, without proper cause, to compensate its insured for a loss covered by the policy." *Gruenberg v. Aetna Ins. Co.*, 510 P.2d 1032, 1037 (Cal. 1973); *see also Major v. W. Home Ins. Co.*, 87 Cal. Rptr. 3d 556, 568 (Cal. Ct. App. 2009) (citing *Gruenberg*, 510 P.2d at 1037) ("In first party cases, the implied covenant of good faith and fair dealing obligates the insurer to make a thorough investigation of the insured's claim for benefits, and not to unreasonably delay or withhold payment of benefits. If the insurer 'without proper cause' (i.e., unreasonably) refuses to timely pay what is due under the contract, its conduct is actionable as a tort.").

For purposes of third-party bad faith, the Supreme Court of California stated that "the insurer must settle within policy limits when there is substantial likelihood of recovery in excess of those limits.... An insurer that breaches its implied duty of good faith and fair dealing by unreasonably refusing to accept a settlement offer within policy limits may be held liable for the full amount of the judgment against the insured in excess of its policy limits." *Kransco v. Am. Empire Surplus Lines Ins. Co.*, 2 P.3d 1, 9 (Cal. 2000).

**Colorado:** The Supreme Court of Colorado stated that "[i]n addition to proving that the insurer acted unreasonably under the circumstances, a first-party claimant must prove that the insurer either knowingly or recklessly disregarded the validity of the insured's claim. This standard of care reflects a reasonable balance between the right of an insurance carrier to reject a noncompensable claim submitted by its insured and the obligation of such carrier to investigate and ultimately approve a valid claim." *Goodson v. Am. Standard Ins. Co. of Wis.*, 89 P.3d 409, 415 (Colo. 2004) (citation and internal quotation omitted); *see also Fincher ex rel. Fincher v. Prudential Prop. & Cas. Ins. Co.*, Nos. 08-1109, 08-1159, 2010 WL 1544361, *8 (10th Cir. Apr. 20, 2010) (applying Colorado law) ("[A]n insurer may challenge claims which are fairly debatable and will be found to have acted in bad faith only if it has intentionally denied (or failed to process or pay) a claim without a reasonable basis."); C.R.S.A. § 10-3-1116(1) ("A first-party claimant as defined in section 10-3-1115 whose claim for payment of benefits has been unreasonably delayed or denied may bring an action in a district court to recover reasonable attorney fees and court costs and two times the covered benefit.").

Turning to the third-party context, the *Goodson* Court stated that "[b]ecause of the quasi-fiduciary nature of the insurance relationship in a third-party context, the standard of conduct required of the insurer is characterized by general principles of negligence. To establish that the insurer breached its duties of good faith and fair dealing, the insured must show that a reasonable insurer under the circumstances would have paid or otherwise settled the third-party claim." *Goodson* at 415.

**Connecticut:** A Connecticut trial court expressly adopted the Supreme Court of California's rule in *Gruenberg v. Aetna Insurance Co.*, 510 P.2d 1032 (Cal. 1973) that allows for recovery of consequential damages where there has been a showing of bad faith by the insurer. *Grand Sheet Metal Prods. Co. v. Protection Mut. Ins.*, 375 A.2d 428, 430 (Conn. Super. Ct. 1977). "Where an insurer fails to deal fairly and in good faith with its insured by refusing without proper cause to compensate its insured for a loss covered by the policy such conduct may give rise to a cause of action in tort for breach of an implied covenant of good faith and fair dealing." *Id.; see also Nationwide Mut. Ins. Co. v. Mortensen*, No. 3:00-cv-1180, 2009 WL 2710264, at *5 (D. Conn. Aug. 24, 2009) (continuing to rely on *Grand Sheet* as authority for a tort action for breach of the duty of good faith and fair dealing); *De La Concha of Hartford, Inc. v. Aetna Life Ins. Co.*, 849 A.2d 382, 388 (Conn. 2004) ("Bad faith in general implies both actual or constructive fraud, or a design to mislead or deceive another, or a neglect or refusal to fulfill some duty or some contractual obligation, not prompted by an honest mistake as to one's rights or duties, but by some interested or sinister motive... . Bad

faith means more than mere negligence; it involves a dishonest purpose.")
(non-insurance case); *Mead v. Burns*, 509 A.2d 11, 18 (Conn. 1986) (holding
that it is possible to state a cause of action under the state's Unfair Trade
Practices Act (CONN. GEN. STAT. ANN. § 42-110a (Westlaw 2009)) for a violation of the state's Unfair Insurance Practices Act (CONN. GEN. STAT. ANN.
§ 38a-816 (Westlaw 2009)).

In the context of third-party bad faith, a Connecticut trial court noted the
lack of Connecticut appellate authority concerning the type of conduct which
would constitute bad faith for failure to settle a claim within the policy limits,
following a demand for settlement. *Hernandez v. Allstate Ins. Co.*, No.
CV040413243S, 2006 WL 2458575, at *3 (Conn. Super. Ct. Aug. 9, 2006). The
court concluded that "'[b]ad Faith' entails more than mere negligence, care-
lessness, or inadvertence. It implies a design to mislead or to deceive another,
or a neglect or refusal to fulfill some duty or contractual obligation, not
promoted by an honest mistake." *Id.* at *4.

**Delaware:** The Supreme Court of Delaware stated that "[i]f a claim arises
concerning a breach of the terms of th[e] [insurance] agreement, whether it
be a dispute over coverage, or an exclusion or delay in payment of a claim, the
remedy should be for breach of contract." *Tackett v. State Farm Fire & Cas.
Ins. Co.*, 653 A.2d 254, 264 (Del. 1995). "A lack of good faith, or the presence
of bad faith, is actionable where the insured can show that the insurer's denial
of benefits was clearly without any reasonable justification." *Id.* (citation and
internal quotation omitted).

In the third-party context, "liability of an insurance carrier to its
policyholder in excess of policy limits is based on the tortious conduct of the
insurance carrier, which under the policy has sole control of the defense."
*Stilwell v. Parsons*, 145 A.2d 397, 402 (Del. 1958); *see also McNally v.
Nationwide Ins. Co.*, 815 F.2d 254, 259 (3d Cir. 1987) (applying Delaware
law) (discussing *Stilwell* and finding that "[w]hen a judgment in excess of the
policy limits might be obtained by the claimant, the good faith standard is
satisfied only if the insurer acts in the same way as would a reasonable and
prudent man with the obligation to pay all of the recoverable damages") (citation and internal quotation omitted); *Gruwell v. Allstate Ins. Co.*, 988 A.2d
945, 949 (Del. Super. Ct. 2009) ("[N]o case has been brought to the Court's
attention which undermines the legal principle for which [*Stilwell*] was cited
by the Third Circuit [in *McNally*]").

**Florida:** FLA. STAT. ANN. § 624.155 created a statutory cause of action for
first-party bad faith and also codified prior Supreme Court of Florida decisions authorizing a third party to bring a bad faith action under common
law. *See Macola v. Gov't Employees Ins. Co.*, 953 So. 2d 451, 456 (Fla. 2006).
The statute authorizes a cause of action against an insurer for, among other
things, "[n]ot attempting in good faith to settle claims when, under all the
circumstances, it could and should have done so, had it acted fairly and honestly toward its insured and with due regard for her or his interests." FLA.

STAT. ANN. § 624.155 (1)(b)(1) (Westlaw 2009). Florida applies a totality of the circumstances approach to bad faith determinations. *State Farm Mut. Auto. Ins. Co. v. Laforet*, 658 So. 2d 55, 62–63 (Fla. 1995). "[A]t least five factors should be taken into account: (1) whether the insurer was able to obtain a reservation of the right to deny coverage if a defense were provided; (2) efforts or measures taken by the insurer to resolve the coverage dispute promptly or in such a way as to limit any potential prejudice to the insureds; (3) the substance of the coverage dispute or the weight of legal authority on the coverage issue; (4) the insurer's diligence and thoroughness in investigating the facts specifically pertinent to coverage; and (5) efforts made by the insurer to settle the liability claim in the face of the coverage dispute." *Id.* The second, third, and fourth factors should be considered in a first-party cause of action. *Id.* at 63; *see also Perera v. U.S. Fid. & Guar. Co.*, 35 So. 3d. 893, 904 (Fla. 2010) (holding that assignee of insured could not recover an excess verdict against a primary insurer where the insured had adequate excess limits, an excess insurer was willing to settle without any contribution from the primary insurer, insured did not face exposure in excess of the limits of the combined policies, and the excess insurer did not bring a bad faith claim against the primary insurer or assign its claim to the underlying plaintiff).

**Georgia:** A Georgia statute provides that "[i]n the event of a loss which is covered by a policy of insurance and the refusal of the insurer to pay the same within 60 days after a demand has been made by the holder of the policy and a finding has been made that such refusal was in bad faith, the insurer shall be liable to pay such holder, in addition to the loss, not more than 50 percent of the liability of the insurer for the loss or $5,000.00, whichever is greater, and all reasonable attorney's fees for the prosecution of the action against the insurer." GA. CODE ANN. § 33-4-6 (Westlaw 2009). "Bad faith for purposes of… § 33-4-6 is any frivolous and unfounded refusal in law or in fact to pay according to the terms of the policy." *King v. Atlanta Cas. Ins. Co.*, 631 S.E.2d 786, 788 (Ga. Ct. App. 2006).

Addressing third-party bad faith, the Supreme Court of Georgia stated that "the insurer had a duty to its insured to respond to the plaintiff's deadline to settle the personal injury claim within policy limits when the insurer had knowledge of clear liability and special damages exceeding the policy limits. Our holding in *Southern General Insurance Co. v. Holt* [416 S.E.2d 274 (Ga. 1992)] was consistent with the general rule that the issue of an insurer's bad faith depends on whether the insurance company acted reasonably in responding to a settlement offer." *Cotton States Mut. Ins. Co. v. Brightman*, 580 S.E.2d 519, 521 (Ga. 2003).

**Hawaii:** The Supreme Court of Hawaii stated that "[t]he breach of the express covenant to pay claims… is not the *sine qua non* for an action for breach of the implied covenant of good faith and fair dealing. The implied covenant is breached, whether the carrier pays the claim or not, when its conduct damages the very protection or security which the insured sought to gain by buying insurance." *Guajardo v. AIG Hawai'i Ins. Co., Inc.*, 187 P.3d 580, 587 (Hawaii 2008) (citation and internal quotation omitted). "[A]n action for the tort of 'bad faith' will lie when an insurance company unreasonably handles or denies payment of a claim... . [C]onduct based on an interpretation of the insurance contract that is reasonable does not constitute bad faith." *Id.* (citation and internal quotation omitted).

In the context of third-party bad faith, a Hawaii District court, following an analysis of the Supreme Court of Hawaii's seminal decision on bad faith in *Best Place, Inc. v. Penn America Insurance Co.*, 920 P.2d 334 (Hawaii 1996), concluded that, for purposes of determining whether an insurer, who does not accept a reasonable settlement offer within policy limits is liable for violation of its duty to act in good faith regarding the interests of the insured, the focus is on the reasonableness of the insurer's actions. *Tran v. State Farm Mut. Auto. Ins. Co.*, 999 F.Supp. 1369, 1372 (D. Hawaii 1998).

**Idaho:** The Supreme Court of Idaho stated that "the mere failure to immediately settle what later proves to be a valid claim does not of itself establish 'bad faith.'... [T]he insured must show the insurer 'intentionally and unreasonably denies or delays payment.' An insurer does not act in bad faith when it challenges the validity of a 'fairly debatable' claim, or when its delay results from honest mistakes." *White v. Unigard Mut. Ins. Co.*, 730 P.2d 1014, 1020 (Idaho 1986) (citations and internal quotations omitted).

In the third-party bad faith context, the Supreme Court of Idaho adopted the "equality of consideration" test to determine whether the insurer breached its duty of good faith in rejecting a settlement offer made by a third party. *Truck Ins. Exch. v. Bishara*, 916 P.2d 1275, 1280 (Idaho 1996). The insurer must give "equal consideration" to the interests of its insured in deciding whether to accept an offer of settlement. *Id.* The court adopted several factors for determining whether an insurer acted in bad faith for failing to settle a claim, including, among others, whether the insurer failed to communicate with the insured concerning compromise offers and the amount of financial risk to each of the parties. *Id.* at 1279–80.

**Illinois:** The Supreme Court of Illinois stated that "[m]ere allegations of bad faith or unreasonable and vexatious conduct, without more,... do not constitute [a bad faith tort action]." *Cramer v. Ins. Exch. Agency*, 675 N.E.2d 897, 904 (Ill. 1996). In such case of insurer misconduct, an insured's remedy is limited to a breach of contract action with a right to recover extra-contractual damages set out in 215 ILL. COMP. STAT. § 5/155. *Id.* "Courts therefore should look beyond the legal theory asserted to the conduct forming the basis for the claim. In cases where a plaintiff actually alleges and proves the elements of a separate tort, a plaintiff may bring an independent tort action, such as common law fraud, for insurer misconduct." *Id.* (citations omitted).

Addressing third-party bad faith, the Supreme Court of Illinois stated that "[t]he duty of an insurance provider to settle arises when a claim has been made against the insured and there is a reasonable probability of recovery in excess of policy limits and a reasonable probability of a finding of liability against the insured." *Haddick ex rel. Griffith v. Valor Ins.*, 763 N.E.2d 299, 304 (Ill. 2001).

**Indiana:** The Supreme Court of Indiana held that Indiana has long recognized a cause of action in tort for a breach of an insurer's duty to deal in good faith with its insured. *Freidline v. Shelby Ins. Co.*, 774 N.E.2d 37, 40 (Ind. 2002). "[A] good faith dispute about whether the insured has a valid claim will not supply the grounds for recovery in tort for the breach of the obligation to exercise good faith. On the other hand, an insurer that denies liability knowing there is no rational, principled basis for doing so has breached its duty. To prove bad faith, the plaintiff must establish, with clear and convincing evidence, that the insurer had knowledge that there was no legitimate basis for denying liability." *Id.* (citations omitted).

Turning to third-party bad faith, in *Catt v. Affirmative Insurance Co.*, No. 2:08-CV-243, 2009 WL 1228605, at *4 (N.D. Ind. Apr. 30, 2009), the Northern District of Indiana noted a split in Indiana law over the appropriate standard for third-party bad faith. Without taking a position, the court cited support for a standard that the insured must prove that the insurer acted with a "dishonest purpose, moral obliquity, furtive design, or ill will." *Id.* (citation omitted). The *Catt* Court also cited support for the "fiduciary duty standard" or "negligence and/or bad faith" standard. *Id.* (citation omitted).

**Iowa:** The Supreme Court of Iowa held that "to establish a claim for first-party bad faith, the insured must prove two facts: (1) that the insurer had no reasonable basis for denying benefits under the policy and, (2) the insurer knew, or had reason to know, that its denial was without basis. The first element is objective, the second subjective. If a claim is fairly debatable, the insurer is entitled to debate it, whether the debate concerns a matter of fact or law. Whether a claim is fairly debatable is appropriately decided by the court as a matter of law." *United Fire & Cas. Co. v. Shelly Funeral Home, Inc.*, 642 N.W.2d 648, 657 (Iowa 2002) (citations and internal quotation omitted).

In the third-party bad faith context, the Supreme Court of Iowa stated: "If the insurer has exercised good faith in its dealings with the insured and if the settlement proposal has been fully and fairly considered and decided against, based upon an honest belief that the action could be defeated or the judgment held within the policy limits, and in which respect… counsel have honestly expressed their conclusion, the insurer cannot be held liable [for an excess verdict] even though there is a mistake of judgment in arriving at its conclusion." *Johnson v. Am. Family Mut. Ins. Co.*, 674 N.W.2d 88, 90 (Iowa 2004) (quoting *Henke v. Iowa Home Mut. Cas. Co.*, 97 N.W.2d 168, 173 (1959)).

**Kansas:** The Supreme Court of Kansas held that the tort of bad faith is not recognized in Kansas. *Spencer v. Aetna Life & Cas. Ins. Co.*, 611 P.2d 149, 158 (Kan. 1980). The court reached this decision on the basis that "[t]he legislature has provided several remedies for an aggrieved insured and has dealt with the question of good faith first party claims. Statutory law does not indicate the legislature intended damages for emotional suffering to be recoverable by an aggrieved insured through a tort of bad faith. Where the legislature has provided such detailed and effective remedies, we find it undesirable for us to expand those remedies by judicial decree." *Id.*

In the third-party bad faith context, the Supreme Court of Kansas rejected the decisions of other courts that have held that an insurer is liable for an excess verdict only if it fails to exercise good faith in considering settlement offers within the policy limits. *Bollinger v. Nuss*, 449 P.2d 502, 508 (Kan. 1969). Instead the court adopted a more stringent standard, holding that "[p]ublic policy dictates that the insured's interests be adequately protechted [*sic*], and we believe this may be best accomplished by holding that both due care and good faith are required of the insurer in reaching the decision not to settle." *Id.* "Something more than mere error of judgment is necessary to constitute bad faith. The company cannot be required to predict with exactitude the results of a trial; nor does the company act in bad faith where it honestly believes, and has cause to believe, that any probable liability will be less than policy limits." *Id.* at 514; *see also Associated Wholesale Grocers, Inc. v. Americold Corp.*, 934 P.2d 65, 90 (Kan. 1997) ("[A]n insurance company should not be required to settle a claim when there is a good faith question as to whether there is coverage under its insurance policy.").

**Kentucky:** The Supreme Court of Kentucky held that "an insured must prove three elements in order to prevail against an insurance company for alleged refusal in bad faith to pay the insured's claim: (1) the insurer must be obligated to pay the claim under the terms of the policy; (2) the insurer must lack a reasonable basis in law or fact for denying the claim; and (3) it must be shown that the insurer either knew there was no reasonable basis for denying the claim or acted with reckless disregard for whether such a basis existed.... [A]n insurer is... entitled to challenge a claim and litigate it if the claim is debatable on the law or the facts." *Wittmer v. Jones*, 864 S.W.2d 885, 890 (Ky. 1993) (citation omitted).

Turning to third-party bad faith, the Supreme Court of Kentucky held that "the 'various factors' to be considered in determining the existence of bad faith are (1) whether the plaintiff offered to settle for the policy limits or less, (2) whether the insured made a demand for settlement on the insurer, and (3) the probability of recovery and of a jury verdict which would exceed the policy limits." *Motorists Mut. Ins. Co. v. Glass*, 996 S.W.2d 437, 451 (Ky. 1997) (citation and internal quotation omitted).

**Louisiana:** A Louisiana statute provides: "An insurer, including but not limited to a foreign line and surplus line insurer, owes to his insured a duty of good faith and fair dealing. The insurer has an affirmative duty to adjust claims fairly and promptly and to make a reasonable effort to settle claims with the insured or the claimant, or both. Any insurer who breaches these duties shall be liable for any damages sustained as a result of the breach." La.

Rev. Stat. Ann. § 22:1973A (Westlaw 2009). La. Rev. Stat. Ann. § 22:1973B sets forth a list of acts which, if knowingly committed or performed by an insurer, constitute a breach of the insurer's duties imposed in Subsection A. *See also Reed v. State Farm Mut. Auto. Ins. Co.*, 857 So. 2d 1012, 1021 (La. 2003) (addressing an "arbitrary, capricious, or without probable cause" standard to prove a statutory violation).

In the context of third-party bad faith, the Supreme Court of Louisiana held that "when an insurer has made a thorough investigation and the evidence developed in the investigation is such that reasonable minds could differ over the liability of the insured, the insurer has the right to choose to litigate the claim, unless other factors, such as a vast difference between the policy limits and the insured's total exposure, dictate a decision to settle the claim." *Smith v. Audubon Ins. Co.*, 679 So. 2d 372, 377 (La. 1996). "The determination of good or bad faith in an insurer's deciding to proceed to trial involves the weighing of such factors, among others, as the probability of the insured's liability, the extent of the damages incurred by the claimant, the amount of the policy limits, the adequacy of the insurer's investigation, and the openness of communications between the insurer and the insured." *Id.*

**Maine:** The Supreme Judicial Court of Maine refused to adopt an independent tort action for bad faith. *Marquis v. Farm Family Mut. Ins. Co.*, 628 A.2d 644, 652 (Me. 1993). The court reasoned that "[i]n view of the broad range of compensatory damages available in a contract action and in view of the statutorily provided remedies of interest on the judgment and attorney fees, we believe sufficient motivation presently exists to stifle an insurer's bad faith tendencies without the further imposition of the specter of punitive damages under an independent tort cause of action." *Id.* (citation and internal quotation omitted); *see also* Me. Rev. Stat. Ann. tit. 24 § 2436-A (listing conduct by an insurer that gives rise to an action by an insured for damages, costs and disbursements, reasonable attorney's fees, and interest on damages at the rate of 1 1/2 percent per month).

Turning to third-party bad faith, "[t]he existence of a cause of action in Maine for damages for an insurer's bad faith failure to settle within policy limits is unsettled." *State Fire & Cas. Co. v. Haley*, 916 A.2d 952, 956 (Me. 2007) (Dana, J., dissenting).

**Maryland:** Historically, Maryland did not recognize a tort action against an insurer for bad faith failure to pay a first-party insurance claim. *Johnson v. Fed. Kemper Ins. Co.*, 536 A.2d 1211, 1213 (Md. Ct. Spec. App. 1988). "Because [a first-party claim]... involves a claim by the insured against the insurer, rather than a claim by a third party against both the insurer and insured, there is no conflict of interest situation requiring the law to impose any fiduciary duties on the insurer. Instead, the situation is a traditional dispute between the parties to a contract." *Id.* at 1213. However, in 2007, Maryland enacted a statute that "provides that a plaintiff can recover expenses and litigation costs, including reasonable attorneys' fees, as well as interest on those costs, in an action seeking 'to determine coverage that exists under [an] insurance policy,' if the plaintiff can show that 'the insurer failed to act in good faith' with respect to the insurance claim." Md. Code Ann., Ins. § 27-1001(e) (2)(ii); Md. Code Ann., Cts. & Jud. Proc. § 3-1701(d)(1)–(2). The statute defines "good faith" as making "an informed judgment based on honesty and diligence supported by evidence the insurer knew or should have known at the time the insurer made a decision on a claim." Md. Code Ann., Cts. & Jud. Proc. § 3-1701(a)(4)." *Schwaber Trust Two v. Hartford Acc. & Indem. Co.*, 636 F. Supp. 2d 481, 484–85 (D. Md. 2009). However, no such action may be brought in court unless certain administrative requirements, as set out in Md. Code Ann., Ins. § 27-1001, are first satisfied. The administrative process can itself result in an award of damages.

Maryland recognizes a bad faith cause of action for an insurer's failure to settle a claim within policy limits. *Mesmer v. Maryland Auto. Ins. Fund*, 725 A.2d 1053, 1062 (Md. 1999) (quoting *State Farm v. White*, 236 A.2d 269, 273 (Md. 1967)) ("[F]or an insurer to measure up to the good faith test, its action in refusing to settle must consist of an informed judgment based on honesty and diligence. Furthermore, the insurer's negligence, if any there be, is relevant in determining whether or not it acted in good faith.").

**Massachusetts:** A Massachusetts statute lists several prohibited unfair claim settlement practices, including refusing to pay claims without conducting a reasonable investigation based upon all available information and failing to effectuate prompt, fair, and equitable settlements of claims in which liability has become reasonably clear. MASS. GEN. LAWS ANN. ch. 176D § 3(9) (d), (f) (Westlaw 2009); *see also Hopkins v. Liberty Mut. Ins. Co.*, 750 N.E.2d 943, 947–48 (Mass. 2001) (addressing MASS. GEN. LAWS ANN. ch. 176D § 3(9)). MASS. GEN. LAWS ANN. ch. § 3(9) is complex and has been the subject of numerous judicial decisions.

In the third-party bad faith context, the Supreme Judicial Court of Massachusetts adopted the following test to determine if an insurer is liable for bad faith for failure to settle a claim within policy limits: "The test is not whether a reasonable insurer might have settled the case within the policy limits, but rather whether no reasonable insurer would have failed to settle the case within the policy limits." *Hartford Cas. Ins. Co. v. N.H. Ins. Co.*, 628 N.E.2d 14, 18 (Mass. 1994).

**Michigan:** Michigan does not recognize an independent tort claim for bad-faith breach of an insurance contract. *Casey v. Auto Owners Ins. Co.*, 729 N.W.2d 277, 286 (Mich. Ct. App. 2006).

However, Michigan does recognize a bad faith cause of action for an insurer's failure to settle a claim within policy limits. In *Commercial Union Ins. Co. v. Liberty Mut. Ins. Co.*, 393 N.W.2d 161, 164 (Mich. 1986) the Supreme Court of Michigan described the standard for liability as follows: "Good-faith denials, offers of compromise, or other honest errors of judgment are not sufficient to establish bad faith. Further, claims of bad faith cannot be based upon negligence or bad judgment, so long as the actions were made honestly and without concealment. However, because bad faith is a state of mind, there can be bad faith without actual dishonesty or fraud. If the insurer is motivated by selfish purpose or by a desire to protect its own interests at the expense of its insured's interest, bad faith exists, even though the insurer's actions were not actually dishonest or fraudulent." (citations omitted). The court then set forth twelve factors for the fact finder to consider in deciding whether or not the insurer's failure to settle was in bad faith. *Id.* at 165–66.

**Minnesota:** Historically, Minnesota did not recognize a cause of action for bad-faith breach of an insurance contract absent an independent tort. *Sather v. State Farm Fire Cas. Ins. Co.*, No. C3-01-1268, 2002 WL 378111, at *5 (Minn. Ct. App. Mar. 12, 2002) (citing *Haagenson v. Nat'l Farmers Union Prop. & Cas.*, 277 N.W.2d 648, 652 (Minn. 1979)). "A malicious or bad-faith motive in breaching a contract does not convert a contract action into a tort action." *Haagenson*, 277 N.W.2d at 652. However, in 2008, Minnesota adopted M.S.A. § 604.18, which provides, in general, that an insured may be awarded one-half of the amount of its claim recovery that is in excess of the amount offered by the insurer at least ten days prior to trial (up to $250,000), if the insurer knew of a lack of a reasonable basis for denying benefits of an insurance policy or acted in reckless disregard of the lack of a reasonable basis for denying such benefits. Further, the insured may also be awarded its reasonable attorney's fees, not to exceed $100,000, to prove such violation.

Minnesota recognizes a bad faith cause of action for an insurer's failure to settle a claim within policy limits. *Short v. Dairyland Ins. Co.*, 334 N.W.2d 384, 388 (Minn. 1983) ("The insurer's duty of good faith is breached in situations in which the insured is clearly liable and the insurer refuses to settle within the policy limits and the decision not to settle within the policy limits is not made in good faith and is not based upon reasonable grounds to believe that the amount demanded is excessive.").

**Mississippi:** The Supreme Court of Mississippi held that punitive damages may not be imposed in "cases in which a carrier is determined to have merely reached an incorrect decision in denying a given claim. The issue of punitive damages should not be submitted to the jury unless the trial court determines that there are jury issues with regard to whether:

1) The insurer lacked an arguable or legitimate basis for denying the claim, *and*

2) The insurer committed a willful or malicious wrong, or acted with gross and reckless disregard for the insured's rights." *Am. Income Life Ins. Co. v. Hollins*, 830 So. 2d 1230, 1239–40 (Miss. 2002) (quoting *State Farm Mut. Auto. Ins. Co. v. Grimes*, 722 So. 2d 637, 641 (Miss. 1998)).

In the context of third-party bad faith, the Supreme Court of Mississippi adopted the following standard: "[W]hen suit covered by a liability insurance policy is for a sum in excess of the policy limits, and an offer of settlement is made within the policy limits, the insurer has a fiduciary duty to look after the insured's interest at least to the same extent as its own, and also to make a knowledgeable, honest and intelligent evaluation of the claim commensurate with its ability to do so. If the carrier fails to do this, then it is liable to the insured for all damages occasioned thereby." *Hartford Accident & Indem. Co. v. Foster*, 528 So. 2d 255, 265 (Miss. 1988).

**Missouri:** A Missouri statute provides that "if the insurer has failed or refused for a period of thirty days after due demand therefor prior to the institution of the action, suit or proceeding, to make payment under and in accordance with the terms and provisions of the contract of insurance, and it shall appear from the evidence that the refusal was vexatious and without reasonable cause, the court or jury may, in addition to the amount due under the provisions of the contract of insurance and interest thereon, allow the plaintiff damages for vexatious refusal to pay and attorney's fees as provided in section 375.420." Mo. Ann. Stat § 375.296 (Westlaw 2009); *see also Hensley v. Shelter Mut. Ins. Co.*, 210 S.W.3d 455 (Mo. Ct. App. 2007) (addressing the proof required to recover under § 375.420).

Missouri recognizes a bad faith cause of action for an insurer's failure to settle a claim within policy limits. *Ganaway v. Shelter Mut. Ins. Co.*, 795 S.W.2d 554, 556 (Mo. Ct. App. 1990) (citing *Zumwalt v. Utils. Ins. Co.*, 228 S.W.2d 750 (Mo. 1950)) (explaining that a bad faith action for refusal to settle sounds in tort, not in contract, and requires a showing that the insurer acted in bad faith, rather than negligently); *see also Shobe v. Kelly*, 279 S.W.3d 203, 210 (Mo. Ct. App. 2009) (discussing factors considered in a bad faith determination); *Johnson v. Allstate Ins. Co.*, 262 S.W.3d 655, 662 (Mo. Ct. App. 2008) ("An insurer's bad faith in refusing to settle is a state of mind, which is indicated by the insurer's acts and circumstances and can be proven by circumstantial and direct evidence. Circumstances that indicate an insurer's bad faith in refusing to settle include the insurer's not fully investigating and evaluating a third-party claimant's injuries, not recognizing the severity of a third-party claimant's injuries and the probability that a verdict would exceed policy limits, and refusing to consider a settlement offer.") (citation omitted).

**Montana:** A Montana statute provides that "(1) An insured or a third-party claimant has an independent cause of action against an insurer for actual damages caused by the insurer's violation of subsection (1), (4), (5), (6), (9), or (13) of 33-18-201 [Unfair claim settlement practices]. (2) In an action under this section, a plaintiff is not required to prove that the violations were of such frequency as to indicate a general business practice. (3) An insured who has suffered damages as a result of the handling of an insurance claim may bring an action against the insurer for breach of the insurance contract, for fraud, or pursuant to this section, but not under any other theory or cause of action. An insured may not bring an action for bad faith in connection with the handling of an insurance claim. (4) In an action under this section, the court or jury may award such damages as were proximately caused by the violation of subsection (1), (4), (5), (6), (9), or (13) of 33-18-201. Exemplary damages may also be assessed in accordance with 27-1-221." MONT. CODE ANN. § 33-18-242 (Westlaw 2009). Some of the prohibited conduct under section 33-18-201 includes "(1) misrepresent pertinent facts or insurance policy provisions relating to coverages at issue;... (4) refuse to pay claims without conducting a reasonable investigation based upon all available information; (5) fail to affirm or deny coverage of claims within a reasonable time after proof of loss statements have been completed."

Montana recognizes a bad faith cause of action for an insurer's failure to settle a claim within policy limits. *Fowler v. State Farm Mut. Auto. Ins. Co.*, 454 P.2d 76, 78–79 (Mont. 1969) ("It has been held that a policy of this type places a fiduciary duty on the insurance company to look after the interests of the insured as well as its own, thus requiring it to consider fairly the insured's liability for the excess when evaluating an offer of settlement within the policy limits. Failure to do so is bad faith and renders the company liable for its breach of fiduciary duty in the amount of any judgment over the policy limits.") (citation and internal quotation omitted).

**Nebraska:** The Supreme Court of Nebraska adopted the following test for bad faith in the context of first-party claims: "To show a claim for bad faith, a plaintiff must show the absence of a reasonable basis for denying benefits of the [insurance] policy and the defendant's knowledge or reckless disregard of the lack of a reasonable basis for denying the claim. It is apparent, then, that the tort of bad faith is an intentional one. 'Bad faith' by definition cannot be unintentional." *Braesch v. Union Ins. Co.*, 464 N.W.2d 769, 777 (Neb. 1991) (adopting the standard in *Anderson v. Cont'l Ins. Co.*, 271 N.W.2d 368, 376 (Wis. 1978)).

Nebraska recognizes a bad faith cause of action for an insurer's failure to settle a claim within policy limits. *Olson v. Union Fire Ins. Co.*, 118 N.W.2d 318, 323 (Neb. 1962) ("If the insurer has exercised good faith in all of its dealings under its policy, if the settlement which it has rejected has been fully and fairly considered and has been based on an honest belief that the insurer could defeat the action or keep the judgment within the limits of the policy, and if its determination is based on a fair review of the evidence after reasonable diligence in ascertaining the facts, accompanied by competent legal advice, a court will not subject the insurer to liability in excess of policy limits if it ultimately turns out that its determination is a mistaken one.").

**Nevada:** "The Supreme Court of Nevada adopted the cause of action called 'bad faith' in *United States Fidelity & Guaranty Co. v. Peterson*, 540 P.2d 1070 (Nev. 1975). The duty to deal fairly and in good faith then is implied by common law. Breach of the covenant of good faith and fair dealing is a tort. An insurer breaches the duty of good faith when it refuses without proper cause to compensate its insured for a loss covered by the policy. An insurer is without proper cause to deny a claim when it has an actual or implied awareness that no reasonable basis exist to deny the claim. Thus, the insurer is not liable for bad faith for being incorrect about policy coverage as long as the insurer had a reasonable basis to take the position that it did." *Pioneer Chlor Alkali Co., Inc. v. Nat'l Union Fire Ins. Co.*, 863 F. Supp. 1237, 1242 (D. Nev. 1994) (citations and internal quotation omitted). Nevada law also permits a cause of action under NEV. REV. STAT. § 686A.310 (Westlaw 2009), which address the manner in which an insurer handles an insured's claim whether or not the claim is denied. *Pioneer Chlor*, 863 F. Supp. at 1243; *see also Turk v. TIG Ins. Co.*, 616 F. Supp. 2d 1044, 1052–53 (D. Nev. 2009) (addressing the elements of § 686A.310).

In the context of third-party bad faith, "the litmus test is whether the insurer, in determining whether to settle a claim, [gave] as much consideration to the welfare of its insured as it [gave] to its own interests." *Landow v. Med. Ins. Exch. of Cal.*, 892 F. Supp. 239, 240–41 (D. Nev. 1995) (citation and internal quotation omitted) (alteration in original) (court's analysis of the standard is minimal but it makes clear that California law provides guidance).

**New Hampshire:** New Hampshire does not recognize a tort action for first-party bad faith. *See Bennett v. ITT Hartford Group, Inc.*, 846 A.2d 560, 564 (N.H. 2004) ("A breach of contract standing alone does not give rise to a tort action; however, if the facts constituting the breach of the contract also constitute a breach of duty owed by the defendant to the plaintiff independent of the contract, a separate tort claim will lie."). "In a given case the [insurer] may in fact have reason to know that its failure or delay in payment will cause the insured severe financial injuries. Whether the defendant had knowledge of the facts and reason to foresee the injury will normally be a question of fact for the jury." *Lawton v. Great Sw. Fire Ins. Co.*, 392 A.2d 576, 579–80 (N.H. 1978).

In the third-party bad faith context, "an insurer owes a duty to its insured to exercise due care in defending and settling claims against the insured, and that a breach of that duty will give rise to a cause of action by the insured." *Allstate Ins. Co. v. Reserve Ins. Co.*, 373 A.2d 339, 340 (N.H. 1977).

**New Jersey:** The Supreme Court of New Jersey adopted the "fairly debatable" standard to establish first party bad faith. *Pickett v. Lloyd's*, 621 A.2d 445, 453 (N.J. 1993). "To show a claim for bad faith, a plaintiff must show the absence of a reasonable basis for denying benefits of the policy and the defendant's knowledge or reckless disregard of the lack of a reasonable basis for denying the claim." *Id.* (citation and internal quotes omitted). "Under the 'fairly debatable' standard, a claimant who could not have established as a matter of law a right to summary judgment on the substantive claim would not be entitled to assert a claim for an insurer's bad-faith refusal to pay the claim." *Id.* at 454.

In the third-party bad faith context, "an insurer, having contractually restricted the independent negotiating power of its insured, has a positive fiduciary duty to take the initiative and attempt to negotiate a settlement within the policy coverage." *Rova Farms Resort, Inc. v. Investors Ins. Co. of Am.*, 323 A.2d 495, 507 (N.J. 1974). The only exception being if the insurer, "by some affirmative evidence, demonstrates there was not only no realistic possibility of settlement within policy limits, but also that the insured would not have contributed to whatever settlement figure above that sum might have been available." *Id.* "The proposed rule is a simple one to apply and avoids the burdens of a determination whether a settlement offer within the policy limits was reasonable." *Id.* at 510.

**New Mexico:** The Supreme Court of New Mexico adopted the following standard for recovering damages in tort for first-party bad faith: "[T]here must be evidence of bad faith or a fraudulent scheme. We further announced that 'bad faith' means any frivolous or unfounded refusal to pay. We have defined 'frivolous or unfounded' as meaning an arbitrary or baseless refusal to pay, lacking any support in the wording of the insurance policy or the circumstances surrounding the claim[.]" *Sloan v. State Farm Mut. Auto. Ins. Co.*, 85 P.3d 230, 236–37 (N.M. 2004) (citing *State Farm Gen. Ins. Co. v. Clifton*, 527 P.2d 798, 800 (N.M. 1974)); *see also* N.M. STAT. ANN. § 59A-16-30 (Westlaw 2009) (authorizing private right of action against insurer for violation of New Mexico's Trade Practices and Frauds Article of the Insurance Code).

In the third-party bad faith context, New Mexico recognizes a common-law cause of action for bad-faith failure to settle within policy limits, but not for negligent failure to settle. An insured must show that the insurer's refusal to settle was based on a dishonest judgment, meaning that the insurer has failed to honestly and fairly balance its own interests and the interests of the insured. *Sloan*, 85 P.3d at 237. "In caring for the insured's interests, the insurer should place itself in the shoes of the insured and conduct itself as though it alone were liable for the entire amount of the judgment." *Id.* (quoting *Dairyland v. Herman*, 954 P.2d 56, 61 (N.M. 1997)).

**New York:** The Court of Appeals of New York held that an insurer that breaches its contract is liable for those risks foreseen or which should have been foreseen at the time the contract was made. *Bi-Economy Market, Inc. v. Harleysville Ins. Co.*, 886 N.E.2d 127, 130 (N.Y. 2008). "To determine whether consequential damages were reasonably contemplated by the parties, courts must look to the nature, purpose and particular circumstances of the contract known by the parties... as well as what liability the defendant fairly may be supposed to have assumed consciously, or to have warranted the plaintiff reasonably to suppose that it assumed, when the contract was made." *Id.* (citations and internal quotes omitted) (alteration in original). The dissent discusses issues related to the insurer's standard of conduct. *Id.* at 133–35 (Smith, J., dissenting); *see also Panasia Estates, Inc. v. Hudson Ins. Co.*, 886 N.E.2d 135 (N.Y. 2008) (companion case to *Bi-Economy* and decided the same day).

On the subject of third-party bad faith, the Court of Appeals of New York rejected the insurer's proposed "sinister motive" standard and instead held that "in order to establish a prima facie case of bad faith, the plaintiff must establish that the insurer's conduct constituted a 'gross disregard' of the insured's interests—that is, a deliberate or reckless failure to place on equal footing the interests of its insured with its own interests when considering a settlement offer. In other words, a bad-faith plaintiff must establish that the defendant insurer engaged in a pattern of behavior evincing a conscious or knowing indifference to the probability that an insured would be held personally accountable for a large judgment if a settlement offer within the policy limits were not accepted." *Pavia v. State Farm Mut. Auto. Ins. Co.*, 626 N.E.2d 24, 27–28 (N.Y. 1993); *see also In re AXIS Reinsurance Co. REFCO Related Ins.*, No. 07-CV-07924, 2010 WL 1375712 (S.D.N.Y. Mar. 7, 2010) (discussing *Pavia* and New York's third-party bad faith standard).

**North Carolina:** North Carolina recognizes a private right of action in general for unfair methods of competition in or affecting commerce. N.C. GEN. STAT. ANN. § 75-1.1(a) (Westlaw 2009). While there is no private right of action against an insurer that engages in unfair methods of competition and unfair and deceptive acts or practices in the business of insurance, in violation of N.C. GEN. STAT. ANN. § 58-63-15 (Westlaw 2009), a court may look to N.C. GEN. STAT. ANN. § 58-63-15(11) (Unfair Claim Settlement Practices) for examples of conduct to support a finding of liability under the broader standards of N.C. GEN. STAT. ANN. § 75-1.1. *Gray v. N.C. Ins. Underwriting Ass'n*, 529 S.E.2d 676, 683 (N.C. 2000) (holding that an "insurance company that engages in the practice of '[n]ot attempting in good faith to effectuate prompt, fair and equitable settlements of claims in which liability has become reasonably clear,' N.C.G.S. § 58-63-15(11)(f), also engages in conduct that embodies the broader standards of N.C.G.S. § 75-1.1 because such conduct is inherently unfair, unscrupulous, immoral, and injurious to consumers") (alteration in original) ("[S]uch conduct that violates subsection (f) of N.C.G.S. § 58-63-15(11) constitutes a violation of N.C.G.S. § 75-1.1, as a matter of law, without the necessity of an additional showing of frequency indicating a 'general business practice,' N.C.G.S. § 58-63-15(11).").

On the subject of third-party bad faith, a North Carolina District Court held that "the duty of the insurer in the exercise of its contract right to settle a pending liability claim or suit, is "to act diligently and in good faith in effecting settlements within policy limits and, if necessary to accomplish that purpose, to pay the full amount of the policy." *Coca-Cola Bottling Co. of Asheville, N. C. v. Maryland*, 325 F. Supp. 204, 206 (D.C.N.C. 1971) (citation and internal quotation omitted). "Although the insurer may be unreasonable as seen in retrospect, it is liable for recovery beyond its policy limits only if it acts with wrongful or fraudulent purpose or with lack of good faith; an honest mistake of judgment is not actionable." *Id.*

**North Dakota:** North Dakota recognizes a cause of action for bad faith if an insurer acts unreasonably in handling an insured's claim by failing to compensate the insured, without proper cause, for a loss covered by the policy. *Hanson v. Cincinnati Life Ins. Co.*, 571 N.W.2d 363, 369–70 (N.D. 1997); *see also Seifert v. Farmers Union Mut. Ins. Co.*, 497 N.W.2d 694, 698 (N.D. 1993) (citing *Corwin Chrysler-Plymouth, Inc. v. Westchester Fire Ins. Co.*, 279 N.W.2d 638, 644 (N.D. 1979)) ("[T]he fact most significant to the question of bad faith was the refusal of the insurer to pay its insured's claim, despite the insurer's knowledge that the insured had incurred a payable loss.").

North Dakota does not appear to have conclusively formulated a bad faith standard for establishing an insurer's liability for an excess verdict following its failure to settle a suit within policy limits. For some guidance, *see Fetch v. Quam*, 623 N.W.2d 357 (N.D. 2001) and cases discussed therein.

**Ohio:** Ohio recognizes a cause of action in tort for bad faith if "an insurer fails to exercise good faith in the processing of a claim of its insured where its refusal to pay the claim is not predicated upon circumstances that furnish reasonable justification therefor. Intent is not and has never been an element of the reasonable justification standard." *Zoppo v. Homestead Ins. Co.*, 644 N.E.2d 397, 400 (Ohio 1994) (citation and internal quotation omitted).

In the third-party bad faith context, an "insurer cannot be held liable in tort for mere negligence on its part in failing or refusing to settle or compromise a claim brought against the insured for an amount within the policy limit, but that to be held liable in tort for its failure or refusal in this respect so as to entitle the insured to recover for the excess of the judgment over the policy limit it must have been guilty of fraud or bad faith." *Hart v. Republic Mut. Ins. Co.*, 87 N.E.2d 347, 349 (Ohio 1949) (citations and internal quotation omitted).

**Oklahoma:** Under Oklahoma law, "[t]he elements of a bad faith claim against an insurer for delay in payment of first-party coverage are: (1) claimant was entitled to coverage under the insurance policy at issue; (2) the insurer had no reasonable basis for delaying payment; (3) the insurer did not deal fairly and in good faith with the claimant; and (4) the insurer's violation of its duty of good faith and fair dealing was the direct cause of the claimant's injury. The absence of any one of these elements defeats a bad faith claim." *Ball v. Wilshire Ins. Co.*, 221 P.3d 717, 724 (Okla. 2009). "If there is a legitimate dispute concerning coverage or no conclusive precedential legal authority requiring coverage, withholding or delaying payment is not unreasonable or in bad faith." *Id.* at 725.

In the third-party bad faith context, the Supreme Court of Oklahoma held that "the minimum level of culpability necessary for liability against an insurer to attach is more than simple negligence, but less than the reckless conduct necessary to sanction a punitive damage award against said insurer." *Badillo v. Mid Century Ins. Co.*, 121 P.3d 1080, 1094 (Okla. 2005). "[T]he insured's interests must be given faithful consideration and the insurer must treat a claim being made by a third party against its insured's liability policy as if the insurer alone were liable for the entire amount of the claim." *Id.* at 1093 (citation and internal quotes omitted).

**Oregon:** Oregon does not recognize a tort action for first-party bad faith. *See Employers' Fire Ins. Co. v. Love It Ice Cream Co.*, 670 P.2d 160, 165 (Or. Ct. App. 1983) ("[A]n insurer's bad faith refusal to pay policy benefits to its insured sounds in contract and is not an actionable tort in Oregon.").

In the context of third-party bad faith, the Supreme Court of Oregon adopted a negligence standard. *Georgetown Realty, Inc. v. Home Ins. Co.*, 831 P.2d 7, 14 (Or. 1992). "The insurer is negligent in failing to settle, where an opportunity to settle exists, if in choosing not to settle it would be taking an unreasonable risk—that is, a risk that would involve chances of unfavorable results out of reasonable proportion to the chances of favorable results. Stating the rule in terms of 'good faith' or 'bad faith' tends to inject an inappropriate subjective element—the insurer's state of mind—into the formula. The insurer's duty is best expressed by an objective test: Did the insurer exercise due care under the circumstances?" *Id.* at 13 (quoting *Me. Bonding & Cas. Co. v. Centennial Ins. Co.*, 693 P.2d 1296, 1299 (Or. 1985)).

**Pennsylvania:** A Pennsylvania statute provides that, "In an action arising under an insurance policy, if the court finds that the insurer has acted in bad faith toward the insured, the court may take all of the following actions: (1) [award interest (as specified in the statute)]. (2) Award punitive damages against the insurer. (3) Award court costs and attorney fees against the insurer." 42 PA. CONS. STAT. ANN. § 8371 (Westlaw 2009). "To prove bad faith, a plaintiff must show by clear and convincing evidence that the insurer (1) did not have a reasonable basis for denying benefits under the policy and (2) knew or recklessly disregarded its lack of a reasonable basis in denying the claim." *Greene v. United Servs. Auto. Ass'n*, 936 A.2d 1178, 1188 (Pa. Super. Ct. 2007) (discussing numerous decisions that have addressed the undefined term "bad faith" in § 8371) (holding that "motive of self-interest or ill will" level of culpability is not a third element required for a finding of bad faith, but is probative of the second element).

The standard in Pennsylvania for third-party bad faith is as follows: "[W]hen there is little possibility of a verdict or settlement within the limits of the policy, the decision to expose the insured to personal pecuniary loss must be based on a bona fide belief by the insurer, predicated upon all of the circumstances of the case, that it has a good possibility of winning the suit. While it is the insurer's right under the policy to make the decision as to whether a claim against the insured should be litigated or settled, it is not a right of the insurer to hazard the insured's financial well-being. Good faith requires that the chance of a finding of nonliability be real and substantial and that the decision to litigate be made honestly." *Cowden v. Aetna Cas. & Sur. Co.*, 134 A.2d 223, 228 (Pa. 1957); *see also Birth Ctr. v. St. Paul Cos., Inc.*, 787 A.2d 376 (Pa. 2001) (addressing damages recoverable for bad faith failure to settle).

**Rhode Island:** A Rhode Island statute permits an action against an insurer that "wrongfully and in bad faith refused to pay or settle a claim made pursuant to the provisions of the policy, or otherwise wrongfully and in bad faith refused to timely perform its obligations under the contract of insurance." R.I. GEN. LAWS § 9-1-33 (Westlaw 2009). "Bad faith is established when the proof demonstrates that the insurer denied coverage or refused payment without a reasonable basis in fact or law for the denial. The standard that this Court employs in making that determination is the 'fairly debatable' standard. According to that standard, an insurer is entitled to debate a claim that is fairly debatable. That inquiry turns on whether there is sufficient evidence from which reasonable minds could conclude that in the investigation, evaluation, and processing of the claim, the insurer acted unreasonably and either knew or was conscious of the fact that its conduct was unreasonable." *Imperial Cas. & Indem. Co. v. Bellini*, 947 A.2d 886, 893 (R.I. 2008) (citations and internal quotes omitted).

Rhode Island sets a low threshold for insureds to establish third-party bad faith: "If the insurer declines to settle the case within the policy limits, it does so at its peril in the event that a trial results in a judgment that exceeds the policy limits, including interest. If such a judgment is sustained on appeal or is unappealed, the insurer is liable for the amount that exceeds the policy limits, unless it can show that the insured was unwilling to accept the offer of settlement. The insurer's duty is a fiduciary obligation to act in the best interests of the insured. Even if the insurer believes in good faith that it has a legitimate defense against the third party, it must assume the risk of miscalculation if the ultimate judgment should exceed the policy limits." *Asermely v. Allstate Ins. Co.*, 728 A.2d 461, 464 (R.I. 1999).

**South Carolina:** The Supreme Court of South Carolina stated that "if an insured can demonstrate bad faith or unreasonable action by the insurer in processing a claim under their mutually binding insurance contract, he can recover consequential damages in a tort action. Actual damages are not limited by the contract. Further, if he can demonstrate the insurer's actions were willful or in reckless disregard of the insured's rights, he can recover punitive damages." *Nichols v. State Farm Mut. Auto. Ins. Co.*, 306 S.E.2d 616, 619 (S.C. 1983). "An insured may recover damages for a bad faith denial of coverage if he or she proves there was no reasonable basis to support the insurer's decision to deny benefits under a mutually binding insurance contract." *Cock-N-Bull Steak House, Inc. v. Generali Ins. Co.*, 466 S.E.2d 727, 730 (S.C. 1996) (quoting *Dowling v. Home Buyers Warranty Corp., II*, 400 S.E.2d 143, 144 (S.C. 1991)).

In the third-party bad faith context, "a liability insurer owes its insured a duty to settle a personal injury claim covered by the policy, if settlement is the reasonable thing to do. An insurer who unreasonably refuses or fails to settle a covered claim within the policy limits is liable to the insured for the entire amount of the judgment obtained against the insured regardless of the limits contained in the policy." *Doe v. S.C. Med. Malpractice Liab. Joint Underwriting Ass'n*, 557 S.E.2d 670, 674 (S.C. 2001) (citations and internal quotes omitted).

**South Dakota:** South Dakota recognizes that an insurer's violation of its duty of good faith and fair dealing constitutes a tort, even though it is also a breach of contract. *Stene v. State Farm Mut. Auto. Ins. Co.*, 583 N.W.2d 399, 403 (S.D. 1998). "[F]or proof of bad faith, there must be an absence of a reasonable basis for denial of policy benefits [or failure to comply with a duty under the insurance contract] and the knowledge or reckless disregard [of the lack] of a reasonable basis for denial, implicit in that test is our conclusion that the knowledge of the lack of a reasonable basis may be inferred and imputed to an insurance company where there is a reckless disregard of a lack of a reasonable basis for denial or a reckless indifference to facts or to proofs submitted by the insured." *Id.* (citation and internal quotation omitted) (alteration in original).

For purposes of third-party bad faith, in the context of an insurer's failure to settle, the Supreme Court of South Dakota has recognized that there are an array of factors to consider in determining whether an insurer's refusal to settle is equivalent to a breach of its good faith duty: "(1) the strength of the injured claimant's case on the issues of liability and damages; (2) attempts by the insurer to induce the insured to contribute to a settlement; (3) failure of the insurer to properly investigate the circumstances so as to ascertain the evidence against the insured; (4) the insurer's rejection of advice of its own attorney or agent; (5) failure of the insurer to inform the insured of a compromise offer; (6) the amount of financial risk to which each party is exposed in the event of a refusal to settle; (7) the fault of the insured in inducing the insurer's rejection of the compromise offer by misleading it as to the facts; and (8) any other factors tending to establish or negate bad faith on the part of the insurer." *Helmbolt v. LeMars Mut. Ins. Co., Inc.*, 404 N.W.2d 55, 57 (S.D. 1987) (quoting *Kunkel v. United Sec. Ins. Co. of N.J.*, 168 N.W.2d 723, 727 (S.D. 1969)).

**Tennessee:** A Tennessee statute provides that, if an insurer refuses "to pay a loss within sixty (60) days after a demand has been made by the policyholder, the insurer shall be liable to pay the policyholder, in addition to the loss, a sum not exceeding 25% on the liability for the loss; provided, that it is made to appear to the court or jury trying the case that the refusal to pay the loss was not in good faith, and that the failure to pay inflicted additional expense, loss, or injury including attorney fees upon the holder of the policy or fidelity bond; and provided, further, that the additional liability, within the limit prescribed, shall, in the discretion of the court or jury trying the case, be measured by the additional expense, loss, and injury including attorney fees thus entailed." TENN. CODE ANN. § 56-7-105 (Westlaw 2009).

For purposes of third-party bad faith, the Supreme Court of Tennessee stated that "[m]ere negligence is not sufficient to impose liability for failure to settle. Moreover, an insurer's mistaken judgment is not bad faith if it was made honestly and followed an investigation performed with ordinary care and diligence. However, negligence may be considered along with other circumstantial evidence to suggest an indifference toward an insured's interest. The question of an insurance company's bad faith is for the jury if from all of the evidence it appears that there is a reasonable basis for disagreement among reasonable minds as to the bad faith of the insurance company in the handling of the claim." *Johnson v. Tenn. Farmers Mut. Ins. Co.*, 205 S.W.3d 365, 371 (Tenn. 2006).

**Texas:** The Supreme Court of Texas held that a "bad faith claimant... [must] prove that a carrier failed to attempt to effectuate a settlement after its liability has become reasonably clear." *Universe Life Ins. Co. v. Giles*, 950 S.W.2d 48, 55 (Tex. 1997) (clarifying the "no reasonable basis for denial of a claim" standard originally adopted in *Arnold v. Nat'l County Mut. Fire Ins. Co.*, 725 S.W.2d 165 (Tex. 1987)); *see also State Farm Fire & Cas. Co. v. Simmons*, 963 S.W.2d 42 (Tex. 1998) (discussing the evidence that supported a jury's finding that an insurer breached its duty of good faith and fair dealing). In addition, a Texas statute provides that "[a] person who sustains actual damages may bring an action against another person for those damages caused by the other person engaging in an act or practice: (1) defined by Subchapter B to be an unfair method of competition or an unfair or deceptive act or practice in the business of insurance." Tex Ins. Code Ann. § 541.151 (Westlaw 2009). Subchapter B includes § 541.060 (Unfair Settlement Practices), which provides, among other things, that it is an unfair method of competition or an unfair or deceptive act or practice in the business of insurance to engage in the following unfair settlement practices with respect to a claim by an insured or beneficiary: failing to attempt in good faith to effectuate a prompt, fair, and equitable settlement of a claim with respect to which the insurer's liability has become reasonably clear. Tex Ins. Code Ann. § 541.060(a)(2)(A).

For purposes of third-party bad faith, the Supreme Court of Texas held that "there must be coverage for the third-party's claim, a settlement demand within policy limits, and reasonable terms such that an ordinarily prudent insurer would accept it, considering the likelihood and degree of the insured's potential exposure to an excess judgment. When these conditions coincide and the insurer's negligent failure to settle results in an excess judgment against the insured, the insurer is liable under the Stowers Doctrine for the entire amount of the judgment, including that part exceeding the insured's policy limits." *Phillips v. Bramlett*, 288 S.W.3d 876, 879 (Tex. 2009) (internal quotation omitted) (citing *G.A. Stowers Furniture Co. v. Am. Indem. Co.*, 15 S.W.2d 544 (Tex. 1929)).

**Utah:** The Supreme Court of Utah held that a violation of the good faith duty to bargain or settle under an insurance contract gives rise to a claim for breach of contract and not a tort action. *Beck v. Farmers Ins. Exch.*, 701 P.2d

795, 798 (Utah 1985). "[T]he implied obligation of good faith performance contemplates, at the very least, that the insurer will diligently investigate the facts to enable it to determine whether a claim is valid, will fairly evaluate the claim, and will thereafter act promptly and reasonably in rejecting or settling the claim. The duty of good faith also requires the insurer to deal with laymen as laymen and not as experts in the subtleties of law and underwriting and to refrain from actions that will injure the insured's ability to obtain the benefits of the contract." *Christiansen v. Farmers Ins. Exch.*, 116 P.3d 259, 262 (Utah 2005) (quoting *Beck*, 701 P.2d at 801) (alteration in original).

In the third-party bad faith context, the Supreme Court of Utah held that "the best view is that [the insurer] must act in good faith and be as zealous in protecting the interests of its insured as it would in looking after its own. Whether it discharges that duty may depend upon various considerations including the certainty or uncertainty as to the issues of liability, injuries, and damages." *Ammerman v. Farmers Ins. Exch.*, 430 P.2d 576, 579 (Utah 1967). "It is therefore essential that the provisions of the contract be given effect and that the company have a reasonable latitude of discretion to decide whether it will accept a proposed settlement. Otherwise the policy limit would mean nothing and it would be all but impossible to determine the correct amount of premiums to be charged and the reserves necessary to cover potential losses." *Id.*

**Vermont:** The Supreme Court of Vermont held that the state "recognizes a claim for tortious bad faith brought by an insured against its own insurer when an insurer not only errs in denying coverage, but does so unreasonably. To establish a claim for bad faith, a plaintiff must show that (1) the insurer had no reasonable basis to deny the insured the benefits of the policy, and (2) the company knew or recklessly disregarded the fact that it had no reasonable basis for denying the insured's claim." *Peerless Ins. Co. v. Frederick*, 869 A.2d 112, 116 (Vt. 2004).

For purposes of third-party bad faith, the Supreme Court of Vermont stated that "[t]he insurer's fiduciary duty to act in good faith when handling a claim against the insured obligates it to take the insured's interests into account. The company must diligently investigate the facts and the risks involved in the claim, and should rely only upon persons reasonably qualified to make such an assessment. If demand for settlement is made, the insurer must honestly assess its validity based on a determination of the risks involved." *Myers v. Ambassador Ins. Co.*, 508 A.2d 689, 691 (Vt. 1986).

**Virginia:** Virginia treats first-party bad faith as a matter of contract and not tort law. *A&E Supply Co., Inc. v. Nationwide Mut. Fire Ins. Co.*, 798 F.2d 669, 676 (4th Cir. 1986) (allowing recovery of foreseeable consequential damages). A Virginia statute allows an insured to recover costs and reasonable attorneys' fees in a declaratory judgment action brought by the insured against the insurer, if the trial court determines that the insurer was not acting in good faith when it denied coverage or refused payment under the policy. VA. CODE ANN. § 38.2-209 (Westlaw 2009). Adopting a reasonableness standard, the Supreme Court of Virginia held that "[a] bad-faith analysis generally would require consideration of such questions as whether reasonable minds could differ in the interpretation of policy provisions defining coverage and exclusions; whether the insurer had made a reasonable investigation of the facts and circumstances underlying the insured's claim; whether the evidence discovered reasonably supports a denial of liability; whether it appears that the insurer's refusal to pay was used merely as a tool in settlement negotiations; and whether the defense the insurer asserts at trial raises an issue of first impression or a reasonably debatable question of law or fact." *Cuna Mut. Ins. Soc'y v. Norman*, 375 S.E.2d 724, 727 (Va. 1989); *see also Nationwide Mut. Ins. Co. v. St. John*, 524 S.E.2d 649, 651 (Va. 2000) (adopting the same standard as *Norman* for purposes of VA. CODE ANN. § 8.01-66.1, which addresses bad faith damages in the context of motor vehicle claims).

For purposes of third-party bad faith, the Supreme Court of Virginia held that "[a] decision not to settle must be an honest one. It must result from a weighing of probabilities in a fair manner. To be a good faith decision, it must be an honest and intelligent one in the light of the company's expertise in the field. Where reasonable and probable cause appears for rejecting a settlement offer and for defendant [*sic*] the damage action, the good faith of the insurer will be vindicated." *Aetna Cas. & Sur. Co. v. Prince*, 146 S.E.2d 220, 228 (Va. 1966) (citation omitted).

**Washington:** Under Washington law, an action for first-party bad faith sounds in tort and in order to establish bad faith, an insured is required to show the breach of duty was unreasonable, frivolous or unfounded. *St. Paul Fire & Marine Ins. Co. v. Onvia, Inc.*, 196 P.3d 664, 668 (Wash. 2008) (citations and internal quotes omitted); *see also Smith v. Safeco Ins. Co.*, 78 P.3d 1274, 1277–78 (Wash. 2003) (addressing reasonableness of the insurer's conduct). In addition, in 2007, Washington enacted the Insurance Fair Conduct Act, which authorizes a cause of action by a first party claimant who is unreasonably denied a claim for coverage. WASH. ADMIN. CODE § 48.30.015. The aggrieved party shall be entitled to recover the actual damages sustained, the costs of the action, including reasonable attorneys' fees and litigation costs. § 48.30.015(1). The court may also award treble damages. § 48.30.015(2). Further, such damages are available if the insurer violates WASH. ADMIN. CODE §§ 284-30-330, 284-30-350, 284-30-360, 284-30-370, and 284-30-380. § 48.30.015(5). In general, these provisions set forth, in detail, a litany of claims handling practices, such as prompt acknowledgment of communications, prompt investigation of claims, prompt settlements, and misrepresentation of policy provisions. *See also Coventry Assocs. v. Am. States Ins. Co.*, 961 P.2d 933, 937 (Wash. 1998) (holding that an insured may maintain an action against its insurer for bad faith investigation of its claim and violation of the Consumer Protection Act (WASH. REV. CODE ANN. § 19.86.010) regardless of whether the insurer was ultimately correct in determining coverage did not exist).

For purposes of third-party bad faith, "[a]n insurer breaches its affirmative duty to make a good faith effort to settle by negligently or in bad faith failing to settle a claim against the insured within its policy limits." *Smith v. Safeco Ins. Co.*, 50 P.3d 277, 281 (Wash. Ct. App. 2002) *rev'd on other grounds by* 78 P.3d 1274 (Wash. 2003); *see also American Best Food, Inc. v. ALEA London, Inc.*, 229 P.3d 693, 700 (Wash. 2010) (holding that the insurer's failure to defend, based upon a questionable interpretation of law, was unreasonable and, therefore, the insurer acted in bad faith as a matter of law) ("An insurer acts in bad faith if its breach of the duty to defend was unreasonable, frivolous, or unfounded. We specifically disapprove of language to the contrary.") (citations omitted).

**West Virginia:** A West Virginia statute sets forth various unfair methods of competition and unfair or deceptive acts or practices in the business of insurance. W. VA. CODE ANN. § 33-11-4 (Westlaw 2009); *see also Taylor v. Nationwide Mut. Ins. Co.*, 589 S.E.2d 55, 59–60 (W. Va. 2003) ("[A]n implied private cause of action may exist for a violation by an insurance company of the unfair settlement practice provisions of [W. VA. CODE ANN. § 33-11-4(9)]... . [P]ast acceptance of an implied cause of action for a statutory violation is deeply ingrained.") (citations and internal quotation omitted).

For purposes of third-party bad faith, the Supreme Court of Appeals of West Virginia held that "wherever there is a failure on the part of an insurer to settle within policy limits where there exists the opportunity to so settle and where such settlement within policy limits would release the insured from any and all personal liability, that the insurer has prima facie failed to act in its insured's best interest and that such failure to so settle prima facie constitutes bad faith towards its insured." *Shamblin v. Nationwide Mut. Ins. Co.*, 396 S.E.2d 766, 776 (W. Va. 1990). The *Shamblin* Court went on to describe the "insurer's burden to prove by clear and convincing evidence that it attempted in good faith to negotiate a settlement, that any failure to enter into a settlement where the opportunity to do so existed was based on reasonable and substantial grounds, and that it accorded the interests and rights of the insured at least as great a respect as its own." *Id.*

**Wisconsin:** The Supreme Court of Wisconsin recognized a bad faith claim sounding in tort, although arising out of a contractual relationship. *Jones v. Secura Ins. Co.*, 638 N.W.2d 575, 579 (Wis. 2002) (citing *Anderson v. Cont'l Ins. Co.*, 271 N.W.2d 368 (Wis. 1978)). "To show a claim for bad faith, a plaintiff must show the absence of a reasonable basis for denying benefits of the policy and the defendant's knowledge or reckless disregard of the lack of a reasonable basis for denying the claim." *Id.* at 579–80 (quoting *Anderson*, 271 N.W.2d at 376).

For purposes of third-party bad faith, the Supreme Court of Wisconsin held that "[t]he insurer has the right to exercise its own judgment in determining whether a claim should be settled or contested. But exercise of this right should be accompanied by considerations of good faith. In order to be made in good faith, a decision not to settle a claim must be based on a thorough evaluation of the underlying circumstances of the claim and on informed interaction with the insured." *Mowry v. Badger State Mut. Cas. Co.*, 385 N.W.2d 171, 178 (Wis. 1986) (citation and internal quotation omitted); *see also Roehl Transport, Inc. v. Liberty Mut. Ins. Co.*, 784 N.W.2d 542, 555 (Wis. 2010) ("For the very reasons our cases have concluded that an insurance company becomes liable for the tort of bad faith when it fails to act in good faith and exposes its insured to liability over policy limits, we likewise conclude that an insurance company may be liable for the tort of bad faith when the insurance company fails to act in good faith and exposes the insured to liability for sums within the deductible amount.") (containing a lengthy explanation and history of third-party bad faith in Wisconsin).

**Wyoming:** The Supreme Court of Wyoming held that an insurer's breach of the duty of good faith gives rise to an independent tort action. *McCullough v. Golden Rule Ins. Co.*, 789 P.2d 855, 855 (Wyo. 1990). "[T]he appropriate test to determine bad faith is the objective standard whether the validity of the denied claim was not fairly debatable." *Id.* at 860. "The tort of bad faith can be alleged only if the facts pleaded would, on the basis of an objective standard, show the absence of a reasonable basis for denying the claim, i.e., would a reasonable insurer under the circumstances have denied or delayed payment of the claim under the facts and circumstances." *Id.* at 860 (citation omitted).

For purposes of third-party bad faith, the Supreme Court of Wyoming held that good faith means "a bona fide belief by the insurer that it had a good possibility of winning the lawsuit or that the claimant's recovery in the lawsuit would not exceed the limits of the insurance policy." *Gainsco Ins. Co. v. Amoco Prod. Co.*, 53 P.3d 1051, 1058 (Wyo. 2002) (citation and internal quotation omitted). "The governing standard is whether a prudent insurer would have accepted the settlement offer if it alone were to be liable for the entire judgment. This is an objective, rather than a subjective, standard." *Id.* (citation and internal quotation omitted).

# CHAPTER
# 21

# The "Reasonable Expectations" Approach to Insurance Policy Interpretation

In contract law generally, one established principle is that contracts should be interpreted in light of the objectively reasonable understanding contracting parties would hold regarding the terms used in the contract. *See* E. ALLAN FARNSWORTH, CONTRACTS § 7.7 (4th ed. 2004).[1] This notion has been part of insurance policy interpretation since at least the early twentieth century. *See,*

---

1. "The concern of a court is not the truth of [contract] language but with the expectations that it aroused in the parties. It is therefore to these expectations, rather than to the concern of the philosopher or semanticist, that we must turn in the search for the meaning of contract language. [However,] [j]udges are not of a single mind in approaching this task of determining the expectations of the parties." *See* Farnsworth, *supra*, § 7.7 at 440. Both laypersons and lawyers commonly refer to a writing as "the contract." But technically, the contract is the agreement of the parties and the written memorialization of the contract is just that—a memorialization of the terms deal that has been made. *See* DAVID EPSTEIN, BRUCE A. MARKELL, & LAWRENCE PONOROFF, MAKING AND DOING DEALS: CONTRACTS IN CONTEXT 1 (2d ed. 2006). Consequently, if there is a "scrivener's error" in recording the terms of the contract, the actual agreement controls over any error in recording. For insurance policies, however, there often is little or no negotiation over many aspects of a standardized insurance policy, making courts more dependent on the written text of the policy than might be the case for other types of contracts. Standard insurance policies in fact have many aspects of a product or thing more than a negotiated agreement, although there is always at least some key discussion over important terms such as policy limits, premiums, and policy periods. *See* Jeffrey W. Stempel, *The Insurance Contract as Thing*, 44 TORT, TRIAL & INS. L.J. 813 (2009). Insurance policies also have aspects of private legislation in that they are for the most part crafted by the insurance industry (although often in response to policyholder demand or legislative or regulatory command). *See* Jeffrey W. Stempel, *The Insurance Policy as Statute*, 41 McGEORGE L. REV. 203 (2010). In addition, insurance policies often are part of an established system of risk distribution and management. *See* Jeffrey W. Stempel, *The Insurance Policy as Social Instrument and Social Institution*, 51 WM. & MARY L. REV. 1489 (2010). Although these additional perspectives can be useful in construing insurance policies, the fact remains that policies remain legally classified as a species of contract, with particular focus on policy text although construction of the policy will often be affected by the purpose of the policy, its function, the

*e.g., Bird v. St. Paul Fire & Marine Ins. Co.*, 224 N.Y. 47, 120 N.E. 86 (1918) (leading opinion authored by Judge Benjamin Cardozo) (using reasonable expectations construction to conclude that explosion rather than resulting fire was cause of loss).

But until the late twentieth century, insurance professionals did not talk of a reasonable expectations "doctrine" or school of thought as such. In two widely noted law review articles, Harvard Professor Robert Keeton (later a federal judge) enunciated the concept based on his reading of case law. *See* Robert E. Keeton, *Insurance Law Rights at Variance with Policy Provisions*, 83 HARV. L. REV. 961 (1970) (Part I) and Robert E. Keeton, *Insurance Law Rights at Variance with Policy Provisions*, 83 HARV. L. REV. 1281 (1970) (Part II).

Keeton focused on insurance coverage decisions that appeared at odds with literal text of insurance policies and concluded that they were not the result of judicial error or inability to read policies but instead represented an interpretative principle, specifically that in construing policies, courts will honor the "objectively reasonable expectations" of the policyholder even though "painstaking" examination of policy text would have negated those expectations. *See* Keeton, *supra*, 83 HARV. L. REV. at 967. Although this notion had hovered in the periphery of insurance law and been recognized in part by other observers,[2] Keeton's article was the first to specifically identify the concept and give it a name.[3]

The consequence was a sharp uptick in reasonable expectations analysis during the 1970s, almost to the point of becoming a fad. A number of courts specifically invoked the doctrine to decide cases. By the 1980s, however, there had been some retrenchment, both because insurers and contract formalists criticized the doctrine and because courts became uncomfortable expressly countermanding clear policy language unless the language was hidden, unfairly surprising, or otherwise deceptive.[4] However, courts also widely embraced the reasonable expectations concept as a means of resolving cases where policy language was ambiguous and have tended to make this assessment before being willing to resolve disputed cases against the

---

parties prior interactions, and questions of public policy. All of these factors also work to inform the limits of the reasonable expectations concept.

2. *See, e.g.*, Edwin W. Patterson, *The Interpretation and Construction of Contracts*, 64 COLUM. L. REV. 833, 852 (1964).

3. Among the prominent cases relied upon by Keeton were *Gray v. Zurich Ins. Co.*, 419 P.2d 168 (Cal. 1966), *Prudential Ins. Co. v. Lamme*, 425 P.2d 346 (Nev. 1967), and *Kievit v. Loyal Protective Life Ins. Co.*, 170 A.2d 22 (N.J. 1961). In addition, prominent insurance coverage cases such as *Gaunt v. John Hancock Mut. Life Ins. Co.*, 160 F.2d 599 (2d Cir.), *cert. denied*, 331 U.S. 84 (1947) (authored by Judge Learned Hand) and *Lachs v. Fidelity & Cas. Co. of New York*, 118 N.E.2d 555 (N.Y. 1954) (providing coverage under flight insurance policy purchased through vending machine despite arguably contrary policy language).

4. Mark Rahdert, *Reasonable Expectations Reconsidered*, 18 CONN. L. REV. 323 (1986).

drafter of unclear policy language (which is almost always the insurance company).

One can today confidently say that almost all states apply the reasonable expectations doctrine in some form for resolving unclear policy provisions. This "moderate" approach is the majority rule. Only a few jurisdictions apply the "strong" or Keeton-style version of the doctrine to overcome clear policy language, and these jurisdictions generally require that the policy language at issue be hidden in the policy's "fine print" or otherwise is unfair if enforced literally. A few states also have rejected the reasonable expectations concept entirely although they arguably let it return in the guise of decisions that refuse to apply policy language if this will lead to an "absurd" result or operate as an "unconscionable" provision.

Consequently, when discussing whether a state follows the reasonable expectations approach or doctrine, one must take care to be specific about whether a state rejects the concept, follows the strong Keeton version of the concept where expectations may trump even clear policy text, or simply uses policyholder (and insurer) expectations as a means of understanding the policy text (what we call the "moderate" approach to the reasonable expectations concept).

In the state-by-state list that follows, states are generally identified regarding their use of the reasonable expectations approach, with leading cases cited and brief explanation. To determine whether policyholder expectations will be a large interpretive factor in a given state, one must pay some attention to the specific precedents and appreciate the facts and equities of a given coverage dispute. Most important: a policyholder's subjective expectation of coverage is not sufficient to establish coverage in the absence of favorable policy text. The test is whether the objectively reasonable average policyholder would hold a given expectation regarding coverage. And, if there is evidence that the policyholder knew there was no coverage, the reasonable expectations concept will be of no avail.

Complete discussion of the reasonable expectations concept and application is beyond the scope this chapter. For more extensive discussion, *see* JEFFREY W. STEMPEL, STEMPEL ON INSURANCE CONTRACTS §§ 4.11, 14.12 (3d ed. 2006 & Supp. 2009); BARRY R. OSTRAGER & THOMAS R. NEWMAN, HANDBOOK ON INSURANCE COVERAGE DISPUTES § 1.03[b] (14th ed. 2008); EUGENE ANDERSON, JORDAN STANZLER, & LORELIE S. MASTERS, INSURANCE COVERAGE LITIGATION § 2.05 (2d ed. 2004); PETER KALIS, THOMAS M. REITER, & JAMES R. SEGERDAHL, POLICYHOLDERS GUIDE TO THE LAW OF INSURANCE COVERAGE § 20.04 (1997 & Supp. 2004); Jeffrey W. Stempel, *Unmet Expectations: The Underutilized Reasonable Expectations Approach and the Misleading Mythology of Judicial Role*, 5 CONN. INS. L.J. 181 (1998–99); Peter Nash Swisher, *A Realistic Consensus Approach to the Insurance Law Doctrine of Reasonable Expectations*, 35 TORT & INS. L.J. 729 (2000); Peter Nash Swisher, *Judicial Rationales in Insurance Law: Dusting*

*Off the Formal for the Function*, 52 Ohio St. L.J. 1 (1991); Stephen J. Ware, Note, *A Critique of the Reasonable Expectations Doctrine*, 56 U. Chi. L. Rev. 141 (1989); Mark C. Rahdert, *Reasonable Expectations Reconsidered*, 18 Conn. L. Rev. 323 (1986); Roger C. Henderson, *The Doctrine of Reasonable Expectations in Insurance Law After Two Decades*, 51 Ohio St. L.J. 823 (1990); Kenneth S. Abraham, *Judge-Made Law and Judge-Made Insurance: Honoring the Reasonable Expectations of the Insured*, 67 Va. L. Rev. 1151 (1981). In addition, of course, a review of Professor Keeton's writing is always helpful for policyholder counsel attempting to assert a strong version of the reasonable expectations concept in the face of contrary policy text.

## 50-State Survey: The "Reasonable Expectations" Approach to Insurance Policy Interpretation

**Alabama:** The Supreme Court of Alabama held that the reasonable expectations doctrine is limited to situations in which the language of the policy is ambiguous. *State Farm Fire & Cas. Co. v. Slade*, 747 So. 2d 293, 311 (Ala. 1999). "[E]xpectations that contradict a clear exclusion are not 'objectively reasonable.'" *Id.* (quoting *Wellcome v. Home Ins. Co.*, 849 P.2d 190, 194 (Mont. 1993)). The court reasoned that "[s]uch a limit on the doctrine of reasonable expectations is necessary. Otherwise, this Court would be faced with the strong temptation to substitute its notion of equity for the unambiguous terms of a contract and the doctrine could be used to invalidate every policy exclusion." *Id.* at 312; *see also Am. Res. Ins. Co. v. H & H Stephens Constr., Inc.*, 939 So.2d 868, 879–81 (Ala. 2006) (alteration in original) (discussing *Slade* in detail and noting its conclusion that, for the reasonable expectations doctrine to apply, "there [must] be, as a predicate, doubts as to the real intent of the policy").

**Alaska:** The Supreme Court of Alaska held that "because insurance policies are contracts of adhesion, they are construed according to the principle of 'reasonable expectations.' Under the reasonable expectations doctrine, '[t]he objectively reasonable expectations of applicants... regarding the terms of insurance contracts will be honored even though painstaking study of the policy provisions would have negated those expectations.'" *West v. Umialik Ins. Co.*, 8 P.3d 1135, 1138 (Alaska 2000) (alteration in original) (internal citations omitted) (quoting *State v. Underwriters at Lloyds, London*, 755 P.2d 396, 400 (Alaska 1988) (quoting Robert E. Keeton, *Basic Text on Insurance Law* § 6.3(a) at 351 (1971)). An Alaska court "need not find the policy ambiguous, however, to construe it under the reasonable expectations doctrine. To determine the parties' reasonable expectations, a court examines (1) the language of the disputed policy provisions; (2) the language of other provisions in the same policy; (3) extrinsic evidence; and (4) case law interpreting similar provisions." *Id.*; *see Dugan v. Atlanta Cas. Cos.*, 113 P.3d 652, 655 (Alaska 2005) (internal quotations omitted) ("[A]mbiguity exists only when the contract, taken as a whole, is *reasonably* subject to differing interpretations. We determine the existence of an ambiguity by determining the reasonable expectations of the contracting parties.").

**Arizona:** The Supreme Court of Arizona adopted the reasonable expectations doctrine "which, in proper circumstances, will relieve the insured from certain clauses of an agreement which he did not negotiate, probably did not read, and probably would not have understood had he read them." *Darner Motor Sales, Inc. v. Universal Underwriters Ins. Co.*, 682 P.2d 388, 399 (Ariz. 1984) (en banc). However, the court recognized that "if not put in proper perspective, the reasonable expectations concept is quite troublesome, since most insureds develop a 'reasonable expectation' that every loss will be covered by their policy... the reasonable expectation concept must be limited by something more than the fervent hope usually engendered by loss." *Id.* at 395. The reasonable expectations doctrine "applies [only] to a limited number of cases in which the boilerplate contract clauses are unambiguous but still operate oppressively. Specifically, those situations are: 1. Where the contract terms, although not ambiguous to the court, cannot be understood by the reasonably intelligent consumer who might check on his or her rights, the court will interpret them in light of the objective, reasonable expectations of the average insured; 2. Where the insured did not receive full and adequate notice of the term in question, and the provision is either unusual or unexpected, or one that emasculates apparent coverage; 3. Where some activity which can be reasonably attributed to the insurer would create an objective impression of coverage in the mind of a reasonable insured; 4. Where some activity reasonably attributable to the insurer has induced a particular insured reasonably to believe that he has coverage, although such coverage is expressly and unambiguously denied by the policy." *Phila. Indem. Ins. Co. v. Barerra*, 21 P.3d 395, 403 (Ariz. 2001) (en banc) (quoting *Gordinier v. Aetna Cas. & Sur. Co.*, 742 P.2d 277, 283–84 (Ariz. 1987)); *see also James v. Burlington N. Santa Fe Ry. Co.*, No. CV05–04106-PCT-NVW, 2007 WL 2461685, at *8 (D. Ariz. Aug. 27, 2007) (recognizing that Arizona courts have yet to address the applicability of the doctrine in the case of sophisticated insureds but holding that "Arizona courts are likely to apply the reasonable expectations doctrine, regardless of the insured's commercial status, where the insured alleges that it did not know and had no reason to know of the existence of an exclusion of coverage in a standardized insurance contract").

**Arkansas:** The Arkansas Court of Appeals held that "[a]mbiguity in an insurance policy must be construed against the insurance company preparing the contract" and that "[c]ourts are to resolve ambiguities in insurance policies in accordance with the reasonable expectations of the insured." *Toney v. Shelter Mut. Ins. Co.*, No. CA 88–305, 1989 WL 72285, at *2 (Ark. Ct. App.

June 28, 1989) (citing *Enter. Tools, Inc. v. Export-Import Bank of the U.S.*, 799 F.2d 437 (8th Cir. 1986)).

**California:** The Supreme Court of California held that "a court that is faced with an argument for coverage based on assertedly ambiguous policy language must first attempt to determine whether coverage is consistent with the insured's objectively reasonable expectations." *Bank of the West v. Superior Court*, 833 P.2d 545, 552 (Cal. 1992); *see also Powerine Oil Co., Inc. v. Superior Court*, 118 P.3d 589, 598 (Cal. 2005) (internal quotation omitted) ("If an asserted ambiguity is not eliminated by the language and context of the policy, courts then invoke the principle that ambiguities are generally construed against the party who caused the uncertainty to exist (i.e., the insurer) in order to protect the insured's reasonable expectation of coverage."); *AIU Ins. Co. v. Superior Court*, 799 P.2d 1253, 1264–65 (Cal. 1990) (citations omitted) ("If there is ambiguity [in policy language] it is resolved by interpreting the ambiguous provisions in the sense the promisor (i.e., the insurer) believed the promisee understood them at the time of formation. If application of this rule does not eliminate the ambiguity, ambiguous language is construed against the party who caused the uncertainty to exist. In the insurance context, we generally resolve ambiguities in favor of coverage. Similarly, we generally interpret the coverage clauses of insurance policies broadly, protecting the objectively reasonable expectations of the insured.").

**Colorado:** The Supreme Court of Colorado held that "when various provisions [of an insurance contract] conflict with each other, [a court] must construe the contract in a manner that protects the reasonable expectations of the insured at the time the insured purchased the policies." *Pub. Serv. Co. of Colo. v. Wallis & Cos.*, 986 P.2d 924, 939 (Colo. 1999). The doctrine only applies when there the policy language at issue is ambiguous. *See, e.g., Spaur v. Allstate Ins. Co.*, 942 P.2d 1261, 1265–66 (Colo. App. 1996) (finding that the doctrine of reasonable expectations did not apply when the terms of the insurance policy were unambiguous). When it does apply it "provides that an insurer who wishes to avoid liability must not only use clear and unequivocal language evidencing its intent to do so, but it must also call such limiting conditions to the attention of the insured. Absent proof of such disclosure, coverage will be deemed to be that which would be expected by the ordinary layperson." *Leland v. Travelers Indem. Co. of Ill.*, 712 P.2d 1060, 1064 (Colo. App. 1985); *see also State Farm Mut. Auto. Ins. Co. v. Nissen*, 851 P.2d 165, 167–68 (Colo. 1993) (en banc) (quoting Robert E. Keeton, *Insurance Law-Basic Text* § 6.3(a) at 351 (1971)) ("'The objectively reasonable expectations of applicants and intended beneficiaries regarding the terms of insurance contracts will be honored even though painstaking study of the policy provisions would have negated those expectations.'").

**Connecticut:** The Supreme Court of Connecticut held that "'ambiguous [policy] language should be construed in accordance with the reasonable expectations of the insured when he entered into the contract,'" and that courts in this situation interpret the policy against the insurer. *Conn. Ins. Guar. Ass'n v. Fontaine*, 900 A.2d 18, 24 (Conn. 2006) (quoting *Metro. Life Ins. Co. v. Aetna Cas. & Sur. Co.*, 765 A. 2d 891, 897 (Conn. 2001)); *see also Cody v. Remington ElecShavers*, 427 A.2d 810, 812–13 (Conn. 1980) ("It is a basic principle of insurance law that policy language will be construed as laymen would understand it and not according to the interpretation of sophisticated underwriters... the policyholder's expectations should be protected as long as they are objectively reasonable from the layman's point of view.").

**Delaware:** In resolving ambiguities in insurance contracts Delaware courts follow two primary rules of construction. *Steigler v. Ins. Co. of N. Am.*, 384 A.2d 398, 400 (Del. 1978). First, language shall be construed against the drafter, typically the insurer. *Id.* at 400–01. Second, to the extent a fair reading of the language will permit, the language should be read in accord with the reasonable expectations of the insured. *Id.* at 401 (citing *State Farm. Mut. Auto. Ins. Co. v. Johnson*, 320 A.2d 345, 347 (Del. 1974)); *see also Alstrin v. St. Paul Mercury Ins. Co.*, 179 F. Supp. 2d 376, 388–89 (D. Del. 2002) (detailing Delaware's rules of insurance policy construction and citing *Steigler* for the proposition that the ambiguous language should be read in accord with the reasonable expectations of the insured).

**Florida:** The Supreme Court of Florida decisively rejected the reasonable expectations doctrine in *Deni Associates of Florida, Inc. v. State Farm Fire & Casualty Insurance Co.*, 711 So. 2d 1135, 1140 (Fla. 1998). *Lenhart v. Federate Nat'l Ins. Co.*, 950 So. 2d 454, 461 (Fla. Dist. Ct. App. 2007); *see Deni Assocs.*, 711 So.2d at 1140 ("We decline to adopt the doctrine of reasonable expectations."); *see also State Farm Fire & Cas. Co. v. Castillo*, 829 So. 2d 242, 247 (Fla. Dist. Ct. App. 2002) (citing *Deni Assocs.*, 711 So. 2d at 1140 for the proposition that "it is the policy's terms which define the coverage, not the insureds' reasonable expectations"). *Deni Associates* stated in dicta that courts will not enforce contract language literally if it produces an "absurd" result. Although the absurd result exception appears seldom invoked in Florida, it might permit consideration of party expectations through the "back door." However, an absurd result would logically be something more troubling than an "unreasonable" result.

**Georgia:** The Supreme Court of Georgia held that "[a]ny ambiguities in [an insurance] contract are construed against the insurer as the drafter... [and] are to be read in accordance with the reasonable expectations of the insured where possible." *Richards v. Hanover Ins. Co.*, 299 S.E.2d 561, 563 (Ga. 1983) (citing *Cincinnati Ins. Co. v. Davis*, 265 S.E.2d 102, 105 (Ga. 1980)); *accord. Owners Ins. Co. v. Smith*, 670 S.E.2d 213, 215 (Ga. Ct. App. 2008); *see also Nationwide Mut. Fire Ins. Co. v. Collins*, 222 S.E.2d 828, 831 (Ga. Ct. App. 1975) ("The test is not what the insurer intended its words to mean, but what a reasonable person in the position of the insured would understand them to mean. The policy should be read as a layman would read it and not as it might be analyzed by an insurance expert or attorney.").

**Hawaii:** The Supreme Court of Hawaii held that insurance "policies are to be construed in accord with the reasonable expectations of a layperson." *Dairy Road Partners v. Island Ins. Co., Ltd.*, 992 P.2d 93, 107 (Haw. 2000) (quoting *Estate of Doe v. Paul Revere Ins. Group*, 948 P.2d 1103, 1112 (Haw. 1997)). In support of this conclusion, the court reasoned that although the terms of an insurance policy should be construed in accord with their plain meaning, unless it is clear that some other meaning was intended, and although the court should not create ambiguity where none exists, because insurance contracts are contracts of adhesion, they must be construed liberally in favor of the insured and in accord with the insured's reasonable expectations. *Id.* at 106–07; *see also Hawaiian Ins. & Guar. Co. v. Brooks*, 686 P.2d 23, 26–27 (Haw. 1984) (quoting Robert E. Keeton, *Insurance Law Rights at Variance With Policy Provisions*, 83 HARV. L. REV. 961, 967 (1970)) ("[T]he objectively reasonable expectations of policyholders… regarding the terms of insurance contracts will be honored even though painstaking study of the policy provisions would have negated those expectations.") (internal quotation omitted).

**Idaho:** The Supreme Court of Idaho "rejected the reasonable expectations doctrine in favor of traditional rules of contract construction." *Ryals v. State Farm Mut. Auto. Ins. Co.*, 1 P.3d 803, 805 (Idaho 2000) (citing *Casey v. Highlands Ins. Co.*, 600 P.2d 1387, 1390–91 (Idaho 1979)). Instead, "[i]ntent is to be determined from the language of the contract itself and 'in the absence of ambiguity, contracts for insurance must be construed as any other and understood in their plain, ordinary and proper sense, according to the meaning derived from the plain wording of the contract.'" *Casey*, 600 P.2d at 1391 (internal citation and quotation omitted).

**Illinois:** Outside the context of uninsured motorist coverage, "[t]he 'reasonable expectations' doctrine is not recognized in Illinois." *El Rincon Supportive Servs. Org., Inc. v. First Nonprofit Mut. Ins. Co.*, 803 N.E.2d 532, 540 (Ill. App. Ct. 2004) (quoting *Zurich Ins. Co. v. Northbrook Excess & Surplus Ins. Co.*, 494 N.E.2d 634, 645 (Ill. 1986)); *see also id.* (recognizing that, in the context of uninsured motorist coverage, "exculpatory language must be read in conjunction with the insured's reasonable expectations relating to uninsured motorist coverage and in conjunction with the public policy underlying the uninsured motorist statute").

**Indiana:** Indiana courts apply the reasonable expectations doctrine in "two circumstances: (1) where the policy at issue is ambiguous…; and (2) [where] the policy provides illusory coverage." *Conseco, Inc. v. Nat'l Union Fire Ins. Co. of Pittsburgh, Pa.*, No. 49D130202CP000348, 2002 WL 31961447, at *15 (Ind. Cir. Ct. Dec. 31, 2002) (citing *Eli Lilly & Co. v. Home Ins. Co.*, 482 N.E.2d 467, 470–71 (Ind. 1985) and *Davidson v. Cincinnati Ins. Co.*, 572 N.E.2d 502, 508 (Ind. Ct. App. 1991)); *see also McGuire v. Century Sur. Co.*, 861 N.E.2d 357, 363 (Ind. Ct. App. 2007) (quoting *Great Lakes Chem. Corp. v. Int'l Surplus Lines Ins. Co.*, 638 N.E.2d 847, 850 (Ind. Ct. App. 1994) ("Even where clauses are unambiguous when read within the policy as a whole, but in effect provide only illusory coverage, the policy will be enforced to satisfy the reasonable expectations of the insured."). When the doctrine applies, courts "must attempt to give effect to the reasonable expectations of the insured and construe the policy to further its basic purpose of indemnifying the insured for its loss." *Cincinnati Ins. Co. v. BACT Holdings, Inc.*, 723 N.E.2d 436, 440 (Ind. Ct. App. 2000).

**Iowa:** In accepting the reasonable expectations doctrine, the Supreme Court of Iowa held that "'[t]he objectively reasonable expectations of applicants and intended beneficiaries regarding the terms of insurance contracts will be honored even though painstaking study of the policy provisions would have negated those expectations.'" *Rodman v. State Farm Mut. Auto. Ins. Co.*, 208 N.W.2d 903, 906 (Iowa 1973) (quoting Robert E. Keeton, *Basic Text on Insurance Law* § 6.3(a) at 351 (1971)); *see also Shelter Mut. Ins. Co. v. Davis*, No. 07–0007, 2008 WL 2200082, at *2 (Iowa Ct. App. May 29, 2008) ("*Rodman*... is the seminal case setting forth the doctrine of reasonable expectations in Iowa."). The doctrine applies when either "an ordinary layperson would misunderstand the policy's coverage, or... circumstances attributable to the insurer fostered coverage expectations." *Grinnell Select Ins. Co. v. Cont'l W. Ins. Co.*, 639 N.W.2d 31, 37 (Iowa 2002) (citing *Krause v. Krause*, 589 N.W.2d 721, 728 (Iowa 1999)).

**Kansas:** The Supreme Court of Kansas held that "[b]efore applying the doctrine of reasonable expectations there must be a finding that the written instrument being interpreted is ambiguous." *Liggatt v. Employers Mut. Cas. Co.*, 46 P.3d 1120, 1127 (Kan. 2002). The reasonable expectations doctrine applies to reform an insurance policy only when the policy is ambiguous. *Id.* If the insurance policy is ambiguous, a Kansas court may utilize one of "two alternatives for interpreting the ambiguous contract: (1) A liberal construction in a way most favorable to the insured and (2) an interpretation consistent with the reasonable expectations of the insured." *Id.* (citing *Penalosa Coop. Exch. v. Farmland Mut. Ins. Co.*, 789 P.2d 1196, 1198–99 (Kan. Ct. App. 1990)).

**Kentucky:** The Supreme Court of Kentucky held that "[t]he doctrine of reasonable expectations is used in conjunction with the principle that ambiguities should be resolved against the drafter in order to circumvent the technical, legalistic and complex contract terms which limit benefits to the insured." *Simon v. Cont'l Ins. Co.*, 724 S.W.2d 210, 213 (Ky. 1986) (internal quotation omitted). "The gist of the doctrine is that the insured is entitled to all the coverage he may reasonably expect to be provided under the policy. Only an unequivocally conspicuous, plain and clear manifestation of the company's intent to exclude coverage will defeat that expectation." *Id.* at 212. Based on this holding Kentucky courts apply the reasonable expectations doctrine only when finding the policy to be ambiguous. *E.g., Frank Shoop, Inc. v. TIG Ins. Co.*, No. 2007-CA-000691-MR, 2009 WL 874535, at *7 (Ky. Ct. App. Apr. 3, 2009).

**Louisiana:** The Supreme Court of Louisiana held that when an insurance policy is ambiguous such "[a]mbiguity will... be resolved by ascertaining how a reasonable insurance policy purchaser would construe the clause at the time the insurance contract was entered." *Breland v. Schilling*, 550 So. 2d 609, 610–11 (La. 1989) (citing *Albritton v. Fireman's Fund Ins. Co.*, 70 So. 2d 111, 113 (La. 1954)); *see also In re St. Louis Encephalitis Outbreak in Ouachita Parish*, 939 So.2d 563, 568 n.9 (La. Ct. App. 2006) (quoting ROBERT E. KEETON & ALAN I. WIDISS, INSURANCE LAW § 6.13 (1988) ("The reasonable expectations doctrine can be capsulized as follows: 'courts will protect the [insured's reasonable expectations] regarding the coverage afforded by insurance contracts even though a careful examination of the policy provisions indicates that such expectations are contrary to the expressed intention of the insurer.'").

**Maine:** The Supreme Court of Maine held that when an insurance "contract is ambiguous, it will be construed against the insurer so as to comply with the objectively reasonable expectations of the insured." *Colford v. Chubb Life Ins. Co. of Am.*, 687 A.2d 609, 614 (Me. 1996) (*Peerless Ins. Co. v. Brennon*, 564 A.2d 383, 386–87 (Me. 1989)). Ambiguity exists, not simply when the insurer and the insured disagree about the meaning of the language of the contract, but where the contract is *reasonably* susceptible to two or more interpretations. *Id.* at 614; *see Patrons Oxford Mut. Ins. Co. v. Marois*, 573 A.2d 16, 19 (Me. 1990) (distinguishing ambiguity from a lack of understanding and stating the former "is created only by converting an insured's hope or assumption that every out-of-pocket payment is covered into a part of the contract language").

**Maryland:** Maryland has not expressly accepted the reasonable expectations doctrine, nor has it expressly rejected it. "Unlike the law of some states which construes insurance contracts against the insurer... [Maryland courts] hold[] that an insurance contract will be construed against the insurer only when an ambiguity remains after considering the intentions of the parties from the policy as a whole and, if necessary, after admitting and considering any relevant parol evidence." *Bailer v. Erie Ins. Exch.*, 687 A.2d 1375, 1378 (Md. 1997). In interpreting a provision of an insurance policy, Maryland courts apply the meaning that a "reasonably prudent layperson" would apply. *Id.* (citing *Pac. Indem. Co. v. Interstate Fire & Cas. Co.*, 488 A.2d 486, 488 (Md. 1985)); *see also Heffernan v. Lumbermens Mut. Cas. Co.*, 2007 WL 603089, at *3 (D. Md. Feb. 21, 2007) (citing *Cheney v. Bell Nat'l Life Ins. Co.*, 556 A.2d 1135, 1138 (Md. Ct. Spec. App. 1989) and noting that Maryland and New Jersey have different approaches when it comes to interpreting ambiguities in insurance policies).

**Massachusetts:** In Massachusetts, the reasonable expectations of the insured are relevant in interpreting a provision of an insurance policy, provided that these expectations are objectively reasonable and consistent with the plain language of the policy. *U.S. Liab. Ins. Co. v. Harbor Club, Inc.*,

No. 06–3938-BLS2, 2008 WL 2121136, at *6 (Mass. Super. Ct. May 8, 2008). "[A Massachusetts] court must consider 'what an objectively reasonable insured, reading the relevant policy language, would expect to be covered.'" *Ruggerio Ambulance Serv., Inc. v. Nat'l Grange Mut. Ins. Co.*, 724 N.E.2d 295, 299 (Mass. 2000) (quoting *Hakim v. Mass. Insurers' Insolvency Fund*, 675 N.E.2d 1161, 1165 (Mass. 1997)). The insured's reasonable expectations are not decisive, but must considered in light of the policy language to produce the interpretation consistent with the objectively reasonable meaning that a reasonable insured would give to the language. *See Aguiar v. Generali Assicurazioni Ins. Co.*, 714 N.E.2d 1046, 1048 (Mass. App. Ct. 1999) (noting that if the insured's reasonable expectations were decisive an insured could argue that one who buys fire insurance expects to be covered for all loss caused by fire even where a policy consists of numerous conditions and exclusions).

**Michigan:** The Supreme Court of Michigan held that "the rule of reasonable expectations should be abolished," in Michigan. *Wilkie v. Auto-Owners Ins. Co.*, 664 N.W.2d 776, 787 (Mich. 2003). The court explained: "[T]he rule of reasonable expectations clearly has no application when interpreting an unambiguous contract because a policyholder cannot be said to have reasonably expected something different from the clear language of the contract." *Id.* Additionally, the court explained that because Michigan already follows the rule that ambiguous language should be construed against the insurer as the drafter, interpreting such language "in favor of the policyholder's reasonable expectations adds nothing to the way in which Michigan courts construe contracts." *Id.*; *accord. Zaremba Equip., Inc. v. Harco Nat'l Ins. Co.*, 761 N.W.2d 151, 164 (Mich. Ct. App. 2008) (citing *Wilkie*, 664 N. W.2d at 786).

**Minnesota:** The Supreme Court of Minnesota first adopted the reasonable expectations doctrine in *Atwater Creamery Co. v. Western National Mutual Insurance Co.*, 366 N.W.2d 271, 277–78 (Minn. 1985). It noted that the doctrine is closely related to the doctrine of adhesion, the policy of which dictates that "[t]he objectively reasonable expectations of [insureds]… be honored even though painstaking study of the policy provisions would have negated those expectations." *Id.* (quoting Robert E. Keeton, *Insurance Law Rights at Variance with Policy Provisions*, 83 HARV. L. REV. 961, 967 (1970)). More recently the Supreme Court of Minnesota clarified the scope of the doctrine in *Carlson v. Allstate Ins. Co.*, 749 N.W.2d 41, 49 (Minn. 2008). The court in *Carlson* explained that the reasonable expectations doctrine should be used both as "a tool for resolving ambiguity and for correcting extreme situations like in *Atwater*, where a party's coverage is significantly different from what the party reasonably believes it has paid for and where the only notice the party has of that difference is in an obscure and unexpected provision." *Id.*

**Mississippi:** No instructive authority. *But see Delta Pride Catfish, Inc. v. Home Ins. Co.*, 697 So. 2d 400, 404–05 (Miss. 1997) (reaching a decision which "best articulate[d] the insured's objectively reasonable expectations about the scope of coverage"); *Brown v. Blue Cross & Blue Shield of Miss.*, 427 So. 2d 139, 141, 141 n.2 (Miss. 1983) (quoting Robert E. Keeton, *Insurance Law Rights at Variance with Policy Provisions*, 83 HARV. L. REV. 961, 967 (1970)) (holding that an insurer was estopped from denying coverage as a matter of public policy where the event by which the policy was terminated was the event for which the insureds sought coverage and providing that when these circumstances exist public policy dictates that the reasonable expectations of the insureds be honored).

**Missouri:** "When construing an insurance policy, [Missouri courts] must give the words their plain and ordinary meaning, consistent with the reasonable expectations, objectives, and intent of the parties." *Bowan ex rel. Bowan v. Gen. Sec. Indem. Co. of Ariz.*, 174 S.W.3d 1, 7 (Mo. Ct. App. 2005). "[W]ords [are] tested in light of the meaning which would normally be understood by the average lay person [and] the layperson's definition will be applied unless it plainly appears that the technical meaning was intended." *Stark Liquidation Co. v. Florists' Mut. Ins. Co.*, 243 S.W.3d 385, 397 (Mo. Ct. App. 2007) (citing *Chase Resorts, Inc. v. Safety Mut. Cas. Corp.*, 869 S.W.2d 145, 150 (Mo. Ct. App. 1993)). This description of the reasonable expectations doctrine applies in Missouri only when an ambiguity exists in the policy language. *Kertz v. State Farm Mut. Auto. Ins. Co.*, 236 S.W.3d 39, 43 (Mo. Ct. App. 2007); *see also Niswonger v. Farm Bureau Town & Country Ins. Co.*, 992 S.W.2d 308, 320 (Mo. Ct. App. 1999) (citing Robert E. Keeton, *Insurance Law Rights at Variance with Policy Provisions*, 83 HARV. L. REV. 961, 967 (1970)) ("The objectively reasonable expectations of [insureds]... will be honored even though painstaking study of the policy provisions would have negated those expectations.").

**Montana:** The Supreme Court of Montana adopted the reasonable expectations doctrine, providing that "[t]he objectively reasonable expectations of [insureds]... will be honored even though painstaking study of the policy provisions would have negated those expectations." *Transamerica Ins. Co. v. Royle*, 656 P.2d 820, 824 (Mont. 1983) (quoting Robert E. Keeton, *Insurance Law Rights at Variance with Policy Provisions*, 83 HARV. L. REV. 961, 967 (1970)). The Supreme Court of Montana reasoned that the use of the doctrine was consistent with Montana's "strong public policy that insurance is to serve a fundamental protective purpose." *Am. Family Mut. Ins. Co. v. Livengood*, 970 P.2d 1054, 1059. The doctrine only applied to honor the reasonable expectations of the insured where such expectations are "objectively reasonable." *See id.* (quoting *Wellcome v. Home Ins. Co.*, 849 P.2d 190, 194 (Mont. 1993) ("The reasonable expectations doctrine is inapplicable where the terms of the policy at issue clearly demonstrate an intent to exclude coverage... . [as] '[e]xpectations which are contrary to a clear exclusion from coverage are not objectively reasonable.'")); *see also Giacomelli v. Scottsdale Ins. Co.*, No. DA 09–0035, 2009 WL 4611126, at *9 (Mont. Dec. 8, 2009) (summarizing the preceding understanding of the reasonable expectations doctrine as applied in Montana).

**Nebraska:** "Under Nebraska law, the reasonable expectations of an insured are not assessed unless the language of the insurance policy is found to be ambiguous." *Ferrell v. State Farm Ins. Co.*, No. A-01–637, 2003 WL 21058165, at *5 (Neb. Ct. App. May 13, 2003) (citing *Cincinnati Ins. Co. v. Becker Warehouse, Inc.*, 635 N.W.2d 112, 120 (Neb. 2001)). When the terms of an insurance policy are clear "the terms are to be accorded their plain and ordinary meaning as the ordinary or reasonable person would understand them." *Becker*, 635 N.W.2d at 120 (citing *Moller v. State Farm Mut. Auto. Ins. Co.*, 566 N.W.2d 382, 386 (Neb. 1997)). Under the reasonable expectations doctrine insureds "'are entitled to the broad measures of protection necessary to fulfill their reasonable expectations.... . [and] should not be subjected to technical encumbrances or to hidden pitfalls and their policies should be construed liberally in favor to [*sic*] the end that coverage is afforded to the dull extent that any fair interpretation will allow.'" *Einspahr v. United Fire & Cas. Co.*, No. A-99–371, 2000 WL 758654, at *5 (Neb. Ct. App. June 13, 2000) (quoting *Heyd v. Chi. Title Ins. Co.*, 354 N.W.2d 154, 156–57 (Neb. 1984)) (internal quotation omitted); *see also Guerrier v. Mid-Century Ins. Co.*, 663 N.W.2d 131, 135 (Neb. 2003) (language in an insurance policy should be construed in accordance with "what a reasonable person in the position of the insured would have understood [the language] to mean").

**Nevada:** The Supreme Court of Nevada held that "[w]hen an ambiguity exists in an insurance policy, the court should consider not merely the language, but also the intent of the parties, the subject matter of the policy, the circumstances surrounding its issuance, and the policy should be construed to effectuate the reasonable expectations of the insured." *Nat'l Union Fire Ins. Co. v. Caesars Palace Hotel & Casino*, 792 P.2d 1129, 1130 (Nev. 1990) (citing *Nat'l Union Fire Ins. Co of the State of Pa., Inc. v. Reno's Executive Air, Inc.*, 682 P.2d 1380, 1383 (Nev. 1984)); *see also Fed. Ins. Co. v. Am. Hardware Mut. Ins. Co.*, 184 P.3d 390, 394, 396–97 (Nev. 2008) (recognizing the reasonable expectations doctrine as established in *Ceasars* and applying it in favor of the insured).

**New Hampshire:** New Hampshire courts "'construe the language of an insurance policy as would a reasonable person in the position of the insured based on a more than casual reading of the policy as a whole,' and... 'will honor the reasonable expectations of the policyholder.'" *A.J. Cameron Sod Farms, Inc. v. Cont'l Ins. Co.*, 700 A.2d 290, 292 (N.H. 1997) (quoting *Town of Epping v. St. Paul Fire & Marine Ins. Co.*, 444 A.2d 496 (N.H. 1982) and *Haley v. Allstate Ins. Co.*, 529 A.2d 394, 396 (N.H. 1987)). However, when a policy is clear and unambiguous, a court need not examine the reasonable expectations of the parties. *Colony Ins. co. v. Dover Indoor Climbing Gym*, 974 A.2d 399, 401 (N.H. 2009); *see also Webster v. Acadia Ins. Co.*, 934 A.2d 567, 570 (N.H. 2007) ("It is well-settled in New Hampshire that an insurer's obligation to defend its insured is determined by whether the cause of action against the insured alleges sufficient facts in the pleadings to bring it within the express terms of the policy. In considering whether a duty to defend exists based upon the sufficiency of the pleadings, we consider the reasonable expectations of the insured as to its rights under the policy.") (internal citation omitted).

**New Jersey:** "Generally an insurance policy should be interpreted according to its plain and ordinary meaning. But because insurance policies are adhesion contracts... . [w]hen a meaning of a phrase is ambiguous, the ambiguity is resolved in favor of the insured, and in line with an insured's objectively-reasonable expectations. Moreover, if an insured's 'reasonable expectations' contravene the plain meaning of a policy, even its plain meaning can be overcome." *Voorhees v. Preferred Mut. Ins. Co.*, 607 A.2d 1255, 1260 (N.J. 1992); *see also Crum & Forster Ins. Cos., v. Mecca & Sons Trucking Corp.*, No. L-847–02, 2009 WL 2917898, at *4 (N.J. Super. Ct. App. Div. Sept. 9, 2009) (quoting *Zacarias v. Allstate Ins. Co.*, 775 A.2d 1262, 1264–65 (N.J. 2001) quoting Robert E. Keeton, *Insurance Law Rights at Variance with Policy Provisions*, 83 HARV. L. REV. 961, 967 (1970)) ("The objectively reasonable expectations of [insureds]... will be honored even though painstaking study of the policy provisions would have negated those expectations.").

**New Mexico:** "When a court interprets the terms of an insurance policy that is unclear and ambiguous, the reasonable expectations of the insured guide the analysis. However, when the policy language is clear and unambiguous, we must give effect to the contract and enforce it as written." *Truck Ins. Exch. v. Gagnon*, 33 P.3d 901, 903 (N.M. Ct. App. 2001) (citing *Ponder v. State Farm Mut. Auto. Ins. Co.*, 12 P.3d 960, 964–65 (N.M. 2000)). This requires a court to construe ambiguous terms in favor of the insured, examining the other terms of the policy and extrinsic evidence to resolve the issue. *Bird v. State Farm Mut. Auto. Ins. Co.*, 165 P.3d 343, 347 (N.M. Ct. App. 2007) (citing *Rummel v. Lexington Ins. Co.*, 945 P.2d 970, 976–77 (N.M. 1997)); *see also Pielhau v. RLI Ins. Co.*, 189 P.3d 687, 694 (N.M. Ct. App. 2008) (declining to apply the reasonable expectations doctrine based on its determination that the policy language was unambiguous).

**New York:** The highest court of New York held that "[t]he tests to be applied in construing an insurance policy are common speech and the reasonable expectation and purpose of the ordinary businessman." *Ace Wire & Cable Co., Inc. v. Aetna Cas. & Sur. Co.*, 60 N.Y.2d 390, 398 (N.Y. 1983). *See also Commercial Ins. Co. of Newark v. Popadich*, No. 08858, slip. Op., 2009 WL 4253729, at *1 (N.Y. App. Div. Dec. 1, 2009). "[T]he reasonable expectations of the average insured upon reading the policy," inform a court's determination of whether a policy provision is ambiguous. *Italian Designer Import Outlet, Inc. v. N.Y. Cent. Mut. Fire Ins. Co.*, No. 21302/06, 2009 WL 4016652, *3 (N.Y. App. Div. Nov. 18, 2009). The ambiguity is then to be construed against the insurer. *MIC Prop. & Cas. Corp. v. Avila*, 886 N.Y.S.2d 186, 187 (N.Y. App. Div. Sept. 29, 2009).

**North Carolina:** The Supreme Court of North Carolina established that "a contract of insurance should be given that construction which a reasonable person in the position of the insured would have understood it to mean and, if the language used in the policy is reasonably susceptible of different constructions, it must be given the construction most favorable to the insured, since the company prepared the policy and chose the language." *Grant v. Emmco Ins. Co.*, 243 S.E.2d 894, 897 (N.C. 1978); *see also N.C. Farm Bureau Mut. Ins. Co. v. Fowler ex rel. Rudisill*, 589 S.E.2d 911, 914 (N.C. Ct. App. 2004) (recognizing *Grant*'s articulation of the reasonable expectations doctrine); *Great Am. Ins. Co. v. C. G. Tate Constr. Co.*, 279 S.E.2d 769, 773 (N.C. 1981) (noting the judicial trend of interpreting insurance policies in accord with the reasonable expectations of the parties).

**North Dakota:** The Supreme Court of North Dakota "has expressly declined to adopt the doctrine of reasonable expectations." *Nationwide Mut. Ins. Cos. v. Lagodinski*, 683 N.W.2d 903, 911–12 (N.D. 2004) (citing *W. Nat'l Mut. Ins. Co. v. Univ. of N.D.*, 643 N.W.2d 4, 13 (N.D. 2002)); *see also Ctr. Mut. Ins. Co. v. Thompson*, 618 N.W.2d 505, 509 (N.D. 2000) ("As we said in *RLI Ins. Co. v. Heling*, 520 N.W.2d 849, 854–55 (N.D. 1994), '[t]he doctrine of reasonable expectations [] is an interpretive tool in the construction of contracts,'" which "has yet to be accepted by a majority of this court.'").

**Ohio:** The Supreme Court of Ohio has declined to adopt the reasonable expectations doctrine. *Wallace v. Balint*, 761 N.E.2d 598, 606 (Ohio 2002); *see also Buckeye Ranch, Inc. v. Northfield Ins. Co.*, 839 N.E.2d 94, 108 (Ohio Com. Pl. 2005) ("[T]he Supreme Court [of Ohio] has not formally adopted the reasonable-expectations doctrine.").

**Oklahoma:** The Supreme Court of Oklahoma adopted the reasonable expectations doctrine in *Max True Plastering Co. v. United States Fidelity & Guaranty Co.*, 912 P.2d 861 (Okla. 1996). *Am. Econ. Ins. Co. v. Bogdahn*, 89 P.3d 1051, 1054 (Okla. 2004). "Under the reasonable expectations doctrine, when construing an ambiguity or uncertainty in an insurance policy, the meaning of the language is not what the drafter intended it to mean, but what a reasonable person in the position of the insured would have understood it to mean." *Id.*; *see also Hall v. Cherokee Nation*, 162 P.3d 979, 983 (Okla. Civ. App. 2007) (declining to apply the reasonable expectations doctrine because the policy was not shown to be ambiguous which is required for the doctrine to apply).

**Oregon:** No instructive authority. However, in a dissenting opinion, Justice Unis of the Supreme Court of Oregon noted: "This court has not explicitly adopted the doctrine of 'reasonable expectation,' at least by name, in any of its forms. Neither has this court explicitly rejected it. Language in at least two of our recent opinions, however, suggests support for the doctrine. In [*Totten v. New York Life Insurance Co.*, 696 P.2d 1082, 1086 (Or. 1985)], this court said: 'We interpret the terms of an insurance policy according to what we perceive to be the understanding of the ordinary purchaser of insurance.' That principle is also stated in [*Botts v. Hartford Accident & Indenity Co.*, 585 P.2d 657, 659–60 (Or. 1978)]. Moreover, various past members of this court have expressed their preference for the 'reasonable expectation' approach, *see, e.g., Lewis v. Aetna Insurance Co.*, 264 Or. 314, 323–24, 505 P.2d 914 (1973) (Bryson, J., specially concurring, joined by McAllister, J.). At some point, this court will have to address this series of conflicting precedents in our cases which today's majority opinion simply ignores." *Collins v. Farmers Ins. Co. of Or.*, 822 P.2d 1146, 1162 (Or. 1991) (Unis, J., dissenting).

**Pennsylvania:** In Pennsylvania, "[t]he insured's reasonable expectations are the focal point in reading contract language." *Winters v. Erie Ins. Group*, 532 A.2d 885, 887 (Pa. Super. Ct. 1987) (citing *Collister v. Nationwide Life Ins. Co.*, 388 A.2d 1346, 1353–54 (Pa. 1978)); *see Collister*, 388 A.2d at 1353–54 ("Courts should be concerned with assuring that the insurance purchasing public's reasonable expectations are fulfilled. Thus, regardless of the ambiguity, or lack thereof, inherent in a given set of insurance documents... the public has a right to expect that they will receive something of comparable value in return for the premium paid."). A Pennsylvania Superior Court noted: "[A] court's focus upon the insured's 'reasonable expectations' is not limited only to situations in which the insurance contract might be deemed ambiguous. In fact, our decisions have affirmed that regardless of the ambiguity, or lack thereof, inherent in a given set of insurance documents insurance transactions are subject to a review of the totality of the underlying circumstances." *Betz v. Erie Ins. Exch.*, 957 A.2d 1244, 1252–53 (Pa. Super. Ct. 2008) (internal quotation and citations omitted). However, "[a]n insured... may not complain that its reasonable expectations have been frustrated when the applicable policy limitations are clear and unambiguous." *Millers Capital Ins. Co. v. Gambone Bros. Dev. Co.*, Inc. 941 A.2d 706, 717 (Pa. Super. Ct. 2007) (citing *Bubis v. Prudential Prop. & Cas. Ins. Co.*, 718 A.2d 1270, 1272 (Pa. Super. Ct. 1998)).

**Rhode Island:** The Supreme Court of Rhode Island noted that its position regarding the interpretation of insurance policy "is consistent with the position adopted in a growing number of jurisdictions that the objectively reasonable expectations of one who enters a contract of adhesion will be enforced, despite the existence of contrary contract provisions." *Elliott Leases Cars, Ins. v. Quigley*, 373 A.2d 810, 814 n.1 (R.I. 1977). A court will not take into account the reasonable expectations of an insured unless it first determines that the policy is ambiguous. *Employers Mut. Cas. Co. v. Piers*, 723 A.2d 295, 298 (R.I. 1999).

**South Carolina:** The Supreme Court of South Carolina has declined to adopt the reasonable expectations doctrine. *Allstate Ins. Co. v. Mangum*, 383 S.E.2d 464, 466–67 (S.C. Ct. App. 1989); *see also Ex parte U.S. Auto. Ass'n*, 614 S.E.2d 652, 654 (S.C. Ct. App. 2005) ("The doctrine of reasonable expectations, which is essentially that the objectively reasonable expectations of insureds as to coverage will be honored even though a careful review of the terms of the policy would have shown otherwise, has been rejected in South Carolina."); *Bankers Ins. Co. v. Prezzy*, No. 2:08–2285-PMD, 2009 WL 3459189, at *1 (D.S.C. Oct. 27, 2009) ("South Carolina courts have continuously refused to incorporate the doctrine of reasonable expectations into South Carolina insurance law.").

**South Dakota:** The Supreme Court of South Dakota "has repeatedly declined to adopt the [reasonable expectations] doctrine." *Culhane v. W. Nat'l Mut. Ins. Co.*, 704 N.W.2d 287, 292 (S.D. 2005) (quoting *Dakota, Minn. & E. R.R. Corp. v. Heritage Mut. Ins. Co.*, 639 N.W.2d 513, 519 (S.D. 2002) (quoting *S.D. State Cement Plant Comm'n v. Wausau Underwriters Ins. Co.*, 616 N.W.2d 397, 407 n. 5 (S.D. 2000)).

**Tennessee:** The Supreme Court of Tennessee established that "[w]ords in an insurance policy are given their common and ordinary meaning, with ambiguous language construed against the insurance company and in favor of the insured.... Policy language should be given its plain meaning, unless a technical meaning is clearly provided in the insurance policy." *Harrell v. Minnesota Mut. Life Ins. Co.*, 937 S.W.2d 809, 814 (Tenn. 1996). The *Harrell* Court read the policy language at issue so as to comply with "the understanding and reasonable expectations of the average insurance policyholder and... [with] the plain meaning of the terms of the contract." *Id.* at 810. *See also Bd. of Trustees of Sumner County Employees' Trust Fund v. Graves*, No. M1997–00069-COA-R3-CV, 1999 WL 1086454, at *4 (Tenn. Ct .App. 1999) (citing *Harrell*, 937 S.W.2d at 810 for the proposition that "courts should construe an insurance policy keeping in mind the 'understanding and reasonable expectations of the average insurance policyholder'"); *Ryan v. MFA Mut. Ins. Co.*, 610 S.W.2d 428, 437 (Tenn. Ct. App. 1980) (using a "reasonable person" standard to resolve ambiguity in the contract language); *Broadnax v. Quince Nursing & Rehab. Center, LLC*, No. W2008–02130-COA-R3-CV, 2009 WL 2425959, at *7 (Tenn. Ct. App. Aug. 10, 2009) ("Contracts of adhesion are not automatically unenforceable. To determine the enforceability of a contract of adhesion, courts generally look to whether 'the terms of the contract are beyond the reasonable expectations of an ordinary person, or oppressive or unconscionable.'").

**Texas:** The Supreme Court of Texas "only [gives] effect to the reasonable expectations of the parties by enforcing the plain language of the insurance policy." *CU Lloyd's of Tex. v. Hatfield*, 126 S.W.3d 679, 684 n.6 (Tex. App. 2004). "Texas law does not recognize the 'Doctrine of Reasonable Expectations' of the insured as a basis to disregard unambiguous policy provisions," *Vandeventer v. All Am. Life & Cas. Co.*, 101 S.W.3d 703, 719 (Tex. App. 2003) (citing *Forbau v. Aetna Life Ins. Co.*, 876 S.W.2d 132, 145 n. 8 (Tex. 1994)), and "an insured may not complain that his or her reasonable expectations were frustrated by policy limitations which are clear and unambiguous." *Tex. Farmers Ins. Co. v. Murphy*, 996 S.W.2d 873, 878 (Tex. 1999) (internal quotation and citation omitted). However, when policy language is ambiguous a Texas court will construe the language "from the view point of the insured," *Republic Nat'l Life Ins. Co. v. Heyward*, 536 S.W.2d 549, 557 (Tex. 1976), giving the language the meaning "which the ordinary person would give to the phrase as a whole, taken in the context of the whole policy." *Bituminous Cas. Corp. v. Maxey*, 110 S.W.3d 203, 213–14 (Tex. App. 2003); *see also Nat'l Union Fire Ins. Co. of Pittsburgh, Pa. v. Hudson Energy Co., Inc.*, 811 S.W.2d 552, 555 (Tex. 1991) ("[I]f a contract of insurance is susceptible of more than one reasonable interpretation, we must resolve the uncertainty by adopting the construction that most favors the insured.").

**Utah:** The Supreme Court of Utah declined to adopt the reasonable expectations doctrine. *Allen v. Prudential Prop. & Cas. Ins. Co.*, 839 P.2d 798, 806 (Utah 1992) (declining to adopt the reasonable expectations doctrine, but continuing to construe ambiguities in favor of the insured); *accord. Alf v. State Farm Fire & Cas. Co.*, 850 P.2d 1272, 1275 (Utah 1993); *see also Kramer v. State Retirement Bd.*, 195 P.3d 925, 931 (Utah Ct. App. 2008) ("[Insurer] could not have violated the reasonable expectation doctrine because such a doctrine does not exist under Utah law.").

**Vermont:** The Supreme Court of Vermont held that "[t]he reasonable expectations of the parties are important in considering the scope of coverage provided in insurance contracts because such contracts, largely adhesive in nature, often contain boilerplate terms that are not bargained for, not read, and not understood by the insureds." *Farm Mut. Auto. Ins. Co. v. Roberts*, 697 A.2d 667, 672 (Vt. 1997); *see also N. Sec. Ins. Co. v. Rosenthal*, 980 A.2d 805, 809 (Vt. 2009) ("The reasonable expectation of the parties is, of course, central to interpreting any contract, and contracts of insurance are no exception."); *Vermont Mut. Ins. Co. v. Parsons Hill Partnership*, 1 A.3d 1016, 1025 (Vt. 2010) (citing strong support for Vermont's adherence to the reasonable expectations doctrine, but noting that, "apart from circumstances where an agent of the insurance carrier promises specific coverage, we have not held that the expectations of an insured can control over unambiguous policy language").

**Virginia:** No instructive authority.

**Washington:** The Supreme Court of Washington has declined to adopt the reasonable expectations doctrine. *State Farm Gen. Ins. Co. v. Emerson*, 687 P.2d 1139, 1144 (Wash. 1984) (en banc); *see also Grange Ins. Ass'n v. Jensen*, No. 51783-0-I, 2003 WL 22683356, at *6 (Wash. Ct. App. Nov. 10, 2003) ("The [*Emerson*] court declined to adopt the [reasonable expectations] doctrine, noting, 'in the absence of ambiguity, there is no reasonable expectation that no exemptions to coverage exist.'"); *Findlay v. United Pac. Ins. Co.*, 917 P.2d 116, 121 (Wash. 1996) (en banc) ("The 'reasonable expectation' doctrine has never been adopted in Washington.").

**West Virginia:** The Supreme Court of West Virginia held that "[w]here the language in an insurance policy is ambiguous... the doctrine of 'reasonable expectations' applies." *Edwards v. Bestway Trucking, Inc.*, 569 S.E.2d 443, 446 (W. Va. 2002) (citing *Nat'l Mut. Ins. Co. v. McMahon & Sons, Inc.*, 356 S.E.2d 488 (W. Va. 1987)). When the doctrine applies "the objectively reasonable expectation of applicants and intended beneficiaries regarding the terms of insurance contracts will be honored even if a painstaking study of the policy terms would negate those expectations." *Id.*; *see also Blankenship v. City of Charleston*, 679 S.E.2d 654, 657 (W. Va. 2009) (quoting *National Mutual* for the rule that the reasonable expectations doctrine applies when the policy language is ambiguous).

**Wisconsin:** The Supreme Court of Wisconsin "read[s] insurance policies to further the insured's reasonable expectations of coverage while meeting the intent of both parties to the contract." *J.G. v. Wangard*, 753 N.W.2d 475, 482 (Wis. 2008) (citation and internal quotation omitted). The reasonable expectations doctrine applies if there exists an ambiguity in the language of an insurance policy. *Blum ex rel. Studinski v. 1st Auto & Cas. Ins. Co.*, 762 N.W.2d 819, 821 (Wis. Ct. App. 2008) (citing *Taylor v. Greatway Ins. Co.*, 628 N.W.2d 916, 920 (Wis. 2001)). Wisconsin courts use the doctrine to "resolve [this] ambiguity by determining what a reasonable person in the position of the insured would understand the words to mean." *Id.*

**Wyoming:** The Supreme Court of Wyoming has repeatedly declined to adopt the reasonable expectations doctrine in the context of clear and unambiguous policy language. *See Ahrenholtz v. Time Ins. Co.*, 968 P.2d 946, 950 (Wyo. 1998) (refusing to "reform" the contract using the reasonable expectations doctrine because the contract was unambiguous); *Pribble v. State Farm Mut. Auto. Ins. Co.*, 933 P.2d 1108, 1113–14 (Wyo. 1997) (same); *St. Paul Fire & Marine Ins. Co. v. Albany County Sch. Dist. No. 1*, 763 P.2d 1255, 1263 (Wyo. 1988) (same); *see also W.N. McMurry Constr. Co. v. Cmty First Ins., Inc. Wyoming*, 160 P.3d 71, 77–79 (Wyo. 2007) (recognizing Wyoming's repeated refusal to adopt the reasonable expectations doctrine in the case of clear and unambiguous policy language). However, the Supreme Court of Wyoming has neither affirmatively accepted nor rejected the doctrine in the context of ambiguous policy language. *See Albany County Sch. Dist. No. 1*, 763 P.2d at 1263 (recognizing that the Wyoming Supreme "Court has never expressly adopted the [reasonable expectations] doctrine," and responding to the insured's argument that "the underpinnings of the doctrine have been accepted by this Court as reflected in the cases of *Sinclair Oil Corporation v. Columbia Casualty Company*, 682 P.2d 975 (Wyo. 1984), and *Wilson v. Hawkeye Casualty Co.*, [215 P.2d 867 (Wyo. 1950)]" by stating: "We agree that those cases, particularly *Sinclair Oil Corporation*, could be read as approving concepts embodied in the doctrine of reasonable expectations," but then refusing to adopt the doctrine in the case because the policy language was clear and unambiguous).

# Table of Cases